KOSOVO

Noel Malcolm was born in 1956, and studied at Cambridge University, where he gained a starred First in English and a Ph.D. in History. Fellow of Gonville and Caius College, Cambridge from 1981 to 1988, he later became Foreign Editor of the *Spectator* and political columnist on the *Daily Telegraph*. His highly acclaimed *Bosnia: A Short History* was published in 1994. He lives in London and is currently working on a biography of Thomas Hobbes.

Also by Noel Malcolm

De Dominis, 1560–1624: Venetian, Anglican, Ecumenist
and Relapsed Heretic

George Enescu: His Life and Music

Sense on Sovereignty

Bosnia: A Short History

The Correspondence of Thomas Hobbes (2 vols.), in the
Clarendon Edition of the Works of Thomas Hobbes

The Origins of English Nonsense

NOEL MALCOLM

KOSOVO

A Short History

PAN BOOKS

First published 1998 by Macmillan

First paperback edition published 1998 by Papermac

This edition published 2002 by Pan Books
an imprint of Pan Macmillan Ltd
Pan Macmillan, 20 New Wharf Road, London N1 9RR
Basingstoke and Oxford
Associated companies throughout the world
www.panmacmillan.com

ISBN 0 330 41224 8

Copyright © Noel Malcolm 1998

3 5 7 9 8 6 4 2

A CIP catalogue record for this book is available from
the British Library.

Typeset by SetSystems Ltd, Saffron Walden, Essex
Printed and bound in Great Britain by
Mackays of Chatham plc, Chatham, Kent

For Melanie

Contents

Acknowledgements

My FIRST DEBT of gratitude is to Alistair Horne, and to the Warden and Fellows of St Antony's College, Oxford, who elected me to the Alistair Horne Fellowship for 1995–6 in order to enable me to complete my work on this book. I am also grateful to Robert Evans and Richard Crampton for letting me try out some of the arguments presented in Chapter 8 at their Central and East European History seminar at Brasenose College.

Anyone who works on Balkan history will know how much time and effort can be spent trying to locate (or acquire) books and articles; there is not a single library, in Western Europe or even in the Balkans, that offers all the relevant materials under one roof. I am grateful to many friends for gifts, loans, copies and other services in this regard: above all, to Bejtullah Destani, whose own knowledge of the sources of Albanian history is extraordinarily encyclopaedic, and to Ahmed Žilić, a generous and ever-resourceful friend. For similar services I should also like to give special thanks to two other friends, D. S. and J. M., as well as to Norman Cigar, Ger Duijzings, Branko Franolić, Timothy Garton Ash, Fra Ignacije Gavran, Ivo Goldstein, Valeria Heuberger, Christine von Kohl, Branka Magaš, Kastriot Myftiu, Luan Malltezi, Željko Mandić, Alexander Shiroka, Aleksandar Stipčević, Yuri Stoyanov, Marian Wenzel, Tadej Zupančič and Isa Zymberi. I am also very grateful to Philip and Anette Goelet for hospitality in Maryland, Berney and Betty Nunan for hospitality in Tirana, and Aleksandra Ivin and Professor M. Rotar for their help at the National Library in Zagreb.

For permission to study and cite manuscript materials in their collections, I am grateful to the Controller of Her Majesty's Stationery Office (representing the Crown) in respect of the Public Record Office,

London, and also to the following: the Archive du Ministère des Affaires Étrangères, Paris; the Archivio della Sacra Congregazione della Propaganda Fide, Rome; the Archivio Segreto Vaticano, Vatican City; the Archivio di Stato, Venice; the Biblioteca Apostolica Vaticana, Vatican City; the Biblioteca Nazionale Marciana, Venice; the Biblioteca Universitaria, Bologna; the Bibliothèque Nationale, Paris; the Bodleian Library, Oxford; the Haus-, Hof- und Staatsarchiv, Vienna; the Istituto per la Storia della Società e dello Stato Veneziano, Fondazione Giorgio Cini, Venice; the Kriegsarchiv, Vienna; the National Archives, Washington, DC; the School of Oriental and African Studies, London; and the Somerset Record Office, Taunton. In addition, I am also grateful to the following libraries and institutions: the Biblioteca Casanatense, Rome; the Biblioteca Nazionale Centrale, Florence; the Biblioteca Nazionale 'Vittorio Emanuele', Rome; the Bibliotekë Kombëtare, Tirana; the British Library, London; the Cambridge University Library; the Institut für osteuropäische Geschichte und Südostforschung der Universität Wien, Vienna; the Nacionalna i Sveučilišna Knjižnica, Zagreb; the Österreichische Nationalbibliothek, Vienna; the Österreichisches Ost- und Südosteuropa-Institut, Vienna; the library of St Antony's College, Oxford; the School of Slavonic and East European Studies, London; the Staats- und Universitätsbibliothek, Hamburg; and the Taylor Institution, Oxford.

Last but certainly not least, I should like to record my gratitude to Tanya Stobbs and Mary Mount for seeing this book so expertly through the press.

A note on names and pronunciations

THE FOLLOWING SYSTEM has been adopted in this book. Its aim is to cater not to the sensitivities of Albanians or Serbs but to the practical needs of English readers. Unfortunately it is not possible to devise any system that will not cause some offence to some or other (or all) of the local inhabitants.

The form 'Kosovo' is used throughout this book (as opposed to the Albanian forms 'Kosovë' or 'Kosova'), simply because it is the form currently used in most English-language publications. As explained in Chapter 1, it is used here for the whole territory of the post-1945 'Autonomous Province'. The confusing usage which also employs 'Kosovo' to refer to one-half of that territory (and 'Metohija' for the other) is not adopted in this book.

For place-names outside Kosovo, the form used in most cases is the one current in the official or principal language of the modern territory to which that place now belongs: thus 'Skopje' (not 'Skoplje' or 'Shkup'), 'Ulcinj' (not 'Ulqin' or 'Dulcigno'), and so on. In some cases, however, other forms of the name are mentioned on the first appearance of the place-name, especially if they are common in the historical literature (e.g. 'Durazzo' for Durrës).

When giving different forms of place-name (or other technical term), I have used abbreviations to indicate the language in each case: 'Alb.' (Albanian), 'Arb.' (Arabic), 'Grk.' (Greek), 'Itl.' (Italian), 'Mac.' (Macedonian), 'Rom.' (Romanian), 'Srb.' (Serbian) and 'Trk.' (Turkish). The term 'Serbian' is used throughout this book for the Serbian form of the language which used to be called Serbo-Croat; this language is, by normal linguistic criteria, a single language which exists in several regional forms (Serbian, Croatian, Bosnian), but for political and cultural reasons most people in the former Yugoslavia now prefer to talk about these forms as if they were separate languages. I have occasionally used the term 'Serbo-Croat' (e.g. when referring to the language spoken by the Catholic Slavs of Janjevo).

For place-names inside Kosovo, it might seem logical to use Albanian forms only, given that Albanian is the language spoken by roughly 90 per cent of the population there. However, this book covers periods of history when the proportion of Albanians in the population was very different from what it is now; and some place-names have particular associations with Serbs or the Serbian Church which it would be perverse to ignore (e.g. the Patriarchate of Peć). So a mixture of Albanian and Serbian forms has been used, with a tendency to use Serbian forms for places with special Serbian associations, but also with some element of random distribution as well. Each time a place-name is mentioned for the first time in the text, the form in the other language is given in brackets. However, once a name has been introduced in this way, it is always thereafter given in the same form, without the bracketed alternative being mentioned again. Thus while the distribution of names between the two languages is partly random, the usage of each individual name is consistent. Readers who wish to find the alternative form of a name can do so using the index. Where no alternative form is given (e.g. with Mitrovica or Prizren) it is because the name is the same in both languages. In many cases, besides, the name is virtually the same, with only slight differences in pronunciation or accentuation (e.g. Alb.: Prishtina; Srb.: Priština).

Every Albanian place-name can be given in either of two forms: with or without the definite article. This article takes the form of a suffix, which may be either an extra vowel or a modification of an existing vowel at the end of the word. Thus: 'Prizren' (indefinite), 'Prizreni' (definite); 'Tiranë' (indefinite), 'Tirana' (definite). Logic should dictate that all names be given in one or other of these forms. However, common usage in English tends to say 'Prizren' and 'Tirana'. Accordingly, I have followed an increasingly common practice in English-language publications on Albania, which is to use the definite form for feminine names and the indefinite for masculine ones. (But 'the Malësi' uses the indefinite, to avoid a duplication of articles.)

One other convention should also be explained here. Throughout this book I have used the names of countries or other territories to refer to their modern (post-1945) geographical areas. This is intended merely as an aid to navigation for the reader. Thus when I describe a seventeenth-century army as crossing northern Bulgaria, I am not implying that there was any geopolitical entity called Bulgaria actually existing at that time; when during the same period I refer to Bar as a port in Montenegro, I am trying only to help the reader who wishes to find Bar on a modern map. In cases where I am referring to historical entities which differ from the modern geographical ones, I use other phrasings to make this clear (e.g. 'the Serbian kingdom').

While there is a useful terminological distinction between 'Serb' and 'Serbian' – the former being a more general ethnic–linguistic–cultural identification, which can be used for Serbs whether or not they live in Serbia – there is no easy equivalent distinction for Albanians. I have therefore used the term 'Albanian' in the general ethnic–linguistic–cultural sense, not in the narrow sense of 'inhabitant of Albania'. For additional clarity, I also use the terms 'Kosovo Serbs' and 'Kosovo Albanians'; from time to time I also employ the term 'Kosovar', which means 'Kosovo Albanian'.

Finally, technical terms are given in Turkish if they are terms for institutions of Islam or the Ottoman Empire (except that where English forms exist, e.g. *spahi* instead of Trk. *sipahi*, I have used them). The term *sancak* is given in its Turkish form, but 'the Sandžak of Novi Pazar' is given in the Serbian form because it is a current term for part of the territory of Serbia and Montenegro. Technical terms for other things are given in the appropriate language: Albanian for Albanian social institutions (*fis*, *vëllazëri*), Serbian for medieval Serbian ones (*meropah*, *župan*), and so on. These words are explained on their first appearance, but there is also a brief glossary after the notes.

Personal names are given in the modern spellings of the relevant language. Foreign-language materials are given in translation; for reasons of space, the original is not given in the notes, except in cases of quotations from manuscripts or other archival sources.

The pronunciation of Albanian is simple and regular: for English-speakers, the following important differences need to be observed:

c	is pronounced	'ts'
ç		'tch' (as in 'match')
dh		'th' (always voiced, as in 'this')
ë		'uh' (like the 'u' in 'radium', or like French 'deux'; virtually silent if it comes at the end of a word)
gj		'dj' (as in 'adjure')
j		'y' (as in 'yellow')
ll		like 'l', but a slightly heavier sound
q		like 'tch', but a slightly thinner sound
rr		like 'r', but a slightly heavier sound
th		'th' (always unvoiced, as in 'thin', not 'this')
x		'dz' (as in 'adze')
xh		'j' (as in 'jam)
y		acute 'u', as in French 'tu' or German 'über'

For the pronunciation of Serbo-Croat:

c	'ts'
č	'tch' (as in 'match')
ć	like 'tch', but a slightly thinner sound
dj	'dj' (as in 'adjure', almost like 'j' in 'jam')
j	'y' (as in 'yellow')
r	when rolled, can fill in between consonants like a vowel
š	'sh'
ž	'zh' (as in 'Zhivago')

And for the pronunciation of Turkish:

c	'j' (as in 'jam')
ç	'tch' (as in 'match')
ğ	is silent, but lengthens the preceding vowel
ı	a light 'uh' (rather like the 'u' in 'radium', or like French 'deux')
ö	long 'uh' (as in French 'peur' or German 'hören')
ş	'sh'
ü	acute 'u' (as in French 'tu' or German 'über')

Maps

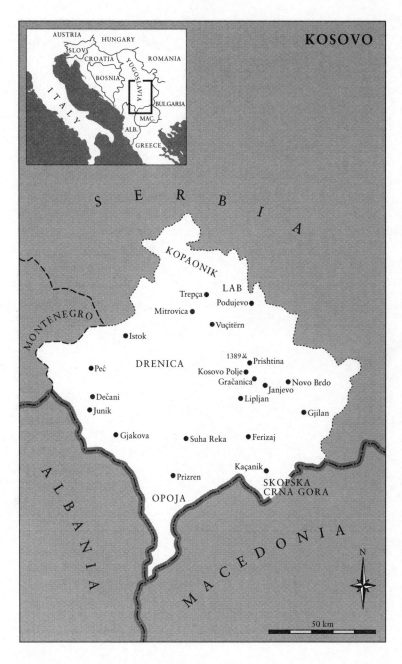

THE WEST-CENTRAL BALKAN REGION

100 km

Niš

Prokuplje

Leskovac

Mitrovica

Prishtina

Vranje

BULGARIA

Sofia

V O

Preševo

açanik

SKOPSKA CRNA GORA

Kumanovo

Skopje

etovo

Vardar

MACEDONIA

Struma

Bitola
(Monastir)

L. Prespa

GREECE

Moravа

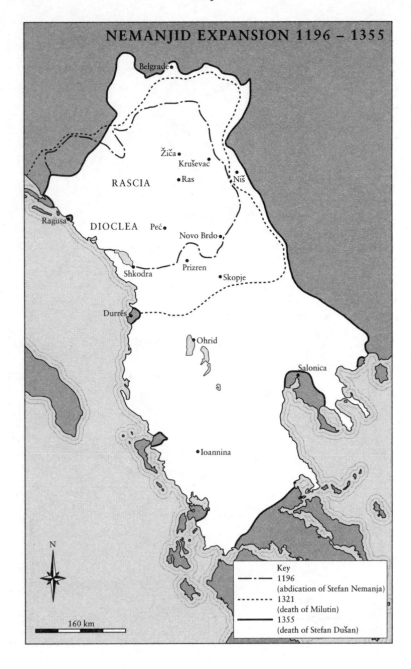

NEMANJID EXPANSION 1196 – 1355

Belgrade

Žiča
Kruševac
RASCIA   Ras   Niš

Ragusa

DIOCLEA   Peć

Novo Brdo

Prizren

Shkodra   Skopje

Durrës

Ohrid

Salonica

Ioannina

N

160 km

Key
— · — 1196
(abdication of Stefan Nemanja)
- - - - 1321
(death of Milutin)
——— 1355
(death of Stefan Dušan)

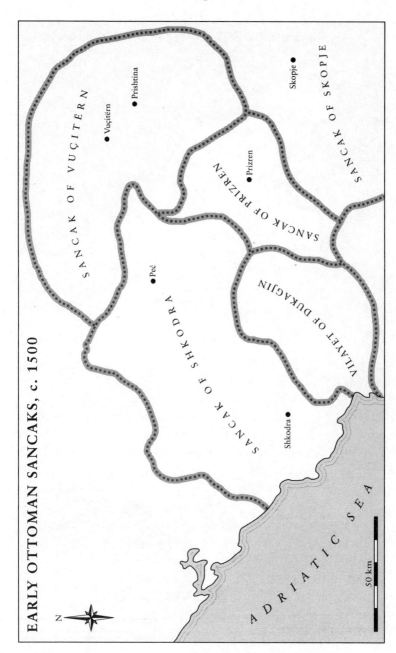

EARLY OTTOMAN SANCAKS, c. 1500

SANCAK OF VUÇITÈRN

• Vuçitèrn

• Prishtina

SANCAK OF SKOPJE

• Skopje

SANCAK OF PRIZREN

• Prizren

VILAYET OF DUKAGJIN

SANCAK OF SHKODRA

• Peć

• Shkodra

ADRIATIC SEA

N

50 km

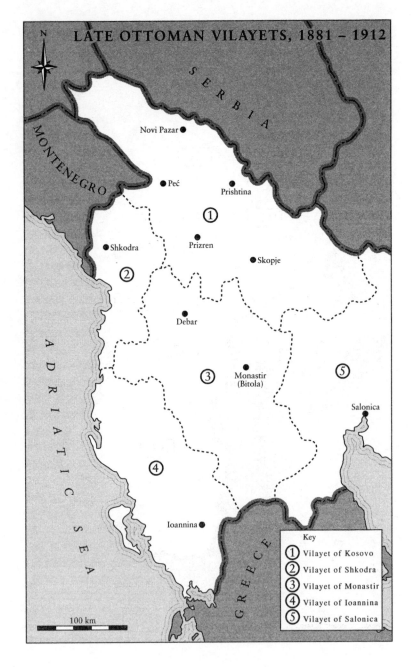

LATE OTTOMAN VILAYETS, 1881 – 1912

N

SERBIA

MONTENEGRO

Novi Pazar ●

Peć ●

Prishtina ●

①

Shkodra ●

Prizren ●

Skopje ●

②

Debar ●

③ Monastir
(Bitola) ●

⑤

Salonica ●

A D R I A T I C   S E A

④

Ioannina ●

GREECE

100 km

Key

① Vilayet of Kosovo
② Vilayet of Shkodra
③ Vilayet of Monastir
④ Vilayet of Ioannina
⑤ Vilayet of Salonica

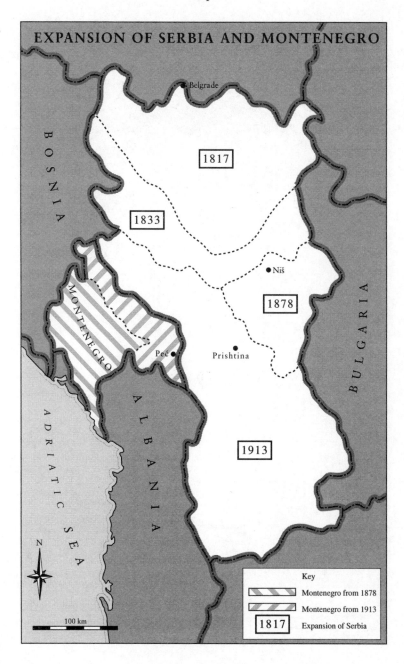

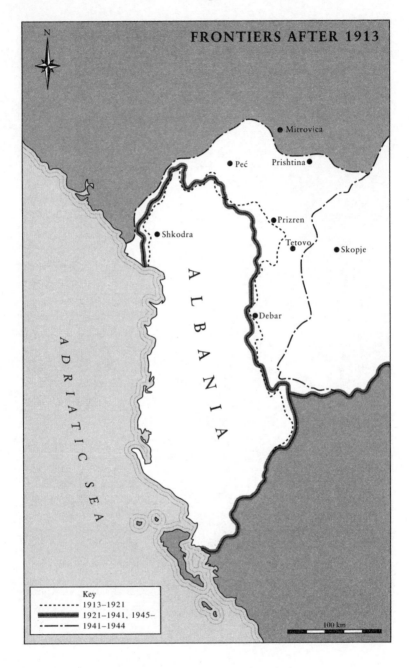

FRONTIERS AFTER 1913

N

Mitrovica

Peć

Prishtina

Prizren

Shkodra

Tetovo

Skopje

A L B A N I A

Debar

A D R I A T I C S E A

Key
1913–1921
1921–1941, 1945–
1941–1944

100 km

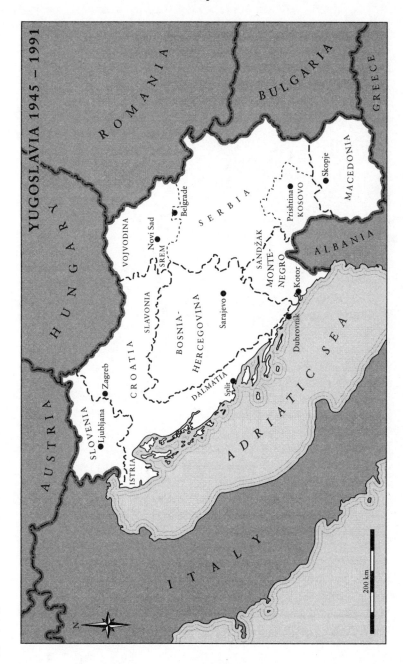

YUGOSLAVIA 1945 – 1991

Preface to the second edition

WHEN I FINISHED WRITING this book, a few months before the first armed clashes in Kosovo, I had both a hope and a fear. My hope was that the intolerance which had characterized Serbian policy towards the Kosovo Albanians might be moderated to some extent, if the Serbs were enabled to gain a more accurate knowledge of the history of the region and a more critical attitude towards some of their national myths. While I knew that any critically minded work of this kind would meet with reflex hostility from some quarters in Serbia, I hoped that thoughtful readers would recognize that my research was based on a wide range of Serbian as well as Albanian sources, and that it dismantled myths on both sides. If more Serbian myths were dealt with than Albanian ones, that was merely because more existed in the first place: my aim in writing this book was not anti-Serb, but anti-myth. The task of defusing historical prejudices is always a slow one, and in present circumstances it may seem to have been entirely overtaken by events. One day, however, the Serbs will need to come properly to terms with their history; and so I continue to hope that some of the materials needed for that fuller understanding may be found in this book.

My fear, on the other hand, was that the political confrontation in Kosovo was moving towards open violence. The Albanians felt increasingly frustrated by the apparent failure of their eight-year-long campaign of passive resistance; and the Yugoslav President, Slobodan Milošević, seemed ever more confident of his own impunity. In late 1997 and early 1998 sporadic acts of armed revolt by Albanians met with severe and sometimes indiscriminate responses from the Serb security forces; the Serbian policy stimulated the growth of the 'Kosovo Liberation Army', the existence of which then formed the pretext for a Serbian campaign of destruction against Albanian villages in the summer of 1998. Against this background, attempts by Western governments to broker a settlement, based on the restoration of autonomy to Kosovo, proved ineffectual. By early 1999 Milošević's military preparations in Kosovo indicated that he was planning a repetition and intensification of the previous year's campaign, which had driven more than a quarter of a million people from their homes. Pressed by Western governments to agree to their autonomy proposal (which included the placing of NATO troops in Kosovo to guarantee the security of the Albanians), and threatened with air strikes if he refused, Milošević refused. Within hours of the first NATO bombs hitting their targets in Serbia, Milošević's forces inside Kosovo had embarked on a campaign of murder, looting and intimidation aimed at driving the bulk of Kosovo's Albanian population out of the territory. The speed of this campaign, and the scale of the human suffering it caused, eclipsed even the 'cleansing' of non-Serbs from northern and eastern Bosnia in 1992. It represented the biggest challenge to Western policy, and to universal moral values, since Milošević first plunged the former Yugoslavia into war in 1991. As I write these words, the NATO bombing campaign continues, but the fate of the Albanians who remain in Kosovo – and, indeed, the eventual fate of Kosovo itself – remains highly uncertain. The main purpose of this Preface, however, is not to predict the future, but to present a few more details about the recent past, taking up the story of Kosovo where it was left at the end of the last chapter of this book and continuing it until the late spring of 1999.

The first significant armed clash between Albanians and Serb forces took place towards the end of 1997. On 25 November Serb police went to serve a court order on an Albanian in the village of Vojnik, in the Drenica region to the west of Prishtina; they were met with rifle shots, and retreated. The next day they returned in a convoy of armoured cars, which also came under fire. As the Serb officers drove back to Prishtina they started shooting indiscriminately at buildings they passed, killing an Albanian schoolteacher in his classroom. A crowd of 20,000 Albanians gathered for his funeral; among them were a few men in military dress, who said they represented the Kosovo Liberation Army (KLA). This was the self-styled army's first public appearance.

Who were, or what was, the KLA? Albanian villagers thought it was a local resistance movement, aimed in theory at 'national liberation' and in practice at protecting their villages against Serb attacks; and because enough of them came to think so, that is what it turned into. The structure and leadership of the organization in its early stages were, however, wrapped in mystery. Outside Kosovo, radical groups among the Albanian diaspora claimed to be directing its activities and issued 'communiqués' on its behalf. Chief among these groupings was the LPK ('Lëvizja Popullore e Kosovës': 'The Popular Movement of Kosovo'), which combined Albanian nationalism with Marxism-Leninism, having campaigned for Kosovo's unification with Albania since the early 1980s, when that country was under hard-line Communist rule. Yet the left-wing ingredients of this ideological mixture held little attraction for ordinary Albanians inside Kosovo; and, as the KLA grew in numbers during 1998, it would acquire local leaderships from a variety of backgrounds, including former army officers and members of the moderate political movement of Ibrahim Rugova. At this early stage, however, Rugova's own attitude to the KLA was quite uncomprehending: when the first KLA attacks on Serb policemen had taken place in 1996 and 1997 he had become convinced that the whole thing was a chimera, invented by Serb *agents provocateurs*. It would be well into 1998 before he changed his mind.

In the eyes of Rugova's critics, this was just another sign of his increasing inability to keep up with the reality of developments in Kosovo. His political reputation had already been damaged in October 1997, when the Albanian student movement in Prishtina had planned a large demonstration, protesting at Milošević's failure to fulfil his promises to restore educational facilities to them: Rugova publicly called on the students to postpone the protest, and they ignored his request. (In the event, the march was halted by a Serb road-block, and the leaders of the demonstration were beaten up by the police.) This issue caused an open disagreement between Rugova and his own Prime Minister, Bujar Bukoshi. Among the general Albanian population Rugova's personal standing remained high; at unofficial elections for the self-styled Kosovo government on 22 March 1998, he was returned unopposed as President. But among members of the political class the growing dissatisfaction with his policy was evident, with several prominent defections from his party; and the reason why he was elected unopposed was that the main

opposition parties boycotted the election, arguing that it was inappro-
priate at such a time of political crisis.

What had caused that crisis was a huge escalation in the use of
military force by the Serbian authorities. Attacks by the KLA on the
Serbian police and other targets had continued during the winter of
1997–8, but on a very limited scale: in the two years up to mid-January
1998, the KLA claimed to have killed five policemen, five other Serbian
officials and eleven Albanian 'collaborators' with the Serbian regime.
Other European countries had experienced similar small-scale campaigns
of politically motivated violence, and had dealt with them using normal
police methods. But the response of the Serbian authorities in this case
was hugely disproportionate; and it was the nature of this response
which, more than anything else, pushed Kosovo into war.

On 28 February 1998, after a fire-fight between Kosovar rebels and
Serb police in which four policemen had been shot dead, the Serbian
authorities launched an attack on two Albanian villages, using military
helicopters and armoured personnel carriers. In one village, Likoshani,
sixteen Albanians were killed; the police also looted the houses they
raided there. A few days later a similar military assault against the village
of Prekaz left fifty-one people dead: the main target of this attack was
the family house of Adem Jashari, a local strongman who was said to be
a commander of the KLA in that region. The Serbian forces killed not
only Jashari but also most of his family; nearly half the victims were
women, children and old men. This action turned Adem Jashari into a
hero and martyr in the eyes of the local Albanians, and encouraged large
numbers of them to join the KLA. Further attacks on other villages in
the Drenica region of central Kosovo during the next few weeks had a
similar effect, while also creating a flood of refugees. The process by
which Milošević's policy acted as the recruiting-master for the KLA was
now fully under way.

Western governments reacted hesitantly and ineptly to these events.
Many observers believed, indeed, that Milošević had actually been
encouraged to launch this campaign by the comments of an American
diplomat, Robert Gelbard, who had denounced the KLA as a 'terrorist
group' on 23 February. On 9 March the 'Contact Group' (USA, Russia,
Britain, France, Germany and Italy) threatened a limited package of
sanctions, such as visa restrictions and the blocking of investment credits,

if Milošević did not change his policy within two weeks; when that deadline was reached, they then extended it by another month. Milošević's only response was to widen the attacks on Albanian villages and increase his military build-up in the region. The threatened sanctions were eventually introduced at the end of April. Meanwhile a resolution of the UN Security Council had imposed an arms embargo, aimed at cutting off supplies to both Yugoslavia and the KLA. (Yugoslavia was, however, a major arms producer, and had recently made a large purchase of arms from Russia; the KLA was equipped mainly with small arms acquired from people who had stolen them from weapons stores in Albania in 1997.)

While the Western politicians debated these measures, Milošević was strengthening his own political position inside Yugoslavia. In March he invited the radical nationalist politician Vojislav Šešelj to join his government; Šešelj was known for his extreme views on the Kosovo question, having publicly advocated a policy of infecting Kosovo Albanians with the AIDS virus. Most of the political spectrum in Serbia (with the exception of the tiny 'Civic Alliance' party) was in any case hostile to the Albanians: a typical example was the commentator Aleksa Djilas (someone regarded in the West as a liberal intellectual), whose main contribution to the debate on Kosovo in April 1998, published in the Belgrade nationalist magazine *Argument*, was entitled 'Whatever Israel Does To The Palestinians, We Serbs Can Do To The Albanians'. During that month Milošević organized a referendum on the question of whether 'foreign representatives' should be allowed to mediate in the Kosovo conflict. The majority, not surprisingly, voted 'no'.

While internal political pressure on Milošević to change his policies was non-existent, Western leverage on him also seemed extremely limited. A display of military force was made on 15 June, when NATO jets flew along the southern borders of Kosovo; and on the following day European governments issued what was described as 'a strong final warning' to Milošević. This warning, like the previous ones, was ignored. Military actions by Serb forces were intensified in two areas: the Drenica region of central Kosovo, and the south-western border area running down from Peć to Gjakova. The official reason for concentrating on this second area was to stop the smuggling of arms to the KLA from Albania; but the tactics used by the Serb forces were aimed mainly at civilian population centres, not at military supply-lines. Towns such as Dečani and Junik were shelled by heavy artillery, and in early June there were reports of villages being bombed by Serbian aircraft. A similar campaign was conducted in central Kosovo, with the ostensible purpose of eliminating the strongholds of the KLA (which had abducted and killed a number of Serb civilians, and was claiming that it controlled a large area of 'liberated territory'). By means of random shootings and artillery bombardments the Serb forces emptied village after village of their inhabitants; the houses were then looted and burnt, and in many cases livestock were killed and crops destroyed in the fields. Over a period of six months, from April to September 1998, more than 300 Albanian villages were devastated in this way; aid agencies estimated that between 250,000 and 300,000 people were driven from their homes. The majority moved to the major towns, while some left Kosovo altogether and others (up to 50,000) sought refuge on hillsides. From the nature of the systematic destruction of houses and livelihoods, it was clear that the main purpose of this entire campaign was not military but demographic: nothing less than the permanent uprooting of a significant proportion of the rural population of Kosovo.

During the summer months the Western powers, despite the urgent 'final warnings' they had issued, remained curiously inactive. Some Western officials apparently believed that the Serbian campaign would increase the chances of an eventual negotiated settlement, by reducing the self-confidence of the KLA and thus forcing the Albanians to climb down from their demand for outright independence. Such a view was gravely mistaken, not only in its acceptance of the idea that the Serbian forces were engaged in a normal 'counter-insurgency' operation, but also in its failure to understand the psychology of the Albanians, whose determination to throw off Serbian rule could only be strengthened by these experiences. While the Albanians became more radicalized, how-ever, they did not become more united politically: criticism of Rugova's moderate policy was intensified, but the KLA failed to put forward any coherent political programme, or to offer any convincing leadership at the political level. American diplomats made several fruitless attempts to persuade the Albanians to come together and form a unified negotiating position. Yet the overall failure of this diplomacy was not very surprising, as the only thing on which all Albanians agreed – the need for full independence from Yugoslavia – was the one option that Western governments ruled out. The Western policy was aimed merely at the restoration of 'autonomy', which meant local self-government under the continuing rule of Belgrade.

At the end of September 1998 world opinion was shocked by the discovery of a massacre near the village of Obrinje in central Kosovo. Sixteen Albanian civilians, including ten women, children and old men, had been killed on a hillside; one elderly man had been left with his throat slit, and with the butcher's knife carefully placed on his chest. The Western powers now renewed their efforts to put pressure on the Yugoslav government, threatening air strikes within days if it refused to halt its campaign. On 16 October the US envoy Richard Holbrooke finally persuaded Milošević to sign an agreement: the text was never made public, but the key provisions included a promise to scale down the Serbian deployment in Kosovo to its pre-February levels, an agreement that all Kosovar refugees could return to their homes, and an acceptance of the presence of an international force of observers to make sure that these pledges were fulfilled.

The Holbrooke-Milošević deal looked, on the surface, like a success for Western diplomacy; but the American envoy had been forced to make important concessions. He had failed to secure free access for investigators from the International War Crimes Tribunal at the Hague, and had conceded that the observers sent to Kosovo should be neither directed nor protected by NATO, but should consist instead of an unarmed 'Verification Mission' under the direction of the OSCE (Organization for Security and Cooperation in Europe). His frequent return visits to Belgrade during these negotiations, and the equally frequent postponements of threatened air strikes, had served merely to illustrate the weakness of the Western negotiating position. The fundamental problem was the West's commitment to autonomy as the maximum that the Kosovo Albanians could be allowed. For Western governments to threaten the military destruction of Serbian forces in Kosovo, while proclaiming that the long-term aim of any such action was to return Kosovo to Serbian rule, was patently illogical: Milošević seems to have recognized this, and therefore to have supposed that whatever pledges he made could later be broken with virtual impunity. Indeed, his willingness to scale down his operations in Kosovo probably reflected nothing more than the fact that his campaign was drawing to a close anyway as the winter approached.

The next two months did see a major reduction in the fighting. Many Serb units were withdrawn at the end of October, and thousands of Albanians were able to return to the burnt-out shells of their homes (which, in some cases, were found to have been booby-trapped with grenades by the Serb forces as they left). The Verification Mission began to operate, though the number of 'Verifiers' fell far below the total of 1,800 agreed in October: there were only 600 of them in Kosovo by the end of the year. During the last week of December, however, the Serb military forces launched a new offensive against KLA positions near the north-eastern town of Podujevo; the battle group used in this attack then remained in place, in further breach of the October agreement, and during the next few weeks an additional force of 15,000 Serbian troops was assembled at staging-posts just outside the Kosovan border. Western monitors concluded that the Serbs were preparing for a new spring offensive against the KLA – which, for its part, had also been re-arming and training since October. However, other evidence suggested that the Serbian authorities were preparing a campaign of destruction and expulsion against the local Albanian population that would be even more far-reaching than the scorched earth policy of the previous summer: in January and February, for example, it was reported that they were seizing official documents and land-ownership registers from Albanian villages, and removing Serbian Orthodox icons and artefacts from museums in Kosovo for 'safe keeping' in Belgrade.

In mid-January 1999 Western diplomacy was jolted once more into action. The immediate cause was not the Serb military build-up, but the discovery of a massacre at the village of Raçak, where forty-five Albanian civilians, including children, had been murdered. Most had been shot in the head at close range with a single bullet, and some of the bodies had been mutilated. When the head of the Verification Mission publicly condemned the Serb forces for this atrocity, the Belgrade authorities demanded his removal; they also refused entry to the chief prosecutor of the International War Crimes Tribunal. Two weeks later the six-nation Contact Group announced that it was summoning the Serbian and Albanian leaderships to a conference at Rambouillet, near

Paris, on 6 February, at which they would be required to agree a negotiated settlement on the political future of Kosovo.

The basis for this negotiation was a proposal which had already been in circulation for many months: known as the 'Hill plan', after the US Ambassador to Macedonia, Christopher Hill (who had been trying to negotiate with the Serbian and Kosovo Albanian sides throughout the previous year), it consisted of a detailed set of constitutional arrangements for an autonomous Kosovo. These included an elected Assembly, a President and a Constitutional Court. In some respects this plan restored elements of the autonomy enjoyed by Kosovo before 1989; but at the same time it introduced new principles which would significantly weaken the power of the Kosovo government. The people of Kosovo were to be divided into so-called 'national communities', which would hold quotas of official posts and would have the power to block any measures in the Assembly that they deemed contrary to their national interests. Also, many governmental powers were to be transferred to the level of the local communes; in 1989 only one out of the twenty-two communes of Kosovo had had a Serb majority, but a subsequent gerrymandering of communal boundaries by the Serbian authorities had created several more, which would now be given substantial powers in areas such as policing. During the second half of 1998 the Albanian politicians had objected to many aspects of this plan; and the Serbian authorities had, in any case, remained hostile to the whole idea of restoring Kosovo's autonomy.

The most important feature of this proposal, however, was its status as a so-called 'Interim Agreement'. In the original versions of the Hill plan, a final clause declared that the agreement would be reconsidered in three years' time; but the phrasing clearly implied that this would be only an 'implementation review', not a re-thinking of the fundamental question of Kosovo's status. The Albanians would not accept this, as it appeared permanently to rule out any further move towards independence. In the version of the plan discussed at Rambouillet in February, this clause was significantly revised: 'Three years after the entry into force of this Agreement, an international meeting shall be convened to determine a mechanism for a final settlement for Kosovo, on the basis of the will of the people . . .' But the Albanians hesitated to accept this as a promise of eventual independence, given that the stated policy of all the Western powers was still set firmly against the independence option. The political representatives of the KLA were also opposed to another key provision of the Rambouillet proposals, the complete disarming of their forces. The Belgrade authorities, for their part, objected to the demand that they withdraw all their troops from Kosovo (with the exception of a small number of border guards); but most of all they opposed the demand of the Western powers that a peace-keeping force of NATO troops be stationed inside Kosovo to police the agreement.

After two weeks of inconclusive negotiation, the Albanian representatives at Rambouillet reluctantly announced their 'conditional' acceptance – the condition being that they needed more time to discuss the proposals with various political and military leaders inside Kosovo. In mid-March the peace talks resumed in France, and on the 18th of that month the Albanians finally signed the agreement. The Yugoslav delegation, on the other hand, boycotted the ceremony and declared its continuing opposition to the plan.

Within Kosovo, meanwhile, the build-up of Serbian military forces had intensified throughout February and early March. New army units and large numbers of tanks had been brought into the province; paramilitary forces controlled by the gangster-politician 'Arkan' were established at a site near the northern Kosovo town of Mitrovica, together with other groups known for their work as 'ethnic cleansers'. Milošević had installed one of his most loyal army commanders, General Nebojša Pavković (a relative by marriage), to direct these forces, and Pavković had immediately begun to integrate his army units with the local special police forces, a move which clearly indicated that something other than a normal military operation was being planned. By 20 March, when the international 'Verification Mission' withdrew from Kosovo, there were more than 26,000 Serbian troops inside the province and another 15,000 stationed just beyond its eastern border. According to some reports, their deployment was in accordance with a strategic plan known as 'Operation Horseshoe', aimed at 'solving' the Kosovo problem. The nature of the plan was not known in detail, but the code-name itself indicated the principle on which it would work: a controlled near-encirclement, designed to force people inside the 'horseshoe' to exit in one particular direction. 'Exit', in this case, would turn out to mean leaving Kosovo altogether, and the aim of the Serbian policy was to ensure that they would never come back.

On 24 March 1999, after the failure of one more attempt at negotiation by Holbrooke and a final rejection of the Rambouillet proposals by the Serbian parliament, NATO forces began their campaign of air strikes against strategic targets inside Yugoslavia. In effect – *de facto* but not *de jure* – the NATO alliance was now at war with Milošević's state. It seemed a classic example of how nations can stumble into war. Milošević, fortified by the knowledge that the Western alliance was still committed to keeping Kosovo as an integral part of Serbia, apparently assumed either that the NATO threats were an outright bluff, or that they would amount, in the event, to no more than a few days of symbolic air strikes. The NATO governments, conversely, seem to have thought that Milošević himself was bluffing, and that a brief period of bombing would force him to climb down – or perhaps even give him a secretly welcome excuse for compliance with their demands. They were not planning a long war: had they done so, they would not have announced, at the outset, that they had no intention of deploying ground forces. Indeed, it would have been hard to get the nineteen-member military alliance to agree to any long-term military commitment at this stage; consensus on the need for immediate air strikes was the most that could be achieved. Although the justification for this action in international law was reasonably clear – on the basis of customary principles of humanitarian law, which permit intervention in cases of extreme humanitarian necessity – some NATO governments were unhappy about the lack of an explicit authorization by the UN Security Council. If Milošević had halted all anti-Albanian actions in Kosovo when the first bombs were dropped, and if he had then concentrated on opening up diplomatic divisions among the Western allies, it is conceivable that NATO's political will might have been dissipated within a week or two. Instead, he decided on a very different policy. It must be hoped, in the interests not only of the Kosovo Albanians but also of the entire civilized world, that this decision will turn out to have been the biggest mistake of his political career.

During the first few days of the air-strike campaign, while NATO confined itself to the use of cruise missiles and high-altitude bombing, the Serbian forces inside Kosovo embarked on a massive campaign of destruction, burning down houses and using tanks and artillery to reduce entire villages to rubble. At first their actions were concentrated in three areas: in the north-eastern corner of Kosovo (securing a wide corridor for the introduction of more forces into the province), in the Drenica region (where the KLA had its main strongholds), and in a broad stretch of south-western Kosovo, near the Albanian border. The significance of this third target soon became obvious: the strategy was to clear a path for the mass expulsion of the Kosovo Albanian population. Two days after the air strikes began, the first waves of deported people began flooding over the southern borders of Kosovo, into Albania and Macedonia. Most had similar stories to tell, of a coordinated operation of 'ethnic cleansing' on a hitherto unprecedented scale. Armed men had arrived at their houses – sometimes special police, sometimes paramilitary gangsters, in many cases accompanied by local Serbs – and had ordered them to leave within minutes. An atmosphere of terror was created by random killings of civilians in the streets; some houses were set on fire as the population was leaving, and the rest would be first looted and then demolished when they had gone. As they left the village they would be funnelled through a cordon of troops, who would rob them of their money and possessions. Finally they would be told which route to take to the border. In many cases, however, not all the inhabitants were allowed to leave: in a development chillingly reminiscent of the seizure of Srebrenica in 1995, men were separated from their families and taken away by Serb forces. By the third week of April the US government was reporting that it had satellite images of many newly dug mass graves; the American diplomat with special responsibility for war crimes issues, David Scheffer, calculated that up to 100,000 men were unaccounted for. Some of these, no doubt, had managed to flee to the hills, where pockets of heavily outgunned KLA fighters were putting up a limited resistance.

The scale of this cleansing operation, and the coordination it displayed between Serbian military and police forces, indicated a high degree of planning. This was clearly not a spontaneous response to the NATO bombardment – though the air strikes may well have given Milošević a welcome opportunity to accelerate and extend the actions he had already planned. The main way in which this campaign of expulsion went beyond the ethnic cleansing of the previous year was in its application to the major towns: the inhabitants of cities such as Prishtina and Mitrovica, whose lives had been largely untouched by the 1998 campaign, were now subjected to the same methods of intimidation and deportation. Thousands of people were forced to board trains at Prishtina, which then took them to the Macedonian border; they were packed so tightly into the waggons that several elderly people died during the journey. By 20 April 1999 it was calculated that nearly 600,000 refugees had left Kosovo in the previous four weeks: 355,000 were in Albania, 127,500 in Macedonia, 72,500 in Montenegro and 32,000 in Bosnia. This was in addition to an estimated 100,000 who had left during 1998. And inside Kosovo, according to NATO spokesmen, there were five large pockets of 'displaced' Albanians, representing a total of 850,000 people.

One especially sinister aspect of the deportation campaign was the confiscation of passports and identity papers; it was reported that municipal registers of births and deaths, and of land ownership, were also being destroyed, and refugees who were allowed to leave the country in cars or tractors were ordered to remove their registration plates before crossing the border. The thinking behind this policy emerged when, after the first week of the NATO campaign, the Russian Prime Minister Yevgeni Primakov obtained a 'peace proposal' from Milošević: this included an offer to allow refugees to return to Kosovo, 'so long as they are Yugoslav citizens'. The idea, clearly, was to eliminate any proof of such citizenship, and then deny these 'non-citizens' re-entry. Serb nationalist propaganda claimed that hundreds of thousands of Albanians had crossed into Kosovo from Albania during and after the Second World War (see pages 313 and 352 of this book); the claim was baseless, but the physical evidence was now being adjusted to fit it. In practical terms, this meant that Milošević was preparing a fallback position: even if he were eventually forced to accept the return of the Kosovars, he would limit their numbers to whatever total he found acceptable. In the last week of April, diplomatic sources in Belgrade reported that Serbian officials were now magnanimously saying that they could 'manage' a population of 600,000 Albanians in Kosovo – less than one third of the previous population.

What those Serbian officials failed to appreciate was that the very nature of the campaign they had launched against the Kosovar population had radically transformed the resolve of the Western powers, making them much less willing to compromise with Milošević and much more determined to break his military machine. The aim of their action, they announced, was to make Milošević withdraw all his forces from Kosovo and permit the return of all refugees. The air campaign continued without pause, and the definition of strategic targets was enlarged to include oil refineries, factories, television transmitters and even Milošević's house in Belgrade. Public opinion in the major NATO countries, shocked by television pictures of hundreds of thousands of destitute refugees, moved firmly behind the bombing campaign; polls suggested that in the USA more than 50 per cent were in favour of sending in NATO ground troops, and the figure was above 60 per cent in both Britain and France. Officially, the governments of those countries remained strongly opposed to such a move; but all military commentators agreed that the conflict could not be decided by air power alone. Given that the Western governments were also reluctant – for reasons that were less clearly explained – to supply arms to the KLA inside Kosovo, it seemed that there was a gap between the announced ends of the NATO campaign, which were absolute, and the apparent means, which were uncertain.

One other (and greater) uncertainty concerned the ultimate political aims of the NATO action. At the outset, the stated purpose had been to force Milošević to accept the terms of the Rambouillet accord – a document which, though it restored some degree of autonomy to Kosovo, still affirmed that it was an integral part of Yugoslavia. Once Milošević had launched his terror campaign against the entire Albanian population, it became abundantly clear that the Rambouillet plan was dead: the Albanians would never return to Kosovo on such terms. Western politicians still shied away, however, from the obvious conclusion, which was that only independence would work. The most commonly stated reason for this reluctance was the claim that granting independence to Kosovo would set a dangerous new precedent: it was argued that if one country's borders were redrawn to reflect ethnic realities, other countries might be forced to do the same. Many states with ethnic minority areas within their borders feared the consequences of such a policy.

This whole argument rested on a misunderstanding of the nature of Kosovo's claim. Independence for Kosovo would involve not setting a new precedent, but following an old one – the precedent of Slovenia, Croatia, Macedonia and Bosnia, which gained their independence in

1991–2. In legal terms (according to the Badinter Commission, a committee of experts advising the European Union at that time), what happened when those states became independent was not secession, not the breaking away of a few branches from a continuing trunk; rather, it was the dissolution of the entire Yugoslav Federation into its constituent units. (The post-1992 self-styled Yugoslavia, often wrongly described as 'rump Yugoslavia', is not the continuation of the old Yugoslavia but a new state, formed by the coming together of two ex-Yugoslav units, Serbia and Montenegro.) Unfortunately, the Badinter Commission had never specified which entities were the constituent units of the old Yugoslavia, and Western governments had simply made a policy decision to regard only the six republics as such – thus treating Kosovo as a wholly owned subsidiary of Serbia. Possibly they were influenced by the fact that, by the time Yugoslavia broke up, Kosovo's autonomous status had already been revoked by Milošević; but this was an act of dubious legality, pushed through the Kosovo Assembly under blatant duress. Kosovo had in fact been a unit of the federal system, with virtually all the powers of a republic and with its own direct representation on federal bodies. When the entire federation dissolved, therefore, Kosovo should also have been offered the right to independence. An independent Kosovo would thus set no new precedent. Its claim would be based on constitutional principles, not ethnic geography, and other countries would become liable to the application of this precedent only if they were federal states in a process of complete dissolution – an extremely rare event in modern history.

Not understanding these facts, some Western politicians and commentators advocated a so-called compromise solution, in which Kosovo would be partitioned: Serbia would acquire the northern part, including the buildings of the Serbian Orthodox Patriarchate at Peć and various other monasteries, while the Kosovo Albanians would be compressed into the southern half of the territory. An element of polite fiction was built into these proposals: the reality was that Milošević's interest in northern Kosovo was not monastic but economic, concerned above all with the mines and power stations of the Trepça district. Partition in this case would not even have an ethnographic basis to it: the northern half of Kosovo is (or was) just as much an Albanian-majority area as the southern half. Those politicians who warn about setting dangerous new precedents should indeed regard these partition proposals with extreme suspicion: the precedent set by such a policy would be that acts of ethnic cleansing and mass terror, if they are sufficiently severe, will be rewarded with at least a portion of the territory so cleansed.

The minimum requirement of Western policy is the safe return of Kosovar refugees to their homes in every part of Kosovo – something that would not be possible if any portion of Kosovo's territory remained under the rule of Belgrade. A simple but fundamental principle is at stake here: the principle that a policy of mass terror against a civilian population should not be rewarded. I believe that the upholding of this principle is something the world owes, not only to the 1,800,000 Kosovars, but also to itself and to future generations.

28 April 1999

Introduction

'THE YUGOSLAV CRISIS began in Kosovo, and it will end in Kosovo.'
One can hear this saying repeated almost anywhere in the former
Yugoslavia; it is one of the few things on which all parties to the conflicts
of the 1990s seem to agree. No one knows how the story will end in
Kosovo. Possible final destinations include autonomy, partition and
independence, and the means of arriving at them range from peaceful
negotiation or international imposition to civil disobedience, violent
intifada and full-scale war. But all parties can agree that the issue of
Kosovo is, quite simply, the most intractable of all the political conflicts
in the Balkans. It is arguably the area with the worst human rights abuses
in the whole of Europe, and certainly the place where, if war does break
out, the killing and destruction will be more intense than anything
hitherto witnessed in the region.

In the West, the popular view of the recent wars in Croatia and
Bosnia was always that these were 'ethnic conflicts', created by the
bubbling up of obscure but virulent ethnic hatreds among the local
populations. This whole approach to the subject was essentially false: it
ignored the primary role of politicians (above all, the Serbian nationalist–Communist Slobodan Milošević) in creating conflict at the political
level, and indeed it ignored the fact that the wars themselves were
launched not by ordinary civilians but by armed forces directed from
above. As a characterization of the history of those regions, talk about
'ancient ethnic hatreds' was in any case grossly misleading: there had
never been ethnic wars in the 'ancient' history of Bosnia or Croatia, and
the only conflicts with a partly ethnic character to them were modern
ones, produced under very special geopolitical conditions (above all, the
Second World War). Some elements of prejudice, linked in some cases

to religious issues and in others to memories of the Second World War, did of course exist. But between low-level prejudices on the one hand and military conflict, concentration camps and mass murder on the other, there lies a very long road: it was the political leaders who propelled the people down that road, and not vice-versa.

Does the same apply to the conflict between Serbs and Albanians in Kosovo? At first sight, this looks much more like a genuine 'ethnic' conflict. The basic division is, in the first place, an ethnic one in the full sense: unlike the different types of Bosnian, who are all Slavs and all speak the same language, the Serbs and the Albanians are linguistically quite separate. Together with the differentiation in language goes a range of other cultural differences, many of them linked to religion: the division between Serb and Albanian roughly coincides with the division between Eastern Orthodox and Muslim. (The exceptions are the small minority of Catholic Albanians, and the Muslim Slavs, who more or less identify with the Bosniacs or Bosnian Muslims.) With both language and religion setting people apart, all the conditions seem to be present for a primary conflict of peoples.

And yet, once we begin to examine both the present political situation and the nature of Kosovo's past, the idea of ethnic or religious hatred welling up from the depths of popular psychology starts to seem less convincing. The Albanians of Kosovo today are in many ways a politically mobilized people, but religion has played almost no role at all in that mobilization. There is no Islamic political movement among the Albanians. Some tensions apparently exist (largely hidden from public view) between Albanian Catholics and Albanian Muslims, yet whatever tensions there may be are not strong enough to inhibit either neighbourly good relations or political cooperation. Where religion is a factor in the present political situation is on the Orthodox side, which constantly employs religious rhetoric to justify the defence of 'sacred' Serbian interests; but this is a classic example of religion being mobilized and manipulated for ideological purposes. If we look further back into Kosovo's past, we can find many examples of mixed religious life involving the Orthodox as well as the Catholics with the Muslims: the syncretistic practices of folk religion, for example, or the tradition of Muslim Albanian 'guardians' of Orthodox religious sites. There were also, on the other hand, many cases of oppression and discrimination against both of the Christian Churches by Muslim Albanian lords and their followers. Religious prejudice was part of the pattern here, but the pattern itself was largely a socio-political one, involving the exercise and abuse of local political power for the sake of financial gain.

As for the supposedly long history of ethnic conflict, this too is a claim that needs to be heavily qualified. There have been many battles and wars in Kosovo over the centuries, but until the last 100 years or so none of them had the character of an 'ethnic' conflict between Albanians and Serbs. Members of those two populations fought together as allies at the battle of Kosovo in 1389 – indeed, they probably fought as allies on both sides of that battle, some of them under Prince Lazar and others under the Ottoman Sultan. Three hundred years later, when an Austrian army invaded Kosovo, both Serbs and Albanians (including even Muslim ones) rose up in sympathy to throw off Ottoman rule: as we shall see, modern historians have had great difficulty trying to distinguish between Serbs and Albanians when analysing the contemporary reports of these events. A later rebellion in support of another Austrian invasion in 1737 also involved a mixed Albanian–Slav group from the mountain areas of northern Albania and Montenegro: the Slav and Albanian mountain clans there had long traditions of cooperation and intermarriage, and, in some cases, legends of common ancestry. And over many centuries in Kosovo the ethnic divisions between Serbs and Albanians were never entirely clear-cut. There was ethnic–linguistic assimilation in both directions; and enough of a shared way of life was established for the Serbian colonists who arrived in Kosovo in the 1920s to feel that the long-established local Serbs were almost as foreign to them in some of their practices as the 'alien' Albanians.

None of this is meant to imply that Kosovo was always a wonderland of mutual tolerance. Conditions for much of its history were far from utopian. Much blame must lie with the rapacious local Albanian lords of the eighteenth and early nineteenth centuries, to whom the property of Christian peasants represented particularly easy pickings. But this sort of exploitation, as already suggested, was not driven primarily by motives derived from religion or ethnicity. Muslim Albanian peasants also suffered grievously. What really turned the division between Orthodox Serbs and Muslim Albanians into a more general and systematic conflict was the politicization of the issue in the nineteenth century, which arose during the growth and expansion of the Slav Christian states in the Balkans.

It was nineteenth-century Serbian ideology that created a cult of the medieval battle of Kosovo as some sort of nationally-defining historical and spiritual event. It was the political role played by protector-powers such as Russia, with their consuls in Prishtina or Mitrovica, that helped to create a new atmosphere of suspicion and hostility on the part of the local Albanians; Ottoman policy in the Crimean War, and the later transplanting of fiercely anti-Russian (and generally anti-Orthodox) Circassians into Kosovo also played an important part in souring Albanian–Serb relations. It was the mass-expulsion of Albanians and other Muslims from the areas conquered by Serbia and Montenegro in 1877–8 that persuaded the Albanians in Kosovo that Serbia – and the Serbs of Kosovo who were claimed as an 'unredeemed' part of the Serbian population – represented a threat to their existence. And, above all, it was the policies imposed from above by the Serbian and Montenegrin governments from the first moment of their conquest of Kosovo in 1912 that created systematic hostility and hatred on a scale that the region had never seen before.

From the Albanian point of view, the experience of that imposition of Serbian–Montenegrin rule (and its reimposition as Yugoslav rule in 1918) was similar to that of many other peoples conquered and colonized by European Christian powers – the Algerians under the French, for example, or the Central Asians (or Chechens) under the Russians. Many aspects of this period of Kosovo's history match just such a 'colonialist' model. There was even, for example, an explicit programme of introducing Serb 'colonists' to Kosovo throughout the inter-war period.

From the Serbian point of view, however, what happened in 1912 was to be understood according to a very different pattern of ideas: it was the ultimate example of a war of liberation to release a captive population (the Serbs of Kosovo) from an alien imperial power (the Turks). And of course there was a real difference between the case of Kosovo and the case of a territory such as Algeria: in the latter example, there was no continuous history of a French population in Algeria going all the way back to a medieval French kingdom there. The trouble with Kosovo, however, was that both of these conflicting conceptual models – the colonialist one, which made sense to the Albanians, and the liberationist one, which made sense to the Serbs – were simultaneously true. The truth as experienced by the Albanians could be described as the more important of the two truths, on the simple grounds that Albanians made up the absolute majority of the population of Kosovo at the time of its conquest. But to reduce the Serb version to a secondary status could not be the same as denying it altogether.

At the time, the Serbian government made great efforts to bolster its case and turn it into the dominant interpretation. A memorandum sent to the Great Powers by Belgrade in early 1913 set out three justifications for Serbian rule in Kosovo: the 'moral right of a more civilized people'; the historic right to an area which contained the Patriarchate buildings of the Serbian Orthodox Church and had once been part of the medieval Serbian empire; and a kind of ethnographic right based on the fact that at some time in the past Kosovo had had a majority Serb population – a right which, according to the memorandum, was unaffected by the 'recent invasion' of Albanians.[1]

Of these three lines of argument, the first was rapidly devalued by the actual behaviour of the Serbian (and, subsequently, Yugoslav) régime in Kosovo. The second was in two parts, one relating to the Serbian Orthodox Church, the other more generally to the medieval empire. Claims are still made today that Kosovo is the 'Jerusalem' of the Serbs; but this has always been something of an exaggeration. In no form of Christianity, including Eastern Orthodoxy, does a 'holy place' play any sort of theological role equivalent to the role of Jerusalem in the theology of Judaism. The seat of the Serbian Orthodox Church was not founded in Kosovo; it merely moved there after its original foundation (in central Serbia) was burnt down. Nor does the Patriarchate have any continuous history as an institution: it was re-created by the modern Yugoslav state in 1920 (having been defunct for 154 years), and since that date the Patriarch has tended to reside mainly in Belgrade. As for the Serbian empire, this was a medieval state which had its origins not in Kosovo but in Rascia, an area beyond Kosovo's north-western border, and most of the important early medieval Serbian monasteries and churches were built outside Kosovo itself. But in any case, the main objection here must be that it makes no sense to base claims of modern political ownership on the geography of long-gone kingdoms or empires. This objection is a simple point, but one which people in the Balkans sometimes find it convenient to ignore. Edith Durham, who knew the region well and witnessed the effects of the Serb–Montenegrin conquest of Kosovo in 1912, later recalled a characteristic exchange: 'I once pointed out to a Serb schoolmaster that we had held Calais at the same time but that did not give us the right to it. He replied: "Why not? You have a fleet." '[2]

Of the three arguments in the Serbian memorandum cited above, the third, about ethnography, is the one that has most bedevilled all historical writing about Kosovo. Looking at some historical works from the region itself, one might almost think that ethnic demography was the only real subject-matter of Kosovo's history. (The present book, it is hoped, will give a different impression.) Some modern Albanian writers argue, quite implausibly, that there was always an Albanian majority in Kosovo, even in the medieval Serbian kingdom; many Serbs believe, equally falsely, that there were no Albanians at all in Kosovo before the end of the seventeenth century. One historical–demographic myth which enjoyed great power in the late nineteenth century was the idea that most of the Albanians in Kosovo were 'really' Slavs; while it is true that ethnic identities have always been fluid to some extent, this claim is simply not justified by the historical evidence. Another myth has grown up around the 'Great Migration' of the Serbs in 1690 which, it is alleged, created a demographic vacuum, subsequently filled by a flood of alien Albanians from outside Kosovo. A closer study of the evidence, presented in this book, will suggest that although there were heavy war losses in 1690, affecting all categories of population, most aspects of the 'Great Migration' story are fanciful. And the evidence also suggests that, while there was a steady flow of Albanians from northern Albania into Kosovo, a major component of the Albanians' demographic growth there was the expansion of an indigenous Albanian population within Kosovo itself.

It is not the purpose of this book to present a case for or against any particular solution to the Kosovo crisis. Some form of self-government for the Albanians there seems, to almost all outside observers, both necessary and right; but there are various different forms that might be attempted. It may be useful, however, merely to point out that the acceptance or rejection of possible solutions for Kosovo will involve different considerations from the ones which have applied to the Bosnian case. Bosnia was a historic unity, a geopolitical entity which had enjoyed an almost continuous history as such (as a unit within Ottoman, Austro-

Hungarian and Yugoslav states) since the Middle Ages. Kosovo is not such a historic unity: there was a vilayet of Prizren from 1868 and a vilayet of Kosovo from 1877 onwards, but those vilayets had a very different shape on the map from modern Kosovo, and before that period Kosovo was divided among several Ottoman administrative units. (These facts have sometimes been grossly misrepresented by Albanian spokesmen: in the memorandum submitted by the Kosovar delegation to the International Conference on the former Yugoslavia in September 1992, for example, it was stated that Kosovo 'has been an autonomous entity since ancient times'.)

On the other hand, Serbia does not have a continuous history either. For several hundred years, Kosovo was not part of Serbia, because there was no Serbia to be part of: during most of the long Ottoman period, Serbia did not exist as an entity at all. Kosovo was annexed *de facto* by Serbia within living memory, in 1912; *de jure*, as is explained in this book, it was not annexed by the Serbian kingdom at all. In modern historical terms, the relation between Kosovo and the rest of Serbia is less close or organic than the relation between any part of Bosnia and the rest of Bosnia. Objections on grounds of historical identity to the partitioning of Bosnia, in other words, need not entail any equivalent objections to the dividing of Kosovo from Serbia.

In terms of ethnic geography, again, the case of Bosnia is very different from that of Kosovo. The three constituent peoples of Bosnia lived mixed together, creating a jumbled ethnic–religious patchwork; in many areas there was no absolute majority group at all. The argument against any division of Bosnia was therefore both practical and moral – practical because there were no clear lines for it on the map, and moral because the only way of creating such lines was to engage in 'ethnic cleansing' and other human rights abuses on a massive scale. Kosovo, on the other hand, offers what by any Balkan standards can be described as a compact mass of ethnically homogeneous people. Of course ethnic homogeneity in itself is neither a necessary nor a sufficient condition for statehood; but it has in fact been treated as at least a natural starting-point for the creation of many modern states, both large and small. Those Serbian politicians who have defended the right of Bosnian or Croatian Serbs to carve out new, artificially homogenized ethnic areas for themselves are especially ill-placed to argue against the claims of the

Albanians, who already constitute roughly 90 per cent of Kosovo's population.

In this Introduction I have concentrated on the present-day Kosovo crisis, and on the historical and pseudo-historical arguments that surround it. I recognize that most readers who already take some interest in Kosovo will have that political crisis constantly in mind when they study Kosovo's history today. And in one sense, of course, a history of Kosovo has to be defined by questions projected back into the past from the political conditions of the late twentieth century, for the simple reason that the precise politico-geographical borders of Kosovo – which form the basic territorial unit of discussion throughout this book – were created for the first time in 1945.

There is indeed something rather artificial about writing the history of a unit of territory, as a unit, when its defining borders have been a political reality only for the last few decades of that history. But the enterprise is not as perverse as it may sound: there are histories of eighteenth-century Italy, although there was no country called Italy at that time; there are histories of Bulgaria which go back many centuries; and there are histories of Greece down the ages, even though the modern borders of Greece were finalized only in 1947. Kosovo does in fact have quite a strong geographical identity, as I have tried to describe in the first chapter of this book. But in any case I have not stuck rigidly to the present-day borders while exploring my more general field of interest in this book; it is not possible to talk about the history of Kosovo without discussing also the Sandžak of Novi Pazar, the upper Morava valley, the Skopje and Debar regions of Macedonia and, above all, the mountains of northern Albania. These areas too are briefly described in the opening chapter; readers unfamiliar with the geography are urged to spend a few moments locating these surrounding places on the map, as such knowledge will provide a useful aid to navigation in what follows.

Even if there were no crisis in present-day Kosovo, however, I still believe that the history of the area would deserve to be written for a whole host of reasons. It is one of the cultural crossing-places of Europe; it was probably central both to the survival of the Albanian language and to the development of the Romanian one; it became the geographical heart of an important medieval kingdom; it was one of the most characteristic parts of the Ottoman Empire in Europe; and it was the area in which the modern Albanian national movement was born, and had its greatest successes and failures.

Many of these aspects of Kosovo's history have also been widely misrepresented, thanks to the national or ideological preconceptions of modern historians. Arguments about the 'ethnogenesis' of the Albanians or the Romanians are notoriously subject to such distortions. The portrayal of the Albanian national movement of the late nineteenth century has also been skewed by modern ideological concerns. And for generations the historians of almost every Balkan country have been basing their accounts of the Ottoman period on some very dubious assumptions, drawn originally from the nationalist historiography of the nineteenth century and adapted to the requirements of Marxist theory – assumptions about the automatically tyrannical nature of Ottoman 'feudal' rule and the equally automatic striving of all subject peoples for 'national liberation'. On the other hand, even historians who have kept broadly within these patterns of thought have been able to do valuable new research on many aspects of Ottoman life: even Communist Albania, with all its restrictions on intellectual life, produced important works of scholarship, such as Zija Shkodra's account of the Ottoman guild system or Petrika Thëngjilli's study of Ottoman taxation, which I have made use of in this book, and which certainly deserve much wider recognition.

At the same time, however, a new wave of important studies relating to the Ottoman Balkans, mainly by Turkish or non-Balkan historians (such as Fikret Adanır and Machiel Kiel), have been completely revising many of the commonest assumptions about how the Ottoman system functioned. I hope that the use I have made of these works will add some further interest to this book; I believe that nowhere in the study of European history are more important or more rapid advances in knowledge being made today than in the study of the Ottoman Empire in Europe. Kosovo is, in many ways, an Ottoman territory *par excellence*; the city of Prizren, where until recently all the street-names were given in Turkish as well as Albanian and Serbian, has always seemed to me one of the most fascinatingly Ottoman places left in the world. It is particularly sad that the rediscovery and re-evaluation of much Ottoman reality by historians should be taking place at the same time as an increasingly virulent rejection and caricaturing of the Ottoman past by the spokesmen of Serbian nationalism, who have encouraged the wholesale destruction of Ottoman monuments in Bosnia. The Ottoman heritage, including the heritage of Islam, is something that belongs to the culture of all the people of the Balkans; to reject it as 'alien', after so many centuries, is as historically absurd as it would be for Irish writers to reject the English language as alien, or South American peasants to reject Catholic Christianity. The same Serbian nationalists who revile the Ottoman heritage have also tried to portray the Albanians of Kosovo as 'aliens'. Kosovo's Muslim Albanian population does indeed bear the imprint of its long centuries of Ottoman acculturation; it merely emphasizes the point I am making to observe that the Albanians are, at the same time, one of the oldest-established populations in Europe. No people could be less 'alien' to the history of the Balkans. And no understanding of Balkan history can be complete without a knowledge of the history of the Albanians, as well as the Serbs, of Kosovo.

1

Orientation: places, names and peoples

A JOURNALISTIC CLICHÉ of the nineteenth century described the Kosovo region as the lost heart of the Balkans. Like many clichés, this one was both slightly foolish and, at the same time, suggestive of a significant truth. Although Kosovo has played a central role in Balkan history, it has remained, during much of that history, mysterious and little known to outsiders. Western knowledge of the whole central Balkan area was confined to the major through-routes until surprisingly recently: European maps of this area contained gross inaccuracies well into the late nineteenth century.[1] Yet it was not only Westerners who knew little of this area. According to a Bulgarian geographer who visited Kosovo during the First World War, parts of the Kosovo region had been, until just a few years previously, 'almost as unknown and inaccessible as a stretch of land in Central Africa'.[2] Political factors are the main reason for the inaccessibility of Kosovo during the last period of Ottoman rule, which was marked by chronic disorder, violent rebellion and even more violent repression. But simple physical geography also matters, helping as it does to explain both the seclusion of the area and, at the same time, its near-central importance.

The present borders of Kosovo – that is, of the 'Autonomous Province' of the post-1945 Yugoslav constitutions – are of course the products of political history. At the same time, they correspond more or less to a physical fact. Kosovo forms a geographical unit because it is ringed by ranges of mountains and hills. The most dramatic of these is the range of the Šar mountains (Alb.: Sharr) which runs eastwards out of the mountain complex of northern Albania and forms much of Kosovo's southern border. Its highest peaks are over 2,500 metres (nearly 8,000 feet), some of them crowned with permanent snow; the high pastures, green and Alpine, are places of breathtaking beauty, grazed in the summer by herds of semi-wild horses, which veer off from the approaching traveller like flocks of starlings on the wing. On the western side of Kosovo, running northwards from the Albanian massif into Montenegro, is another range, the 'Accursed Mountains' (Srb.: Prokletije; Alb.: Bjeshkët e Nemura), so called because of their fierce impenetrability: rivers have sliced through their dry limestone like wires through cheese, creating a network of vertiginous gorges. The borders of Kosovo continue (still moving clockwise) along another mountain range until, at their northernmost extension, they cross a different massif: the Kopaonik range, which pushes down into Kosovo from the highlands of central Serbia. On the eastern side of Kosovo the circuit of mountains softens, with a string of summits less than half the height of those of the south and west, until we come back, in the south-eastern corner of Kosovo, to the easternmost extension of the Šar mountains – a range of hills known as the Skopska Crna Gora (Alb.: Karadak, from the Turkish for 'Black Mountain'; this is also the meaning of Srb. 'Crna Gora').[3]

Within this ring of peaks and hills, the interior of Kosovo is raised up, its plains qualifying as plateaux, 1,200 feet or more above sea level. Some idea of the elevation, and the near-central position of Kosovo in this Balkan region, can be gained from the curious fact that rivers run out of Kosovo into each of the three coastlines of the Balkans: the Aegean, the Black Sea and the Adriatic.[4] One, the Lepenac, runs south through the Kaçanik (Srb.: Kačanik) gorge into Macedonia, where it joins the broad river Vardar on its slow journey to the Greek coast near Salonica. Another, the Ibar, flows northwards out of the eastern half of Kosovo and passes through central Serbia into the river Morava, which joins the Danube near Belgrade. The valley of the Morava is the main south–north axis of Serbia, and its most important head-waters, near the Serbian–Macedonian border, are streams which flow out of the south-eastern corner of Kosovo. Finally, on Kosovo's western flank, there is a river whose name recurs constantly in the history of the region: the Drin (Srb.: Drim). This is the river which flows westwards through the mountainous territory of northern Albania, entering the Adriatic a little way past the city of Shkodra (Srb.: Skadar; Itl.: Scutari). At a point just inside Albania, 10 miles west of the border with Kosovo, two contributary rivers join to create the united Drin: one, the White Drin, has flowed southwards through the western half of Kosovo, while the other, the Black Drin, has never quite touched Kosovo territory, flowing northwards from Lake Ohrid, first through Macedonia, then through Albania itself.

Running from north to south through the middle of Kosovo is a lesser range of hills which divides the whole territory into two roughly equal halves: streams running off the eastern side of these hills will flow into the Ibar and the Danube, while the western side sends its waters to the White Drin and the Adriatic. The two halves of Kosovo have their own traditional names, which for various reasons, political and geographical, have been sources of both friction and confusion. The western half of Kosovo is known to Serbs as the Metohija. This is derived from *metochia*, a Byzantine Greek word for monastic estates, and reflects the fact that many Orthodox monasteries were granted rich endowments here (farmland, orchards and famously fine vineyards) by medieval Serb rulers. Kosovo Albanians, on the other hand, resent the use of this name, since it seems to imply that the identity of the territory itself is bound up with Serbian Orthodox land-ownership. Their own name for this part of Kosovo is Rrafsh i Dukagjinit, the 'Dukagjin plateau' – Dukagjin being a medieval Albanian ruling family which also gave its name to a broad swathe of territory in northern Albania.

Where Kosovo's eastern half is concerned, confusion arises because this sub-division of Kosovo is itself known simply as 'Kosovo'. (Historically, the confusion happened the other way around: it is this area which gave its name to the entire territory, rather in the way that Holland, one of the component territories of the Netherlands, has become a commonly used name for the whole country too.) Thus the official name for the administrative unit of Kosovo during most of the Titoist period was 'Kosovo and Metohija', sometimes compressed into a made-up single word, 'Kosmet'. Quite how and why Kosovo became the name of this component territory is a little unclear; it was never used as a territorial name under the medieval Serbian kings, and first appears in accounts of the great battle of 1389, which took place on Kosovo Polje, the 'Kosovo field (or plain)'. *Kos* means 'blackbird' in Serbian (the *-ovo* is an adjectival ending): hence Germans know the battle-site as the 'Amselfeld', and Latin chronicles call it *campus merulae*. (Kosovo is not an uncommon place-name in the Balkans: there are various villages or districts called Kosovo, unconnected with this one, in Dalmatia, Bosnia and Albania.)[5] Geographically, Kosovo Polje (Alb.: Fusha e Kosovës) can describe not just the battlefield but the whole rolling plateau which extends to the north and south of the territory's capital, Prishtina (Srb.: Priština); there is also a town named Kosovo Polje on that plateau, just to the west of Prishtina, on the main railway line. Early sources show that there was also once a small mining town called 'Kosovo' somewhere in this region; its precise whereabouts are uncertain, as are those of a minor administrative sub-division called 'Kosovo' in the early Ottoman period.[6] And, just to add a final touch of complication, a sub-region to the north of Prishtina is also known as Malo Kosovo (Alb.: Kosova e Vogël), 'little Kosovo'.

In order to hold some of these confusions at bay, a simple rule will be adopted in this book. The term 'Kosovo' will refer to the entire geographical region in accordance with its post-1945 borders (the so-called Kosovo and Metohija). The western half of Kosovo will be called Western Kosovo; the eastern half will be called Eastern Kosovo. (This differs from the usage of some modern Kosovo Albanian writers, who use 'Eastern Kosovo', misleadingly, to refer to a small area to the east of Kosovo itself.) The names of a few sub-regions of Kosovo will be mentioned from time to time, and explained on their first appearance. The term 'Kosovo Polje' will be used either for the immediate area of the battlefield or (where the context makes this clear) for the small modern town of that name to the west of Prishtina; and 'the Kosovo Polje plateau' will refer to the wider area (corresponding to what geographers know as the 'Kosovo depression') running north and south of Prishtina.[7]

Geography, or rather geology, supplies one essential reason for the enduring historical importance of Kosovo – particularly of its eastern half. It contains the greatest concentration of mineral wealth in the whole of south-eastern Europe. The Trepça mine (Srb.: Trepča; near Mitrovica, 30 miles north of Prishtina), developed by a British company in the 1920s, became in the post-war period one of Europe's largest suppliers of lead and zinc; this mining area, including another important mine south-east of Prishtina, was estimated in the 1960s to contain 56 per cent of the reserves of those metals in Yugoslavia, and 100 per cent of the nickel. It also supplied half of the country's production of magnesite (of which Yugoslavia was the third largest producer in the world).[8] Important too are the deposits of bauxite and chrome in Western Kosovo; and there are large coal-mines in both halves of the territory, as well as some copper and iron ore. Kosovo's mineral riches have made the territory a special target for conquest by many armies, from the Romans to the Nazis: when Hitler divided this area into occupation zones with his Axis allies after the conquest of Yugoslavia in 1941, he took care to create a special German zone to include the Trepça mine and its nearby mines and factories. Within three months, Trepça was sending a daily train-load of 500 tons of lead and zinc concentrate to supply the war industries of the Reich.[9]

But of all the mineral assets of Kosovo, the most important for much of its earlier history was its wealth of silver. There was mining in this area in pre-Roman times, and both silver and lead (and, probably, some gold) were mined extensively during the Roman period.[10] The medieval Serbian kingdom drew much of its wealth from the mines of Kosovo, especially from the area south-east of Prishtina. Novo Brdo (Alb.: Novobërda), the town which processed the ore and minted the coins, became one of the richest places in southern Europe.[11] Production remained strong throughout the early Ottoman period: at the end of the sixteenth century this whole mining region (including the mines of the Skopje area and the rich Zaplana mine near Trepça) was producing more than 800,000 troy ounces of silver per year.[12] During the next century production steeply declined, thanks in large part to Ottoman mismanagement and the terrible disruptions of the Austro-Turkish war. And for the last two centuries of Ottoman rule the underground wealth of Kosovo remained almost completely neglected: it is a pathetic commentary on the economic incompetence of the Ottoman state that the only sign of mineral extraction noticed by one traveller through this region in 1858 was the panning of river-sand for specks of iron ore. (So rich were the local ore-beds that this method alone supplied enough for six small foundries in the villages of one valley; the metal so obtained was then used mainly by Gypsy smiths and farriers.)[13]

Geography also explains why the possession of this territory has always been important for strategic reasons. Despite its ring of mountains, Kosovo has always been a crossing-place for both merchant caravans and armies. It is true, admittedly, that the most important routes in the western and central Balkans lay elsewhere – which is why Kosovo's position was described above only as 'near-central'. The main route into the Balkans from Austria or Hungary went southwards from Belgrade, up the Morava valley to Niš. From there, travellers to Constantinople could turn east and take the road through Bulgaria; those who were going to Salonica could continue due south to the range of hills which separates Serbia from Macedonia, crossing it just to the east of the Kosovo border. The most important east–west route from the Adriatic coast to Salonica, the ancient Via Egnatia, also missed Kosovo, and by a wider margin: it went from Durrës (Itl.: Durazzo) across the middle of Albania to the northern side of Lake Ohrid, and then across Macedonia into Greece.

But Kosovo did possess two routes of real importance. The first linked it with the city of Shkodra, a major trading centre in north-western Albania (connected by a short stretch of navigable river to the Adriatic coast). From Shkodra an old caravan track, based partly on a Roman military road, wound through the mountains of northern Albania, crossing into Kosovo on the bank of the White Drin and arriving shortly thereafter at Prizren. This connection with a Mediterranean port made Prizren a commercial centre for the entire Kosovo region – until the 1870s, when a railway joined the towns of Eastern Kosovo to Salonica, drawing trade away from Prizren and bringing in cheap goods made in Manchester and Birmingham. After Prizren, travellers from Shkodra could continue northwards to Peć (Alb.: Peja) or eastwards to Prishtina; both of those towns were connected with a network of other routes through Kosovo and neighbouring parts of inner Serbia. And from Prishtina a main road led due south, through the Kaçanik gorge, to Skopje and on down to Salonica.

The second important long-distance route, also connecting Kosovo to the Adriatic coast, began in Ragusa (modern Dubrovnik). This extraordinary commercial city-state, at the southern end of modern Croatia, was in some periods the main rival of Venice in the trade of the Eastern Mediterranean, and gained a privileged trading relationship with the Ottoman Empire. Unlike Venice, it never tried to conquer territory. Existing only on its wits (and its money), Ragusa might be described as the Hong Kong of the Ottoman Balkans. Huge quantities of Ottoman imports and exports passed through Ragusan hands; the Ragusans had so-called 'colonies' (communities of merchants) in many inland towns, and organized the transport of goods between all parts of the Balkans and their mother-city. One of their main routes went up from Ragusa through the south-eastern corner of Bosnia–Hercegovina to Foča, and then turned eastwards to the town of Novi Pazar (Trk.: Yeni Pazar: meaning 'New Market' in both languages); a few miles beyond that town, it crossed into the northern part of Kosovo. From there traders could either continue eastwards to Niš, where they joined the Belgrade–Sofia–Constantinople route, or turn southwards through Kosovo, passing through Prishtina and down into Macedonia. Because of these connections, Prishtina was also an important trading centre, and the road from Niš via Prishtina to Skopje was in some periods just as frequented as the more direct Serbian–Macedonian route.[14]

Trading-routes can play a great role in history; but the strategic importance of Kosovo is not a question of roads alone. A glance at the map of the Balkans will show why Kosovo mattered so crucially to the Ottoman sultans. Whoever held Kosovo would control their strategic access to Bosnia and northern Albania, and could threaten to cut the link between Serbia and the Macedonian–Aegean region. The conquest of Kosovo was a key element in the ambitious Austrian strategy of 1689, which aimed at prising the whole of Serbia, Kosovo and Bosnia free from the grip of Ottoman rule. Similarly, it was in Kosovo that a force of Bosnian rebels met the Ottoman army in 1831: there they inflicted a heavy defeat on the Turks, in a battle which, had a canny Grand Vizier not succeeded soon afterwards in sowing political dissension among the rebels, might have altered the course of modern Balkan history. In the course of three centuries, Kosovo has been either the turning-point or the choke-point for four major withdrawals by German-speaking forces (in 1690, 1737, 1918 and 1944), and one massive and terrible retreat in the opposite direction, southwards into Kosovo and then over the Albanian mountains to the sea, by the defeated Serbian army in 1915. And, of course, no brief tally of Kosovo's military history would be complete without mentioning the medieval battles: the famous battle of Kosovo of 1389, and the much less well-known 'second battle' of 1448.

Some of the links between Kosovo and its surrounding territories have now been briefly sketched; it may be helpful to add a few more details here about those neighbouring areas, which have been connected with

Kosovo not only by trade and war but also by overlapping populations. Just to the north and north-west of Kosovo lies the historic territory of Rascia (Srb.: Raška), the original nucleus of the medieval Serbian state. (The town of Ras, its early capital, was a few miles from the site of Novi Pazar.) The central Serbian territory due north of Kosovo remains, in every sense, a Serb heartland. But the broad swathe of land stretching north-westwards from Novi Pazar to the Bosnian border underwent a special development in the final Ottoman period. This was the 'Sandžak of Novi Pazar'; which is often called simply 'the Sandžak'. A *sancak* (Srb: *sandžak*; Alb.: *sanxhak*) was an administrative division of the Ottoman Empire, and this sancak was originally just one of many; but it gained a peculiar status in 1878 which brought it to the attention of the outside world, and has been referred to simply as 'the Sandžak' since that date. Like Kosovo, the Sandžak passed from Ottoman to Serbian and Montenegrin rule only as late as 1912; and as in Kosovo the majority of its population consists (or consisted until very recently) of Muslims. But unlike the people of Kosovo, the Sandžak Muslims are mainly Slavs, like the Muslims of Bosnia: for much of the eighteenth and nineteenth centuries, the Sandžak was treated as part of the administrative unit of Bosnia. There is an ethnic Albanian minority in the Sandžak, and there were larger concentrations of Albanians there in the past; but these two Muslim populations stand somewhat apart from one another, divided by national consciousness as well as language.

Moving clockwise round Kosovo again, one comes to the upper Morava valley, the area of Serbia south of Niš. This region too had a large Muslim Albanian minority in the later Ottoman period, until the wars of the 1870s and the territorial changes of 1878 enabled the Serbian authorities to expel the Albanians *en masse*. Only a handful remained after that date; but since 1912, when Kosovo was mainly absorbed by Serbia, there has been some eastwards expansion of the Albanian population again, particularly in the region of the Preševo pass (where the main route crosses from Serbia into Macedonia) and round the little town of Vranje. (This is the area now referred to by some Kosovo Albanian writers as 'Eastern Kosovo', a usage which will not be followed in this book.)

Passing westwards along the Kosovo–Macedonian border, one finds at first, in the hills of the Skopska Crna Gora, a fairly clear ethnic frontier between Albanians and Macedonians. The Macedonians are Slavs whose language is quite distinct from Serbian and closely related to Bulgarian. In the past, populations have spilled over this line of hills in both directions; nineteenth-century travellers found villages inside Kosovo whose people spoke 'Bulgarian' (i.e. Macedonian) rather than Serbian, and some linguists (particularly, of course, Bulgarian ones) noticed 'Bulgarian' influences on the Serbian speech of southern Kosovo.[15] Where the political and ethnic frontiers begin seriously to diverge, however, is further to the west, along the Šar mountain range. Here a substantial Albanian population extends well over the range into Macedonia, including the predominantly Albanian town of Tetovo (Alb.: Tetova; Trk.: Kalkandelen) and, further to the south and west, the town of Debar (Alb.: Dibra). These two towns have been linked, for much of their history, with Kosovo. A road over a mountain pass connected Tetovo with the trading centre at Prizren, and another route led from Prizren up a river valley to Debar. The people of Debar and its surrounding villages (which include, almost uniquely among the northern Albanian population, a cluster of adherents to the Orthodox Church) were famously independent-minded, and this was often the last area to be subdued when Albanian rebellions were crushed by Ottoman armies.

To the north-west of Debar lie the great mountain massifs of northern Albania. Inhabited by powerful clans (many of them Catholic) who jealously guarded their territory and lived by their own customary law, this area enjoyed a kind of semi-autonomy for much of the Ottoman period. As one English traveller in the late nineteenth century put it: 'To say that the Turks have subjugated the Arnauts [i.e. Albanians] is not strictly correct. Their position is something like that of the French in the remoter parts of Algeria. They hold certain towns, the intervening country being occupied by independent tribes, governing themselves.'[16] For most British readers, a closer parallel might be with the Scottish Highlands up to the eighteenth century; and as we shall see, this is not the only resemblance between northern Albania and 'North Britain'. An inhabitant of this mountainous Albanian region is known as a *malësor* (from *mal*, meaning mountain), which translates precisely as 'highlander'; the whole complex of mountains can be referred to by the general name of the Malësi, the Highlands.[17] (Within this region, there are smaller ranges with their own particular names: of these the most important in relation to the history of Kosovo are the Malësi e Gjakovës, the Gjakova Highlands, which lie inside Albania to the west of the Kosovo town of Gjakova, and the Malësi e Madhe, the Great Highlands, which run to the east of Shkodra along the Montenegrin frontier.) This entire region has enjoyed a peculiarly close relation to Kosovo, and very many of the Kosovo Albanians are descended from these mountain clans. To say that the Malësi and Kosovo are umbilically connected might even be to understate the case: until a frontier was created between them after the war of 1912, the two areas had been – at least so far as the Albanian population was concerned – parts of a single, continuous ethnic realm.

Finally, north of the Malësi, there are the mountains of Montenegro. The Montenegrins are generally regarded, in ethnic terms, as a type of Serb, and their adherence to the Orthodox Church has indeed aligned them closely to the Serbian cultural world, rather than to the Croatian or Bosnian.[18] But Montenegro has led a very separate life from Serbia for much of its history, becoming contiguous with it only in 1912 and united with it in the Yugoslav Kingdom only in 1918. The inhabitants of the Montenegrin mountains just to the north of Albania, known as *brdjani* (sing.: *brdjanin*; 'highlander' in Serbian, from *brdo*, meaning 'mountain'), do in fact share many characteristics – customs, traditional laws and forms of social organization – with their Albanian malësor neighbours. In past centuries, there were strong and specific links between Albanian and Montenegrin highland clans: some were long-standing allies in war, others had traditions of each taking brides from the other clan, and some had legends of common ancestry. Long-term patterns of what might be called ethnic osmosis took place: some of the Montenegrin clans may originally have been off-shoots from Albanian families, and some of the Albanian ones may have Slav ancestry too.[19]

As these details may already have suggested, the two main ethnic groups whose history will dominate this book – Serbs and Albanians – are far from being homogeneous blocs of humankind. There are many variations within each of them, different ethnic roots, regional varieties and different cultural and religious alignments.

Generalizations about 'the Serbs' or 'the Albanians' are always slightly suspect, and statements about 'national character' are of no explanatory value to the historian. But some characteristics – social practices, inherited traditions – can be broadly described, and a few words about them may be of some use to readers unfamiliar with this part of Europe.

The Serbs of modern Kosovo come, as we shall see, from many different stocks, some of which migrated to Kosovo from Dalmatia or Bosnia or northern Serbia. Within Kosovo, however, their differences of origin were largely discarded, and they shared a common way of life, touched to some extent (in matters of clothing, for example) by the influence of their Albanian neighbours, but broadly similar to the lifestyle of the Serbs to the north of them in the central Serbian territory. A mainly agricultural population, they based their society on the community of the village and, within it, the community of the family. The self-image of the Serbs is of a naturally egalitarian people; it is true that there is no hereditary aristocracy in Serbia, but that is more easily to be explained as a consequence of the Ottoman conquest (which eventually eliminated the Serbian nobility) than by innate tendencies in the Serbian soul. Similarly, romantically-minded Serb historians, influenced by nineteenth-century Russian theories about the village commune as an ancient Slav institution, have made much of the role of the self-governing village community in Serbian life. But modern scholars have demolished the Russian theory, and it seems that self-reliant villages can better be explained simply as a practical response to periods of insecurity or weak government.[20]

The same factors help to explain the famous *zadruga* or family commune, which involves several generations of the same family living together (usually in a group of houses protected by an outer wall) and functioning as a single economic unit. The zadruga died out in most parts of Serbia in the late nineteenth century, but it seems to have lasted a little longer among the Serbs of Kosovo: Edith Durham, travelling across Western Kosovo in 1908, saw many 'typical Servian zadrugas, family groups of houses enclosed in huge palisades'.[21] Within the zadruga there is a kind of equality of the male heads of the component families, who form a council to decide important matters, subject to the final authority of the ruling 'elder'. However, modern research has shown that there is nothing peculiarly Serbian, and perhaps nothing even peculiarly south-Slav, about the zadruga. It is just a product, found in many parts of Europe, of two common factors: conditions of insecurity, which put a premium on mutual defence, and a patrilinear social system, which identifies family with sons.[22] A third factor, pastoralism, may also play a part: the management of large flocks or herds, and the control of grazing-grounds, also puts a premium on large cooperative groups. That probably explains why the zadruga has survived longest in mountain regions, which depend more on pastoralism than on settled agriculture. In fact, the last surviving zadrugas in Kosovo are not among the Serb population but among the Albanians, whose way of life has been more dominated by pastoral traditions.[23]

There are many other aspects of the traditional way of life of the Serb peasant which can be found mirrored in his Albanian counterpart. Some may be historical products of shared centuries of Ottoman rule; others may reflect a common heritage at a far deeper level. Codes of honour, respect for military prowess, a strong tradition of hospitality (anyone who has visited Serbian villagers in their homes will testify to the strength and warmth of this last characteristic): all these are common features of traditional rural societies in this part of Europe.

Of the things that differentiate Serbs and Albanians, the most obvious is language. But although the Serbian language clearly separates Serbs from Albanians, it does not so clearly constitute Serbs as Serbs: the type of dialect and pronunciation used in Serbia shades off – in Bosnia, for example, and in Montenegro – into other varieties of what used to be called Serbo-Croat, as spoken by Croats and Bosnian Muslims. Another key factor is needed to determine Serbian-ness; and that factor, historically the most powerful one in building a Serb identity, is the Serbian Orthodox Church. This Church first acquired an autonomous status within the Greek Orthodox Church in the early thirteenth century, and became fully independent in 1346; since then its independence has been intermittent, but its use of the Slavonic liturgy and its key role in Serbian cultural life have been continuous. When modern concepts of nationhood began to be propagated in the nineteenth century, membership of this Church supplied a ready-made category of Serbian-ness.

However, although Serbian Orthodoxy may in this way have a national–political dimension to it, Western readers should be reminded that the type of Christianity found in the Orthodox Church is in some ways much further removed from social and political matters than is the case with Protestantism or Roman Catholicism. In Western Europe, the churches have always been actively engaged in social and political thinking: the arguments debated in the major Western texts of political theory have many of their roots in works by medieval Franciscans and Dominicans. There is nothing really equivalent to this in the Eastern Orthodox tradition (at least not since the early Byzantine period). The intellectual energies of Orthodoxy have been devoted to mystical theology, and the real focus of religious life is placed, to an extent which West Europeans must make an effort of the imagination to understand, on just one thing: the celebration of the liturgy. To explore the implications of this would take a book in itself. But one rather paradoxical suggestion can be touched on here. It is sometimes claimed that the political traditions of many Orthodox countries (including Serbia) suffer from a Byzantine legacy of 'caesaro-papism', meaning a fusing together of temporal and spiritual rule, and that this is the root cause of their occasional tendencies towards a kind of mystical or fanatical politics. If the argument sketched here is correct, the problem is the other way round: far from fusing themselves with politics, the Orthodox Churches withdrew from social and political engagement into a realm of contemplation and liturgical celebration. As a result, the cultures of their countries had fewer chances to develop the habits of critical social and political thinking which were generated in the West by the Catholic Church and its Protestant offshoots. This may help to explain why the Serbian people have been, at some moments in their history, persuaded to follow political causes with an uncritical and absolute loyalty.[24]

These issues are relevant to any study of the Kosovo question, not only because of the quasi-religious fervour of some Serbian writers and politicians on this subject, but also because the Patriarchate of the Serbian Orthodox Church is located at the Western Kosovo town of Peć. Let the last word on the general question of the Serbs and their religion go to a distinguished Serbian diplomat and historian, Čedomil Mijatović, whose remarks, written at the beginning of the twentieth century, may be equally valid at its end:

The religious sentiment of the Servians [i.e. Serbians] is neither deep nor warm. Their churches are generally empty, except on very great Church festivals, and on political festivals. The Servians of our day consider the Church as a political institution, in some mysterious manner connected with the existence of the nation. They do not allow anyone to attack her, nor to compromise her, although, when she is not attacked, they neglect her.[25]

No religion, on the other hand, unites the Albanians. There is an autocephalous Albanian Orthodox Church, but it gained its autonomy from the Greek Church only as recently as 1923; its members are all in the southern half of Albania (or in the émigré community), and it has played no part in the history of Kosovo. Overall, the modern Albanian population (i.e. the Albanians of Albania, Kosovo, Macedonia and Montenegro) divides, in terms of religious background, into roughly 80 per cent Muslim, 12 per cent Orthodox and 8 per cent Catholic. The word 'background' is essential here: since religion was heavily suppressed in the Albanian state after 1945 and officially abolished in 1967, whole generations have grown up there knowing little or nothing about the religious practices of their ancestors. And in Kosovo, where religion was never formally banned, urban Albanians are just as secularized as their Muslim counterparts in the towns of Bosnia. The proportions in Kosovo are roughly 95 per cent Muslim and 5 per cent Catholic.

The other division in the overall Albanian population is between the Gegs, who live in northern Albania and Kosovo, and the Tosks, who live in southern Albania. (There are also two smaller southern groups who are considered distinct from the Tosks, the Çams and the Labs, but these can be ignored here.) The differences between Gegs and Tosks are a matter partly of language, partly of way of life. In the north the highland clans developed their special social system; in the less mountainous landscape of the south, whatever quasi-clans that may have existed were more or less swept aside, and the countryside was dominated by feudal or Ottoman landowners.[26]

The linguistic differences between Gegs and Tosks are striking, but not large enough to get in the way of mutual intelligibility; in most respects the gulf is no greater than that between Scotland and the south of England. To the outsider, the most obvious differences are in the pronunciation of certain vowels (nasalized in Geg speech), and in the Geg use of the consonant 'n' in some words where Tosk has 'r'. This last detail helps to show that Geg has retained an earlier form of the language: it is Tosk speech which has changed 'n' into 'r', in a process known to linguists as 'rhotacism'. (Thus the Albanian town whose name comes from the Greek 'Aulôn' and the Latin 'Avlona' or Italian 'Valona' is Vlona in Geg, and Vlora in Tosk.)[27] When a standardized version of the language, known as 'unified literary Albanian', was finally codified in Tirana in 1972, it was based – partly for political reasons – much more closely on Tosk than on Geg. (The Communist leader Enver Hoxha and many of his inner circle were Tosks; and they felt a special hostility towards not only the traditional clan leaders of the north, but also the Catholic priests of Shkodra, who had developed the Geg literary language.) As a result, the type of Albanian now found in almost all printed works, including books printed in Kosovo, diverges from the spoken language of Kosovo and the other northern regions.[28] For simplicity's sake, the standard Albanian forms are used in this book.

The basis of the traditional Geg social system, as mentioned already, is the clan. The Albanian word for this, *fis*, is also sometimes translated 'tribe' (like the Serbian word *pleme*, which refers to the Montenegrin equivalent). Northern Albanian society was strictly patrilinear, which means that descent was calculated only through the male line. The official theory or myth of each fis was that all its members were descended from a common male ancestor, the founder of the clan – rather in the way that all MacGregors might romantically suppose that they were descended from a single Gregor. In some cases there may well have been one original founder, whose direct descendants supplied at least the dominant element in the clan; but in the formative stages of these clans it is likely that unrelated groups who lived in close proximity came together for mutual protection.

A smaller collective sub-group within an Albanian clan – or, at least, within most of them – was the *vëllazëri*, or brotherhood (Srb.: *bratstvo*), which did indeed consist of a group of blood-related families (again, only through the male line). The vëllazëri was like a looser version of a zadruga: the family structure was similar, but it did not live in a single set of buildings and did not pool its earnings and expenditure in a single budget. In the Malësi, each clan had its own territory, consisting of its grazing-lands and an inhabited valley or group of valleys. In Kosovo, where members of different clans intermingled, this territorial principle could seldom be applied, and clan loyalties were somewhat eroded. So while in the Malësi blood-feuds could reach the point of pitting one whole clan against another, in Kosovo the basic unit of cooperative retribution was not the fis but the family.[29]

In between those two collective identities, large and small, some other groupings also existed. Some of the larger clans were divided into (or had been composed of) several smaller clans. With their belief in patrilinear descent, the malësors regarded any relative on the paternal side as the same blood, and marriage to such a relation as incestuous. The clans were therefore 'exogamous', acquiring their brides from other clans.[30] But in a few cases the sub-clans of a large fis were seen as sufficiently unrelated (or their supposed common ancestor was thought sufficiently distant in time) for them to exchange brides with one another. In some cases also one sub-clan might convert to Islam, while other components of the same overall fis remained Catholic; their mutual loyalty as fellow clan-members would remain unaffected by their religious differences.

The other important grouping was the *bajrak*, a word derived from the Turkish for a banner or military standard. This institution, which became a more or less organic part of the clan system, was originally an alien administrative device, imposed on the area by the Ottomans from the seventeenth century onwards. Its purpose was to single out local leaders who could supply fighting men, when called on, and who would gain status and privilege in return; and its basis was territorial, not tribal. Roughly speaking, a large clan's territory might be divided into several bajraks, each under its own *bajraktar*, a medium-sized clan might constitute one bajrak, and several small clans might be lumped together; but there were also less neat arrangements, with just some members of one clan included in another clan's bajrak. (As a result of this, the first Westerners who tried to describe and classify the Albanian clan system were faced with all kinds of difficulties, and produced very conflicting accounts.)[31] In Kosovo, because of the geographical dispersal of the clans, the bajrak became an important unit, and the bajraktars wielded great local power as administrators, military leaders and settlers of disputes.[32]

One sign of the alien origin of the office of bajraktar was that it was a hereditary title. Most of the Albanian clans, despite their obsession with male genealogy, had not regarded the authority to rule as an inheritable good. (The main exception was the Mirdita, the largest and most untypical of the Catholic clans, which had its own hereditary ruling family.) Decision-taking, at each of a series of levels – village, clan and inter-clan – was made by councils of elders. For important matters, such as going to war against another clan, a general assembly of all the elders of the clan was held; this was known as a *kuvend* (from the Latin *conventum*). And on special occasions assemblies were called of all the clans of the region: there are important historical examples of this from as early as the beginning of the seventeenth century.[33]

No such system of local self-government could subsist without a strong framework of customary law. Large-scale assemblies were infrequent, and were usually aimed at getting agreement on action or policy, not at legislation. All the essential rules of human life – relating to marriage, inheritance, pasture rights, criminal acts, and so on – were laid down in traditional codes of law, transmitted from memory to memory; the job of the elders was not to make new laws but to interpret the facts of any particular case in the light of the laws they knew. Over time, of course, the codes of different geographical areas diverged on some points; several regional law codes have survived into the twentieth century. Of these, the only one which matters for the history of Kosovo, and for most of the Malësi, is the most famous of them all: the Kanun of Lek Dukagjin. The name 'Kanun' is derived (via Arabic and Turkish) from the Greek word which gives us 'canon'. Lek Dukagjin is commonly identified with a fifteenth-century member of the Dukagjin family ('Lek' or 'Lekë' being an abbreviated Albanian form of Alexander).[34] The attachment of this nobleman's name to the law may be spurious: some scholars have suspected that it was originally known just as the law of Dukagjin, referring to the territory, not the family.[35] But even if a fifteenth-century individual did put together this code, it is clear that he was codifying many customary practices which went back much further into the past.[36] The Kanun remained unwritten until the nineteenth century, when summaries of it by non-Albanian writers began to appear in print.[37] The fullest and most authoritative text was compiled by a Catholic Albanian priest, Father Shtjefën Gjeçov, and issued first as a sequence of articles in a Catholic journal; it was eventually published as a book, four years after his murder by Serb extremists in 1929.[38]

The importance of the Kanun to the ordinary life of the Albanians of Kosovo and the Malësi can hardly be exaggerated. 'Whenever in the

mountains I asked why anything was done,' wrote Edith Durham in the
1920s, 'I was told, "Because Lek ordered it." ... "Lek said so" obtained
more obedience than the Ten Commandments, and the teaching of the
hodjas [Muslim clerics] and the priests was often vain if it ran counter
to that of Lek.'[39] Anyone who has read Ismail Kadare's novel *Broken
April* will associate the Kanun above all with the archaic and terrible
laws of the blood-feud; and some news reports on the revival of the
blood-feud in post-Communist Albania have given the impression that
the Kanun, which is now being implemented again in the Malësi, is
nothing more than a system of vendettas. But the Kanun covered most
aspects of human life (there are sections, for example, on the duties of
blacksmiths and millers); it specified the system of assemblies, judges
and juries; and it laid down punishments for a range of criminal offences
(fines for minor ones, and execution, plus the burning down of the
offender's house and the expulsion of his family, for serious crimes).[40]

One leading scholar has summed up the basic principles of the Kanun
as follows. The foundation of it all is the principle of personal honour.
Next comes the equality of persons. From these flows a third principle,
the freedom of each to act in accordance with his own honour, within
the limits of the law, without being subject to another's command. And
the fourth principle is the word of honour, the *besë* (def.: *besa*), which
creates a situation of inviolable trust.[41] Gjeçov's version of the Kanun
decrees: 'An offence to honour is not paid for with property, but by the
spilling of blood or a magnanimous pardon.' And it specifies the ways of
dishonouring a man, of which the most important are calling him a liar
in front of other men; insulting his wife; taking his weapons; or violating
his hospitality.[42] The reference to hospitality here is important: entering
a man's house as his guest creates, like the word of honour, an inviolable
bond between the two, and there are stories of Albanians sacrificing
their lives to protect a perfect stranger who had taken shelter with them
for one night. The reference to weapons should also be noted: the history
of Kosovo and northern Albania is punctuated by a series of revolts
caused by ill-starred official attempts to disarm the population. In the
words of one English traveller of the 1880s: 'The pride of a farmer in his
livestock, or of a collector in his specimens, is nothing to the pride of an
Albanian in his weapons. They are ... the guardians of his hearth, the
object of his admiration, and his perpetual glory.'[43]

As several details will already have suggested, this was very much a man's world. The reference to 'equality of persons' above needs some qualification. Women had their honour, but it existed through, and was defended by, men. Of all the proverbial sayings in the Kanun, few will offend modern sensibilities as sharply as the statement, 'A wife is a sack for carrying' – meaning that her *raison d'être* is simply to bear her husband's children.[44] A woman had a hard life in this society, engaged in ceaseless housework and labour in the fields, and forbidden to have contacts with the world outside the family, at least until she was old. The only permitted escape from such a life was to become a 'sworn virgin', which involved renouncing all prospects of marriage, dressing in man's clothes and leading the life of an honorary man; but this was a rarity, caused either by extreme revulsion at an arranged marriage, or by a desire to look after a father who had no sons.[45] Of course, as is usual in rigidly patriarchal societies, there were some compensations: the strongest taboo of all concerned the murder of women, and any woman could walk through raging gunfire in the knowledge that she would never be shot at. Edith Durham, a close observer of life in the Malësi, summed up her impressions thus:

A woman in the mountains, in spite of the severe work she is forced to do, is in many ways freer than the women of Scutari. She speaks freely to the men; is often very bright and intelligent, and her opinion may be asked and taken. I have seen a man bring his wife to give evidence in some case under dispute. I have also seen the women interfere to stop a quarrel, but where the family honour is concerned they are as anxious that blood should be taken as are the men.[46]

Which brings us back, finally, to the blood-feud. This is one of the most archaic features of northern Albanian society, resembling the codes that govern other isolated societies in the Mediterranean region (such as Corsica) or the northern Caucasus. What lies at the heart of the blood-feud is a concept alien to the modern mind, and more easily learned about from the plays of Aeschylus than from the works of modern sociologists: the aim is not punishment of a murderer, but satisfaction of the blood of the person murdered – or, initially, satisfaction of one's own honour when it has been polluted. If retribution were the real aim, then only those personally responsible for the original crime or insult would be potential targets; but instead, honour is cleansed by killing any male member of the family of the original offender, and the spilt blood of that victim then cries out to its own family for purification.

Since honour is of the essence, there are strict rules for every step of the feud: one who 'takes blood' to satisfy his (or his family's) honour must announce that he has done so; a formal truce or besë for a set period must be agreed to, if requested for a proper reason (this is a special use of 'besë', the general term for a man's word of honour); and so on. The person who has the right to claim satisfaction for a killing is known as 'Zot i Gjakut', 'Lord of the Blood': in some clan areas there were procedures to enable him, with the encouragement of the bajraktar or other elders, to settle a feud in peace.[47] But such procedures, though urged by both Ottoman administrators and Catholic priests, were of limited popularity. At the end of the Ottoman period it was estimated that 19 per cent of all adult male deaths in the Malësi were blood-feud murders, and that in an area of Western Kosovo with 50,000 inhabitants, 600 died in these feuds every year.[48] One mid-nineteenth-century vendetta in the Malësi began when two men quarrelled over four cartridges which one had promised and not delivered: within two years it led to 1,218 houses being burnt down and 132 men killed.[49] This is an extreme example, of course, and the days of entire clans becoming involved in such wholesale feuding are unlikely to recur. And yet the tradition of the blood-feud has never died out in Kosovo: innumerable small-scale feuds have continued in the remoter villages, and not all of them were ended by the great series of mass reconciliations arranged by an inspirational settler of blood-feuds, Anton Çetta, in the early 1990s.

Only if we bear in mind the whole system of the feud and the Kanun can we make sense, finally, of the very conflicting reports which have come down to us on the Kosovar and Northern Albanian character. In the writings of some past visitors to the Balkans, Kosovo was a place of anarchy and terror, where even children carried guns and murders were everyday events. Those who understood the rules (such as Edith Durham) saw, on the other hand, that a strict system of law was usually at work. However, the law applied only to Albanian clansmen, and, in some respects, only within the clan. As with many other warlike pastoral societies – Scotland, again – stealing cattle from outsiders might be seen as an exploit rather than a crime. Many of the Serbs of Kosovo suffered grievously on this principle. In the words of the handbook on Albania issued by the British military in the Second World War:

> Our own Army Act draws a distinction between stealing the property of a comrade, and stealing from one of the public, but the Albanian would hardly recognize any similarity between the two. Where the limits of social obligation are so sharply defined as in tribal society, the same man may be loyal, generous, and hospitable to all those within the bond, but haughty, morose, suspicious, and untrustworthy to those beyond it.[50]

The traveller, brought 'within the bond' by the sacred duties of hospitality, could more easily experience the best of the Albanian character. As one Austrian who visited Kosovo in the bloodiest period of its final revolt against Ottoman rule declared: 'If you observe the customs of the land, you can travel more safely in Albania than in any other country in the world.'[51]

2

Origins: Serbs, Albanians and Vlachs

ALL ORIGINS BECOME mysterious if we search far enough into the past. And almost all peoples, when we look at their earliest origins, turn out to have come from somewhere else. Before embarking on these origin quests, it is good to keep a few qualifying principles firmly in mind. First, it can never be said too often that questions of chronological priority in ancient history – who got there first – are simply irrelevant to deciding the rights and wrongs of any present-day political situation. Secondly, accounts of the earlier movements of peoples or tribes give a very misleading impression when they treat them as if they were unitary items, with unchanging identities, being transferred from place to place in a game of ethno-historical pass-the-parcel. In many cases (such as the migrations of the Franks in early western Europe) it is the movement of a people into a new territory or society that gives it an identity it did not previously have. Identities continue to develop over time: 'Serb' was a tribal label in the sixth century but not in the sixteenth, so that to treat 'the Serbs' as an unchanging category is as foolish as trying to identify Jutes and Angles among the subjects of Queen Elizabeth I. And thirdly, we should never forget that all individual ancestries are mixed – especially in this part of Europe. When a Serb today reads about the arrival of the early Serbs, he may not be wrong to suppose that he is reading about his ancestors; but he cannot be right to imagine that *all* his ancestors were in that population. The equivalent is true for the Albanians, and indeed for every other ethnic group in the Balkans.

While most details about the movement of the early Slavs into the Balkans are unclear, the basic facts are known. A large tribal population of Slavs – among whom the Serbs and the Croats were two particular tribes, or tribal groupings – occupied parts of central Europe, north of the Danube, in the fifth and sixth centuries AD. The Serbs had their power-base in the area of the Czech lands and Saxony, and the Croats in Bavaria, Slovakia and southern Poland. This central European location was not the earliest known home of the Serbs; most of the evidence points to an earlier migration from the north and north-eastern side of the Black Sea. At that earlier period the Serbs and Croats seem to have lived together with more warlike Iranian tribes, and their tribal names may derive from Iranian ruling elites: Ptolemy, writing in the second century AD, located the 'Serboi' among the Sarmatians (an Iranian grouping) on the northern side of the Caucasus. Little is known about the Slavs' way of life in these earlier periods. The first descriptions we have of them are by Byzantine writers, who portray them as a wild people, more pastoral than agricultural, with many chiefs but no supreme leader.[1]

For a tribal population with a fairly low level of material culture, reaching the line of the Danube and looking south was the equivalent of a hungry man pressing his face against the window of a grocery. The Balkans, fully restored to Byzantine control under the energetic Emperor Justinian (527–65), contained many flourishing towns and cities, supported by productive agriculture and active trading routes. The Slavs were not the first to cross the Danube in search of better things. Germanic Goths had done so (with Byzantine permission, at first) in the fourth century, and had gone raiding as far as Greece and the Albanian coast thereafter; Huns, under Attila, had attacked in the 440s, and Bulgars (a Turkic tribe) had started raiding at the end of that century.[2] But none of these earlier invaders left any imprint on the Balkans comparable to that of the Slavs. Indeed, by the time that the Turkic-speaking Bulgars came to settle permanently in the Balkans in the seventh century, the Slav element was already so well established there that the conquering Bulgars were eventually to lose their own language and be absorbed by their Slav-speaking subjects.[3]

The first major Slav raids took place in the middle of Justinian's reign. In 547 and 548 they invaded the territory of modern Kosovo, and then (probably via Macedonia and the Via Egnatia across central Albania) got as far as Durrës on the northern Albanian coast.[4] More substantial invasions took place in the 580s, bringing Slavs deep into Greece. Historians used to think that it was only these later invasions that involved any permanent settlement; but there is evidence of Slav place-names in the Balkans – particularly along the river Morava – by the 550s, which suggests a more continuous process of infiltration.[5] One factor which may have turned the southward movement of Slavs from a trickle to a flood was the arrival, in the north-western part of the Balkans, of an especially warlike Turkic tribe, the Avars, who subjugated or coopted some Slavic tribes but drove many others away. By the early seventh century the Avar armies were raiding as far as the walls of Constantinople, and threatening the very existence of the Byzantine Empire.

It was at this point, in the 610s or 620s, that the Emperor of the day (according to a detailed but somewhat confused account by a later Emperor-cum-historian, Constantine Porphyrogenitus) invited the Croats to come down from central Europe and deal with the Avar threat.[6] This they did, bringing with them their neighbours, the Serbs. Both populations then settled in the territories abandoned by the Avars: the Croats in modern Croatia and western Bosnia, and the Serbs in the Rascia area on the north-western side of Kosovo, and in the region of modern Montenegro. In some of these areas they supervened on an already existing Slav population, which, as a result, must gradually have taken on a 'Croat' or 'Serb' identity. The Serbs did not have anything like a state at this stage, but they developed several small tribal territories, each called a *župa* and ruled by a tribal chief known as the *župan*.[7] By the mid-seventh century, Serbs (or Serb-led Slavs) were penetrating from the coastal lands of Montenegro into northern Albania. Major ports and towns such as Durrës and Shkodra held out against them, but much of the countryside was Slavicized, and some Slav settlers moved up the valleys into the Malësi. By the ninth century, Slav-speaking people were an important element of the population in much of northern Albania, excluding the towns and the higher mountainous areas (especially the mountains in the eastern part of the Malësi, towards Kosovo).[8] Slav-speaking people lived in the lowlands of this area, gradually becoming a major component of the urban population too, until the end of the Middle Ages.[9]

What had happened to the local populations of the western and central Balkans during and after the Slav invasions? Something is known about the urban inhabitants, but much less about the people in the countryside. Despite the apocalyptic tone of early Byzantine writers, who give the impression that all civilization came to an end here in about 600, there is good evidence that the main cities survived (or were revived), just as they had done after earlier sackings. Refugees from central Balkan towns such as Niš and Sofia fled to the safety of Salonica at first, but many must have gone back home later.[10] The main towns on the Dalmatian and northern Albanian coastline, too, retained their Latin-speaking populations and stayed under Byzantine rule. (For naval and commercial reasons, Durrës was the most important Byzantine possession on the entire Adriatic coast of the Balkans.)[11] But outside the major cities there are signs of decline and contraction; typical of the seventh to ninth centuries are the remains of small townships based on hill-forts, such as the one at Koman in the mountains of north-central Albania, where a Christian and probably Romanized (Latin-speaking) population must have led a rather limited existence.[12]

As for the rural population, which was also mainly Latin-speaking in most of the territory of Yugoslavia and north-western Bulgaria, it is assumed that large numbers of people were driven southwards by the Avars, Croats and Serbs. Some evidence from place-names suggests a flow of such refugees down the Dalmatian coast into northern Albania; and a folk tradition set down by a later Byzantine writer referred to a large movement of native people southwards and eastwards away from the area of the Danube and the Sava – that is, from northern Bulgaria, northern Serbia and Croatia.[13] No doubt Latin-speaking peasants and farmers continued to live in many of these areas, especially where they were in contact with a large town or city. But sooner or later the majority of them were Slavicized, and the towns in the interior of the Balkans filled up with Slav-speakers too.

Only the remnants of a Latin-speaking population survived in parts of the central and west-central Balkans; when it re-emerges into the historical record in the tenth and eleventh centuries, we find its members leading a semi-nomadic life as shepherds, horse-breeders and travelling muleteers. These were the Vlachs, who can still be seen tending their flocks in the mountains of northern Greece, Macedonia and Albania today.[14] The name 'Vlach' was a word used by the Slavs for those they encountered who spoke a strange, usually Latinate, language; the Vlachs' own name for themselves is 'Aromanians' (Aromâni). As this name suggests, the Vlachs are closely linked to the Romanians: their two languages (which, with a little practice, are mutually intelligible) diverged only in the ninth or tenth century.[15] While Romanian historians have tried to argue that the Romanian-speakers have always lived in the territory of Romania (originating, it is claimed, from Romanized Dacian tribes and/or Roman legionaries), there is compelling evidence to show that the Romanian-speakers were originally part of the same population as the Vlachs, whose language and way of life were developed somewhere to the south of the Danube. Only in the twelfth century did the early Romanian-speakers move northwards into Romanian territory.[16]

Finally, before turning to the most mysterious problem of all – the origin of the Albanians – it is worth looking once more at the pattern of settlement in the Kosovo area during the early Slav centuries. Kosovo did not fall within the Serb territory of Rascia, which was further to the north-west: the Serbian expansion into Kosovo began in earnest only in the late twelfth century. About the other early Slav settlers in this part of the Balkans we have much less information. Byzantine sources just referred generally to 'Sklaviniai', Slav territories, in the Macedonian region; in the few cases when they made more localized references they often used names derived from rivers, so that it is not clear whether these were the names of Slav tribes or just geographical labels. The 'Moravoi' or 'Moravlians', for example, who are first mentioned in the ninth century, lived somewhere near the river Morava, but that is all we know about them. Historical map-makers, who do not like leaving too many blank spaces, place these Moravlians over much of south-eastern Serbia from as early as the sixth century, with arrows showing them passing into Kosovo; real evidence for this is lacking.[17]

Obviously some Slavs did spread through all these areas sooner or later. But there is one intriguing line of argument to suggest that the Slav presence in Kosovo and the southernmost part of the Morava valley may have been quite weak in the first one or two centuries of Slav settlement. If Slavs had been evenly spread across this part of the Balkans, it would be hard to explain why such a clear linguistic division emerged between the Serbo-Croat language and the Bulgarian–

Macedonian one. The scholar who first developed this argument also noted that, in the area dividing the early Serbs from the Bulgarians, many Latin place-names survived long enough to be adapted eventually into Slav ones, from Naissus (Niš), down through the Kosovo town of Lypenion (Lipljan) to Scupi (Skopje): this contrasts strongly with most of northern Serbia, Bosnia and the Dalmatian hinterland, where the old town names were completely swept aside. His conclusion was that the Latin-speaking population, far from withering away immediately, may actually have been strengthened here (and in a western strip of modern Bulgaria), its numbers swelled, no doubt, by refugees from further north. These Latin-speakers would have thus formed 'a wide border-zone between the Bulgarians and the Serbs'.[18] Kosovo's protective ring of mountains would have been useful to them; and the Roman mountain-road from Kosovo to the Albanian coast – along which several Latin place-names also survive, such as Puka, from 'via publica' – might also have connected them with other parts of the Latin-speaking world. (The hill-top town of Koman, mentioned earlier, is only a few miles from Puka, and may well have had a Latin-speaking population too.) If this argument is correct, we might expect many of the ancestors of the Vlachs to have been present in the Kosovo region and the mountains of western Bulgaria; it may have been in these uplands that they developed their pastoral skills.

Only in the ninth century do we see the expansion of a strong Slav (or quasi-Slav) power into this region. Under a series of ambitious rulers, the Bulgarians – a Slav population which absorbed, linguistically and culturally, its ruling elite of Turkic Bulgars – pushed westwards across modern Macedonia and eastern Serbia, until by the 850s they had taken over Kosovo and were pressing on the borders of Rascia. Soon afterwards they took the western Macedonian town of Ohrid; having recently converted to Christianity, the Bulgar rulers helped to set up a bishopric in Ohrid, which thus became an important centre of Slav culture for the whole region. And at the same time the Bulgarians were pushing on into southern and central Albania, which became thoroughly settled by Bulgarian Slavs during the course of the following century.[19] Kosovo was to remain under Bulgarian or Macedonian rulers until the period 1014–18, when the Macedonian-based Tsar Samuel died, his empire broke up, and Byzantine power was fully re-established by a strong and decisive Emperor, Basil 'the Bulgar-killer'. For nearly two centuries after that, Kosovo would stay under Byzantine rule.[20]

One key element is missing from the picture presented so far. While the origins of the Vlachs are obscure enough, the origins of the Albanians have been the subject of a much more bewildering mass of conflicting claims and theories. The two main rival theories that have emerged identify the early Albanians as either Illyrians or Thracians: in pre-Roman and Roman times, Illyrians lived in the western half of the Balkans and Thracians in the east. Albanian historians, who like the idea that Albanians have always lived in Albania, prefer the Illyrian theory. Romanian scholars, who have to deal with the awkward fact that there are strong early links between the Albanians and the Vlachs, prefer to put them on the Thracian side of the divide (the ancient Dacians, who lived in Romania, were part of the Thracian group), and in this they are sometimes supported by Bulgarian experts. But there is really no point in going into this labyrinth of historical debate unless one is prepared to discard all national prejudices at the entrance.

The Albanians first emerge in the historical record in 1043, when Albanian troops appear fighting alongside Greeks in the army of a rebel Byzantine general. They are mentioned at Durrës in 1078, and again in 1081, when they joined the Byzantine forces resisting an invasion there by the Norman adventurer Robert Guiscard.[21] (Bizarrely, a garbled list of Albanian place-names, picked up by the Normans on this expedition, was soon afterwards incorporated into the *Song of Roland*: one manuscript of that poem includes a reference to 'Albanie', implying that it was a place or area just north-east of Durrës.)[22] Over the next two centuries the references to Albanians gradually increase, until by 1281 we have a mention in an Italian document of a 'duca Ginius Tanuschus Albanensis', who ruled an area between Durrës and Shkodra: 'Ginius' must be the Albanian 'Gjin' (John), and this 'duca Gjin' is presumed to be the founder of the famous 'Dukagjin' family.[23] By the early fourteenth century there are also signs of a long-established Albanian presence in the mountains of Montenegro, and as far north as the Ragusan hinterland.[24]

The name used in all these references is, allowing for linguistic variations, the same: 'Albanenses' or 'Arbanenses' in Latin, 'Albanoi' or 'Arbanitai' in Byzantine Greek. (The last of these, with an internal switching of consonants, gave rise to the Turkish form 'Arnavud', from which 'Arnaut' was later derived.) Nor is there any mystery about the origin of this name. In the second century Ptolemy referred to a tribe called the 'Albanoi', and located their town, 'Albanopolis', somewhere to the east of Durrës. Some such place-name must have survived there, continuously if somewhat hazily, ever since; there was an area called 'Arbanon' in north-central Albania in the eleventh century, and in the early twentieth century 'Arben' was the local name for a region near Kruja (which lies just north of Tirana).[25] Linguists believe that the 'Alb-' element comes from the Indo-European word for a type of mountainous terrain, from which the word 'Alps' is also derived. (So too, coincidentally, is the Gaelic word for Scotland, 'Albainn', which classicizing eighteenth-century Scots sometimes turned into 'Albania'.)[26]

The continuity of this name is a striking fact; but it does not amount to proof that the Albanians have lived continuously in Albania. Place-names can endure while populations literally come and go. In any case, the Albanians do not use this word to describe themselves: in their language, Albania is Shqipëria, an Albanian is a *shqiptar*, and the language itself is *shqip*. (The only Albanians to use the 'Alb-' root are the ones who emigrated to Italy in the fifteenth century, who call themselves 'Arbëresh'.)[27] The origins of shqiptar, which first crops up as a personal name in late-fourteenth-century documents, are completely obscure: some think it means 'he who understands', from a verb *shqipoj*, while others connect it with the word for an eagle, *shqipojnë*, which may have been the totem of an early tribe.[28]

Is there any way to bridge the gap between the 'Albanoi' of the second century and the medieval Albanians? The historical record is utterly silent: there is one apparent reference in a medieval document to 'Duchagini d'Arbania' warring against a king of Bosnia in the seventh century, but it must be discounted, as the document's chronology is completely unreliable.[29] For some scholars, the argument from silence carries a certain force of its own; it is suggested that any large-scale migration of the early Albanians into Albania would surely have been remarked on by Byzantine authors.[30] But the truth is that those authors were interested in alien tribes only when their actions impinged, militarily or politically, on the Empire. A small pastoral population, moving away from them into some remote mountain region, might never have attracted their notice. Some Albanian archeologists have tried hard to show that the Koman hill-town culture of the seventh and eighth centuries is the essential proof of Illyrian–Albanian continuity; but material remains do not tell us what language people spoke (unless they include inscriptions, which these do not), and the main cultural affinities here seem to have been with the Latin-speaking Romano-Byzantine towns of the previous centuries.[31] And one other line of argument, which tries to find striking similarities between Albanian social practices and what classical authors tell us about the Illyrians, must also be described as inconclusive. Certainly the tribes of the ancient Illyrians, political groupings covering large areas and heavily stratified with a powerful ruling caste, were quite different from the modern Albanian clans.[32]

If there is any chance at all of solving this mystery, it lies in the study of the Albanian language. Historical linguistics is a complex science and not, in some of its activities, a very exact one. But by sifting through the evidence of vocabulary and place-names, and sorting out different layers of borrowings from other languages and cultures, linguists can often construct quite a detailed chronology, just like an archeologist examining different layers of wood-ash and broken pots. They can point out, for example, that the Albanian names for the fauna and flora of the high mountain regions are purely Albanian, while the low-altitude vocabulary borrows heavily from Slav; the words for ploughing are mainly Slav, and so are many words for weaving, masonry and milling. Much of the vocabulary of medieval government and society is also Slav-based.[33] This strongly suggests that the early Albanians led a mainly pastoral life in mountainous regions, before settling in lowland areas after the Slavs had extended their culture and rule. And the evidence of place-names shows that Albanian–Slav contacts in the northern Albanian region must have happened before 900 at the latest: a vowel-shift in the Slav language took place by the end of the ninth century, and some Albanian borrowings from Slav preserve the pre-shift form of the vowel.[34]

We have now got back to the ninth century, but that still leaves seven centuries unaccounted for. The most direct way of bridging the gap with the Roman world would be for the historical linguists to demonstrate a

link between Albanian and one of the 'barbarian' Balkan languages of
the region – either Illyrian or Thracian. It is clear that Albanian is indeed
the only surviving representative (apart from Greek) of an ancient
Balkan language: it belongs to the Indo-European family of languages,
but exists in a sub-section of its own, with no immediate relatives. If
either Illyrian or Thracian could be identified as its parent, this would at
least set some fairly clear geographical limits to the early home of the
Albanians: Illyrians lived in Albania and most of Yugoslavia, Thracians
in Bulgaria and part of Macedonia, and the boundary between them ran
approximately along the Morava valley and down the eastern side of
Kosovo.[35] (Kosovo itself was part of the tribal land of the Dardanians,
who almost certainly belonged to the Illyrian grouping.)[36]

Unfortunately, working out the relation between Albanian and Illyrian
or Thracian is like trying to solve an equation with too many unknowns.
We do not possess a single text in Illyrian. We have two short texts in
what is presumed to be Thracian, but no one knows what they mean.
The longer one, consisting of sixty-one Greek letters without any word-
divisions, has been subjected to eighteen speculative and somewhat
comically divergent translations: one version says 'I, Rolisteneas, son of
Nereneas, eat the sacrificial meal; Tylezypta, originally from Arazea,
attached the golden objects to me', while another comes up with 'O
Rolisten, I, Nerenea Tiltea, die peacefully next to you, my quietly
deceased one, I who raised the children.'[37] The linguists who have offered
these translations from the Thracian have at least fared better than the
one who interpreted an 'Illyrian' inscription as 'Consecrated to the
goddess Oethe': it was later pointed out that this inscription, if read
from bottom to top, produced a perfectly normal Greek phrase, 'Lord
help Anna'.[38]

Apart from inscriptions, there are a few 'glosses' (comments explain-
ing the meanings of words) in classical authors: here the evidence is too
slight to be conclusive. One Illyrian word, *rhinon*, glossed as 'mist', does
resemble an old Albanian word for cloud, *ren*. A Thracian word for a
blackberry, *mantia*, resembles the Albanian for a mulberry, *man*, and the
Thracian for 'camomile' could perhaps be linked to the Albanian for
'sweet-tasting'; but those are the only clear resemblances, and the names
of edible plants are in any case famously mobile across linguistic
frontiers.[39]

Otherwise, the only evidence available consists of proper names: place-names, personal names and tribal names, preserved in Latin or Greek inscriptions and the works of ancient historians. There are several thousand such names altogether; but the difficulties of interpretation are immense. Trying to extract a language from such evidence is rather like some linguists of the distant future trying to work out the true nature of the English language on the basis of 'Edinburgh', 'Lancaster', 'Whitby', 'Grosvenor', 'Gladstone', 'Victoria' and 'Disraeli'. Place-names are often the remnants of an earlier language; personal names may reflect cultural influences (it has been observed that if future linguists knew only the names 'Carlo' and 'Lodovico', they would assume that the Italian language was a type of German); and in any case we have no reason to suppose that the ancient Balkans were any less of a linguistic hotch-potch than they have been for most of the rest of their history.[40] On balance, there are more examples of plausible links between Illyrian names and Albanian words than there are in the case of Thracian (though there are some of both, and some names were common to the two ancient languages). Most of these relate to place-names in the area of central and northern Albania, such as the river Mat (Alb.: *mat*, river-bank) or the town of Ulqin or Ulcinium (Alb.: *ujk* or *ulk*, wolf), or indeed the early name for the Kosovo area, 'Dardania' (Alb.: *dardhë*, pear).[41]

The strongest evidence, however, comes not from the meaning of the proper names (which is always open to doubt) but from their structure. Most Illyrian names are composed of a single unit; many Thracian ones are made of two units joined together. Several Thracian place-names end in *-para*, for example, which is thought to mean 'ford', or *-diza*, which is thought to mean 'fortress'. Thus in the territory of the Bessi, a well-known Thracian tribe, we have the town of Bessapara, 'ford of the Bessi'. The structure here is the same as in many European languages: thus the 'town of Peter' can be called Peterborough, Petrograd, Peters-burg, Pierreville, and so on. But the crucial fact is that this structure is impossible in Albanian, which can only say 'Qytet i Pjetrit', not 'Pjetërqytet'. If *para* were the Albanian for 'ford', then the place-name would have to be 'Para e Bessëve'; this might be reduced in time to something like 'Parabessa', but it could never become 'Bessapara'. And what is at stake here is not some superficial feature of the language, which might easily change over time, but a profound structural principle. This is one of the strongest available arguments to show that Albanian cannot have developed out of Thracian.[42]

Other linguistic arguments which have been deployed in this Illyrian versus Thracian debate are more technical. Much ink has been spilt, for example, on the question of whether Illyrian was a *satem* language or a *centum* language. This is a traditional classification of all Indo-European languages according to their underlying patterns of consonant development. (The labels are taken from the Old Iranian and Latin for 'a hundred'.) Albanian is a satem language, and Thracian is thought to have been one too. Most scholars believed that Illyrian was a satem language, until linguists analysed the surviving inscriptions in Venetic, a language of north-eastern Italy which was assumed (on the authority of ancient authors) to be related to Illyrian. This turned out to be definitely centum, and persuaded some experts that the whole Illyrian group must therefore have been centum too – in which case Albanian could not have come from Illyrian.[43] However, more recent research has shown that Venetic had nothing to do with Illyrian.[44] (Similar problems caused by another language thought to be related to Illyrian, the Messapian language of southern Italy, have also been resolved in the same way.)[45] Illyrian was probably satem after all. And in any case, it is increasingly apparent that the whole satem/centum classification system does not correspond to the fundamental distinguishing features of the Indo-European languages: it may be the linguists' equivalent of one of those classifications of mammals by eighteenth-century biologists, which modern scientists have had to discard.[46] Another technical (and much more speculative) argument for identifying early Albanian with Thracian was put forward by the Bulgarian linguist Georgiev, who divided Thracian into two languages, one north-western, the other south-eastern, and argued on the basis of consonantal changes that Albanian must have come from the north-western one. But his arguments (at least in relation to the supposed Albanian connection) have been thoroughly dismantled by other scholars.[47]

Other linguistic arguments are more closely linked to geography. The place-names of the northern Albanian region offer a valuable linguistic testing-ground. We know what many of them were called in Roman times; it should therefore be possible to tell whether their modern

Albanian form derives from a continuous Albanian tradition going back to contact with the Romans, or whether it is derived from the Slav form of the name. If the latter, then this might suggest that the Albanians entered this area only after the Slav immigration of the seventh century. The fact that Slavs developed their own forms of the urban names directly from the Latin (Skadar from Latin Scodra, for example, where the Albanian form developed as Shkodër/Shkodra) is not in itself significant; their contact in the urban areas would have been mainly with Latin-speakers anyway. But if, on the other hand, the Slav names for rivers or mountains show that they were borrowed from Albanian forms of those names, this would indicate that there were Albanian-speakers in the countryside when the Slavs first arrived.

The evidence is in fact very mixed; some of the Albanian forms (of both urban and rural names) suggest transmission via Slav, but others – including the towns of Shkodra, Drisht, Lezha, Shkup (Skopje) and perhaps Shtip (Štip, south-east of Skopje) – follow the pattern of continuous Albanian development from the Latin.[48] (One common objection to this argument, claiming that 'sc-' in Latin should have turned into 'h-', not 'shk-' in Albanian, rests on a chronological error, and can be disregarded.)[49] There are also some fairly convincing derivations of Slav names for rivers in northern Albania – particularly the Bojana (Alb.: Buena) and the Drim (Alb.: Drin) – which suggest that the Slavs must have acquired their names from the Albanian forms.[50]

Finally, one more common-sensical linguistic and geographical argument should also be mentioned: the claim, by the pioneering German Balkanologist Gustav Weigand, that the early Albanians must have lived a long way to the east of the Adriatic coast, because most of the Albanian words for fish, boats and coastal features are borrowed from other languages.[51] Sterling efforts have been made by Albanian scholars to find authentic Albanian fish-words, but the tally, though not insignificant, is still rather poor.[52] However, Weigand's argument could not be very powerful even if its basic observation were correct (as it may in fact be). A pastoral population might have lived only 50 miles inland in the Albanian mountains without having any contact with fishing or sailing; it is not necessary to push its location eastwards all the way to Thrace.[53] Of course Illyrians did once live on the coast, and would presumably have had their own maritime vocabulary. But if Illyrian survived as

Albanian, it did so only by means of physical contraction, withdrawal and isolation, which naturally would have taken place in mountain terrain. This is why the purest element of Albanian vocabulary refers to mountains, high-altitude plants and shepherding: the point is not that the proto-Albanians had never lived any other sort of life, but that the only ones who survived as Albanian-speakers did so precisely because that was the sort of isolated and independent life they led, probably for several centuries. The Illyrians who lived on the coastal plains were Romanized, like the ones on the Dalmatian coast and indeed in most areas of Yugoslavia. By the time the Slavs began arriving in the sixth century, there were only scattered pockets of speakers of the old 'barbarian' languages left anywhere in the Balkans, and all of them were in mountainous regions.[54]

Of these, the only population considered important enough to be mentioned by name in early written sources was the Thracian tribe of the Bessi, who lived in the western and southern mountains of Bulgaria. We know that their version of the Thracian language was still being spoken in the second half of the sixth century, and we also know that they had been converted to Christianity: the most striking piece of evidence refers to monks speaking 'Bessan', as well as Latin and other languages, in a monastery on Mount Sinai in the 560s.[55] Until very recently, this was treated by most scholars as just an intriguing oddity, a last lingering survival which must have been extinguished before long. However, a dazzling new piece of research and speculative reconstruction by the German scholar Gottfried Schramm has proposed that these Thracian Bessi were none other than the real ancestors of the Albanians.

According to Schramm, the Bessi must have moved out of their western Bulgarian homeland and into the northern Albanian region in the early ninth century, probably to escape the persecution of Christians by the still pagan Bulgar khans.[56] The early conversion of the Bessi to Christianity is indeed, in Schramm's view, the key to the entire question of how and why Albanian survived as a language. We know that the Bessi were converted by an enterprising bishop, Nicetas, in the late fourth century, and from the writings of a friend of Nicetas who celebrated this event we also know that he learned their language and taught them to practise their Christianity in it – in other words, that Bessan was used as a liturgical language. (The evidence of the Bessan-speaking monks supports this point.) Nicetas, whose own mother-tongue was Latin, may also have translated parts of the Bible; the obvious model – or competition – that he must have had in mind was the work of a heretical bishop, Ulfilas, who was using the Germanic Gothic language for liturgy and Bible-translation among the nearby population of Goths in northern Bulgaria. And, as comparison with other linguistic survivals (such as Armenian or Coptic) shows, nothing helps a language to survive quite so much as its use from a very early stage in a kind of national church.[57]

One thing is quite certain: the Albanians did acquire their Christianity from a Latin-speaking teacher or teachers. The Albanian language contains much Latin-derived vocabulary anyway, having obviously absorbed words from nearby Romans or Romanized barbarians from the second century BC onwards; but the Latin element is especially rich in the area of Christian belief and Christian practice. Thus we have *meshë* (mass), from *missa*; *ipeshk* (bishop), from *episcopus*; *ungjill* (gospel), from *evangelium*; *mrekull* (miracle), from *miraculum*; and a great number of other words, extending far into the vocabulary of psychology, morality and even the natural world (such as *qiell*, meaning heaven or sky, from *caelum*).[58]

Many of the words that would need to be put on such a list, in fact, are not special ecclesiastical terms, for which a non-Christian population would have no equivalent of its own; they are simple words such as 'spirit', 'sin', 'pray', 'holy', and so on, for which most languages, even in pre-Christian times, have their own vocabulary. When other early evangelizers translated the Bible or the liturgy into Armenian, or Gothic, or Anglo-Saxon, they used local words for these things – that, indeed, is what is implied by the whole idea of translation. Why should Nicetas, translating into proto-Albanian, have simply transferred huge quantities of Latin words? Schramm notes the oddity of this in passing, and suggests unconvincingly that there must have been some special cultural reasons.[59] But the oddity is more overwhelming than he admits. For example, even the word for a flock, as used in Christian discourse, was taken from the Latin (*grigjë*, from *grex*) – of all the things in the world, the one for which a shepherding population must surely have had its own word already.[60]

The solution to this puzzle is blindingly simple. These elements of

Latin vocabulary have undergone exactly the same sorts of sound-changes, compressions and erosions as all the other Latin words which entered the Albanian language over several centuries; and the reason why those words entered the language was that the Albanians were in contact, over a long period, with people who spoke Latin. The existence of large quantities of such Christianity-related Latin vocabulary does not show that someone 'translated' Christian discourse into early Albanian. It shows the precise opposite – namely, that Albanians were for a long time exposed to the conduct of their religion not in translation but in the original Latin. This can even be demonstrated grammatically. The term for 'Holy Trinity', *Shëndërtat*, bears a final 't' and an accent on the last syllable: this shows that it developed from the accusative, *sanctam trinitatem*, not the nominative, *sancta trinitas*. That is in fact the normal pattern of development in Romance languages, which gives us, for example, Spanish *ciudad* from *civitatem* (not from *civitas*), or French *mont* from *montem* (not from *mons*). (There are many other Albanian examples too, such as *grigjë*, mentioned above, which is really from *gregem*, not *grex*.) What this phenomenon reflects is a pattern of usage in spoken Latin: these words were heard much more often as the objects in sentences than as the subjects. If Nicetas had been coining new Albanian words out of Latin for the purposes of his translation, he would surely have taken them from the nominative form. These words entered Albanian because Albanians heard them, over and over again, in spoken liturgical Latin.

Schramm's theory fails, therefore; and in so doing it performs a signal service. Thanks to Schramm, the Thracians can now be eliminated from these enquiries. His research into Nicetas's activities does indeed show that the Bessi received their Christianity, so to speak, in translation; this must force us to conclude that the Albanians, who received theirs in the original Latin, cannot be identified with the Bessi. The language of the Bessi must eventually have perished. Since the Bessi were the only Thracian tribe known to have kept their language as late as the sixth century (and Byzantine sources are naturally more detailed on the Thracian areas, which for them were closer to home, than on the Illyrian ones), it is impossible to find any other Thracian candidates. The origins of the Albanians must be sought, therefore, on the Illyrian side of the divide – particularly in the mountains round Kosovo, in the Malësi, and in the tangle of mountains stretching north from there through Montenegro.

The Latin elements in Albanian help to confirm this location. From the fact that so much general vocabulary was absorbed into Albanian from Latin, and so little from Greek, it is clear that the proto-Albanians lived some way to the north of the Latin–Greek linguistic divide. This language frontier ran from the Adriatic coast near Lezha across the middle of Albania, then up to the line of the Šar mountains, curving southwards to take in Latin-speaking Skopje, and then running north-wards roughly along the Serbian–Bulgarian border.⁶¹ At the same time, the fact that the proto-Albanians never actually lost their language indicates that they were somewhat isolated from the main areas of Roman settlement – which included the lowlands and the major roads. One influential theory therefore places the early Albanians in the part of northern Albania which (according to archeological evidence and place-names) was the most untouched by Roman influence: the 'Mat' district north-east of Tirana and west of Debar. From there, according to this theory, the early Albanians were able to expand to fill the region bounded by the river Shkumbin, the Black Drin, the united Drin and the coast.⁶²

What this theory fails to account for, however, is another key aspect of the Albanian language's connection with Latin: its intimate involve-ment in the development of the Vlach–Romanian language. Linguists have long been aware that Albanian and Romanian have many features in common, in matters of structure, vocabulary and idiom, and that these must have arisen in two ways. First, the 'substratum' of Romanian (that is, the language spoken by the proto-Romanians before they switched to Latin) must have been similar to Albanian; and secondly, there must have been close contact between Albanians and early Romanian-speakers over a long period, involving a shared pastoral life. (Some key elements of the pastoral vocabulary in Romanian are borrowed from Albanian.)⁶³ The substratum elements include both structural matters, such as the positioning of the definite article as a suffix on the end of the noun, and various elements of primitive Balkan pre-Latin vocabulary, such as *copil* ('child' in Romanian) or *kopil* ('bastard child' in Albanian).⁶⁴ If the links between the two languages were only at substratum level, this might not imply any geographical proximity – it would merely show that proto-Albanian was similar to other varieties of Illyrian spoken elsewhere. But the pastoral connections do indicate that Albanians and early Romanians lived for a long time in the same (or at least overlapping) areas.

This has some geographical implications. Late Latin developed in two different forms in the Balkans: a coastal variety, which survived as a distinct language (known as Dalmatian) until the end of the nineteenth century, and the form spoken in the interior, which turned into Romanian and Vlach.[65] From place-names it is clear that the coastal form, spoken also in Shkodra and Durrës, penetrated some way into the northern Albanian mountains.[66] There are some traces of this variety of Latin in Albanian, but the Albanian language's links with the inland variety of Balkan Latin are much stronger. This suggests that the centre of gravity of Albanian–Vlach symbiosis lay a little further to the east.[67]

When and how did that symbiosis take place? Presumably the Latin-speaking proto-Romanians came to pastoralism later than the early Albanians. If they had been doing it for as long as the Albanians, and in similar areas, they would – just like the Albanians – have escaped Latinization altogether. Some historians have decided that the proto-Romanians must have been Latin-speaking city-dwellers, who somehow extricated themselves from their towns in the early Slav centuries and became long-distance travellers or shepherds instead; but this seems inherently implausible.[68] (Had they come from the towns, their Latin would surely have been closer to standard Latin in its structure, too.) There is in fact enough Latin agricultural vocabulary in Romanian – words for sowing, ploughing, harrowing, and so on – to show that they were farming in Roman times.[69] The shift towards pastoralism was probably quite gradual. One particular factor that may have helped to promote it was the practice of horse-breeding, which was, or at least became, a Vlach speciality: the medieval records are full of Vlach muleteers and Vlachs leading caravans of pack-horses.[70] Such an occupation requires contact with towns (where the trade is), and may be combined with some farming in the towns' vicinity; but it also involves a form of stock-breeding, which could have given the early Vlachs an entrée into the higher-altitude world of Albanian flocks and herds.

The main area of the Balkan interior where a Latin-speaking population may have continued, in both towns and country, after the Slav invasion, has already been mentioned: it included the upper Morava valley, northern Macedonia, and the whole of Kosovo. It is, therefore, in the uplands of the Kosovo area (particularly, but not only, on the western side, including parts of Montenegro) that this Albanian–Vlach symbiosis probably developed.[71] All the evidence comes together at this point. What it suggests is that the Kosovo region, together with at least part of northern Albania, was the crucial focus of two distinct but interlinked ethnic histories: the survival of the Albanians, and the emergence of the Romanians and Vlachs. One large group of Vlachs seems to have broken away and moved southwards by the ninth or tenth century; the proto-Romanians stayed in contact with Albanians significantly longer, before drifting north-eastwards, and crossing the Danube in the twelfth century.[72]

Having reached these conclusions, it may be possible, finally, to draw some further implications from them that point back to a much earlier period of Kosovo's history. The point is a very simple one. If Albanian-speakers were able to live in this area without losing their language during the period from the sixth century to the twelfth, is there any reason to think that they could not have been there in the previous six centuries or more? The Roman province of Dardania contained some Roman towns and several large estates, but it was far from being utterly and homogeneously Romanized: frequent Roman references to Dardanian bandits and robbers, and the presence of many forts and watch-towers, suggest that it was never completely under control.[73] References to Dardanian cheese, a famous and widely exported product, also testify to a large shepherding population.[74] And if the shepherds in the hills were speaking proto-Albanian, then perhaps that is what the ordinary Dardanians had spoken in the valleys too, before the Romans came. This is more a speculation than a conclusion; and it is not meant to exclude other areas in the Albanian (or Montenegrin) mountains further to the west, given that 'Dardania' was, essentially, a tribal division, not a linguistic one. Once again it must be emphasized that such ancient history can have no implications for modern politics. Nevertheless, the idea that the Illyrian Dardanians were ancestors of the Albanians may be of some sentimental interest to Kosovo Albanians today.

3

Medieval Kosovo before Prince Lazar:
850s–1380s

THE PREVIOUS CHAPTER brought the political history (if such it may be called) of Kosovo up to the final period of Bulgarian–Macedonian rule, before the territory of Tsar Samuel was reconquered by the Byzantine Emperor Basil the Bulgar-slayer. Medieval Kosovo is often referred to in general terms as the 'cradle of the Serbs', as if it had been a Serb heartland from the outset; but the reality was rather different. Just over 800 years separate the arrival of the Serbs in the Balkans in the seventh century from the final Ottoman conquest in the 1450s: out of those eight centuries, Kosovo was Serb-ruled for only the last two-and-a-half – less than one-third of the entire period. Bulgarian khans or tsars held Kosovo from the 850s until the early eleventh century, and Byzantine Emperors until the final decades of the twelfth.

Unfortunately there is very little direct evidence about conditions in Kosovo during those earlier centuries of Bulgarian and Byzantine rule. We can assume that the Slav population that had settled in Kosovo was brought within the cultural realm of the Bulgarian Empire, which means that it would have been included in the Bulgarian dioceses of the Orthodox Church. Thanks to the work of Saints Cyril and Methodius (and their followers) in the ninth century, the Slavs had a liturgy and other texts in their own language, written in either of two newly invented alphabets: Cyrillic and Glagolitic. The western Macedonian town of Ohrid developed strongly as a cultural and religious centre in the ninth and tenth centuries, and by the end of Tsar Samuel's reign the archbishopric of Ohrid included bishoprics in Skopje, Lipljan (Alb.: Lipjan; a town just south of Prishtina) and Prizren.[1] Although the formal division of the Christian Church into Roman Catholic and Eastern Orthodox did not occur until 1054, it would not be anachronistic to describe this Bulgarian Christianity as Eastern in the ninth and tenth centuries; the roots of the conflict between East and West went back a long way. (The Slav liturgy was at first violently rejected by the Roman Church, on the grounds that God spoke only three languages: Hebrew, Greek and Latin.)

As early as the eighth century a Byzantine Emperor had transferred authority over the dioceses in most of the territory of modern Yugoslavia from Rome to Constantinople, and the power of the Pope in this part of the Balkans had contracted westwards, towards the coast.[2] From bases in Dalmatia and the territory of Dioclea (modern Montenegro), the Roman Church continued to operate in northern Albania, where it coexisted and competed – in the end, successfully – with the Orthodox for most of the Middle Ages.[3] Rome also influenced the Montenegrin area: some of the Serbs of Dioclea were brought under the Roman Church, and the ones in Rascia were subject at first to conversion from both sides, West and East (there is a church with a ninth-century Latin inscription near Prijepolje, well inside Rascian territory).[4] Albanians in the mountains round Kosovo presumably kept up their contact with the Roman Church through the bishoprics of northern Albania; there are also two shadowy references to a Roman bishop of Skopje, once in the late ninth century and again in 1204.[5] Later in the Middle Ages there were Catholic churches in Prizren and elsewhere. So it seems that some separate Roman Catholic tradition did survive throughout this period, albeit with a thoroughly second-class status. And this religious division may have corresponded to some extent to the linguistic divide between Albanian and Slav.

Not long after the Byzantine reconquest of Macedonia and Kosovo in the early eleventh century, a Greek from Constantinople was appointed bishop of Ohrid, and a steady process of cultural Hellenization got under way. By the end of the century, an energetic Greek bishop of Ohrid was shutting down Slavic schools and putting pressure on local churches to abandon the Slavic liturgy.[6] Highly educated Greeks served as bishops of Prizren in the eleventh and twelfth centuries; and Skopje became, to a significant extent, a Greek-speaking town.[7] We can assume that this Byzantinization of the region was accompanied by social changes too, with the introduction of the type of Byzantine feudal estate known as a *pronoia*. Large private land-holdings had spread throughout the Byzantine Balkans from the ninth century to the eleventh, squeezing out the earlier free village communities: independent peasants were turned into serfs, and entire villages became the possessions of the large estates. By the eleventh century, Byzantine emperors saw that they could not stop this development; so they regularized these land-holdings on a new basis, through the institution of the pronoia. In theory, a pronoia was an estate held on strictly conditional military–feudal terms; the holder had to bring soldiers to war, and did not have the right to sell or bequeath the land. In practice the pronoias became hereditary, and supported the growth of a powerful land-based aristocracy.[8] From the later documents of the Serbian kings it is clear that they found many such estates in the territories of Kosovo and Macedonia when they conquered them, and that the pronoia system continued under Serbian rule.[9]

Of the Serb powers to the north and west of Kosovo during these Byzantine centuries, Rascia (the nucleus of the future Serbian state) was at first overshadowed by its powerful neighbour to the west, Dioclea (Montenegro). Rulers installed as Dioclean vassals in Rascia soon broke free, however, and in the early twelfth century Rascia gained the upper hand. Rascian expansion was checked for a while by a heavy military defeat at the hands of the Byzantine army in 1150.[10] But in the 1160s a new Rascian ruling family emerged, which was to dominate the history of the region for the next 200 years. Its leading founder-member (there were several co-ruling brothers to begin with) was called Stefan Nemanja, and the dynasty he created is known as the Nemanjids. ('Nemanja' is a Serbian name derived from a Greek version of the biblical name 'Naaman'; the '-id' termination is a traditional way of referring to a dynasty, using a suffix from classical Greek.)

Stefan Nemanja inherited one part of the Rascian territory, on the northern flank of Kosovo. Within a few years, after some fierce fraternal in-fighting, he took over the whole of Rascia and was declared 'Grand Župan'. Then, during the 1180s, taking advantage of an enfeebled Byzantine Empire (which was fending off attacks elsewhere by Hungarians and Normans), he extended his rule in all directions: westwards into Dioclea and northern Albania, north-eastwards as far as Niš, and (in 1184–5) southwards through parts of Kosovo and down into northern Macedonia. Before long, a Byzantine counter-attack forced him to give up some of his conquests, including Niš in the north and the Skopje region in the south.[11] According to a biography of Nemanja written by one of his sons, he had also conquered 'the district of Prizren', a phrase which may refer to some part of the Prizren diocese in Western Kosovo rather than the town itself.[12] If he did conquer Prizren and other areas of Western Kosovo, then he must have given them up again soon afterwards.[13] But by the time Nemanja abdicated in 1196, the Rascian state (which from now on can be referred to as 'Serbia') had absorbed the whole of Eastern Kosovo.

Nemanja's abdication was for the good of his soul; he became a monk, and two years later went to join his youngest and most pious son, Sava, on Mount Athos. His successor in the main Serbian territories was another son, Stefan, who had a long and successful reign until his death in 1227. The most shocking event of this entire period in the Balkans was the seizure of Constantinople by the adventurers of the Fourth Crusade in 1204; it was probably as a direct result of that political upheaval that Stefan was able to take over most of Western Kosovo (excluding the area round Prizren), some time before 1208. A few years later (by 1216 at the very latest) he had also taken Prizren itself.[14] The whole territory of Kosovo was now under Serbian rule.

Stefan was not the only ruler to take advantage of the new instability in the Balkans. For much of his reign he was kept busy fending off various land-grabbing Bulgarian armies, and protecting his interests on the coast. This brought him into more contact both with Catholic powers (he married a granddaughter of the formidable old Doge of Venice – and chief architect of the Fourth Crusade – Enrico Dandolo), and with the Catholic Church in Dioclea. Despite the Orthodox piety of his father and younger brother, Stefan seems to have had no qualms about these Catholic connections; and it may be no accident that he mentions, in his own biography of his father, that Nemanja had actually received a Catholic baptism at his Montenegrin birthplace.[15] In 1217 Stefan was crowned King of Serbia by a papal legate, who had been sent from Rome specially for this purpose. He is thus known in Serbian history as Stefan 'Prvovenčani', the 'First-crowned'.

Stefan's brother Sava, who had spent the last ten years as the senior Orthodox churchman in Serbia, was so angered by this obeisance to Rome that he returned to Mount Athos. Two years later, however, Sava was able to make a spectacular deal, which was to have enormous long-term effects on Serbian history. Up until then the Serbian bishoprics (including those in Kosovo) had remained under the Archbishop of Ohrid, in the hierarchy of the Greek Orthodox Church. Sava's achievement in 1219 was to persuade the Patriarch to grant 'autocephaly' (autonomous status) to the Serbian Church. It may be wondered why any Patriarch should agree to surrender any rights over such a large part of his Church. But the answer is very simple: the Archbishop of Ohrid was in revolt against the Patriarch, and this move was a way of cutting half the Archbishop's territory from under his feet. Sava returned in triumph to Serbia, kicked out the Greek bishops from Kosovo, and set about reorganizing the Church with himself as autocephalous Archbishop – a position he held until 1233. (He died in 1235, and was canonized soon thereafter.)[16]

Despite Stefan's Catholic coronation and occasional opportunistic promises by several of his successors to transfer their allegiance to Rome, it is clear that the Orthodox Church played an important role in the dynastic ideology of the Nemanjids.[17] With both Nemanja and Sava canonized and revered, a royal cult developed which greatly strengthened the family's hold on power. (Originally this cult seems to have been modelled on the cult of an earlier ruler of Dioclea, St Jovan Vladimir; the Nemanjids must have been very envious of Dioclea's Pope-crowned dynasty and miracle-working royal saint.)[18] But at the same time the personal piety of Nemanja and Sava cannot be doubted. It was Sava, for example, who laid down the strict rules of Serbian monastic life, adapting them from those of a Greek monastery just outside the walls of Constantinople: they forbade all private possessions, the keeping of servants and all communication with family and friends. On their frequent fast-days the monks were limited to the consumption of bread, fruit, and hot water flavoured with caraway seeds.[19]

While the life may have been strict, however, the settings for it were lavishly expensive, in a great series of Nemanjid-founded monasteries. Although the architecture was provincial in style to begin with, no expense was spared on the decoration of these buildings. After the fall of Constantinople in 1204 many of the best fresco-painters had to go looking for employment elsewhere; they found it in Serbian territory, where they produced Byzantine work of the highest quality.[20] The earliest foundations were mainly in the old nucleus-territory of Rascia, to the north of Kosovo: Studenica, Nemanja's most important foundation, which still survives today, and a monastery dedicated to St George, the ruins of which (near Novi Pazar) are known as 'Djurdjevi Stupovi', 'George's Pillars'. Further to the north, near the central Serbian town of Kraljevo, the monastery of Žiča was founded by Stefan the First-crowned; this was chosen by Sava as the seat of his autocephalous Church. (Only at the end of the thirteenth century, when Žiča had been burnt down by a raiding expedition of Tatars and Cumans, did the seat of the archbishopric move to Peć in Western Kosovo.)[21] After Studenica, the second most important Nemanjid monastery was Mileševa, founded by Stefan the First-crowned's successor: this was much further to the west, towards the Bosnian border. And the main foundation of the next-but-one Serbian king was at Sopoćani, which lies just to the west of Novi Pazar. In other words, the cradle of Serbian monasticism in the first two or three generations of Nemanjid rule was located where the cradle of the Serbian state had been: not inside Kosovo, but further to the north and west. It was only later, with the development of the Patriarchate buildings at Peć, and the fourteenth-century foundations of Gračanica, Dečani and the monastery of the Holy Archangels in Prizren, that Kosovo gained any real importance for the Nemanjid church-building programme.

Stefan the First-crowned's successor-but-one, Stefan Uroš I, consolidated Serbian power in the mid-thirteenth century. His reign coincided with the end of the long Latin interlude at Constantinople and the restoration of the Byzantine Empire in 1261, which regained its Macedonian territories and thus bordered with Serbia again. Despite all the troubles and humiliations they had been through, the Byzantine Greeks still retained a sense of lofty cultural superiority. One Byzantine envoy who visited Stefan Uroš I's court in 1268 reported sneeringly that 'The Great King, as he is called, lives a simple life in a way that would be a disgrace for a middling official in Constantinople', that his daughter-in-law (Princess Catherine of Hungary) 'works at her spinning-wheel in a cheap dress', and that the royal household 'eats like a pack of hunters or sheep-stealers'.[22] Since the religion, culture, canon law and institutions of the Serbian kingdom were mainly derived from the Byzantine world, it is not surprising that this feeling of Constantinopolitan superiority was, to some extent, reciprocated by the Serbian rulers, with an attitude of deference and eager emulation.

Of no one is this more true than of Stefan Uroš I's younger son, Milutin, who took over the main part of the kingdom from his elder brother (in what seems to have been a peaceful coup) in 1282.²³ Some time thereafter (perhaps in the 1290s) he seized Skopje, an important town with a more Greek character than any of his other possessions: this became his capital.²⁴ In 1299 he realized a long-standing ambition by marrying a daughter of the Byzantine Emperor: as a dowry, Milutin received imperial permission to keep the large part of Macedonia he had conquered. By 1315, when Milutin had subdued his elder brother in the northern Serbian territories and occupied the Adriatic coast as far south as Durrës, he was the most powerful monarch in the Balkans. Enriched by his new lands and by the growing exploitation of Kosovo's mines, he had embarked on a colossal church-building programme, not only within the Serbian state, but also at Mount Athos, Salonica, Constantinople and Jerusalem. (Fifteen foundations were listed by one early biographer; only three of these were in Kosovo, but they included the extraordinarily compact and complex architectural masterpiece of Gračanica.)²⁵ At the same time he was engaged in a determined programme of Byzantinizing Serbian institutions, with elaborate imitations of Byzantine officialdom and court life.²⁶ Milutin was thus laying the foundations, psychologically as well as territorially, for the declaration of a Serbian 'Empire' by his grandson, Dušan. The Greeks were impressed – but only up to a point. Although one Byzantine official who visited Milutin in 1299 was struck by his clothing (covered in jewels, pearls and gold thread) and his furnishings (all made of silk and gold), he nevertheless reported: 'there are many people around him who are vile and ill-natured; the people of these regions are barbarous, uncouth and ignorant.'²⁷

The reign of Milutin's son, Dečanski (so called because he commissioned another architectural masterpiece, the monastery of Dečani, south of Peć) was shorter and more troubled. That he was able to succeed to the throne at all was due to luck: Milutin had had him blinded – a disqualification for kingship – as a punishment for leading a rebellion, but it seems that this was incompetently done, and he retained enough sight to get by.[28] Dečanski further extended Serbian power, by inflicting a heavy defeat on Bulgarian forces in 1330. But in the following year family history repeated itself: his own son, Dušan, rebelled against him. For some time Dušan had been based in Shkodra, governing the Serbian kingdom's Montenegrin and northern Albanian territories. It was from there that he marched with his own army – including, it can be assumed, large numbers of Albanians – and attacked his father at Nerodimlje in Kosovo. Dečanski was defeated, imprisoned, and, not long afterwards, strangled. Dušan was crowned King in September 1331.[29]

The reign of Dušan brings the medieval Serbian state to its apogee. It was a short-lived glory: his main territorial conquests were in the 1340s, and the empire he created began to break up soon after his death in 1355. Yet, while it lasted, the phenomenon was extraordinary. Dušan took advantage of a long-running civil war in the Byzantine Empire to conquer a huge stretch of territory, including the whole of southern Albania and most of northern Greece. In this way he built up a multilinguistic empire, extending from the Danube to the Gulf of Corinth. Albanians played a major role: the army Dušan used to conquer northern Greece consisted mainly of Albanians, who were taking revenge on the Byzantines for earlier attacks on their territory, and this conquest was followed by the migration into Greece of large numbers of Albanians and Albanian Vlachs.[30]

The capital of this empire was Skopje, and it was there, in 1346, that Dušan made two important changes in status. First, with the assent of the Bulgarian Patriarch and the monastic leaders of Mount Athos, the Serbian autocephalous Archbishop was raised to the rank of Serbian Patriarch.[31] The Serbian Church, which up till then had remained at least theoretically part of the Greek Church, was now fully independent. Next, on Easter Day, the new Serbian Patriarch crowned Dušan as 'Emperor of the Serbs and the Greeks'. (He is thus known as Tsar Dušan, using the Slav word for emperor, *car.*) The symbolic threat to the Byzantine Empire was obvious: Dušan imitated Byzantine ritual (wearing, for example, imperial purple shoes at his coronation), and distributed to his followers various grand-sounding titles, such as 'despot', which only an Emperor could bestow.[32] He also issued an imposing new code of law, modelled mainly on Byzantine practices. At various times in his career, Tsar Dušan seems to have thought seriously about seizing

Constantinople and taking over the whole of the Byzantine Empire; but this was not to be. He died, aged forty-six, in 1355.

The break-up of the Serbian Empire under Dušan's son, Tsar Uroš, was fairly rapid. The Greek and southern Albanian territories fell into the hands of local noblemen; part of Macedonia was taken over by a Serb called Branko (father of the famous Vuk Branković); and even within the areas that were technically under Uroš's rule, *de facto* power was exercised by local dynasties, such as the Balsha (Srb.: Balšić) family of north-western Albania and Montenegro.[33] Tsar Uroš was also obliged to share power with one of his senior administrators, a man of Hercegovinan origin called Vukašin; eventually he gave Vukašin the subsidiary title *kralj* (king), which is why Vukašin's son, a popular hero of Slav folk epics, is known as Marko Kraljević.[34] Also important was Vukašin's brother, who took over a large area on the modern Greek–Bulgarian border. And among other noblemen who vied for power in a Serbian civil war in the 1360s, one requires special mention: Lazar Hrebeljanović (the future hero of the battle of Kosovo), son of a senior court official, who acquired a territorial base in north-central Serbia centred on the town of Kruševac.

In 1371 two events happened which hastened the collapse of the Serb state: a Serbian army under Vukašin and his brother was annihilated by Ottoman Turkish forces at a battle on the river Marica in Bulgaria, and Tsar Uroš died. The second of these events marked the end of the Nemanjid dynasty (Uroš was childless), and prompted a further territorial shake-up: the Balsha family seized part of south-western Kosovo, including Peć and Prizren, and Lazar moved south to take Prishtina. By the end of the decade, however, those three towns (and all the territory in between) had been taken over by Lazar's chief rival, Vuk Branković, whose family estates were in north-central Kosovo, between Peć and Prishtina. But Lazar still held all the northern part of Serbia (which he extended further), and the eastern strip of Kosovo, including the rich mines of Novo Brdo. This made him the dominant ruler in the Serb lands, as those territories entered their final decade of full independence.[35]

From this brief survey of the Nemanjid period, it is clear that Kosovo played an important role in the Serbian state. It was, or became, central

– at least in the geographical sense. A dynastic territory which had begun on the northern side of Kosovo was extended southwards (under Milutin) beyond Kosovo's southern border: Kosovo thus became the geographical heart of the kingdom. With Serbian rule extending to Montenegro and northern Albania for most of this period, the trading routes through Kosovo from the coast were also important. (Prizren developed strongly as a commercial centre in the fourteenth century, with its own colony of Ragusan merchants.)[36] And it was of course the mines of Kosovo that provided much of the wealth of the Nemanjids.

However, if we move from geography and economics to politics, the centrality of Kosovo becomes much less apparent. The medieval Serbian state never had an official capital, but most of these rulers tended to have one main centre of residence and administration: from Nemanja's reign to the mid-thirteenth century this was at Ras (near Novi Pazar), the old centre of Rascia, and from Milutin onwards it was at Skopje. Prizren and Prishtina were sometimes used, and from the late thirteenth century the kings had a number of lakeside courtly residences in south-central Kosovo.[37] But for important ceremonies (Milutin's marriage, Dušan's coronation), only Skopje would do. And the ruler with whom the fate of Kosovo is most strongly associated, Prince Lazar, had his own centre of administration at Kruševac, much further to the north. As we have seen, Kosovo was not the main focus of the church-building activities of most of these rulers, although important churches and monasteries were built there, particularly in the fourteenth century. One factor only made Kosovo central to the Serbian Church: the location of the seat of the Archbishopric, and then Patriarchate, in Peć. This was largely the consequence of a chance attack on the monastery of Žiča in the 1290s by a marauding force of Tatars and Cumans. Had those raiders taken another route, perhaps Kosovo would never have acquired the significance which it has gained for modern Serbs.

The church-founding activities of the Nemanjids performed one useful service for the historian: when they granted income-yielding estates to the monasteries, they described them in great detail in special charters or 'chrysobulls'.[38] From these and a number of other texts (the most important being the early royal biographies and Dušan's code of laws), it is possible to build up quite a detailed picture of life in Nemanjid Kosovo. Society was heavily stratified, with a two-level noble class, corresponding roughly to the barons and knights of western Europe. (The system may well have been influenced by Western models, having apparently developed among the Serbs as late as the twelfth century.) Only a nobleman could own a fully freehold property. The Serbian kings established the basic feudal principle that all land not in full freehold ownership was theirs, and they also continued the type of conditional military–feudal property, inherited from the Byzantines, known as a pronoia (Srb.: *pronija*).[39]

Further down the social scale was the peasant or *meropah* (from the Greek word *merops*), who was tied to the land, and below the level of the meropahs there was a significant population of slaves. The documents refer very occasionally to 'free men', who may have been independent peasants; but most were on the feudal estates, where their duties (according to Dušan's law code) included labouring two days a week on their lord's land, cutting his hay and working in his vineyard, and paying him six gold francs per year.[40] Other taxes and impositions included obligatory labour on royal land or the building of forts or palaces, fodder for royal horses and other transport services, a state tithe, a 'hearth-tax', customs duties (paid in the market, not at the border), and several other taxes in money and kind.[41] Direct comparison between the level of taxation and forced labour in medieval Kosovo and the level in the early Ottoman period is difficult to make, but some scholars believe that conditions were better under the Ottomans (at least to begin with), since many of the labour services were then commuted into a single monetary tax.[42]

Social divisions were strictly maintained by Tsar Dušan's criminal laws. A nobleman who raped a noblewoman would have his hands cut off; a commoner who raped a noblewoman would be hanged. If, however, a noblewoman fornicated with a peasant, both would have their hands cut off and their noses slit. Anyone who 'plucked the beard' (presumably a symbolic insult) of a lord would lose his hands; anyone who beat a judge's cook would be imprisoned and stripped of all his property. Brigands would be hanged, thieves blinded, and the villages in which they were found would be destroyed. And the punishment for any meropah who absconded from his master's estate was to slit his nose and brand him.[43] (This last provision, again, contrasts with the Ottoman system, in which only a monetary penalty was applied.) That brigands

and thieves were a constant problem is confirmed by frequent references
to 'watches' or guard-posts on the roads of medieval Kosovo.[44] If these
laws were strictly applied, blinded or mutilated men must have been a
frequent sight in the Kosovo countryside. But of course it is always
difficult to deduce actual conditions from the formal provisions of a
legal code. A similar problem arises when reading that St Sava, preaching
with tears in his eyes, begged his flock to refrain from adultery,
homosexuality and bestiality: as the great Slavic scholar Konstantin
Jireček noted somewhat drily on this passage, 'He would not have done
that without a reason.'[45]

Of particular interest in Dušan's code are the articles relating to
religion. There is one which lays down punishments for people uttering
a *babunska reč* or 'heretical word'; the term *babunski* is usually taken as
referring to the Bulgarian Bogomil heresy, although this was almost
extinct by the time Dušan's code was promulgated.[46] More important,
probably, are the articles on the 'Latin heresy' (Roman Catholicism),
which order punishment for those who fail to 'return to Christianity',
and decree: 'If any heretic be found living among the Christians, let him
be branded on the face and driven forth.'[47] As we have seen, the early
Nemanjids had had some Catholic connections of their own; Stefan the
First-crowned received his kingly title from the Pope, and some of them
also married Catholic princesses. Milutin's wife, Queen Helen, was from
a French family (probably Anjou), and her confessor was a Franciscan
friar specially recommended to her by the Pope. By 1303 there were at
least two Catholic parishes in Kosovo, Trepça and Gračanica (Alb.:
Graçanica). Various popes urged Milutin to convert to Catholicism, or
Helen to convert him, and in 1308 Milutin even sent two envoys to
discuss the matter in Rome. But nothing came of that, and it is evident
that within the next ten years he was actively persecuting Catholics.[48]
This policy seems to have continued under his two successors; and yet
the first references to specific Catholic churches in Kosovo – at Prizren,
Trepça, Janjevo (Alb.: Janjeva) and Novo Brdo – come from the middle
of Dušan's reign.[49]

The explanation of this paradox is probably very simple. These
churches were permitted because they were patronized by privileged
communities of outsiders: above all, Ragusan merchants and 'Saxon'
miners. It must have been principally for the benefit of these commun-

ities that a series of Catholic bishops of Prizren were appointed from the 1330s to the 1380s. (Whether these bishops actually visited their diocese, however, is not recorded; one was an English friar from Notting-hamshire, Robert of Worksop.)[50] The Ragusans, who had their own commercial treaties with the Serbian kings, have already been mentioned; they had a formal right to worship in their own churches, and were supplied with priests from Kotor (in Montenegro) or Albania. There is a record of one Ragusan merchant from Novo Brdo who died in 1387 and left money for the completion of a Catholic church in Prishtina.[51]

The 'Saxons' (Srb.: 'Sasi') were Germans, not from Saxony but from Transylvania or northern Hungary. Experts in mining, they were encour-aged to settle in the Serbian lands from the mid-thirteenth century onwards, and were granted wide-ranging privileges. They had their own courts, consisting of *purgari* (from the German, *Bürger*, burghers), and they seem to have preserved their language until the sixteenth century. Thanks to their technical skills, and the capital and commercial links of the Ragusans, the production of silver, gold and lead boomed from the late thirteenth century onwards in the three main mining centres of Kosovo: Trepça, Janjevo and Novo Brdo. It has been claimed that between 1350 and 1450 Novo Brdo was 'the best-known town in the Balkans'.[52] The Serbian kings also minted their own coins at Novo Brdo and Prizren, although Milutin's first venture in coin-production has earned him an unenviable place in literary history. He produced imitations of Venetian silver coins containing only seven-eighths of the silver; Venice banned them, and Dante denounced 'the King of Rascia' as a counterfeiter in his *Divine Comedy*.[53]

Finally, two other categories of people also received special treatment in Nemanjid Kosovo: Vlachs and Albanians. These are mentioned several times in Dušan's code, usually together. For example, 'When a Vlach or an Albanian ['Arvanas'] stays in a village, other herdsmen who come after them may not stay in the same village.' From such references, it is clear that the terms 'Albanian' and 'Vlach' refer to semi-nomadic shepherds; there are also rules about payments to landlords for winter grazing rights, and so on. One intriguing article declares: 'All shepherds of my Empire who have actions among themselves touching murder, brigandage, theft, killing, harbouring or land, shall appear before the judges of the court.' One scholar suggests that this was to stop local lords from arrogating the right to judge their peasantry; but if that were so, it would have been logical to refer to all land-workers, not just the shepherds.[54] It is tempting to speculate that this article was an early attempt to clamp down on the self-administered customary law of the mountains, as later codified in the Kanun of Lek Dukagjin. (If so, this would be the earliest evidence that such customary laws were in operation.) Certainly these pastoral people were seen as particularly liable to violence or revenge. One article sets out a scale of penalties as follows: 'A brawl between villages, fifty perpers [one perper was worth six gold francs]; but between Vlachs and Albanians, one hundred perpers.'[55]

From the details of the monastic estates given in the chrysobulls, further information can be gleaned about these Vlachs and Albanians. The earliest reference is in one of Nemanja's charters giving property to Hilandar, the Serbian monastery on Mount Athos: 170 Vlachs are mentioned, probably located in villages round Prizren. When Dečanski founded his monastery of Dečani in 1330, he referred to 'villages and katuns of Vlachs and Albanians' in the area of the White Drin: a *katun* (Alb.: *katund*) was a shepherding settlement. And Dušan's chrysobull of 1348 for the Monastery of the Holy Archangels in Prizren mentions a total of nine Albanian katuns.[56] More than once these chrysobulls refer to a special 'law of the Vlachs', relating mainly to taxation: they paid a lower rate of state tithe, and were meant to hand over one sheep and one lamb per annum for every 100 (or, sometimes, every fifty) in their flock.[57] One curious statement in Dečanski's chrysobull is that a Serb must not marry a Vlach: if he does, he must become a meropah (peasant tied to the land) – a puzzling requirement, since most Serbs were meropahs anyway.[58]

Serbian historians have often argued that the word 'Vlach' was not an ethnic category at all, and that it merely referred to a pastoral way of life. Its usage may have blurred in that way much later in its history, but in this period it clearly indicated more than just a shepherd: otherwise why specify Vlachs and Albanians, when shepherding was their common occupation? In fact, the sources clearly show that 'Vlach' could be used in an ethnic-linguistic sense. A charter of 1280 for a monastery near Shkodra, for example, alluded to 'other noblemen, whether Serb, Latin, Albanian or Vlach'; and in any case, several of the documents mention individuals with obviously Vlach names, such as 'Surdul'.[59] But with the exception of those putative noblemen in the charter, the term seems in medieval Serbia to have been used almost always to describe people who were *both* ethno-linguistically Vlach *and* engaged in shepherding, horse-breeding, caravan-leading and so on. It could be argued that Vlachs engaged only in those occupations, and never turned to any others (apart from soldiering, which was a tradition among most mountain peoples). But since we know that some Vlachs have drifted into town life and settled agriculture in almost all places and periods, it seems more reasonable to suppose that this happened in medieval Serbia too, and that when it did so, they became assimilated to the Serb population and ceased sooner or later to be described as Vlachs.

Which prompts the question of whether the same process was happening to Albanians – and, if so, to what extent. There is some evidence that Albanians were more apt to turn to settled agriculture than the Vlachs: the rule against intermarriage mentioned above did not apply to Albanians; Dušan's chrysobull for the monastery at Prizren has different taxation rules for Vlachs and Albanians, with the Albanians performing agricultural labour-service like the Serbs; and one of Milu-tin's charters also puts Albanians and Serbs in the same category.[60] If Albanians began to live like Serbs, perhaps after some time they would cease to be described as 'Albanians' in the official documents.

Modern Albanian writers have made much of the fact that the chrysobulls demonstrate the presence of people described as Albanians in medieval Kosovo; but if the evidence of these documents is all that can be relied on, then the conclusion must be that the Albanians were a declining minority. Certainly a tabulation of all the personal names mentioned by these medieval charters shows a majority of Slav Orthodox names.[61] In the earliest charters, the majority is strong, but not over-whelming: Stefan the First-crowned's charter for Žiča, of *c*.1210, gives 154 Serb names and fifty-four non-Serb, most of which are clearly either Albanian or Vlach (such as 'Mik', 'Doda', 'Bukor' and 'Šarban'). This ratio gradually changes: in the Banjska charter of 1313–14, for example, it is 444 Serb to 117 non-Serb names. The scholar who first presented this evidence drew the natural conclusion that it represented a steady process of Serbianization.[62]

A few recent works by Albanian historians have suggested that many of the bearers of those Serbian Orthodox names were also ethnic Albanians – a hidden ethnic mass whose re-emergence in the early Ottoman period explains an otherwise puzzling 'Albanianization' of the area.[63] Most of this argument is based on evidence from the early Ottoman centuries: it will therefore be discussed in Chapter 6. Here it can only be observed that this line of argument makes some good points, but fails to establish its case for the medieval period. One valid point is that evidence which is drawn from grants of property to Orthodox monasteries may well be rather skewed: first, because such endowments were more likely to include agricultural villages and exclude the harder-to-tax semi-nomadic shepherds, and secondly, because being controlled by a famous monastery must have encouraged a closer identification with Serbian Orthodoxy among the villagers themselves. (Several of the chrysobulls are confirmations of grants, dealing with villages which have already been monastic property for some time.)

Another valid point is that personal names – which are all the evidence we have – are not very reliable guides to ethnic identity. This was demonstrated by the Serbian scholar Stojan Stanojević as long ago as 1929. Sifting through the names in the Dečani charters, he found many cases where the father had an Albanian name, and the son a Serbian one; or vice-versa; or stranger combinations involving three generations. Thus we have a father called Tanush (Alb.), whose son is called Boljko (Srb.); a father called Bogdan (Srb.), with a son called Progon (Alb.); and several pairs of brothers such as Gon (Alb.) and Drajko (Srb.). Stanojević's explanation is twofold: intermarriage, and sheer fashion.[64] Some features of the evidence he collected – particularly, the cases of Serb-named fathers producing Albanian-named sons, which are slightly more numerous than the converse – weigh against any simplistic explanation in terms of a rapid one-way process of assimilation, from Albanian to Serb. And yet, given the dominance of Serbian Orthodoxy and the Serb language in medieval Kosovo, it is reasonable to think that the overall flow of assimilation must have been in that direction, whatever the minor swirls and eddies. The main conclusion has to be that, whatever quantity of assimilation was involved, it worked: many of the people who underwent this process must have lost the Albanian language and become Serbs. The idea that the great mass of the Kosovo population, behind the cover of their Serbian Orthodox names, were Albanians who continued to speak Albanian, is simply not credible. If that were true, then the names of most of the towns and villages in Kosovo would have been Albanian; whereas in fact the great majority of them are Slav. Albanians have certainly had a continuous presence in this region. But all the evidence suggests that they were only a minority in medieval Kosovo.

4

The Battle and the Myth

THERE ARE TWO popular assumptions about the great battle of Kosovo in 1389: that it was this Turkish victory that destroyed the medieval Serbian empire, and that the defeated Serbs were immediately placed under Ottoman rule. Both are false. The first assumption ignores the fact that the Serbian empire had disintegrated soon after the death of Tsar Dušan in 1355. And Serbian statehood did survive (as we shall see in the next chapter) for another seventy years, with only a limited degree of Ottoman interference for some of that time. As for the significance of battles, many historians believe that the earlier Turkish victory at the river Marica in Bulgaria in 1371 had much more far-reaching effects than the battle of Kosovo: it was Marica, arguably, that opened the way to the overall Ottoman conquest of the Balkans.[1] The battle of Marica must also have had a severe effect on the Serbs: a large Serbian army was entirely wiped out by a surprise night-time attack there, and this defeat resulted in the loss of the important Serb-ruled territories in Macedonia. (The son of the dead 'kralj', Marko Kraljević, was installed there as a tribute-paying vassal by the Turks.)[2]

However, for the Serbian heartlands it does make sense to regard the battle of Kosovo as an important turning-point, the event which ensured that Serbian statehood would be extinguished sooner or later. And in any case, the significance of this battle to the Serbian people is not to be measured simply in terms of its politico-strategic consequences. The story of the battle of Kosovo has become a totem or talisman of Serbian identity, so that this event has a status unlike that of anything else in the history of the Serbs. To call this ideologically charged story 'the myth of Kosovo' is not to suggest that everything in it is false, but rather to indicate the talismanic way in which it operates. Yet some aspects of the myth of Kosovo probably are false, and it is the proper job of historians both to try to set down a more accurate account, and to explain how and why the myth itself arose.

By the late 1370s, as we have seen, the former Serb-ruled lands were divided into a patchwork of principalities. The largest patch was that of Lazar Hrebeljanović, based on the central Serbian town of Kruševac and including a strip of eastern Kosovo. With his control over the richest mines of Kosovo and central Serbia, Lazar was the most powerful of the Serb rulers; he also took the leading role as sponsor of the Serbian Church, with the Patriarch residing once again at Žiča, in his territory.[3] Most of Kosovo was held by Vuk Branković; he had pushed out the Balsha family from Peć and Prizren, but they still controlled much of Montenegro and northern Albania. The greatest power in the whole region was the King of Bosnia, Tvrtko, who had joined Lazar in carving up the territory of another ruling family in western and central Serbia. Tvrtko and Lazar enjoyed generally good relations. Lazar also tried hard to bind his neighbours in a network of family alliances, marrying off two of his daughters to Vuk Branković and one of the Balshas. But it was difficult to keep all relationships equally in good repair, given that the Balshas and Tvrtko were frequently at war with each other, as they struggled for territory on the Adriatic coast.[4]

In 1385 the ruling Balsha lord had been killed in a battle against a Turkish raiding force in central Albania. Before long his successor, Gjergj II Balsha, had agreed to become a Turkish vassal.[5] He may have thought this not merely a prudent arrangement, but a positively advantageous one: it gave him more military muscle with which to oppose not only the threat of Bosnian expansion, but also his various rebellious local magnates (including the Dukagjin family, and the Thopia family of Durrës, which had invited the Turks in to attack the Balshas in the first place).[6] Modern Balkan writers tend to view anyone who cooperated willingly with the Turks, or invited them as allies into the area, as guilty of the most heinous treachery against their nation and their identity. But this way of looking at the past is highly anachronistic. Every medieval ruler made use, when possible, of other people's armies; and drawing in a potentially threatening power to divert it against one's enemies was also normal practice. Strange soldiers speaking unknown languages were nothing new: Balkan rulers had long been making use of Hungarians,

Germans, Catalans and others. The only thing that was obviously different about the Turks was that they were not Christians. That may not have seemed very important at the time: after all, they were in the area to fight, not to preach, and they were not making any attempt to convert their new vassal territories in the Balkans to Islam.

In fact the entire history, up to that point, of Turkish expansion in the Balkans had been a history of cooperation with Christian rulers. The first Turkish soldiers who crossed into Europe did so on the invitation of a Catalan commander in 1305. Several years later, after they had split up with the Catalans, they entered the employment of the Serbian King Milutin, who hoped to use them in a campaign against the Byzantine army; eventually he settled them on Serbian territory.[7] (Possibly this settlement of 1,500 Turks in Milutin's kingdom explains an otherwise puzzling reference in a Ragusan document of 1353 to a slave-girl from Kosovo, 'Yeni of Lipljan', bought from 'Yunan, a Turk'.)[8] Milutin also had a large force of Turkic Cumans, and Tsar Dušan employed Turks in his army.[9] The Byzantine civil war of the 1340s, which enabled Dušan to embark on his own great programme of expansion, revolved around the use of Turkish forces: the Emperor who was struggling to regain his throne, John Cantacuzenus, depended for several years on the army and navy of a western Turkish emir. When that ally went home, Cantacuzenus turned instead to the most powerful of the Turkish emirs, the Ottoman ruler, Orhan, and gave him his own daughter in marriage. It was at Cantacuzenus's instigation that the Turks plundered several towns to the west of Constantinople, and it cannot have surprised him greatly when the Ottomans, having occupied a large stretch of the coastline in 1354, refused to give it up.[10] This was the Ottoman foothold in Europe. In 1360 Orhan was succeeded by his younger son Murat, who embarked on an energetic campaign of expansion in Thrace, Bulgaria and Macedonia, capturing the key town of Adrianople (Edirne) in 1361 and winning his decisive victory at the river Marica ten years later.

By the 1380s Serbia and Bosnia, both prosperous areas with highly productive silver mines, were the most obvious choice for the next target. In 1386 Murat attacked Lazar's territory and seized the town of Niš, which, with its position athwart the river Morava and at the junction of two major roads, was of great strategic importance. Many historians have said that Lazar agreed to become a tribute-paying vassal of the

Turks at that point; but the only evidence for this idea is an account by an influential early-sixteenth-century Ottoman historian, Neşri, who tried to justify Murat's campaign of 1389 as retribution against Lazar for breach of promise. Since there is other evidence of a military skirmish between Lazar's and Murat's forces soon after the taking of Niš, the claim about vassalage should probably be rejected.[11] In Gjergj Balsha's case, however, the evidence is stronger. It was probably with Balsha's cooperation that a large raiding force of Turks attacked the southern tip of Bosnia in 1388. (A minor Ottoman raid on Kosovo, probably associated with this expedition, is also recorded for that year.)[12] But the expedition ended in failure, with a crushing defeat at the hands of one of King Tvrtko's military commanders, Vlatko Vuković.[13] To avenge this humiliation, and to secure the intervening territory between his existing possessions and the long-term target of Bosnia, Murat assembled his army and advanced on Kosovo in the summer of 1389. Lazar called on the Bosnians for help, and was sent a large contingent of soldiers under Vlatko Vuković. Lazar's son-in-law, Vuk Branković, whose own territory was directly in the line of the Ottoman advance, came with another large body of troops. And so it was that the forces of these three leaders (with some other contingents too), under the general command of Prince Lazar, were drawn up on Kosovo Polje, a few miles to the north-west of Prishtina, at the confluence of the rivers Lab (Alb.: Llap) and Sitnica, on the morning of 15 June 1389.

The few things that are known with real certainty about this battle can be stated in very few words. The fighting was intense, and there were heavy losses on both sides. Both Lazar and Murat were killed. At the end of the battle the Turks were left in possession of the field. Murat was succeeded by his son Bayezit, who was commanding some of the Turkish forces at the battle; he then took what remained of his army back to the Ottoman heartlands to secure his succession. Lazar was succeeded by his young son Stefan Lazarević, who, acting under the guidance of his mother, the widowed Queen Milica, later agreed to become a Turkish vassal. Everything else about the battle of Kosovo is uncertain: who took part, how large the armies were, what the order of battle was, what the key turning-points in the fighting may have been, how and when Lazar and Murat met their deaths, and whether, in the end, it should be characterized as a victory or a draw.

There is widespread disagreement about the composition of the armies. Serbian historians, for example, make little or no mention of Albanian forces in Lazar's army, while Albanian historians give them a prominent place. There is one valuable piece of evidence that Albanians did take part: an early-sixteenth-century family history of an Albanian noble family, the Muzaka (or 'Musachi'), records that Teodor Muzaka brought 'a large band of Albanians' to join Lazar's army, together with 'other Albanian lords', and that he was killed in the battle.[14] Many of the other details in this memoir are verifiably accurate, so this claim may well be trustworthy too. On the other hand, Albanian history books claim that the Serbo-Albanian Gjergj Balsha, whom they treat as a purely Albanian figure, also took part, and this is almost certainly false. The only basis for this claim is the account of the early Ottoman historian Neşri, whose justification for Murat's campaign of 1389 involved an elaborate story of broken promises and a conspiracy between Balsha, Lazar and Tvrtko. As we have seen, this story is doubtful in Lazar's case, and the known hostility between Tvrtko and Balsha makes it even harder to believe. In any case, it was demonstrated nearly a century ago that Balsha must have been at Ulcinj, on the Montenegrin coast, on the day of the battle.[15]

The earliest Ottoman accounts, written in the fifteenth century, do refer to Albanians in Lazar's army; they also list many other ethnic components. One refers to mercenaries from Serbia, Albania, Bosnia and Hungary; another adds to that list soldiers from Wallachia (part of Romania), and Bulgarians, Czechs and 'Franks' (western Europeans); Neşri, synthesizing several earlier versions, includes all of the above.[16] But on the other hand the Ottoman writers were evidently eager to build up the size and significance of Lazar's army, which they described as vastly outnumbering Murat's, in order to add to the glory of the Turkish victory: the earliest of these accounts simply says that Lazar drew his forces from 'all those that live in the West.'[17] According to Neşri, Lazar had gathered such a huge host, three times the size of the Ottoman army, that his men were utterly confident of victory and spent the night before the battle getting blind-drunk.[18] These Ottoman claims are not to be trusted. Of course there may have been people from many countries in Lazar's army; the Serbian rulers had long depended on mercenaries for their campaigns (Dušan's large private guard of Germans being a famous example). The participation of Hungarians seems especially likely, given that Lazar had long had close relations with his northern neighbours and had married one of his daughters to a Hungarian nobleman. But the main components of his force were probably his own men, Vuk Branković's, and those of the Bosnian general, Vlatko Vuković.

As for the Ottoman army, it may well have contained substantial contingents of non-Turkish soldiers. Two Serbian rulers of nearby Macedonian and Bulgarian territories, Marko Kraljević and Konstantin Dejanović, were Ottoman vassals, and a prime condition of their vassalage was the requirement to supply troops: this they presumably did, and many historians assume that either or both of them took part in person on the Turkish side.[19] An early Italian chronicle, written perhaps seventeen years later, emphasized the presence of 'Greek and Christian' soldiers in the Turkish army, and concluded: 'The reason for Murat's victory lies in the 5,000 Christian crossbowmen he had in his pay, among the Greeks and the Genoese, and many other soldiers on horseback.'[20] This reference to Genoese soldiers, apart from reflecting the chronicler's own prejudices (he was a Florentine), may contain an element of truth. We know that a claimant to the Byzantine throne, John VII Palaiologos, had accepted Turkish vassalage, and had visited Genoa (presumably with Murat's permission) in May 1389 to get support for an attack on his grandfather, John V. That attack was indeed carried out in the following spring, when John VII besieged Constantinople with a combined force of his own men, Genoese soldiers and Turks.[21] So it is surely quite possible that the same combination was operating in Kosovo in June 1389.

The earliest Serbian chronicle, written probably within a few years of the battle, says that Murat's army included Greeks, Bulgarians and Albanians.[22] The first two categories have now been accounted for; but the identity of the Albanians is harder to establish *a priori*. Two of the most warlike Catholic tribes of the Malësi, the Mirdita and the Këlmendi, were to claim many centuries later that they had fought on the Turkish side at this battle, and had been granted important privileges as a result.[23] Such claims have to be treated with great caution: for the sake of tax privileges, people can falsify oral history just as thoroughly as medieval corporations used to falsify their charters (and with less danger of disproof). Yet, given the confused political situation in the whole

Albanian region, and the degree of Ottoman influence already established in some parts of central and northern Albania, it is quite possible
that some Albanians did fight on the Turkish side.

On the question of total numbers there is simply no reliable information. Neşri says first that Lazar's army was innumerable, then that it
contained 500,000 men; the first statement was obviously more truthful
than the second. An earlier (mid-fifteenth-century) Turkish chronicler,
Uruc, puts Murat's army at 60,000, but even this is very high for the
period.[24] Ottoman writers describe their own side as outnumbered; the
Serbian tradition makes the same claim for the Serbs. Since the Turks at
least supply some figures, their version has had more influence on many
modern historians: common estimates are 40–60,000 for Murat's army
and 100,000 for Lazar's.[25] But this last figure is impossibly high. Serbian
military historians have both reversed the proportions and lowered the
figures: 40,000 under Murat versus 25,000 under Lazar, or 27–30,000 for
Murat and 15–20,000 for Lazar. The latter estimate is accepted by the
leading Western authority on the medieval Balkans.[26]

On the disposition of the forces, direct evidence is also lacking. But
the chroniclers' claims are at least more plausible, being in line with the
general military practice of the day. It is supposed that Murat commanded the centre; his European troops were on the right under his
younger son Bayezit and his most trusted commander, Evrenoz; and his
elder son, Yakup, commanded the Anatolian troops on the left. Neşri
also includes a detailed and perhaps partly fanciful account of a
discussion about tactics between Murat and Evrenoz before the battle,
in which Murat was keen to place camels in the front in order to terrify
the Serbian horses; Evrenoz finally persuaded him to place them a little
further back.[27] This does at least accord with one of the earliest
documents relating to the battle, a letter sent from the senate of Florence
to the Bosnian king (replying to, and commenting on, a message he had
sent about the outcome of the conflict) in October 1389, which mentions
'chained camels' stationed in front of Murat. It also chimes with what
we know about the general military practice of the period: Ottoman
armies tended to form defensive positions, while the Serbs, like other
Europeans, put heavy cavalry in front, which was not suited to defensive
fighting.[28] As for Lazar's army, it is said that he commanded the centre;
Vuk Branković was on the right; and all the foreign contingents were

gathered on the left, under the Bosnian general and (according to Neşri) a certain Dimitri, son of Yund – of whom more will be said later.[29]

Where the overall course of the fighting is concerned, we are again dependent on much later accounts. There is not a single description of the battle by any of its participants. Two letters apparently written by Bayezit, Murat's son and successor, have been taken as genuine by some modern scholars; but there is abundant evidence that they are forgeries, produced by a Turkish official of the late sixteenth century who engaged in the wholesale falsification of documents.[30] The most detailed version we have, once again, is the one presented by Neşri, according to which the Serbs broke through the Ottoman left wing, there was fierce fighting in the centre, and the decisive turning-point was an advance by Bayezit (followed by Evrenoz) on the right, which caused the Serb-led forces to break and run.[31] Since Bayezit succeeded to the throne, one would hardly expect the story to have been told in any other way.

All accounts of the course of the fighting in this battle have to deal with three particularly tangled topics: the alleged treason of Vuk Branković, the time and manner of Murat's death, and the time and manner of Lazar's. The story of Vuk Branković's betrayal of Lazar can be seen developing gradually in the aftermath of the battle. A Serbian monastic chronicle, written perhaps thirteen years after the battle, says rather hesitantly: 'I do not know what to say in truth about this, whether Lazar was betrayed by one of his own or whether God's judgement was fulfilled.'[32] Also within a few years of the battle, a rather different story had been picked up by a Catalan writer, who blamed Lazar's son-in-law (Vuk Branković) not for a conspiratorial act of treachery, but simply for abandoning the field after Lazar had been killed: 'he returned to his territory to be lord.'[33] A Bulgarian-born historian, who spent some time at the court of Lazar's son before writing his account in the 1430s, made no mention of betrayal; but he did say that Lazar's son received no support from many of the Serbian lords after the battle, because Lazar 'from the beginning had trampled them under his feet'.[34] And a Serbian ex-Janissary, writing a strongly anti-Turkish text in the 1490s, blamed the defeat on certain Serb noblemen who had watched the battle 'through their fingers'.[35]

Another writer of the same period, an anonymous Venetian or Dalmatian, named a treacherous captain, Dragoslav Probišić, who was

said to have turned his men round to fight the Serbs, and alleged that
the Bosnian general, on hearing this news, had withdrawn his own
troops from the field. Probišić's name appears in no other account, and
some historians have doubted whether he existed. But coins struck by
Probišić have been found, and they bear a close resemblance to the ones
minted by Vuk Branković; so it is now assumed that he was one of
Branković's own vassals.[36]

The first written source to name Vuk Branković as a traitor was an
influential history book published in 1601 by a Ragusan monk, Mavro
Orbini. 'As some say', he noted, Branković had had secret negotiations
with the Turks before the battle, and had agreed to betray his commander.[37] Orbini's whole account of Kosovo was deeply influenced by
the folk epic tradition, and it is clear that by this time, more than 200
years after the battle, what we are looking at is a highly stylized and
mythologized version of events, determined by folk–literary requirements rather than historical analysis. The story of a scheming traitor has
its analogues in other epics, such as the *Song of Roland*; and this oral
epic tradition, like the early French one, had seized on the dramatic and
psychological interest of a clash between two lords, one of them loyal
(the hero who assassinated Murat) and the other treacherous. In several
surviving poems, it is Vuk Branković, the traitor, who accuses Miloš
Kobilić, the hero, of disloyalty before the battle, and it is because Miloš
is so stung by this false accusation (which is given credence by Lazar)
that he vows to go and assassinate the Turkish Sultan.[38] The idea that
these were two sons-in-law of Lazar who had long been vying for his
favours also had a pleasing symmetry and psychological force; this aspect
of the story was picked up by a German writer who lived in Hercegovina
in the 1450s, which helps to confirm that the folk-epic tradition was well
under way by then.[39]

By 1601, however, the folk tradition may also have been influenced
by accounts of the second battle of Kosovo, which took place on Kosovo
Polje in 1448 between a Turkish army and an invading force led by a
Transylvanian nobleman, János Hunyadi (Rom.: Iancu de Hunedoara).
Hunyadi's campaign was sabotaged by the then ruler of most of Serbia,
Djuradj Branković (Vuk's son), who tried to stop Hunyadi passing
through Serbian territory, probably informed the Sultan of his move-
ments, and threw him into gaol afterwards. It is quite likely that the

identification of Branković *père* as a traitor in the Kosovo songs was partly the result of a popular confusion between these two battles. Certainly the Dalmatian-born Archbishop of Bar, Marin Bizzi, writing in 1610, put both 'Gianco' (Iancu de Hunedoara) and 'Milos Cobilich' (Miloš Kobilić, the assassin of Murat) together in his account of Kosovo; and many of the folk epics mingle characters promiscuously from different periods.[40]

The highly stylized folk–literary character of the epics is in itself a reason for not taking the story of Vuk's conspiracy as historical truth. A glance at the historical evidence confirms this; but at the same time it suggests what the original foundation may have been on which these over-elaborate accusations were later built. If Vuk Branković had made a secret deal with Murat, one would expect him to have emerged, after the battle, as the most prominent and most privileged of Bayezit's vassals in the area. Instead, he seems to have held out against becoming a vassal at all. He kept some continuing territorial autonomy, and was only forced to relinquish his prized possession of Skopje three years later; although he finally agreed to become a Turkish vassal in 1392, he did not take part in Bayezit's later Balkan campaigns of 1395 and 1396 (as Lazar's son, and other vassals in the region, did); and he was finally deposed by the Turks and put into prison, where he died.[41] This is not the record of a pro-Turkish conspirator.

But on the other hand, the desire for autonomy and personal power can be traced back before 1389 too, in various political clashes or tensions (particularly over the control of the Serbian Church) with Lazar.[42] Branković may not have been pro-Turkish, but perhaps he was not very strongly pro-Lazar either. Leaving aside the story about his man Dragoslav Probišić (where the evidence is too slender to support much weight), we can still note that several early accounts suggest both a lack of enthusiasm on the part of some of Lazar's lords, and a turning-point in the battle caused by the withdrawal of one large body of troops. Perhaps the Catalan writer, who stated merely that when Vuk Branković saw that Lazar was dead he had no wish to continue the battle and 'returned to his territory to be lord', was closest to the truth.

The Ottoman sources say nothing about a Serb traitor; but this is not surprising, since such an explanation of the Serbs' defeat would hardly add to the glory of the Turkish army. On the question of the death of

Murat, on the other hand, the Ottoman writers have a great deal to say. All of them are agreed that Murat was killed by a solitary Christian soldier, who was able to get close to the Sultan either by luck or by guile. The earliest Turkish writer, Ahmedi, who worked in the household of Bayezit's son and died in 1412, described what happened after the Serbian enemy had broken and fled:

> Much of the army went to pursue the enemy, and only the ruler and a few of his courtiers stayed in one place ... But an unbeliever was lying there, covered in blood from head to foot. He was hidden among the corpses, but he could easily see the heroic Khan. As fate willed, he rose up from where he lay, jumping up with his dagger and stabbing the ruler.[43]

Other writers, such as Uruc (in the mid-fifteenth century), told a similar story but placed it in the middle of the battle, not at the end. They also added an element of deceit: the unbeliever had asked to kiss the hand of the Sultan, which Murat had graciously permitted. In this way it was explained how his courtiers or bodyguard could have made the fatal mistake of allowing the Christian soldier to get so close to Murat.[44] The first scholar to compare all these accounts, Aleksej Olesnicki, concluded that the Ottoman writers simply did not know what had happened; this would explain why none of them said what became of the assassin afterwards, or gave any other details about him. All that could be deduced, he suggested, was that Murat had been left briefly unattended by his guard (probably during the battle, not after it), and had been found dead thereafter.[45]

The tradition which developed on the Serbian side also hinged on a solitary deed and a deception; but it differed in every other way. In the final version of the story, as presented in the folk-poetry, the deed was carried out by Miloš Kobilić before the commencement of battle. Stung by Vuk Branković's taunts, and/or grieved by Lazar's reproaches, Miloš rode out on the morning of the battle-day to Sultan Murat's tent, where he announced that he had decided to join the Turkish side. The Sultan asked him to perform the ritual obeisance of kissing his foot (or knee). In the words of the earliest recorded song:

> Before the Sultan Miloš bowed,
> And he leaned o'er to kiss his knee,

His golden dagger drew, and struck.
And underfoot he trampled him . . .[46]

As with the story of Vuk Branković's treason, and indeed the whole drama of rivalry between Vuk Branković and Miloš Kobilić, this story bears all the signs of having been moulded by a literary tradition. It has been suggested that the idea of riding into the enemy's camp and performing a cunning feat may have arisen from traditional songs about bride-seizing, where the hero enters enemy territory and performs the abduction through a daring act of trickery.[47] If the story of Miloš Kobilić is largely the product of a literary formula, then the formula was at work from an early stage. The Bulgarian-born historian Konstantin, writing in the 1430s, already had all the main elements of this story: a falsely accused nobleman who tricked his way to the Sultan and killed him in order to clear his own name.[48] We know that it has long been the practice of Serb folk-poets to turn events almost immediately into poetry. (One memorable example of this was given by the poet–peasant Ante Nešić, who was a member of the Serbian National Assembly in 1873–4: he would emerge each day from the Assembly and convert the entire debate on the Monetary Reform Bill, and the Budget, into blank verse for an admiring audience.)[49] Konstantin had been at the court of Lazar's son since 1411; no doubt he had heard the story many times from courtly minstrels there. And other elements of the epic tradition (not the Miloš Kobilić episode, but the heroic speech made by Lazar before the battle) can be seen to have influenced an even earlier text, a memorial oration composed probably in the 1390s by the Serbian Patriarch.[50]

The epic tradition was a powerful one, and eventually it took over completely. But during the first century after the battle it had to compete with a different version of events, which was also current among Christian writers. This version, attributing Murat's death to a daring attack in the middle of the battle, first appears in one of the very earliest documents, the comments (sent in October 1389) by the senators of Florence on the report of the battle which they had received from King Tvrtko of Bosnia:

> Fortunate, most fortunate are those hands of the twelve loyal lords who, having opened their way with the sword and having penetrated the enemy

lines and the circle of chained camels, heroically reached the tent of
Murat himself. Fortunate above all is that one who so forcefully killed
such a strong war-lord by stabbing him with a sword . . .[51]

Most historians have regarded the details here as fanciful; the figure of
twelve loyal men seems suspiciously symbolic, and one leading scholar
simply dismissed this account as an oddity or 'special case'.[52] But the
fact remains that this Florentine document is the closest thing we have
to the events themselves: it is a direct comment on a report which was
sent within a few months of the battle by a ruler whose own men had
been participants in it. The circumstantial detail about a line of chained
camels matches other accounts; and whether or not the figure of twelve
was a piece of deliberate symbolism, the central idea of a small band
of knights attacking Murat is not such a 'special case' after all. The
anonymous Florentine chronicler, probably writing less than twenty
years after the battle, gave a slightly more elaborate version of the same
story: according to him, it was Lazar himself and a band of twelve men
who attacked Murat's tent (after the Turks had defeated Lazar's army on
the field) and killed him with a blow from a lance.[53] Elements of this
story also appear in another account, by a Sienese merchant who lived
in Ottoman territory until 1402 and published a historical work in 1416.
In his version of the story, Lazar and a few loyal men rushed at Murat's
tent, but were stopped and captured; then, when they were brought into
the Sultan's presence, one of them managed to stab him to death.[54] At
this point we can see the two stories – knightly attack, and deceitful
stabbing – being fused into one.

Of all the early accounts, however, none is so detailed or so compelling
as the one by the anonymous Catalan author, who must have been
writing before 1402. Most historians of Kosovo have paid little or no
attention to this account of the battle, because it comes at the end of a
mainly fictional text, a sentimental romance full of fabulous inventions.
The work itself is a romanticized biography of Yakup, the elder son of
Murat who was killed by Bayezit after the battle in order to secure
Bayezit's own succession to the throne. (The final paragraph of the book
describes Bayezit as still ruling, which dates the text to before his defeat
and imprisonment by Timur Leng in 1402.) And yet, as many Catalan
scholars have noticed, the description of the battle of Kosovo which

forms the final section of the book is quite different in kind from the fanciful romance which precedes it: it seems to be based quite closely on one or more historical accounts, written perhaps by a Byzantine Greek or by a Turk who belonged to an anti-Bayezit lobby. And throughout the book, the anonymous author shows an unusually exact knowledge of place-names, Ottoman customs and historical details.[55]

According to this author, Lazar's forces (26,000 infantry and 4,000 armed cavalry) included 'many Germans and many Hungarians'. One of the knights on horseback, 'a big Hungarian man', asked Lazar to place him at the front of the troops; permission was granted, and he was given command over one entire section of the army (the other commanders being Lazar himself and 'his son-in-law', i.e. Vuk Branković). The author then gives various details about the two armies, including the fact that Murat arranged his camels in three lines, one in front of the other, 'chained together with great chains'. (This is a noteworthy detail, since it matches so closely the remark about chained camels in the Florentine senators' letter.) During the battle a group of German knights broke through the line of camels, penetrating deep into the Turkish army. In the confusion which followed, the Hungarian knight, who had sworn to fight personally with Murat, spurred his horse straight towards the Sultan. Undeterred by the arrows which were fired at him by Murat himself,

> he made his way, with his lance at the ready, and struck him such a blow
> with the power of his horse, that the shield and the cuirasses which Murat
> was wearing were all penetrated, and the tip of the lance pierced his side
> to the depth of four fingers' breadth, and Murat fell very badly wounded
> to the ground.

The Hungarian knight himself was immediately brought down by a hail of arrows; Murat died soon afterwards from his wound.[56]

This identification of Murat's killer as a Hungarian knight is worth taking seriously. As we have seen, Lazar would almost certainly have had a Hungarian contingent in his army; his son-in-law, Nicholas Garai, was one of the most powerful noblemen in Hungary, and much involved in Balkan affairs.[57] Garai himself was not present at the battle, but any senior knight sent by him would have had an honoured place. The symmetry of two sons-in-law, which appears in the epic tradition, may have something to do with this. Another feature of the epic tradition could also have a Hungarian explanation. Several of the most famous songs describe the exploits of the nine Jugovićes, a band of brothers who fought valiantly and were all killed in the battle. According to the folk tradition, they were the brothers of Lazar's wife, Queen Milica; but their existence is unknown to historical science. It often happens, however, that names in epic poetry have some basis, however far removed, in reality: even the most ornate pearls of epic invention may have grown round some small element of historical grit. (An example of this from another culture has already been mentioned: the Albanian place-names which, in distorted forms, found their way into the *Song of Roland*.) In the earliest recorded Kosovo song, the name which later writers were to record as 'Jugović' was actually given as 'Ugović', and the very first line to include that name linked the Ugović brothers with 'ugarski', i.e. Hungarian, lords.[58] Possibly the original Ugovići were 'ugarovići', sons of Hungarians – a small group of knights sent by Lazar's Hungarian relative. The connection with Garai might explain why, in the epic, they were regarded as some sort of in-laws of Prince Lazar. And, to extend the speculation just a little further, it may be that it was such a group of élite Hungarian knights who, led by the 'big Hungarian man' of the Catalan account, charged towards Murat, and were later commemorated as twelve loyal knights in the early report sent to Florence by King Tvrtko of Bosnia.

None of the other early Christian sources can match the Catalan account for circumstantial detail. But there is one other text, a Bulgarian chronicle written in the period 1413–21, which not only gives (very briefly) a version of the knightly story, but also adds one important extra element: it names the knight who killed Murat. 'And there was among the warriors a man of great courage, named Miloš, who drove his spear through the unbeliever Murat, just as St Demetrius did...'[59] Towards the end of the fifteenth century one finds the full name given as Miloš Kobilić or Kobilović; and over the next couple of centuries it crops up repeatedly in a Chinese-whispers-style profusion of varieties: Milois, Miloss Kobyla, Milos Cobilith, Milossus Kobyliczh, Milosch Khobilovitz, Milo Comnene and Minkos Koplaki.[60] In the folk-epic tradition it is always Miloš Kobilić – or rather, it always was, until an interfering editor in the eighteenth century decided to 'improve' it by converting it into 'Obilić', in order to suggest the word *obilje* (meaning 'abundance' or 'riches').[61] 'Obilić' is the form used by all modern Serbian writers; strangely, even serious historians and literary scholars continue to use it, although they are well aware that it is a completely spurious emendation.

Can anything be deduced from the original form of this name? The answer, unfortunately, is that a great many things can or could be deduced, none of them with certainty. If we assume that this was the actual name of a real person, then the evidence of the chrysobulls would suggest that he probably came from Western Kosovo, where 'Miloš' was a popular name during this period. Although Miloš nowadays sounds quintessentially Serbian, names ending in -oš or -uš were not so common in the Middle Ages, and may have reflected an Albanian influence; while Miloš was popular in Western Kosovo, it was absent from areas further north. Similarly, 'Kobilić' or 'Kobilović' may have arisen from the Vlach and Albanian word 'copil' or 'kopil', which, as already mentioned, means 'child' or 'bastard child'. 'Kopil' appears in some medieval records as a Vlach personal name; and there is also a village called Kobiliće or Kopiloviće in north-western Kosovo. For all these reasons, it has been claimed that Miloš Kobilić had a Vlach–Albanian background.[62]

A different etymology, however, derives 'Kobilić' from *kobila*, which means 'mare' in Serbian: 'Kobilić' would therefore mean 'son of the mare'. This was the sense in which popular tradition understood the name: according to legend, Miloš had been nursed by a mare in his infancy.[63] So it is worth noting again that the Ottoman historian Neşri mentioned a leading knight on the Serbian side called Dimitri, the 'son of Yund' (Yund-oğlu): *yund* is in fact an old Turkish word for 'mare'.[64] Why he called him Dimitri and not Miloš is unclear; perhaps he had confused 'Miloš' with 'Mito' (a diminutive of Dimitri), or perhaps there was some interference from a popular comparison with St Demetrius (as made by the Bulgarian chronicler, mentioned above). But the significant point here is that this 'Yund-oğlu' is described as commanding part of Lazar's left wing, where foreign troops were stationed – which exactly matches the account given by the anonymous Catalan.

If we take this as reinforcing the credibility of the Catalan version, then perhaps we should look for a Hungarian origin for the knight's name. It may be speculative to suggest that 'Miloš' was originally 'Miklos' (the Hungarian for 'Nicholas'), and it is probably too fanciful to suppose that 'Kobilović' was originally *koborlovag* ('knight-errant' in Hungarian). A more likely line of explanation runs through the concept of a 'mare's son', rather than the sound of the name. Rural Hungarian society at this time was still deeply influenced by the traditions of shamanism which the Magyars had brought with them from Central Asia. These traditions were especially strong in the military: Hungarian soldiers of this period, for example, wore magical bones on their costumes (a design which survives in the form of the lines of gold braid on the uniform of a modern hussar). Nor was it only peasant soldiers who espoused these beliefs; art-historical evidence suggests that Hungarian noblemen were deliberately adopting local 'ethnic' costumes and practices during this period. And among the various totem-animals used by Hungarian shamans, the horse was the most powerful and the most popular. Every shaman, it was believed, had a magical white horse which would carry him to heaven. So, although the overall identification of Miloš Kobilić with a Hungarian must remain uncertain, it is interesting to note that Hungary, more than any other country in the region, had a culture which might produce a charismatic warrior claiming a magical connection with a mare.[65]

Of course, if the Catalan author's whole account is correct, then it does become difficult to explain why the Ottoman historians developed such a very different story of the Sultan's death. Here again, several explanations are possible. For a Sultan to die in battle was an unprecedented event; perhaps the idea of a deceitful murder was less wounding to Ottoman self-esteem than that of sheer incompetence in battle. Perhaps the Sienese writer's combination of the two stories – cavalry charge, capture of the knights, and then an opportunistic murder by one of them – was closer to the truth. Or perhaps the charge by the Hungarian knight ended in failure, and the killing of Murat was a separate, later event: Christian sources may have recorded only that the knight was last seen bearing down on the Sultan, and that the Sultan was later reported to be dead. Without further evidence, the precise truth may never be known. But in the present state of knowledge, it is reasonable to think that Murat was in fact killed by someone, quite possibly a Hungarian, whose name either was, or sounded like, or was later adapted into, or meant the same as, Miloš Kobilić.

The death of Lazar has also been the subject of many competing stories; here too the literary requirements of the folk-epic have also played a large part. In some versions of the epic, a final dramatic confrontation takes place between a captured Lazar, who is about to die, and Murat, who has already received his fatal wound.[66] The Ottoman historians, more simply, have a captured Lazar brought to Bayezit at the end of the battle, and executed on his order; and the earliest Serbian chronicle gives a very similar account.[67] Those versions of the story which make Lazar the knight who killed Murat have, naturally, a different story-line; but these rather transparent attempts to give Miloš's role to Lazar can be discounted. Once again, the most prosaic account is given by the Catalan, who merely says that within a short time of the death of Murat, Lazar was killed, 'having got involved in a part of the battle against Ayna bey' (a commander of the Anatolian cavalry on the Ottoman left wing).[68] If this was the plain truth, then it is understandable that the Serbian people should have yearned for a rather different story-line, in which Lazar had the opportunity to make at least one more heroic speech before he died.

The question of whether this battle was a victory for the Turks or merely a draw may seem a strange thing to ask about the most famous defeat in Serbian history. And yet some of the early sources make a claim which is much stranger: they describe the battle as a Serbian victory. The letter from the Florentine senators leaves no doubt that King Tvrtko had informed them of a great victory over the Turks; the same impression was given a few years later in a book by a French author, Philippe de Mézières; and the first reaction of Byzantine writers was to acclaim the battle of Kosovo as a humiliation for the Turks. Some early Serbian religious texts about Lazar, written in a form known as a *pohvala* or eulogy-commemoration, say that Murat was defeated. And the popular epics heard by a Slovene traveller through Kosovo in the 1530s celebrated the killing of Murat by Miloš Kobilić and concluded: 'When the Turks had lost their leader, they took flight. In this way the Margrave [Lazar], his army and his country were delivered from the Turks.'[69]

Obviously there were two main reasons for the development of such ideas. The first was the fact that a Sultan had been killed in battle: this was what captured the interest of Byzantine writers, who would otherwise care little about what happened in (or to) a far-off Slav principality.

And it was also what mattered most to the writers of the Serbian pohvalas, who, concentrating on Lazar, viewed all the events of the battle in personal, rather than military–strategic terms: their favourite comparison was with David and Goliath, who of course had fought as individuals, not as generals. And the second reason must have been that, immediately after the battle, the Turkish army made no further attempt to conquer Serbian territory and rapidly withdrew to Anatolia (in order to secure Bayezit's succession). This may have given the impression at the time that the Turks had been successfully repelled. Whether King Tvrtko of Bosnia had some further, ulterior reason of his own for spreading the news of a victory – for example, to gain military or financial support from Italian powers, who might otherwise have given it to Hungary instead – can only be guessed at.

One other feature of the battle that must have influenced these reports is the fact that the Turks too had sustained heavy losses. With grievous losses of men on both sides, there were some grounds for regarding the whole battle as an expensive draw. One early Serbian religious text concluded: 'Both sides were exhausted, and the battle stopped'; and several early chronicles, Italian and Ragusan, gave more or less that version of the outcome.[70] Most modern historians are willing to describe the battle as substantially similar to a draw, but with two important qualifications. The first is that, in technical military terms, the battle can still be described as an Ottoman victory, because it was the Serbian army which broke and ran and the Turkish one which ended the day in possession of the field. And the second is that, while the Serbs had expended all their military strength, the Turks were able to come back again and again in later years with ever-larger armies. In the long run, therefore, it can be correctly regarded as an important defeat for the Serbian side. And there is in fact good evidence that it was seen in that way by people in the territory of Kosovo within the next one or two generations: the Bulgarian writer Konstantin, who was at the court of Lazar's son from 1411, definitely described the battle as a Turkish victory, and so did the Catholic bishop Martino Segono, who was brought up in Novo Brdo in the first half of the fifteenth century.[71]

But did the views of scholarly writers such as Konstantin and Segono represent public opinion in general? To this there can be no certain answer. Each account of the battle that has come down to us was composed under the pressure of various special influences – religious, literary and political. There is no way of getting behind these texts and sources to carry out some sort of imaginary opinion poll among the local population. All we can do is try to distinguish and trace some of the early strands of tradition which were eventually to be woven together into the popular, modern (mainly nineteenth-century) 'myth of Kosovo' which dominates Serbian thinking today.

The most distinctive early strand was that of the Serbian Orthodox cult of Prince Lazar. Within roughly one year of the battle, Lazar's body was reburied in the monastery which he had founded at Ravanica, between Niš and Belgrade. Religious texts were written, proclaiming him a martyr, and a special liturgy was composed for the annual commemoration on 15 June, including a narrative of his life and death. The main emphasis in this and other monastic texts, however, was on his acts of piety: much more space was given to his endowment of Ravanica than to his final conflict with the Turks.[72] The only important contribution made by these writings to the later Kosovo myth was the inclusion, in some of them, of a speech allegedly delivered by Lazar to his troops before the battle, in which he told them, using stock rhetorical formulae, that 'It is better to die in battle than to live in shame ... We have lived a long time in the world; in the end, we seek to accept the martyr's struggle and to live forever in heaven.'[73]

As we have already seen, some of these religious writings (but only a minority of them) described the battle as Lazar's 'holy victory'. The standard format for celebrating saints involved reciting achievements, not sufferings; there was a strong tradition of royal sainthood in the Serbian Church, but no tradition of royal martyrdom. So it is not surprising that the commemorations of Lazar consist mainly of recitals of his virtues and achievements – of which the killing of Murat was naturally seen as the final one. Celebration is more important than grieving in these texts; and although the deaths of Serbian soldiers at Kosovo are mentioned, there is little sense at this early stage of any emerging myth of national catastrophe. Nor should that surprise us; when these texts were written, during the first decade or two after the battle, Lazar's son was securely ruling the Serb lands, and, what is more, was doing so as a loyal vassal of the Sultan. For monks dependent on his patronage to describe the current state of affairs as a catastrophe for his people would have been highly imprudent – even if they had in fact seen it in those terms, which is far from certain.

This early liturgical celebration of Lazar's death on 15 June of each year (28 June according to the modern calendar) may seem like proof of a continuous tradition of Kosovo-commemoration from 1390 to the present. But the continuity is in fact very tenuous. The cult of Lazar continued at Ravanica, of course; all monasteries maintained the cults of their saintly founders. By the seventeenth century, however, Ravanica was the only place where the cult of St Lazar was celebrated.[74] A few churches here and there may have commemorated 15 June as St Vitus's Day ('Vidovdan'); but in the official calendar of the Church this day was dedicated to the Old Testament prophet Amos, and it was only in the late nineteenth century that St Vitus was formally promoted to the calendar. The whole idea of a national–religious celebration of this day is, in fact, a nineteenth-century invention.[75]

For a more widespread and popular continuous tradition, we have to turn to the folk-epics. The earliest written versions of these songs relating to Kosovo come only from the second half of the eighteenth century; but there is clear evidence (from travellers' reports, and from the visible influence of the songs on other written texts) of continuous transmission and development, stretching all the way from the earliest years after the battle.[76] Careful study of the early evidence yields the conclusion that, very soon after the battle, two main songs had been formed: 'The Death of Lazar' and 'The Death of Murat at the hands of Miloš Kobilić'.[77] A common story-line was developed which connected the two, and other songs, such as the one about Queen Milica and her brothers, the Ugovićes or Jugovićes, were also added. From as early as the mid-fifteenth century, however, it is quite clear that the most popular of all these songs was the one about Miloš Kobilić. (This was the song to which, as we have seen, the Slovene traveller Benedikt Kuripešić devoted his account in 1530, treating it as such a celebration of Serb derring-do that the whole battle was regarded as a defeat for the Turks.)

Some of the songs about Lazar did include lines which portrayed the battle as a historic defeat for the whole Serbian people; but even in these songs the main focus was on Lazar's fate as a personal hero-martyr, not on the national destiny of the Serbs. No doubt, during the long centuries of Ottoman rule, there would have been many Serbs who understood these songs as expressing something about the historical origins of their predicament as subjects of the Turks. And yet the folk-song tradition can hardly be used as direct evidence of 'public opinion' on political matters: if it were to be interpreted in that way, we should have to draw a very different conclusion from the fact that the most popular hero of the folk poetry – much more popular than Lazar, and probably more popular even than Miloš Kobilić – was Marko Kraljević, the Ottoman vassal who almost certainly supplied troops for Murat's army, and may even have fought in it himself.

The idea that this folk-poetic tradition supplied the essence of a special type of historical–national self-consciousness for the Serbs is, in fact, a product of the nineteenth century. It was nationalist writers and nation-builders such as Vuk Karadžić (the influential early-nineteenth-century folksong collector and dictionary writer) and Petar Petrović Njegoš (the poet and princely ruler of Montenegro, whose famous epic poem, *The Mountain Wreath*, was published in 1847) who took the elements of the popular Kosovo tradition and transformed them into a national ideology.[78] Nor is this very surprising. The nineteenth century was the period in which national identities were developed in many parts of Europe; and in Serbia's case, the very idea of forming an independent national territory necessarily involved the idea of rebelling against, or making war on, the Ottoman Turks. A national myth centring on the symbolic moment of Turkish conquest both focused attention on the enemy, and reminded Serbs of a glorious pre-Ottoman past. As a subsidiary ideological purpose, a renewed cult of Lazar also focused attention on the idea that the Serbs should be led by a princely ruler – a useful ploy for the aspiring dynasties of nineteenth-century Serbia. After the proclamation of a 'Kingdom' of Serbia in 1882, special efforts were made by the government to turn the anniversary of the battle in 1889 into a celebration of national unity, national aspirations and royal destiny. And in the earliest film ever made on Serbian soil, *The Coronation of King Peter the First* (1904), the English cinematographer Frank Mottershaw was persuaded to include a historical pageant of actors in medieval dress, representing Miloš 'Obilić', the nine 'Jugović' brothers and, of course, Prince Lazar himself.[79]

Of all the elements of the Kosovo myth which was formed in the nineteenth century, none has been more powerful than the 'Kosovo covenant'. This is the idea that Lazar was offered a choice between an earthly kingdom and a heavenly one, and that he chose the latter; because of this decision, described as a covenant with God, the Serbs are often said to consider themselves as a 'heavenly people'. In the folk tradition, the story appears in a song collected by Vuk Karadžić, called 'The Downfall of the Serbian Empire', where St Ilija (Elijah) appears to Lazar before the battle in the form of a falcon, and offers him the choice between the two kingdoms.[80] Some of the other songs express a similar idea, in the speech which Lazar is said to have made to his army before the battle. The earliest known version of this speech comes not in a song but in a liturgical text which was probably influenced by the folk-singers; as already quoted, Lazar declares that 'It is better to die in battle than to live in shame.' A later and more elaborate version (by the Ragusan monk Orbini), also written under the influence of the folk tradition but employing many standard rhetorical techniques, includes the question, 'Is it not better to die gloriously than to live in disgrace?'[81] As literary historians know, all these antitheses were just rhetorical commonplaces, which could have been drawn from any one of a wide range of classical and Christian sources: the line 'Better an honourable death than a shameful life', for example, can be found in the best-known work of pre-Kosovo Serbian literature, the Serbian version of the highly popular medieval *Romance of Alexander*.[82]

There is simply no evidence to suggest that any Serb ever drew the idea of a special 'Kosovo covenant' out of these common rhetorical figures before the nineteenth century. Even then, the application of this 'heavenly kingdom' concept must have been somewhat problematical, given that the national ideology to which it was harnessed was concerned very much with the territorial extension of an earthly kingdom – indeed, concerned above all with its extension as far as Kosovo itself. And yet today, whether it makes sense or not, the 'Kosovo covenant' is the object, in some quarters, of an almost religious faith. In the words of one prominent Serbian historian: 'The Kosovo covenant – the choice of freedom in the celestial empire instead of humiliation and slavery in the temporal world – ... is still the one permanent connective tissue that imbues the Serbs with the feeling of national entity.'[83] 'Permanent' is perhaps not the most obvious choice of word for such a very recent product of nationalist ideological history.

5

The last years of Medieval Serbian Kosovo: 1389–1455

STEFAN LAZAREVIĆ, Prince Lazar's son, was only fourteen or fifteen years old in 1389. So it was his widowed mother, Queen Milica, who had to take charge after the battle. There was, it seems, no immediate submission to Ottoman overlordship; the Turkish withdrawal had been too rapid for that. Milica's troubles were compounded when, three months later, the northern part of her territory was invaded by King Sigismund of Hungary, who was seizing the opportunity to take back lands which the Hungarians had once controlled south of the Danube. Milica appealed, unsuccessfully, to Ragusa for help. Then an envoy from Bayezit arrived and proposed terms which, in the circumstances, were impossible to refuse. In return for Turkish protection against the King of Hungary's forces, Milica accepted – on behalf of her son – Ottoman vassalage, which meant paying an annual tribute and supplying troops, when requested, for Ottoman campaigns. This agreement, made in 1390, was endorsed by a council of the Serbian Orthodox Church.[1] Stefan Lazarević then travelled with the Serbian Patriarch to Edirne (Adrianople) to make his formal submission to Bayezit.

With him, as tradition relates, Stefan took his sister Olivera, whose fate had also been determined by the vassalage agreement. Serbian historians always describe the giving away of Olivera in lurid terms: they say that she was sent 'to join Bayezit's harem', as if this part of the deal were a deliberately gross indignity, the reducing of a noble princess to a kind of sexual slavery. The truth is quite different: Olivera was joined to Bayezit in a formal and honorific ceremony of marriage.[2] In principle, therefore, this was no different from the alliance-binding dynastic marriages which had been the fate of almost all medieval princely daughters, including the other daughters of Prince Lazar. Far from being a humiliation for Lazar's children, it was if anything intended as a special honour. All the early Ottoman historians record that Bayezit grew especially fond of Olivera, and never forced her to convert to Islam; and one modern study based on Turkish sources concludes also that 'his brother-in-law Stephen in turn was a devoted and steadfast friend.'[3]

Stefan Lazarević attained his majority in 1393; his mother, as befitted someone whose late husband had been officially declared a saint, retired into a nunnery. Two years later we find Stefan joining the Turkish army which attacked the prince of Wallachia (southern Romania) at the battle of Rovine; also on the Turkish side were the two other Serbian vassals, Marko Kraljević and Konstantin Dejanović, who may both have fought against Lazar at the battle of Kosovo. The Turks were defeated at Rovine; both Marko and Konstantin were killed, but Stefan Lazarević survived. In 1396 he joined another Ottoman campaign to oppose the King of Hungary, who had gathered a large crusading force and had crossed the Danube into northern Bulgaria: there, at the battle of Nikopolis, the Hungarians were heavily defeated.[4] Stefan's early biographer, the Bulgarian-born Konstantin, insisted that Stefan took part in these campaigns 'not out of free will, but out of compulsion'.[5] But Konstantin was writing at a time (in the 1430s, after Stefan's death) when Serb–Ottoman relations had greatly deteriorated. Apart from this assertion in his biography, there is no evidence of reluctance on Stefan's part to cooperate with his powerful brother-in-law.

One person who showed real reluctance, on the other hand, was Vuk Branković, who held most of the territory of Kosovo. As has been mentioned already, he held out against the Turks until 1392, when they forced him to give up his most prized possession, the city of Skopje; he appears to have accepted vassalage later that year, but he failed to appear at a gathering of Balkan vassals in 1393–4 and did not take part in the battle of Rovine. There is also evidence that during these years he was moving large quantities of silver to Ragusa for safe-keeping.[6] Bayezit's patience was eventually exhausted: in 1395 or 1396 Vuk was driven out of his lands, and within another one or two years he was dead, probably in a Turkish gaol.[7] Most of the Kosovo territory which Vuk had ruled was transferred at first to Bayezit's loyal ally, Stefan Lazarević; a few years later it was returned to Vuk's sons – who were also Stefan's nephews – Grgur (Gregory) and Djuradj (George) Branković, who had agreed to become Ottoman vassals.[8] However, one or two strategically important places, such as the fortress of Zvečan in northern Kosovo, received Turkish garrisons; from 1399 there is evidence that Zvečan was controlled by a Turkish governor called Feriz. These were the first steps in a slow process of infiltration by Ottoman military and civilian administrators: as early as 1396 there was a Turkish *kadı* (judge) at the mine of Gluhavica (near Novi Pazar), and by 1410 there were Turkish officials operating alongside Serbian ones in the mining town of Trepça.[9] But the Serbian vassals remained substantially in control of their lands, and it was possible to regard the vassalage relationship as working to mutual advantage.

The main advantage for Bayezit was the large supply of troops which his Balkan possessions gave him. He needed all the soldiers he could muster when, in 1402, he faced the greatest challenge of his life: an invasion deep into Anatolia by the Central Asian warlord Timur Leng (Tamerlane, Tamburlaine), who had already conquered Iran, Iraq, Syria, and much of the Caucasus region. The large army which Bayezit gathered to oppose him included forces led by Stefan Lazarević and Stefan's nephew Djuradj Branković; these troops, from Serbia and Kosovo, were placed at the front of the Ottoman army.[10] But Timur Leng's war horde was superior both in numbers and in fighting skills. At the battle of Ankara, in July 1402, the Ottomans were massively defeated. In the words given to Tamburlaine by Christopher Marlowe: 'But come, my lords, to weapons let us fall. / The field is ours, the Turk, his wife and all.'[11] Early chronicles relate that Bayezit was kept imprisoned in an iron cage, and that his beloved wife Olivera 'in a state of nudity served the Tartar conqueror with wine at his feasts'; Stefan Lazarević's offer of a ransom for her was rejected.[12] Stefan himself, who had fought doughtily in the battle, returned to Constantinople, where the reigning Byzantine Emperor awarded him the title 'Despot'. (His territory, until the final Ottoman takeover, is therefore known as the Despotate.)[13] But Stefan could not afford to linger for long in the Byzantine capital. The defeat at Ankara had caused a shake-up of power throughout the Ottoman dominions, and more than ten years of civil war now lay ahead.

There were in fact two civil wars: one between the sons of Bayezit, who squabbled over the remains of their empire, and the other between Stefan Lazarević and his own relations. Stefan quickly fell out with his nephew Djuradj Branković; on his return to Kosovo in November 1402 he found his route barred at Gračanica by a joint force of Djuradj's men and a Turkish army. Stefan fought his way through successfully, but Djuradj later continued to oppose him, and Stefan also had to face a rebellion by his own brother. Stefan turned to the King of Hungary for help, becoming his vassal; he also remained, in theory, a vassal of the Ottomans, making an agreement to continue that arrangement with Bayezit's son Süleyman. By 1409, however, Süleyman was supporting the revolt of Stefan's brother; war raged over the territory of Kosovo, and a Hungarian army, in support of Stefan, raided as far as Prishtina. Eventually Stefan's rebellious brother was seized and executed by Süleyman's own brother and rival, Musa, in 1410.[14] Having had Süleyman strangled in the following year, Musa then turned against Stefan Lazarević and attacked his domain: in 1412 Novo Brdo was subjected to a long Turkish siege, but resisted with success. In the following year Musa was defeated in turn by his other brother, Mehmet, who had won the support of Stefan, the Byzantine Emperor, and several other Balkan lords and vassals.

Stefan had no further trouble from the Turks for the rest of Mehmet's reign; and when Mehmet died in 1421 he was quick to give his support to the new Sultan, Murat II. Confident of his good relations with the Ottomans, Stefan also seized an opportunity in 1421 to conquer a large part of Montenegro (from Venice). But the main focus of Stefan's interests was further north, in the region of Belgrade; and he was becoming more actively involved in Hungarian affairs as a vassal of the Hungarian king. Eventually the Ottomans grew suspicious of this attachment to a power outside their empire, and attacked Stefan's territory in 1425. Help was forthcoming from Hungary, and in the following year, when Stefan drew up the arrangements for his succession, he agreed to hand over some of his northernmost territories to the Hungarian crown. As successor he appointed his nephew Djuradj Branković.[15] Djuradj had been reconciled to his uncle after their earlier conflict, and had continued to govern most of the territory of Kosovo, also on terms of Ottoman vassalage. (Turkish garrisons in key fortresses in Kosovo remained in place; in 1423 there was an Ottoman law-court in Prishtina, and from three years later there is evidence of Turkish customs officials operating on the road between Prishtina and Novi

Pazar.)[16] Stefan Lazarević died in 1427. Under his successor, Djuradj Branković, Kosovo was now united as part of a larger Serbian territory, extending northwards as far as the Belgrade district which Lazar had ceded to Hungary.

From such a brief survey, it might seem as if Stefan's reign had been little more than a maelstrom of military expeditions, battles and sieges. And yet in the cultural history of the Serbian people this period was something of a golden age. Stefan himself was a generous patron of the arts, and a keen book-lover with a special interest in Greek literature; he invited several monks from Athos to come and copy manuscripts for him. He is also thought to have written two texts himself, a eulogy of his late father and a memorial inscription about him.[17] The most important writer patronized by Stefan was the Bulgarian Konstantin, known as Konstantin the Philosopher, whose biography of Stefan is the leading source of information about his life; Konstantin also composed a 'treatise on writing', as well as some shorter texts on cosmography and geography. Other Slavic writers under Stefan's patronage included two men of Greek origin: Nikon, who wrote a history of the Church of Jerusalem, and Andonje Rafail, who penned another eulogy of Lazar. It is clear that a Byzantine literary culture survived with real vitality in the town of Novo Brdo, where it was stimulated by the flow of refugees from Constantinople after 1453 and continued even after the final Ottoman conquest in 1455: one author who lived there, Dimitrije Kantakuzin, was from a famous Byzantine family, and a Greek manuscript of Pindar and Aeschylus, written (perhaps for Kantakuzin) in 1474, remained in Novo Brdo until the following century (it is now in the state library in St Petersburg).[18]

The mining town of Novo Brdo, which was in Stefan's part of Kosovo, was in fact the key to the prosperity of his entire state. Other mines, such as Rudnik in central Serbia, were also important, and for a short time he also held the Bosnian silver-mining town of Srebrenica. But Novo Brdo was the jewel in his crown: as Konstantin the Philosopher put it, 'in truth, a city of silver and gold'.[19] A French traveller who visited Serbia six years after Stefan's death heard glowing reports of Despot Djuradj's town of 'Neuberg' (a version of its name which reflects the continuing dominance of German-speaking miners in Novo Brdo), and recorded that it gave Djuradj 200,000 ducats per year: this was apparently the sum which Ragusa paid him for a licence to run the mines there.[20] The Ragusan colony in Novo Brdo had grown steadily in importance, to the point where it had its own 'consul' and its own court of law. Most of the noble families of Ragusa were represented in the town, and there were some Venetian traders too.[21] One valuable surviving document is the account-book of a Ragusan trader who was active in the Novo Brdo region in the 1430s: it shows that there was an extensive commercial and financial network connecting Novo Brdo to a range of other towns in Eastern Kosovo. (It also shows that many of the people in these towns, including quite a few identified as miners, bore Albanian names such as 'Gin', 'Gon', 'Tanus', 'Progon' and 'Lecha'.)[22]

Thanks partly to its proximity to Novo Brdo, Prishtina also developed rapidly as a commercial centre. The focus of activity for Ragusan merchants in Kosovo had shifted decisively away from Prizren, which had been their base in the fourteenth century. (During the period of the Despotate Prizren completely lost its colony of Ragusans, though their merchants continued to be active in the villages of Western Kosovo.)[23] The number of Ragusans resident in Prishtina rose from thirty-nine in 1414 to ninety-seven in 1420 and 157 in 1424. Not all of these were traders; some were goldsmiths, leather-workers, or even carpenters or bakers. There were also merchants from the Dalmatian towns of Split and Zadar, several members of a noble Albanian family from Ulcinj, and several Turkish merchants as well as the resident Turkish officials.[24] Indeed, this period saw a continuing Serbian–Turkish osmosis in terms of trade and people. Turkish coins circulated in Novo Brdo alongside Serbian ones; as early as 1426 there was a small Turkish *mahalle* or quarter in the mining town of Trepça; and the construction of the first mosque in Prishtina also began during the final period of Serbian rule.[25]

Djuradj Branković's official relations with the Ottomans were, how-ever, much more troubled than those of his predecessor. When he succeeded to Stefan's lands, he also immediately inherited his latest quarrel with the Sultan about the Serbian relationship with Hungary. While Djuradj cemented his own deal with the Hungarian king in 1427, Ottoman forces raided deep into Serbian territory, seizing several of the major towns (but not Novo Brdo, which once again withstood a lengthy siege). In 1428 Djuradj bowed to this pressure and agreed to fulfil all the duties of an Ottoman vassal. Five years later he married off his daughter

to the Sultan, Murat II. And yet the Ottoman raids continued, dismantling his territory bit by bit, until by 1439 Djuradj controlled only the city
of Novo Brdo and part of Montenegro: all the rest was under direct
Turkish rule, and was starting to experience the introduction of the
Ottoman administrative and feudal system. The final blows came in
1441, when Murat, suspecting the Branković family of plotting against
him, had both of Djuradj's sons blinded, and then brought another siege
of Novo Brdo, at long last, to a successful conclusion. Djuradj fled to
Hungary; if he had not been plotting against Murat before this point, he
must certainly have wanted to do so now.[26]

His chance came in 1443, when King Vladislav of Poland, who had
now become king of Hungary too, launched a multinational crusade to
drive the Turks out of Europe. Djuradj Branković contributed a force of
800 Serbian soldiers, and there were also German, Bosnian and Croatian
contingents.[27] The most important commander among the Hungarians
was János Hunyadi (Rom.: Iancu de Hunedoara), who had been made
military governor of Transylvania and had won two major victories
against Ottoman armies there in the previous year.[28] These combined
Christian forces entered Serbia, drove the Ottomans out of Niš and then
penetrated as far as Sofia, which they also seized; but by early 1444 they
had proceeded no further, and some of their contingents were starting
to drift homewards. (During their advance in late 1443 they had also
taken part of Kosovo from the Turks, but were driven out of that
territory by a small Ottoman force in January.)[29] In the spring of 1444
Murat II sent envoys to Djuradj, informing him that he would have all
his Serbian territory restored to him if he withdrew from the campaign.
Djuradj promptly agreed, and the brief initial period of direct Turkish
rule over Serbia (1439–44) was thus brought to an end. The King of
Hungary also made a peace treaty with the Sultan; but then he reneged
on the deal. Since Djuradj, reinstalled as a vassal ruler, now refused to
grant passage to the Hungarian army through Serbia, the King and his
chief commander, Hunyadi, crossed the Danube into Bulgaria and
marched to Varna on the Black Sea coast. There, in November 1444, the
Christian army was utterly destroyed by superior Ottoman forces;
Hunyadi managed to escape, but the Polish–Hungarian king met his
death.[30]

The Varna crusade was a disaster for Hungary, but it did act as the catalyst for a vital development in Albanian history: the revolt of Skanderbeg. Skanderbeg (meaning 'Lord Alexander'; Alb.: Skënderbeu) was the Turkish name given to an Albanian nobleman, Gjergj Kastriot, whose family, originally from Western Kosovo, controlled extensive lands in north-central Albania. His father, Gjon, had become an Ottoman vassal and had sent his son to be brought up as a hostage at the Ottoman court. Popular tradition has always believed that Skanderbeg was sent by the Sultan to take part in the defence of Niš against the Varna crusade in 1443, and that he then deserted with his contingent of Albanian cavalry, rode to the fortress of Kruja in northern Albania, tricked the Ottoman governor there into handing him the keys of the fortress, declared himself a Christian and raised his revolt. Modern research, however, has shown that he was already in an administrative post in Kruja as early as 1438.[31] But his revolt did indeed start in 1443, and it must have been the Hungarian advance through Serbia and Bulgaria that provided the opportunity for it.

Skanderbeg was to keep up his resistance to Ottoman forces for an extraordinary twenty-five years, until his death in 1468. His campaigns would have little direct military impact on Kosovo, though they did of course increase the strategic importance of the Kosovo territory as a base or staging-post for some of the Turkish armies that were sent to attack him. But the greatest military significance of Skanderbeg for the history of Kosovo is a negative one: it consists of his narrow failure to join up with the army of János Hunyadi, which penetrated as far as Kosovo Polje in 1448 and was destroyed there by the Turkish Sultan.

Hunyadi had long wished to revenge himself for the humiliating defeat at Varna. Acting as regent of Hungary (for an infant king), he gradually rebuilt the Hungarian army. From early 1447 he was trying to put together an alliance of Balkan and Danubian rulers, and during that year he sent requests for help to the Pope, to Venice, and to the King of Aragon and Naples, but with no success. According to some early chroniclers he also sent envoys to Skanderbeg, who did agree to cooperate with him.[32] In July 1448 Murat II brought a large army into Albania to crush Skanderbeg's revolt: this provided just the opportunity Hunyadi had been waiting for. In July and August he gathered an army of at least 30,000 – and perhaps as many as 72,000 – men, consisting mainly of Hungarians, but including also a Wallachian (Romanian) contingent of 8,000 soldiers, as well as German and Czech mercenaries.[33]

During these final stages of preparation Hunyadi seems also to have tried to persuade Djuradj Branković to join him; but the Serbian Despot was determined not to get involved, and even forbade him to pass through Serbian territory. (Relations between Hunyadi and Djuradj Branković were in any case not good: they were locked in a bitter dispute about some estates in southern Hungary which Hunyadi had seized from Branković in 1445, after the latter's reinstatement in Serbia by the Sultan.)[34] The early Ragusan chronicler Mavro Orbini recorded rumours that Djuradj actually passed on intelligence reports about Hunyadi's army to Sultan Murat. Some modern historians have been sceptical about this, but one such report does in fact survive: it is a detailed description of Hunyadi's army, sent from Hunyadi's camp on 11 September 1448 by a Ragusan, Pasquale de Sorgo, who was in the service of Djuradj Branković.[35] De Sorgo's report also included the information that messengers had arrived from Skanderbeg, promising 20,000 armed men. But of the various details supplied by de Sorgo, few can have been more galling to Djuradj than the news that many people from Serbia itself had come 'with great alacrity' to join Hunyadi's army.[36]

At the end of September Hunyadi crossed into Serbia and, ignoring Djuradj's requests, marched his army southwards, up the Morava valley. Murat II, informed of Hunyadi's plans, had broken off his siege of Skanderbeg's stronghold of Kruja in mid-August, and had withdrawn his army to a waiting position near Sofia. Having established (probably with Branković's help) that Hunyadi was now moving due south, he brought his army to Kosovo in order to block his advance. And so it was that, on 17 October 1448, Hunyadi's army found itself drawn up in front of a larger Ottoman force, on almost exactly the same spot as Lazar had chosen for his final battle against the Turks in 1389.[37]

Unlike Lazar, Hunyadi had one potential advantage: he was expecting, any moment now, the arrival of significant reinforcements, in the form of an Albanian army. Skanderbeg had not forgotten his promise; but, unfortunately for Hunyadi, he had meanwhile become embroiled again in a long-running struggle against Venice for possessions in north-western Albania. On 4 October the Venetians finally submitted, agreeing to pay Skanderbeg a tribute of 1,400 ducats a year. He asked for a speedy down-payment, because he was now hurrying with his army, as the official document put it, 'to join the lord János'.[38] But the delay was fatal. While Skanderbeg marched eastwards, the second battle of Kosovo had already begun. Hunyadi fought, according to the early historians, for three days. On the third day (19 October) one entire section of his army was surrounded and destroyed; there are also reports that the Wallachian commander deserted to the Turkish side. The Hungarian army began to flee, and Hunyadi was obliged to flee with it. Just 20 miles from Kosovo Polje, Skanderbeg encountered Hungarian soldiers hastening away from the battlefield, and learned that all was lost. He quickly turned his army round and returned to his mountain domain.[39]

This second battle of Kosovo is one of the great might-have-beens of Balkan history. If it is true that the battle lasted for three days, this must indicate that the forces were quite evenly balanced. The arrival of a large and fresh Albanian force, under a charismatic leader with five years of experience in anti-Ottoman campaigns, might well have been decisive. An even greater might-have-been concerns the role of Djuradj Branković: after all, if he had joined this campaign instead of sabotaging it, there would have been a military alliance against Murat stretching all the way from Wallachia and Transylvania, through Hungary and the whole of Serbia, down to the Albanian coast. But on the other hand the general history of this period teaches that anti-Ottoman alliances were always liable to break up under their own internal strains and rivalries; and the Ottoman rulers could draw, as the next few centuries would show, on huge reservoirs of manpower in Asia as well as in their European territories. That the battle might have been turned by Skanderbeg's arrival is quite likely; that the whole of Balkan history might have been changed by an Ottoman defeat at this stage is much less easy to imagine. It is quite possible that Djuradj Branković had a surer grasp of the political and strategic realities than Hunyadi or even Skanderbeg, and the sheer romanticism of those two commanders' stories should not, in the end, be allowed to obscure that possibility.

Branković had his revenge on his Hungarian rival. While returning northwards, Hunyadi was captured by a Serbian band and brought before the Despot, who put him in gaol. He was later released, after agreeing to various conditions and pledges: he was obliged to pay a large ransom, to promise not to cross Serbian territory again, and, it is said, to marry his son (the future King of Hungary, Matthias Corvinus) to Branković's niece.[40] Djuradj Branković devoted the next few years to consolidating his state, and even extending it in the area of Montenegro. He did his best to placate the new Sultan, Mehmet II (known in Ottoman history as Mehmet Fatih, 'Mehmet the Conqueror'), who came to the throne in 1451: two years later, when Mehmet was engaged in the final siege of Constantinople, Branković fulfilled his duties as a vassal by sending 1,500 Serbian cavalry to take part in the operation.[41] But the conquest of this last outpost of the Byzantine Empire in Europe – the imperial capital itself – seems to have prompted a change in approach by the Sultan: as the controller of an empire with its own seat of imperial administration, he had no need of indirect methods of government, such as semi-independent vassal states, when he could govern directly himself. And, in addition, he distrusted the Serbian Despot, who had made a new alliance with Hungary and was also suspected of entering into negotiations with the Pope to organize a new crusade.[42]

In 1454 Mehmet sent a large force against the elderly Djuradj Branković, who retreated to his northern fortresses and called on Hunyadi for assistance. By the end of the year, much of southern and central Serbia had been seized by the Turks. In 1455 Mehmet assembled a larger army; moving through eastern Macedonia, it headed straight for the fortified town of Novo Brdo. When the town's commander refused to surrender to Mehmet's general, Novo Brdo was put under siege, and over the next forty days its walls were gradually demolished by the Ottoman artillery. Finally, on 1 June 1455, a treaty of surrender was agreed. Mehmet, who by this time had come in person to direct the campaign, promised that the inhabitants would be allowed to keep their possessions, and that their women and boys would not be enslaved; but it seems that the initial refusal of the city to surrender had cancelled, in his mind, any further moral obligations. No sooner was Novo Brdo in his hands than he broke his promise: seventy-four women were (in the words of one eye-witness) 'distributed among the heathen', and 320 boys were taken off to be trained as Janissaries in Anatolia.[43] Other towns in Kosovo were also taken: Prizren surrendered on 21 June.[44] The entire territory of Kosovo was brought under direct Ottoman rule, and would remain so until the early twentieth century.

The Despotate of Serbia lasted just four more years. In 1456 a massive Ottoman siege of Belgrade ended in failure, thanks to an extraordinarily energetic defence of the citadel by Hunyadi; but he died of plague soon afterwards, and the octogenarian Djuradj Branković also died at the end of the year. Branković's sons then quarrelled over the succession, and the broken remains of the Despotate became easy pickings for the Turks. Belgrade itself would stay in Hungarian hands for another sixty-odd years; but Smederevo, the last northern fortress held by the Serbs, surrendered to Mehmet without a fight in 1459.[45] This was the final extinction of the medieval Serbian state.

6

Early Ottoman Kosovo: 1450s–1580s

IN MOST BALKAN countries, the popular view of Ottoman rule is almost entirely negative. The Ottomans are depicted as Asiatic barbarians who destroyed, in each of their possessions, a flourishing national culture. They imposed an utterly alien system of rule; they cynically suppressed all sense of national identity; they colonized large areas of the Balkans with Turkic settlers; they reduced the Christian peasantry to a condition of helpless serfdom; they introduced barbaric practices such as slavery, torture and mutilation; they put intolerable pressures on the local Christian Churches and forced people to convert to Islam; and they showed a fanatical devotion to the principles of the *şeriat*, the Islamic sacred law. Or so we are told.

All these claims are at best misleading and at worst completely false. It is of course understandable that, in countries which were fighting to free themselves from Ottoman rule in the nineteenth and early twentieth centuries, historians, like most other intellectuals, should have been drawn into the anti-Ottoman struggle. It is also true that in the last two centuries of Ottoman power there were many cases of arbitrary rule, violence and oppression. But to project the conditions of that final period further back into the past, and to characterize the entire 'Ottoman system' from its earliest stages as chaotic and tyrannical, is to commit a crude anachronism. The Ottoman government of the Balkans in its early years (that is, at least until the end of the sixteenth century) was a well-regulated system of rule, and the conditions of life it produced compared favourably in many ways with those of the rest of Europe.

Far from imposing an utterly alien system, the Ottoman Empire did in fact preserve and develop many of the features of life – administrative, social, ceremonial and so on – which it found in its conquered Christian states. The claim that it suppressed national identities in this early period is almost meaningless, since our modern concept of 'national' identity had not yet begun to appear in this part of Europe. Mass-colonization by Turkic settlers was an exceptional thing in the Balkans, confined to a few areas of Bulgaria, Thrace and Macedonia; it did not touch Kosovo, Albania or any of the Slav lands further north. Far from being reduced to serfdom, the Balkan peasants actually enjoyed an improvement in their rights vis-à-vis their landlords. Slavery did exist under the Ottomans, but it had also existed under the previous Christian rulers; and where torture and mutilation were concerned, the Ottoman law-codes were in fact more humane than the ones they superseded. The local Orthodox Churches were allowed to continue to minister to their flocks. Some restrictions were imposed, and Christians in general certainly acquired a second-class status; but forcible conversion to Islam was extremely rare. As for the şeriat law and Muslim fanaticism, the Ottoman Empire never became a narrowly Islamic state, and even the sacred Koranic law was only one element in a complex legal system.

This is not meant to imply, however, that the Ottoman Empire was just a larger and better version of a normal western European Renaissance state. There were of course some deep-rooted differences. Some of these flowed from the Ottomans' commitment to Islam; but the most fundamental characteristics of the Ottoman Empire were connected not with religion but with war. The innermost dynamic of the Ottoman state was one of military expansion – a dynamic that can be traced back, through the earlier stage of Ottoman rule as a frontier statelet in Anatolia, to its original basis in the practices of a nomadic war-horde. (The English word 'horde' comes, in fact, from the Turkic *ordu*, which referred originally to an encampment of nomadic warriors, and means 'army' in modern Turkish.) The powers of an Ottoman ruler had developed originally out of those of a tribal chief whose essential role was military command: everything, including life and death, could be determined by his decision. Hence the personal absolutism of the Ottoman system, and its extreme slowness to develop anything like the constitutionalism of western Europe. And yet, by a curious paradox, the same underlying conditions also produced what might be called the tolerationist aspects of Ottoman rule. Because of its essential dynamic of military expansion, the Ottoman state was concerned above all with two things:

men to fight wars, and money to pay for them. So long as those requirements were met, it cared little about many other aspects of people's lives; thus, for example, the Orthodox Churches and the Jews were allowed to maintain their own courts and judges, applying their own laws to their communities in a whole range of civil matters. To put it in an aphorism: state control existed for the sake of war, not war for the sake of state control.

The two fundamental requirements of the state were reflected in its basic division of people into two classes: those who fought in its wars, and those who paid for them. In the early period of the Empire this was a much more important distinction than the one between Muslims and non-Muslims. The people who belonged to the Sultan's military–administrative machine were known as *askeri*, the soldier-class (Trk.: *asker*, soldier): this category included all those who exercised power delegated to them by the Sultan, such as judges and clerks, as well as the Muslim clergy. All these were exempt from state taxes. The tax-paying class, on the other hand, was known as *raya* (Trk.: *reaya*, from an Arabic word meaning 'flock'). In the later stages of Ottoman rule in the Balkans the term raya was used only for the Christian peasantry; but its original meaning was wider than that, and independent of religious identity. Muslim peasants were raya too, and so were all people who paid taxes to the Sultan and did not fight on his behalf.[1]

The fighting forces of the Empire fell into two main categories: those who received salaries, and those who were given feudal estates. The former category included naval forces and some salaried cavalry, but its most important component was the Janissary corps. This was the Sultan's personal standing army, formed originally out of 'slaves of war' (captured soldiers or other young male prisoners, usually Christians); the 320 youths of Novo Brdo who were taken away when the city fell in 1455 were all sent to join the Janissaries. During the fifteenth and sixteenth centuries a more systematic method of recruitment was developed: the *devşirme* or 'collection'. Every seven years (or more often, in periods of frequent war) officials would tour the Christian villages of the Balkans, forcibly recruiting teenage boys. According to one sixteenth-century regulation, the levy was of one boy from every forty households. These were then taken off to Istanbul and Anatolia, converted to Islam, taught to speak Turkish, and trained to serve either as soldiers or as servants in the imperial household. Since the household was at the same time the imperial administration, and all officials of the imperial government were servants of the Sultan, this was in fact the road to advancement to the highest offices in the state. Many of the Ottoman Grand Viziers, and other members of the Divan (the Sultan's council of state), began their careers in this way.[2]

Although the devşirme was a cruel infliction on Christian parents, it nevertheless provided the main form of upward social mobility in the early Ottoman system: this was the route by which raya children became members of the askeri class. While some may have lost touch altogether with their families, there are many cases of successful members of the devşirme intake re-establishing contact with their areas of origin and extending their patronage towards them.[3] So sought after were the advantages that could flow from Janissary status that the Slav Muslims of Bosnia asked for, and obtained, the special privilege of sending their own sons to join this otherwise entirely Christian intake.[4] But among the Christian villagers the devşirme was understandably unpopular; in 1565 there was an uprising against it in Albania, and some areas, such as the mining district of Novo Brdo, were granted exemption from the devşirme as a special privilege.[5] Albanians were particularly prized by the devşirme collectors for their physical toughness and fighting skills. Many also turned out to be canny administrators who rose to the highest offices of state: two fifteenth-century Grand Viziers, Gedik Ahmet pasha and Davut pasha, are known to have been of Albanian origin, and the total number of Albanian Grand Viziers in the history of the Empire – including many Albanians from Kosovo – is put at forty-two.[6] Apart from creating upward mobility, the devşirme was also important in two other processes of social change: it played a part in spreading Islam in the Balkans, and it also ensured that the Ottoman ruling class became an ethnic mélange of all its subject peoples. (For this reason, although the word 'Turks' was used to describe the original conquerors of the Balkans, the term 'Ottomans' will be used from now on.)

The other main element of the military system was the class of knights, known as *spahis* (Trk.: *sipahi*, cavalryman), who were granted feudal estates. The estates were in two categories, according to size: the basic type was called a *timar* (and this is used as the general term for all these military–feudal properties), while the larger type was called a *zeamet*. (A third and even bigger type, the *has*, was reserved usually for members of the imperial family and high-ranking pashas.) The basic duty of a spahi was to join the Sultan's military campaigns, bringing with him men and equipment in proportion to his income, according to a fixed scale. If he failed to answer the military summons, he could be ejected from his timar. The ultimate owner of the land was the Sultan; the timars were in practice handed down from father to son, but the son could inherit only if he accepted all the military obligations of the estate. In fact, strictly speaking, the timar was not a piece of land but merely the right to certain feudal incomes which in most cases were derived from peasants working the land: in exceptional cases, a timar could consist of a designated income from taxation without any land at all.[7] When the spahi was not on campaign he lived on his estate; usually one part of the land, known as his *çiftlik*, was for his direct personal use, and would be farmed for him by his peasants. (Some aspects of this arrangement are similar to those of the pre-Ottoman pronoia estates.) Early Ottoman legislation required the spahi to stay in his local military–administrative area. Spahis did not perform all the feudal functions of their western European equivalents; there were no manorial courts, for example. But they did play one key administrative role: they collected all the taxes from their raya, retaining a certain proportion for their own benefit and passing on the rest to the state.

In the early stages of Ottoman expansion the spahis had been free Muslim warriors who fought as volunteers and were rewarded for their valour with conquered land. During the conquest of Balkan territories in the fifteenth century, however, many local Christian knights were accepted as spahis, on condition that they performed military service for the Sultan. The existence of these Christian spahis – who are assumed, in most cases, to have been local landowners before the arrival of the Ottomans – is striking proof that the early Ottoman state was not based on the distinction between Muslims and non-Muslims. In the first surviving set of registers for Albania (from 1431), fifty-six out of the 335 timars were held by Christians; a register of 1455 for Skopje, Tetovo and parts of Kosovo listed fifty Christian spahis; and a register of the same year for 'the vilayet of Vuk' (i.e. a tax district made out of Branković territory, corresponding roughly to Eastern Kosovo) listed twenty-seven Christian spahis out of a total of 170.[8] Interestingly, a handful of these

Christians were described in the last two documents as 'old spahis', meaning not that they had been feudal land-holders under the Christian régime, but that they had already been installed as Ottoman spahis before the final Ottoman takeover of 1455.

Christians continued to be granted new timars during the second half of the fifteenth century; sometimes estates were transferred to them from Muslims.[9] Most Christian spahi families converted to Islam within a few generations, and this category of spahi disappears from the Ottoman records before the end of the sixteenth century. But the last generation must have lingered on into the seventeenth, as we know from the evidence of the patronage of Christian churches. Christian spahis sponsored a new monastery building at Pljevlja (in the Sandžak of Novi Pazar) in 1592, and a spahi paid for paintings in the church of the Holy Apostles in the Patriarchate complex at Peć in 1633; as late as 1642 the Serbian Patriarch remembered two old spahis called Miloš and Stoiko.[10] These, probably, were the very last of their kind.

Apart from the spahis, the main representative of the Ottoman state system at the local level was the *kadı* or judge; each kadı was responsible for an administrative area called a *kadılık* or *kaza*. The kadı was always a Muslim: his responsibilities included administering the şeriat or Islamic sacred law. But most of the criminal law was contained in separate codes, known as *kanuns*, which were derived not from the Koran but from the will of the Sultan. Apart from the general criminal code there were also local kanuns, which often incorporated the traditional laws or practices of conquered lands; all these codes were renewed or added to by each Sultan in turn.[11] The fullest surviving criminal code from this period is traditionally called the kanun of Süleyman the Magnificent, and probably dates from 1534–45, the middle years of his reign. Compared with the law-code of Stefan Dušan, it is positively humane: although there are some punishments involving death or mutilation (hanging for burglars, branding for pimps, and the amputation of a hand for those guilty of major thefts), most of the penalties consist of fines or floggings – even for morally serious offences such as fornication. Interestingly, the fines for 'unbelievers' (Christians and Jews) are set at one-half of the fines for Muslims.[12] Christians did suffer one serious disability in Ottoman legal practice: their testimony could not be used against a Muslim in court. But there are, on the other hand, many records of Muslims witnessing in favour of Christians, against other Muslims.[13] Modern scholars are convinced that the kadıs had a high standard of integrity in the fifteenth and sixteenth centuries, and concur with the judgement of the Kosovo-born historian Celalzade Salih Çelebi (1499–1570), who wrote that in the reign of Süleyman the Magnificent 'the gates of oppression and aggression were fastened with the nails of the kanuns.'[14]

The next level of government above the kadılık was a military–administrative district known as a *sancak* ('banner'), which was governed by a *sancakbeyi* (Trk.: *bey*, lord). A number of sancaks formed an *eyalet* (not to be confused with a vilayet, which at this stage was a much smaller taxation district), governed by a *beylerbeyi* or lord of lords. Most of the European provinces of the Empire were part of a single eyalet, the eyalet of Rumeli; for some short periods in the 1540s, 1560s and 1570s Bosnia and part of Kosovo were included in the eyalet of Buda (i.e. Budapest), and Kosovo seems to have been included in this eyalet again for part of the early seventeenth century. Otherwise, the entire territory of Kosovo was in the Rumeli eyalet. The administrative units of Kosovo varied during the first two centuries of Ottoman rule, but the main division was between three sancaks: the sancak of Vuçitërn (Srb.: Vučitrn), which included Prishtina and most of Eastern Kosovo; the sancak of Prizren, which at first covered a smaller area centring on Prizren but later in the sixteenth century expanded northwards to Novi Pazar; and the sancak of Shkodra, which stretched from the Adriatic coast across the northern Albanian Malësi to include the area of Kosovo round Peć. Smaller slices of Kosovo were also included in other neighbouring units: in particular, the sancak of Dukagjin, which covered part of north-central Albania and in some periods included the Kosovo town of Gjakova (Srb.: Djakovica) with its nearby district of Altun-ili; and the sancak of Skopje, which included the south-eastern Kosovo town of Kaçanik.[15]

From the early Ottoman tax registers for these sancaks it is possible to make a rough calculation of the total population of Kosovo. In 1490 there were 64,328 Christian tax-paying households in the areas corresponding to Kosovo: the usual multiplier used by Balkan historians is five people per household, and to this one must then add a small number of Muslims and some non-tax-paying Christians, as well as making some allowance for those inhabitants (particularly the pastoral ones) who may have slipped through the Ottoman net. Possibly the total was in the region of 350,000.[16] The great majority of these tax-paying Christians lived in the countryside: it has been calculated that only 3.5 per cent of all Kosovo households in the late fifteenth century were in towns.[17]

Most of the peasants would have been working on some sort of feudal estate before the Ottoman conquest, and their overall conditions of life would not have changed very much. A peasant living in an Ottoman feudal domain owned his own house, a small vegetable garden and perhaps a vineyard; these could be inherited or sold. He also had a plot of arable land called a *çift*, which means 'pair' in Turkish: originally it was the area of land that could be worked by a pair of oxen (the Byzantine *zeugarion* or 'yoke-land'). His ownership of this was not absolute, but has been defined as a hereditary tenantship in perpetuity.[18] In some cases these lands were not enough to live on, so the peasants would also work other lands which were part of the timar estate. The basic taxes paid by a peasant were the tithe on his produce (not necessarily one tenth, but often a greater proportion, which varied according to the nature of the crop) and a fixed annual tax related to the land he worked, known as *ispence* for Christian peasants and *resm-i çift* for Muslim peasants.[19] Both this fixed tax and the tithe had existed in pre-Ottoman times; the ispence was simply a version of what the Byzantines had called the *zeugaratikion*.[20] There were some other minor feudal dues, and a tax on things bought and sold at market. In addition there were several state taxes, including the poll-tax on non-Muslims (which will be discussed later) and some so-called extraordinary taxes, which in fact became quite regular, to support the Empire's military campaigns.[21]

The main difference, however, between the Ottoman system and its predecessor was that the feudal status of the peasants underwent a real improvement. The duty of *corvée* or obligatory labour on the estate-holder's lands was greatly reduced – in some cases, from two days per week to just three days per year.[22] Several of the old feudal obligations were commuted into cash payments. Although the Ottoman system required peasants to stay on the land, the punishment for leaving (for example, to become an artisan in a nearby town) was merely a fine to compensate the spahi for his lost income, not the mutilations of the medieval Serbian code; and after a time-limit of fifteen years the spahi lost all his claims over an absconding peasant.[23] In this early period, the Ottoman state seems to have taken more care to protect the rights of the peasants than its Serbian predecessors had done. A law for the Skopje area in the 1560s, for example, decreed: 'Those who administer justice should not interfere in the raya's affairs and should not torment him. Let him possess the lands as he wishes, until his death. When he dies, let his sons take his place...'[24] Such laws would not need to have been promulgated, of course, unless there had been some spahis who were abusing their powers. But the overall benefits of the Ottoman system were clear: during the fifteenth and sixteenth centuries there were many cases of peasants migrating from unconquered regions to settle in Ottoman territory.[25]

For at least the first century of Ottoman rule, rural life in Kosovo seems to have flourished. The disruptions of the conquest had not been very severe; the first register in 1455 recorded only forty-two abandoned villages out of a total of more than 600.[26] Grain production was in a healthy state for most of this period; from studies of other parts of the Ottoman Balkans we know that it was common in the sixteenth century for peasants to produce a surplus which they took to market, and until the mid-sixteenth century Ragusan grain merchants were buying direct from peasant farmers in Kosovo, Albania and neighbouring areas. Only in the latter part of that century did the Ottoman government sometimes prohibit such exports, after a number of poor Balkan harvests.[27] Apart from the standard crops (wheat, barley, rye, oats, millet), Kosovo also yielded some specialist products such as saffron and silk-worms; Western Kosovo was also famous for its fruit. Stock-breeding was of course important, and another Kosovo speciality was bee-keeping: in the *nahiye* (administrative sub-district) of Vuçitërn in 1455 more than 2,000 houses had beehives.[28] Grapes and wine were major products: in 1485, 197 out of the 261 villages in the nahiye of Peć had vineyards. And despite the formal prohibitions of the law, it was not unknown for Muslims to make wine. Roughly ten hectares of vineyard were in Muslim ownership in the Peć nahiye in 1582.[29]

Not all Christian subjects were simple peasants on feudal estates. Apart from the spahis already mentioned, there were several other

groups of more or less privileged Christians. Some of these performed
military duties, such as the type of paid soldier known as a *martolos*
(from Grk.: *armatôlos*, armed man), who was considered a member of
the askeri class. There were also Christian soldiers (cavalrymen in some
cases) known as *voynuks*, many of whom were Vlachs: these were exempt
from the poll-tax and some other dues. Martoloses and voynuks were
mainly used in frontier regions, such as Bosnia, but they were also given
some internal security duties, guarding roads and mines in areas such as
Kosovo. They maintained their privileged position until the late sixteenth
century, when the martoloses were reduced to raya and the voynuks lost
their tax-exemptions altogether.[30]

Also privileged, and important in the Kosovo region, were the *derbend*
villages (from a Persian-derived Turkish word for a mountain pass),
which enjoyed special tax advantages in return for maintaining the
security of mountain roads. In the 1450s, just before the final Ottoman
conquest of Kosovo, nine villages in the Kaçanik district had this special
status; it was later extended to other areas, such as the Rugovo (Alb.:
Rugova) district in north-western Kosovo, and the Këlmendi villages of
northern Albania. By the end of the sixteenth century a large swathe of
the Malësi, from near Shkodra across to Peć, was declared *derbend* and
freed from many state taxes.[31] Other groups of privileged Christians
included artisans who manufactured arms and ammunition for the
Ottoman army; falconers who bred birds for the Sultan and the local
lords (there were fifteen falconer households in villages round Prishtina
in 1477, and twenty-four in villages near Prizren); and miners, who
continued to enjoy special tax advantages.[32]

The Ottoman rulers were well aware of the economic value of the
mines of Kosovo, and the incompetence which marked their later
management of the mines was not immediately apparent. Although the
women and young men of Novo Brdo were enslaved when the town was
captured in 1455, the miners were encouraged to remain.[33] Miners
retained some rights of self-administration, electing their own governing
councils, and their tax privileges included exemption from both the poll-
tax on non-Muslims and the 'extraordinary' taxes; not being peasants,
they paid no tithes or ispence. (Villagers in mining areas who performed
auxiliary tasks for the mines, such as transportation, could also have
these privileges.)[34]

One document which survives from 1463 is a letter from the Grand Vizier to a Ragusan, Franko Bobanić, asking him to continue to work at the mines of Novo Brdo just as he had done in the time of the Despot: presumably he was an overseer or financial manager.[35] The Ragusan community did not disappear from Novo Brdo: its numbers in the second half of the fifteenth century were smaller, but still significant (as many as seventy-nine). But on the other hand it was a general principle of Ottoman government that precious metals should not be exported; the bullion trade to Ragusa, which the Ottoman officials in Kosovo had been trying to halt since the 1420s, was thus brought to an end. Silver mined in Kosovo was either minted at Novo Brdo or sent to Istanbul.[36] The Ottomans made real efforts to encourage mining in the late fifteenth century, and even started a new silver mine near Prizren; they also took care to reissue and codify the old 'Saxon' mining laws, and added a new law in 1536 giving greater freedom to prospectors.[37] Although the population of Novo Brdo contracted during the sixteenth century, which suggests an overall decline in activities, the town was still a major producer in the 1580s: its mines then yielded more than 33,000 ounces of silver per year, while those of Trepça produced nearly 29,000.[38]

Apart from precious metals, most commodities were still freely traded; only occasionally would the Ottoman government ban the export of things it needed, such as arms, gunpowder, lead and copper. Non-precious metals and agricultural products such as hides and wool were the main international exports of the Kosovo region, and most of them went to western Europe via Ragusa. In return, textiles, sugar, spices, and exotic manufactured goods such as mirrors were imported into the area by Ragusan merchants resident in Novi Pazar, Skopje and, just to the south of Prishtina, the mining town of Janjevo.[39] While a few towns, such as Novo Brdo and Peć, may have contracted, the general pattern was one of steady urban expansion under the Ottomans: between the late fourteenth and late fifteenth centuries, the town population of the Kosovo region grew by at least 70 per cent.[40] Two towns in particular, Vuçitërn and Prizren, were stimulated by their new roles as administrative centres; and the latter, despite its lack of a Ragusan colony, also became an important centre of trade and economic life. One rich Muslim from Prizren, Mehmet Hayredin Kukli bey, who set up a religious–charitable foundation in the 1530s, owned 117 shops, six mills and one caravanseray.[41]

Some of these shops were also artisan workshops where goods were made; a total of fifty-five crafts are known to have been practised in early Ottoman Kosovo, and forty-five of them are recorded for Prizren alone.[42] This was the main economic mechanism drawing people from the villages into the major towns. Many of the crafts involved processing agricultural products: leather-working, for example, or silk-weaving. Some craftsmen, such as armourers and smiths, served the needs of the Ottoman military, and gunpowder was being produced in Prishtina as early as 1485.[43] New crafts introduced by the Ottomans, such as soap-making, were practised only by Muslims, but a dozen popular crafts, including those of the silversmiths, dyers and saddle-makers, remained partly or wholly in Christian hands.[44]

Towards the end of the sixteenth century a formal – and increasingly elaborate – system of craft guilds emerged, which was to dominate urban life in Kosovo for the next three centuries. (This system will be described in the next chapter.) One of the unsolved puzzles of this area of Balkan history is the question of whether these organizations had developed continuously out of pre-Ottoman types of guild, either Byzantine, medieval Serbian or Italian-influenced. We know, for example, that the cobblers of Prizren had been organized under a leader with the Byzantine-derived title of *protomajstor* in 1348, and it is a suggestive fact that the Christian quarters of several Kosovo towns in the Ottoman period were named after Serbian medieval crafts (such as the 'Lukar' and 'Pojasar' quarters of Prishtina, meaning 'bow-maker' and 'belt-maker').[45] A form of Roman-style *collegium* had survived in Albanian coastal towns, undergoing both Byzantine and Italian influences; and the governing council of an Ottoman guild was called a *lonca* (Alb.: *llonxha*), which is derived from the Venetian *loggia*. Although the Ottoman guilds are not mentioned in Albania until the 1580s or in Kosovo until the early seventeenth century, there are traces of fifteenth-century Ottoman guilds in Sarajevo.[46] So, while there is no direct evidence of continuity in the Kosovo towns, the indirect evidence is quite strong.

As several details will already have suggested, there was a close connection between urban life and the spread of the Islamic faith. Apart from the spahis on their estates, most of the askeri class – which was

overwhelmingly Muslim – lived in the towns; and many of the institutions of the towns were bound up with those of Islam. Particularly
important was the religious–charitable foundation, of the sort endowed
by Kukli bey, known as a *vakıf* (Alb. and Srb.: *vakuf*). Under Islamic law,
property given to endow a vakıf could never be taken from it, and its
income was meant to be tax-free; many rich Muslims would appoint
their descendants as salaried administrators of these endowments, thus
creating in effect a financially advantageous family trust. (In practice,
however, the Ottoman state continued to demand some taxes from vakıf
endowments.)[47] But the benefits of the vakıf were public as well as
private: these foundations could be dedicated to the upkeep of a mosque,
a school, an *imaret* (soup-kitchen for the poor) or a *hamam* (public
bath), or even to the maintenance of bridges and inns.

Several important vakıfs operated in Prizren, and by the mid-sixteenth
century the town possessed seven or eight mosques (one of them with a
library), a *medrese* (Muslim seminary), several elementary schools, a
hamam (with separate sections for men and women) and a handsome
stone bridge.[48] As the presence of schools and libraries suggests, it was
possible for Muslims from Kosovo to gain access to the world of
Ottoman literary culture. Kosovo produced several well-known writers
in this early period, including Priştinasi Mesihi (1470–1512), who
composed a famous 'divan' (poetry collection) and is thought to have
written the first humorous poem in Turkish literature; Prizrenasi Suzi
Çelebi (d. 1524), founder of an important vakıf in Prizren, who became
secretary to a famous general and wrote a 3,000-line poem celebrating
his exploits; and the historian Celalzade Salih Çelebi (1499–1570), born
in Vuçitërn, whose chronicle was cited above.[49] Other important connections which bound town life to Islam included the links between the
craft-guilds and the dervish orders. The latter certainly existed in this
first century of Ottoman Kosovo (Kukli bey's endowment deed mentions
a dervish lodge in Prizren), but there is so little information about them
in this period that the discussion of them will be held over, like that of
the guilds, to the next chapter.[50]

The growth of Islam in Kosovo, during the early Ottoman period, was
an almost exclusively urban phenomenon. The figures for the countryside are minimal: in the 1480s the villages round Prizren contained no
Muslims at all; in the 1530s the nahiye of Morava (in the south-east of

Kosovo) had 1,020 Christian households, and just six Muslim ones; and in 1566/7 the 1,000-odd villages of the sancak of Vuçitërn contained only forty-six Muslim households, scattered through thirty villages.[51] Compared with other neighbouring regions, Kosovo possessed quite a dense network of towns; and yet the process of Islamicization was not rapid there either. Novo Brdo in 1488/9, for example, had thirty-eight *mahalles* (Alb.: *mëhallë*, Srb.: *mahala*, usually translated 'quarter', but in fact only a small urban sub-division of perhaps forty houses), all of them Christian; in 1525 there were forty-two Christian ones and four Muslim; and in 1544 thirty-eight Christian and five Muslim.[52] In the entire sancak of Vuçitërn in 1530/1 there were just four mosques, located in the towns of Vuçitërn, Prishtina, Trepça and Novo Brdo, and ten *mescids* (smaller places of worship); the total Muslim population of the sancak was only 496 households.[53] Towns which served as Ottoman administrative centres, such as Vuçitërn, Prishtina and Prizren, were Islamicized more quickly. Those which had strong communities of miners and merchants, many of whom were Catholic (either the 'Saxon' Germans, or the Ragusans and other Dalmatians, or Catholic Albanians) were slower to change.[54] The pace of Islamicization increased in the second half of the sixteenth century, and by the period 1582–91 the percentages of Muslims in the major towns were as follows: Peć ninety; Vuçitërn eighty; Prishtina sixty; Prizren fifty-six; Novo Brdo thirty-seven; Trepça twenty-one; Janjevo fourteen.[55]

How and why did this growth occur? The historical evidence is frustratingly insufficient in some ways – there is almost nothing from this early period, for example, to show what any individual actually thought about becoming a Muslim – but it does enable us to make some deductions, and to rule some theories out altogether. It is clear, for example, that the growth of a Muslim population was not caused by any kind of mass settlement of Muslims from outside.[56] The number of Muslim spahis brought in to the territory at the outset cannot have been more than a few hundred. Other soldiers, administrators and merchants must have settled in Kosovo, both now and in later periods (there are families today in Kosovo which trace their descent from Anatolian Turks), but as a proportion of the total population this element would be quite insignificant. And although some parts of Macedonia were settled by semi-nomadic Turkic Muslims known as Yürüks, that was a phenomenon which hardly touched the territory of Kosovo itself; just a handful of Yürüks are mentioned as people employed to guard mines in Kosovo during this early period.[57]

The overwhelming majority of the Muslims in early Kosovo must have been produced by the conversion of local people from Christianity. To some extent this can be traced in the records, because of a convention by which new converts would either take the name of 'Abdullah' (which means 'slave of God') or give it as their father's name. A study of the tax registers of the Skopje and Tetovo regions in the sixteenth century shows that the proportion of new converts among Muslim heads of households rose from a quarter in the 1520s to a third in the 1540s and almost one half in the late 1560s.[58] Forced conversions were rare; one German traveller did record in 1555 that prisoners of war were being forcibly converted in Istanbul, but this was never a general practice.[59] Similarly, Ottoman officials were occasionally instructed to promote the conversion of certain districts as a pacification measure: in 1573 the kadı of Elbasan was ordered to carry out this policy in the Reka district, north of Debar, and by 1582 170 Muslim heads of household were recorded there, 160 of them new converts.[60] But this too was unusual.

Whether converts in this early period were persuaded by anything that might be called theological argument is impossible to say, though there is some evidence of that in the following century. Probably the main reasons were more to do with worldly affairs – involving questions of status as well as economic interest. Those who had most to gain were slaves (usually prisoners of war) who were brought to work the private estates of Ottoman lords or the lands of the religious–charitable foundations: the usual pattern was that they would convert to Islam, lose their slave status, and be installed on the land as peasants.[61] This may have happened in Kosovo, although, as we have seen, the growth of Islam in the countryside was particularly slow. The expanding towns also provided employment for converted and liberated slaves, particularly in those crafts which became Muslim monopolies.

For those who chose to become Muslims, the immediate economic benefit was a reduction in taxation: above all, they were freed from the *cizye*. This was a special tax on non-Muslims, based on the teachings of the Koran about the tribute payable by Christians and Jews. The cizye had become combined with another such tax, the *haraç*, which was originally a tax on land; by the sixteenth century the cizye was a graduated poll-tax, levied annually on each adult male and collected on a household basis.[62] In the middle of the century an average household would pay roughly 50 akçes, the equivalent of two sheep.[63] Other taxes, such as the peasants' ispence or resm-i çift, were set at a slightly lower rate for Muslims. But on the other hand Muslims had to pay the *zekat* or alms-tax, which was not paid by Christians; and, as we have seen, the fines on Muslims in the criminal courts were twice as heavy. The explanation given for this last fact in the law-code of Bayezit II (ruled 1481–1512) is particularly instructive: the Christians pay lower fines, it says, 'so that the poll-tax payers shall not vanish'.[64] Neither economic interest nor religious duty compelled the Ottoman state to convert its subject peoples; and when large tax increases in the seventeenth century did in effect put strong pressure on Christian tax-payers to convert, the motive on the Ottoman government's part was simply a desperate wish for money, not a desire to gain souls.

Under traditional Islamic law it was of course meritorious at an individual level to convert people to Islam; but Christians and Jews in general were *zimmi* (Arb.: *dhimmi*, 'people of protection'), which meant that their status was subordinate but protected by law. They had various legal disabilities; they were not allowed to bear arms (a prohibition widely disregarded in the Albanian lands); and they were forbidden to wear certain Islamic items of dress. There were also more strict prohibitions against insulting the Islamic faith or trying to convert people from it. So long as they accepted these restrictions, the Christians were allowed to get on with their own religious lives, maintaining their own churches and even, as mentioned above, their own civil courts.[65]

Lurid stories about the treatment of Christians are sometimes told in connection with the conquest of Christian territory; but that was always a special case. Under traditional Islamic rules, which were generally observed by the Ottomans, Christians who surrendered were immediately awarded the rights of zimmi, and only those who resisted were given punitive treatment. This is particularly noticeable where the treatment of church buildings is concerned. In towns which conquered after refusing to surrender, churches could be converted into mosques: this happened, for example, to the 'Saxon' church of Novo Brdo in the 1460s. (Two churches in Prizren were converted in this way at an early stage, and one in Peć.)⁶⁶ But even in these cases there was no systematic takeover of all church buildings. The city of Ohrid, for example, which was (and still is) packed with medieval Orthodox churches, had just one church confiscated after its conquest in the fourteenth century and one other in the fifteenth; even after the population of Ohrid had become mainly Muslim in the sixteenth century, the authorities left the existing churches alone and built new mosques instead.⁶⁷

According to standard Islamic regulations, Christian communities were permitted to maintain existing church buildings, but not to extend them without special permission. Such permission, for extensions or even completely new churches, was in fact given quite frequently: there was widespread rebuilding of churches and monasteries in the area of the Patriarchate of Peć in the second half of the sixteenth century.⁶⁸ Generally speaking, monasteries were allowed to keep their estates, and in some cases they were even granted some of the tax privileges associated with vakıf status.⁶⁹ The pictures of Serbian monastic life supplied by foreign travellers during this period are strikingly positive. The Italian envoy Pigafetta, visiting Ravanica (Lazar's foundation) in 1568, observed that the monks lived freely and that the Ottomans had never touched the monastery; and the French traveller Palerne, visiting Mileševa (in the Sandžak of Novi Pazar) in 1582, was impressed by this 'very beautiful monastery of kaludjers [Orthodox monks], which is rich, and well endowed, and where many relics and silver caskets can be seen ... all nations are well received there, and given hospitality for a whole day, free of charge.'⁷⁰

The Serbian Orthodox Church was in fact enjoying a particularly favoured position at this time, after the re-establishment of the Patriarchate of Peć in 1557. Quite what had happened to the Church during the previous century is, however, a question which has puzzled many historians. The last cleric to bear the title of Patriarch, Arsenije II, had died in 1463. It used to be believed that, soon after the final Ottoman conquest of Serbian lands in 1459, the whole territory of the Serbian Orthodox Patriarchate was taken over again by the Archbishopric of Ohrid; later, in the 1520s and 1530s, a bishop from the northern territory of Smederevo tried to break away from Ohrid's jurisdiction, and several formal meetings of the Church were held in Ohrid to denounce his 'rebellion'. This version has been rejected by most modern historians. It now seems clear that Ohrid did not gain any general control over the Serbian Church in 1459; the Metropolitans of Hercegovina, for example, remained independent of Ohrid until the final conquest of Hercegovina in the 1480s. Before 1459, the ecclesiastical administration of the Patriarchate of Peć had already moved northwards, probably to Smederevo; as a result of this, there was some *de facto* takeover by Ohrid of bishoprics in the south of the Serbian Orthodox territory. In the 1520s the Archbishop of Ohrid persuaded the Ottomans to grant him general rights over the Serbian Church; this was resisted by Serbian bishops in the north, and Bishop Pavle tried to persuade the Sultan formally to reinstate the Patriarchate of Peć, with himself as Patriarch. That was the so-called 'rebellion' which the Archbishop of Ohrid successfully crushed, forcing Pavle to appear as a penitent at meetings which he had packed with his own supporters.[71]

The seed which Pavle had planted in the minds of the Ottoman rulers bore fruit in 1557, when one of the senior viziers, Mehmed Sokolović (Trk.: Mehmet Sokollı), officially reinstated the Patriarchate at Peć. Sokolović was from an Orthodox family in Hercegovina; taken to Istanbul in the devşirme, he rose rapidly in government service, becoming an admiral, then Beylerbeyi of Rumeli (1551–5), then a member of the council of viziers, and finally Grand Vizier (1565–79). He furnishes conclusive proof that boys seized in the devşirme did not lose all their family links, since the person he appointed Patriarch, a Serb archimandrite on Mount Athos, was his own brother, Makarije. But we need not suppose that Mehmed Sokolović's principal motive was either nepotism or secret Christian sentiment: there were good political reasons for this move. It was clearly in the interests of the Ottoman state to enjoy better relations with its Orthodox subjects, now that the main enemy powers ranged against the Empire in the West were all Roman Catholic. A Patriarch dependent on Ottoman good will would be a useful instrument of control, especially in sensitive areas with mixed Catholic–Orthodox populations, such as parts of Montenegro. And the choice of Makarije was evidently also a good one: all the evidence indicates that he was a serious and energetic man who furthered the interests of his Church.[72] One example of his successful efforts is given by a document of 1570/1 (shortly before Makarije resigned on health grounds; he died in 1574), preserved in the Istanbul archives: it refers to the properties of an abandoned monastery near Peć which had become 'scattered', and declares that 'they have now been joined to the property of the monastery of the Saviour and given in usufruct to the said monk Makarije.'[73]

By the time the Patriarchate was re-established at Peć, the town of Peć itself may already have gained an absolute majority of Muslims. At the same time, there is an increasing volume of evidence that parts of Western Kosovo had a significant ethnic Albanian population, evidence which goes beyond anything that can be demonstrated for the medieval period. Some modern Albanian scholars have put these phenomena together – the growth of Islam and the apparent growth of an Albanian population – to argue that what we are seeing in both cases is the emergence of a previously invisible mass of ethnic Albanians, who had been disguised in the records under Slav Orthodox names. It is claimed that the loss of authority by the Peć Patriarchate in this area between 1455 and 1557 had made it possible for these Albanians to detach themselves from Serbian control; and that while ethnic Serbs would have felt a continuing (and, after 1557, a revived) attachment to their Church which would have prevented them from turning to Islam, the ethnic Albanians would have felt no such scruples about adopting this new religion. Thus, it is suggested, the people who became Muslims were nearly all of them ethnic Albanians, and the creation of a Muslim majority was at the same time merely the revelation of an already existing Albanian majority.[74]

Some aspects of this argument are unconvincing on *a priori* grounds. Ethnic Albanians are unlikely to have felt estranged from the Serbian Church merely because it was not their 'national' Church; this is to project a modern idea of 'national' loyalties a little too far into the past. Orthodox Albanians in southern Albania and Greece, for example, remained loyal to the Greek Church and its liturgy for many generations, even though they may have spoken only Albanian in the home. Nor, conversely, were Slavs incapable of converting to Islam: it was happening all the time in the neighbouring territories of Macedonia and Novi Pazar, as well as in Bosnia and Hercegovina. (As early as 1580 the 6,000-odd households of the Novi Pazar district were almost entirely Muslim.)[75] Many of the Albanian names which crop up in the early Ottoman

registers for Kosovo are Catholic Albanian Christian names, such as
'Gjin' (John) and 'Doda' (a diminutive of Dominic); and it is not clear
why Albanians who had long been Serbian Orthodox should have
regarded the Catholic Church, with its Latin liturgy and Italian-trained
priests, as more deserving of 'national' loyalty than a Church based in
their own locality.

On all these grounds, one might feel tempted to reject this argument
entirely. Those who do so (and this includes almost all Serbian historians) explain the growth of an Albanian population in Kosovo during
the early Ottoman period in terms of physical immigration: it is
suggested that Albanians from the Malësi were encouraged by the
Ottomans to settle in Kosovo, that many of these turned to Islam to gain
the advantages of superior status, and that those Slavs who became
Muslims were not merely Islamicized but, sooner or later, Albanianized
as well.

Although the Albanian historians' argument seems unconvincing for
general reasons, it nevertheless comes buttressed with some intriguing
evidence from the Ottoman registers. The Ottoman officials usually
noted which heads of family were 'new arrivals' in their places of
residence; out of 121 new arrivals in the nahiye of Peć in 1485, the
majority had Slav names. In the sancak of Prizren in 1591, only five new
arrivals out of forty-one bore Albanian names; and in a group of Kosovo
towns in the 1580s and 1590s there were twenty-five new Albanian
immigrants and 133 with Slav names – several of them described as
coming from Bosnia.[76] This evidence counts strongly against the idea of
a mass immigration from northern Albania. Other more general arguments against that idea are based on relative population sizes and rates
of growth. The population of Kosovo during this period was much
bigger than that of northern and central Albania, and its rate of growth
was actually lower. This is not what one would expect if a large overflow
from the Albanian Malësi were flooding into Kosovo.[77]

All arguments which depend on identifying Slav or Albanian names
are of course subject to doubts about whether the names really did
indicate ethnic–linguistic identity – which is, of course, one of the key
points at issue. In a previous discussion of this question (in Chapter 4)
it was suggested that although names are not very trustworthy in any
particular case, the broad pattern probably does indicate both the nature

of the dominant culture and the direction of flow of any tendencies to assimilation. On that basis it is reasonable to say that a Serbian Orthodox culture was overwhelmingly dominant in Eastern Kosovo: the first Ottoman register, of 1455, yields only a small minority of Albanian names, and many of these involve an Albanian-named father and a Slav Orthodox-named son ('Radislav, son of Djon'; 'Radovan, son of Djin').[78] Many of the Albanians in this register are identified as 'Arbanas' or 'Arnaud', which suggests that their Albanian identity was a distinguishing feature, setting them apart from most of the surrounding population. In the 1570s there was a mahalle (quarter) of Janjevo called 'Arbanas'; roughly half of its heads of families had Slav or mixed Slav–Albanian names.[79] According to some Albanian historians, this shows that many apparent Slavs were really Albanian-speaking Albanians. A simpler explanation, surely, would be that the small Albanian minority in Janjevo was gradually being assimilated to the Serbian-speaking majority.

On the other hand, there is clear evidence of Orthodox names appearing in Albanian-language forms – which implies that adherence to the Orthodox Church did not necessarily involve assimilation to a Serbian-language culture. While the majority of the Albanian names in Western Kosovo were Catholic, a significant minority were Orthodox, including several of the fifteen Orthodox families that constituted the entire Orthodox population of Peć in the 1590s. (Also in Western Kosovo in this period were 'Gjon, son of an Orthodox priest', and 'Gjonja, an Orthodox monk').[80] Again, Albanian historians argue from this that most of the Orthodox population of Kosovo was in fact Albanian; it would surely be simpler to suppose that the majority of the Orthodox (who do have Slav names) were Serbian-speaking and a minority Albanian-speaking, and that the Albanians were not assimilated linguistically because there was also a significant population of Catholic Albanians in Western Kosovo – as the other Albanian names clearly show.

The evidence scrupulously presented by one leading Albanian historian, Selami Pulaha, does not really support the argument which he then tries to build on it. In 1591, for example, in the nahiye of Hoça (north of Prizren), there were 883 heads of family with Slav or other Orthodox names, 196 with mixed Albanian–Slav names and 248 with purely Albanian names; Pulaha's conclusion is that the area was 'completely Albanian'. A group of Kosovo towns in the same period yields 330 purely Slav Orthodox names and 217 mixed Albanian–Slav or purely Albanian; Pulaha deduces that the urban population was 'almost completely Albanian'.[81] Similarly, the claim that only Albanians became Muslims can be argued only on the basis of the prior assumption that all people with Slav names were really Albanians. Of the Muslims of Hoça in 1591, fifty-four had Albanian names and nineteen Slav names; of those in the Has district (near Gjakova) in 1571, 166 had Albanian names and thirty-seven Slav names.[82] What this suggests is not that Slavs never became Muslims, but that a higher proportion of Albanians did so; and the reason for that may be that Catholic Albanians were even less well supplied with priests in the early Ottoman period than they had been under Serbian rule.

What a straightforward reading of all this evidence would suggest is that there were significant reservoirs of a mainly Catholic Albanian-speaking population in parts of Western Kosovo; and evidence from the following century suggests that many of these eventually became Muslims. Whether Albanian-speakers were a majority in Western Kosovo at this time seems very doubtful, and it is clear that they were only a small minority in the east. On the other hand, it is also clear that the Albanian minority in Eastern Kosovo predated the Ottoman conquest.[83]

Finally, one other social process was taking place in this period which is also relevant to arguments about the migration of Albanians into Kosovo: the formation of the northern Albanian clans. As was mentioned in the first chapter, these clans appear to have been formed out of groups of pastoral families in the Malësi from the late Middle Ages onwards: the main stimulus must have been the requirement of self-protection after the old system of powerful land-owning families (Balshas, Dukagjins, and so on) had been broken up by the Ottoman invasions and the disruptions of the fifteenth-century revolts. Some of the oldest clans preserve detailed family trees in their oral tradition, going back to founder-ancestors in the fourteenth or fifteenth centuries; others were formed from sub-branches of these older clans.[84]

The key development, it seems, was the adaptation of the social structures of pastoral life to the purposes of territorial self-defence. With several of the clans of the northern Malësi, the process by which vëllazëris (brotherhoods) came together to form clans can be traced, through Venetian and Ottoman documents, to the period between 1455 and 1485: what happened in these cases was that the members of the dominant brotherhood would impose their name on the whole clan, and on the territory which the clan defended. And at some time in the sixteenth century the Ottoman authorities gave up even trying to impose their normal administrative or feudal system in those areas, letting the clans run their own affairs in virtual 'zones of self-government' instead.[85] Curiously, the development of the clan system in Scotland was taking place at precisely the same time, and for much the same reason: a breakdown of central power and feudal structures in the fifteenth and sixteenth centuries. Scottish clans also developed the idea of common ancestry: 'at first this relationship might clearly be seen as fictitious or honorary, but in time the metaphor of kinship tended to be converted into belief that real blood kinship existed.'[86]

Thus, increasingly, Albanians from the Malësi would bear the name of their clan as a kind of surname: Berisha, Këlmendi, Shala and so on. There are many people with these names in modern Kosovo, and it is clear that, from the early seventeenth century onwards, at least some of their ancestors must have come into Kosovo as immigrants from the Malësi. ('At least some' is a necessary qualification, because we cannot assume that the process of agglomeration – of people joining a clan and taking its name – never took place on Kosovo soil.) However, there are also many Kosovo Albanians who do not bear clan names. Serbian writers sometimes argue that all these Albanians must therefore be Albanianized Serbs, as if all genuine Albanians would originally have belonged to clans. But since we know that there were non-clan Albanians in Kosovo as early as the fifteenth century, that clans were only formed in areas which (unlike Kosovo) lacked governmental security, and indeed that many of the clans in the Malësi were still only in the process of formation at that time, this particular version of the argument about 'Albanianized Serbs' can simply be dismissed.

7

War, rebellion and religious life: 1580s–1680s

IN 1585 THE Ottoman government reduced the silver content of the coins it minted by more than 40 per cent, while claiming that they still had just the same value. Four years later the Janissary corps in Istanbul was given its wages in these new debased coins; it promptly revolted, and was pacified only when the Sultan agreed to execute the Chief Treasurer, the Master of the Mint and the Beylerbeyi of Rumeli.[1] If a symbolic event (or pair of events) is needed to mark the beginning of the decline of the Ottoman Empire, this devaluation and ensuing revolt is ideally suitable, combining as it does the essential elements of administrative incompetence, violent rebellion and, above all, an insatiable hunger for cash.

The theme of Ottoman decline has preoccupied chroniclers and analysts from the sixteenth-century Ottomans onwards. Some modern historians have turned against this tradition; they argue that it is unrealistic to judge all Ottoman institutions by the standards of the reign of Süleyman the Magnificent (1520–66, usually seen as the golden age of Ottoman statehood), and point out that a more sensible comparison for the following century would be with other European states, which had their own seventeenth-century rebellions and structural problems.[2] It is true that regional revolts and price-inflation were not peculiar to the Ottomans. It is also true that some of the changes of this period – for example, the decay of the timar system, as Ottoman armies became more and more dependent on large bodies of paid infantry – resulted from progress in military technology, which could hardly be reversed. (During the Habsburg–Ottoman war of 1593–1606 the Ottoman commanders complained that their spahis were useless against Austrian musketeers, and asked for paid infantrymen with firearms instead.)[3] And yet the conclusion cannot be avoided that there was a general decline in standards, as government at most levels became less competent and more rapacious.

Money was at the root of many of these evils. The legal system, for example (in which the judges' incomes came mainly from the fines they imposed), became notably more corrupt after the mid-sixteenth century.[4] The behaviour of regional administrators was bluntly described in a 'Justice Decree' issued by the Sultan in 1609: 'You are not making the rounds of your provinces doing your duties. Instead you are going round taking money from the people unlawfully.'[5] While the local pashas imposed new forms of requisitioning and arbitrary fees and fines, the state did the same thing on a larger scale, with a number of 'extraordinary' taxes which rapidly became both ordinary and heavy.[6] More taxes were demanded in cash, and the collection of the taxes was itself sold on a tax-farming basis; the sale of offices of state was also becoming more common. By the late seventeenth century, many spahis were simply bribing their way out of doing military service.[7] The whole land-owning system was gradually changing, and not only because feudal cavalrymen were losing their military value or buying exemptions: timars were being sold off as private estates, and when this happened the peasants lost the protection of the feudal system. (The new private estates were called *çiftliks*, and the peasants on them *çiftçis*. This development was, however, very slow to occur in Kosovo and the Serbian lands.)[8]

The driving force behind most of these changes was the government's need for cash to pay for its military campaigns. An empire which had grown by war was now being gradually eroded by the expenses of war itself. Under the two great conquering Sultans, Mehmet II and Süleyman the Magnificent, the Empire had expanded to include Bosnia, almost the whole of Greece, all of Romania and most of Hungary. During the sixteenth century the Ottomans had also fought a number of costly wars against the Persians, and had taken over the Holy Cities of Mecca and Medina: these events promoted a stronger identification of Islam (and, in particular, Sunni Islam) with the official ideology of the Ottoman state. So it is not surprising that, while tax burdens in general were raised, those on Christian subjects were increased disproportionately.

Writing for Sultan Murat IV in the 1630s, the Albanian-born courtier and chronicler Koçi-bey declared: 'Before, the haraç [i.e. cizye, tax on non-Muslims] was small. Its application was such that the Christians were not oppressed. It was not demanded in such a way that people were forced to sell their clothes, their cattle, their sons or their daughters...'[9] This sounds a little over-rhetorical; modern research suggests that tax levels in the Ottoman Balkans at this time were still low compared with those in western Europe. But it is clear that, since grain prices fell and taxes were collected increasingly in cash, a higher proportion of the peasants' own produce was now being taken in taxes.[10] And it is also clear that the relative burden on the Christians was increasing. Particularly resented was the practice of making Christian villages communally responsible for a fixed-sum cizye payment, so that each time a peasant absconded, or converted to Islam, the tax burden on each of the others went up. In 1669 a British diplomat was told by the haraç-collector in an area near Istanbul that 'there were 1,700 persons that pay'd Harrach before the Venetian Warr, & that now there were but 700 left all the rest having abandoned their Houses, and Vinyards, & that those which remaine fly daily because they must pay not only for themselves, but for the whole 1700.'[11]

Wars against Christian powers, such as this war against Venice over Crete, always tended to produce both an overall increase in taxation and a tightening of official policy against the Ottoman state's Christian subjects. When the town of Bar (in Montenegro) fell to the Ottomans in 1571, the fact that its defence had been led by the Catholic Archbishop caused special resentment; Catholics in Kosovo suffered harsher treatment as a result.[12] Twice during the 1640s the Catholic Archbishops of Bar tried to organize conspiracies to deliver the city of Shkodra to the Venetian army; on both occasions the plan was betrayed, and fierce persecution of Catholics followed. According to a report from Prizren, heavy new taxes on Catholics were imposed in 1652.[13]

Some of the events which prompted these repressions, such as the Archbishops' plots, can properly be described as attempts to liberate territory from the Ottoman Empire. There were also many local revolts, some of them in or near the Kosovo territory; not all of these can seriously have aimed to throw off Ottoman rule altogether. In the past Albanian and Serbian historians have tended to lump all such actions together under the heading 'national liberation struggle'. Most Balkan countries also cherish romantic traditions about the popular *hajduks* or outlaws who took to the hills and lived by brigandage: these too are regarded as resistance fighters in a struggle for liberation. But a few critical distinctions need to be made. Some rebellions did aim at throwing off Ottoman rule; others were ordinary tax revolts, or protests against particularly oppressive officials, the aim of which was to restore the previous or official Ottoman practices; and some brigands were simply brigands.

There is no reason to suppose that the 'brotherhoods' of robbers called Bilejić and Tuvaćević which attacked Ragusan caravans near Novo Brdo and Kaçanik in the early sixteenth century, for instance, had anything to do with a national liberation struggle.[14] (The Kaçanik pass was a particular trouble-spot; eventually, at the end of the sixteenth century, the Ottomans had to build and garrison a fort there.) Similarly, modern Albanian historians make much of the 'revolt' of 1560 in the Peć area by Pjetër Bogdani (possibly a direct ancestor of Archbishop Pjetër Bogdani, of whom more will be said later); but all we know of his revolt is that he robbed a caravan, killed some traders, and was captured and executed.[15] A rising by 2,000 villagers in the Debar area in 1580 was a tax revolt over the *cizye*, which had recently been increased; and a rising which took place in much of Western Kosovo in 1585 may also have been aimed merely at restoring a previous level of taxation.[16] The phenomenon of the hajduk can be found also in areas of the Empire, such as Anatolia, where there were no thoughts of 'national liberation'; it arose partly from the traditional conflicts between pastoral societies and settled ones, but also partly from the Ottoman practice of employing the more mobile or rootless raya men as casual paid soldiers, and giving them firearms for that purpose. (Indeed, the very word *hajduk* – from the Hungarian *hajtó*, cattle-drover – developed as a term for a sort of freebooter soldier used on the Hungarian and Serbian sides of the Habsburg-Ottoman frontier.)[17]

Some of the Albanian and Montenegrin mountain clans, which were employed from time to time as auxiliary forces by the Ottomans, used their manpower and their firearms to mount large raiding expeditions into the lowlands. The Këlmendi (also referred to as Klimenti or Clementi) were especially feared; they regularly seized livestock and goods in Western Kosovo, and according to one report in 1614 their raiding expeditions sometimes penetrated as far as Bulgaria.[18] In the spring of 1638 the inhabitants of Peć, Vuçitërn, Novi Pazar and other towns complained in a petition to the Sultan that the Këlmendi, with other Albanian and Montenegrin clans, were robbing caravans from Ragusa and Sarajevo, killing roughly fifty travellers and merchants per annum, and stealing 20–30,000 sheep; as a result, the Novi Pazar road was disused, and the raya had fled from 150 villages. A large expedition was mounted against the mountain clans in 1638, involving more than 15,000 soldiers; eventually the raya were able to return to fifty villages, and the Novi Pazar road was reopened.[19] Although some modern historians are tempted to present this conflict purely in terms of a liberation struggle against the Ottomans, that is probably not the way it seemed to many of the local inhabitants.

And yet at the same time there is strong evidence to show that large-scale political projects for the ejection of the Ottomans were present in the minds of some people, including many of the leaders of the mountain clans, from the late sixteenth century onwards. Not only did they hold formal meetings of clan chiefs to plan for a general uprising, but they also sent appeals to western European powers for assistance. They were no doubt aware that, ever since the Cyprus War of the early 1570s (with the battle of Lepanto in 1571, which raised hopes in western Europe, and the Ottoman conquest of Bar and Ulcinj in the same year, which dashed them in the northern Albanian region), various plans had been circulating in Venice and other centres of power for a military action against the Ottomans which would begin with a general revolt in the western Balkans. One typical proposal was drawn up by the Pope's Apostolic Visitor to the Balkans, Aleksandar Komulović, who had travelled there for several years in the 1580s: it involved a grand alliance of Italians and Austrians, and its starting-point was meant to be a revolt by the people of Albania.[20] Within the Balkans, it was usually the Catholics who took a particular interest in such projects, all of which required the assistance of the three major Catholic powers in the region: Austria, Venice and Spain (which held the Kingdom of Naples). But some of the senior Orthodox clergy also got involved – including the Patriarch of Peć, Jovan, in the 1590s and 1600s. Especially active were the Orthodox Archbishops of Ohrid: one wrote a letter to Don Juan of Austria (the victor at Lepanto) in 1576, and another appealed to Olivares, the Viceroy of Naples, for help, organized a revolt by the people of

Himara (on the southern Albanian coast) and even travelled all the way
to Madrid to put his case, but with no success.[21]

The sequence of formal gatherings of Albanian and Montenegrin clan
chiefs began in 1594 at a monastery in north-central Albania. Others
followed in 1598, 1601, 1602, 1608 (in a monastery near Shkodra, with
the Serbian Patriarch presiding) and 1614; and in 1620 a meeting was
held in Belgrade which included the chiefs of the Këlmendi and Kuçi
clans, as well as leaders from parts of Croatia and Serbia.[22] The meeting
in 1602, which decided to offer Albania to the Venetians and sent
ambassadors to Venice with a pledge to raise 100,000 fighting men, was
attended by four leading Albanians from Kosovo, one of them a Catholic
priest.[23] An Albanian Catholic bishop, Nikoll Mekajshi, was involved in
many of these projects; a detailed proposal sent by him to the Pope in
1610 promised that the 'Albanesi', both Catholic and Orthodox, could
raise 50,000 men, and suggested getting the King of Spain to raise troops
among his own population of Albanian émigrés in Apulia.[24] At first these
appeals were sent only to the major powers and the Pope, but from 1606
onwards requests for help were also being sent to smaller Italian states,
such as Savoy, Tuscany, Mantua and Parma.[25]

It is against this background that we must set the activities of one of
the most extraordinary characters of this period of Balkan history – in
fact, one of the most extraordinary in all of seventeenth-century Europe.
Though he had various names, the title by which he is best known – to
those few historians who know of him at all – is Sultan Jahja; many
details of his life have come down to us only from a biography compiled
by an admiring friend, which no doubt contains numerous exaggerations.
But whenever contemporary records do intersect with Sultan Jahja's life
story, they tend to confirm his biographer's claims; and if only half those
claims were true, this would still make a life story stranger than the most
extravagant of historical novels.[26]

Jahja was born in 1585. His mother was from the Byzantine Comnenus
family of Trebizond, and his father was Mehmet, the eldest son of Sultan
Murat III; Jahja was the third of Mehmet's five sons. When Mehmet
succeeded as Sultan in 1595 he followed the Ottoman imperial custom
of killing all his own brothers, to eliminate potential rivals for the
throne. Jahja's mother, fearing that he would eventually undergo the
same fate, smuggled the boy to Greece; she entered a nunnery in

Salonica, and a loyal eunuch, who was of Bulgarian origin, took Jahja into Bulgarian-speaking territory further north, where he was placed in an Orthodox monastery and baptized. Eight years later he left the monastery and went travelling in the Balkans with his faithful eunuch, both of them disguised as dervishes. Meanwhile the eldest of Jahja's brothers had died and the second-born had been executed; at the end of 1603 it was Jahja's younger brother Ahmet, the fourth-born, who succeeded to the throne. Jahja felt bitterly cheated: from this moment, his life would be devoted to a great series of plots, rebellions and diplomatic activities to gain the Sultanate for himself. In 1608 he went to seek help from Rudolf II in Prague; in the following year he visited Cosimo II of Tuscany, who was caught up in some grandiose plans to foment revolts against the Sultan in the Middle East. (Jahja led a small Florentine naval expedition to Syria; but the local uprising had been crushed before they arrrived.) For most of the next five years Jahja stayed in Italy, lobbying the Medici, the Duke of Savoy, the Pope and the King of Spain. Then, in late 1614, he took a boat to Greece, and travelled, disguised as an Ottoman spahi, first to Macedonia, then to Kosovo.[27]

Jahja was aware that the previous Patriarch of Peć, Jovan, had also been actively seeking support from Western powers; one of Jovan's envoys had met him in Florence in 1609 and had invited him to come and organize an uprising in Serbia.[28] Jahja received no encouragement, however, from the new Patriarch, Paisije; but he did meet Jovan's nephew, Bishop Visarion (Bessarion), who was eager to raise a revolt. Together, they gathered 1,200 Këlmendi and 'Serbians' (probably Montenegrin mountain clansmen) and raided the Eastern Kosovo town of Janjevo; Visarion and Jahja then attacked Novo Brdo with a smaller band of men, before retiring with their booty into the Šar Mountains. There they met a famous half-Albanian and half-Greek bandit, Vergo, and recruited him and his *vojvods* (chieftains) to their cause. A general revolt was now planned, with Jahja as its charismatic leader; for this purpose Visarion persuaded him to change his name to Alexander, in order to be the new Alexander of Macedon. Vergo claimed that he and the clan chiefs could raise huge numbers of men, but said they lacked firearms; and Visarion pointed out that Patriarch Jovan had previously obtained a promise of weapons from Prince Maurice of Orange (in

Holland). He suggested that Jahja travel to western Europe to get the weaponry they needed, while he and Vergo waited with their men in Kosovo.[29]

It was to be a long wait. Jahja went first to Venice and Mantua, then to the Elector Palatine in Heidelberg, and was ill for three months in Antwerp before finally meeting Prince Maurice in Holland and getting permission to buy weapons from the merchants of Amsterdam. The deal was that arms for 100,000 men would be supplied within one year, and paid for by goods from the Balkans, such as silk and beeswax, with one quarter of the price put up in advance. (Although this figure of 100,000 seems wildly exaggerated, its origin may be explained by one of Jahja's written proposals from this period: he stated that he had 12–15,000 armed men already, and that a general rising would draw in up to 100,000 men, who could then march all the way to Istanbul.)[30] To obtain that advance, Jahja then embarked on a series of negotiations with the Duc de Nevers in Paris and the Archduke Ferdinand in Graz, but without success.[31]

From Austria he made his way back through Serbia (disguised as an Orthodox monk) to Kosovo, where he explained to Visarion and Vergo that they had to find the money themselves. Vergo, who was aged seventy-two, announced that he was retiring to a monastery, and gave Jahja all his accumulated booty. Also during this visit, in November 1616, Jahja organized a large meeting of clan chiefs and local leaders in the town of Prokuplje, just to the north-east of Kosovo; this produced yet another plan for a general rising in support of an invasion, details of which were then sent to the Duke of Parma and the King of Spain.[32] Jahja's main base at this time seems to have been the Këlmendi and Kuçi territory of the northern Malësi; he also claimed to have been acknowledged as leader of the mountain people of Montenegro and Hercegovina. In the spring of 1617, according to a letter he wrote later that year to the Grand Duchess of Tuscany, he took 17,000 men 'into the plains of Kosovo and Bosnia', seized 60,000 head of livestock and attacked Novi Pazar, Prishtina, Novo Brdo and Skopje.[33]

Jahja's next trips to northern and western Europe – to Krakow, to persuade the Grand Chancellor of Poland to send arms via Gdansk, to Florence, to organize the shipment of Vergo's booty to Italy and obtain muskets from the Tuscan Grand Duke, and once more to Poland and

Germany – were all ultimately fruitless. He also visited the Khan of the Crimean Tatars, entered the service of a rebellious pasha in eastern Turkey, took a band of Polish mercenaries to the Ukraine, gained the support of the Ukrainian and Russian Cossacks, mounted with their help a large-scale naval campaign in the Black Sea and attacked Istanbul with 130 ships; the authorities were so alarmed that they deployed the great harbour-chain last used by the Byzantine Emperor in 1453. This was as close as Jahja ever came to his goal. After that he travelled again through Russia and Central Europe, and spent many more years negotiating with General Wallenstein, the Austrian Emperor, the Pope and the Duke of Savoy. In 1643 he returned briefly to Novo Brdo; six years later he went to Montenegro and joined the abortive attempt, organized by Catholic bishops, to take the cities of Bar and Shkodra. He fell ill and died there, on the Montenegrin coast, in 1649.[34]

Sultan Jahja was by far the most colourful propounder of these schemes of liberation, but he was not the only one. Increasingly, during the seventeenth century, it was the Catholic clergy who were putting forward such proposals. One Albanian Catholic priest, Pjetër Budi, submitted a plan to an influential Roman Cardinal in 1621; another was offered by the Archbishop of Bar, Gjergj Bardhi, in the mid-1630s; the plots of the 1640s have already been mentioned; and in 1685 the Archbishop of Skopje, Pjetër Bogdani, included detailed figures for the Ottoman garrisons in Kosovo in his report to Rome, noting that Novo Brdo was guarded by only forty Janissaries and adding that 'my Albanians' had offered to seize it.[35]

Whilst the position of ordinary Catholics in Kosovo had deteriorated during this period, one thing which had significantly improved was the organization of the Church itself. The few sixteenth-century documents which survive suggest that it had been in a pitiful state. Since the early fifteenth century the Catholics of Kosovo had been in the Archdiocese of Bar; after the fall of Bar to the Ottomans in 1571 the Archbishop moved up the coast to reside even further away from Kosovo. A letter sent by the Catholics of Eastern Kosovo in 1578 told a sorry story of neglect, scandals and apostasies; it also reported, bizarrely, that a 'Lutheran' had passed himself off as a Catholic priest and had spent six months in Kosovo, celebrating Masses. Claiming to speak on behalf of 15,000 Catholics, the signatories of this letter warned that many were now converting either to Serbian Orthodoxy or to Islam.[36] For several decades to come, one of the main themes of all reports from the Kosovo region was that souls were being lost because of the lack of priests.[37]

Gradually, the Church tried to strengthen its activities in the Kosovo area. One important development was the creation in 1622 of a new body in Rome, the Congregatio de Propaganda Fide, with responsibility for supporting Catholicism in areas ruled by 'infidels'; the regular sequence of detailed reports sent by the local clergy to this body constitutes the richest single source of information about conditions in Kosovo from the seventeenth century to the nineteenth.[38] Another important move was the decision in the mid-1630s to send a Franciscan mission to northern Albania; one friar reached Gjakova in 1637, and in the 1640s friars were established in seven *ospizi* ('hospices', i.e. friars' houses), including one near Prizren.[39] The bishopric of Prizren was reinstated in *c.*1618; and in 1656 the whole area of Kosovo was removed from the archdiocese of Bar and placed within a newly constituted Archbishopric of Skopje. An able Albanian from Western Kosovo, Ndre (Andrea) Bogdani, was appointed Archbishop; when he resigned in 1677 he was succeeded, in 1679/80, by his nephew – also born in Western Kosovo, at the village of Has i Gurit – Pjetër Bogdani.[40]

A series of educational measures improved both the supply and the quality of Albanian Catholic priests. The most important of these was the founding of an 'Illyrian College' by the Jesuits at Loreto (near Ancona) in 1574, at which Albanians as well as Catholic Slavs were educated: both the Bogdanis received their training there. Another such college, the Clementinum, was founded in Rome in the 1580s. A plan for an Albanian college in Bologna in the 1640s fell through; but in 1663 another 'Illyrian College', run by non-Jesuits, started up in Fermo, with pupils from northern Albania and Kosovo among its intake. (It was not without its disciplinary problems, however: several students absconded, and one, a Dalmatian, 'Giovanni Podbiovich', tried to assassinate the Rector.)[41] Inside Kosovo there were at least two Catholic schools. One, at Peć, was run by a Ruthenian missionary (from the western Ukraine), and, presumably because of his own linguistic limitations, did its teaching in Serbian or Croatian. The other, at Janjevo, was probably also using the Slav language: a list of its pupils from 1670 yields twenty-one Slav names and only four Albanians.[42] This does not mean, however, that the

Albanian language was not used for religious purposes. In his reports to the Propaganda Fide, Pjetër Bogdani recorded which languages he had preached in on his episcopal visits: Albanian was the language he used in the whole of Western Kosovo.[43]

Nor was Albanian merely a spoken language. The priest Pjetër Budi published an Albanian translation of the Cathechism in 1618; another Albanian cleric and alumnus of Loreto, Frang Bardhi, had a Latin–Albanian dictionary printed in 1635; Ndre Bogdani produced a Latin–Albanian grammar (now lost); and another dictionary (also apparently lost) published by a Franciscan, Fra Leo da Cittadella, was, according to a later Franciscan chronicler, 'extremely welcome to the local inhabitants'.[44] But the leading figure of Albanian Catholic culture during this century was Pjetër Bogdani, who composed a theological treatise which was the first major prose work to be written in Albanian. It was published eventually with a parallel Italian translation, under the Latin title *Cuneus prophetarum* (roughly, 'The Vanguard of the Prophets'), in Padua in 1685; a subsequent Italian-only edition was called *L'infallibile verità della cattolica fede* ('The Infallible Truth of the Catholic Faith'). Adhering closely to the orthodoxies of Catholic doctrine, Bogdani also displayed wide classical learning and a moral and aesthetic approach which several modern scholars have described as 'humanist'.[45]

While some Catholic culture was kept alive in Kosovo, the general state of the Church was not good. Complaints about the lack of priests continued well into the seventeenth century. (One report of 1630 said that 'thousands' of Catholics in the Prizren area were being lost for this reason.)[46] Some of the clergy were of poor quality: according to the Franciscan who visited Gjakova in 1638, Catholics were converting to Islam not merely because of the absence of priests, but because of the negligence or ignorance of the ones who were there.[47] In 1661 Pjetër Bogdani reported that the parish priest of Prizren, Gregor Mazrreku, 'spends too much time boozing, drinking to the point of complete unconsciousness'.[48] Sixteen years later even Bogdani's uncle, the Archbishop, was criticized as 'rather negligent' by the secretary of the Propaganda Fide. (He also noted that the bishop of the northern Albanian diocese of Pulat had been imprisoned for many years in Rome, 'for having been unruly, and because of doubts about his faith'.)[49]

The Catholic Church in Kosovo was poor, and was frequently under

pressure not only from the Ottoman authorities but also from the Orthodox Church, which tried to force the Catholics to pay it ecclesiastical
dues. Within one year of the reinstatement of the Serbian Patriarchate,
the new Patriarch Makarije had obtained an imperial *firman* (decree)
that all Christians in his territory must pay their church taxes to him.[50]
Such moves by the Orthodox Church, which were always eventually
reversed by the diplomatic efforts of the Catholic powers in Istanbul,
were a recurrent feature of Orthodox–Catholic relations: a similar firman
was granted, for example, in 1661 and only withdrawn in 1665/6, thanks
to the efforts of a Scottish general, Walter Leslie, who was acting as an
envoy of the Austrian Emperor.[51] A letter survives from Ndre Bogdani
in Janjevo in 1664, complaining bitterly about this; he said that the
Patriarch, who resided in the nearby monastery of Gračanica, was trying
to extract a tribute of 100 scudi (roughly 15,000 akçes) from the
Catholics, and described the Orthodox – who he said were protected by
the Ottomans – as the Catholics' worst enemies.[52]

It is certainly true that the Orthodox Church was looked on with less
suspicion by the Ottoman government: the Catholics owed their religious
allegiance to a foreign power, the Papacy, whereas the Serbian, Bulgarian
and Greek Orthodox Churches all lay within the territory of the
Empire.[53] The finances of the Serbian Church were also linked with
those of the state: as early as the 1570s the practice had grown up of
Patriarchs paying a large annual 'gift' to the Sultan (120,000 akçes in
1578) for the continuance of their rights. This would lead eventually to
wholesale simony, the submission of huge financial bids to the Sultan
for the privilege of being appointed Patriarch. The money was recouped
from an annual tax paid by each Orthodox household (twelve akçes for
the Church, twelve for the Patriarch in person); parishioners paid taxes,
and charges for religious services, to their priests, and the priests paid a
tax to their bishops. One Catholic cleric wrote of the Orthodox priests
in the Peć Patriarchate in 1640: 'they are extremely grasping, and will
not administer the sacraments without payment; they also require money
for giving absolution on the point of death, and they bargain for
payment for giving the viaticum [eucharist for the dying]'.[54]

Compared with the Catholic Church, the Serbian Orthodox Church
in Kosovo was certainly much larger, richer, more established and more
privileged. This helps to explain why a much lower proportion of its

members converted to Islam. It was also apparently skilful in using its family connections with the Ottoman administration (most of them, probably, resulting from the devşirme system): one Catholic report in the early seventeenth century commented that the monks of Peć were all related to beys and sancakbeyis.[55] And yet, as we have seen, there were Patriarchs such as Jovan (1592–1614) who were so determined to throw off Ottoman rule that they willingly turned to Catholic powers for help. This move happened to coincide with a new enthusiasm in the Papacy for forming 'Uniate' or 'Greek Catholic' Churches – that is, Orthodox Churches which acknowledged the primacy of the Pope and were accepted into the Catholic Church, while retaining many of their own practices and liturgies. The first of these was the Ruthenian Uniate Church, created in 1596 (hence the Ruthene missionary–schoolteacher in Peć in the 1640s); a Serb Uniate Church was set up in Hungary and Croatia in 1611; and there were frequent attempts to win round the Patriarchs of Constantinople.[56] Not surprisingly, therefore, Patriarch Jovan's appeals for Italian help got mixed up with the pursuit of this policy, and a series of delicate (and, in the end, fruitless) negotiations began over the transfer of the entire Serbian Orthodox Church to Rome. Such discussions were resumed several times in the 1640s and 1650s; but the Patriarch insisted that he would recognize the Pope only as the 'founder' of the Monastery of Peć, not as the head of the Christian Church.[57]

Apart from the creation of Uniate Churches, there were simpler ways of gaining souls: straightforward conversion. The early Franciscan missions converted several people from Orthodoxy to Catholicism; one of the friars, Fra Cherubino, even tried to win over the monks in the Orthodox monastery of Dečani; and in the 1640s a Franciscan in Dalmatia scored a great coup by converting the local Orthodox Archbishop, plus two bishops and most of their flocks.[58] In places with Ragusan colonies, all the Catholics would contrive to claim the same privileges as the Ragusans, and to gain those advantages many of the local Orthodox would convert to Catholicism.[59] But overall there was a bigger flow in the opposite direction. As we have seen, the Catholics of Eastern Kosovo were drifting to Orthodoxy as well as Islam in 1578. A report of 1599 also said that the lack of priests was driving some to become Muslims and others Orthodox; and in 1638/9 it was said that because the Catholics of Trepça had no priest, most of them would probably join the Serbian Church.[60] Against the background of such competition, as well as the struggle between the two Churches over financial rights and dues, it is not surprising to find many expressions of open hostility between the Orthodox and Catholic hierarchies – especially on the part of the Catholic priests, who sometimes complained that they were more oppressed by the Orthodox than by the Muslims.[61] And yet it is also possible to find examples of genuinely friendly relations between the two hierarchies: Pjetër Bogdani described the Patriarch in 1661 as 'learned and well-disposed', for example, and Andrija Zmajević kept up cordial relations with several Orthodox bishops.[62] Most strikingly, Francesco de Leonardis reported after a visit to Peć in 1645:

> Although they are very fixed in their own rite, neither their clergy nor their laity has that hatred for our religious practices which the original Greek Church has ... In these districts, not only do they visit and frequent our churches, coming to Masses and other services and listening to sermons; but also they kneel down and receive the sacraments from our priests, taking off their hats and observing many of our rituals.[63]

When reading accounts such as this, it is always necessary to bear in mind that the main function of religion for ordinary people in this kind of society was quasi-magical: religion was a set of practices for warding off evil, curing illnesses, ensuring good harvests and so on. (Holy unction was particularly popular for these purposes among the Orthodox: as de Leonardis reported in 1640, they would use it when building a house, planting a vineyard, celebrating a wedding, or undertaking any other 'solemn action'.)[64] In areas where two or three religions intermingled, people would of course want to make use of all available forms of magically efficacious remedy or protection. The cure-working tomb of King Stefan Dečanski in the monastery of Dečani, for example, was visited by Catholics as well as Orthodox; and there are other reports of Catholics adopting some Orthodox religious practices.[65]

This syncretism (mixing-together) of rituals and folk-beliefs also included the Muslims. Christian baptism was especially popular among them because of several beliefs about it: that it would give them a longer life, protect them from being eaten by wolves, guard them against mental illness, or (a strange but widespread idea) prevent them from smelling like dogs.[66] The fact that so many practices could be shared helps to explain a common lack of religious hostilities at the ordinary personal level. Fra Cherubino reported disapprovingly after his visit to Kosovo that the Catholics were getting Muslims to act as godfathers for their children, and that they were letting the Muslims use holy chrism on their own children because it would guard them against diseases of the eye. In a village outside Gjakova he and his companion had been welcomed into one house with the words 'Come in, Fathers: in our house we have Catholicism, Islam and Orthodoxy'; in shocked tones, Fra Cherubino reported that 'they seemed to glory in this diversity of religions.'[67] Some of the practices used in the common folk-religion were clearly of pagan origin. The parish priest of Prizren in 1651 complained that many of his flock, when sick, would go to 'the Gypsy women and the Muslim women, who are very great necromancers', and that these would 'breathe with their mouths on the places which hurt ... while saying certain words brought up from the bottom of hell; and I have even found some Christian women who perform this practice.'[68]

While the Catholic clergy might inveigh against some of these forms of folk religion, they happily presided over the most dramatic example of all: the great two-day festival on a mountain-top to the west of Prizren, to celebrate the Assumption of the Virgin Mary. The mountain had three peaks; more than 1,000 people would gather there, and say vespers on the two lower ones. Then, in the words of Pjetër Bogdani's visitation report of 1681,

> They spend all the night there, with drums, whistles, dancing and singing.
> After midnight they begin a mixed procession – Muslims, Serbians and
> Greeks with lighted wax candles, their length proportionate to each
> person's age. They walk round the peak of the highest mountain for three
> hours in bare feet (with some of the leading Muslims on horseback).

In the morning, Bogdani held a service on the mountain-top, preaching in Albanian to 'a numberless crowd of all sorts of people', and was taken to lunch afterwards by the Orthodox Bishop of Prizren.[69] This cult of mountain-tops was evidently a pagan survival; what makes it a peculiarly fascinating example of syncretism is the fact that in later periods it was subsumed under two different interpretations, Muslim and Orthodox. One of the many tombs of the legendary Muslim holy man Sarı Saltık was located there, with celebrations on Ali's day, 2 August; and the Orthodox in Prizren in the late nineteenth century had their own version of this story, in which the grave of St Pantaleimon was on the summit – also with appropriate celebrations taking place over a whole night in the summer.[70]

Syncretism is an important part of the background to the whole issue of conversion to Islam. To modern eyes it may seem strange that Catholics, if driven to abandon their faith by a lack of priests, did not automatically switch to Orthodoxy, thereby at least preserving their Christianity. Syncretist folk religion supplies part of the answer; with so many practices either shared or replicated between the faiths, these people probably did not notice such a dramatic difference in kind between all forms of Christianity on the one hand and Islam on the other. But a large – and increasing – part of the explanation lay in the economic and social disadvantages of non-Muslim status. While most of the earliest Catholic reports mentioned only the absence or ignorance of the clergy as a cause of apostasy, by the middle of the century they almost always referred to the burden of taxation too. Evidently it was the increases in the cizye, the poll-tax levied on non-Muslim men, which weighed most heavily; we can deduce this from the fact that in many places the men converted to Islam while their wives and daughters remained Christians. In 1637, for example, Gjergj Bardhi found that the men and women of a village near Gjakova had divided in this way. In 1651 Gregor Mazrreku reported that all the men in Suha Reka (Srb.: Suva Reka), where there had previously been 160 Catholic households, had gone over to Islam, but that thirty-six or thirty-seven of their wives were still Catholic; twenty years later another priest, Shtjefën Gaspari, found 300 Christian women but no Christian men at all in the Has district near Gjakova.[71]

Mazrreku's report of 1651 also contains an early reference to a phenomenon which developed among some of the Catholics of Kosovo and lasted into the twentieth century: crypto-Christianity.

Some of the men (and there are very many of these) say: 'We are Christians in our hearts, we have only changed our religious affiliation to get out of paying the taxes which the Muslims imposed on us', and for this reason they say ... 'dear Reverend, come and give us confession and

Holy Communion secretly'. But I have not done this up till now, nor does it seem right to me ...[72]

This is not quite the first definite reference to such a request; something very similar was recorded by Archbishop Bizzi in 1618.[73] The phenomenon of crypto-Christianity in Kosovo eventually involved whole communities behaving outwardly as Muslims, while retaining a secret adherence to Catholicism. (The secret was in some cases more or less public knowledge, and there was even a popular Albanian word for a crypto-Christian: *laraman*, meaning parti-coloured or piebald.) Much remains obscure, however, about both the origins of crypto-Christianity and its long-term transmission. Some references to people leading a kind of amphibious religious life can be found as early as the sixteenth century: an Ottoman document of 1568 noted disapprovingly that Muslim villagers in the Debar area were taking their new-born children first to the priest, who gave them Christian names, and only afterwards to the Muslim clergy.[74] But, as we have seen, baptism could have a simple practical–magical purpose; and the use of double names later became quite common in the northern Malësi, without involving crypto-Christianity.[75]

We get a little closer to the idea of crypto-Christianity in the first years of the seventeenth century: one general account of the Ottoman Empire noted that there were many Muslim converts in Istanbul 'who say they are Christians internally', and a visitation report from northern Albania in 1603 mentioned people who think they can profess Islam and at the same time 'retain the Christian faith in their hearts'.[76] Many people who had converted for prudential reasons might say (and think) such things; but some further mechanisms were needed to transform such first-generation feelings into a tradition so tenacious that it could last for ten generations or more.

One possible mechanism in the early stages may have been the division between men and women which was referred to earlier: it was not unknown in Ottoman society for Muslim men who married Christian women to allow their daughters to be brought up too as Christians.[77] This could have preserved Christianity as a more private, domestic form of religious life for several generations; and, indeed, the villagers who asked Mazrreku to minister to them secretly in 1651 also said that they would marry Christian girls 'so that the name "Christian" does not die out completely in my house'.[78] With women in the family who were officially Christian, it became possible for priests to enter their homes in order to minister to them. Once there, they could minister in secret to the menfolk as well.

Some social mechanisms may also have been at work: crypto-Christianity developed not in towns, where there was both greater mobility and the possibility of closer surveillance by the Muslim clergy, but rather in cohesive villages – particularly in ones which, like the mining villages of the Skopska Crna Gora, had enjoyed some communal privileges or exemptions. But the most important mechanism was a straightforward religious one: the complicity of the local clergy, who continued to administer the sacraments to these ostensible Muslims even though the Church strictly forbade it. The first decree against this was issued by Andrija Zmajević, Archbishop of Bar, in 1674; his nephew and successor-but-one Vicko Zmajević re-promulgated this at an 'Albanian National Synod' in 1703; additional stern injunctions were issued by Pope Benedict XIV in the 1740s and 1750s.[79] And yet, as one report by an Apostolic Visitor in Kosovo confirmed in 1743, the bishops and priests had continued and did continue to administer the sacraments to these people.[80] If they had not done so, the phenomenon would surely have come to an end – and thousands of souls, some of whose descendants did re-emerge publicly as Catholics in the nineteenth and twentieth centuries, would have been lost to the Church.

A general background of syncretist practices in the population at large may have been one of the things that made life easier for crypto-Christianity; but the two things are quite different in their essential natures. Crypto-Christianity is not the same as an easy-going religious amphibianism. It must be based on the idea that the two faiths are radically opposed, and that one (the secretly held Christian faith) gives salvation while the other does not. Interestingly, one of the main arguments used by Muslim proselytizers was that Christianity and Islam were hardly opposed to each other at all. In the words of one Franciscan report:

Those impious people also said that the difference between them and the Christians was small; 'After all,' they said, 'we all have only one God, we

venerate your Christ as a prophet and holy man, we celebrate many of
the festivals of your saints with you, and you celebrate Friday, our festive
day; Mohammed and Christ are brothers...' And this error was so
widespread, that in the same family one person would be Catholic, one
Muslim and one Orthodox.[81]

Similarly, a report of 1650 noted that 'the Muslims preach to them that
everyone can achieve salvation in his own religion'.[82] This argument,
which seems at first sight to strengthen the case against changing one's
faith, was in fact a subtle first step towards converting Christians to
Islam: the important move was to get them to accept the idea that
Muslims too would achieve eternal life. Discussions of Islamicization by
modern historians concentrate so heavily on economic or social factors
that theological arguments are sometimes entirely ignored. And yet there
is plenty of evidence of Catholic priests reconverting people away from
Islam and using theological arguments to do so; we should not exclude
the possibility that some sort of preaching and theological persuasion
had sometimes helped to draw people to Islam in the first place.[83]

Where the preaching of Islam was concerned, a special role was
played by the Sufi or dervish orders. These religious orders contributed
hugely both to the intellectual life of Islam and to popular folk-religion;
but they have often been rather neglected in standard accounts of the
Islamic faith, since they operated outside the 'official' structures of the
medreses (seminaries) and the mosques. They had their own dervish
lodges or *tekkes* (Alb.: *teqe*; Srb.: *tekija*), in which they would meet for
fellowship, prayer and, in some cases, ritual movements, the most
famous of which are the 'whirling' movements of the Mevlevi dervishes.
(To English ears, the word 'dervish' may conjure up an image of
unworldly fanatics or wandering mendicants; but most members of these
orders were, and are, ordinary lay people, rather like the members of lay
fraternities in some Catholic countries.) Many of the orders developed
varieties of mystical theology which drew not only on Sunni doctrine
but also on Shiism, Judaism (including the theories of the cabbala),
Neoplatonism and Christianity; traces of pre-Islamic Asian shamanism
have been found in their religious practices, and in the countryside they
also fostered a cult of local saints and their tombs. The most heterodox
order of all was the Bektashi, which became the official order of the

Janissaries: no doubt it had a special appeal to soldiers who had been brought up as Christian children, given that Bektashi adherents would drink wine and ignore the fast of Ramadan, and that their version of Muslim theology included a quasi-Trinitarian doctrine. And throughout the Ottoman Empire, the dervish orders were actively engaged in proselytizing among non-Muslims.[84] One holy dervish, for example, Veli Baba, was based in a tekke in Prizren and spent all his time travelling round the towns and villages, teaching Islam to the people; his *türbe* (tomb) later became a special place of veneration, to which mothers would take their children to be cured.[85]

The evidence of dervish tekkes in Kosovo is only fragmentary for this period. We know, for example, that in the early sixteenth century Kuklibey had endowed a tekke at his place of residence south of Prizren, but we do not know which order it belonged to. In Prizren itself there was a tekke of the Sinani branch of the Halveti order (the Halveti and the Bektashi became the two largest and most active orders in the Balkans), also from the same period. When the Turkish traveller Evliya Çelebi visited Kosovo in 1662 he found Bektashi centres at Mitrovica, Vuçitërn and Kaçanik; the tekke at Kaçanik was probably founded by the great Albanian-born general Sinan Pasha, the 'Conqueror of the Yemen', who ordered the building of the fort at Kaçanik in the 1580s, and who may also have been responsible for founding the first recorded Bektashi tekke in Albania.[86] No doubt there were other tekkes too, although it is clear that many of the orders developed in Kosovo only in the eighteenth and nineteenth centuries.

Some of the dervish orders were bound up with the economic life of the towns, through their connections with the craft guilds. These institutions, known as *esnafs* (from the plural of an Arabic word meaning order, rank or class), were self-elected but state-regulated bodies which controlled standards, maintained fixed prices, limited competition, acted as banks granting loans to their members, and played a powerful role in the internal politics of the towns. The majority were Muslim, but some were Christian, with their own elected Christian councils. Joining an esnaf was a three-stage process: junior apprenticeship (lasting 1,001 days), senior apprenticeship (lasting four to five years), and mastery. Only a master was a full member of the esnaf, with the right to set up a workshop of his own.

Apart from regulating their own businesses, the esnafs also maintained roads, fountains, inns and other buildings. The Muslim esnafs looked after the tekkes of most of the dervish orders, just as the Christian ones played a special role in furnishing and maintaining the churches. The Bektashi order had connections with the sword-smiths, gunstock-carvers, wool-workers and skullcap-makers; but the strongest link was between the Kadiri order of dervishes and the tanners. Of all the esnafs, the tanners (and associated leather-workers and cobblers) were the most powerful, thanks not only to the importance of hides in the local economy but also to their special links with the military (in particular, the cavalry, who needed saddles and bridles). From an early stage, every tanner esnaf had had a spiritual leader called an *ahi* or *ahi-baba*: this was a type of dervish associated with the early Ottoman army. And each ahi-baba of the tanners was officially a representative of the Kadiri tekke in Anatolia, which received an annual payment from every tanner esnaf in the Empire. Prizren was famous for its tanners in the early sixteenth century; by the eighteenth century there were forty-three tanning shops in Prizren, fifty in Peć and sixty in Gjakova.[87]

Urban life continued to flourish in Kosovo for most of the seventeenth century. Prizren was the leading city, with an estimated 8,600 houses in 1610 and 10,000 in 1670. The Ottoman style of urban life impressed Archbishop Bizzi in 1610: he noted that nearly all the houses 'have their courtyards, in the style of a *villa rustica* in Italy', and that the whole city was 'irrigated by fountains and other running waters, which turn the water-mills, and make the city pleasant and delightful'. Prishtina was much smaller, with roughly 2,000 houses, but the traveller Evliya Çelebi was equally pleased in the 1660s by its fine gardens and vineyards. And in Gjakova (also *c.*2,000 houses) he was impressed by the town's splendid public baths, its 300 shops and two important mosques, and commented: 'Since the climate of the place is pleasant, the inhabitants look very handsome and good-natured.' The Muslim proportion of the urban population was continuing to grow: Prizren in 1624 was reported to have 200 Catholics, 600 Orthodox and 12,000 Muslims, 'almost all of them Albanians'.[88] One of the big social changes of the seventeenth century was that the Janissaries were settling in the towns as a kind of hereditary social caste, a process which began when their own sons started to be accepted as Janissary recruits in addition to (and, by the second half of the century, instead of) the devşirme boys. As one Western observer noted in 1683: 'They no longer live by the strict rule of their former discipline, because most of them are allowed to go into business and live with their families.'[89]

The only Kosovo towns contracting during this period were the ones dependent on mining, such as Novo Brdo. The decline of the Kosovo mines is a complex issue; probable causes include the withdrawal of foreign miners, the lack of any technological improvements, the ban on exports of bullion, and the growing insecurity of transportation. The greed of local lords, who imposed heavy extra taxes, was also an important factor. Physical causes may also have played a part: reports from Trepça said that the main silver lodes there were running out in 1624, and that the mines had completely failed by 1642. And yet some production clearly continued: Pjetër Bogdani reported in 1685 that the Pasha of Skopje resided in Prishtina in order to supervise the mines, and since he also noted that the Pasha bought his position for 100,000 reals (c.1,500,000 akçes), we are presumably meant to deduce that much of the income with which he recouped his outlay came from the mines of Kosovo.[90]

Finally, the surviving reports also enable us to draw some conclusions about the ethnic composition of Kosovo in the seventeenth century. Most of this evidence comes from Catholic sources, of course, and its main focus is on the Catholic minority: of this small section of the population, it can confidently be said that those in Western Kosovo spoke Albanian while most of those in Eastern Kosovo spoke Serbo-Croat.[91] The Muslim population of the towns seems to have been mainly Albanian: Pjetër Mazrreku's reference to the Albanian Muslims of Prizren has already been noted, and a similar impression is given by Evliya Çelebi's account of the administrative town of Vuçitërn, where, he said, the population (2,000 houses) did not speak 'Bosnian' (Serbo-Croat), but only Albanian and Turkish.[92] The distribution of the Serbian Orthodox is a little harder to specify; the Catholic reports mention the Orthodox in towns where Catholics lived, but take little interest in Orthodox peasants. Bizzi did note in 1610 that his journey from Prizren to Janjevo took him through a plain 'entirely full of Orthodox villages'. One report of 1577 stated that on the five-day journey from the Albanian port of Lezha to Novo Brdo the first four days were through Catholic territory, and only the last through Orthodox. We know that the equivalent journey from Shkodra to Prishtina via Prizren took forty-five hours of travel, with the last stretch, from Prizren, lasting eleven or twelve; at a calculation of nine hours' travel per day, this suggests that the transition from Catholic to Orthodox took place a few hours' journey to the east of Prizren.[93] But of course there would also have been Orthodox villages in the western part of Kosovo too.

Some of the Catholic documents also note cases of Albanians moving into Kosovo from northern Albania. Pjetër Mazrreku reported from Prishtina in 1624: 'not long ago ten Catholic families came from Albania to live in this area'; in Suha Reka in 1637 Gjergj Bardhi found fifteen Catholic families who had fled there from the Dukagjin mountains because of 'assassins'; and Gregor Mazrreku found several Albanians at a nearby village in 1651, who had also 'fled from the mountains'.[94] Gregor Mazrreku noted that most of these had become Muslims since their arrival. It seems likely that people fled from the Malësi either because of blood-feuds or because they had been punished under the Kanun of Lek Dukagjin (which, it will be recalled, said that people guilty of serious crimes should have their houses burnt down and be expelled). Such people, arriving in a new area, would naturally feel more unattached to the local Catholic community, and would be more easily tempted to make the switch to Islam. Larger groups emigrating together were much more rare; but in these cases there was more religious cohesion. A group of thirty-five Catholic Albanian families from Albania was noted at the mining town of Kratovo, east of Skopje, in 1637; they were already learning the Slav language, and it is likely that they were eventually assimilated by the local Slav-speaking Catholic community.[95] Overall, however, one conclusion is certain: the number of people migrating into the Kosovo area from northern Albania during this period was, relative to the already existing Albanian population of Kosovo, extremely small. The Malësi was almost entirely Catholic; the reports by the Catholic priests in Kosovo are thorough and very detailed; and it is not possible to imagine that many thousands of Catholic immigrants could have escaped their notice – even (or, perhaps, especially) if they did not remain Catholic for long.

8

The Austrian invasion and the 'Great Migration' of the Serbs: 1689–1690

THE OTTOMAN–HABSBURG war of 1683–99 marks one of the turning-points in European history. When it began, with the advance of a huge Ottoman army towards the Austrian heartland, there was a real possibility that Vienna would fall; after a ten-week siege, however, the Ottomans were driven off by a combined Imperial (i.e. Habsburg) and Polish force, and their withdrawal quickly turned into a rout. When the war ended, at the peace of Karlowitz in 1699, Ottoman rule was restored in the areas to the south of the Danube, but all the Sultan's former Hungarian possessions passed to the Habsburg crown. From this point onwards, the history of the Ottoman Empire would be a story of territorial contraction and loss.

For the history of Kosovo, this war has a very special significance. In the autumn of 1689 a small Imperial army invaded Kosovo, drove off the local Ottoman forces and established Austrian control over the whole area. Many of the inhabitants of Kosovo pledged their loyalty to the Austrian Emperor; some of them even enlisted as auxiliary troops. But in the first days of 1690 the Austrians hastily withdrew, and a mixed Ottoman and Tatar army poured into Kosovo, killing and plundering on a large scale. Later in 1690 the Austrians were forced to retreat further northwards, abandoning first their headquarters at Niš and then, after a short siege, the key fortress-city of Belgrade. With the retreating Austrians went a large number of Serb refugees; by the end of the year there were thousands of these living in a state of almost complete destitution in central Hungary. And with them too had gone the Patriarch of Peć, Arsenije III Črnojević. He would never see Peć again; the Austrian Emperor Leopold I granted him the right to exercise his jurisdiction over the Serbs on Hungarian territory, where he, like many of his flock, remained until his death.

For many Serbian historians, it has been an article of faith that the exodus of the Serbs from Kosovo – known as the 'Velika Seoba' or 'Great Migration' – was on a huge scale. Popular nineteenth-century paintings depict the Patriarch riding at the head of an immense mass of suffering humanity. It has often been claimed that 37,000 families joined Arsenije on this epic march, and many writers have assumed that some or all of these were not ordinary families but zadrugas, extended family units. Estimates have ranged as high as 400,000 people, or between 400,000 and 500,000, or 500,000 'if not more'.[1] The significance of this relates partly to arguments about the ethnic–demographic history of Kosovo: it is claimed that before 1690 the Albanians were an insignificant minority in Kosovo (or perhaps not there at all), and that only after the exodus of the Serbs did Albanians come flooding in to fill the vacuum they had left. But the significance of the Velika Seoba cannot be confined to demographic arithmetic: it is also an essential element of Serbian national–religious mythology. Serbian Orthodox writers have often compared the defeat of the Serbs at Kosovo in 1389 to the crucifixion of Christ. There is a three-part theological parallel at work in the Serbian national myth; the second phase, corresponding to Christ's death and burial, is the withdrawal of the Serbian people from Kosovo in the Velika Seoba, and the third phase, corresponding to the resurrection, is the reconquest of Kosovo by Serbian forces in 1912.

Against the Serbian nationalist claims, a different interpretation of the events of 1689–90 has been put forward in more recent years by Albanian historians. It may be useful, before entering the sequence of events, to pick out the strongest claims from these two opposing versions of history and place them side by side. The maximal Serb claim is that the inhabitants of Kosovo who rose up in support of the invading Austrians were all Serbs: any Albanians in the area either took no part in the revolt or fought for the Ottomans. It is also claimed that the Albanian Catholic archbishop, Pjetër Bogdani, had nothing to do with rousing or organizing the people; the only religious leader to do that was Patriarch Arsenije, who met the Austrian general on his arrival in Prizren in November 1689. Maximal claims about the numbers who left with the Patriarch have already been mentioned; but another important contention is about the Patriarch's reasons for taking them on to Hungarian soil. It is claimed that he had received an official '*Invitatorium*' or 'Invitation' from the Emperor Leopold, which promised the Serbs not only that their religious rights would be respected, but also that they would enjoy a kind of semi-autonomy under their own vojvods (chiefs). This, it is said, is the origin of the so-called 'Vojvodina', which became part of the new Yugoslav state in 1918.[2]

The main Albanian claim is that the local rebels against Ottoman rule were almost all Albanian. It is said that the religious leader who met the Austrian general in Prizren in November was Archbishop Bogdani, and that the Serbian Patriarch was not even in Kosovo at the time. It is also claimed that the number of Serbs who eventually migrated with the Patriarch was not very large (certainly not large enough to have a major effect on the demographic balance in Kosovo), and that the refugees included Albanians too.[3] The question of the Emperor's 'Invitation' has not greatly interested Albanian historians; there the debate is between two opposing lines of thought on the Serbian side, and the counter-claim to the one given above is that the 'Invitatorium' was not an invitation to emigrate, but merely an exhortation to continue the revolt.[4]

The military sequence of events begins, for our purposes, in July 1687, with the decisive victory of Habsburg forces over an Ottoman army at Mohács in southern Hungary. (This had also been the site of a famous Ottoman victory 161 years earlier.) The Ottoman Empire was under attack on most of its northern and western border, in a great arc from Poland down to Greece. Venetian forces were aiming to take Athens – where, later that year, their artillery would ignite an Ottoman powder-store in the Parthenon – and had sent expeditionary forces to Montenegro and deep into the Dalmatian hinterland. As usual in times of war, new Ottoman taxes had been imposed and bread prices had soared; the Catholics of Janjevo had seriously considered fleeing from Kosovo altogether in 1683, and a tax register for the Vuçitërn district in 1686 lists one third of the previous year's cizye-payers as fugitives.[5] In many parts of the Empire, famine and plague were combined with violent social unrest. One rebel leader in Anatolia, Yeğen Osman pasha, had become so powerful that the Sultan felt obliged to woo him with offers of high command in the Ottoman army; and when a new Sultan came to power in November 1687 (Süleyman II), Yeğen was appointed Beylerbeyi of Rumeli and commander-in-chief on the Hungarian front.

Yeğen pasha proceeded to treat the whole of Rumeli, which included Kosovo, as a personal fiefdom, ranging through the territory with large numbers of his armed retainers and raising arbitrary extra taxes wherever he went. A vivid picture of conditions at this time comes in a letter from Pjetër Bogdani, written in May 1688. Under Yeğen's rule, he said, 'the churches were locked up, the priests dispersed, and the people fled'; he himself, 'followed by a large crowd of the faithful, fled into the mountains and had the snow for a mattress'.[6] This shows how unsettled the Kosovo region was more than a year before the Austrian invasion; it also suggests how accustomed people may already have been to taking to the hills for days or weeks at a time, before returning to their homes. The position of the Orthodox Church was not much better. In the same letter, Bogdani said that a disgruntled monk, angry at being disciplined by Arsenije, had burgled the Patriarchate's treasury at Gračanica, making off with 100,000 thalers (12 million akçes); Yeğen eventually got hold of the money and, in addition, imposed a fine of 10,000 thalers on the Patriarch.[7]

Yeğen's star waned, however, in late 1688. Süleyman II had found a new source of military power, in the form of the Khan of the Crimean Tatars, and now felt confident enough to crush his unruly pasha – who, in response to the first moves made against him, issued a formal declaration of rebellion. After several months of near-anarchy in the Kosovo region, Yeğen was finally driven back and forced to seek shelter with the pasha of Peć, Mahmut Mahmutbegolli (from the Trk.: 'Mah-mutbeyoğlu'; Srb.: 'Mahmutbegović'), a personal friend. Mahmutbegolli then received a lapidary order from the Sultan: 'Başı bizim, malı sizin', 'His head is ours, his treasure is yours.' Yeğen's head was duly delivered to Istanbul on 19 March 1689.[8]

What had led to Yeğen's downfall was the abysmal performance of the armies under his command against the Imperial troops. In September 1688 the Austrians had captured the vital fortress of Belgrade, which gave them an entrée to the whole of the central Balkans. In the following summer they resumed their advance, led by an experienced commander, Margrave Ludwig of Baden. Their next breakthrough was the seizure of

Niš in late September, where Baden caught the Ottoman army by surprise in its encampment in front of the town.[9] According to reports from the British envoy in Istanbul, this defeat 'putt ye Ottoman Court into very great Feare & Confusion'; the Ottoman military commander was strangled, and the Grand Vizier, who was so fearful of a mutiny that he dismissed most of the remaining soldiers from the army, was himself turned out of office. In his place came one of the most effective Grand Viziers the Empire ever saw: Mehmet Köprülü, a member of a powerful Albanian dynasty of Ottoman public servants. As the British envoy reported: 'He is esteemed a verie strict & just person, greately skilld in their Law & a rigid observer of it, free from Covetousness & Extortion ... The former Vizir is allready as much spoken against, as a Man given to Sodomie & Wine.'[10]

Baden now divided his troops and, in mid-October 1689, sent a force of 5,000 men – including two cavalry regiments, and a body of soldiers described as 'Rascians' – southwards, to Kosovo.[11] Its leader was Count Eneo Piccolomini, a scion of a famous Italian family which had supplied several distinguished commanders to the Habsburgs. Already in the spring of that year Piccolomini had come quite close to Kosovo, raiding southwards through central Serbia as far as Novi Pazar and driving off the pasha of Peć, Mahmutbegolli.[12] But the purpose of his expedition in October went beyond mere raiding. As Baden explained in the formal instructions sent to Piccolomini's successor in the following month, the strategic aim was to seize a broad swathe of territory from Kosovo to the Adriatic coast, thus completely cutting off the Ottoman territory of Bosnia; and if (as became increasingly clear) the Austrian troops were not sufficient for this task, then the aim was at least to keep control of Kosovo by holding all the passes and fortified places.[13]

Piccolomini's first experiences in Kosovo were entirely positive. Mahmutbegolli, who had advanced to meet him with 10,000 men, promptly retreated; many of the soldiers in his army were Orthodox, and most of these, it seems, deserted him.[14] According to a report by one of Piccolomini's officers, the local Muslims had fled by the time the Austrians arrived.[15] Piccolomini was impressed by the country he had entered: he described it as 'abundant in foodstuffs for men and horses'.[16] Many of the local peasants had also fled, but, in the words of the Venetian envoy in Vienna (who was being given the gist of Piccolomini's despatches), 'By means of good discipline, and other enticements, he was managing to draw the inhabitants back to that area: they were coming back again, and giving their oath that they would be loyal to the Emperor, the majority of them being members of the Orthodox Church.'[17] An early account of this campaign, based on original documents, also states that before Piccolomini had even reached Prishtina, the local Orthodox inhabitants had offered him their homage, through their bishops.[18] These early references to the Orthodox population are what one would expect, given that the part of Kosovo which Piccolomini was entering was a Serb Orthodox-majority area; they disprove the maximal Albanian claim that only Albanians supported the Austrians.

The Catholic Archbishop also hurried to meet the advancing Austrian troops. A letter written two months later by his nephew, the priest Gjin Bogdani, explains his reason: 'when the victorious army of our Emperor arrived suddenly in these parts, he went in person to meet it and to restrain the arrogance of the soldiery so that they would not go so far as to rob or massacre the Catholics; and he was completely successful.'[19] Similar requests would no doubt have come from the Orthodox: it is significant that the summary of one of Piccolomini's despatches, quoted above, said he was drawing the population back to the area by means of 'good discipline, and other enticements'. One section of the original text of a despatch from Piccolomini clearly identifies the problem: 'I am making arrangements to stop atrocities by the Slav hajduks, and other gangs of soldiers, who oppress these poor people, and force them to flee.'[20]

These hajduks were not local brigands but members of Piccolomini's army: as we have seen, the term hajduk had developed in Austria and Hungary to refer to a semi-controlled martial frontier population (similar to the Cossacks of Russia and the Ukraine), which in Hungary was predominantly Slav. In addition, thousands of Serbs from Ottoman territory had crossed into the Habsburg lands after 1683 and had been recruited into the army. Out of these immigrants and the existing hajduks a 'Rascian regiment' had been formed, which took part in the invasion of Ottoman Serbia; after further recruits had been made in the Niš area in the autumn of 1689, it consisted of ten *četas* (bands) of 300 hajduks each.[21] This supplied the 'Rascians' who came with Piccolomini's two Austrian regiments into Kosovo. The reputation of all such auxiliary forces was well known. In June 1689 the Catholic bishop of Nikopol (whose flock, in Bulgaria, was also at risk) had sent a special petition to the Emperor: 'In Your Sacred Majesty's army there are many Serbs or Rascians ... who, as they are all greedy for plunder, will commit atrocities not only against the Turks but also among themselves and against the peasants ...'.[22]

This term 'Rascian' requires a little explanation. Deriving originally from the medieval territory of Rascia (Raška), the early heartland of the Serb state, it had been largely superseded by the word 'Serb' within the Serb lands themselves, and was more widely used by outsiders. Early waves of emigrants from the Serb lands to the north had either brought the term 'Rascian' with them, or had it applied to them: one sixteenth-century Italian account of the Ottoman Empire said that the Rascians were people from 'Serbia and Rascia' who had fled from the Turks and now lived to the north of the Danube.[23] Although some writers tried to maintain a geographical distinction between 'Serbia' and 'Rascia', any distinction between the people bearing those names became very blurred. Thus Hans Dernschwam in 1550 described Serbia as the region between Belgrade and Niš, but added that the Rascians (*die ratzen*) call themselves Serbs.[24] In seventeenth-century Austrian usage, the term 'Rascian' referred most commonly to the Serbs who lived in Habsburg territory, then more generally to Orthodox Serbs, wherever they lived, and then more generally still to speakers of Serbian or Serbo-Croat. The Emperor's so-called 'Invitatorium' in April 1690, for example, was addressed to Arsenije as 'Patriarch of the Rascians'; but Austrian court style also distinguished between 'Catholic Rascians' (mainly people who emigrated from Hercegovina during this war) and 'Orthodox Rascians'.[25] The documents relating to the Austrian campaign in Kosovo refer frequently to 'Rascian' soldiers; given the presence of a large 'Rascian regiment' among the Austrian forces, it can be assumed that many of these references are to the Serbs, also known as hajduks, who had been brought from Austria or recruited in Niš. But some of these 'Rascians' were probably local Serb Orthodox recruits.

The town of Prishtina was taken without resistance. Its normal population was roughly 15,000, and the overwhelming majority of these were Muslims. Many had fled, as the report mentioned above indicates; but one early account states that 'in Prishtina 5,000 Arnauts, having thrown off the Turks' pledged their loyalty to the Austrians.[26] ('Arnauts' was a term commonly employed by Western writers to refer to Albanians, usually Muslim ones, and especially ones who were used as soldiers by the Ottomans.) Piccolomini now attacked the Ottoman garrisons at Novo Brdo and Kaçanik; Novo Brdo surrendered, and Kaçanik was taken on 23 October.[27] He also reported to Baden in late October that he was expecting 'the Orthodox Patriarch, together with some of the chiefs of that territory' to come and see him within the next few days; as we shall see, he had sent an officer to Peć to summon Patriarch Arsenije to him.[28]

Meanwhile, learning that Mahmutbegolli had retreated to Skopje, he pursued him there and attacked his encampment outside the city. Mahmutbegolli's army consisted of 6,000 men, mainly 'Rascians and Albanians'; these were completely routed, and 2,000 of them were killed.[29] Many waggon-loads of booty and provisions were now added to the Austrians' supplies. Skopje was by far the biggest and richest city in the region; however, deciding that it could not be defended, Piccolomini put the entire city to the flames and took his small army back to Kosovo. Here, south of Prishtina in the small town of Lipljan, he divided his army into three forces, to cover all the main entry-points to Kosovo. Taking one small force himself, he then marched westwards to Prizren, which he reached on 6 November.[30]

The historian Camillo Contarini, whose account, published in 1710, seems to have been based on original documents, described Piccolomini's arrival at Prizren as follows. 'Near Prizren, as he was approaching, the inhabitants came out to meet him with festive shouts: they were 5,000 in number and were led by their Archbishop, holding a banner with the image of the Holy Cross. With three salvos of musket-fire they received him into the city.'[31] As mentioned above, Serbian historians have claimed that this 'Archbishop' was the Serbian Patriarch, while Albanian writers have insisted that it was Bogdani, the Albanian Catholic Archbishop. Other historians have noted, however, that there are some early printed accounts which say that both the Archbishop and the 'Patriarch of the Këlmendi' ('der Climentiner-Patriarch') were present on this occasion.[32] Some Albanian writers have suggested that the 'Patriarch of the Këlmendi' was just another current name for the Catholic Archbishop, given that the Këlmendi were a Catholic clan; but there is ample evidence that, in the rather vague geographical thinking of the Austrians at this time, 'Climenti' referred to the whole area of quasi-independent mountain clans stretching northwards and north-eastwards from the Këlmendi and Kuçi to cover a large part of the Montenegrin highlands, where clans were Orthodox. In any case, Bogdani did not have the title 'Patriarch' (a rarity in the Catholic Church), and the use of plural verbs in these early texts clearly shows that two different people were intended.[33]

For many historians, the conclusive proof that both men were present has come from a manuscript in the Austrian military archives, a narrative in German describing the campaign in Kosovo and entitled 'Annotationes und Reflexiones der Gloriosen Kayserlichen Waffen, im Jahre 1689' ('Notes and Reflections on the glorious Imperial arms in 1689').[34] All historians who have used this source have assumed that it is a written-up version of a campaign diary kept by one of Piccolomini's officers: as such, it is given priority over almost any other evidence. Since it too clearly states that both the Archbishop and the 'Climentiner-Patriarch' met Piccolomini at Prizren, this has been regarded as settling the matter.[35] What no one has noticed, however, is that this manuscript is simply a German translation of one short section from a much longer work, a history of the Ottoman–Habsburg war, which was written in Italian and of which a manuscript copy survives in the French Foreign Ministry archives. From various inaccuracies and authorial uncertainties it is clear that the author of this work was not writing from first-hand experience, but merely synthesizing a mass of other materials, some of which he may not fully have understood. His name is nowhere given, but his constant attempts to draw moral or theological lessons, and his frequent references to the Austrian forces as 'the Catholics', strongly suggest that he was a Catholic priest.[36]

In fact there is – as we shall see – conclusive evidence to show that Patriarch Arsenije was not and could not have been in Prizren on 6 November 1689. Evidently the confusion was originally caused by someone who thought, quite wrongly, that 'Patriarch of the Këlmendi' was another title of the Catholic Archbishop, and put the two titles together in a grammatically ambiguous way. (In Latin, for example, which has no definite article, 'Archiepiscopus et Patriarcha Climentinorum' could refer to one person or two.) The despatch containing this ambiguous reference was sent from Kosovo on 29 November: the French ambassador in Vienna saw it, and noted that Piccolomini was 'received by the Archbishop and the Patriarch' in Prizren. However, in the very next sentence he showed that he understood this to refer to one person: 'Il conclut le traité avec le dit archevesque et patriarche...' ('He concluded the treaty with the said Archbishop–Patriarch').[37] The anonymous Italian account, similarly, goes on to talk about only one religious leader in Prizren, the Catholic Archbishop.

The nature of the 'treaty' was as follows. The local volunteers, and half the inhabitants, would be organized in Austrian-style regiments; the other half would stay at home; and all of them would be under the protection of the Austrian Emperor.[38] The soldiers thus raised amounted to 20,000 men. As the Italian historian noted, Piccolomini 'did not fail to consult with the Archbishop, and the other German [i.e. Austrian] leaders', about the wisdom of putting his trust in such a force; but he was reassured by the Archbishop.[39] Bogdani seems to have played a leading role in organizing this pro-Austrian movement; also prominent was a Catholic priest, an Albanian from the Skopska Crna Gora, called Toma Raspasani. Trained in Italy, he had been appointed parish priest in Prizren in 1679; Bogdani evidently thought him both trustworthy and energetic, and made him 'Vicar' first of the dioceses of Prizren and Pulat (the latter being in northern Albania) and then of his own Archbishopric.[40] General Veterani, who was appointed Piccolomini's successor, later wrote that Raspasani was 'the person whom Piccolomini made use of to induce loyalty in Albania'. Later, in mid-December, when the Austrian recruiting officer in Prishtina was called away, Raspasani officially took over his position.[41]

Who exactly were the local people who volunteered, or were persuaded, to join the Austrian forces? Given the prominent role played by Bogdani and Raspasani, it is reasonable to assume that many Catholics took part; these, in the Prizren area, were almost all Albanian-speaking. But the Catholic population was very small: one of Bogdani's own recent reports to Rome had stated that the total for the whole of Kosovo was only 1,000 households, and that they could raise at most 3,000 fighting men. (He also said that, with the addition of 'the Serbians', this number would increase to 10,000.)[42] When the anonymous Italian writer refers to the local recruits, the term he uses most frequently is 'Albanesi'; he does also mention 'Rassiani', but most of those references are probably to the Rascian auxiliaries the Austrians had brought with them. At one point he writes 'Rassiani, ò siano Albanesi' ('Rascians, or Albanians'), which might mean that he thought the terms were identical, or that he thought they were different but did not know which was the correct description in this case; or the 'ò siano' might be better translated as 'or rather'.[43] The word 'Albaneser' often cropped up in the documents from which this Italian author was working: thus, for example, Baden's report to Vienna on 29 October said that Piccolomini had already got the support of some of the 'Albaneser'.[44]

For most Albanian historians, the mere fact that this word was used is enough to prove that the local volunteers were Albanians. But the issue is not as simple as that. While some writers in the early modern period did use the term 'Albanian' to distinguish, in a linguistic–ethnic sense, Albanians from Slavs, others used it geographically, to mean the inhabitants of an area described as 'Albania'. And where geographical boundaries were concerned, there were no universally agreed lines on the map. The most common categorizations were based partly on memories of pre-Ottoman kingdoms, and partly on the ecclesiastical provinces of the Catholic Church: according to Catholic priests, therefore, most of Kosovo was in 'Serbia'. Pjetër Bogdani, writing in 1685, described the White Drin as the border between Serbia and Albania, but then added that Prizren (which is on the eastern side of the Drin) is also 'in Albania'. And although his archdiocese was, in ecclesiastical terms, part of 'Serbia', he was often referred to by the Austrians as 'Archbishop of Albania'. The anonymous Italian writer called Prizren the 'capital city of Albania'.[45] Count Marsigli, an adviser to the Austrian army who was regarded as an expert on the Balkans (though his knowledge of Kosovo and Albania was in fact very hazy), wrote rather uncertainly that 'Kossovopolje' was a region 'between Serbia and Bulgaria'; in another text he wrote first that Kosovo was part of 'Rascia', but then that 'I think part of this territory could belong to Albania rather than to Serbia.'[46]

Most writers regarded 'Albania' as including not only the Malësi but also the mountains adjoining it to the north, in Montenegro. All this mountain-clan territory made up the so-called 'free Albania' (as opposed to 'Turkish Albania', the areas under full Ottoman administration, further south). It is clear that some of the Orthodox clans in the

Montenegrin part of that territory were described in Austrian documents, for geographical reasons, as 'Albanians'; and it is also clear that
the Austrians were keen to get the support of these Orthodox clansmen,
whom they knew to be good fighters. One modern Serbian historian,
Rajko Veselinović, has therefore decided that all the 'Albanians' recruited
in Kosovo were Orthodox Montenegrins.[47] However, there is other
evidence (as we shall see) about the activities of these Orthodox clans,
and it does not support the idea that large numbers of them had gone
to join the Austrians in the Prizren area. Veselinović was influenced by
the idea that the religious leader who met Piccolomini was the Orthodox
Patriarch; but since it can be shown that he was nowhere near Prizren at
the time, this element of the case also fails.

Better evidence of the identity of the volunteers can be drawn from
the early summaries of the Austrian documents. Describing Piccolomini's
arrival on 6 November, the anonymous Italian wrote: 'There stood
outside Prizren 6,000 and more Albanians, including the same ones who
were previously paid wages by the Turks, and who are called "Arnauts".'
These were the men, he said, who fired the three salvos. Later, the same
writer described Bogdani as the person who 'kept all these people [or
'peoples'], and most of the Arnauts, under control, and loyal to His
Imperial Majesty'.[48] One of the early German narratives painted a very
similar picture of the welcome at Prizren: '5,000 Arnauts, who were
some of them Christian and some of them Turkish [i.e. Muslim]
Albanians, stood in two lines with their guns and ... fired three salvos
one after the other.' And the original despatches to Vienna were
summarized by a papal envoy on 28 November 1689, who reported that
'the Albanians, Arnauts and other peoples of those regions, as much the
Turks [i.e. Muslims] as the Christians, were negotiating with General
Piccolomini'.[49] Descriptions of later military actions often refer to
'Arnauts', and sometimes, significantly, to 'Albanian Arnauts': this is
significant because it shows that if 'Albanian' was used for the inhabitants
of a territory, 'Arnaut' had a more specific meaning.

The Arnauts were, as mentioned above, usually Albanian-speakers
who were used as fighters by the Ottomans: 'Arnaut' was simply the
Turkish word for an Albanian, *arnavut*, and normally had an
ethnic–linguistic as well as a geographical connotation. Some local
Serbian-speakers may have volunteered too; we know that the Orthodox

had welcomed Piccolomini in Eastern Kosovo. But Prizren was a large town (c.50,000 inhabitants) with an overwhelmingly Muslim and Albanian-speaking population. Some of these would have been only first-generation converts, and perhaps not immune to Archbishop Bogdani's rhetoric; others may just have thought life would be better under Austrian rule. As for the Christian Arnauts who had been receiving payments for military service from the Ottomans, there is evidence that this was quite a common practice: a report from Kosovo in 1638 said that the pasha of Bosnia had used 'the Christians and Muslims of these plains' for his campaign against the Këlmendi, and in 1692 the pasha of Peć had in his army 'many Albanians, from the plain as well as the mountains, their main strength consisting of Catholics'. Other Catholic Albanians, from the clans of the nearby Malësi (in the districts of Gashi, Puka, Fandi and others) also joined the revolt, as an Ottoman document of February 1690 shows.[50]

Piccolomini's diplomatic success at Prizren crowned his military triumph at Skopje; but he did not live long to enjoy it. Before he reached Prizren he already had a swelling under his arm, which turned out to be a plague bubo, and on 9 November he died. Pjetër Bogdani, who had given him the last rites, carried on his work, but eventually he too was infected; he was taken to Prishtina, to receive the best treatment available from Austrian doctors, but died there on 6 December, having been given the last sacrament by a German Jesuit. He was buried in the 'Imperial' Mosque of Murat I (the Fatih-xhami), which the Austrians had deftly converted into a church and dedicated to the Jesuit saint, Francis Xavier.[51] Piccolomini was officially succeeded as commander in the region by General Veterani; but Veterani was far away, and operational command in Kosovo passed to the next most senior officer in Piccolomini's force, Duke Christian of Holstein. Several minor military actions were mounted, all of them successful; one in particular, a raid in the direction of Tetovo, was designed to test the willingness of the 'Albanian Arnauts' to fight. (They passed.)[52]

But in other ways Holstein was less successful than his predecessor. After repelling an Ottoman force which had advanced towards Prizren from the Luma district (which lies to the south, on the eastern side of the Black Drin), he then tried to get the allegiance of the inhabitants of that area, who were Orthodox Slavs; when they declared that they still

supported the Ottomans, and fired at his men, he put more than thirty
villages to the flames.[53] This created a reputation for harshness. The
Albanian recruits, meanwhile, were becoming discontented; they resented the 'avarice and arrogance' of their Austrian officers. According
to the papal envoy in Vienna, Holstein failed to keep the bargain made
with the Arnauts by Piccolomini, imposing exorbitant taxes and execut-
ing those who resisted. His final mistake was not only to demand taxes
from the Arnaut soldiers, but also to try to disarm some of them –
something, as the Italian writer observed, 'intolerable for this free and
warlike people'. The result was that by the end of the year, out of the
20,000 Arnauts raised by Piccolomini, only 3,000 were left.[54]

Holstein needed all the support he could get. There were greater
forces mustering against him now than the ineffective army of the pasha
of Peć. The Sultan had ordered Halil pasha, governor of the Morea
(southern Greece), to bring his army, plus 3,000 Arnauts, to Skopje. (It
is a sign of the decay of Ottoman discipline that Halil agreed to do so
only on condition that he were sent 200 *yüks* of akçes – one yük was
roughly 100 kilograms.) Also in the Skopje area was a large force of
Crimean Tatars under the command of Nureddin, a son of the Khan.[55]
The first Tatar raids began in late December: 3,000 Tatars penetrated
Kosovo and burnt down many villages in the south-eastern corner of the
territory. Before that, Holstein had already called a council of war in
Prishtina on 22 December, at which it was decided to remain in Kosovo
but to concentrate the Austrian forces. Whatever detailed plans he made,
however, were disrupted on 30 December by the news that the fort
commanding the vital pass of Kaçanik was now under siege: there were
only 100 musketeers in it, and a large Tatar–Ottoman army was
approaching. Holstein ordered one of his officers, Colonel Strasser, to
take a small force southwards and join up with 500 men from the
Piccolomini regiment, who would come to meet him from Prizren;
together, they would then march to the relief of Kaçanik. Strasser had
(according to the Italian writer) 1,300 Austrian troops (900 cavalry and
400 infantry), plus 1,500 'Rascians and Arnauts'.[56] They set out from
Prishtina on 1 January 1690; on the following day, Strasser would lead
them to a catastrophic defeat, and within hours the Austrians would
abandon Kosovo.

Also on 1 January Holstein sent a report to Vienna, which was later summarized by the papal envoy in Austria as follows:

> The Patriarch of that territory had just arrived there [i.e. in Prishtina]; admitted into the presence of His Highness [the Duke of Holstein], he made a request for a passport to enable him to travel to the Imperial Court, and explain to it the state of that territory and the intentions which those people are forming towards Catholicism.[57]

This is, at it happens, the first record in the Austrian (or Austrian-derived) documents of any meeting with Patriarch Arsenije in Kosovo. He had probably been in the territory for a number of weeks, and one later account by a German author suggests that he had negotiated with Holstein for some time; a modern historian claims that he was part of Holstein's council of war on 22 December, but the statement that he had 'only just' arrived before 1 January counts against this.[58]

Significantly, the papal envoy's report shows that Arsenije was preoccupied with the question of relations between his Church and that of Rome. It was an issue which had troubled him for several years. The spirit of the Counter-Reformation was particularly strong in Austria: it was on Austrian territory that the Serbian Uniate Church functioned, and Arsenije had good reason to think that he would be pressed to submit to Rome if ever the Serb lands came under Austrian rule. In 1688 he sent a Serbian archimandrite, Isaias, to Moscow to ask the Tsar for assistance: Isaias told the Russians that the Austrian forces tried to 'uproot and expel the Orthodox clergy' in the towns they seized, and that if Austria conquered the Balkans 'the Orthodox Christians will fall into a worse situation than under the Turks'. (On his return through Transylvania in March 1689, Isaias was arrested by the Austrian authorities.)[59] At the same time, the Venetian military actions in Montenegro and parts of Hercegovina, as well as the Austrian successes, obliged Arsenije to enter into some delicate negotiations on the Catholic side: he sent friendly letters to the Pope in October 1688 and to the Catholic Archbishop of Bar in September 1689.[60]

Faced with a choice between Austria and Venice, the Patriarch definitely preferred the latter: the Venetians had a long tradition of religious quasi-autonomy, and in one famous episode in the early seventeenth century the whole of Venice had even been put under an 'interdict' (denial of the sacraments) by the Pope. Although Venice and Austria were allies in this war, their traditional hostility remained strong; and it had been intensified in 1684 by the decision of Ragusa, Venice's commercial rival, to drop its pro-Ottoman stance and side with the Habsburgs. By the summer of 1689, with Venice established in central Montenegro and the Austrians advancing towards Novi Pazar, a desperate competition was developing to see who could gain the loyalty of the territories in between.[61] In early May the Venetian official in Kotor was discussing the possibility of a pro-Venetian uprising with two Orthodox bishops; later that month he reported that he was trying to woo the mountain clans, especially the Këlmendi, Kuçi, Piperi and Bjelopavlić; and in July he made an urgent request for money to give out as bribes to those local clan chiefs who had already submitted to Venice, because of 'the approach of the Emperor's army, whose commanders do not fail to apply both flatteries and threats' to win them over from Venice. By October, the Venetians at Kotor were even holding seven prominent people from the mountain clans (some Slav, some Albanian) as 'hostages', to ensure their clansmen's loyalty.[62]

During this period Patriarch Arsenije became resolutely pro-Venetian. Some time in early September, when an Ottoman official came to Peć to take Arsenije and his treasury to Istanbul, the Patriarch slipped out of his monastery and went to Montenegro. Touring his flock there, he apparently encouraged them to pledge their support to Venice. But in early October, while he was residing at the monastery of St Luke in Nikšić (in the area which was now officially under Venice), he was startled to receive a visit from an Austrian 'Rascian' army captain, who had been sent by Baden with two documents for him. One was a personal letter, asking him to raise his people in revolt in support of the Austrians; the other was a general proclamation telling them to do so and threatening that if they did not, Baden would treat them as rebels and 'persecute them to the point of their destruction'. Arsenije immediately sent copies of these papers to the Venetian *provveditore* (governor–commander) on the coast, assuring him that he still intended to keep the local population loyal to Venice.[63]

Although the Venetians were told that Arsenije had united all the mountain clans (including the Këlmendi and Kuçi) in a great 'confederation', there is little evidence of coordinated action on their part. Until September some of the malësor clans (Këlmendi, Hoti, Kastrati and others) had been serving in the army of Süleyman pasha, the governor of Shkodra: it was a Venetian official who persuaded them to withdraw from it.[64] Even after Arsenije had cast his lot with the Austrians, the attitude of these clans remained unclear. By 1 December rumours had reached Istanbul that the Këlmendi and other clans had revolted, but ten days later the Venetian envoy in Vienna wrote that reports that the Këlmendi clans had sent their chiefs to submit to the Austrians were untrue. A later Venetian report from Montenegro said that the four Këlmendi chiefs did go to negotiate with the Austrians in Peć, but came back discontented because they had not been given suitable presents.[65] No coordinated rising of the Këlmendi and their Orthodox Montenegrin allies emerges from this evidence; instead, it seems that there were some local actions, such as the sending of a joint Këlmendi-Kuçi force to help the Austrians near Bijelo Polje (in the Sandžak of Novi Pazar) in mid-November. The general pattern was probably the one described by the Venetian provveditore in March 1690: 'The peoples of these mountains are still standing at the ready ... Some of them, who are in the vicinity of the Austrian troops, join in their raiding parties against the Ottomans; others make raids for their own benefit.'[66]

What finally persuaded Patriarch Arsenije to go over to the Austrian side was a desperate letter from his monks at Peć. They informed him that an Austrian officer had come to the Patriarchate and demanded Arsenije's return; if he were not back in Kosovo within one week, the officer had said, the Austrians would appoint someone else in his place. The monks also reported that 'the Orthodox people, having taken the Emperor's side', did not want to be without their chief pastor any longer. Their letter was dated 28 October O.S. (Old Style: the Julian calendar, used by the Orthodox Church, was ten days behind the Gregorian calendar used by the Catholics); unfortunately, by the time its bearer reached Nikšić, Arsenije had already left, on his way to a meeting with the Venetian provveditore on the coast. The courier caught up with him at Cetinje; the Patriarch turned round immediately, sending off a hasty letter of apology (dated 4 November 'alla Vechia', i.e. Old Style) to the Venetians.[67] The Patriarch must have been close to panic at this point; already, seven days had passed since the Austrian threat was issued, and the journey back to Peć would take several more. He did, however, have one other lifeline: he had been corresponding with the Austrian Resident in Ragusa, who had been bidding hard for his favours. Although direct proof is lacking, it seems likely that he got some kind of official document from the Austrian envoy to protect his status, before returning to Peć.[68]

One thing, therefore, is quite certain: while the Patriarch was in Cetinje on 14 November (New Style), Piccolomini had already been dead for five days. (His date of death, 9 November, comes from Austrian records, which always used New Style.) The two men can never have met. How quickly the Patriarch got back to Kosovo is, however, very unclear. One puzzling piece of evidence is a letter sent by a Venetian officer to the provveditore on 22 November (12 November O.S.), which not only discussed Arsenije's dealings with Ragusa but stated that he was still in Montenegro: 'At the moment, the Patriarch is at Nikšić'; and another letter, from an Orthodox monk in Cetinje on 29 November, said that the weather was so bad that 'I do not believe that the Patriarch himself will be able to travel.'[69] All we can be certain of is that he was in Prishtina immediately before 1 January; from there, having presumably obtained his passport, he went back to Peć, perhaps to make preparations for his journey. Just as he was returning to the Patriarchate monastery, however, the entire military situation of the Austrians in Kosovo underwent a disastrous change.

Colonel Strasser, the leader of the small force heading for the relief of Kaçanik on 1 January, was an impatient man. Instead of waiting for the troops from Prizren to join him – as he had been instructed, and as one of his senior officers, Prince Karl of Hanover, begged him to do – he pressed on. Just before Kaçanik, on the following day, his scouts brought the first news of the size of the Ottoman forces waiting for him, which numbered more than 11,000 men. When one of his chief Arnaut captains warned him to proceed no further, Strasser laughed at him and called him a coward; an angry exchange of insults followed, which ended with Strasser shooting the man in the arm. Strasser then arranged his troops in an open field, with undefended flanks, and the Ottoman–Tatar forces began their attack. Before long the Austrians were completely overwhelmed, and the battle turned into a massacre. Most of the officers, including Prince Karl of Hanover (a younger brother of the future King George I of England), were killed.[70]

All these details come from the account compiled by the anonymous Italian writer. A handful of Austrian soldiers did escape from the field, and all accounts of the battle which reached Vienna presumably derived from their testimony. But there was great confusion: it was not known, for example, whether Strasser had been killed or captured. Much emphasis was put in the Austrian reports on the idea of treachery by the Arnauts: it was said that their chiefs had entered into secret contracts with the Ottomans, and that they fled at the start of the battle.[71] By a lucky historical fluke, however, it is possible to get a different perspective on the battle of Kaçanik. In the following month, a Greek employee of the English embassy in Istanbul happened to be in Edirne when the first Austrian prisoners from Kaçanik were brought in. The two surgeons and a Lieutenant-Captain that he interviewed described the performance of the 1,200 Austrian troops, but made no mention of an Arnaut betrayal: 'After a battle lasting six hours, the 400 of those troops who were on horseback fled, and left 800, who were the infantry; these, being unable to resist such a large enemy army, also tried to flee, and were pursued . . .'[72]

Learning of this disaster, Holstein seems simply to have panicked. He immediately withdrew his men from Prishtina, parting in such haste that all the provisions, a large quantity of ammunition and several artillery pieces were left behind.[73] The 500 soldiers from Prizren, who had been meant to rendezvous with Strasser, reached the battlefield on 3 January and had to fight a rearguard action on their rapid retreat to Prishtina: they found it abandoned, and hastened on towards Niš. Soon afterwards, the Tatar and Ottoman troops arrived in Prishtina and took what revenge they could. As the priest Gjergj Bogdani, another nephew of the Archbishop, later recorded: 'My uncle, being found already dead and buried, was nevertheless dug up from his grave, and put out as food for the dogs in the middle of the square in Prishtina, with his mitre on his head.'[74] Those troops which remained in Prizren, consisting of the rest of the Piccolomini regiment and a number of 'Rascians' and Arnauts, had to make their escape by a different route; they travelled north, via Peć and Novi Pazar, closely pursued by the Tatars. With them went the

Arnaut-recruiter and Vicar, Toma Raspasani, who later wrote: 'I escaped from the Turks by the skin of my teeth, on horseback; they made a special attempt to capture me.'[75]

Also departing in great haste, presumably just ahead of Raspasani, was the Serbian Patriarch. According to one Venetian report he fled northwards with ten horse-loads of 'rich furnishings', and was robbed of them by 'Rascians' en route; the city of Peć, meanwhile, was quickly reoccupied by its pasha, Mahmutbegolli. A monk who escaped from Peć in early February said that the monastery was sacked; some of the monks had gone with Arsenije, but two of those who remained were 'chopped to pieces'.[76] Clearly, the speed of the Patriarch's flight means that the traditional image of him leading a great exodus out of Kosovo itself is quite false; if he did ever lead a mass of people, it must have been a mass that he joined up with much later. Almost no one else had time to escape from Western Kosovo: Raspasani, writing in April 1690, explained that 'Nobody was able to get out of Prizren or Peć; they all remained there as prey to the barbarian.' Overall, he said, 'The country and its people were indeed destroyed, massacred by the barbarians, and enslaved.'[77] Other early reports confirm this miserable picture. As early as 18 January, the English agent in Edirne wrote that the Tatars had caused enormous damage to the people in Kosovo, 'from which perhaps they will never recover, or at least not for a very long time'. The Papal envoy in Vienna reported similarly on 5 February that the Ottoman forces in Kosovo were 'burning and ruining the country'; in the following month he wrote that the Ottomans and Tatars had 'barbarously butchered those poor inhabitants and taken a great number of them away into slavery'.[78]

Holstein's headlong flight was stopped by General Veterani, who reimposed discipline and, in February and March 1690, began to recover some ground. The anonymous Italian writer even claims that he regained all the former Austrian positions, including Kaçanik; but this is obviously a confusion, and no such claim was made by Veterani in his memoirs. All he could manage was a number of raiding expeditions against targets such as Novo Brdo and Peć. In April a Venetian officer in Montenegro reported that all the rumours of large-scale reoccupation by the Austrians were false; he also wrote that 'Kosovo, destroyed by the two armies, was lying deserted between them; in the countryside you could not see a soul.'[79] One member of Veterani's staff made a more factual and slightly less bleak analysis. He noted that all the villages (roughly 360) in the Vuçitërn and Trepça area were deserted, and the majority of the 360 villages in the district of Prishtina; but his detailed figures for many other districts, including Novo Brdo, Suha Reka, Prizren, Gjakova and Peć, gave a total of 671 villages, all of which were still inhabited.[80] The pattern fits what one might expect: the north-eastern shoulder of Kosovo was the area from which people could most easily escape, travelling towards the Austrian-held territory of Niš.

Veterani did still hope to reconquer Kosovo; but Baden was advising the Emperor to order a further withdrawal. To counter this, Veterani sent Count Marsigli to Vienna to represent his case. Marsigli submitted a memorandum he had written, arguing that the mountain clans of what he called 'Albania' (the northern Malësi and highland Montenegro) could be persuaded to rise up if an Imperial declaration were made promising them the continuation of all their privileges, their freedom of religion and their right to elect their own chiefs or vojvods. He also suggested that the Emperor send a letter to the 'Patriarch of the Rascians' inviting him to 'animate his people in Albania and Rascia to take up arms against the Turks'.[81]

It was in response to this that the Emperor issued the document dated 6 April 1690 which some Serbian historians have described, quite wrongly, as an 'invitation'. This text was not inviting the Patriarch to bring his people to Hungary; on the contrary, it was urging him and his people to rise up against the Ottomans, so that Austrian rule could be extended all the way to 'Albania'. For that purpose, it guaranteed (as Marsigli had suggested) that Habsburg dominion over their territory would not infringe their religious freedom or their right to elect their own vojvods. The original manuscript of this document was endorsed: 'An exhortation to the Patriarch of the Rascians, to rouse his people to rebel against the Turks'; and a key passage in the text said: 'Do not desert your hearths, or the cultivation of your fields.' Some nineteenth-century historians of a romantic Serbian persuasion dealt with this passage in a wonderfully economical way: instead of printing the correct text, which says *non deserite* (do not desert), they simply omitted the 'non'.[82]

By the summer of 1690, however, all such plans for reconquest were abandoned. The Ottomans, under their competent Grand Vizier, had built up their forces, and the military tide had definitely turned. A massive Ottoman army advanced on Niš and besieged it; it surrendered on 6 September. The Imperial garrison was allowed to leave, but a large number of 'Rascian' soldiers (400 in one account, 4,000 in another) were taken out and killed.[83] In the last week of September, Belgrade was under siege; it held out for just twelve days, before an Ottoman shell hit the fort's main powder-store on the night of 8 October, blowing the whole citadel to smithereens.

By September Belgrade had become the natural destination of a large number of refugees. One modern historian estimates that there were 40,000 there; many of these would have come from the Niš region, and the region between Niš and Belgrade – areas which had been under Austrian administration for a whole year.[84] But among them also would have been some of the people who had fled from the Prishtina–Trepça–Vuçitërn area of Kosovo. Their Patriarch had reached Belgrade much earlier in the year. In June he had gathered a large assembly of Serbian religious and secular leaders there, to discuss further negotiations with the Emperor over the question of religious autonomy in the areas still under Austrian control. The list of dignitaries who attended includes churchmen from the monasteries of Studenica and Sopočani, and 'kapetans' from Krupa and Kragujevac; not a single person from Kosovo is mentioned, however, apart from the Patriarch himself.[85]

How – and exactly when – the Serb refugees in Belgrade escaped into Hungary is not clear. Few of those who remained there during the siege can have survived; the early reports all state that only a few hundred people escaped when the city fell. Those inhabitants and soldiers who were not captured or killed were drowned as they tried to swim across the Danube; just a small number of soldiers managed to get into the boats which were tied up below the citadel.[86] An early Serb chronicler recorded that all the Serbs fled from Belgrade in 10,000 boats; no doubt some of those who left before the siege began did so by river, but this figure seems highly fanciful.[87]

Nevertheless, whatever the means and the timing, a large number of Serbs did travel north into Hungary, including the Patriarch. The conditions most of them had to live in, as they camped out in the central Hungarian region in the winter, were atrocious. Before the end of the year Patriarch Arsenije sent a petition to the Emperor Leopold begging for assistance for these people; he also gave an explicit estimate of their numbers. 'There have come to Esztergom, Komárom and Buda men with their wives and children, completely destitute and bare, coming to a total of more than 30,000 souls.' Much later, in 1706, Arsenije made another estimate in a letter to Leopold's successor: he said he had come to Hungary with 'more than 40,000 souls'. These statements – each of them clearly specifying souls, not families – are confirmed by a news-sheet of 1696, which said that after the fall of Belgrade 30,000 people had come to Hungary.[88] The popular tradition of 37,000 families derives from a single source: a Serbian monastic chronicle which was written many years after the event and contains several other errors. Such evidence can be given little weight, when compared with the clear testimony of documents written by Patriarch Arsenije himself.[89]

It is reasonable to assume that the total Serb emigration to Hungary did not consist only of this wave of people in October 1690; some had come before then, and perhaps others trickled in afterwards. On the other hand we know that many died of hunger, exposure or disease, and that a significant number (as we shall see in the next chapter) eventually returned home. The Austrians, who were desperately short of military manpower, recruited as many of these people as they could, forming a new 'Rascian militia'; but the maximum number of troops they formed, from these and from other 'Rascians' in the area, was only 10,000 men (2,000 of them recruited by Arsenije himself in April 1691), which is roughly what one might expect from an overall population of 40,000. By 1693 the main concentration of Serbs was at Szent Endre, near Budapest; according to one report there were 24,000 there and 6,000 in Pest itself.[90]

As has been suggested already, not all of these people were from Kosovo. The largest element must surely have come from the Niš region, the Morava valley and the area of Belgrade. (A comparison between the Ottoman tax registers before and after the period 1688–90 for the sancak of Belgrade shows that the non-Muslim population there fell by seven-eighths.) Other parts of central Serbia must also have contributed their refugees, as the geographical spread of the Serb dignitaries who met in June 1690 – and much other evidence besides – suggests.[91] It is hard to believe, therefore, that more than one-quarter of the total refugee population came from Kosovo itself. No doubt many more had fled;

many of those trying to travel long distances may have died en route, but some were probably just taking refuge in the hills, as they had done at previous times of crisis, to return home sooner or later. And of those who did get as far as Hungary, a minority (perhaps only a small one) were either Slav-speaking Catholics, or Albanian-speaking Catholics, or Albanian-speaking Muslims, or even Muslim Slavs. Toma Raspasani, writing in 1693 about the Catholics of Kosovo, observed that many had gone to the district of Budapest, 'where most of them died, some of hunger, others of disease'.[92] Austrian military records mention 'Arnauts in Imperial service' in December 1690 and March 1691; and a document of February 1693 states that on the island of Szent Endre there are 'a large number of Rascians, among whom are there apparently also Turks [i.e. Muslims]'.[93] These pro-Austrian Muslims and Arnauts deserve, one may feel, a little more recognition from the history books than they have hitherto been allowed to receive.

9

Recovery and decline: 1690–1817

ALL FOUR HORSEMEN of the Apocalypse had entered Kosovo with the Tatar cavalry. Many people were killed, or taken away as slaves; the plague continued to rage in 1690, and such was the destruction of food stocks that people were reduced to eating horses and dogs.[1] But although the terrible reprisals carried out by Ottoman and Tatar forces were part of a deliberate policy of intimidation, it was not in the long-term interests of the Ottoman state to depopulate its own territory: it needed the food those people grew and the taxes they paid. In late March 1690 the Sultan issued a firman (edict) to halt the killing of the raya, and promised protection for all those who had not actively joined the Habsburg forces. (A second firman, in September, offered a full amnesty, but was addressed only to the raya of the area between Niš and Belgrade.)[2] In the following year the Sultan permitted the appointment of a new Patriarch in Peć to replace Arsenije: this move may also have been intended to stabilize the position of the Orthodox Serbs and prevent any further migrations northwards. The new Patriarch, Kalinik or Kallinikos, came from Skopje but was probably Greek by birth; his appointment was, however, generally accepted by the Serbs. Since Arsenije also retained the title until his death, there were two patriarchs of the Serbian Church between 1691 and 1706. Thereafter, Arsenije's successors on Habsburg soil – who were based in Sremski Karlovci, close to Novi Sad – took the title of Metropolitan; there was some rivalry between the two centres, but a fair degree of cooperation was maintained.[3]

In fact, during the negotiations in 1699 for the Treaty of Karlowitz (Sremski Karlovci) which ended the Habsburg–Ottoman war, Arsenije sent a request to the Sultan to be allowed to return to Peć. But he was informed that his presence was not desired, because he had 'meddled in civil affairs'.[4] He was not the only Serb who had wanted to go back. Many had returned to Ottoman territory in the first half of 1691, having resented the hostile treatment they received from the Austrian nobility, the local authorities and the Catholic Church. Arsenije had made a formal complaint about one military commissar in the Osijek region, whose treatment of the Serbs had been so harsh that 649 families returned to Ottoman soil. And Leopold himself admitted that in the period 1693–7 alone, 3,000 Serbs had fled from the Vukovar area.[5] Conversely, there are many complaints in the Austrian records about 'Rascian robbers' and their 'great insolences', about Serb traders breaking local laws, about the theft of livestock, gold and church goods, and acts of violence against Catholics.[6] One jaundiced Austrian official would go so far as to state in 1724 that the 'Rascians' actually preferred to live under Ottoman rule, because the Ottoman punishment for murder was only a fine, whereas in Habsburg territory murderers were executed.[7]

While the Ottoman authorities applied the rudiments of a conciliatory policy in Kosovo, their hostility and suspicions towards their Christian subjects there – above all, towards the Catholics, who were the Austrians' coreligionists – did not disappear overnight. A new wave of Islamicization seems to have taken place during the first couple of decades after 1690. It has sometimes been suggested that this was the result of a deliberate policy decision in Istanbul, using conversion as a pacification measure. But the evidence suggests that conversion was caused by a variety of factors, rather than a single overriding policy. One story, for example, is told in a Franciscan source: it says that by 1692 Mahmut-begolli was once more employing large numbers of Catholics (from both the highlands and the plains) in his army, and that the Grand Vizier was horrified when he learned that some of the soldiers were roasting pigs in their camp. Mahmutbegolli, threatened with death by the Vizier, tried hard to persuade the Catholics, especially the Këlmendi, to convert to Islam, but most of them kept their faith.[8] Mahmut Mahmutbegolli died in 1695; his successor in Peć, Hudaverdi pasha (also of the Mahmut-begolli family), did impose heavy new taxes on the Christians in 1700, and during the next few years the Archbishop of Bar, Vicko Zmajević, would complain repeatedly that this was driving large numbers of people to convert to Islam. Yet at the same time Zmajević confirmed (as we shall see) that Hudaverdi was friendly and protective towards the Catholic Church.[9]

The only clear statement about a policy of pacification-by-conversion comes in a report sent to Rome by Zmajević in 1702; but here Zmajević was referring specifically to the area to the west of Kosovo itself. He said that in the sensitive frontier zone of northern Albania and Montenegro new taxes were being imposed 'to force the Catholics either to become Muslims, or to leave the province and move to another part of the Ottoman realm, or to submit to paying the tribute'.[10] This reference to forcing people to move is also significant, in the light of Hudaverdi's policy towards the Këlmendi. Although this warlike Catholic clan had been used from time to time by local pashas in their military campaigns (possibly as recently as 1698), its habit of robbing lowland towns and villages, or demanding 'contributions' from them, was strongly resented by the authorities – including Hudaverdi, whose own family's house in Peć had once been sacked by Këlmendi raiders.[11]

In 1700 he decided to deal with them once and for all. Having persuaded some of the other Christian clans of the Malësi to support him, he surrounded the Këlmendi in their mountain stronghold near Gusinje and eventually starved them into submission. One group of clansmen was allowed to stay there, because its chief, Hudaverdi's brother-in-law, had promised to convert them to Islam; but the main body of the Këlmendi, consisting of roughly 2,000 people, was forcibly moved to the plains of Pešter (north of Peć, in the Sandžak of Novi Pazar), to be kept under surveillance and control.[12] This was the most dramatic instance of Hudaverdi's policy of transplanting mountain clans, but it was not the only one: in the area round Gjakova, south of Peć, Archbishop Zmajević also noted the arrival of 'colonies of Albanians from the mountains, forced to migrate there by the Turks, both to take away their opportunity to rob, and to populate the country, which had been destroyed by the wars'.[13]

One optimistic Ottoman decree in 1702 said that most of the Këlmendi had now converted to Islam, and suggested that they might now be given land in Kosovo itself.[14] But the records of the Catholic Church show that the exiled Këlmendi were quickly supplied with two priests; and when the Archbishop of Skopje visited them in 1706 he found a strong Catholic population of 2,000 souls.[15] In the following year, tiring of their exile, more than half of these proud highlanders decided to fight their way back to their mountain homes. There were only 400 fighting men among them, so they were joined in arms by 300 of their wives; together they fought their way through an Ottoman army of 6,000 men. Four years later they sent out a large raiding force to rescue some of the remainder of their population, and came back with fifty families – to the delight of the Archbishop of Bar, who thought that the residue had been on the point of going over to Islam. But a significant number did remain in the Pešter plains, without apparently changing faith.[16]

The general position of the Catholics in Kosovo, since the restoration of Ottoman rule in 1690, had not been good. Their priests had either fled, like Raspasani, or been killed, like Gjin Bogdani; during the immediate aftermath of the Austrian invasion just one remained in the whole of Kosovo, and his life was preserved only because he gave Mahmutbegolli all his possessions, including his house.[17] The person appointed by Rome to succeed Pjetër Bogdani as Archbishop in 1690 was an Italian professor of Arabic, a former Franciscan missionary in Egypt, who never even attempted to set foot in the archdiocese; and by the summer of 1692 there were still only three priests in the whole ecclesiastical province of 'Serbia', which included Kosovo and all the Serb lands to the north.[18] Things improved slightly in 1702, when the absentee Archbishop was transferred to Smyrna and was succeeded by a local man, Petar Karadžić (born in Novo Brdo), who had previously been bishop of a see in northern Albania.[19]

Immediately, the biggest problem Karadžić had to deal with was the attitude of the Orthodox Church: Patriarch Kalinik had resumed the traditional policy of trying to force all Christians in the territory, including the Catholics, to pay their ecclesiastical taxes to him. Kalinik needed all the money he could get: the large sums he was having to pay annually to Istanbul strongly suggest that he had followed the common practice of buying his office with a promise of subsequent payments. (Archbishop Zmajević reported in 1703 that the monasteries of Peć and Dečani, which used to have 150 monks between them, now had precisely ten, because Kalinik had seized all the revenues.)[20] In his drive to extract money from the Catholics too, Kalinik had two great advantages: he possessed a firman from the Sultan, stating his rights over the Christians in rather general terms, and he also enjoyed the protection of a powerful Greek at the Sultan's court. In 1703 Archbishop Zmajević listed the Patriarch's various demands, beginning with the expulsion of a Catholic mission and ending with a string of new taxes on Catholics: he noted that the first demand had been blocked by Hudaverdi pasha, and said that he would have blocked the others if he had felt able to do so, 'both because of the friendly feeling he bears towards our Catholics, and because of the hostility he feels towards the Patriarch, were it not for the fact that the latter is backed up by the protection of Mavrokordatos, the Chief Dragoman, a man of great authority at Court.'[21]

The explanation Zmajević gave for Hudaverdi's benevolence towards the Catholics is a rather touching one: he said that a Catholic priest who practised medicine in Peć had won the gratitude and confidence of Hudaverdi's mother, and that on her death-bed she had solemnly required her son to give him all possible assistance.[22] Nor was this the only example of indulgence towards the Catholics by local lords. When Archbishop Petar Karadžić came to live in his archdiocese he settled in the Catholic village of Zumbi, in the Has district near Prizren. His reason for doing so was that the village was owned by a powerful lord, to whom the Catholic peasants paid their tithes, and no other pashas dared attack them: 'I give him twenty scudi [*c*.2,000 akçes] a year, and he defends me from other Ottomans and barbarians.' Apart from this monetary payment, other sweeteners were also required: 'I have to give him good presents for our Easter, and St George's Day, and for their Bayram ... I order from Venice so many candlesticks, large mirrors, candies, sugar-loaves, and fine drinking-glasses.'[23] But on the other hand Hudaverdi's successor as pasha of Peć was a bitter enemy of the Catholics; and when war resumed with Venice in 1714, instead of expelling all Italian priests (as the Sultan had ordered), he arrested and tortured them, demanding a large payment for their release.[24]

When Austria, the other great Catholic power, joined the war in 1716, Ottoman policy hardened even more against the Catholics; and hostility was further intensified by a pro-Venetian rebellion of several Albanian Catholic clans, including the Këlmendi, the Gashi and the Mirdita.[25] After the Austrian capture of Belgrade in 1717, some of the Serbs in Eastern Kosovo also rose up. No special reprisals are reported after the end of the war in 1718; but the tax burden continued to grow, and eight years later even an Ottoman report noted that the tax rises had been so steep that many of the richer raya from Eastern Kosovo were emigrating. The kadı of Janjevo complained to the authorities in Istanbul that the local lord was setting the ispence (the variety of land-tax for non-Muslims) at 80 akçes, when the official rate was only 32. And although the new Serbian Patriarch, Arsenije IV Šakabenta, obtained a firman confirming all his rights and possessions in 1731, it also confirmed that he had to pay 70,000 akçes per annum to Istanbul. Soon after his election as Patriarch, he had had to write to the Metropolitan of Karlovci (his counterpart on Habsburg soil), begging for money.[26]

So it is not surprising that when the Austrians started making diplomatic overtures to the religious leaders in this region in 1736, they met with a very positive response. Austria had been dragged into a Russian–Ottoman war by its alliance with Moscow, and was now planning a large-scale invasion to conquer the whole of Bosnia, Serbia and northern Albania. In the summer of 1736 the new Catholic Archbishop of Skopje, Mikel Suma (who had succeeded Karadžić in 1728), began secret negotiations with the Austrians. Somehow the Ottoman authorities found out about Mikel Suma's activities, and he was forced to flee to Austria at the end of 1736.[27] But the Serbian Patriarch continued to negotiate, giving the Austrians every encouragement. In March 1737 he sent one of his senior monks to meet an Austrian general in Belgrade (which had been in Austrian hands since the end of the previous war in 1718): the monk urged him to advance on Kosovo, because all the Ottoman soldiers had gone to fight in the Russian campaign and the defence of the country had been left to 'Gypsies, and people with no military experience'.[28]

In June 1737 the Austrian commander, Field-Marshal Seckendorf, began his advance southwards from Belgrade. He also sent two detachments of 'Rascian militia' towards Novi Pazar to make contact with the Patriarch and local clan chiefs; they brought with them copies of a manifesto printed in Serbian, calling on all Christians to revolt. On 24 July the Patriarch came with a group of local chiefs (representing Albanian Catholic clans, such as the Këlmendi, and Montenegrin Orthodox ones, such as the Bratonožić) to meet the Austrian field-marshal near Niš; they promised their support but asked also for more

Austrian troops to be sent to their area. Everything seemed to be turning in the Austrians' favour: four days later Niš surrendered to them, and at the same time their 'Rascian militia', together with a force under a local Serb leader, seized the important town of Novi Pazar. According to one Bosnian–Ottoman chronicle, as soon as Novi Pazar was taken, the Austrians sent word, via those Këlmendi who were still living in exile in the Pešter plains, to the other Albanians in the mountains, telling them to begin the revolt. And in early August a larger force of 2,300 Austrian soldiers was sent into Kosovo, where it penetrated as far as Prishtina. It must have seemed, once again, that a general conquest of Kosovo was just about to happen. The Austrian mood was euphoric: on 4 August a special Te Deum was sung in Niš to celebrate its occupation, and a large banquet was held there for all staff officers.[29]

In fact the tide of war had turned disastrously on that very day, with the heavy defeat of another Austrian army at Banja Luka in northern Bosnia. Instead of operating a pincer movement which would bring two Austrian forces together in the Sandžak of Novi Pazar, Seckendorf now found that he had a dangerously over-extended position in Kosovo; the victorious Ottoman troops were moving from Bosnia towards Novi Pazar, while another Ottoman army was also advancing against him from the Bulgarian side. In mid-August the expeditionary force in Kosovo was pulled back towards Niš, and on 24 August the Austrians abandoned Novi Pazar.

Just a few days earlier the Patriarch had begun his own military action with 3,000 men from the mountain clans. They reached Novi Pazar only hours after the Austrians had left; Arsenije was alarmed, and hurried on after them. Most of the highland clansmen followed him, while a few returned to their homes. For the next two months these clansmen – a mixed Slav-Albanian group, in which the Këlmendi were the largest component – took part with the Austrian forces in a desperate attempt to hold a position in west-central Serbia; then, in October, the whole Austrian front broke. Niš was abandoned, and the Patriarch, who had been staying there in September, fled northwards. The Këlmendi and other clansmen were also in flight (with their families and all their flocks) up the north-western side of Serbia, towards Belgrade; 3,000 were captured or killed in a successful ambush by an Ottoman army, but a few survivors did get through to Habsburg territory, where they were joined by two of their chiefs, who had been with the Patriarch in Niš.[30] It has always been assumed that the Catholic Archbishop, Mikel Suma, had stayed in Belgrade throughout the period of the Austrian invasion and withdrawal. But a paper by him in the Vatican Archives suggests that he too had gone out to the Novi Pazar and Pešter region, and had taken part in the retreat: 'With the missionaries of Pešter I retreated to Austrian territory when the Imperial troops withdrew; so did the chaplaincy of Novi Pazar, and many other Catholics who were able to flee.'[31]

Eventually the Këlmendi who reached Habsburg territory were incorporated as soldiers in the Austro-Hungarian 'Military Frontier'; they and their families were given two villages to live in, Hrtkovci and Nikinci, in the Srem or Srijem region to the west of Belgrade. With the help of a succession of Albanian-speaking Catholic priests they would maintain their language and culture there for generations, only gradually being transformed into Croats.[32] The census in 1900 recorded fifty-five elderly Albanian-speakers in the two villages, and in 1968 an Albanian researcher from Kosovo heard one of the old women of Hrtkovci recite an Albanian lullaby. In 1992, however, Serb extremists mounted a campaign to drive out the 'Croats' from Hrtkovci, changing the name of the village to 'Srbislavci' ('Serb-glorifiers'). As a result, most of the descendants of the Këlmendi highlanders, who had risked their lives in 1737 to fight under the Patriarch of the Serbian Orthodox Church, were expelled from Serbian soil.[33]

The events of late 1737 are often referred to by historians of Kosovo as the 'Second Migration'; but, as we have seen, the main body of emigrants came not from Kosovo itself but from the area just to the north-west. Nevertheless, there were probably also many who fled (though not in an organized way) from the Prishtina region, where once again false expectations had been raised by an Austrian army and dashed by its hasty withdrawal. One Ottoman report in 1738 said that Janjevo, Novo Brdo, Prishtina and Vučitërn were all destroyed, and that the people there had either fled or been killed; Catholic sources confirm that many were murdered, some were sent into exile and a large number of men and women were taken off into slavery.[34] Many of the events of the period after 1690 were now repeated. There was an edict telling the Christian peasants to return to their homes in 1740; there were punitive expeditions against some of the highland clans; one of these, part of the Orthodox Montenegrin Vasojević group, was forcibly transplanted into Western Kosovo; and a new Patriarch, of Greek origin, was installed once more in Peć.[35]

The Patriarchate now entered its final years of corruption and decline. With its senior posts filled by 'Phanariot' Greeks (so called from the Phanar quarter of Istanbul, where prominent families of Greek merchants, dragomans and administrators lived), it was absorbed into the patronage system of the Greek Patriarchate of Constantinople. Earlier in the century a French traveller had described how that system worked. When a new Greek Patriarch was installed, having paid the Sultan 60,000 scudi for the post, he would calculate very carefully how much each Metropolitan (senior bishop) could afford to pay him. 'He taxes them, and tells them very explicitly to send the allotted sum. Otherwise, he says, their own posts will go to the highest bidder. The prelates, who are used to this commerce, do not spare their suffragan bishops, and the suffragans squeeze the priests ...'.[36] By 1760, according to a Catholic report, the Patriarch in Peć was paying 10,000 scudi per annum to the Greek Patriarch.[37] In 1766, pleading the burden of the payments they had to make under this system, the bishops of many Serb sees, including Skopje, Niš and Belgrade, together with the Greek-born Patriarch of Peć himself, sent a petition asking the Sultan to close down the Serbian Patriarchate and place the whole Church directly under Constantinople. Some Serbian historians insist that the closure of the Patriarchate was an act of force; but there is good evidence that the closure was carried out canonically, by a decision of a Serbian synod.[38] The primary cause of this event was not the attitude of the Ottoman state (harsh though that was at times) but the financial oppression of the Greek hierarchy. In the Habsburg domains, meanwhile, the Serbian Church based in Karlovci continued to operate, keeping up its *de facto* autonomy. But although some nineteenth-century Metropolitans of Karlovci called themselves 'Patriarch', the title would not have any official basis until the Patriarchate of Peć was formally restored in 1920.[39]

To the Catholics in Kosovo, the abolition of the Patriarchate seems to have made little difference: attempts by the Orthodox hierarchy to force them to pay taxes continued unabated. Under the new arrangements, the Orthodox bishoprics of Kosovo were gathered under a Metropolitan of Prizren; the Catholic Archbishop, Matija Mazarek, still referred to this man as the 'Patriarch', as in a report of 1774 when he described yet another dispute over taxation. Mazarek had appealed to a local lord, 'Mehmet aga, my great friend', for help, and Mehmet had arranged a theological disputation between the two prelates. (The Greek Metropolitan began with what he evidently considered a knock-out question: did Jesus Christ wear a beard?) Finally Mehmet asked the Greek whether his firman, authorizing him to demand taxes of Christians, specifically mentioned the Catholics; he answered that it did not. 'Well then', said Mehmet aga, 'in that case, Patriarch, mind your own business, and stop trying to cheat.'[40]

Contrary to the impression given by this anecdote, however, the Catholics did not enjoy a protected position in late-eighteenth-century Kosovo. The reports sent back to Rome by Matija Mazarek (who was Archbishop of Skopje for most of his adult life, from 1758 to 1807) form a dismal catalogue of complaints and lamentations. Three issues crop up again and again: the immigration of lawless Albanians into Kosovo; the question of conversion to Islam (and, in particular, the dilemma posed by the crypto-Catholics); and the problems created by the local Ottoman–Albanian lords, with their imperious demands and their increasing resort to mutual violence.

Whether from prejudice or from experience, Archbishop Mazarek developed a strong antipathy towards the Albanian migrants from the Malësi. There is a certain irony about this, given that he was himself from a well-known Albanian religious family, the Mazrrekus, who seem originally to have migrated to Kosovo. But although he could speak Albanian, it was not his mother-tongue, and he did not identify with Albanians at all: he thus supplies an example of ethnic-linguistic assimilation from Albanian to Slav, disproving the common assertion that in this period all the assimilation in Kosovo was in the opposite direction.[41] His own complaints about the Albanians were made with real feeling in his first visitation report, of 1760:

All the time, many Catholic families come from the mountains of Albania; being hot-natured, irascible and proud, and very much given to murdering people, they refuse to be trampled underfoot by the Turks, as the holy Gospel teaches. Not submitting to the Ottoman taxes, they go around

armed all the time, day and night, and indeed kill one another for the
slightest affront in word or deed. . . .[42]

Usually, he observed, they would convert to Islam soon after their arrival
in Kosovo, in order to live a more untrammelled life. Thirty-one years
later, Mazarek was denouncing these 'renegade' Albanians with even
greater passion: they had 'filled and taken over' the whole of Serbia, he
said, and committed numerous outrages against the Christians, both
Orthodox and Catholic. He also complained, in terms which would be
echoed in anti-Albanian writings of the next two centuries, that they
were 'the race which breeds fastest', and that one family would create 'a
hundred households' in a few years. Although the detailed demographic
evidence of tax registers is not available for this period, it seems clear
that there was a steady flow of Albanians into Kosovo during these years,
and it also seems likely that those who converted to Islam and came
under the patronage of local Albanian–Ottoman lords did enjoy real
advantages. But on the other hand Mazarek's mental state, by this stage,
should probably be described as clinically paranoid. In the same report
of 1791 he also said of the Albanians: 'At night, they get intelligence and
supply information to one another about everything that is said and
done by day throughout the world; all night long they meet in one house
of each city or village, and hold their conventicles and councils . . .' And
he ended his report by saying that he wanted to add to the liturgy an
extra prayer: 'Ab albanensibus libera nos Domine.'[43]

Some of the Albanians who converted to Islam on arrival, according
to Mazarek, regarded their new faith as a mere formality, to be used just
as a passport to social privilege. But the local Muslim religious teachers
would immediately take charge of them, insisting on their circumcision
and requiring them to make a public profession of faith.[44] There are
many references to crypto-Catholics during this period, in reports by
Mazarek and others; most of them seem to refer to villages which had
been part of the long-established Catholic population in Kosovo, rather
than these recent arrivals. (In a village near Gjakova in 1784, for
example, Mazarek found 'five houses of large crypto-Catholic families'
who had acted as Muslims for eighty years.)[45] Outward conformity to
Islam had probably become more common after 1690; it is significant
that the first ecclesiastical decrees against it dated from 1703. As has

already been suggested, it was the willingness of Catholic priests to give these people the sacraments (in defiance of those decrees) that kept the phenomenon of crypto-Catholicism alive. In 1728 one priest from Kosovo reported that apart from the 4,695 official Catholics in the archdiocese, there were 'many other believers scattered among the homes of the Muslims, and we administer the sacraments to them'; another report in 1743 confirmed that the bishops and priests did give these people the sacraments, against the rulings of the synod of 1703, and it asked Rome for further instructions.[46] Those instructions, however, took the form of an utterly uncompromising papal encyclical in 1744, restating the official line. Despite this, sixteen years later Mazarek was still willing to give the sacraments to crypto-Catholics so long as they made four promises: not to eat forbidden foods during Christian fasts, not to circumcise, not to enter mosques and not to allow Muslim burials for their dead.[47]

The eighteenth-century reports from Kosovo help to fill in a little more detail about how crypto-Catholicism worked in practice. As was suggested in Chapter 7, the custom of allowing women to practise Christianity openly while their menfolk formally adopted Islam played an important part: this was what enabled the priests to enter the homes of these families, where the men could secretly receive the sacraments too. In some of the villages near Prizren, the open Catholics were almost all female.[48] The men would be Muslims in public, circumcising their sons and attending the mosques; but in their homes they would baptize their children, confess, take Holy Communion, observe vigils and Lent, and say Masses for the dead. More problematically, some of the men would marry Muslim girls and then secretly convert them to Christianity; these would thus become female crypto-Catholics.[49] But in cases where the men were genuine converts to Islam (or if the priests refused to give the sacraments to the outwardly Muslim menfolk), husbands would often try to stop the Catholic clergy from visiting their wives at all. As one priest explained: 'Being deprived of the sacraments themselves, they want their wives to be deprived of them as well, saying, "Where we are going, it's good that our wives should come too." '[50] And several reports observed that when the priests obeyed instructions from Rome and refused the sacraments altogether, the crypto-Catholics became bitter enemies of the clergy. One priest was threatened with death by disgruntled crypto-Catholics, and Mazarek noted that when these people were shunned by the Church in this way, they turned into 'the worst persecutors of the Catholics'.[51]

These were not the only problems Mazarek had on his mind. Although he enjoyed the patronage of a few benign local lords, it came at a price: he had to keep them constantly supplied with presents (the usual fancy goods from Venice), and attend to their various whims. One powerful lord summoned him to Peć because he wanted an exorcism to cure him of impotence; the governor of Novo Brdo ordered him to give holy oil and water to his wife, who suffered from 'a certain curious female malady'; and to placate local Muslims the Archbishop was also required to 'visit their sick and even exorcise and bless their animals'.[52] Maintaining good relations with all the local pashas must have required great skills of diplomacy, given that they were involved in frequent clashes and power-struggles among themselves. In 1785 Mazarek wrote that 'terrible wars among the Turks' had been going on since the 1750s; and for the next six years he was unable to travel through his archdiocese because of 'the continual and general bloody civil wars between the Ottoman governors of almost every city in Serbia'.[53] As in many other parts of the Ottoman Empire in the eighteenth century, real power in the Kosovo region had devolved upon men from prominent local families with large private armies of retainers. In the case of Kosovo, the local dynasties went back a surprisingly long way: the Mahmutbegolli family, for example (known also just as Begolli) had supplied governors of Peć in the late sixteenth century, and claimed descent from the Dukagjin family of medieval Albania.[54] Other important families were the Rotul dynasty, which ruled Prizren from the 1770s to 1836, and the Gjinolli family whose members ruled Prishtina and Gjilan (Srb.: Gnjilane), becoming so powerful in the early nineteenth century were they were called the 'second rulers' of Kosovo after the Sultan.[55]

In the late eighteenth century, however, there was just one local dynasty that could rival – and did in fact openly challenge – the Sultan: the Bushati or Bushatli family of Shkodra. 'Old Mehmet' Bushati became governor of the sancak of Shkodra (which included Peć) in 1757, and then gradually extended his rule over the whole of northern Albania. His ambitions of becoming an independent prince were cut short by his death in 1775, but his younger son Mahmut had similar plans; in 1785 he conquered parts of southern Albania and much of Kosovo too. Modelling himself (it was said) on Skanderbeg, he set up a 'Confederation of Illyria', based in Montenegro, and called on both Slavs and Albanians for support. Popular history in the West has taken too little interest in this extraordinary man, compared with the attention it has lavished on his southern counterpart, Ali pasha, the 'Lion of Ioannina'; Mahmut suffers from the fact that he was never visited by Romantic English travellers. Twice the Sultan sent a large army against him; twice he withdrew to his fortress at Shkodra, survived the siege and then destroyed the besieging forces.[56]

Several times he campaigned in Kosovo: in 1795, for example, he took his army to Prizren, smashed the forces put up against him by the local Rotul dynasty, and installed his own nephew as governor of the town. The Catholic chronicler who recorded these events was enthusiastic in his praises of the man: 'I would go so far', he wrote, 'as to compare him to a Maccabaeus, and even to the venerated Skanderbeg; if only he had been a Catholic, in my opinion he would have been the equal of either of them.'[57] Archbishop Mazarek wrote that he was a just ruler, good to 'Christians' and very active against robbers, and that his protection of the Christians was one of the things the Ottoman authorities held against him. Like other Catholics of this period, however, Mazarek used 'Christian' to mean 'Catholic' only; he also wrote that Mahmut 'has taken countless purses of money from the Serbians, and has robbed them of all their possessions, food and livestock, and has taken the lot to Shkodra'. And in general Mazarek observed that many of the civil wars between the various lords of Kosovo were stirred up by Mahmut Bushati, as part of a deliberate policy of divide and rule.[58]

Mahmut's death in 1796 came just as he was embarking on his most ambitious plan of all: a conquest of much of the western Balkans as an independent ally of the revolutionary French army. The younger brother who succeeded him, however, abandoned all such plans. The lords of Kosovo were able to extend their own local power once more. Their rule was arbitrary, and largely uncontrolled from Istanbul; and the decades of fighting in the region had taken their toll on the population and the economy. A French officer who travelled through Kosovo in 1813 observed north of Prishtina that farming and village life had retreated to the hills; to the south of the town he noted that 'this country has only a quarter of the population it should have.' Prishtina itself, he said, looked impressive from a distance, but 'close up, it is a mass of muddy streets and houses made of earth.' Kaçanik pleased him even less: 'May my enemies', he exclaimed, 'live and die in Kaçanik!'[59]

Not until the late nineteenth century would the major towns of Kosovo recover the population levels they had enjoyed before 1690. Prishtina in 1812, for example, had just over half the number of inhabitants it had had in the 1680s.[60] Mining, which had originally supported the economy of several of them, declined almost to vanishing point: one early-eighteenth-century Ottoman attempt to revive mining operations at Trepça ended fairly quickly in failure.[61] Nevertheless, commerce did continue (Venetian records for 1741–1800 reveal contracts with six local Muslim merchants in Gjakova, for example), and traditions of urban life, such as the guild system, were kept up. Indeed, it was the powerful guildsmen, such as the tanners, who supplied political support – and bodies of armed men – to the local dynastic rulers.[62] The dervish orders expanded their activities considerably in the eighteenth century: the Halveti order, for example, made Prizren one of its main centres from 1713 onwards, and the Sa'di order, having founded its first tekke in Gjakova in 1699, extended its influence through south-western Kosovo. It is said that the dervishes were particularly active in missionary work among the crypto-Catholics.[63] Once again, there are signs that conversion to Islam could involve theological persuasion, as well as economic pressure: Mazarek commented in 1760 on the 'subtle arts' of those Muslims who persuaded Catholics to join their faith on the grounds that the principles of Islam were already contained in the Gospels.[64]

For the life of the Orthodox community during this period the evidence is very scanty, compared with the rich documentation of the Catholics. Despite all their tribulations, the Orthodox Slav population did keep up some minimal cultural life, based on the institutions of their Church. It seems likely that they maintained some small schools, since we know that there were literate Serbs in Prizren (not only priests) in the eighteenth century; but the detailed evidence has not survived.[65] Some modern Serbian writers present this period of Kosovo's history as an unremitting sequence of oppressions against the Serbs, with their status being reduced to the lowest place in the pecking order, and their numbers being gradually swamped by immigrant Albanians. As we have seen, there is plenty of evidence of oppressions against the Serbs, and there is also evidence of steady Albanian immigration. But such an account of their sufferings needs to be qualified on several points.

First, the privileged status enjoyed by the Orthodox vis-à-vis the Catholics continued for a long time; as late as 1791 Archbishop Mazarek could report that he was taunted by 'proud Orthodox and schismatic people' in Prizren, who asked if he came accompanied by an honorary guard of Janissaries, as their Patriarch did.[66] Secondly, the outrages perpetrated by local rulers and armed gangs were not usually aimed at Serbs *qua* Serbs: all Christians were easy prey, and Muslim peasants were also robbed and oppressed. In 1772 Mazarek wrote that the Catholics and Orthodox were suffering equally, 'and so do the Muslims themselves, who devour one another, kill one another, and pillage one another'; all the villages, he exclaimed, 'Catholic and Orthodox and Muslim, have indeed been exterminated and depopulated'.[67]

Thirdly, the idea that a fixed but gradually eroded Serb population was swamped by a tide of Albanian immigration is misleadingly schematic. There was flux and emigration, settlement and resettlement, in all sectors of the population. Waves of Orthodox people also migrated into Kosovo: the forced migration of one body of Vasojević clansmen has already been mentioned, and a large group of Orthodox Vlachs, most of whom would eventually be assimilated into the Serbian Orthodox population, came in the 1770s. (These will be discussed in Chapter 11.) Just as Catholic Albanian highlanders moved into Kosovo from the Malësi, so Orthodox Slav ones from the mountains of Montenegro moved into the Sandžak of Novi Pazar; from there, many also spread into northern Kosovo. Members of all the Montenegrin clans took part in this population drift, though they tended to be lumped together under the clan-name 'Vasojević'.[68] Their reasons for moving were just the same as those of the Albanians: a search for better land or grazing, and a desire to escape from vendettas. One French traveller in Kosovo noted in 1911 that some parts of northern Kosovo which had lost their Serbs in the eighteenth century had regained a Slav population not long afterwards: villages near Vuçitërn which had been entirely 'Albanianized' up to 100 or eighty years ago, he wrote, had then become completely repopulated by Slavs. Part of the explanation for this, he said, was that these Slav highlanders (like their Albanian equivalents) had a very high birth-rate.[69] Possibly Archbishop Mazarek was referring to something similar when he wrote in 1772 that countless Orthodox people had been killed, 'but they have become numerous once again.'[70]

Orthodox people moved to Kosovo not only from Montenegro, but from all the other surrounding areas too. In the 1930s a Serb researcher took down details of the oral family traditions of all the households in several areas of Eastern Kosovo. He recorded that only a small proportion of Serb families had been living in the same place for 200 years or more. In one large section of Eastern Kosovo, running north and south of Prishtina, he was able to categorize the Serb households as follows: leaving aside the 1,437 colonist families who had come after 1912, there were 706 households of 'old inhabitants' and 1,819 households of 'immigrants'. The family traditions of the latter recorded that 780 of them had come from Macedonia, northern Albania, Montenegro, Bosnia–Hercegovina and central or northern Serbia, while the rest had moved from other parts of Kosovo. In the Gornja Morava district (the south-eastern corner of Kosovo) the Serb population consisted of 1,143 households of 'old inhabitants' and 1,205 of 'immigrants', fewer than 200 of whom had migrated from other parts of Kosovo.[71] Of the Albanian families he investigated in these areas, only a small minority were 'old inhabitants'. The proportions would have been different if he had done his research in Western Kosovo; but in any case the whole debate which pits fixed Serbs against mobile Albanians is, as his researches demonstrate, rather bogus. Most of the families in any part of Kosovo are known to have come from somewhere else.

Finally, this period also marks the first opportunity Serbs in Kosovo had to emigrate in order to live in a modern Serbian state. In 1804 the Serb revolt began in north-central Serbia, the first step on the road to an independent Serbian kingdom. Several Serbs from Kosovo were active in the Serbian cause: one, a well-known merchant from Prizren called Andrija, organized the smuggling of weapons and gunpowder to the rebels in Belgrade. (Some Albanians also took part on the Serb side, including the prominent fighter Kondë Bajraktari.)[72] In the first five years of the revolt the fighting spread southwards as far as the Sandžak of Novi Pazar, close to the Kosovo border; there was unrest in northern Kosovo, and some Serb četas (bands) penetrated there. The pashas of

Kosovo and northern Albania raised armies and fought several battles against the Serb forces in 1809; the pasha of Prishtina seems also to have adopted a policy of moving Serb peasants out of the sensitive Lab region of north-eastern Kosovo, and replacing them with Albanians.[73] Although Ottoman forces did eventually reconquer the whole Serbian territory, a renewal of the revolt persuaded the Sultan to agree, in 1815, to give extensive powers of self-administration to a Serbian statelet under its own *knez* or prince. This small state, formally set up in 1817, covered only the district of Belgrade (not extending as far south as Niš); it was still under Ottoman sovereignty, and Ottoman garrisons remained in place.[74] But its degrees of autonomy would grow, until in 1878, when it was already the most powerful Christian state in the Balkans, its full independence would finally be recognized.

10

Reform and resistance: 1817–1878

THE POPULAR VERSION of nineteenth-century Balkan history is extremely simple: it is a story of people struggling to be free on the one hand, and an illiberal, autocratic Ottoman state trying to suppress them on the other. The reality was more complicated. Starting in the reign of Sultan Mahmut II (1808–39), the Ottomans introduced an ambitious sequence of reforms, designed to turn the Empire into a modern (which meant, in many respects, Westernized) state. Much of the original impetus for reform came from observing how effective Western armies were in the Napoleonic period, and realizing that the Ottomans had a huge amount of catching up to do. The military reform programme – which included suppressing the Janissaries and introducing Western-style uniforms (1826), sending officers to be trained in France (1827) and abolishing the obsolete timar system (1831) – may not have been in itself either liberal or illiberal; but other reforms which followed later, such as the development of a state education system and the proclamation of equal rights for non-Muslims, could be called liberalizing measures.[1] In order to implement any of these reforms, however, it was necessary for the central administration in Istanbul to win back real power from the local lords who had usurped it in most provinces of the Empire. And the move to centralize power, while it may have been the strategic ally of a liberalization programme, was sometimes indistinguishable at the tactical level from sheer brutal oppression.

For those in the provinces, therefore, various different responses were possible. Those with the strongest reason to oppose the central power of the Ottoman state were the provincial rulers, who fought hard to retain their own little local empires. If they maltreated their own subjects, those suffering subjects might find themselves taking the side of the Sultan, or at least appealing to him for support. (The Serbian revolt of 1804 had begun like that, with Christian Serbs protesting against a local coup by senior Janissary officers who refused to carry out the Sultan's pro-Serbian reforms.) Among the Christian populations of south-eastern Europe the spread of nationalist ideas made it possible in this period to envisage a radically different solution: throwing off Ottoman rule and creating independent national states. Those who favoured this option would usually be opposed both to the local pashas and to Istanbul. But among the Muslim populations of the Balkans – above all, in Bosnia and the Albanian lands – such an option was at first almost unthinkable. Observing how the nascent Christian states killed or ejected their Muslim subjects (not only the Turkish-speaking ones), and knowing that those states had much wider territorial ambitions, they regarded membership of a still powerful empire as their only guarantee against being conquered and expelled themselves. Yet at the same time, although they may have suffered under their local rulers, they resented the reforming and centralizing programme imposed by Istanbul: they disliked the new obligations it imposed (taxes and conscription), and they saw the gradual extension of equal rights to the Christian subjects of the Empire as a series of concessions to pressures from Christian powers, which might lead eventually to the handover of their territories to the new Christian states in the region.

All these conflicting tendencies can be seen in the history of nineteenth-century Kosovo. Modern writers do not do justice to the complexities of that history if they treat it either as a tragic story of Serbs being systematically oppressed by Albanians, or as a heroic story of Albanians fighting consistently for national liberation. One event, for example, which fits neither of those patterns was the great protest march of 1822, in which 3,000 people tried to walk from Kosovo to Istanbul to demand the removal of the tyrannical Maliq pasha Gjinolli, who resided in Prishtina. Christian raya did take part in this protest, but its organizers were the local Muslim notables, including five landowners and the imams (prayer-leaders) of twelve mosques: the kadı of Prishtina, forwarding their earlier petition to Istanbul, had described them as 'all the learned men, all the clerics, all the noble and honourable people, all the powerless people, the raya and the rest'. The protest was in the end unsuccessful; although the Grand Vizier was in favour of granting its main demand, he was overruled by others on the state council, and most of the protestors were simply arrested en route. Its significance lies not in its consequences but in what it tells us about the political understanding of ordinary people at this stage: their response to local oppression was not rebellion, but appeal to higher authority.[2]

This episode also reveals that Muslims as well as Christians suffered under some of the local rulers. The main complaints in the first of several petitions were that Maliq and his nephew Jashar had murdered fifty Muslims, stolen their property, seized Christian girls, and forced Muslim girls to marry their followers. (These forced marriages were a common ploy, involving brotherless girls whose husbands could then inherit their fathers' property.) Jashar did show real hostility to Christianity: he is said to have demolished four churches.[3] But on the other hand there are warm accounts, by Kosovo Serbs, of some of the local pashas of this period. Rustem pasha Rotul, who ruled in Prizren from 1801 to 1806, was remembered by the Serbs there as having been 'very well-disposed' towards them; in general, local Serb tradition recalled that all the Rotul dynasty dealt strictly with wrong-doers and maintained 'complete security of property' for the inhabitants. The most important of the Rotul in Prizren, Mahmut pasha, who ruled from 1809 to 1836, was a benevolent and quirky man who kept two Serb villagers in his household as court fools: they were permitted to make criticisms of him that no one else would have dared express. In his attitude to religion he was 'very tolerant' (according to local Serb tradition), and he was irritated when over-zealous followers persuaded one of his favourite tenants, an Orthodox Serb, to convert to Islam. His approach to religious disputes was also rather original: once, when he asked a village priest and a hoca (Muslim teacher) to conduct a theological argument in front of him, and they bashfully refused, he made them have a wrestling match instead.[4]

Once again, the most powerful ruler in the whole region was a Bushati lord of Shkodra. When war broke out between the Ottoman Empire and Russia in 1828, Mustafa Bushati (a nephew of the Francophile Mahmut) was much courted by the Sultan, who needed his assistance in raising troops: for this purpose, more than half of Albania was put under his personal administration. He did bring an army to the front (in northern Bulgaria), but took little part in the fighting, and was welcomed by local

Ottomans as an independent force opposed to the Sultan's reforms.[5] After the war most of his Albanian territories were officially transferred (in early 1831) to the Grand Vizier. Mustafa was also ordered to accept a garrison of the new regular army in Shkodra, and to disarm the local Albanians. With the backing of all the Shkodran notables and many of the pashas of Kosovo he decided to reject these instructions; but by that time the Grand Vizier was already marching with an army against him. Mustafa turned to two potential allies. One was Prince Miloš of the semi-autonomous Serbian state; Miloš received his envoy, promised him the sum of 25 million akçes (which was never delivered), and then sent an envoy of his own to the Sultan to inform him of Mustafa's movements. The other was a charismatic rebel leader in Bosnia, Husein of Gradačac, who had just overthrown the official governor there. Husein was, like Mustafa, a local ruler who resented the new military and administrative reforms and wanted more autonomy; so the two agreed to work together.[6]

Unfortunately for Mustafa, their actions were poorly coordinated. He himself marched through Kosovo, gathering support as he went from the pashas of Peć, Gjakova, Prizren and Prishtina, and then took over the whole of northern Macedonia and parts of western Bulgaria. But in mid-April, while his ally Husein was just gathering his own army in Bosnia, Mustafa Bushati was defeated in a sequence of three battles with the Grand Vizier in Macedonia, and was forced to flee to Shkodra. The Grand Vizier decided to deal leniently with Kosovo. Hoping that such treatment would conciliate the Bosnians, he took a few pashas as hostages but made no heavy reprisals, and raised some local troops. Bosnian forces meanwhile were moving into the Novi Pazar district in May, and by June they numbered at least 20,000 men; they then advanced into Kosovo, and on 16 July 1831 Husein's army fought a major battle against the Grand Vizier's troops at Lipljan, at the southern end of the Kosovo Polje plateau. At the critical moment, the Albanians recruited in Prizren abandoned the Grand Vizier and went over to Husein's side. The Ottoman army was routed; the Vizier's chief commander was killed, and the Vizier, himself wounded, fled to Skopje.[7] This encounter deserves to be known as the third battle of Kosovo; if only Husein had followed up his victory, it might have changed the whole history of Bosnia, Kosovo and Albania. But instead he allowed himself to be fobbed off with concessions and promises, while Ottoman statecraft cleverly set his supporters against one another. He returned to Bosnia, from where, in the following year, he was expelled by an Ottoman army. Mustafa Bushati, meanwhile, had been besieged in Shkodra and had surrendered in October 1831.

The main consequence of this episode for Kosovo was the ending of uncontrolled rule by local dynasties. The Grand Vizier spent the summer of 1832 in Kosovo, and only in September of that year did he report that the rebellion there had finally been crushed.[8] Some of the local rulers, such as Jashar pasha and Mahmut pasha Rotul, stayed in place for a while, but were kept more directly under supervision by Istanbul; in 1836 Mahmut Rotul was arrested and sent into exile on suspicion of supporting another rebellion in Shkodra, and by the end of that year several of the other local lords had been deposed and executed.[9] Although the most troublesome paşalıks, Prizren and Peć, were now placed under direct military rule, this probably had little effect outside the towns where the garrisons were stationed. Conscription was resisted; those who did perform military service rebelled against the Western-style uniforms; and there were numerous local revolts, including a large uprising in Prizren in 1839 which drove the governor out of the town.[10]

That year saw the promulgation of a major new series of reforms by the new sixteen-year-old Sultan, Abdülmecit. The widely abused system of tax-farming was abolished, military recruitment was put on a new basis, and equal security and legal rights were proclaimed for all subjects, regardless of religion. Other reforms in the early 1840s included a new penal code and (after much pressure from the British Ambassador in Istanbul) a declaration in 1844 that Muslim converts from Christianity who wanted to revert to the Christian faith would no longer be subject to the death penalty.[11]

All these measures were much easier to announce in Istanbul than to put into effect in unruly territories such as Kosovo. The first attempt to impose the new conscription system in Kosovo and northern Albania was made in 1844; accompanied by new taxes and some attempts to disarm the local population, it was intensely unpopular. A revolt in Prishtina and Skopje was quickly crushed by the Ottoman army, but in the following year a larger force had to be sent to deal with an uprising in Western Kosovo (centring on Gjakova) and all the neighbouring areas

Kosovo

of the Malësi. Many of the Kosovo chiefs were imprisoned, and some sort of order was imposed; guns were confiscated, and conscription and tax-collection were carried out, though only while the army was present.[12] After 1845 there were no major revolts in Kosovo for a decade. Military rule seems to have been relaxed, and most of Kosovo was joined with Skopje in an eyalet (administrative province), governed first from Skopje itself, and later from Prizren.[13] The Archbishop of Skopje would write in 1853 that a long period of civil war in Kosovo had come to an end in 1845; but he added that killings were still so frequent that 'These districts may be regarded as being in a state of permanent revolution and anarchy.'[14]

A dramatic example of the gap between promise and performance, where the Ottoman reforms were concerned, arose over the crypto-Catholics of Kosovo. When the Ottoman army commander imposed order in Gjakova in the summer of 1845 and began conscripting the local men, the call-up was applied only to Muslims. (This was the traditional Ottoman policy, although the new army law of 1843 did in principle make Christians liable for military service too.)[15] A group of crypto-Catholics from nearby villages went to the Catholic church in Gjakova and declared themselves as Christians; and the same happened soon afterwards in Peć. Seventy of these men then made a public declaration of Christianity in the army camp. This was an act of some bravery: everyone in this part of Kosovo would have remembered the fate of a group of Catholics in Rugovo, a village west of Peć, who had Muslim names but professed Catholicism openly, and were executed by the local pasha in 1817.[16] The crypto-Catholics who declared themselves in 1845 were also put into prison, but the army commander did at least order an inquiry, at which the Catholic priests were allowed to make their case. When they argued that these people had only simulated Muslim beliefs in order to avoid oppression, the local Ottoman officials raised the counter-example of the Fandi, a warlike Catholic clan (and sub-branch of the Mirdita) who had moved into the area west of Gjakova in recent decades. 'Why is it that the Fandi have never been disturbed in their religious affairs?' they asked, rhetorically. The parish priest of Gjakova replied that they were a powerful clan who could defend themselves, whereas his crypto-Catholics were 'scattered among completely Muslim villages'. After six weeks in gaol (during which two died of dysentery), the Catholics were released, on payment of a fine. Fifty more heads of family promptly came out as Christians, bringing the total to more than 150.[17]

Later that year, and in the spring of 1846, more crypto-Catholics declared themselves in the villages of the Skopska Crna Gora. The treatment they received was harsher: both they and their priest were thrown into prison, and when they failed to pay the allotted fine (despite, or perhaps because of, the confiscation of all their property), they were sent into exile in Anatolia. Roughly 150 people (twenty-five families) underwent this punishment, with their priest; twenty of them perished on the way to Anatolia, and at least seventy more died in exile before they were finally permitted to come home two years later.[18] Similar problems involving the conscription of crypto-Catholics arose again in 1849 and 1850.[19] But the position of the Catholic Church did generally improve, and the leverage exerted by Western diplomats in Istanbul was enormously increased during the period of the Crimean War, when the Ottoman state was allied with European powers against Russia. In 1856 another important reform decree was issued declaring full equality of rights among Muslim and non-Muslim subjects and full freedom of religion; this decree, which included a remarkable clause against hate-speech (forbidding officials to use words or expressions 'tending to make one class of my subjects inferior to another class on account of religion, language or race'), also confirmed that apostasy from Islam was no longer punishable by death.[20] After this, the persecution of the Kosovo crypto-Catholics seems to have ceased. But many families would retain their Muslim camouflage for several generations to come.[21]

Although the principles of the Ottoman reforms were often heavily diluted by the time their effects reached Kosovo, these decades do show a steady growth of cultural and educational activity by all the communities there. A new system of Turkish-language state schools was introduced from the 1830s onwards: by the mid-1860s Prizren, for example, had seventeen elementary schools for boys, seven for girls, and one secondary school. There were also medreses (Islamic seminaries) in six Kosovo towns.[22] The Serbs opened two elementary schools in Prizren in 1836, and by 1848 they had schools in Gjakova, Peć, Vuçitërn and Gračanica too; the Catholics had schools in Prizren, Gjakova, Peć, Janjevo and Stublla (Srb.: Stubla; a village near Gjilan), with teaching in

Italian.[23] According to the reform decree of 1856, every community had the right to set up public schools; the Ottoman state allowed the funding of these to come from outside powers, such as Austria–Hungary, Serbia and Russia. A later 'School Law' of 1869 also declared that teaching could be in the local language. (This right had long been granted to the Serbs, but the Ottoman state would nevertheless continue to deny it to the Albanians.)[24] The Kosovo Serbs were able to set up religious–cultural societies, such as the 'Society of St Basil', founded in 1860 to restore an old church of that name; in 1856 they started to build a new church in Prizren, dedicated to St George; and in 1871 they opened an Orthodox seminary there as well.[25]

Many of these activities of the Serb community received financial support either from the increasingly autonomous Serbian state, or from Russia, its chief protector on the international stage. This could be a source of some friction, since the Orthodox hierarchy in Kosovo was still under Greek control. The Greek Metropolitans, who sold bishoprics for up to 8 million akçes each, were widely disliked by their flock; they were also highly suspicious of the Serbian Church to the north, whose efforts in support of religious life in Kosovo they interpreted as attempts to undermine their own authority. One Serbian teacher who came to Prizren in 1857, Nikola Musulin, had trained in the Serbian Orthodox seminary at Sremski Karlovci, and was keen to spread Serb national–religious ideas; this led to such a clash with the Metropolitan of Prizren that he was placed under an anathema by the Patriarch of Constantinople, and expelled in 1859.[26]

These Serbian-sponsored activities were not, of course, purely religious in their aims. Musulin's teachings included a call for 'national emancipation', meaning a pro-Serbian revolt against Ottoman rule. Ilija Garašanin, a Serbian minister and one of the chief ideologists of Serbian nationalism, took a special interest in Serb cultural life in Kosovo, and sent two Serbian schoolteachers to Prizren in 1866. A committee was formed in Belgrade to organize Serb propaganda (not only to rouse Serbs against the Ottomans, but also to compete against Bulgarian propaganda for the loyalties of the Macedonian Slavs); it managed to set up sixty-one schools in 'unredeemed' areas to the south of the then Serbian state. In 1873 one of its members, Miloš Milojević, opened a school in Belgrade for children from those territories, at which speeches celebrating Serbian history were declaimed every Sunday; and when war broke out between Serbia and the Ottoman Empire in 1876, Milojević led a detachment of his pupils into battle.[27]

Serbian politicians such as Garašanin had other, more subtle political strategies for undermining Ottoman rule in the Albanian-inhabited lands. They knew that they could not appeal directly to the Muslim Albanians: the treatment of Muslims in Serbia from 1804 onwards had been too notoriously violent and hostile for that. (Prince Miloš, who ruled from 1815 to 1839, had taken special trouble to expel Muslim Albanians from his territory.)[28] But with the Catholics of northern Albania Garašanin pursued an elaborate political courtship, corresponding in Latin from 1846 onwards with a Catholic priest, Gaspër Krasniqi. Through him he made contact with the leader of the powerful Mirdita clan, and discussed sending money via the prince-bishop of Montenegro to support a Mirdita rebellion in Albania. Nothing came of these plans, although it is noteworthy that the Mirdita refused to respond to the Ottoman call-up during the brief Ottoman–Montenegrin war of 1862. After that war the contacts were renewed, first with Krasniqi and then with his successor as abbot of the Mirdita, Prenk Doçi (whose secret dealings with Montenegro became sufficiently well known for him to be first imprisoned by the Ottomans, and then sent to cool his heels for six years in New Brunswick by the Vatican).[29] The lure which the Serbian politicians dangled in front of the Mirdita, the idea of an independent northern Albanian Catholic principality, did have some psychological effect. But of course its purpose, so far as the Serbs were concerned, was simply to encourage a diversionary rising, which would help them to seize territory elsewhere. And by the time the Serbian state was strong enough to conquer Kosovo, its territorial ambitions would extend to most of northern Albania too.

Conditions in mid-nineteenth-century Kosovo, although unstable, were not so intolerable as to drive people automatically to rebel. An English traveller who visited Prizren in 1850 was struck by the prosperity of the place, 'if we may judge from the costly wares in the bazaar, the well-supplied markets, the quantity of meat exposed for sale and the number of cook-shops and coffee-houses, always filled with well-dressed men'. He noted that groups of Orthodox villages could elect their own Christian mayor or *hoca-başı*, who dealt with the authorities on their behalf and also settled all civil and criminal cases in his community. And he also observed that the Patriarchate monastery at Peć was 'held in high estimation by the inhabitants, both Christian and Mahometan'.[30]

The syncretism of folk religion ensured that the most important Christian churches were generally respected by ordinary Muslims; but there was also a special tradition in Kosovo of Albanian families with the hereditary title of *vojvods* or 'guardians' of particular church buildings. Peć, Dečani, Devič and other important monasteries all had Albanian guardians of this sort (some paid, some unpaid); the fact that these families had become Muslims had not in any way affected the fulfilment of their hereditary role.[31] One elderly Serb from Gračanica whose reminiscences were recorded in 1914 said that conditions in the 1850s had been good: his family, which had some large properties in the area, had lived peacefully and without fear among the Albanians. He dated the deterioration in relations to 1864, when Circassians (Muslims driven out of the Caucasus by the Russians: see Chapter 11) were settled by the Ottomans in Kosovo, as part of a deliberate policy of building up an anti-Orthodox bulwark in the region.[32] Anti-Russian feeling at the time of the Crimean War seems also to have hardened the attitudes of the Ottomans against their own Orthodox subjects. When a revolt against taxes and conscription broke out in the Peć area in 1855, the military commander in the region used the monastery of Dečani as his head-quarters, and engaged in the forced recruitment of many local Serbs.[33]

The best years, probably, were the 1860s and early 1870s. By then Kosovo itself was fairly peaceful; the only area of chronic unrest was the Debar region, just to the south, where resistance had been encouraged by local leaders of the Bektashi order of dervishes. (The Bektashi order had been officially abolished along with the Janissaries in 1826. This made it hostile to Istanbul, but its religious unorthodoxy ensured that it could not be aligned with a narrowly traditionalist religious reaction to the reform programme. For these reasons it would later play an important part in the Albanian national movement.)[34] In 1860 the Grand Vizier – who, incidentally, had married the widow of Byron's doctor – went on a tour of inquiry round several Balkan towns, including Prishtina, with a joint Muslim–Christian commission. The commission concluded that although there was no systematic oppression of Christians, there were various problems: Christian testimony was still being rejected in court, Ottoman officials were often corrupt, and the Greek Orthodox hierarchy was guilty of great injustices.[35] In the following year an energetic governor, Midhat pasha, was put in charge of one of the main European provinces, the eyalet of Niš. He was a reformer with Western ideas, and the eyalet under his governance became a showpiece of the reformist movement. The first two problems he tackled were those of communications and security: he started a road-building programme, and set up a system of block-houses to stop the incursion of armed bands from Serbia. In the words of a laudatory biography of him later written by his son, 'He organized a *gendarmerie*, secured the peaceful collection of taxes, and put an end to all religious persecution; schools, too, were established, and hospitals for members of all religious denominations without distinction.'[36]

So successful were Midhat's reforms that they helped to inspire a complete reworking of the Ottoman administrative system. In 1864 his backers on the council of state decided that the old eyalets would be replaced by a new type of large-scale unit called a *vilayet*. (This word had been used in earlier periods, but only for a small administrative division for taxation purposes.) Each vilayet, governed by a *vali*, would be divided into sancaks, each governed by a *mutesarif*, and each of those would be divided into kazas, governed by *kaymakams*; below them would be the mayors of communes, elected by the people. At each of the three main levels of rule, there would be mixed Muslim–Christian consultative councils, some of whose members were elected by the religious communities.[37] The first vilayet to be set up was run for some time as an experiment by Midhat pasha: called the 'Danube' vilayet, it included the former eyalet of Niš (to which the eyalet of Skopje, including the whole of Kosovo, was joined in early 1865) as well as much of Bulgaria.[38] During the next three years Midhat carried through a large programme of school-building and other public works, as well as introducing a provincial newspaper.[39] In Kosovo he formed a special commission of local notables to end the violence of the Albanian blood-feuds: they agreed to impose a system of fines instead.[40]

In 1867 the system of vilayets began to be extended, with frequent revisions and adjustments, to other areas of the Empire.[41] Kosovo was at first divided between two vilayets, but in 1868 a new vilayet of Prizren was created, consisting of four sancaks: Prizren itself (a large

administrative area including almost the whole of Kosovo, plus Tetovo
and the Gusinje area which now lies on the Montenegrin side of the
Albanian–Montenegrin border), Debar, Skopje and Niš. Since there were
sizeable Albanian elements in the populations of the two last sancaks as
well, the Muslim Albanians were the strongest component of this vilayet;
but there was also a large Orthodox Slav population. Ottoman administrators usually preferred to create mixed units in this way, to reduce any
risks of national state-formation. In the period 1866–9 the Ottomans
seriously considered creating a single 'Albanian' vilayet to include the
whole of Albania and Kosovo, most of Macedonia and part of Bulgaria:
the aim would have been to restrain Slav nationalisms, and the fact that
this area would have united most of the Albanian population did not
seem to trouble the authorities at this stage.[42] Such a united Albanian
vilayet would become, however, one of the key demands of Albanian
leaders later in the century.

Before this Prizren vilayet was put in place there was one last rebellion
over taxation and conscription in Western Kosovo, which broke out in
1866 and was heavily suppressed by the Ottoman army in the winter of
1866–7.[43] Thereafter there would be no major revolt in Kosovo for just
over a decade (though a particularly unpopular kaymakam in Peć was
driven out by the people of that town in 1869).[44] Many of the reforms
pioneered by Midhat bey were introduced in the vilayet of Prizren,
including the novelty of an official local journal. The first issue of *Prizren*
came out in August 1871, with facing pages in Turkish and Serbian: it
enjoyed great success, and attracted subscribers throughout the vilayet
and beyond. The vali of the Prizren vilayet, Safet pasha, was well
disposed towards the Serbs: his decision to print half the journal in
Serbian was warmly welcomed by them, and he also encouraged the
setting up of the Orthodox seminary in Prizren (one of the professors of
which was appointed editor of the journal's Serbian section). Publication
came to an end in 1874, however, when the seat of the vilayet was moved
to Prishtina. Three years later, when the vilayet was enlarged, reorgan-
ized, and renamed the vilayet of Kosovo, a new journal was started in
Prishtina in a Turkish-only format under the title *Kosova*.[45]

By the mid-1860s there were already telegraph lines connecting
Prizren, Peć and Prishtina with Salonica and Istanbul.[46] At the end of
that decade the Ottoman government signed a contract with a Belgian

financier, Baron de Hirsch, to complete a number of projected railway lines, including one from Salonica to Prishtina. The plan was later changed to a line from Salonica via Skopje to Mitrovica, passing rather inconveniently six miles to the west of Prishtina; this railway was opened to public traffic at the end of 1874.[47] One of the reasons for building this line was military: it provided a way of getting troops and artillery quickly to a sensitive area, and Mitrovica soon became a major garrison town. Unfortunately, once Bosnia and part of the Sandžak of Novi Pazar were under Austrian control (after 1878), military–strategic fears overruled the long-cherished plan to extend this line from Mitrovica through Bosnia to western Europe. A through-route was built instead in the 1880s via Skopje, Vranje and Belgrade; this skirted round Kosovo, which thus had to remain something of a commercial backwater. Nevertheless, the fact that goods unloaded at the docks of Salonica could now be in Kosovo on the following day did have some economic effect; it also shifted Kosovo's commercial centre of gravity away from Prizren, towards Prishtina and the two railway towns of Mitrovica in the north and Ferizaj (Srb.: Ferizović, later renamed Uroševac) in the south.

The towns of Western Kosovo were still important producers of leather, sheepskins and silk-worm cocoons, exporting large quantities to Austria and Italy; and the skilled craftsmen of Prizren and Gjakova remained famous throughout the Balkans for their metalwork, their filigree silver and, above all, their guns (many of them exported to Serbia).[48] The conditions of economic life were gradually modernized and Westernized: the esnafs lost their monopoly powers and gave way to chambers of commerce, and prices were liberalized by a new Ottoman commercial code. As early as 1865 the new trades to be found in the bazaar at Prizren included eleven European-style tailors, three pharmacists, four watch-makers and no fewer than sixty-five liquor-stores.[49] Nor did Prizren suffer a rapid commercial decline: the bazaar, which had 1,200 shops in 1863, would still contain more than 1,000 in 1891. But the first small factories, saw-mills and motorized flour-mills would all be in the eastern towns of Mitrovica and Prishtina.[50]

This period saw the first attempts at modern statistical surveys of the population of the Kosovo region. It also saw the first stirrings of nationalist ethnographic arguments: such disputes, about who was in the majority, and about what the real ethnic identity was of so-called

Muslims or even of so-called Albanians, have continued with unremitting acrimony to this day. There is much room for manoeuvre in these arguments, as the evidence which has come down to us suffers from many inadequacies. The most general problem is that the Ottoman state classified people not by language but by religion: 'Muslim', 'Greek' (i.e. Greek Orthodox), and so on. Another limitation is that we know very little about how the Ottoman statistics were gathered on the ground; statistics for the towns were fairly easy to compile, but many Muslim villagers would have tried hard to escape being counted, in order to avoid military service.

Some official census figures do exist for the early 1870s, but they are of limited use: they appear to list all inhabitants, male and female, for the regions of Kosovo, but in fact they do so for the major towns only. Putting the six principal towns of Kosovo together, this gives a total of 90,893 Muslims and 39,874 non-Muslims: a proportion of 70:30 per cent.[51] For more reliable totals for the whole population we have to wait until the 1890s, when an Austrian study was published, based on a careful analysis of Ottoman statistics. Taking the administrative units of Prishtina, Peć and Prizren, and omitting those areas (such as Luma) which lie outside Kosovo itself, this study yields a total of 246,450 Muslims and 93,750 non-Muslims: again, a proportion of 72:28 per cent.[52] (The proportion is probably more reliable than the absolute figures, which can be presumed to be underestimates.) Since we know that between the 1870s and the 1890s there had been an influx of perhaps 50,000 Muslim refugees and a similar (probably slightly smaller) outflow of Serbs, we can guess that the overall figures in the 1870s would have been closer to a ratio of 60:40 per cent. These overall figures conceal a regional imbalance. An estimate for the paşalıks of Western Kosovo in the 1830s gave a total of 114,000 Muslims and 81,000 Christians: a ratio of 58:42 per cent.[53] In the western part of Kosovo the Muslim proportion certainly strengthened as the century progressed: the detailed surveys of villages conducted by the Russian consul Yastrebov from the 1870s onwards, for example, suggest a heavy preponderance of Muslims.[54] But in parts of Eastern Kosovo, especially to the south and east of Prishtina, Orthodox Serbs probably formed a majority in the countryside.[55]

We can assume that most of the non-Muslims were Serbs. There were roughly 500 Jews, 2–3,000 Orthodox Vlachs (who were being gradually Serbianized), perhaps a few thousand Orthodox Gypsies and, by the 1870s, about 11,000 Catholics, of whom at least two-thirds were Albanian-speakers.[56] (The others were Slav-speakers but did not identify themselves as Serbs, since they were descended mainly from immigrants from Dalmatia.) There was also a small number of Orthodox families in Peć who had Albanian as their mother tongue.[57] Taking all these together, the total number of Serbs would be the total of non-Muslims minus approximately 18,000.

Similarly, not all Muslims were Albanians. By the 1890s, when the Austrian statistics were published, there were roughly 6,000 Circassians and at least 10,000 Muslim Gypsies. Many of the latter, however, spoke Albanian in the home. More difficult to distinguish are the urban families identified as 'Osmanlı', i.e. Ottoman Turkish; some of these, especially in Prizren, were Albanian families which had sent their sons off to be educated in Istanbul and had become fully bilingual. Altogether there were probably no more than 5,000 genuine 'Turks' in Kosovo, excluding temporary residents such as soldiers in garrisons.[58] Even more problematic, however, are the Muslim Slavs. It is natural to assume that many Slavs did convert to Islam during the Ottoman period, just as they did in neighbouring areas such as Macedonia and the Sandžak; but it is often difficult to locate or identify these people using the existing historical evidence. The best-attested group of Slav-speaking Muslims in Kosovo consisted of the inhabitants of the Gora, a mountain region to the south of Prizren containing roughly thirty villages with 2,600 households. According to local tradition, the main reason why these people had converted to Islam was the neglect or hostility shown to them by Greek bishops after the closure of the Serbian Patriarchate in 1766 (though some may already have become Muslims by then).[59] Two other areas of rural Muslim Slavs contained roughly 1,100 households; and there were also some Slav-speaking Muslims in the towns of Prizren and Prishtina.[60] The Austrian analysis published in the 1890s gave a total of 57,300 'Muslim Serbs' in Kosovo; but this included many refugees who had come to Kosovo in 1878, when Bosnia was occupied by Austria and other territories were handed over to Serbia and Montenegro.

All these Slavs are usually enlisted, for the sake of historical–ethnographic polemics, in the ranks of the Serbs in the 'Serb versus

Albanian' debate; but the Muslim Slavs, although clearly aware that they
had a different ethnic identity from the Albanians, did not identify with
the Orthodox Serbs. On the contrary, there are many reports that the
Slav Muslims (above all, the refugees who had fled to avoid living under
'infidel' rule) were much more hostile to the Orthodox Serbs than the
local Muslim Albanians were. Some, indeed, were so reluctant to be
identified in any way with the Serbs that they claimed to be descended
from Jews instead.[61]

Having made all these statistical adjustments, it is still possible to say
with reasonable certainty that the population of Kosovo contained
an absolute majority of Albanian-speakers over Slav-speakers in the
mid-nineteenth century. At this point in the argument, however, the
advocates of a Serb majority introduce a claim which was first made
during precisely this period, and which has dogged all debate on this
topic ever since: the 'Arnautaš' thesis. This is the thesis which says first
that many of the so-called Albanians were in fact Albanianized Slavs (for
whom there was a special word, 'Arnautaš' instead of 'Arnaut'), and
secondly that they should therefore be counted on the Serb side of the
equation. The second half of this thesis can be rejected as an indefensible
argument about how to categorize people: it admits that these Albanian-
speakers lost the use of the Serbian language and identified themselves
with other Albanian-speaking Muslims, and yet it still insists that they
be regarded as Serbs. On those grounds any Englishman called Beau-
champ or Beaumont would have to be reclassified as a Frenchman, on
the grounds that his ancestors were Normans (and perhaps they would
then be re-classified in turn as Norwegians, since the Normans were
originally Norsemen). Earlier in this book it was suggested that if
medieval Albanians were so Serbianized that they stopped speaking
Albanian, then it was reasonable to say that they had stopped being
Albanians and had become Serbs. The converse must surely also apply
to Serbs who became Albanians.

The first part of the Arnautaš thesis, however, is a factual claim, which
asserts that many Slavs in Kosovo had been culturally and linguistically
Albanianized. There is nothing implausible about this in principle. Even
the existence of a special word, 'Arnautaš', suggests that some such
process of Albanianization took place, although it must be said that the
word is hard to find outside the texts written by Serbian authors

propounding the 'Arnautaš' thesis. (It is not in the standard dictionary of the Kosovo Serbian dialect, nor was it listed by the great lexicographer Vuk Karadžic, though he did include *arnaućenje*, meaning 'turning into an Albanian'.)[62] Some specific examples are quite well attested in the historical literature. The best known is the case of the Luma district, which lies just outside Kosovo, to the south-west. Here all sources agree that the Luma villages first converted to Islam and then, mainly in the eighteenth century, shifted linguistically from Slav to Albanian.[63] Another area where the same is believed to have happened is the Opoja (Srb.: Opolje) district south of Prizren. At the end of the century the Serbian consul Branislav Nušić also observed this process happening in Orahovac (north of Prizren), where more than half the population of 500 households were Muslim Slavs who were beginning to speak Albanian because they married Albanian girls. And ten years later another writer noted that some of the 'Bošnjaks' (Muslim Slavs) from the Sandžak who had settled in the Mitrovica area of northern Kosovo were beginning to adopt the Albanian language.[64]

No ethnic groups in the Balkans ever lived in completely watertight compartments: there has been assimilation in almost every direction across ethnic and linguistic barriers. The conversion of Albanians into Serbs in the Middle Ages has already been noted; the case of the Slavicized Archbishop Mazarek, from the Mazrreku family, supplied a later example; and in nearby areas such as the Sandžak the Slavicization of Albanians continued well into the twentieth century. (Some of the bilingual singers of folk epics recorded there by Albert Lord and Milman Parry in the 1930s came from villages, or families, which had once been Albanian but were now becoming mainly Slav-speaking.)[65] So the question in the case of the Albanianization of Kosovo Slavs is not 'Did it happen?' (to which the answer is evidently 'Yes'), but 'How widespread a phenomenon was it?'

Apart from the areas mentioned above, there is no evidence for any Albanianization of entire Slav districts in Kosovo comparable to what happened in the Luma area. On the contrary, the example of the Gora villages and other Slav Muslim districts suggests that it was quite possible to be Islamicized without being Albanianized too. Marriage to Albanian women did not automatically create Albanian-speaking households: Slav-speaking Catholics who married Albanian girls, for example, made them speak Serbo-Croat in the home, and in any case relations between the Muslim Slavs and the Muslim Albanians were generally quite distant, with only limited inter-marriage.[66]

Lacking direct evidence to support their claims, many Serbian writers have depended on an indirect argument: they suppose that any trace of folk-religious practices with Orthodox origins among the Kosovo Albanians is sufficient proof that they were originally Orthodox Slavs. Thus the cult of popular saints such as St George or St Nicholas, or the celebration of a family patron saint's day (the so-called *slava* of the Serbs), or the ceremony of cutting a special Yule-log at Christmas, are all adduced as proof that the Albanians are 'really' Slavs.[67] Such an argument begs many questions. Of course it must be true that the ancestors of the Muslims were originally Christians, whether Orthodox or Catholic. Some may have been Albanian-speaking members of the Orthodox Church: a group of villages in the Reka district north of Debar consists of Orthodox Albanians to this day. Others would have been Albanian Catholics. To suppose that the celebration of an Orthodox saint's day or some other Orthodox religious practice implies descent from Orthodox Serbs (or even, as is sometimes claimed, consciousness of such descent) is to misunderstand the whole nature of folk-religious syncretism in the Balkans. And the claim that practices such as the celebration of the slava or the Yule-log are peculiar markers of Serb identity is quite false. The slava, which has pre-Christian origins, was popular among Catholics and Muslims in northern Albania as well as Catholics in Dalmatia, Bosnia and Slavonia, and has been found among the Orthodox as far afield as eastern Bulgaria and Moldova; and the Yule-log is a pagan survival which has been noted in many countries, including Greece, Bulgaria, Italy, Portugal, France, Britain and Belgium.[68]

To take these Serbian claims to their logical conclusion would involve redescribing most, or all, of the Kosovo Albanians – or indeed all of the people of northern Albania too – as 'really' Serbs. Such a conclusion, the *ne plus ultra* of the Arnautaš theory, was in fact put forward by some of the Serbian writers of the nineteenth century. The growth of this whole 'Arnautaš' thesis can be traced from its starting-point in the 1830s, when an Austrian official, Joseph Müller, implied that the majority of the Albanian-speaking Muslims in the Peć district were in fact of Slav origin. A manuscript draft of this part of his book, which survives in the

Austrian military archives, adds an important detail not contained in the book itself: namely, that one of his main sources of information for the demography of Kosovo was the Orthodox Metropolitan of Prizren.[69] Later in the century the theory was evidently an article of faith among Serb intellectuals in Kosovo, who buttressed it with whatever ethnographic evidence they could find.

The first writer to make the sweeping claim that all Gegs (northern Albanians) were in fact Albanianized Serbs was Miloš Milojević, whose activities as school-teacher and military commander have already been mentioned. His argument about the Gegs was presented in 1872; in the following year he read a paper to the Serbian Royal Academy arguing that all the Macedonians were really Serbs too. This time he was trounced by the distinguished scholar Stojan Novaković, who demonstrated that much of his evidence was forged. But his argument about the Albanians continued to exert real influence, and even those who described him as a 'propagandist', such as the influential geographer Jovan Cvijić, would fall under its spell.[70] The most energetic propounder of this argument, however, was a man called Spiridion Gopčević, who has been described as 'the father of Serbian political ethnography'. His book about the ethnography of Macedonia and Kosovo declared that almost all the Albanians there were 'Albanianized Serbs'; and a later book on Albania insisted that all Gegs were really Serbs as well.[71] The first of these books was so congenial to Serbian policy that a lavishly produced German translation (printed in Vienna in 1889) was paid for by the government in Belgrade. It was, however, described by the leading German expert on the Balkans, Gustav Weigand, as 'a mass of crude lies', and several critics demonstrated that the journey through Kosovo which Gopčević described had never actually taken place: he had simply copied material from other books, embroidering and falsifying as he did so.[72]

The political passions which led to such inventions are easily understood. By the last quarter of the nineteenth century all Balkan politicians (and many foreign diplomats) were making calculations about how the maps could be redrawn. Serbia and Montenegro hoped to take over not only the whole of Bosnia–Hercegovina but also all the territory to the south of the Serbian state, at least as far as Macedonia. A large revolt in Hercegovina in 1875, which spread to much of Bosnia, seemed to offer a first opportunity to move against the Ottomans; but the Serbian government, aware of its own military unpreparedness, was cautious at first. Pressure built up both from Serbian public opinion and from Russian pan-Slavists, who began sending money and volunteers to Belgrade; and public opinion throughout western Europe turned against the Ottomans in the early summer of 1876, when news came out of the brutal suppression of an uprising in Bulgaria. And so, at the end of June, Serbia and Montenegro decided to launch their attack. Their first strategic aim was to break through the Sandžak of Novi Pazar, linking their territories; they would then push southwards into Kosovo. The Serbian army given this task was commanded by a Czech artillery instructor (and former travelling companion of the great Albanologist von Hahn), General Zach: he entered the Sandžak north of Novi Pazar, but was quickly driven back by a small Ottoman force under the military commander in Kosovo, Mehmet Ali pasha. Zach was then replaced by a Russian general, who was also defeated by the Ottomans in late October.[73] By this stage the whole Serbian campaign had disastrously collapsed. A complete Ottoman reconquest of Serbia might have followed had it not been for the diplomatic intervention of Serbia's patron, Russia, which imposed an armistice in November.

Although Serbia made its peace with the Ottomans, Russia, which had larger plans for the whole Balkan region, declared war in its own right against Istanbul in April 1877. The Russian armies met stiff Ottoman resistance in Bulgaria, and by the end of the year Russia was asking the Serbs to go to war again. This they did in mid-December. Preoccupied with their Bulgarian campaign, the Ottomans had depleted their garrisons further to the west: this enabled the Serbian army to capture the important stronghold of Niš within seven weeks. An Ottoman force which had been going to the relief of Niš then fell back towards Prishtina to cover the railway, and the Serbian army now moved southwards to encircle it, dividing into two forces which entered Kosovo from the north-east and the south-east. The first captured Podujevo (Alb.: Podujeva); the second seized Gjilan and Kaçanik, and had just got as far as Prishtina (stopping en route at Gračanica to hold a service of thanksgiving) when the fighting was ended by a Russian–Ottoman armistice on 31 January 1878.[74] Some Serbian troops stayed on in the south-east of Kosovo for several months, where they came under frequent guerrilla attacks from local Albanian fighters.[75] But in the end they were forced to withdraw, in accordance with the new lines drawn by the Great Powers on the map.

There were two very different geopolitical settlements. The first, worked out between Russia and the Ottoman Empire alone (the Treaty of San Stefano, March 1878), would have created an enormously expanded Bulgarian state, stretching all the way into central Albania; Serbia would have gained the whole region of Niš, plus most of the districts of Vuçitërn and Mitrovica in northern Kosovo.[76] So many aspects of this treaty were unacceptable to the other Great Powers that a congress was called in Berlin to revise it. And so it was that in July 1878 a Treaty of Berlin was agreed which would determine the shape of the Ottoman possessions in the western Balkans until the final destruction of Ottoman rule. Bulgaria was cut down to size, with Macedonia restored to the Ottomans; Serbia was allowed to keep the whole Niš area, but not any territory in Kosovo itself; Bosnia-Hercegovina was handed over to Austrian administration, and Austrian garrisons were also permitted in the Sandžak of Novi Pazar; and some territory was given to Montenegro, including the Gusinje area (to the north of the modern Albanian border) which had been part of the vilayet of Kosovo.[77] That last concession, allowing the hand-over of an Albanian-inhabited area to a Slav state, caused intense and widespread resentment in Kosovo itself. This was the spark that lit a movement of resistance in Kosovo, first to the Treaty of Berlin and eventually to Ottoman rule itself; and within thirty-four years the conflagration it caused would be one of the principal reasons for the downfall of the Ottoman Empire.

11

Kosovo's other minorities: Vlachs, Gypsies, Turks, Jews and Circassians

SOME OF THE other peoples who have lived in Kosovo have been mentioned in passing already. This chapter will discuss each of the main groups in turn, bringing together some details about them which might otherwise get dispersed or lost in a general chronological treatment of Kosovo's history.

The first of these populations to exist in Kosovo, the Vlachs, has now disappeared as a distinct group: its members have either become Serbs or moved away. Possibly this is not the first time the Vlachs of Kosovo have exited from history; the ones who were there in the nineteenth century seem to have consisted entirely of recent immigrants from further south, and there may have been no continuity between them and the Vlachs who had preceded them in the late medieval period.

It was argued in Chapter 2 that Kosovo and its surrounding upland areas may have been the crucible in which the Vlach and Romanian peoples were originally formed. Nomadic or semi-nomadic Vlachs spread southwards into northern Greece from the tenth century onwards; others stayed longer in contact with Albanian-speakers and spread out northwards and eastwards, crossing the Danube into Romania in the twelfth century. Many Vlachs remained, however, in the area of Kosovo, Montenegro and Hercegovina. As we have seen, special provisions were made for pastoral Vlachs in the law code of Stefan Dušan, and Vlachs played a key role as packhorse-leaders in the trade of medieval Serbia and Ragusa. The presence of Vlachs in Kosovo is attested to in several place-names, such as Vlaško Groblje ('Vlach grave') in the Čičavica (Alb.: Çiçavica) range of central Kosovo; the folk traditions of many northern Albanian clans also recalled that there had been Vlachs in the mountains before the coming of the Turks.[1] When the Ottomans compiled detailed tax-registers in the late fifteenth century, they recorded large numbers of Vlach households in Kosovo: in 1488/9 there were 481 in Prizren, 870 in Prishtina and 1,008 in Peć, and two years later another register also referred to a special tax-district for Vlachs near Vuçitërn.[2]

In the early Ottoman period the Vlachs retained the special tax status which they had enjoyed under the Serbs: pastoral Vlachs would pay one sheep and one lamb per household on St George's Day each year. They were also used as military auxiliaries, and in Kosovo, as an extension of that role, some of them were used to guard the mines.[3] During the first two Ottoman centuries, however, the Vlachs simply fade out of the records in Kosovo. We know that large numbers of them in Hercegovina, northern Serbia and north-western Bosnia were gradually Slavicized, thanks mainly to the cultural influence of the Serbian Orthodox Church, so it seems reasonable to suppose that this is what happened to most of them in Kosovo.[4] But the Vlachs have always been a very adaptable people, capable of assimilating to any local language or culture: there are a few references to Islamicized Vlachs in the early Ottoman registers for Kosovo, and in Albania many Muslim Albanian families would later preserve traditions of Vlach origins.[5]

More generally, it seems that a wide swathe of Vlach-populated country extended originally from the mountains south of Prizren, through the Debar area and all the way down the eastern side of Albania: while Vlachs retained their language and identity in the southern part of this strip (in the area to the south-west of Lake Ohrid), the ones further north turned either into Slav-speakers (the Mijaci, north of Debar, and perhaps the Gora villagers too) or into Albanian-speakers (in the Debar area).[6] One rather unlikely skill developed by Vlachs in this region was the craft of stone-masonry – unlikely, that is, given their pas-toral–nomadic traditions. Nevertheless, there were Vlach villages whose men specialized in masonry, and travelled far and wide to build houses, bridges and aqueducts. In the Ottoman period these crafts were also practised by Christian Albanians from eastern and central Albania: above all, Debar, Berat and Gjirokastra. All these areas had Vlach populations; whether the stone-building skills passed originally from Albanians to

Vlachs or vice-versa is not clear, but it is possible that many of the Albanians who plied these trades were themselves Albanianized Vlachs.[7]

At the lower end of this swathe of Vlach-inhabited territory, to the south of Lake Ohrid, a town developed in the seventeenth century which became, for a while, the most important Vlach centre in the Balkans: Moschopolis (Alb.: Voskopoja). By the early eighteenth century this flourishing town may have had 20,000 inhabitants (popular tradition would later credit it with as many as 12,000 houses, implying a much larger population); it also had a famous school and (from 1731) a printing-press. Both Vlach and Greek were spoken there; Vlach trading-houses in Moschopolis had branches in Italy, Austria and Hungary, and most of the 'Greek' merchant community in Vienna consisted in fact of Moschopolitan Vlachs.[8] All this came to an end, however, in the late eighteenth century, when bands of local Albanian Muslims (encouraged, it seems, by the Ottoman authorities in a wave of anti-Orthodox feeling during the Russian–Ottoman war of 1768–74) repeatedly pillaged and burned the town. The inhabitants fled to many other towns in Greece, Albania and Macedonia; some went to join their merchant relatives in Austria or Hungary (where a church near Budapest has frescoes by a Moschopolitan painter); and one large group moved to Prizren.[9]

No doubt there had been occasional influxes of Vlachs into Kosovo before this. Vlach traders would have come to the big annual fairs at Prizren and Prishtina, and pastoral Vlachs from northern Macedonia might also have brought their flocks into the south-eastern corner of Kosovo; a few Macedonian Vlachs had settled in the southern town of Ferizaj.[10] The popular word for a 'Vlach' among the Prizren Albanians was 'Gog', which means 'stone-mason': this too suggests a tradition of contact with the Vlachs of the Debar region. But it was the arrival of the refugees from Moschopolis that created a distinctive Vlach population, which seems to have attracted other Vlach migrants in the early nineteenth century from northern Greece and Macedonia, and which would retain its identity for much of the century. A few settled in villages near Prizren, but most led an urban life: by the 1830s there were roughly 2,000 Vlachs, most of them in Prizren, but some in Gjakova and Peć.[11] In Prizren the Vlachs settled in the Serb part of the town, where they created a 'Gog quarter' (*Gogska mahala*), and were given a Serbian Orthodox church, Sveti Spas (Holy Saviour), for their own use. Under the malign influence of the Greek Orthodox bishops of the period, however, relations between the Vlachs (who used the Greek liturgy) and the Serbs deteriorated. In the 1860s the Prizren Vlachs set up their own school, with teaching first in Greek and Serbian, then in Greek only; and when the Serbs tried to claim back their church in 1869 the Vlachs set fire to the iconostasis (icon-screen), the most distinctively Serbian thing about it.[12] By the early twentieth century, however, the Metropolitan (senior bishop) of the area was a Serb, and the boot was now on the other foot: in 1907 a small Greek-language school in Lipljan, run by the tiny Vlach community of that town – consisting of just nine families – was shut down on the Metropolitan's orders.[13] But all the while, the Vlachs in Kosovo were being gradually Serbianized. Gopčević, ever the optimist, reported that they were 'three-quarters' Serbianized by the 1880s; the Russian consul Yastrebov found at the end of the century that there were just 137 Vlach households in Prizren; and a Bulgarian writer noted that this number had gone down to 120 by 1916.[14] The church of Sveti Spas was returned to the Serbian liturgy after the conquest of Kosovo by Serbia in 1912, and since then the Vlachs of Prizren have been, so far as one can tell, Serbianized completely.

Taking Kosovo's minorities in their order of historical appearance in the region, the next group was almost certainly the Gypsies. These nomadic people had moved from their original home in northern India and had reached the European part of the Byzantine Empire as early as the eleventh century, where there are references to them as fortune-tellers and bear-leaders; by 1362 there were Gypsies in Ragusa, in 1373 they were mentioned in Zagreb, and a document of 1378 referred to villages of sedentary Gypsies in western Bulgaria.[15] Given this geographical spread, it is reasonable to assume that Gypsies had also reached the Kosovo area in the fourteenth century. Clear and direct evidence is lacking, however: the only phrase which was once thought to refer to Gypsies in medieval Serbian Kosovo, a reference to *cingarije* in Prizren in 1348, is now thought to be just a word for cobblers.[16] On the other hand, historians have paid little attention to the term *magjupci* which appears in one of the Dečani chrysobulls of the same period: the Slavic scholar Konstantin Jireček glossed this as a word for 'bakers' (from Grk.:

magkipoi), but did not comment on the fact that this term was virtually identical with a common later word for a type of Gypsy, *magjup*. As early as 1455 there was a village in north-central Kosovo called Magjupci, which one modern historian has confidently identified as a Gypsy village.[17]

In the early Ottoman period Gypsies are occasionally mentioned, but they seem to have been a tiny minority in the Kosovo region. A few Christian Gypsies in the districts of Prizren and Vuçitërn are listed in a register of 1491; smithing was a typical occupation, and their general skills in metal-working must have brought them into closer association with the mining towns.[18] A clearer picture emerges in the 1520s, when a Gypsy census was carried out in the eyalet of Rumeli, the main European province of the Empire: this yielded a total of 17,000 Gypsies, of whom 60 per cent were Christian and 40 per cent Muslim. In Kosovo itself the census revealed 164 Gypsy households in Prishtina, 145 in Novo Brdo, and smaller numbers in a few other towns; the majority were Christian, and all of these had Serbian Orthodox names such as Jovan and Dimitrije. The degree of Serbian Orthodox acculturation helps to con-firm that many of these Gypsies had been there before the arrival of the Ottomans.[19]

During the early sixteenth century the Ottoman government placed the Gypsies in a Gypsy sancak, an administrative unit rather than a geographical one. They paid a standard rate of annual tax: 22 akçes for Muslim households (a version of the land-tax, resm-i çift), and 25 for Christian ones, plus an additional charge on the Christians of 6 akçes. The law also prohibited the Muslim ones from having social intercourse with the Christians – a strange ruling, since there was nothing like it for Muslims and Christians in general.[20] Overall, the treatment of Gypsies in the Ottoman Empire was not severe, and compared well with the situation in northern Europe, where punitive laws were enacted against them. In the Ottoman Balkans they enjoyed all the basic legal rights of town-dwellers (though they were often pushed out to the edge of town), and in the seventeenth and eighteenth centuries they continued to enjoy some tax exemptions, such as relief from the so-called 'extraordinary' taxes.[21]

We have already caught some glimpses of Gypsies in the reports of seventeenth-century Catholic clerics, complaining about their 'necromancy' and folk medicine. Evidently the sedentarized Gypsies were by now a special but accepted part of local society, performing functions such as smithing, fortune-telling, doctoring and so on. The seventeenth-century English traveller Edward Browne (son of the famous prose-writer, Sir Thomas), who passed briefly through Kosovo, noted that the Gypsies 'are in most Towns, and live by labour, and handy-crafts Trades'; having to make a hurried exit northwards from Prishtina, where he had enountered the plague, he took a Gypsy guide with him.[22] Gypsies could also be used as military auxiliaries; an Ottoman decree of 1566 calling up extra forces in Macedonia for a military campaign classified the Muslim Gypsies as 'Yürüks', the term used for pastoral but quasi-military Turkic tribesmen.[23] When (as mentioned in Chapter 9) a Serbian monk reported to the Austrian commander in 1737 that the defence of Kosovo and southern Serbia had been left in the hands of Gypsies, he meant what he said; and in 1788 the Bosnian Gypsies played a large part in the Ottoman defence against another Austrian invasion.[24] Presumably these services to the state were carried out mainly by sedentary Gypsies; the entirely nomadic ones would have been too hard to pin down.

From the early nineteenth century onwards, writers on Kosovo offered some estimates of the number of Gypsies there, at least in the main towns. In the early 1840s Joseph Müller noted a settlement of 240 Gypsy huts on the side of the citadel hill at Prizren; in the 1850s the Catholic Archbishop reported that there were more than 3,000 Gypsies in Prizren in 603 houses; and in the following decade the French diplomat Émile Wiet found 3,000 in Prizren, 2,000 in Peć, 1,700 in Gjakova and 1,000 in Prishtina.[25] Once again, the nomadic ones remained uncounted. By this stage the difference between the settled and wandering Gypsies was linguistic as well as social. Only the nomadic ones retained the Gypsy language, Romany; in Kosovo most of them were also fluent in Albanian, and their area of travel would include parts of Albania too. They supported themselves by begging, basket-weaving, sieve-making, horse-dealing, bear-leading (the bears not only danced, but also trod on people's backs to cure back-ache) and doctoring: a German visitor to Prizren in 1910 noticed Gypsies in black tents on the outskirts of the town, 'giving quack remedies to the doctorless Albanians'.[26] The sedentary Gypsies in Kosovo were mainly Albanian-speaking and Muslim; this type, known as *magjups*, lived by iron-working, music-making and performing menial tasks in the towns such as donkey-driving, brick-making and portering. Some also worked as day-labourers on the larger farms. A small minority of the non-nomadic Gypsies, mainly in Eastern Kosovo, were Serbian Orthodox, and in towns such as Prishtina and Mitrovica they were Serbian-speakers; in rare cases they would inter-marry with ordinary Serbs.[27] Both Orthodox and Muslim Gypsies would celebrate saint's days such as St George's Day, and all Serb Gypsies would also celebrate their *slava* or family saint's day – a point con-veniently ignored by those Serbian ethnographers who argued that this was an infallible sign of Serb ethnic origins.[28]

One other type of Gypsy may also have been present from the early nineteenth century onwards: semi-nomadic Gypsies speaking both Romany and Romanian, who had recently spread out from the Roman-ian lands. In 1858 the Austrian Albanologist von Hahn noticed a group of what he called 'Linguri' (Rom.: *lingurari*, 'spoon-carvers', one of the main classifications of Romanian Gypsies) near Vranje, just to the east of Kosovo.[29] Vranje itself became a major Gypsy centre, with a large population of Serbian-speaking Muslim Gypsies. After the nineteenth-century expulsions of Muslim Slavs and Muslim Albanians from the Serbian state, these Gypsies were virtually the only Muslims permitted to remain on Serbian soil: in 1910 there were 14,335 Muslims in the whole kingdom of Serbia (6,089 of them in Vranje), and roughly 90 per cent of the urban Muslims were Gypsies.[30] A campaign by the Orthodox Church did succeed in converting more than 2,000 of them in the 1890s; but in general Serbian attitudes to the Gypsies have combined social contempt (of the sort expressed by all Balkan peoples towards them) with an element of tolerance or even indulgence.[31] Although there were no official campaigns against Gypsies as such in the Yugoslav state between the two World Wars, Albanian-speaking Gypsies did suffer under the anti-Albanian policies which were applied in Kosovo, and many of them fled into Albania.[32] During the Second World War, when many thousands of Gypsies were murdered by the Ustaša authorities in Croatia and (as Muslims) by Serb extremists in Bosnia, Kosovo remained largely free from such pogroms: only 1,000 Kosovo Gypsies, approxi-mately, are thought to have been killed. The first census after the war recorded a total of just over 11,000 Gypsies in Kosovo; by the 1991 census this had grown to nearly 43,000.[33] But all such figures, based on self-classification, tend to underestimate the true numbers of the Gypsies, many of whom prefer to identify themselves as Albanians, or Turks, or Serbs – or even, in the most recent and most picturesque self-reclassification, 'Egyptians'.[34]

A precise date for the advent of Kosovo's Turkish minority would be hard to fix. As we have seen, some Turks were settled in this region by King Stefan Milutin in the early fourteenth century; on these grounds the Turkish presence in Kosovo should probably be dated to before the coming of the Gypsies. But on the other hand we have no evidence of a continuously existing Turkish-speaking community stemming from that first settlement. So it makes more sense to trace the origins of Kosovo's Turkish population to the period 1389–1455, when officials, soldiers, traders and their families began to settle in some of Kosovo's towns. It has already been pointed out that there was no policy of mass coloniza- tion in this area; the northernmost settlement of the Turkic tribesmen known as Yürüks was in Macedonia. Just a few Yürüks were introduced to guard mines in Kosovo; by the end of the seventeenth century there were also Yürüks in Montenegro, and a small number in the Sandžak of Novi Pazar.[35]

Ethnic categorizations are often imprecise where the Ottoman 'Turks' are concerned. The term 'Yürük' was, or became, more a social–military category than an ethnic one: Tatars and other ethnic types (including, as mentioned above, Muslim Gypsies) could be included in it. And in any case the 'Turkish' spahis and soldiers who came to Kosovo in the early Ottoman period may have had a variety of ethnic origins, such as Kurdish or Arab. The military guard of Novo Brdo in 1455, for example, contained one Tatar and one Laz: the Laz are a population in north- eastern Anatolia whose language is related to Georgian.[36] And one Turkish-speaking family in Janjevo, called Spahijović, traces its origins to a Syrian spahi who settled in Kosovo in the reign of Süleyman the Magnificent.[37] Conversely, many local Kosovo families who converted to Islam – Albanians, predominantly, but probably some Slavs too – became so absorbed in the Ottoman Turkish culture of the towns that they used Turkish as their language of preference, even in the home. In the 1930s all the old Muslim families of Janjevo were Turkish-speaking, though their family traditions (apart from the one just mentioned) recorded that their ancestors had been local Christians, both Catholic and Orthodox.[38] Since they remained bilingual, however, it is a moot point whether they should be described as having become Turks.

Because of the role played by Ottoman Turkish-language culture in urban life, it is hardly possible to talk about the history of a distinct 'Turkish community' in Kosovo during the Ottoman centuries: a fully Ottomanized Albanian would be both Albanian and Turkish. To give just one example: the poet Mehmet Akif or Aqif (1873–1936) was the son of an Albanian villager (from Shushica, near Peć) who had become a schoolteacher in Istanbul. Mehmet was born and educated in the Ottoman capital, and in 1921 he wrote the *Istiklâl marşı* ('March of Independence') which became the Turkish national anthem; Turks naturally regard him as a Turkish poet, but he thought of himself as an Albanian.[39]

In Kosovo itself, the only meaningful way of distinguishing 'Ottoman Turks' ('Osmanlı') from the rest would have been to single out those families who both spoke Turkish and recorded in their family traditions that they had come originally from Anatolia. (Both these criteria are necessary, since some families with Anatolian origins were assimilated to Albanians, and became monoglot Albanian-speakers.)[40] On this basis, it is possible to say that the Turkish minority in Kosovo was very small, and almost entirely urban: just three small Turkish villages are recorded in the whole of Kosovo.[41] Joseph Müller, in the 1840s, thought there were sixty-two Ottoman Turkish families in Peć, 4–500 people in Prizren, and 180 people in Gjakova; von Hahn, two decades later, found no more than fourteen Ottoman Turkish households in Prishtina, all of them members of one family, called Emir, which had originally settled in Novo Brdo.[42] By the end of the century, as we have seen, there may have been no more than twenty Ottoman Turkish families left in Prizren.[43]

Many of these were old land-owning families, which means that after the Serbian–Montenegrin conquest of Kosovo they would have suffered economically as well as politically. There was, as we shall see, large-scale emigration to Turkey during the inter-war period, and the Turkish-speaking Kosovars were naturally the ones who found it easiest to start a new life there. The Serb authorities, indeed, were keen to classify as many Albanians as possible as 'Turks', in order to facilitate their removal.

The proportion identifying themselves as Turkish in the censuses was, however, small: 27,920 in 1921 and 23,698 in 1931. In the early post-war censuses the figures fluctuated rather wildly, according to changes in political pressures and/or calculations of advantage, but since 1971 the figure has remained fairly static, in the region of 11–12,000.[44] Turkish culture has not entirely disappeared: until the 1990s there was a Turkish-language newspaper published in Kosovo. But most of the speakers of this language are probably best described as bilingual Albanians, and few of them are the direct descendants of Anatolian Turks.

Historical evidence places the arrival of the Jews in Kosovo in the fifteenth century. It is very likely that Jews had had contacts with Kosovo long before that, in Roman times, but no direct evidence of their presence there has survived from that period. We do know, however, that there was a synagogue in Stobi, a Roman town south-east of Skopje, in the third and fourth centuries, and a Jewish gravestone from the same period has been found in Montenegro.[45] The most important town of the Macedonian region, Salonica, had a Jewish community with a continuous history from the second century BC onwards; its population of 'Romaniot' (Greek-speaking) Jews was the main reservoir which filled or replenished the Jewish communities of northern Macedonia in the late medieval or early Ottoman periods, starting with the building of the first synagogue in Skopje in 1361. And on the Albanian coast there were several towns with Jewish communities, also Romaniot but culturally Italianized, in the Middle Ages: a Jewish merchant from Durrës is referred to in a document of 1281.[46]

The first specific mention of a Jew in Kosovo comes in 1442, when two merchants in Prishtina, one Jewish, one Genoese, are described as holders of the tax-farm for silver production.[47] It is significant that this date falls within the brief period when Kosovo was under full Ottoman occupation, before its restoration to Djuradj Branković's rule: the significance lies in the fact that the Jews were generally much better treated by the Ottomans than by Christian states, and found it easier to attain prosperity, and high social positions, under Ottoman rule. Given that so many of them had suffered under Christian governments, they tended to be trusted more than Christians were by the Ottoman authorities, who only began to apply all the conditions of the *zimmi* (bearers of non-Muslim status) to them in the late sixteenth century. Even then they suffered no special penalties (of the sort that were imposed again and again by Christian rulers), and their skills as traders, entrepreneurs and administrators were highly valued.[48] For this reason the Ottoman lands became a refuge for several waves of Jewish refugees from further north and west, starting with the Jews expelled from Hungary in 1360. Another wave of 'Ashkenazi' Jews (from central and north-eastern Europe) came in the 1470s, and after the expulsion from Spain and Portugal in 1492 roughly 90,000 Spanish-speaking 'Sephardic' Jews flooded into the Balkans, where they quickly outnumbered the existing Romaniot population.[49]

By 1498/9 there were six Jewish households in Novo Brdo: some of them were coin-minters, and may have been brought in by the Ottomans specifically to help with such specialist tasks. Whether any of these were refugees from Spain is not known, though there is evidence that the Ottoman state did direct groups of those refugees to particular towns. Another Ottoman tax register in 1569/70 recorded the same number of households in Novo Brdo, and categorized them as a *cemaat* or religious community, 'Cemaat-i Yahudan'.[50] There are occasional references to Jews in other documents of the sixteenth and seventeenth centuries, from which it appears that three families (Bahar, Ruben and Salamon) moved from Novo Brdo to Prishtina; and a Jewish merchant in Prizren is known to have traded in the 1580s with a wide network of other Jews in the Balkans. Indeed, the Albanian coastal trade, which handled many of the agricultural goods exported from Kosovo, was largely in the hands of Jews, in both Lezha and (especially) Vlora, which had a majority Jewish population in the sixteenth century.[51] The dominant town for the Kosovo Jews was Skopje, and any rabbis who visited the Kosovo community would presumably have come from there. Skopje's Jewish community grew rapidly, from thirty-two families in 1544 to a reported total of 3,000 people in the 1680s, but the entire Jewish quarter was destroyed when Piccolomini set fire to the city on 26 October 1689.[52]

Despite the upheavals of 1690 and 1737, the Jewish community seems to have survived in Kosovo. By the mid-nineteenth century there were Jewish merchants in Prizren, 600 Jews in Gjakova, a Jewish community in Prishtina and ten Jewish households in the small town of Prokuplje, just to the north-east of Kosovo.[53] Other writers at the end of the century noted that there were 305 Jews in Prishtina, and that the community there was Spanish-speaking; by 1910 there may have been as many as 3,000 in the whole of Kosovo.[54] Soon after the Serbian–Montenegrin conquest in 1912 some of these emigrated to Turkish territory. They were no doubt aware that the Serbs had traditionally regarded the Jews in Ottoman territory as adjuncts to Ottoman rule, and had often given them the same harsh treatment that they meted out to Muslims in the territories they conquered; there had also been anti-semitic legislation in Serbia which had only been rescinded after Western diplomatic pressure in 1889.[55] But in 1913 the Chief Rabbi of the Sephardic Jews of Belgrade, Isak Alkalaj, came to Prishtina and persuaded many not to leave, promising them that Jews would enjoy full civic rights.[56] For much of the inter-war period this promise was fulfilled, and some of the Kosovo Jewish families became very prosperous. But the atmosphere changed in the late 1930s, when the Serbian fascist party 'Zbor' campaigned openly on an anti-semitic platform; Chief Rabbi Alkalaj was ejected from the Senate in 1938, and various legal restrictions on Jews were introduced in 1939 and 1940.[57]

After the Axis conquest of Yugoslavia in April 1941 most of Kosovo was occupied by the Italians, who did not share the German authorities' obsession with racial purity. In the Italian zone racial laws were proclaimed but not enforced: there was no curfew for Jews and no wearing of yellow stars. Many Serbian Jews fled to Kosovo for the comparative safety it offered; some were interned in an abandoned school in Prishtina. The local Italian commander at first resisted German pressure to send these people back, but in March 1942 a total of fifty-one Jews were handed over to the Germans. Of the remaining Jewish refugees and local residents in Prishtina, at least 281 would later be arrested by Albanian collaborationists in May 1944 and given to the Germans: of these more than 200 died in Belsen. Most of the local Jewish men, meanwhile, had been sent off by the Italians for internment in central Albania. After the Italian capitulation in September 1943 the internees fled from their camps; some joined the Partisans, while others were given refuge by Albanian villagers. Altogether, out of the 551 Jews known to have been living in Kosovo before April 1941, 210 had died by the end of the war.[58] Thereafter, many of the rest emigrated to Israel; there is no functioning synagogue in Kosovo today.

The last and in some ways the strangest minority to enter Kosovo was the small population of Circassians, settled there by the Ottoman state in the 1860s. Strictly speaking, they were not the first Circassians (also called 'Cherkess'; Alb.: Çerkez; Srb.: Čerkez) to set foot in Kosovo: among the ethnically mixed 'Turks' who settled there in the sixteenth century there was at least one Circassian spahi.[59] The Circassians, who lived in a rich and fertile area of the north-western Caucasus, only came under direct Ottoman rule in the late eighteenth century, but long before that they had been supplying fighting men – and famously beautiful women – to the Ottoman sultans. Also in the eighteenth century the Circassians converted to Islam; and during the first half of the nineteenth century this large and resilient Muslim population was one of the main bulwarks against the Russian advance in the Caucasus. But in 1864 the Russian armies finally overwhelmed Circassia, and most of the population fled to Ottoman territory. The precise figures are unknown, but the scale of the exodus was colossal: more than one million left the Caucasus region, and of that number the Circassians were the largest component.[60] There are thought to be as many as a million people of Circassian descent in modern Turkey, of whom roughly 50,000 have preserved their highly complex language; and compact groups remain in many ex-Ottoman countries, such as Jordan, where they keep up a strong tradition of supplying army officers.[61]

Since these warlike people would willingly fight against any further advance by Christian states into Muslim-ruled territory, the Ottoman authorities settled large numbers of Circassian refugees (a mass which probably included members of several other nationalities, such as the Abkhaz) in their Balkan territories. The total seems to have been between 150,000 and 200,000 people, distributed in areas of what are now Greece, Bulgaria, Macedonia and Serbia.[62] In Kosovo roughly thirty new colony-villages were created for them, all of them in the Eastern half of the territory. A couple of these were large settlements of a hundred houses, but the majority were quite small, with forty or fifty at most; the Circassians' own tradition said that 2,000 families came to Kosovo, and the total number of people was probably not higher than 12,000.[63] Conditions were hard, however, and after the destitution they had endured during their exodus many were killed by epidemics. Although the settlers in Kosovo were given tax exemptions, they still found it difficult to make a living; some of them even staged a rebellion, but were driven back to their villages by the Ottoman army. Not being accustomed to farming, they mainly engaged in two trades: metalwork (specializing in fine silver in the Russian 'Tula' style, for ornamenting gun-stocks and whip-handles), and horse-breeding.[64] In connection with this last activity, they also acquired a reputation as horse-thieves.

The local Albanians and Serbs regarded the Circassians as wild, primitive people, and were particularly shocked to find that they ate horse-meat. It was also widely believed that they took their children to market and, as one elderly Albanian recalled in the 1920s, 'sold them like cattle'. A more careful inquiry into this question in 1925 yielded the following explanation. Those families which had been rich in their native land had brought with them the slaves whom they had kept in their households; some had entire slave families, and it was their normal custom to sell slave children in the market. But because the Ottoman authorities were trying to stamp out slavery in the late nineteenth century, they pretended (in a curious attempt to make their action appear less blameworthy) that the children were their own.[65]

The Kosovo Circassians were used as auxiliary forces in the suppression of the Bulgarian uprising in 1876, and again in the campaigns of 1877–8. After that date, the smaller number of Circassians who had been settled in the Niš region were expelled by the Serbs and went to live in Asia Minor and Syria; many Kosovo Circassians decided to join them. By the late 1890s the numbers in Kosovo had come down to roughly 6,400.[66] Larger exoduses followed after 1912 (when Circassians left most of the other conquered areas in the Balkans) and again after 1918. By 1931, when an Austrian anthropologist went in search of the Circassians in Kosovo, he found just fifty families of 'blue-eyed Caucasians' in the village of Donje Stanovce, between Prishtina and Vuçitërn; he noted that they all spoke Circassian, Turkish, Albanian and Serbian, and he also recorded that the men were 'models of masculine beauty'.[67] Fifty years later, the number of families (in that village and the nearby village of Miloševo) was almost precisely the same, and the total population was estimated at between 600 and 700. They have preserved their immensely complex language, making occasional adaptations from other tongues (the Kosovo Circassian for 'telephone', for example, is *telebzeguhatz'-yk'u*); and some, poignantly, still retain a hazy recollection of the name of the village in Circassia from which their forefathers fled.[68]

12

From the League of Prizren to the Young Turk revolution: 1878–1908

BETWEEN THE EARLY months of 1878, when the military actions of Russia and her Slav allies in the Balkans came to a halt, and the final months of 1912, when Serbian and Montenegrin forces invaded Kosovo, lies the period known in Albanian history as the *Rilindje kombëtare*, the 'national rebirth' or 'national renaissance'. For November 1912 saw not only the triumph of Slav armies in Kosovo but also the declaration, made in the Albanian coastal town of Vlora, of an independent Albanian state. This is a crucial period in Albanian history; and many of the most important events which led to the declaration of Albanian independence took place not in Albania itself (as its frontiers were eventually defined) but in Kosovo, whose history therefore has a peculiar importance for all Albanians.

Albanian historians not only regard the setting up of an Albanian state as the culminating achievement of the whole period, but have also tended to see everything that preceded it as part of a national striving which always had independence as its goal. Albanian history books refer constantly, when dealing with this period, to 'the national movement' or 'the national liberation movement', phrases that conjure up the idea of a single political force, at once historically continuous, socially cohesive and ideologically consistent. To point out that such an image is simplistic is not to belittle the extraordinary way in which the leaders of the Albanians, acting in very difficult circumstances, did achieve a high level of mutual agreement and cooperation in both their demands and their actions. But a true history of this period cannot be written if we just begin by assuming that all the Albanians – apart from a few traitors or 'reactionaries' – were automatically striving to throw off Ottoman rule and create a fully independent state of their own.

Looking at the period immediately before 1878, we can distinguish three different sorts of political demand or project. The first was an attempt by the malësors (people of the Malësi) to defend, or even extend, their traditional rights of virtual self-government in the face of the Ottoman reform programme. Thus in the 1860s the highlanders of the paşalıks of Prizren and Peć had demanded that the Ottoman authorities should continue to use local chiefs and not try to introduce officials from outside; that instead of forced recruitment to the new regular army, the Malësi should keep its old custom of supplying troops (raised by its own bajraktars) in times of war; and that there should be no new taxes.[1] Such demands, which can best be described as politically conservative (in the sense that they aimed at the preservation of the old system), were common to both Muslim and Catholic malësors, and were attractive to the lowlanders of Kosovo as well as the men of the mountains. As early as 1840 one observer, trying to answer the question 'What do the Albanians want?', had written: 'They want to enjoy the same privileges, the same independence, as are enjoyed by the free districts of the mountains. They are quite willing to serve the Turks, but only as volunteers, and cannot bear the idea of compulsory recruitment.'[2]

A second and rather different political project, however, was toyed with by some of the Catholic mountain clans, above all the Mirdita: this was the plan (already mentioned in Chapter 10) to create an autonomous or fully independent Catholic Albanian principality. The idea found favour with the leader of the Mirdita, Prenk Bib Doda – not least because he would be the automatic choice of prince, as he was the only hereditary clan chief and the Mirdita were by far the most powerful of the Catholic clans. In 1876 Prince Nikola of Montenegro was trying hard to encourage this ambition, since a Catholic rising against the Ottomans would make it easy for his own troops to conquer much Albanian Muslim territory; Italy and Austria-Hungary, as Catholic protector-powers, also took an interest for their own purposes, and a delegation from an Arbëresh committee in southern Italy offered support and weapons. In April 1877 Prenk Bib Doda did lead a rebellion, and sent a request to Montenegro for arms and money, but the rising was suppressed by Ottoman troops. Undeterred by this setback, he gathered the leaders of several neighbouring Catholic clans and sent a joint petition to the Congress of Berlin in June 1878, asking it to create an autonomous Mirdita principality.[3] The similarity between this project and the more general political conservatism of the Malësi was that both appealed to traditions of quasi-autonomy and customary law: if the Mirdita had gained their principality, they would certainly have continued to live by the Kanun of Lek Dukagjin. The difference was that the Mirdita project was, by definition, exclusive to Catholic areas, whereas the general appeal for a return to the old ways could be extended to all Albanian territory.

A third project, full independence for an overall Albanian state, was not unthinkable in the period before 1878; some people did think it. But most of them were outsiders, members of intellectual circles in the various Albanian émigré communities. The most radical were the Arbëresh in Italy; having just experienced their own country's Risorgimento, the more enthusiastic of them were keen to repeat the experience in Albania. In 1876 an 'Italian–Albanian Committee for the Liberation of the Albanians in the East' was set up in Milan, and an active subcommittee in the Calabrian town of Cosenza issued an appeal for Albanian independence in September of that year.[4] For a long time the intellectual development of the Albanians had been dependent on émigré circles, especially the ones in Romania and Bulgaria; other Albanian communities, as far afield as Egypt, were also important.[5] In the earliest phase of the Albanian Rilindje, the most radical calls for virtual or full independence tended to come from these outside sources. Thus in 1879, for example, one of the leading Albanians in Bulgaria, Jusuf Ali bey, published a brochure which, although modestly entitled 'Current discussions, worthy of attention', was nevertheless a clarion call for Albanian independence.[6] Most of the Albanian-language material that was produced during this period was printed in these émigré communities; not surprisingly, therefore, they placed a special emphasis in their political projects on the establishment of Albanian schools, in which children would be taught to read their own language (in a yet-to-be-standardized alphabet).

The most important of all the Albanian communities was the one in Istanbul; it was also the one most constantly and directly in contact with the Albanian lands, whose social and political elite would conduct much of their business there. Foremost among them during this period was the Frashëri family of southern Albania: three Frashëri brothers came to play an essential role in Albanian political and intellectual history. Highly educated and well-read in French, as well as being fluent in Albanian, Turkish and Greek, they all had 'progressive' ideas about such matters as education, law and social policy, which would set them some distance apart from the more traditional of the lords and clan chiefs of Kosovo and the Malësi. Naim Frashëri (1846–1900) became Albania's leading poet; he also wrote an important text celebrating the values of the Bektashi dervish order. Sami Frashëri (1850–1904) was a prolific author who also edited an influential Turkish daily newspaper in Istanbul. And the eldest brother, Abdyl (1839–92), became the intellectual leader of an Albanian autonomist movement, carefully adapting his demands to a variety of audiences and circumstances.[7] However he altered his position, however, two themes remained constant: he wanted the Albanians to be united among themselves, and he wanted them to be free from direct Ottoman rule.

In 1877 Abdyl Frashëri set up a secret 'Albanian committee' in Ioannina (Trk.: Yanina), the town, now in north-western Greece, where he had been educated and for which he was elected to the Ottoman parliament later that year. Of all the documents produced during the period of the Rilindje, the one which deserves to be called the foundation of the entire autonomist programme was a memorandum sent by this committee to the Ottoman government in the spring of 1877. It called for the uniting of the Albanian provinces in a single vilayet, the employment of Albanian officials there, the establishment of Albanian-language schools, and the limiting of military service to within the territory of the vilayet.[8] On the committee's behalf Frashëri also had secret discussions with Greek officials over the idea of a joint Greek–Albanian revolt; but the Greeks were unable to break his resolve that the Albanians should administer their own territory, rather than becoming subject to Greece.[9] In early 1878, as soon as the territorial proposals of the Treaty of San Stefano became known, he established another committee of Albanian intellectuals and politicians (including Muslims, Orthodox and Catholics) in Istanbul, which called itself the 'Central Committee for the Defence of the Rights of the Albanian Nation'. It sent appeals to Western statesmen to stop the carving-off of Albanian-inhabited lands; it issued a proclamation to 'all Albanian patriots', calling on them to oppose any annexations; and it encouraged local committees to send off their own petitions and protests.[10] In May Abdyl Frashëri organized a meeting of southern Albanian leaders in his home town of Frashër (where they met in the Bektashi tekke), and in June he travelled to Prizren for a larger gathering of notables, religious leaders and clan chiefs.

The idea of a great gathering of chiefs tapped a deep vein of Albanian history: as we have seen, such meetings had been held in different parts of northern Albania in the early seventeenth century. There was also a strong tradition of inter-clan councils or *kuvends* which might, for example, agree on joint action and the suspension of blood-feuds at times of invasion. The powerful clan chief Ali pasha of Gusinje, whose territory was allotted to Montenegro under the terms of the San Stefano treaty, had already formed a 'league' of local clans to resist any annexation; in the eyes of most of the chiefs and notables in Kosovo and northern Albania, the gathering at Prizren was probably just an extension of that idea, having little to do with the plans of a secret committee in Istanbul.[11]

Partly because of the speed of events, it was not possible to bring together representatives of all the Albanian lands; most of the delegates who met in Prizren on 10 June 1878 were from Kosovo or the Malësi, and only five of them were Christians. Abdyl Frashëri was one of only two representatives from the south of Albania. He was recognized as one of the most eloquent speakers, and was invited to give the opening address, a short fragment of which survives.[12] But the general character of the gathering was not attuned to the advanced political thinking of a metropolitan intellectual such as Frashëri. The first set of formal decisions issued by this meeting (on 18 June) said nothing about reforms, nothing about schools, nothing about autonomy, nothing even about the unification of the Albanian lands in one vilayet. Instead, it announced the formation of a military-defensive organization to be known as the 'League', the aim of which was simply to stop any territory from being occupied by foreign troops. It declared the League's loyalty to the Sultan, and it said that, in accordance with the şeriat (Islamic law), the League would defend the life, property and honour of all the Sultan's loyal subjects, including non-Muslims.[13]

The next few months would see an ideological tug-of-war between the Muslim traditionalists on the one hand, who dominated the League in Kosovo at this stage, and the intellectuals, autonomists and reformists such as Frashëri on the other. Outside Kosovo there was more sympathy for Frashëri's ideas in the League committee that sprang up in Shkodra, which contained a balance of Muslims and Catholics; the Mirdita pledged their support and were very active in the Shkodran committee, bringing their own autonomist sympathies with them.[14] But observers who looked just at the League in Kosovo in these early days regarded it as essentially a Muslim religious movement, whose veneration of the Caliph-Sultan was obviously quite genuine; and since its campaign against territorial changes served the interests of the Ottoman state, many foreign diplomats also assumed that it was little more than a puppet of Istanbul. Thus a British officer who travelled through Kosovo in late 1878 reported: 'The movement is rather religious than secular, and is led by the Muftis, Ulemas, Cadis ... I think it is clear that the Porte and the League are now on good terms, and working for the attainment of a common object – the defence of the province.'[15] The Ottoman authorities had in fact been quite sympathetic towards the League at first, and had placed no obstacles in the way of its formation.[16] But the limits of Istanbul's tolerance were quickly reached.

The Congress of Berlin, as we have seen, agreed to hand over to Montenegro part of the north-western corner of the Vilayet of Kosovo, including the Albanian-inhabited district of Gusinje. On 25 August 1878 a senior Ottoman official, Mehmet Ali pasha, arrived in Prizren, on his way to supervise the work of the joint Ottoman–Montenegrin Boundary Commission. A marshal in the Ottoman army, he was originally a German called Karl Detroit, from a Huguenot family in Magdeburg, who had jumped ship in Istanbul as a young man and joined the Ottoman military. He had been one of the Sultan's chief negotiators at Berlin (where Bismarck referred to him dismissively as 'der Magdeburger'), and had in fact worked hard to oppose any cessions of territory.[17] Part of his mission now, however, was to meet the local leaders in Western Kosovo and persuade them to accept the Congress's decisions. The reception he was given in Prizren was very hostile: according to one account, when he tried to read the Sultan's decree about the Berlin decisions at the Barjakli mosque he was shouted down. (He was doubly unpopular in Kosovo, as he had directed one of the Ottoman army's periodic campaigns to disarm the population there seven years before.)[18]

Mehmet Ali continued on his way towards Gusinje, and spent the night of 1 September in Gjakova as a guest of the governor of the town, Abdullah pasha. On the next day a large crowd of angry Albanians – some of them led, it was said, by Ali pasha of Gusinje – surrounded the house and called on Abdullah to hand over the 'infidel'. When he refused, shooting began which continued until the following evening, when the house was set alight; Mehmet Ali, Abdullah and their small personal guard then moved into a *kullë* (fortified stone tower), where they kept up the fight for another three days. Finally this too was set on fire; Mehmet Ali emerged and, according to one report, tried to trick his way out with a white flag before shooting eight Albanians with his revolver. He was killed, together with Abdullah and most of their guard, and his head, 'stuck on a pike, was paraded in triumph through the town's bazaars'. It was estimated that 280 people had died in the fight, with a total of 300 wounded.[19]

This event had enormous repercussions. It ended (for the time being, at least) all cooperation between the League and the Ottoman government; it strengthened the resolve of local Albanians to resist any cession of territory; and it brought 'the Albanian question' forcefully to the attention of Western governments and newspaper-readers. Seizing this opportunity, Abdyl Frashëri published an article in his brother's Istanbul paper, in which he set out what he described as the demands of the Albanian League: a single vilayet, Albanian-speaking officials, elected local councils of Muslims and Christians and an elected assembly for the whole vilayet, and Albanian-language schools. At the top of this list he added a commitment to the defence of territory and of the Sultan's rights; otherwise this was a liberal autonomist programme significantly different in character from the aims of the Leaguers in the Kosovo region.[20] But the influence of Frashëri's ideas was growing: he had already persuaded the southern committee of the League to adopt such a programme in Ioannina, and in October – helped, probably, by his Bektashi connections – he won over the important and independent-minded Debar region too.[21]

During the following year the issue of the Montenegrin annexation of Gusinje remained unresolved: the Ottoman government was clearly happy to have the process delayed, and Ali pasha of Gusinje remained in place with his armed men. Montenegrin army units were sent to dislodge him in November 1879 and January 1880, but were repulsed. Eventually, as a result of Ali pasha's defiance, the Great Powers changed their minds about the annexation and decided to give Montenegro the coastal district of Ulcinj (which also had an Albanian population) instead.[22] Meanwhile, in October 1879, a meeting of the League in Prizren had agreed to accept the autonomist programme of Abdyl Frashëri and the southern League committee. Most of the Kosovo Leaguers probably did not want, at this stage, anything more than a degree of self-administration within the Ottoman Empire: their main aim, according to one report, was to have their own courts in which only the Kanun of Lek Dukagjin would be applied. An interesting picture of the League's attitudes was given by a French official in Skopje, who had had a long conversation with Ali Draga, one of the leaders of the League, in October 1879. Draga said the League had 300 members, fifty of whom represented Catholic clans; they remained faithful subjects of the Sultan, but no longer believed that the Empire was competent to protect them. They wanted their own vilayet, within which an Albanian army would be created, with Albanian officers: it would remain, nevertheless, at the service of the Ottoman government, since the Albanians were willing to fight against any enemy of the Empire. On all further questions of autonomy or institutional reform, the Frenchman wrote, this notable of the League had only the most hazy of notions.[23]

Others had more definite ideas: a strong declaration in favour of an autonomous principality was made by a joint Muslim–Catholic meeting in Shkodra in April 1880. And the basic demand of a unified Albanian vilayet was now being made more forcefully by the Leaguers in Kosovo. They probably did not realize how close they came to achieving this objective. It had some diplomatic support in Britain, which was taking (unusually) an active role in the international diplomacy on the Albanian question: a senior official, Lord Edmund Fitzmaurice, wrote from Istanbul to the Foreign Secretary commending the idea.[24] And on 30 May 1880, after several long debates, the Ottoman Council of Ministers did agree, in principle, to grant the Albanians their wish. Just three weeks later, however, the Council began to change its mind after receiving a telegram from the governor of Prizren warning that the Albanians would regard the creation of a united vilayet as just a step towards complete autonomy; he advised the government to begin a crack-down in Kosovo, with arrests and other military actions. Two months later he was urgently requesting up to twenty battalions from Anatolia: by now the constant refusals of the Ottoman authorities were hardening the attitudes of the Leaguers in Kosovo, who were beginning to expel judges and officials, and threatening to seize the barracks as well.[25]

It is not clear that the governor's analysis of the League's intentions was correct; at this stage, the aims of the League in Kosovo were still essentially conservative rather than radical. As one British report from a consular agent in Kaçanik put it in August 1880: 'They want to be governed according to the old system – i.e. a Pasha, Cadi, Mufti and local Medjliss [advisory council] and no one else. The National Albanian Costume is to be obligatory – No more pantaloons and frock coats!'[26] Nor can we be sure that the governor's warnings were the only thing that persuaded Istanbul to change its approach. When an Ottoman army commander made a final attempt to dissuade the League in January 1881, the proclamation he issued contained some darker hints. It warned that the creation of an Albanian vilayet would lead to the disappearance of Albania, and observed: 'In this piece of land that is called Albania there are so many different interests, the essence of which you would not be in a position to comprehend.' Hinting more openly, it added: 'The fact that the laws, way of life and national characteristics of some areas are incompatible with those of others completely validates this point.'[27] The implication seems to have been that an autonomous Albanian vilayet would have been torn by conflicts between Muslim and Christian Albanians, and that this would have given outside powers (not only the Slav states, but also Italy and Austria-Hungary) an excuse to intervene.

This analysis was also questionable. Although the League in Kosovo had a strongly Muslim character, and although there were occasional reports of mistreatment of Christians, most observers were struck by the good public order which the League enforced, from which Christians also benefited. One British official who visited Kosovo in May 1880 commented: 'The Albanian League has, curiously enough, succeeded in establishing a better feeling between the Mussulmans and the Christians of North Albania.' Robbers who stole from the Christians were, he said, promptly punished by the League. And in February 1881 another British diplomat observed that the League was trying hard to retain the good will of the Christian inhabitants: 'It seems that the Chiefs of the League are doing their best to maintain order and tranquillity; and pursuing a conciliatory policy towards those inhabitants of the Vilayet.'[28]

By the time that last report was sent, the League was in full control of Kosovo, and was running the territory as a *de facto* government. This development had begun in the autumn of 1880, when the League installed a committee of its own to administer Prizren in place of the governor. In January three of the League's commanders marched with a small force to Skopje, where the Muslim population welcomed their authority; the chief commander, Sulejman Voksh from Gjakova, then went to Prishtina and occupied the town.[29] One month later the British consul in Salonica reported that conditions in Kosovo had greatly improved as a result: 'The blood-feuds ... are in abeyance, brigands and other lawless characters no longer roam about with impunity, and the taxes are regularly collected under the authority of the League.' But he also wrote that Abdyl Frashëri had addressed a big meeting in Prizren in mid-February, at which he urged the League to move further towards complete independence. In the words of one reported extract from his speech: 'The Porte will do nothing for Albania ... The Porte will probably give up a part of Albania under European pressure ... Let us think and work for ourselves. Let there be no difference between Toscas and Ghegas. Let us be Albanians and make one Albania.' Perhaps as a result of such exhortations, it was reported in early March that the League was forming an army of 12,000 men, which would march first on Monastir (Alb., Trk.: Manastir; modern Bitola), the administrative capital of southern Macedonia, and then on Shkodra and Ulcinj.[30]

Such news must have strengthened the Ottoman government's resolve to crush the League once and for all. In late March 1881 an army of 20,000 men was sent to Skopje; its commander, Marshal Derviş pasha, secured the railway and brought more than 10,000 of his troops, plus artillery, to Ferizaj, from where he began the march to Prizren. The League had raised 4–5,000 men, who tried to ambush Derviş pasha's force at Shtimle (Srb.: Štimlje), north-west of Ferizaj; but the marshal quickly deployed his artillery and drove them off the hills. Prizren was captured in April, and Gjakova and Peć in May.[31] Special efforts were made to hunt down Abdyl Frashëri, who was finally captured in central

Albania, near Elbasan, and brought back to Prizren in chains. There a tribunal sentenced him to death; this was later commuted to life imprisonment. (After three years of incarceration in Prizren, from which his health never recovered, and nearly two years of internment in Anatolia, he was allowed to live in Istanbul on condition that he abstained from all political activities: he died there, aged fifty-two, in 1892.)[32] Altogether Derviş pasha arrested more than 4,000 people: many were deported to Asia Minor, one other leader (Sulejman Voksh) was sentenced to death, and the deputy secretary of the League (Shuajip aga Spahi) died later in prison.[33]

The Ottoman action was crudely effective. Although there would be various uprisings in Kosovo during the next three decades, some of them with quite fierce fighting, all would be localized revolts, not involving organized resistance throughout Kosovo, and most were short-lived. An attempt would be made to set up a revived Albanian League in the last years of the century, but its aims were in some ways more limited, and it never brought about a Kosovo-wide rebellion. For much of this period the business of arguing and campaigning for autonomy or independence was carried on by the émigré communities, especially the ones in Bulgaria and Romania: in 1896, for example, the 'Dëshira' society of Sofia prepared a petition demanding a united Albanian vilayet and the employment of Albanian officials in it, and the 'Dituria' society of Bucharest sent a memorandum with the same demands to the ambassadors of the Great Powers in 1897.[34] Also during this period, with support from the émigré communities, a few token Albanian-language schools were allowed to be set up in southern Albania. There is some evidence too that the Catholic schools in Kosovo were at last permitted to teach in Albanian as well as Italian.[35]

The general conditions in Kosovo in the 1880s and 1890s were very poor. After the changes imposed by the Congress of Berlin the Ottomans had made a new vilayet of Kosovo, incorporating the old vilayet (which included the Skopje region: the capital of the vilayet was moved to that city in 1888) and much of the former Sandžak of Novi Pazar, which had previously belonged to the vilayet of Bosnia. (The Austrians were allowed to keep garrisons in the Sandžak, but otherwise it remained under Ottoman government.)[36] In theory the administrative structures of the Ottoman reform programme were all now in place: since 1876 these had included the provisions of a new Ottoman Constitution, which offered a bill of rights, elected members of parliament, an independent judiciary and all other modern political amenities. But the parliament was dissolved in 1878, and the key elements of the constitution were simply suspended by the new Sultan, Abdülhamit II. As for the Kosovo vilayet, as one Austrian observer put it, describing conditions in 1892, 'The administration functions not at all, or in utterly inadequate ways; and, what is worse, it does so with an attitude which is pernicious and demoralizing. The government has no authority – or, at best, a purely nominal one.' A similar Austrian report seven years later noted that officials could function only if they belonged to a local clique, and that those who crossed it were harshly dealt with: in Prizren the tax-collectors were expelled, and in Peć the governor had been burnt to death in the government building.[37]

This period also saw a deterioration in relations between the Muslims and Christians of Kosovo. The prime cause of this was the mass expulsion of Muslims from the lands taken over by Serbia, Bulgaria and Montenegro in 1877–8. Almost all the Muslims (except, as we have seen, some Gypsies) were expelled from the Morava valley region: there had been hundreds of Albanian villages there, and significant Albanian populations in towns such as Prokuplje, Leskovac and Vranje. A Serbian schoolmaster in Leskovac later recalled that the Muslims had been driven out in December 1877 at a time of intense cold: 'By the roadside, in the Gudelica gorge and as far as Vranje and Kumanovo, you could see the abandoned corpses of children, and old men frozen to death.' Precise figures are lacking, but one modern study concludes that the whole region contained more than 110,000 Albanians. By the end of 1878 Western officials were reporting that there were 60,000 families of Muslim refugees in Macedonia, 'in a state of extreme destitution', and 60–70,000 Albanian refugees from Serbia 'scattered' over the vilayet of Kosovo.[38] Albanian merchants who tried to stay on in Niš were subjected to a campaign of murders, and the property of those who left was sold off at one per cent of its value. In a petition of 1879 a group of Albanian refugees from the Leskovac area complained that their houses, mills, mosques and tekkes had all been demolished, and that 'The material arising from these demolitions, such as masonry and wood, has been sold, so that if we go back to our hearths we shall find no shelter.'[39]

This was not, it should be said, a matter of spontaneous hostility by local Serbs. Even one of the Serbian Army commanders had been reluctant to expel the Albanians from Vranje, on the grounds that they were a quiet and peaceful people. But the orders came from the highest levels in Belgrade: it was Serbian state policy to create an ethnically 'clean' territory. And in an act of breath-taking cynicism, Ivan Yastrebov, the vice-consul in Kosovo of Serbia's protector-power, Russia, advised the governor of the vilayet not to allow the refugees to return to Serbia, on the grounds that their presence on Ottoman soil would usefully strengthen the Muslim population.[40]

All these new arrivals were known as *muhaxhirs* (Trk.: *muhacir*; Srb.: *muhadžir*), a general word for Muslim refugees. The total number of those who settled in Kosovo is not known with certainty: estimates ranged from 20,000 to 50,000 for Eastern Kosovo, while the governor of the vilayet gave a total of 65,000 in 1881, some of whom were in the sancaks of Skopje and Novi Pazar.[41] At a rough estimate, 50,000 would seem a reasonable figure for those muhaxhirs of 1877–8 who settled in the territory of Kosovo itself. Apart from the Albanians, smaller numbers of Muslim Slavs came from Montenegro and Bosnia: a village of Montenegrin Muslims from Nikšić was created near Prishtina, for example, and Prizren acquired a small Bosnian quarter, known as the *muhadžirska mahala*.[42] The Bosnians were not expelled by the Austrians, but chose to leave because they did not want to live under 'infidel' administration; since they constituted a self-selected group of particularly uncompromising Muslims, they brought a new level of anti-Christian feeling to the areas where they settled. Another wave of such Bosnian Muslims would arrive after 1908, when Austria fully annexed Bosnia-Hercegovina. According to some sources, the muhaxhirs were resented – whether they were Albanian or Slav – by the local Muslim Albanian population, which had to pay for the building of new houses for them. All sources are agreed that the muhaxhirs, for their own part, were particularly hostile to the local Christians, especially to the Orthodox Serbs.[43]

Partly as a result of this, there was a steady emigration of Serbs from Kosovo during this period. Local hostilities were not the only cause: the general stagnation and poor administration of the vilayet were good enough reasons for wanting to live elsewhere, and the attractions of life in Serbia (a fully independent country from 1878, and a kingdom from 1882) must have been very strong. There was no Ottoman state policy of expelling Serbs, and therefore no symmetry in principle between these migrations of Serbs and the uprooting of the Albanians in Serbia.

Precise numbers, once again, are lacking. Most of the figures which are commonly quoted are estimates made by Serbian diplomats or nationalist ethnographers of the period, who were all keen to demonstrate that conditions had become so intolerable in Ottoman Kosovo that it must be put under Serbian rule as quickly as possible. Thus the ethnographer Niko Županić, writing under a pseudonym, declared that 150,000 Serbs left Kosovo between 1876 and 1912 – a figure for which he presented no evidence at all, and which may have exceeded the total number of Orthodox Serbs in Kosovo at the starting-date.[44] More detailed estimates exist for particular areas and periods. In the 1890s, for example, the Serbian official Branislav Nušić compiled statistics for villages in the Peć region, from which he concluded that 15,756 Serbs had left in the period 1870–95.[45] In late 1879, a French official wrote that 25,000 Serbs had recently left from the *arrondissement* of Prishtina; but this total, given to him perhaps by local Serb activists or Serbian diplomats, looks improbably high, given that the kaza of Prishtina had a population of only 11,500 Orthodox Serbs in 1878 (and 15,268 in 1902).[46] Once again, only a rough estimate is possible for the total figure: 60,000 seems a reasonable assumption for the period 1876–1912. The combined effect of the Serbian emigration and the influx of Muslim Albanian refugees did further depress the proportion of Serbs in Kosovo: Austrian statistics of 1903 for the sancaks of Prishtina, Peć and Prizren gave the Orthodox Serbs as 25 per cent of the population, and Ottoman statistics of 1912 put it at 21 per cent.[47]

The activities of Serbian (and Russian) diplomats played an ever more important role during this period. While Russia had had a consulate in Prizren since the 1860s, Serbia was able to open such diplomatic offices only after it had become, formally speaking, an independent state: the first Serbian consulate in the region was established in Skopje in 1887, and Prishtina acquired a Serbian consulate two years later. Many Muslim Albanians viewed these developments as the first steps towards a Serbian annexation: the Serbian consul in Prishtina, Luka Marinković, was killed in 1890, and his assassins were never found.[48] Serbian diplomats were naturally concerned to protect the interests of the local Serbian Orthodox community; and more generally, all the outside powers had been given an opportunity to lobby diplomatically for the better treatment of Christians in Kosovo by a rather open-ended article inserted into the Treaty of Berlin. This article, number 23 in the treaty, would form the pretext on which Serbia and Montenegro invaded in 1912. It stated that for areas such as Kosovo and Macedonia a new administrative system would be adopted by the Ottoman government, and that the system, although 'adapted to local needs', would be broadly similar to the so-called Organic Statute introduced in Crete in 1868 (which had set up a mixed Christian–Muslim administration). But the Ottoman authorities dragged their feet, eventually producing only a vaguely worded decree in 1896 promising tax reforms, more schools and the better administration of justice.[49]

A new factor in the 1890s was the growth of a Slav Macedonian nationalist movement, campaigning for autonomy under the slogan 'Macedonia for the Macedonians'. The Serbian government regarded this as a Bulgarian ploy; and there were many Serbian officials who, convinced by the bogus ethnography of writers such as Milojević and Gopčević, believed that the Macedonian Slavs were all really Serbs. The language spoken by the Macedonians was certainly different from Serbian; but, on the other hand, many Slavs in this whole region of the Balkans did not have any strong sense of national identity at this stage. As the geographer Jovan Cvijić noted, the Slavs in the southern Morava valley had 'a very vague national consciousness' before 1878, and were only taught to think of themselves as Serbs thereafter. Slav speakers in the Kosovo region would refer to their language simply as *naš jezik* or *naški*, 'our language'; if they were members of the Serbian Orthodox Church they would call themselves Serbs, but this was a religious identification more than a national one.[50] Much effort was made by the Serbian consuls and Serbian-trained schoolteachers to instil a 'national' consciousness into these people. As late as 1912, one scandalized report by Milojević (who had become Serbian consul in Prishtina) said that some of the Serbs of Mitrovica were identifying themselves not as Serbians but as 'Kosovci', Kosovans, and had adopted the slogan, based on the Macedonian model, of 'Kosovo for the Kosovans'.[51]

By the late 1890s the agitation in Macedonia had entered a new phase,

with frequent raids by members of the 'Internal Macedonian Revolutionary Organization'. After the Ottoman–Greek war of 1897 the Western
powers also renewed their pressure on Istanbul to introduce the long-
overdue administrative reforms in Macedonia and the Albanian lands. A
congress of Macedonians and Bulgarians in Geneva was arranged for
January 1899, to demand the creation of an autonomous Macedonia
that would include the vilayets of Monastir and Kosovo.[52] It was in
reaction to such developments that a group of Albanian notables in
Kosovo started campaigning more actively for the old idea of uniting the
four vilayets with Albanian populations (Kosovo, Monastir, Ioannina
and Shkodra) into a single Albanian province. Some of the leaders of
this movement had been members of the League of Prizren: the most
charismatic of them, a fiery Muslim cleric called Haxhi Zeka, had been
on its central council. In 1893 Haxhi Zeka had led a revolt in Kosovo,
together with a young ex-officer called Bajram Curri, which was
suppressed by the Ottoman army; in 1897 there was more fighting in
Western Kosovo, and Haxhi Zeka began organizing meetings with the
aim of reviving the League, an activity that was continued throughout
the following year.[53]

As before, however, there were tensions within the movement. While
Haxhi Zeka wanted a large degree of autonomy (in order, apparently, to
insulate the Albanians from Istanbul's Westernizing reforms), he was
counterbalanced by an influential landowner from Western Kosovo, Riza
bey Kryeziu of Gjakova, who wanted the movement's efforts to be
directed only against the Sultan's enemies, not against the Sultan's own
authority. At the end of 1897 Riza bey went to Istanbul and held
discussions there in which he promised to defend the Sultan's interests:
in an interview in January 1898 he declared that 'All the Albanians,
without exception, are and remain devoted to the Sultan.'[54] The
summoning of a national gathering was organized by Haxhi Zeka: leaders
were invited from all the Albanian lands, but most of the 500 who
gathered in Peć in late January 1899 were from Kosovo. There it was
agreed to form a league which would function throughout the four
Albanian-inhabited vilayets: its first concern was to create a general *besë*
(truce, suspension of blood-feuds) among all the Albanians of those
areas, and for that reason it became known simply as 'Besa' or 'Besa-

Besë'. It is also commonly referred to as the League of Peja (the Albanian name for Peć).

Albanian history books give a rather misleading picture of the League of Peja. The image they present is of Haxhi Zeka on the one hand, striving for reforms, progress and independence, and the followers of Riza bey Kryeziu on the other, exerting a sinister reactionary influence; the outcome of the meeting is presented as something of a compromise between these two, but with a strongly progressive 'autonomist' element to it.[55] In fact there was little conflict here between autonomism and socio-political conservatism. As one of Ali Draga's sons put it in early January, the aim of the meeting would be 'to unite everyone in a general besë in order to be able to stand up to the Bulgarians, Serbs and Montenegrins, and reject all other sorts of reforms'.[56] In the previous month a Serbian official had had a conversation with Bajram Curri, Ferat bey Draga and his brother Ajdin, who all expressed the same wish: 'We want to restore the old Albania.' The reason for desiring some degree of autonomy was not to proceed more rapidly with social reforms but, on the contrary, to hold such innovations at bay: they wanted their courts, for example, to judge only by the Kanun of Lek Dukagjin. Interestingly, they thought this would be welcomed by the local Serbs, because public order would improve (as it had done under the League of Prizren). The only 'progressive' measure that appealed to them, it seems, was the introduction of Albanian-language education. They said that they read books printed in Albanian in Brussels or Bucharest 'with intense pleasure'; it is as if they had not noticed the difference between the modernizing and Westernizing programmes of the émigré presses and their own more traditionalist concerns.[57]

The final decisions of the meeting at Peć concentrated simply on territorial defence. A list of twelve points was agreed, beginning with loyalty to the Sultan, and the general besë was then sworn, according to a report by the Austrian consul, 'on the Koran, with a festive oath'. Autonomy was not mentioned in this list; the only implicitly autonomist elements of the programme were the treatment of the four vilayets as an overall Albanian unit, and the decision to set up local Muslim committees which would guard public order and enforce the şeriat and the customary law (the Kanun of Lek).[58] A few months later, armed

Albanians did force the governor of the vilayet of Kosovo to dismiss twelve officials; there was also a tax revolt in the Peć region, combined with calls for Albanian-language schools. But the Ottoman government defused the crisis, replacing the governor of the vilayet in 1900 and making various other concessions. Further local protests were organized by Haxhi Zeka in 1901, this time against the proposal to allow an Austrian railway line to extend from Bosnia to Mitrovica; the line was never built, however, and in the following year Haxhi Zeka was assassinated by an Albanian gendarme who was almost certainly in the pay of Belgrade.[59]

By now the Great Powers were intensifying their pressure on the government in Istanbul to make reforms in the Macedonian region. In early 1903 Russia and Austria-Hungary presented a joint proposal to the Sultan for changes in the vilayets of Salonica, Monastir and Kosovo: the key reform was to be the creation of a new gendarmerie, supervised by foreign officers, to which local Christians as well as Muslims would be recruited. (Later in the year a revised version of this plan was agreed by those two Great Powers at Mürzsteg, south-west of Vienna: it is therefore known as the Mürzsteg Accord.) Since this plan also involved disarming the population, the whole proposal was bitterly resented by the leaders of the Kosovo Albanians, who saw it, once again, as a step towards subjection to one of the Christian states.[60] Unfortunately the first announcement of the Austro-Russian plan coincided with the arrival of a new Russian consul in Mitrovica. A large force of Albanians, led by a local strongman, Isa Boletin, vowed both to oppose the reforms and to eject the new consul: on 30 March 1903 more than 2,000 of them attacked the Ottoman garrison in Mitrovica, which defended itself with artillery fire. During the fighting the Russian consul toured the Ottoman army positions on horseback. On the following day, when the fighting had died down, he was out visiting the soldiers again when one of them (an Albanian, who wished to avenge the death of one of his family) shot him; he died of his wounds ten days later.[61] Partly as a result of this murder, when the Mürzsteg programme began to be put into effect in the summer of 1904 it was decided not to apply the reforms in areas with majority Albanian populations.[62]

As these events show, the pressure exerted by the Great Powers on the Ottoman state tended to increase the suspicions and hostilities of

Albanian Muslims towards their Christian neighbours. The general deterioration in relations between them during this period should probably be blamed mostly on external developments of this sort. Isa Boletin, for example, was not a Christian-hater by nature. He had been employed as recently as 1898–9 to guard the Serbian Orthodox community in the Mitrovica region, and had been given a medal by the Serbian consul for his services as 'protector of the raya'; he would be noted for making further efforts on their behalf in 1912.[63] Similarly, the tradition of Albanian 'guardians' protecting the monastery of Dečani survived as late as 1898. In the next four years, however, there were several attacks on the monastery by mountain clansmen; the Metropolitan then hit on the idea of introducing Russian monks there, which greatly intensified the hostility of the Muslims.[64] Even the Serbian diplomats began to be irritated by the degree of Russian interference in Kosovo: one junior consular official, the talented young writer Milan Rakić, noted in 1905 that Serb villagers in the Dečani region were beginning to describe themselves, absurdly, as Russians.[65]

Rakić's letters from Kosovo provide a useful corrective to the wilder claims of the Serbs – some of which, as he observed, were promoted by his own boss, the consul. As Rakić pointed out, Serb peasants would exaggerate their sufferings 'in order to get some help, or money, or a rifle or revolver', and the number of Serb deaths was constantly overstated. In the first five months of 1905, he noted, twenty-five Serbs were killed in Kosovo, four of them by other Serbs and three by unknown hands. 'Is that number so desperately large? In Serbia many more people were killed in the same period,' he wrote. 'And why is it that we, for example, categorically assert in our daily bulletins that there are one or two murders every single day, when we know perfectly well that there are only twenty-five in five months?' Discussing ways of helping the Serb community in Kosovo, Rakić noted that the Foreign Ministry in Belgrade had accepted the idea of paying Albanian 'guardians' of Serb villages; he thought this was a workable strategy, so long as the deals were struck with the leading Albanian chiefs. But he advised against another scheme which the consul, Spalajković, had put forward: stirring up feuds between the Albanians. 'Of all the ways of helping our people here,' Rakić wrote, 'this is the most expensive and the most worthless.'[66] One other strategy, discussed by Spalajković but also strongly criticized by Rakić, was the sponsoring of Serb *četas* (armed bands). It was in fact the policy of the Belgrade government to encourage such bands, not to fight in Kosovo, but to oppose the Macedonian or Bulgarian četas in Macedonia and create a pro-Serbian movement there. Some of these bands were also active in the territory of Kosovo, however, where they occasionally fought pitched battles with local Albanians. Two such incidents became *causes célèbres* (the 'Velika Hoča affair' of 1905 and the 'Pasjan affair' of 1907), significantly harming relations between Albanians and Serbs.[67]

By 1908 nothing had changed in Kosovo: there were the usual sporadic revolts against taxation and conscription, including strong resistance in the spring and summer of that year to recruitment for an Ottoman campaign in the Yemen.[68] But important changes were under way in Ottoman political life. Since the 1890s a number of secret groups and semi-secret movements had been planning and campaigning for a radical overhaul of the Ottoman system. They were known collectively as the Young Turks; their membership was strongest among young army officers (such as Mustafa Kemal, later known as Atatürk), and their main political organization was called the Committee of Union and Progress. It was a title which aptly summarized their main aims. They wanted to unify the Ottoman Empire on the basis of a kind of Ottoman nationalism (this was not as paradoxical as it sounds: all citizens of the Empire had been declared Ottoman 'nationals' by a Nationality Law in 1869), and they wanted to subject the Empire to a crash programme of modernization and reform, starting with the full restoration of the suspended Constitution of 1876.[69] Such aims were almost the precise opposite of the wishes of the Kosovo Albanians, who wanted less centralization or unification, and were opposed to most varieties of Westernizing or modernizing reform (with the sole major exception of Albanian-language schools). In theory, therefore, Kosovo should have been a bulwark against the Young Turks. In practice, it played a key role in bringing them to power. The support of the Kosovo Albanians was won, quite simply, by a huge deception.

The Young Turks had not been without some contacts and support among the Albanians. One member of the influential Draga family, Nexhip, had been involved with them from the 1890s. There were local Young Turk committees in Prizren, Mitrovica and Ferizaj; the town of

Debar – thanks, perhaps, to the strong identification of the Bektashi with the Young Turk cause – was a particular centre of support. And the main strength of the Young Turks was in the officer corps (especially in the Third Army Corps, stationed in Macedonia), in which Albanians were well represented.[70] When the Young Turks led a large-scale mutiny in the Third Army Corps in early July 1908, they used what contacts they had to try to win over the leaders of the Kosovo Albanians to their side. Almost the only strong common interest was the desire to resist the encroachments of foreign powers on the territory of the Empire: and by a lucky coincidence for the Young Turks, Kosovo was already in a ferment over just that issue.

In early 1908 the old plan to extend the Austrian railway line from Bosnia to Mitrovica had been officially revived, and a commission of engineers had been sent to Kosovo in March; at the same time the Serbian government was discussing a plan for a railway that would pass through Kosovo and northern Albania to the Adriatic. These proposals, especially the Austrian one, were regarded with intense hostility in Kosovo.[71] During the first days of July rumours began to spread (whipped up, according to the Austrian consul, by 'Serb agitators') of an imminent Austro-Hungarian invasion. Thanks to a ludicrous misunder-standing about a special excursion train which had been arranged for the students of the railway training school at Skopje, the idea sprang up in Kosovo that the Austrian army was about to invade, by rail, from the south. Thousands of armed Albanians promptly descended on Ferizaj, the first main stop in Kosovo: by 5 July there were 3,000 men there, and the numbers were constantly growing.[72] The authorities sent the gen-darme chief from Skopje to disperse the gathering; they were unaware that he was in fact the leader of the local Young Turk committee, and had very different plans.

With the help of Nexhip Draga and Bajram Curri he persuaded the Kosovar leaders to summon yet more men – by mid-July the number reached 30,000 – and he brought in more delegates of the Young Turks to bombard the Albanians with rhetoric and win them over to the cause. The pledges they made in their speeches were grotesquely at variance with their real political programme: they promised to respect the traditional rights of the Sultan, implement the şeriat, and allow the Albanians all their old privileges, including (above all) the right to bear arms. The Kosovo chiefs accepted these promises, and informed their people, in the words of one Austrian consular report, 'that they had obtained everything they wanted, i.e. the exclusive re-imposition of the şeriat, the abolition of prisons, and the cancellation of all innovations and reforms'. On the strength of such pledges the Kosovo leaders signed a telegram, drafted by the Young Turks and addressed to the Sultan, demanding the restoration of the constitution of 1876. This telegram from the Ottoman bastion of Kosovo, as the Albanian statesman Ismail Qemal Vlora later recalled, had a stronger effect on the Sultan than the complaints of all the Turks or the Great Powers. He gave in to the Young Turks on 24 July, and restored the constitution.[73]

In the northern Albanian lands the news was received with triumph and euphoria. The men who returned to Prizren from the gathering at Ferizaj were met by a festive welcoming committee of Muslims and Christians, including the Christian clergy. The non-Muslims thought they would gain new rights; the Muslims thought their old privileges would be restored; and some of the Young Turk officers from the garrison spent the evening marching through the streets, singing the Marseillaise. How much understanding there was among ordinary people of the real nature of this suddenly famous 'constitution' is very uncertain. Two years later, when a French traveller asked some local dignitaries whether they had demanded the constitution, and, if so, whether they were satisfied with it, he received the reply: 'We don't know what the constitution is; we have heard of it; but we don't know what it is. What we want is the şeriat.'[74] A similar degree of ignorance, or naivety, was noted by Edith Durham, who attended the triumphant celebrations of the new 'Constituzi' (as it was adapted to local tongues) in Shkodra on 2 August. 'The Moslem band played outside the cathedral, and Christian and Moslem swore brotherhood on the Koran and a revolver. "Ah! la bella cosa, la libertà" cried a man to me. "We are united. Albania is free!"'[75] It would not take the Albanians of Kosovo long to discover just how grossly they had been deceived.

13

The great rebellions, the Serbian conquest and the First World War: 1908–1918

ALBANIAN SATISFACTION WITH the new régime was short-lived. For six months or so there was what might be called a honeymoon period, at least between the Young Turks and the more radical and intellectual Albanian circles – which operated mainly in Istanbul, Salonica and Albanian areas outside Kosovo. At the new elections for the Ottoman parliament twenty-five Albanian deputies were chosen; Albanian cultural and quasi-political societies known as 'clubs' sprang up in many Albanian towns (but not in Kosovo); a dozen new Albanian newspapers and journals appeared (none of them produced in Kosovo); and in November a pan-Albanian conference in Monastir finally agreed on a modified Latin alphabet for the Albanian language.[1] Some new Albanian-language schools were opened in Kosovo, but the Latin alphabet offended many of the Muslim clergy there, who wanted only the Arabic script to be used. The muftis of Prishtina and Debar issued proclamations against the 'infidel' alphabet; in this they were supported by the Young Turk committee in Salonica, which wanted to retain the Arabic script as a unifying factor for the whole Ottoman Empire.[2]

For ordinary Kosovars, however, most of whom were illiterate, there were other things to worry about. From an early stage it was made clear that military conscription, far from being abolished under the new dispensation, would be more strictly enforced. Edith Durham, who travelled through Kosovo soon after the proclamation of the constitution, found that this was the Albanians' main concern. 'Already in September I found distrust of the Turk all through Kosovo vilayet. The Moslems who had gathered at Ferizovitch [Ferizaj] and demanded the Constitution of Abdul Hamid saw they had been tricked.' As for the leaders of the Serb community there, they 'frankly lamented the Turkish revolution, and looked on it only as a frustration of all their schemes. A well-governed Turkey was the last thing they wished for, as it would prevent the creation of Great Serbia.'³ On that point, at least, their fears were unjustified. There were no significant improvements to the system of administration, beyond some ineffective attempts to enforce on the Albanians the old and much hated measures of disarmament, tax-collection and conscription.⁴

Confidence in the new régime was greatly weakened in October 1908 by two events: the annexation of Bosnia (which had remained up till then officially under Ottoman suzerainty) by Austria-Hungary, and the declaration of complete independence by Bulgaria. Muslim traditional-ists felt that the Young Turks were merely hastening the break-up of the Empire. In early 1909 there was an attempted coup, supported by such Muslims (particularly Albanian soldiers of the First Army Corps in Istanbul); when Riza bey Kryeziu, who had been interned in Aleppo, heard the news he wrote to his followers in Gjakova urging them to help overthrow the Young Turks. But the coup failed, and in its aftermath the Young Turks deposed the Sultan, sent him off to internal exile in Salonica, and installed a new and compliant successor. This act of *lèse-majesté* shocked many of the ordinary Albanians of Kosovo, who had been told at Ferizaj that the rights of the Sultan would remain inviolate. One person who was especially unhappy with the removal of Abdülhamit was Isa Boletin, who owed his position to the Sultan's patronage: in 1902 he had been appointed head of the Sultan's personal 'Albanian guard', with the title of *bey* ('lord'), and he had spent four years in Istanbul in that post. By late April 1909, when the Sultan was deposed, several areas of Kosovo were already rebelling against new taxes imposed by the Young Turks, and the rebellion was now intensified.⁵

To quell it a force of more than 5,000 men was sent to Kosovo, equipped with artillery batteries and machine-gun units. The com-mander was an energetic thirty-nine-year-old Circassian officer, Cavit pasha, who had a particular hatred of the Kosovo Albanians, having undergone a humiliating defeat by them in a previous campaign. With his small army he toured the Peć and Gjakova regions, enforcing a range of unpopular measures: gathering a backlog of two years' taxes, confis-cating arms, registering the population and destroying a total of sixty kullës (fortified tower-houses). By July he had returned to the garrison at Mitrovica; but local opinion was not impressed. Vice-consul Rakić reported that 'Cavit pasha had to come back without achieving anything, and all has stayed as it was.' Sure enough, he had to undertake another campaign against a more widespread rebellion in September, which had started in the Luma region south-west of Prizren. One Albanian writer commented that the Luma people would willingly have responded to a call to arms to defend the Empire, but that they would never tolerate being either disarmed or press-ganged. Cavit pasha caused fierce resentment by such actions as attacking a wedding party, because it was celebrating in the traditional way by firing in the air. By the end of his campaign the resistance was so intense that he was forced to retreat from Western Kosovo altogether.[6]

In the spring of 1910 another tax revolt broke out, this time starting in northern and north-eastern Kosovo: troops sent from Prishtina to deal with it were defeated in battle, and the revolt spread to many parts of Western Kosovo too. Now, for the first time since 1881, a large-scale coordinated rising was planned by Albanian chiefs from all parts of Kosovo. In late March the leaders of twelve clans of Western Kosovo met near Peć and agreed on joint action; Isa Boletin, who controlled the Mitrovica area, also coordinated his plans with a chief from the Skopska Crna Gora in the south, Idriz Seferi, who had taken over the town of Gjilan. Meanwhile the Ottoman authorities, alarmed by the scale of the revolt, gathered an army of 16,000 men and sent it to Skopje, under another Circassian commander, General Şefket Torgut pasha. The first action of the rebels was to send a force of 9,000 men under Idriz Seferi to Kaçanik, to block the railway line: they held it for several days, but were eventually driven back by the army, with heavy loss of life. The next military encounter was at Carraleva (Srb.: Crnoljevo), on the road from Ferizaj to Prizren, where Isa Boletin and Idriz Seferi tried to halt the westward advance of the Ottoman troops. But they were outnumbered and outflanked by the army (which had been given the assistance of local Serb villagers and schoolteachers to guide it through the mountains), and had to withdraw. By mid-May the army had seized Prizren, and the rebels had mainly retreated to Gjakova and Peć; those towns too were taken by the end of June, when the revolt was finally crushed. Boletin and Seferi escaped, but thousands were less fortunate: many were imprisoned or interned, and there were daily hangings in the bazaar at Prizren. Thousands of Albanians were press-ganged into the army and sent to Anatolia, and weapons were confiscated on a huge scale.[7]

Şefket Torgut pasha assembled more troops, up to a total of 40,000 men, and pushed on quickly through northern Albania to Shkodra, where he arrived in early July and declared martial law. The same measures were now enforced throughout the Malësi. No action could have been better calculated to embitter the entire population than this disarmament programme, which, by early September, had collected 147,525 guns; the official proclamations also demanded the handing in of all knives except bread-knives.[8] One unintended consequence of this policy was that it greatly strengthened the power of Montenegro over northern Albanian affairs, since the Albanians (both Catholic and Muslim) now depended on Montenegro to replenish their stock of arms. Many of the leaders of the revolt in Kosovo, including Isa Boletin, took refuge in Montenegro, where the government paid for their food and lodging: by the spring of 1911 it was estimated that there were nearly 5,000 Albanian rebels there, with 100 chiefs and bajraktars. Some of the Catholic clansmen of the Albanian–Montenegrin border region also moved into Montenegro, while arms were smuggled in the opposite direction to Catholics who stayed put in the Malësi.[9] Nikola of Montenegro was a man of ever-expanding political ambitions; symbolically, it was during 1910 that he elevated his own rank from 'Prince' to 'King'. What was new about his tactics now was his willingness to support Muslim rebels as well as Christian ones. But his basic strategy, clearly, was the same as before: to stimulate unrest in northern Albania and north-western Kosovo, to the point where he could intervene and annex more territory for Montenegro.

Serbian policy, on the other hand, was more cautious at this stage. The crisis in relations between Serbia and Austria-Hungary after the latter's annexation of Bosnia had made the Serbian government less hostile to the Ottoman state, not least because it now depended on the port of Salonica for its own arms imports: a high-level Serbian delegation went to Istanbul to make new trade agreements in 1910. Fear of Austria-Hungary was the dominant factor in Serbian policy, and although the Austrians had now removed their garrisons from the Sandžak of Novi Pazar, it was thought that they would seize any opportunity to march in again and annex that territory, and perhaps even Kosovo and Macedonia too. So when King Nikola of Montenegro asked the Serbian government to join him in a more active anti-Ottoman policy in the region based on a division of 'areas of interest' (most of Kosovo and Skopje for Serbia, Peć and northern Albania for Montenegro), the Serbs warned against it. And when a committee of Albanian rebels sent an emissary to Belgrade in March 1911 to ask for help, the Serbian Foreign Minister recorded in his notes that Serbia had no interest in assisting a full-scale rebellion in Kosovo, which might lead to the creation of an autonomous Albanian state, but that continual unrest might be useful.[10] In most ways, however, the thrust of Serbian policy was directed quite actively against the Albanians, to the point of giving direct support to the Young Turk régime – as the instructions to Serb schoolmasters to assist Şefket Torgut pasha's campaign in 1910 clearly showed.

One other sign of this was the creation of an 'Organization of Ottoman Serbs', set up in Skopje with Young Turk approval in 1908 under the leader of the *četniks* (fighters in Serb četas or armed bands), Radenković. It had branches throughout Kosovo and Macedonia, published a newspaper (*Vardar*) and generally supported the Young Turk programme: in 1910 it joined a virulent new Young Turk campaign against the use of the Latin alphabet by the Albanians. The Orthodox Metropolitan of Skopje also signed a decree for the suppression of this alien script. There were links between the Organization of Ottoman Serbs and the new Serb nationalist paramilitary movement, the 'Narodna Odbrana'; in late 1910 an Ottoman envoy met the leaders of that movement in Belgrade, who agreed to help the Young Turks, in return for more freedom of action for the Organization of Ottoman Serbs in its campaigns against Albanians and Macedonians.[11]

In March 1911 the Catholic clansmen who had taken refuge in Montenegro crossed back on to Ottoman soil to begin a new revolt. The Muslim Kosovar Isa Boletin seems to have been involved in this rebellion from an early stage, but the initial action was confined to the northern Albanian Catholic clans, who were getting arms and encouragement from Montenegro. By April the revolt had spread to the Mirdita area, further to the south-east. A radical Arbëresh lawyer from Calabria, Terenzio Tocci (Terenc Toçi) was also touring the region, calling on the clan chiefs to rise up; in late April, with the support of the Mirdita and some of the local Muslim clans, he announced the creation of a 'Provisional Government' there, under the slogan 'Albania for the Albanians'.[12] Various committees of Albanian activists issued declarations: the one which achieved widest circulation was a so-called 'Red Book' published by Ismail Qemal bey in Montenegro, a proclamation which began by making a statement of loyalty to the Sultan, and went on to present the by now familiar autonomist demands in a list of thirteen points: Albanian-speaking officials, military service to be local only, tax revenues to be reserved for local use, respect for religious and traditional customs (i.e. the şeriat and the Kanun of Lek), official recognition of Albanian nationhood, Albanian-language schools, and so on.[13]

But the 1911 rising in northern Albania suffered from weaknesses and divisions. In the Shkodra region the authorities succeeded in persuading the local Muslim Albanians that it was part of an 'infidel' plot against the Empire (which, so far as Montenegro's involvement was concerned, it was). And just as the general Kosovo rising of 1910 had not been supported by the Malësi, so this large revolt in the Malësi in 1911 was not coordinated with any significant rising in either Kosovo or the south of Albania. After some successes by the Ottoman army, an armistice was declared. Concessions on several of the thirteen points were offered (though only to the Malësi, not to all the Albanian lands); the Catholic clansmen, suddenly abandoned by Montenegro, were obliged to accept in early August.[14]

The Young Turk government had decided to take a conciliatory line with the Albanians, and for that purpose it had also organized a visit to Kosovo by the Sultan, Mehmet V, two months earlier. He arrived in Prishtina on 15 June, where he was welcomed by the choir of the Serbian Orthodox Seminary, serenading him with Turkish songs; vice-consul Rakić had gathered a large contingent of Serbs, but the Albanians of many areas of Kosovo boycotted the event. On 16 June the Sultan, accompanied by the Grand Vizier, went to the tomb of Sultan Murat at the site of the battle of Kosovo. There a proclamation was read, announcing an amnesty for all those who had taken part in the revolt in 1910.[15] The Kosovo Albanians were still demanding compensation for the destruction of their homes and the confiscation of their weapons, and when news came of the concessions to the Malësi in August there were some uprisings in Kosovo by people demanding the same privileges for themselves. But a declaration of war by Italy against the Ottoman Empire in September, followed quickly by the Italian seizure of Tripoli and much of the Libyan coast, made the Kosovo leaders feel that any revolt would only facilitate conquests by Christian states in the Balkans too. So they decided to bide their time.[16]

New elections were announced for the Ottoman parliament in early 1912. In an attempt to improve the image of the Young Turk administration, a high-ranking government commission (including a British official, Mr Graves) was sent to Kosovo and Albania to inquire into conditions there and make promises of reform: it was widely viewed, however, as nothing more than a piece of cynical electioneering, issuing promises about schools and road-building programmes that were unlikely ever to be fulfilled.[17] Meanwhile the Young Turks were making great efforts to ensure that none of the Albanian deputies who had become such troublesome voices of opposition in the parliament would be re-elected. Foremost among the deputies from Kosovo was Hasan bey Prishtina (so called because he had been elected to represent Prishtina in 1908; his family name was Berisha). He had studied at the French lycée in Salonica and had originally joined the Young Turks, before joining an opposition group led by Ismail Qemal Vlora in 1909. He had become a very popular figure in Kosovo, thanks to his campaign for Albanian-language schools and his widely reported speeches in the Istanbul parliament denouncing the brutalities of the Ottoman army in Kosovo in 1909 and 1910.[18] Hasan Prishtina was a man in the tradition of Abdyl and Sami Frashëri, a Westernized intellectual rather than a pious Muslim traditionalist; the incompetence and intolerance of the Young Turk administration had convinced him that the Albanian lands must seek more or less full autonomy, but, like Abdyl Frashëri before him, he had to adjust his demands and his rhetoric to the concerns of those Kosovo traditionalists – such as Isa Boletin – who retained a deep loyalty to the old Sultan and to the idea of the Ottoman Empire.

An interesting account of Hasan Prishtina's position was given by the British vice-consul in Skopje, who received a visit from him in late April 1912. 'He assured me', the diplomat reported, 'that the general revolt in Albania is imminent. Albanians will demand annulment of elections throughout Turkey ... Failing this they will demand complete autonomy for Albania . . .' Asked about the form this 'complete autonomy' would take, Prishtina said that 'He aspired to complete fiscal and military separation and to an Albanian republic whose connection with the Porte should be merely nominal.' But, the vice-consul noted, 'He did not appear to have a cut-and-dried programme of the minimum which would be accepted.'[19] Prishtina's preference for virtual independence was later toned down for the benefit of cooperation with other rebel leaders in Kosovo. Thus a 'manifesto' signed by him, Isa Boletin, Riza bey Kryeziu and Bajram Curri at the end of June began by declaring that 'The Albanians are, and always will be, firmly attached to the Caliphate and the Ottoman Fatherland with a fidelity which nothing can shake'; it explained that they were rebelling only because the 'accursed and execrable policy' of the Young Turks was ruining the Empire and would lead, if unchecked, to a foreign invasion.[20] But elsewhere, especially in central and southern Albania, there were other leaders whose ideas were closer to Hasan Prishtina's. One such leader, a member of the shadowy 'Albanian Committee', gave a frank assessment to an Italian writer in 1912: he agreed that ordinary Albanians had remained loyal to the Ottoman Empire until a few years before, and he also admitted that they had a clearer idea of what they were fighting against (Young Turk oppression) than of what they were fighting for. 'But', he added, 'those who are directing the movement, on the other hand, know perfectly well what their aims are . . .'[21] By the end of the year those aims would be fulfilled, after a fashion, in Albania, but thwarted, disastrously for the Albanians, in Kosovo.

The revolt began in the spring of 1912 in parts of Western Kosovo, especially round Gjakova and Peć. In late May several thousand rebels met at Junik, between those two towns, where their leaders swore a general besë and vowed to overturn the Young Turk régime. Those present included Hasan Prishtina, Nexhip Draga (who had also dissociated himself from the Young Turks by now), Bajram Curri, his old rival from Gjakova Riza bey Kryeziu, and Isa Boletin (who, rumour said, was particularly angry with the Young Turks because they had cut off the pension he used to receive from the Sultan). Together they drew up a twelve-point programme, based on the thirteen-point 'Red Book' of the previous year, and sent it off to Istanbul.[22] According to Hasan Prishtina's later account, there was some backsliding by some of the local beys; so he decided to begin military action immediately. The first operation, an attempt to seize the whole town of Peć on 30 May, was unsuccessful, and two Ottoman divisions drove the Albanian fighters out of Junik; but by late June the revolt had spread to many other parts of Kosovo – as well as to much of Albania, including the Mirdita area, Tirana and Shkodra – and there were widespread desertions by Albanian soldiers in the army.[23]

The reaction of the Ottoman authorities was cack-handed at first. Their arrest and internment of the wives of some of the rebel leaders was regarded by the Albanians, who had a strict code of honour where women were concerned, as a peculiarly despicable act. The revolt continued to grow, until by the end of July the rebels had taken over Prishtina, Mitrovica, Vuçitërn and Ferizaj, and the governor of Prizren had fled in disguise over the mountains to Tetovo (where Albanians searched for him in one of the inns, and finally discovered him 'cowering in the water-closet').[24] With more than 25,000 armed men assembled in Prishtina, and another 20,000 covering the south-eastern corner of Kosovo, this rebellion had reached the point where the authorities could no longer contemplate a military solution; so in the last week of July they sent a high-ranking commission, followed by a new acting governor of Kosovo, to parley with the rebels. The Albanians' first demand was the dissolution of the new parliament, which they regarded as gerrymandered and fraudulently elected; this was granted on 5 August.[25]

Four days later the Albanian leaders in Prishtina (who had now been joined by representatives from many parts of Albania) presented a further list of fourteen demands, which became known as the 'Fourteen Points' of Hasan Prishtina. Several slightly different versions of this list were being circulated. The most striking new demand was for the impeachment of various recent government ministers; but otherwise, broadly speaking, the Fourteen Points were the standard list of demands which went back to the 'Red Book' of 1911 (and, on some points, all the way back to the demands of Abdyl Frashëri in 1878 and 1877): the treatment of the Albanian lands as a unit, Albanian schools and officials, military service in Albania except in times of war, and so on. The word 'autonomy' was not used, but the substance of it was there, even though the text was vague about the actual borders of the proposed Albanian unit. And at the same time, to satisfy the traditionalists, there was a demand that the 'religious and national laws' of the Albanians (the şeriat and the Kanun) should be kept in place.[26]

Receiving no immediate reply from Istanbul, the rebels decided to pile on more pressure: they sent their troops to occupy Skopje. This was done without bloodshed, and by 14 August there were 16,000 armed Albanians in and around the city; Hasan Prishtina, Riza Kryeziu and the other leaders joined them over the next two days. The men were kept under strict discipline, and the British vice-consul was able to report that 'Public order here has been good, the Albanians have even, with rare exceptions, refrained from their favourite amusement of firing their rifles in the air.'[27] To the government in Istanbul, which was still fighting a war against Italy and was facing a new revolt in the Yemen, the fact that they were dealing with a disciplined force and not with some mere rabble of tribesmen must have weighed heavily in the balance. They were probably aware that some of the traditionalists among the Kosovo leaders, such as Isa Boletin and Riza Kryeziu, were in favour of continuing their southwards march all the way to Salonica, to free and restore the deposed Sultan. And so it was that, on 18 August, the authorities agreed to grant almost all of the fourteen demands. They demurred on the request for impeachment, and hedged on one or two other points; a further dilution was made later, in a somewhat sneaky way, when the Ottoman government published the text of the Fourteen Points in an altered wording which avoided the use of the terms 'Albania' or 'Albanian' except in the preamble. But the overall concessions were large enough to satisfy Hasan Prishtina, who accepted the deal; the idea of a march to Salonica was abandoned, and the Albanian fighters began to return home.[28]

This was the high, culminating point of all the various struggles for national recognition by the Albanians since 1878. At long last a framework had been agreed for an Albanian quasi-state, within the Ottoman Empire, in which a national culture and national institutions for all the Albanians could have developed over time. But there was no time. Within two months the Ottomans would be driven out of most of their European possessions; and indeed it was the upheaval of the Albanian revolt in 1912 which both persuaded the Balkan states that the time was ripe for an anti-Ottoman war, and so fatally weakened the Ottomans that the war was quickly won. As the English traveller and politician Aubrey Herbert put it six years later in a memorandum on the Albanians: 'In the end, like Samson in the Temple of Gaza, they pulled down the columns of the Ottoman Empire upon their own head. It was the Albanians and not the Serbs or Bulgars or Greeks who defeated the Turks.'[29]

But if long-term responsibility for this outcome needs to be apportioned, it must surely lie in the first place with those Ottoman policy-makers who had so doggedly resisted the Albanian demands over the previous thirty-four years. The psychology of their refusals is not hard to understand, of course. The Young Turks were trying to create a more centralized and unified Ottoman national state; decentralizing in favour of people who had traditionally been viewed as loyal Ottomans was the last thing they intended. More generally, 'autonomy' in Ottoman Europe was associated with the gradual emancipation of Christian states, the chrysalis stage they went through before fluttering off as independent countries. This process was grudgingly accepted where the Christians were concerned, but Ottoman rulers found it an unthinkable thing to happen to their Muslim subjects. The mistake, however, was theirs. If autonomy had been freely granted to the Albanians it might eventually have paved the way to independence; but that path would have been a long one, and in the meantime the Albanians of Kosovo would have formed a strong bastion against any further encroachments on the Empire. Aubrey Herbert, who visited Kosovo during these last months of Ottoman rule, summarized the desires of the Albanians very simply: 'The real complaint, first and last, is that their honour and freedom are not sufficiently considered.' The word 'freedom' here meant not political independence, but freedom to live by their own values and traditions. Similarly, when he asked Isa Boletin if the ordinary Albanians wanted autonomy, he received a plain reply: '"No," he said, "they did not; what they wanted was not to be interfered with."'[30] Interference, nevertheless, was what the Albanians of Kosovo would experience for a very long time to come.

Serbian plans for an anti-Ottoman war had begun to be formed in early 1912. In March Serbia made a 'treaty of friendship' with Bulgaria; a secret annex to that treaty set out the terms of possible joint military action against the Ottoman Empire, and agreed that Serbia would have rights over all territory to the north of the Šar mountains.[31] Bulgaria, acting under Russian guidance, now became the centre of a diplomatic network of alliances. Greece joined in May; Montenegro (whose relations with Serbia were quite frosty) joined the Bulgarian alliance in August, and finally made a secret military agreement with Serbia in September.[32] King Nikola revived his former contacts with Catholic clansmen in northern Albania, while the Serbian government spent the summer delivering arms to the Kosovo region – not only to Serb leaders there, but also to those Albanian chiefs whom it thought it could influence or control. In early 1912 Serbian officials had offered arms to the Albanians under the strict condition that they must then act only under Serbia's instructions. But as the summer wore on the conditions were relaxed, as Belgrade realized that it could benefit from almost any way that the weapons were used: at the same time as it was arming Albanians, it was running a publicity campaign complaining of Albanian 'lawlessness' against a defenceless Serb population. Serbian agents had several meetings with Bajram Curri, and Nexhip Draga also visited Belgrade.[33] But the main contact was with Isa Boletin, who was known to be well disposed towards Serbs: various Serbian envoys were sent to parley with him, including the notorious Colonel Apis of the nationalist 'Black Hand' movement. Large quantities of weapons were delivered to Boletin in August and September 1912, and it was also rumoured that Serbia paid him a large monthly subsidy; but, as events would show, his honour was not so easily bought.[34]

During August and September Montenegro arranged 'incidents' on its southern border, and Serbia increased the activities of its četnik bands on the frontier with Kosovo. The propaganda war was also stepped up: Western consuls were given a new list of Albanian 'atrocities' in mid-September. (The British vice-consul in Skopje investigated twelve cases on the list, and concluded: 'Some of the cases reported were untrue, and in others ... the responsibility rests with the Serbs.')[35] On 28 September Serbia complained that the Ottoman army was 'mobilizing', although the truth was the precise opposite: three Ottoman regiments completed their withdrawal from Kosovo on that very day. Just two days later, Serbia, Bulgaria and Greece began their own general mobilization. In response to this, the Ottoman War Ministry did begin mobilizing on 1 October, but its strength in the Macedonian region had been sapped by desertions during the Albanian revolt, as well as by a subsequent purge of 'unreliable' elements. Reservists and completely untrained recruits were called up in the Kosovo vilayet; many were then sent home again because there was not enough money for provisions.[36] On 13 October Serbia, Bulgaria and Greece presented an ultimatum to the Ottoman Empire, referring to article 23 of the Treaty of Berlin and demanding an immediate grant of autonomy to all its European Christian subjects; five days later they made their declaration of war. But Montenegro had already declared war on its own account, and begun its invasion, as early as 8 October. Rumour had it that King Nikola broke ranks in this way in order to make a killing on the Paris stock exchange.[37]

The advance by the Serbian Third Army into Kosovo began before Serbia's declaration of war, on 16 October. There were 76,000 men in the Third Army; facing it were disorganized Ottoman army units of approximately 16,000 men. Of the Kosovo Albanians, some had not responded to the official call-up: a few did not want to fight at all, but most, apparently, were willing to fight so long as they did so in their own traditional formations. A report from Skopje on 12 October said that several thousand armed Albanians had arrived there, and had asked to be sent to the front line; other bajraktars had telegraphed to promise tens of thousands of men. On 16 October the French consul reported that Isa Boletin, 'who people said had been bought by Serbia, is making strenuous propaganda against that country, and has armed 1,000 of his people with good Mauser rifles', 800 of whom he had sent to defend the frontier.[38] A Serbian journalist who was with the Third Army confirmed that Boletin's men put up a stiff resistance in north-eastern Kosovo: he estimated Boletin's force, which included men under the veteran fighter Idriz Seferi, at 20,000 men (probably an exaggerated figure, to magnify the Serbian victory), and also noted the disappointment of the Serbian strategists who thought they had bought Boletin's services. The Serbs fought their way through, destroying Albanian villages as they passed, and reached Prishtina, which they took on 22 October; by then they had lost 1,448 dead and wounded. Boletin went back to Mitrovica to get more men, but the fighters he gathered were persuaded by the Ottoman garrison commander to stay there, on an assurance that a large Ottoman force was coming to Kosovo: in fact the commander merely wanted them to cover his own retreat, which he promptly effected. After this delay Mitrovica itself came under Serbian attack, and Isa Boletin had to fall back first to Gjakova, then to Prizren, then into Albania.[39]

Meanwhile Boletin's comrade in arms, Idriz Seferi, organized more resistance in his home area of Ferizaj: this was where the fiercest fighting in Kosovo took place. But the Albanians were forced by superior numbers and firepower to retreat into the hills; and, at the same time, a major encounter between the Serbian First Army (132,000 men) and the Ottoman army outside Kumanovo ended, after two days' pitched battle, in a massive Ottoman defeat. While the First Army continued deeper into Macedonia, the Third Army now turned westwards across Kosovo, to finish the conquest of the territory and to press on through northern Albania to the coast.[40] When they reached the outskirts of Prizren on 31 October they found a large Ottoman force, equipped with artillery and machine-guns, which had withdrawn from the Montenegrin front. The local Albanians begged its commander to stay and defend the city, but he ignored them and continued his retreat southwards to Debar. Prizren thus surrendered without a fight on 3 November; Gjakova was attacked simultaneously by Serbian and Montenegrin forces on the following day, and was strongly defended by 5,000 Albanians under Bajram Curri, until heavy artillery fire forced them to head for the hills; and Peć had already fallen to the Montenegrin army on 30 October. The conquest of Kosovo was now complete, and the Serbian army pressed on through the Malësi to the Adriatic coast.[41] Meanwhile a group of Albanian politicians led by Ismail Qemal Vlora had decided to proclaim a new independent Albanian state. They travelled to his home town, the southern Albanian port of Vlora, and made their proclamation on 28 November. But by then most of northern Albania, and large parts of the south as well, had been occupied by foreign troops.

The reaction in Serbia to the Ottoman defeat was understandably euphoric. The Serbian press had been full of references to medieval history and the battle of Kosovo: in its ideological justification of the war to its home audience, the government relied much more on medieval history and folk poetry than on article 23 of the Treaty of Berlin. A special commemoration was held on the battle-site of Kosovo Polje on 23 October, and three days later the Crown Prince made a visit to Skopje, which was now constantly referred to as the capital of Stefan

Dušan's empire.[42] Most Western commentators were touched by this historical romanticism (a typical example was the British historian G. M. Trevelyan, who visited the area as a guest of the Serbian army in 1913), and were also persuaded by the argument that Serbian rule would introduce a higher level of civilization to the region; the latter idea also satisfied many radicals on the European left. But there were a few dissenting voices. One journalist who covered the war, the Vienna correspondent of the Ukrainian newspaper *Kievskaia Mysl*, Lev Bronshtein (better known in history as Leon Trotsky), was shocked by the evidence he encountered of atrocities by Serbian and Bulgarian forces. One Serbian officer told him that the worst of these were committed not by the regular army but by the paramilitary četniks: 'Among them were intellectuals, men of ideas, nationalist zealots, but these were isolated individuals. The rest were just thugs, robbers, who had joined the army for the sake of loot.' But further evidence convinced Trotsky that the killing of Albanians and the destruction of their villages was the product of something more than private initiative: he concluded that 'The Serbs in Old Serbia, in their national endeavour to correct data in the ethnographical statistics that are not quite favourable to them, are engaged quite simply in systematic extermination of the Muslim population.'[43] A few radicals in the Serbian Social Democratic Party, notably Dimitrije Tucović, did protest at the Serbian policy, and an Austrian Social Democrat, Leo Freundlich, collected evidence of Serb atrocities which he published in 1913 under the title *Albaniens Golgotha* (Albania's Golgotha).[44] But it was not only the radicals of the left who noticed that something was wrong.

Edith Durham was in Montenegro during October 1912, and when the fighting was over in Kosovo the British military attaché asked her to go with him on a visit to Prizren; but the trip was forbidden by the authorities. As she later recalled: 'I asked wounded Montenegrins why I was not to be allowed to go and they laughed and said "We have not left a nose on an Albanian up there!" Not a pretty sight for a British officer.' Later she did visit one northern Albanian outpost, where she saw captured Ottoman soldiers whose noses and upper lips had been cut off.[45] Most foreign journalists were forbidden to enter Kosovo, but some news did emerge: a Danish journalist in Skopje reported that 5,000 Albanians had been killed in Prishtina after the capture of that city, and wrote that the Serbian campaign had 'taken on the character of a horrific massacring of the Albanian population'. Some information reached the outside world through the Catholic Church: it was from a local Catholic priest that the *Daily Telegraph* learned of a massacre at Ferizaj, where the Serbian commander had invited the Albanian men to return to their homes in peace, and where those who did so (300–400 men) were then taken out and shot. The fullest and most chilling account was given by Lazër Mjeda, the Catholic Archbishop of Skopje, in a report to Rome of 24 January 1913. He said that in Ferizaj only three Muslim Albanians over the age of fifteen had been left alive; that the Albanian population of Gjilan had also been massacred, although the town had surrendered without a fight; and that Gjakova had been completely sacked. But the worst case was Prizren, which, like Gjilan, had peacefully surrendered:

> The city seems like the Kingdom of Death. They knock on the doors of the Albanian houses, take away the men, and shoot them immediately. In a few days the number of men killed reached 400. As for plunder, looting and rape, all that goes without saying; henceforth the order of the day is: everything is permitted against the Albanians – not merely permitted, but willed and commanded. And despite all these horrors, the military commander, Božo Janković, forced the city notables, with his revolver in his hand, to send a telegram of thanks to King Peter!

Altogether, the Archbishop estimated the total number of Albanians killed in Kosovo by this stage at 25,000. This was in agreement with other reports in the European press, which had given an estimate of 20,000 in early December.[46] In 1914 an international commission of enquiry set up by the Carnegie Endowment published its own findings. It did not hazard a guess as to the total number of Albanians killed, but it did conclude that something in the nature of a systematic policy had been at work: 'Houses and whole villages reduced to ashes, unarmed and innocent populations massacred ... such were the means which were employed and are still being employed by the Serb–Montenegrin soldiery, with a view to the entire transformation of the ethnic character of regions inhabited exclusively by Albanians.'[47]

One special feature of the Serbian and Montenegrin policy was the forced conversion of Muslims and Catholics to Orthodoxy. This was applied with peculiar vigour by the Montenegrins, who controlled the

Peć region; by May 1913 the Austrian consul in Prizren reported that 2,000 Muslim families in the town of Peć had been converted, and that those who refused were tortured or shot. The whole population of the Lug i Baranit district (a group of Muslim Albanian villages south-east of Peć) was brought into the town by the army for compulsory baptism, and each family was then given an Orthodox godfather. Catholics in the Montenegrin zone were also put under pressure: a Catholic priest in Gjakova, Fra Luigj Palaj or Palić, was unable to save his parishioners from forced conversion, and was then bayoneted to death for refusing to make the Orthodox sign of the cross. By late March 1913 Archbishop Mjeda was complaining that 1,200 of his flock there had been forcibly converted to Orthodoxy.[48] In the Serbian zone the policy was less severely applied; but the chief of the Prishtina district proudly informed Belgrade in May 1913 that 195 Muslim Albanians there had converted, and it was also reported that the Slav-speaking Catholics of Janjevo had come under strong pressure to change to Orthodoxy.[49]

The immediate reason for all these measures was, as some of the reports quoted above clearly recognized, to change the population statistics and thereby strengthen the diplomatic case of the Serbian and Montenegrin governments for the right to incorporate these conquered lands. The leaders of the Balkan states had felt confident enough to start the war against the wishes of most of the Great Powers; but once the fighting was over, they knew that their territorial expansion would be subject to the approval of those countries, just as it had been in 1878. At first, the overriding concern of the Serbian government was to obtain an outlet to the sea. Prime Minister Pašić told the *Times* in November: 'It is essential that Serbia should possess about fifty kilometres from Alessio [Lezha] to Durazzo [Durrës]. This coastline would be joined to what was formerly Old Serbia' – in other words, Serbia would extend from Kosovo through most of northern Albania. Similarly, the former Serbian consul in Prishtina, Branislav Nušić, told a British diplomat in November that Serbia's southern frontier would run from Lake Ohrid and along the river Shkumbin (which flows westwards across the middle of Albania) to the sea. It was, however, a fixed principle of Austro-Hungarian foreign policy that Serbia should not become an Adriatic power; Italy agreed on this, and Britain gave its support, first because it did not want to provoke a crisis with Austria-Hungary, and secondly because it could see no ethnographic justification for giving such a swathe of Albanian territory to the Serbs.[50] It was because they knew that such ethnographic questions were bound to be raised that the Serbian authorities were keen to reduce, minimize or reclassify the non-Serb population in areas they had conquered. Thus the census which they carried out in Kosovo in early 1913 recorded no Albanians at all in the town of Prishtina – even though a Russian journalist noted that half the population of the town was Albanian in 1915, and a Bulgarian census managed to find 11,486 of them there in 1916.[51]

The Great Powers (Austria-Hungary, Britain, France, Germany, Italy and Russia) discussed the territorial changes at a conference in London which started in December 1912. It was quickly agreed that Serbia would not extend to the coast, and that an autonomous Albania would be created: Austria-Hungary argued that all Albanian-inhabited lands should be included in it, but was opposed by France and, most strongly, by Serbia's protector-power, Russia. Much haggling then ensued, with Austria-Hungary first of all claiming Ohrid, Debar, Prizren, Gjakova and Peć for the new Albanian state, but then yielding them in a series of concessions to Russia. In return, Russia conceded Shkodra to the Albanians, and also the Luma district to the south-west of Prizren. The last town on Austria-Hungary's list to be given up was Gjakova, which was yielded on the specific condition that there would be effective protection for the Albanian and Catholic minorities in the new Serbian and Montenegrin territories.[52]

The borders of the new Albanian state were described in a text which the Great Powers finalized in March 1913; a commission of officers from those six countries was then assembled to mark out the frontier on the ground. It travelled to Lake Ohrid in October, and worked northwards from there, reaching Prizren on 1 December. Unfortunately the wording of the text they were meant to implement was ambiguous: it said the frontier should pass between 'the district of Prizren' and 'the district of Luma', but did not specify the type of district (geographical area, Ottoman sancak, Ottoman kaza of 1910, or Ottoman kaza of pre-1910). The Russian and French representatives insisted on exploiting these ambiguities to gain more land for Serbia, and the commission's work ended in deadlock in mid-December. All that Austria-Hungary could suggest was that the disputed area should be treated, for the time being, as a 'neutral zone'.[53] By this time one other dispute, between Serbia and Montenegro over the apportioning of the conquered land, had at least been settled: in November 1913 they agreed that Montenegro could keep Peć, Dečani and Gjakova. There was something paradoxical about this outcome: Serbia had declared to the world that one of its prime reasons for the conquest of Kosovo lay in the historic rights of the Patriarchate of Peć, but it now conceded the seat of the Patriarchate itself to a foreign state.[54]

Meanwhile the conditions of life for the majority Albanian population in Kosovo had not improved. In December 1912 the Serbian King issued a personal decree placing the region under military rule; the Albanians were warned that they must hand in all weapons or be regarded as enemies and hunted down. Another royal decree-law for the 'liberated areas' in August 1913 was based on a law of 1885 for the 'liquidation of bandits': it allowed for the deportation of entire villages, and contained clauses against gatherings of more than five people in the evenings, and against any form of 'propaganda against the state'. An even more draconian 'Decree on Public Security', issued in September, said that anyone resisting the authority of the state would be punished by five years' hard labour, and that 'the decision of the police authorities ... is sufficient proof of the commission of crime'; anyone declared a criminal by the police who did not give himself up within ten days could be killed by any state official, civil or military.[55]

As these decrees may suggest, resistance had continued in some areas. In the summer of 1913 small bands of Albanian rebels, known as *kaçaks* (an Albanian term for rebels or bandits, from a Turkish word meaning 'fugitive'), were active in the Peć and Gjakova region. All forms of resistance were severely dealt with. In September, after a Serbian officer had tried to rape an Albanian woman and had been shot dead by her husband in the village of Fshaj, that village and two others were destroyed and thirty-five Albanians burnt to death. Also in September a large rebellion was organized in the Luma region and the mountains west of Gjakova, with Isa Boletin, Bajram Curri and other leaders coming from inside Albania to direct it; the Serbs shot many of the Albanian notables in Gjakova *pour encourager les autres*, assembled an army of more than 20,000 men, and launched a campaign deep into Albanian territory. They had almost reached Elbasan when an ultimatum from Austria-Hungary obliged them to stop.[56]

A detailed report by the Austrian consul in Prizren in January 1914 summed up conditions in Kosovo at that time. He noted that none of the Serbs' promises of equal treatment for Muslims and Albanians had been kept. Of the thirty-two mosques in Prizren, thirty had been taken over by the army as barracks, ammunition stores and hay-barns. The local administration now consisted mainly of former Serb četniks, and the degree of corruption, he observed, was far worse than anything experienced under the Turks. The ordinary Serbs of the city were also dissatisfied: they had hoped for economic progress, but experienced only higher taxes which even the Orthodox had to pay, albeit at lower rates than the Catholics or the Muslims. Some of the Muslims intended to emigrate to Turkey, Albania or Bosnia, he wrote, but most of the Albanians were determined to stay, believing that Serbian rule in Kosovo would turn out to be only a temporary oppression.[57] Many did in fact leave, but the figures are very uncertain. Roughly 11,000 are thought to have fled into Albania from Gjakova and the hill country to the west of it by September 1913. Montenegrin and Austrian figures suggest that more than 16,000 Muslims left the 'liberated areas' of Montenegro for Turkey in the first half of 1914, but only a small proportion of these came from inside Kosovo.[58] An Austrian official recorded in 1913 that 20,000 men from the Gjakova district and 30,000 from Prizren had fled into Bosnia, together with 21,000 from the Muslim clans of those areas. Altogether, the total number of Albanians who left Kosovo in the period 1913–15 has been put as high as 120,000, though this is probably an over-estimate.[59]

Those Albanians who had calculated that Serbian rule would be only temporary must have begun to think they were right when, on 28 July 1914, Austria-Hungary declared war on Serbia. Orthodox Serbs from Kosovo were called up to fight, but the Muslim Albanians were officially exempt under the terms of an agreement between Serbia and the Ottoman state. (Nevertheless, it is recorded that 8,481 Albanians from Kosovo were enlisted, and that by late 1915 this number had grown to 50,000.)[60] For more than a year the Serbian army succeeded in driving back the Austrian forces that were launched against it from the north and west. Not only did it repulse the attacks on those fronts; it also used the opportunity the war provided to conquer part of central Albania, seizing Elbasan and Tirana in June 1915.[61] Only during the next four months, with a new joint Austrian–German offensive and the entry of Bulgaria into the war as an ally of those powers, did Serbia's position become untenable. The Bulgarian army attacked on a broad front in October: its main aim was to take over Macedonia, cutting the Serbs off from the Salonica area, where the British and French armies had their toe-hold in the Balkans. On 21 October the Bulgarians entered south-eastern Kosovo, and on the following day they took Skopje; the Serbian division which had been stationed in Macedonia withdrew northwards into Kosovo. One of its officers recorded that in addition to Bulgarian attacks, the Serbian troops also had to contend with frequent raids by Albanian kaçaks; at the same time he noted that his own men were committing numerous 'disorders and robberies' against the local population.[62]

Meanwhile the main body of the Serbian army was being pushed relentlessly down through central Serbia by the Germans and Austro-Hungarians. By 18 November, when a council of Serbian generals was held (in an atmosphere of bitter mutual recrimination) near Novi Pazar, they had lost 60,000 men (35,000 of them captured), 450 artillery pieces and almost all their transport. On the next day the Austro-Hungarians entered the Sandžak, where the local Muslims, apparently with fond memories of the Austrian garrisons there before 1908, greeted them as liberators.[63] The Serbian government, which was in flight with its army, knew that the only options were retreat or surrender, but hoped to continue southwards to Salonica; that possibility was now excluded, with the news that Bulgarian forces had reached western Macedonia. And so it was decided to evacuate the entire Serbian army over the mountains to the Adriatic coast, using the narrow and, in winter snows, almost impassable roads that went through northern Albania and Montenegro. The decision was made on 20 November; but because of the congestion of Serbian forces in Kosovo, and the speed of the enemy's advance on several fronts, many thousands of Serb soldiers were captured as the Austro-Hungarian and Bulgarian armies took Mitrovica, Prishtina and

Prizren in quick succession. By 29 November, when Prizren fell, the total number of captured Serbian soldiers during this campaign had reached 150,000.[64]

For those dignitaries who had good horses and escorts, the journey over the mountains did not take too long: Prime Minister Pašić managed it in four days, and Crown Prince Aleksandar in two-and-a-half. But for the ordinary soldiers, exhausted, ill-shod and completely unsupplied with food, it was a terrible ordeal. The mountain tracks became lined with the bodies of those who had perished of cold and hunger: some of the horses that died were eaten raw, and cases of cannibalism were also reported. There are complaints in some Serbian accounts about the reluctance of the local Albanians to give food to these soldiers as they passed through. They could have expected worse treatment than that, however, and the comment later made by Edith Durham was probably a fair one: 'That they suffered great hardships on the way, is because they fled through districts which they had completely pillaged and devastated barely two years before. That the Albanians spared the lives of the retreating Serbs who had previously shown them no mercy, is to their honour.'[65]

The Austrians stayed longer in Kosovo this time than on their previous visits in 1689 and 1737. They occupied the northern half of the territory, while the south was held by the Bulgarians. After the experiences of the last two years, ordinary Albanians were clearly glad to see the Austrian army: early communiqués from the War Ministry in Vienna reported that 'numerous Arnauts' took part on the Austrians' side during the initial fighting between Mitrovica and Peć, and that the local population joined 'enthusiastically' in the victory celebrations on 2 December. The Albanian political leaders would also have been aware that Austria-Hungary, more than any other power, had favoured the creation of an Albanian state. So it is not surprising that local leaders such as Hasan Prishtina and Ferat Draga cooperated willingly with the new occupier: Prishtina organized the recruitment of 2,000 Albanian volunteers to go with Austrian forces deeper into Albania, and Draga recruited 1,000 men who were sent off to Austria-Hungary's eastern front.[66] (Of the other leaders, Bajram Curri was in Albania, where he had spent 1915 trying to persuade the government to take a more pro-Austrian position; Isa

Boletin had been interned in Montenegro, and was killed in a shoot-out there as the Austrian army approached.)[67]

The Austrian authorities installed Albanians in the local government, allowed them to use the Albanian language in their work, and positively encouraged the setting up of Albanian-language schools. The same policy was applied in northern and central Albania in 1916; there the Austrians even set up two Albanian teacher-training schools, and established an 'Albanian literary commission' to standardize spellings and publish Albanian books in cheap popular editions. The official policy of the Austrian Foreign Ministry towards Albania itself was that it was a friendly neutral country, not a conquered land; the Austrian military thought this an unreal attitude and argued for partition, with the northern part, plus Kosovo, being annexed by Austria-Hungary, but their policy was never applied. The Austrian Foreign Minister, Burián, was in favour of adding most of Kosovo to an independent Albanian state (while subtracting territory from southern Albania and giving it to Greece); this policy was not implemented either. Kosovo and Albania were not reunited, and Albanians needed special permission to cross from one to the other.[68]

As well as being separated from Albania, Austrian-occupied Kosovo was also divided from the Bulgarian-occupied zone. This division was the cause of serious political friction between the two powers. When the Bulgarian Army's Third Division had taken both Prishtina and Prizren in November, it had gone beyond the limit of Bulgarian expansion agreed by the two governments in advance; but instead of handing over these areas to the Austrians, the Bulgarians had left some troops there and installed a civil administration, which they then extended to the Gjakova district too. King Ferdinand of Bulgaria was quick to visit the area, and by February he was assuring the Austrians that 'a large part of the population is Bulgarian'. In April 1916 the Austrians gave in, allowing Bulgaria to occupy Prishtina and Prizren and requiring only their withdrawal from Gjakova.[69] Conditions of life under Bulgarian rule were significantly worse than in the Austrian zone: compulsory labour service was introduced for such projects as railway-building in Macedonia, there was heavy requisitioning of food and materials, and severe famine developed in 1916 and 1917. According to Archbishop Mjeda, in 1917 roughly 1,000 people died of hunger in Prizren. The Serbs, many of whom were interned under Austrian rule, suffered even worse under the Bulgarians, thanks partly to the long-running rivalry between the Bulgarian and Serbian Churches: the Serbian Orthodox Metropolitan of Skopje, who took refuge in Prizren, was taken away and murdered by Bulgarian soldiers. And just as the Serbs had carried out a policy of Serbianization in Kosovo and Macedonia during 1913–15, so the Bulgarians now forcibly Bulgarianized the Macedonians and the Serbs.[70]

In these circumstances, those Albanians who had welcomed the Bulgarian advance in 1915 were quickly disillusioned, and many reacted to the new occupier in their traditional way. In the Skopska Crna Gora the old local leader Idriz Seferi, who had taken part in every rebellion since 1878, organized several kaçak bands: in one action near his home village of Sefer they killed twenty Bulgarian soldiers. Later in 1916 he was captured by the Bulgarians; he would be released at the end of the war, aged seventy-one. There was some resistance too in the Austrian zone: particularly active here was a charismatic young Albanian from north-central Kosovo, Azem Bejta (also known as Azem Galica, from the name of his village), whose young bride, Shota, joined him as a comrade-in-arms and became a famous fighter in her own right. Azem Bejta cooperated with local Serbs against the Austrian army, and in early 1918 he even had discussions about joint actions with the leader of the main četnik organization, Kosta Pećanac, who had daringly entered occupied Serbia by aeroplane.[71]

By the summer of 1918 it was quite clear that the Austro-Hungarian forces in the Balkans, already sapped by mutinies and desertions, were heading for defeat. In September the Allied army at Salonica (which had been joined by the remnants of the Serbian army after the retreat through Albania) began its advance through Macedonia; and at the end of that month Bulgaria signed an armistice with the Allied powers, which made the Austrian and German position in the Kosovo region quite untenable. Serbian and French troops were approaching Skopje, and a joint French–Italian force was pushing up through western Macedonia towards Tetovo. On 1 October the German and Austrian soldiers received the order to withdraw northwards from Macedonia; the commanders of the Central Powers realized that the Kosovo Polje plateau was indefensible, and so a further withdrawal, to Kruševac in central Serbia, was ordered five days later. Azem Bejta's men did capture a large number of Austrian and German soldiers, but one officer who encountered a band of Albanians to the north of Prishtina was more fortunate: he was allowed to go on his way with the words, 'Germans good, Bulgarians no good.' By the end of October the French 11th Colonial Division had taken Prishtina and Mitrovica, and the Italian 35th Division had entered Prizren and was pursuing the remnants of the Austrian army northwards through Gjakova and Peć. Some Serbian units stayed to occupy Kosovo; the rest of the seven Serbian divisions that formed part of this allied army pressed onwards towards Belgrade. Their victory was assured. Kosovo was now back under Serbian rule.[72]

14

Kaçaks and colonists: 1918–1941

THE NEW YUGOSLAV state was proclaimed on 1 December 1918. Officially called 'The Kingdom of Serbs, Croats and Slovenes', it brought together the Serbian kingdom, the kingdom of Montenegro (from which Nikola and his dynasty were deposed) and several parts of Austria-Hungary, including Slovenia and the Croatian territories. Serbia was the dominant element, not only because of its size and its victorious army, but also because the ruler of Serbia, Crown Prince Aleksandar Karadjordjević (who had been made Regent in place of his father in 1914), became king of the new state – which, for simplicity's sake, will henceforth be referred to as 'Yugoslavia', even though that became its official name only in 1929. As for Kosovo, it was carried along in this process because it was regarded simply as an integral part of the Serbian kingdom. All commentators at the time, and all subsequent historians, seem to have accepted this as a plain statement of legal fact. And yet the truth – so far as legal facts are concerned – is very different. Kosovo had never been legally incorporated into the Serbian state.

When Kosovo was conquered in 1912–13, Serbia was operating under its constitution of 1903. Article Four of that constitution clearly states that no change to the frontiers of Serbia can be valid unless it has been agreed by the Grand National Assembly – not the 'Ordinary Assembly' or parliament, but a special enlarged assembly summoned to deal with constitutional matters. No such Grand National Assembly was ever convened to discuss or ratify the extension of Serbia's borders to include Kosovo and Macedonia.[1] Some might wish to argue that, even if the correct procedures were not followed so far as Serbia's internal constitutional requirements were concerned, nevertheless the territories were properly annexed in terms of international law under the treaty-making powers of the king. But the strange truth is that Kosovo was not legally incorporated into Serbia by the standards of international law either.

When territory passes from one state to another by conquest in wartime, the transfer has to be recognized by a treaty between the two belligerents after the war. Such a treaty, the London Treaty of 1913, was drawn up between the Balkan allies (Serbia included) and the Ottoman state at the end of the war between them; but it was never ratified by Serbia, and therefore had no legal force where the new Serbian territories were concerned. Another treaty, the Treaty of Bucharest of 1913, was signed at the end of the Second Balkan War in that year (a war which broke out among the victorious Balkan allies, pitting Bulgaria against the rest); this treaty did contain statements about territorial changes, at least in Macedonia, and it was both signed and ratified. But the Ottoman state was not a party to it; so its statements about recently conquered ex-Ottoman territory could not legally validate that conquest itself. In March 1914 Serbia and the Ottoman state drew up a new treaty, the Treaty of Istanbul, which said that they would regard the non-ratified Treaty of London as ratified in those matters which concerned them. Unfortunately, this treaty could not do the trick because it itself was never ratified, being overtaken by the declaration of war between the two states in October 1914. And the problem is not directly solved by later treaties between Yugoslavia and Turkey, such as the Treaty of Sèvres of 1920, which became null and void, or the Treaty of Ankara of 1925, which, although it involved the mutual recognition of the two states, made no specific mention of the territories taken from the one by the other in 1912–13.[2]

Only in a rather roundabout and pragmatic way could a case for the new political ownership of Kosovo be made in legal theory. Both Yugoslavia and Turkey joined the League of Nations, and were committed under Article Ten of the League of Nations Pact to guaranteeing each other's territorial integrity. This in itself, strictly speaking, would not prove anything, since the territorial integrity referred to was a matter only of those territories that were legally possessed: if a state was illegally occupying some part of another country when it joined the League, no other states would be thereby obliged to defend that illegal occupation. But if this point about the League of Nations Pact is combined with the pragmatic observation that Turkey did behave as if it regarded those conquered territories as belonging to Yugoslavia – not only did it lodge no formal objections, for example, but it eventually opened a consulate in Skopje – then some kind of legal case can be made, and extended on the same basis, perhaps, to the Treaty of Ankara of 1925. One point, however, is quite clear. This legal case concerns Turkey's recognition that Kosovo was part, not of Serbia, but of Yugoslavia, the state which joined the League of Nations and signed the Treaty of Ankara.

Similarly, the Albanians of Kosovo had not become Serbian citizens, but they did eventually become Yugoslav ones. The only pre-war treaty to discuss the nationality of the Kosovars ('nationality' in the legal sense, i.e. national citizenship) was the Treaty of Istanbul, of which Article Four said that 'Individuals resident in the territories ceded to Serbia will become Serbian subjects'; but this treaty, as we have seen, never acquired any legal force. The official policy of the Serbian Kingdom had been to exclude the Kosovo Albanians (and other Muslims in Kosovo and Macedonia) from the call-up in the war; even though this policy was widely breached, the fact that it existed at all confirms that these people were thought of as being in a different category from ordinary Serbian citizens. In fact the first law to regulate their citizenship was the Yugoslav Nationality Law of 1928, which did not claim that it was confirming some already existing national status, but clearly said that it was creating that status for the first time: the Albanians who had lived in Kosovo between 1913 and the establishment of Yugoslavia in 1918 were described (in paragraph 4 of section 55 of the law) as 'the non-Slavs who have become nationals of the Kingdom by virtue of the second paragraph of this section'.[3]

Obviously the legal facts had got somewhat out of joint with many of the day-to-day realities. Since 1918 the Kosovo Albanians had in many ways been treated as Yugoslav citizens; they had been given the vote for the elections to the Constitutional Assembly and subsequent parliaments, they had been called up for military service, and so on. And when the Constitution (an essentially centralist scheme, favoured by Serbs and rejected by the main Croatian party) was finally put to the vote in 1921, the Kosovo Albanian deputies, led by Nexhip Draga, voted in favour – though this was mainly because they were landowners who had extracted, as the price of their support, some valuable concessions on the question of the dismantling of the old Ottoman feudal estates.[4]

But in some significant ways the majority Albanian population of Kosovo was not permitted to enjoy all the rights of ordinary Yugoslav citizens. The most important restriction concerned the Albanian language. Under the Treaty for the Protection of Minorities, which it signed reluctantly in 1919, Yugoslavia promised to supply primary education in the local language in all areas where 'a considerable proportion' of the population had a language other than the official one (which was Serbo-Croat). In addition, minorities had the right under this treaty to establish at their own expense 'schools and other educational establishments, with the right to use their own language and to exercise their religion freely therein'. And, more generally, Yugoslavia undertook to assure 'full and complete protection of life and liberty to all inhabitants of the Kingdom without distinction of birth, nationality, language, race or religion'.[5]

These pledges, especially the one about language, were openly disregarded. The schools which had been set up during the Austrian occupation were closed, or converted to Serbian-only education. A few *mektebs* (Islamic elementary schools) and private 'Turkish schools' were permitted, on the understanding that their teaching would be in Turkish. By 1930 there were no Albanian-language schools, except for a few utterly clandestine ones, in the whole of Kosovo; nor was there a single Albanian-language publication on sale there, though almost every other minority in Yugoslavia (including Germans, Hungarians, Czechs, Turks and even Russians) had newspapers of its own. Among the official reasons given for this state of affairs were the claims that most Albanians were illiterate, and that it was difficult to find any schoolteachers who spoke the language; but these were disingenuous excuses. Seventy-five per cent of the population of Montenegro had been illiterate in 1918, but that had not stopped the development of education and publications there. In 1930 a detailed testimony deposited at the League of Nations by three Catholic priests from Kosovo listed twenty-seven Albanian teachers whose schools had been forced to close by the authorities: some of these were distinguished figures in Albanian cultural life, such as the Prizren schoolmaster Lazër Lumezi, who wrote plays in Albanian as well as textbooks, and also made translations from Molière. The truth, as the three priests explained with much supporting evidence, was that the Albanian language was energetically suppressed. One of them was even warned by a Serb schoolmaster not to teach the Catholic Catechism in Albanian; and the mayor's office in each Albanian-inhabited town bore a poster prohibiting people from speaking any language except Serbian.[6]

The official Yugoslav position was not without its ambiguities. On the one hand it tried to get round the general obligations of the 1919 Treaty on the Protection of Minorities by saying that there was no such thing in Kosovo as an Albanian national minority. A statement drawn up by the Yugoslav delegation at the League of Nations, in response to Albanian criticisms in 1929, plainly said: 'Our position has always been that in our southern regions, which have been integral parts of our state or were annexed to our kingdom before 1 January 1919, there are no national minorities. That position is still our last word on the question of the recognition of minorities in Southern Serbia.' On the other hand, the Yugoslav census of 1921 did record figures for Albanian-speakers: 439,657 in the whole of Yugoslavia, of whom 288,900 were in Kosovo.[7] These figures were, however, regarded as underestimates, not only by Albanian representatives but also by foreign observers: the Italian expert on Albania Antonio Baldacci, for example, thought there were at least 700,000 Albanians in Yugoslavia in the 1920s, and by 1931 the Romanian geographer Nicolae Popp put the total at 800,000. Had the Yugoslav census-takers found just 67,000 more Albanian-speakers, the Albanians would have been listed as the second-largest linguistic minority in the country after the Slovenes, beating the Germans (505,790) and the Hungarians (467,658).[8]

How could the authorities list hundreds of thousands of Albanians, and say that no national minority existed in Kosovo and Macedonia? The answer to this conundrum is that they did not regard Albanian-speakers as being Albanians in an ethnic or national sense: they were merely Albanian-speaking Serbs. The Arnautaš thesis, as developed by Milojević and Gopčević in the late nineteenth century, had become entrenched in the official ideology, first of the Serbian kingdom, and then of the Yugoslav one too. A flood of books produced in 1912–13 to justify the Serbian conquest had emphasized this theme, although it was often blithely combined with the claim that the Albanians were sub-human. Thus Vladan Djordjević, for example, a former President of the Council of Ministers in Serbia, had written that there were almost no real Albanians apart from a few clans in remote areas of the Malësi, and that Skanderbeg himself was a Serb; but he also claimed in all seriousness that until recently the Albanians (whom he compared to Gypsies and 'Phoenicians' – the latter being a sort of contemptuous code-word for Jews) had had monkey-like tails.[9]

The suppressing of their language and the denial of their existence as a national minority were not the only forms of pressure the Albanians of Kosovo came under. There was also a large-scale programme of colonization, settling Slav-speakers in Albanian-inhabited areas: this will be discussed in detail later in this chapter. And associated with the colonization process were various forms of harassment, such as the confiscation of land from Albanian villagers, which seemed designed to encourage the tendency to emigrate to Albania or Turkey. To all these pressures the Albanians could respond in a variety of ways, legal and illegal, ranging from above-board political action through clandestine self-help to open and violent rebellion.

The legal political party set up to represent the interests of Albanian Muslims in both Kosovo and Macedonia was created at a conference in Skopje in December 1919. Popularly known as Xhemijet or Bashkim (both terms meaning 'association', the latter being the Albanian word, the former the Turkish word in Albanian spelling), its full name was 'Islam Muhafaza-yı Hukuk Cemiyeti', 'Islamic Association for the Defence of Justice'. There had at first been a plan to unite with the political party of the Bosnian Muslims, the Yugoslav Muslim Organization (founded in Sarajevo in February of that year), but the degree of fellow-feeling between Slav-speaking Muslims and Albanians was not strong enough to sustain such common action. (Differences between these two communities would become more visible during the next few years, as the Belgrade government tried to Slavicize the Islamic institutions of Kosovo by introducing pro-Serbian Slav Muslims, who were rejected by the Albanians.) Nevertheless, the Muslims of Kosovo, Macedonia and Bosnia–Hercegovina did agree on a number of policy demands at the conference in Skopje: full religious autonomy, the continuation of şeriat courts for civil matters, the preservation of the vakıfs, 'free use and official use of the respective mother-tongue, where non-Serb, in the schools', and the protection of the beys' estates from the new agrarian reforms.[10]

In the elections for the Constituent Assembly in 1920 Xhemijet won three out of the eighteen seats in Kosovo (and two in Macedonia). The other seats were won by nation-wide Yugoslav parties: nine by Democrats, three by Radicals and three by Communists. Out of the eighteen Kosovo deputies, ten were Serbs and eight were Albanians. But the electoral base on which these people were elected was quite slender: although all male citizens over the age of twenty-one could register to vote, only 85,159 did so in Kosovo, and of those only 46,561 actually voted.[11] Shortly after this election, the Communist Party (which was regarded in Macedonia as a cover for Macedonian and/or Bulgarian nationalists) was formally banned. The two major national parties, the Radicals and Democrats, would dominate Yugoslav political life throughout the 1920s, and the Muslim Albanian politicians would cooperate with both of them at different times, sometimes sharing the same electoral 'list'; in the early years this cooperation was particularly strong between Xhemijet and the Radicals. The difference between the two major parties was, in any case, not crystal-clear. An American political scientist who asked to have it explained to him in the late 1920s received various answers, including: 'The Radicals are conservative and the Democrats are radical', 'The Radicals are fundamentally Serbian and the Democrats are Yugoslav', and 'There is no basic difference between the parties ... They are all seeking government jobs.' The main difference was that the Radicals were an essentially Serbian party which stood for a centralized state governed from Serbia, while the Democrats wanted to minimize or destroy the distinctions between the historic regions and create a new, homogenized and unitarist Yugoslavia.[12]

Many of the initial political strivings of the Xhemijet deputies in Belgrade were aimed at protecting the large estates of ex-Ottoman landowners; for this reason the organization is often dismissed as little more than a 'beys' party'. But its deputies (and other Muslim deputies from Kosovo, formally attached to the Radicals or Democrats) did also campaign and protest, from time to time, about the general conditions of life in Kosovo. In February 1921 the Muslim deputies complained in the Assembly about arbitrary arrests and police violence, claiming that the police in the Prishtina district 'treat the innocent Muslim population in a manner reminiscent of the inquisition of the Middle Ages'. In April of the following year, at its third party congress, Xhemijet publicly asked the government to permit refugees to return to their former properties. Before the elections of 1923 the leader of the Radicals, Nikola Pašić, went to Skopje to woo the Xhemijet politicians: they demanded the opening of Albanian schools, and some general promises were made. When the votes were counted it was found that the Radicals could form a government only with the support of the Xhemijet deputies and the ethnic German party, which was given; and yet the promises made by Pašić on the question of Albanian rights were never kept. Later that year, in September, Xhemijet also sent in a formal request to stop the colonization programme, which was also ignored. Finally, in 1924, the Xhemijet deputies voted against the budget, when they found that no provision had been made in it for any of the things (above all, Albanian schools) they had asked for.[13]

From now on relations between Xhemijet and the Radicals deteriorated quickly. The leading Xhemijet politician, Ferat Draga, wanted to break with them altogether: he had already complained, in the previous year, of Serb terror in Kosovo, including a death threat against himself. He now decided to make Xhemijet part of an anti-Belgrade opposition alliance, and even visited the party congress of the Croat People's Peasant Party – the strongest anti-centralist political force in the country – in October 1924. But one wing of Xhemijet refused to follow him in this policy, and the party split.[14] In late 1924 Pašić sent his Montenegrin confidant and strongman, Puniša Račić (who in 1920 had actually stood as a joint Radical-Xhemijet candidate in Tetovo) to Kosovo to meet local Serb officials and prepare the ground for a campaign of obstruction and intimidation to undermine Xhemijet in the province. In January 1925, two weeks before a general election, Ferat Draga was arrested together with other prominent activists, including journalists from the Turkish-language Xhemijet paper, *Hak*; on the eve of the election Draga was sentenced to twenty years' imprisonment. (He was later released from prison and invited to Belgrade to make a political deal with Pašić; but nothing came of this, and on the eve of the next election, in 1927, he was arrested again and given another sentence of twenty years.) The Xhemijet party, weakened by this attack as well as its own internal split, collapsed, and ceased to exist as a political force. Its journal, *Hak*, was closed down; several more of its leaders were arrested; and one, the prominent intellectual Nazim Gafuri, was assassinated in May 1927, apparently because he had publicly criticized the methods of intimidation used during the local elections by Serb officials.[15]

Apart from this public engagement in Yugoslav politics – which, it must be said, achieved almost nothing for the Albanians of Kosovo – there were other more private activities of cultural self-help. Although its publications were issued only in Turkish or Serbian, Xhemijet did also encourage the setting up of some private schools in people's homes, where children were taught in Albanian. Some Xhemijet members did continue this activity after the collapse of the party; but the increasing tendency of middle-class Albanians was to send their children to be educated in Albania. There were also various sports clubs, youth groups and humanitarian organizations in Kosovo which engaged in more or less clandestine educational and cultural work, and in the early 1920s an underground group called 'Agimi' ('The Dawn') imported and distributed Albanian books from Albania. One organization which played an important role was the Catholic Church, which ministered to a mainly Albanian-speaking flock. It supported a society in Peć known at first as the 'White Drin' and then legalized as a religious-charitable association under the name of the 'Society of St Catherine'. The Catholic priest Shtjefën Gjeçov, an enthusiast for Albanian literature and culture (whose studies of the Kanun of Lek Dukagjin appeared as a series of articles and were later collected into a book, which became the standard work), moved to a parish in Western Kosovo in 1926 and became an active member of this association. His activities, including his teaching of the Catechism in Albanian, incurred the displeasure of local Serb officials, and in 1929 he too was assassinated.[16]

For many Albanians in Kosovo the preferred response was open rebellion. It would, however, be misleading to present this simply as a considered and delayed reaction to specific policies such as the closing down of Albanian schools. Some Albanians had taken up arms against the Serb authorities from the first moments of the reimposition of Serbian rule; and it was the continuing existence of armed rebellion in the area that gave the authorities the excuse or justification they needed for many of their draconian methods. Nor should we forget that large numbers of ordinary Albanians did cooperate with the authorities and take low-level jobs in the local administration; some of these were, consequently, also targeted by the rebels. In official communiqués from Belgrade, the rebels, referred to by both sides as kaçaks, were simply bandits, engaged in thieving and plunder. No doubt there were some crimes of that sort committed, from time to time, under the colours of the kaçaks; and some local blood-feuds may also have become inter-twined with their activities. But it is clear that, overall, the kaçak movement was a political phenomenon, directed against Serbian rule as such, and it is also clear that the anti-Albanian policies of the government and local authorities (including the whole colonization programme) were a powerful stimulus to the rebellion.

The earliest resistance seems to have been a spontaneous reaction to events during the reimposition of Serbian rule: some of the Serb soldiers who entered Kosovo in October 1918 took their revenge for the hostile attitude of the Albanians at the time of the Serbian withdrawal in 1915, and several armed clashes now took place. Albanians also resisted the immediate attempts of the Serbian army to disarm them; many took to the hills, and villages which refused to hand over their rifles were bombarded by Serbian artillery. More than 200 Albanians were killed by such operations in the Peć area (where, incidentally, Montenegrins also joined the Albanians in resisting the Serbian forces), and armed resist-ance spread in many parts of northern and Western Kosovo in the early months of 1919. Serb reprisals were extremely severe. According to a detailed set of statistics later published in Italy, 6,040 people were killed by Serbian troops in Kosovo during January and February 1919, and 3,873 houses destroyed.[17]

Most of the wartime political leaders of Kosovo had left the territory by this time; a group of them, led by Hasan Prishtina, gathered in Shkodra in November 1918 and formed a 'Committee for the National Defence of Kosovo', known more simply as the Kosovo Committee. Prishtina was actively lobbying the American government for the inclu-sion of Kosovo in a new Albanian state, and in February the Committee sent a protest letter to the Paris Peace Conference about the killings of Albanians in Kosovo. But little attention was paid to Albanian interests at the Peace Conference: the Albanian government was denied represen-tation there, and although Albania had not been a belligerent state, the redrawing of its frontiers was under discussion. In February a request was submitted by Yugoslavia for the annexation of the whole of northern

Albania; this was later withdrawn, but until 1921 the Serbian army was allowed to occupy a broad strip of Albanian territory to the west of the 1913 frontier.[18]

In practice, the Kosovo Committee devoted most of its energies to supporting and, to some extent, directing the kaçak movement inside Kosovo. In early 1919 it drew up a general set of rules for the movement, beginning with the following two points: '1: No rebel will dare to harm the local Serbs, but only those who stand with weapons in their hands against the will of the Albanians. 2: No rebel will dare to burn down a house or destroy a church.' It also issued an appeal to the population to begin a general revolt on 6 May. Large-scale actions did start around that date, especially in the Drenica region of north-central Kosovo, where the charismatic kaçak leader Azem Bejta had many followers. It is estimated that there were 10,000 active rebels at this time. But the kaçaks, only half of whom had rifles, were no match against the machine-gun units and artillery batteries of the Yugoslav army, which drove them off towards the mountains near Peć, destroying many villages as it did so and carrying out further reprisals afterwards. Many of the kaçaks retreated into Albania, but Azem Bejta stayed on in Kosovo. In October he and some other kaçak leaders had a meeting with a senior Serb official, at which he presented a set of eight demands – a list which, more than anything else, demonstrates that his was not a 'bandit' movement but a politically motivated campaign. He asked the Serbs to recognize the Kosovo Albanians' right to self-government; to stop the killing of Albanians; to stop taking their land; to stop the colonization programme; to stop army actions carried out on the pretext of disarma-ment; to open Albanian schools; to make Albanian an official language of administration; and to stop interning the families of the rebels.[19]

In the following year (1920) more local revolts were prompted by the two traditional bugbears of the Kosovo Albanians: a renewed disarmament campaign and a drive to conscript eighteen- to twenty-five-year-olds into the army. A new tactic employed by the authorities was the formation of četas (armed bands) out of the local Serbs; established četnik leaders, such as Kosta Pećanac (who had held friendly discussions with Azem Bejta only two years previously), were also brought in to conduct anti-kaçak operations. One consequence of this policy was that kaçaks began to attack some of the Serb villages too. Finally, in

November 1920 a well-coordinated operation by army and gendarme units (plus a plane from the Skopje squadron of the Yugoslav Air Force) succeeded in defeating a large force of kaçaks in the Drenica region. Many of the kaçak leaders, including Azem Bejta and his warrior-wife Shota, now fled to Shkodra.[20]

In January 1921 the Yugoslav authorities decided to step up the pressure. A proclamation was issued, calling on all rebels to give themselves up by 10 March. It offered an amnesty for crimes committed between November 1915 and August 1919 (excluding, therefore, the last one and a half years of intensive rebellion), and said that deserters would not be punished so long as they completed their military service; but those who failed to respond would be 'killed or arrested and their families removed'. It also imposed new collective penalties: 'The villagers will be obliged to indemnify all the damage caused within the limits of their village by the kaçaks.' And it authorized the general distribution of arms to the Serbs of Kosovo, a move which severely reduced any chances of peaceful coexistence between the Serb and Albanian populations there. The deadline was later extended to 20 March; by the 16th roughly 2,000 Albanians had surrendered, but most of these seem to have been deserters from military service rather than active kaçaks. Immediately after the expiry of the deadline, the authorities carried out their threat, rounded up the women and children of suspected kaçaks and sent them to internment camps in central Serbia.[21] This last move, predictably, stiffened the resolve of the rebels. Indeed it may have created new ones, since some of the women who were taken away were the wives of Kosovo chiefs who had gone into exile in Albania and had sent messages urging restraint to their followers during 1920. As the British envoy in Durrës reported: 'This passive attitude does not suit Serbia as it gives no excuse for harsh measures. Consequently they have now laid hands on women which they know no Albanian mountaineer will endure.' A large group of these exiles returned to fight in April. Azem Bejta also went back to Kosovo then and led an active campaign throughout the summer. By late May one prominent commentator in the Belgrade press was complaining that 'the hills are fuller than ever of brigands', and calling for 'a plan of action against brigands and against the Albanians in general'.[22]

A plan of action was in fact being formed. The government in

Belgrade had been constantly irritated, ever since the start of the kaçak rebellion, by the support given to these rebels from inside Albania itself. Several of the Kosovo activists there had achieved public positions. Hasan Prishtina had been elected to the Albanian parliament; another leading member of the Kosovo Committee, Hoxha Kadri, was Minister of Justice; and Bajram Curri became Minister of War in 1920.[23] The key to suppressing the revolt in Kosovo, therefore, seemed to lie in controlling or neutralizing Albania. One proposed way of gaining leverage was to seize Shkodra the moment Allied troops were withdrawn from it in early 1920; but this planned Yugoslav action was forestalled by the energetic young Albanian Minister of the Interior, Ahmet Zogolli (he later removed the suffix '-olli' – the Turkish '-oğlu', 'son of' – and became simply Zog), who immediately occupied the city. So in the summer of 1921 the Yugoslav government revived the old Montenegrin tactic of manipulating the Catholic Malësi: it persuaded one of the leaders of the Mirdita to go to war against the Albanian state. This he did in July, when a telegram, ostensibly sent by him from Prizren but almost certainly prepared by the Yugoslav authorities, was circulated by the Yugoslav Press Bureau, proclaiming (yet again) a 'Mirdita Republic'. In an initial campaign Zogolli's forces drove him off into Yugoslavia; but he came back, supported by Yugoslav troops (together with members of General Wrangel's White Russian army, who had settled in Yugoslavia and were paid by Belgrade), and retook a large area of north-eastern Albania. At this point the Great Powers, whose peace conference was still under way, decided that the Albanian–Yugoslav border must be settled as quickly as possible. A formal Albanian request made in the previous year to transfer Prizren, Gjakova and Peć to Albania was disregarded, and the line was finally drawn in October and November, following the 1913 division quite closely with the exception of a substantial area to the south and west of Prizren which was transferred to Yugoslavia.[24]

One by-product of this speedy settlement of the frontier question was that a 'demilitarized zone' was set up on the western fringe of Kosovo, centring on the village of Junik (south of Peć and north-west of Gjakova). This became a haven for Azem Bejta and many other kaçaks, who used it not only as a refuge but also as a base for other operations in 1922. But although this neutral zone gave the rebels what seemed to Belgrade like an unfair advantage (it was in fact heavily attacked by the Yugoslav army in June 1922), its existence may in fact have weakened the kaçaks' operations by localizing them and cutting them off, to some extent, from their supporters elsewhere. More decisive in undermining the kaçak movement, however, was a political upheaval in Albania. The Kosovo politicians fell out with Zogolli at the end of 1921: Hasan Prishtina, who became Prime Minister of Albania in December, tried to dismiss Zogolli but had to resign himself when Zogolli quickly marched on Tirana with his troops. Two months later he almost turned the tables on Zogolli, when he and Curri brought their own army to Tirana: fighting started in the streets, and Zogolli's men seemed to be losing, when the British envoy, Sir Harry Eyres, succeeded in persuading one of Prishtina's commanders to withdraw his men. This feat of diplomacy saved Zogolli, but was fatal to the long-term interests of the kaçaks in Kosovo.[25]

Zogolli had by now become a sworn enemy of all the Kosovo rebels and irredentists. He put Azem Bejta on trial *in absentia* and had him sentenced to death; and at the end of January 1923 he sent the Albanian army into the Junik 'neutral zone', driving out all the kaçaks and setting up joint Albanian–Yugoslav patrols to stop them from coming back. The kaçak movement was seriously weakened now, and there was a wave of surrenders to both national authorities during the summer of that year. Azem Bejta himself negotiated a besë with the local authorities of his home district, under which he was allowed to live undisturbed so long as he stayed within a group of three villages; meanwhile a few of his comrades continued their activities elsewhere in Kosovo. This arrangement continued until the summer of 1924, when conditions were once again changed by political events in Albania. Zogolli (now called Zog) was driven from power by an alliance of his opponents, including Bajram Curri; he withdrew into Yugoslavia, and took up residence in the Hotel Bristol in Belgrade; and the Yugoslav authorities, fearing that the new pro-Kosovar régime in Albania would reactivate the kaçaks, moved quickly to eliminate Azem Bejta. In a surprise attack on his village they killed most of his men and wounded him severely; he escaped to a cave in the mountains, but died there on 25 July. A few of his followers continued to fight during the rest of the year, but in December Zog returned to Albania at the head of a force of 2,000 Yugoslav soldiers (dressed as Albanians) and 800 Russian mercenaries, and regained power. Bajram Curri was hunted down and killed in the following spring. Almost the last active kaçak leader in Kosovo was Shota, Azem Bejta's widow: she kept up the fight until July 1927, when, badly wounded, she crossed over into Albania and died there, aged only thirty-two.[26]

The armed resistance of the kaçaks, like the political actions of the Xhemijet party, in the end achieved very little in concrete terms. None of Azem Bejta's eight demands was satisfied. Many people were killed, and it became impossible to say what proportions of the deaths (and of the destructions of houses) were attributable to direct actions against the kaçaks, or to subsequent reprisals and secondary actions, or to unrelated and unprovoked government oppression. The number of those killed is very uncertain; figures claimed for specific places or short periods seem more reliable than any overall totals. Thus the Albanian Government informed the League of Nations in April 1921 that 2,000 Albanians had been killed in Kosovo since the beginning of the year; and four months later the head of the Islamic community in Bosnia, Reis ul-ulema Čaušević, told a British diplomat that 5,000 people had been killed in the Prishtina district since November 1918. As for general totals, a document drawn up by the Kosovo Committee in 1921 calculated that up till then 12,371 had been killed, 22,110 had been imprisoned, and roughly 6,000 houses had been burnt down.[27] Even if these figures were overstated then, they would probably have been not only reached but widely surpassed by the end of the kaçak rebellion. And it should not be forgotten that many people, besides, were killed by the kaçaks: soldiers and gendarmes, Albanians who cooperated with the authorities, and Slav colonists. In the final analysis, the kaçaks achieved just two things. First, they made a strong symbolic demonstration of the fact that many Kosovo Albanians did not accept the legitimacy of Serbian or Yugoslav rule. And secondly, they did in fact seriously obstruct the colonization programme, to the point where many would-be settlers were reluctant to go to Kosovo, and many who went returned home.[28]

The colonization programme was a complex phenomenon, serving a variety of aims: the overriding, long-term purpose was to change the national composition of the population in Kosovo (and in Macedonia, which was also colonized), but other factors were also involved. One such factor was a desire to stop the outflow of people from Serbia and

Montenegro who were emigrating to North America, by offering them grants of free land closer to home. Another was the policy of punishing kaçaks by confiscating their property: the most effective way of enforcing this punishment was to give their land to new settlers. Security policy also influenced the general pattern of location of the colonies: new villages of Serbian or Montenegrin settlers were concentrated strategically along the main communication routes, and efforts were made (not very successfully) to establish such colonies in the sensitive border area adjoining Albania. There was even a plan (seriously discussed in Belgrade in 1921, but never carried out) to settle 7,000 of General Wrangel's Russian soldiers in Kosovo – a Serbian counterpart to the Ottoman policy of placing warlike Circassians in strategically important regions. Finally, the factor which was most commonly appealed to as an explanation and justification of the colonization programme was the policy of 'agrarian reform', the breaking up of the old Ottoman estates. But this was the one factor which had no necessary connection with colonization: the land taken from these estates could all have been redistributed to the local peasants, without bringing in a single new settler from outside. Kosovo was, in fact, already the most densely populated area in the whole of Yugoslavia.[29]

The first attempts at colonization were made before the First World War. By a 'Law-decree on the settlement of the newly liberated areas' of February 1914, the Serbian government promised colonists nine hectares (1 hectare = 2.47 acres) of land for each family, plus two hectares for each male member of the family above the age of sixteen; it also offered free transport to the region by rail, and a three years' holiday from taxes. Some attempts were made to persuade Serbian emigrants in the United States to come back and settle in Kosovo. Other Serbs, who were not intending to settle there, were also allowed to buy confiscated land at highly advantageous prices: the Serbian politician Nikola Pašić bought 3,000 hectares near Prishtina in this way. Montenegro also introduced a law on colonization in early 1914. But the total number of settlers who responded in 1914–15 was small: in the Montenegrin-occupied areas, roughly 300 families arrived during this period. Most of these, it is thought, went back to their original homes during the Austro-Hungarian and Bulgarian occupation in 1916–18.[30]

Only after the reconquest of Kosovo in late 1918 did the colonization programme get seriously under way. A decree on 'preliminary measures for agrarian reform' in February 1919, which announced the break-up of the large estates and the nationalization of forests, included provisions for the grant of land to Serbian soldiers and volunteers: a further decree in December defined as 'volunteers' all those who had joined the Serbian army of their own accord before 18 November 1918, and gave them the right to claim 5 hectares of arable land. Two years later another decree added extra categories of potential colonists, such as volunteer fighters in the Balkan Wars, and members of četnik organizations (who were entitled to 10 hectares in Kosovo or Macedonia). Meanwhile a 'Decree on the colonization of the new southern lands' in September 1920 had set out the basic types of land that could be given to these colonists. These included vacant land in state ownership, communal land which was not being cultivated, privately owned land which was uncultivated or 'abandoned', and all land confiscated under the 'preliminary measures' of February 1919.[31] Under a new law in 1931 (which was in fact the first full law on colonization, as opposed to 'decree-laws' and so-called 'preliminary' or 'provisional' measures), the land of all those who had participated in kaçak rebellions could also be seized and colonized; in fact such confiscations had been taking place for many years already, with the land merely being classified as 'abandoned'.[32]

Official presentations of this entire policy by Serbian writers concentrated on the expropriation of big estates, as if the colonization programme were simply a by-product of agrarian reform; but in fact only a quarter of the land distributed to colonists came from that source. Most of the çiftlik estates were, in any case, not very big: out of the 6,973 estates in the whole of Kosovo, the Sandžak and Macedonia, three-quarters were smaller than 50 hectares and half were below 20 hectares: the owners were allowed to keep a maximum of 15 hectares, and much of the remainder was distributed among their existing farm-workers.[33] Altogether, 14,000 families of local peasants received land in this way, at an average of 4.1 hectares per family. The local Albanian peasants were not excluded from this process, but the system seems to have been skewed in favour of the Slavs: it is estimated that only 4,000 out of those 14,000 recipient families were Albanian. And even the local Slavs who did receive land became dissatisfied when they saw that larger parcels were given to the incoming settlers: the average grant to a colonist family was not 4.1 hectares but 7.2. Because of such dissatisfactions, the local Serb peasants were often openly hostile to the colonists: one official in charge of the colonization programme in Kosovo noted in 1928 that they tended to form a 'united front with the Albanians against the settlers'.[34]

The colonists enjoyed a wide range of advantages and incentives. The land itself was entirely free: they were required to occupy it within one year of the grant being made, and would acquire full ownership of the property – including the right to sell it – after ten years. All costs of moving to the place of settlement were covered, including the transportation not only of flocks, but even of wood and other materials for building a house. Once installed, the colonists would join an agricultural association, which gave them subsidies and interest-free loans.[35] Foreign organizations also subsidized some of these projects: American and British pro-Serbian charities paid for the building of roughly 700 houses on the road from Peć to Mitrovica, including the important colony-village of Vitomirica. Many completely new villages were built, and given suitably uplifting names from Serbian mythology (such as 'Devet Jugovića', 'The Nine Jugovićes', after the legendary brothers-in-law of Prince Lazar). But some colonists moved into existing villages from which local Albanians had been driven out: there were some cases where the Albanians had not even been informed of the decision to expel them when the colonists arrived to take over their homes. (The local commissions for sequestration and colonization did not publicize their decisions; and even if the decision happened to become known immediately, the Albanians had only two weeks in which to appeal against it.)[36]

Large sums of money were spent on this colonization programme. In Western Kosovo alone during the years 1928–9, the expenditure came to 10 million dinars (roughly $180,000 at the time). The claim made by some modern Serbian writers that the Yugoslav state failed to keep its promises on matters such as Albanian-language education merely because it had no money to pay for such things seems peculiarly unconvincing in the light of the large budget allocated for colonization.[37] And the scale of the operation was indeed impressive: during the entire inter-war period just under 200,000 hectares of agricultural land (three-quarters of which was arable) were taken from their original owners, and half of that land was distributed to the colonists. (In the whole of

Kosovo there were only 584,000 hectares of agricultural land, of which 400,000 were arable.) The total number of colonists who came to Kosovo was just over 13,000 families: perhaps 70,000 people altogether, equivalent to more than ten per cent of Kosovo's entire population. Writing in 1928, the Serbian official Djordje Krstić described the colonization programme as a great 'success' in demographic terms: whereas, he said, 'we' were only 24 per cent of the population of Kosovo in 1919, the figure had now risen to 38 per cent.[38]

Despite all the money spent on them and all the advantages they enjoyed, however, the general experience of the colonists was not a happy one. Many found that the provisions made on paper did not correspond to the reality that awaited them in Kosovo. They suffered from a lack of agricultural implements, tools for house-building, draught animals and seed; they also complained bitterly of the incompetence and corruption of local Serbian officials. Until the mid-1920s attacks by kaçaks were a strong disincentive; thereafter, small-scale local hostilities continued. Health care was minimal, and many of the colonists suffered badly from malaria.[39] Of all the settlers, those who found it hardest to adapt to local conditions were the Serbs from the Vojvodina, whose way of life had developed under the comparatively advanced conditions of Austria-Hungary. To them, the local Serbs in Kosovo seemed just as alien as the local Albanians: one study of the Vojvodinan colonists summarizes the problems they encountered as 'differences in mentality between the Albanians and old Serb inhabitants on the one hand, and Vojvodinans on the other', giving as an example the tendency of both Albanians and local Serbs to settle their disputes by shooting. As a result, many of the Vojvodinan colonists returned home during the mid-1930s.[40] They were not the only ones to give up and go home. Figures from the district of Peć and the nearby district of Istok (Alb.: Istog) show that of those who had arrived by 1931, between 18 and 21 per cent had returned home by 1935. The agricultural depression of those years was one reason, but not the only one. A letter sent to the Yugoslav government by a group of Serbs from America in the early 1930s said that 3,000 American Serbs, having come back to Europe to settle in Kosovo, had now returned to America: it blamed this new exodus mainly on the local Serbian officials' insatiable hunger for bribes.[41]

While the conditions for the Serb colonists were far from good in the

1930s, they worsened dramatically for the local Albanian population. The political climate had become even more intolerant than before: following the murder of the Croatian leader Stjepan Radić in the Yugoslav parliament in 1928, the king suspended the constitution and imposed a much more unitarist and authoritarian system of rule. In January 1929 Yugoslavia was divided into nine new *banovinas* or governorships, which were carefully designed to cut across previous administrative or historical borders. Kosovo's territory was shared out between three banovinas: Vardarska, which included Macedonia and had its provincial capital in Skopje; Moravska, which covered much of eastern Serbia and had its capital in Niš; and Zetska, based on Cetinje, which included all of Montenegro. The governors of these banovinas, who had wide-ranging arbitrary powers, were drawn from the ranks of hard-line military men and Serbian nationalists: Vardarska was governed by Žika Lazić, a former head of the Serbian secret police (described in an émigré socialist publication as a 'bourreau' or executioner), and Zetska was put in the hands of General Krsto Smiljanić, one of the leaders of the 'White Hand' nationalist-terrorist organization.[42] And at the national level a new generation of politicians was emerging who were both nationalist and authoritarian – men such as the fiercely anti-Albanian Vojislav Marinković, who was Prime Minister from 1932 to 1934, Milan Stojadinović, whose own political movement imitated elements of fascism, and the extremist Dimitrije Ljotić, who was an open admirer of Hitler.

From 1935 onwards, a wave of confiscations of land from Albanians built up, on the basis of a new rule that all land should be treated as state property unless the farmer had a Yugoslav document to prove his ownership – something that had hardly ever been issued to Albanians. In just one example of this process, the entire Albanian population of twenty-three villages in upper Drenica (6,064 people) was dispossessed in 1938. The official policy was to allow such people only 0.4 hectares per family member. As a Serbian policy document of the previous year noted: 'This is below the minimum for subsistence. But that is and has been our aim: to make their life impossible, and in that way to force them to emigrate.'[43]

Such calculations were in keeping with the ideas of many Serbian officials and intellectuals. During the years 1937–9 there were frequent discussions on this topic among senior civil servants at the 'Serbian Cultural Club' in Belgrade. According to the minutes of these debates, the head of the Yugoslav statistical service declared that although the Albanians were 'passive' now, they could become 'an active national group, extraordinarily dangerous for our national and state interests'; he demanded that an 'effective plan' to deal with them must be formed. One member of the club, Orestije Krstić, proposed: 'The land must be bought from the Albanians, but of course only when it cannot be taken from them without compensation'; another, Djoka Perina, thought it necessary to create a 67.5 per cent majority of Serbs in 'Southern Serbia', for which purpose he advocated introducing 470,000 colonists and expelling 300,000 Albanians.[44] One of the most distinguished members of this club was Vasa Čubrilović, a former member of the 'Mlada Bosna' group of young terrorists who planned the assassination of Archduke Franz Ferdinand in 1914; he was now a respected historian at Belgrade University. His own contribution to this debate took the form of a long policy paper which he submitted to the Yugoslav government in 1937. Recognizing the limitations of the colonization programme, he wrote: 'If we assume that the gradual displacement of the Albanians through our progressive colonization is ineffective, then we are left with only one course – that of their mass emigration.' As he pointed out: 'At a time when Germany can expel tens of thousands of Jews ... the shifting of a few hundred thousand Albanians will not lead to the outbreak of a world war.' Čubrilović proposed a whole range of methods to induce them to leave:

> The law must be enforced to the letter, to make staying intolerable for the Albanians ... such as punishment for smuggling, for cutting the forest, for damaging agriculture, for leaving dogs unchained ... any other measure that an experienced police force can contrive. From the economic aspect: the refusal to recognize the old land deeds ... the requisitioning of all state and communal pastures ... dismissal from state, private and communal offices ... When it comes to religion, the Albanians are very touchy. Therefore, they must be harassed on this score too. This can be achieved through the ill-treatment of their clergy, the destruction of their cemeteries ... There remains one more means, which Serbia had employed very successfully after 1878: secretly burning down Albanian villages and city quarters.[45]

Some of these measures were indeed carried out: apart from the refusal to recognize Ottoman land deeds, the next few years also saw a huge increase in police harassment. One report in 1939 noted that the police in the Gjakova district had issued 1,500 summary penalties to Albanians, imposing, for example, fines of 50 dinars if a horse or cow committed the crime of defecating on a 'national road'. As for the harassment of Muslims, this had been an element of official policy ever since the reconquest of Kosovo in 1918, when many mosques were turned into stables and the Muslim graveyard outside Mitrovica was deliberately destroyed. A confidential report by the commander of the Yugoslav Third Army (based in 'Southern Serbia') in 1922 stated that the conversion of mosques to cavalry stables or ammunition depots was a way of putting pressure on the Muslim Albanians to emigrate.[46]

Plans for the total expulsion of the Albanians might seem at first sight to have belonged to the realm of pure fantasy; but the fantasy came very close to becoming a reality. From 1933 onwards there were serious discussions between the Yugoslav and Turkish governments over the deportation to Turkey of huge numbers of Muslim Albanians. Officially these people were described as 'Turks'; in 1935 the Turkish government offered to take 200,000 of them, a figure which, although well below the Yugoslav government's target, was way above the official total of Turkish-speakers (150,000) recorded in the 1921 census. In a new round of negotiations in 1938 Stojadinović's government offered to pay Turkey 15,000 dinars for every family; after much haggling, the text of an inter-governmental agreement was eventually drawn up and initialled on 11 July 1938. According to this agreement, Turkey would take 40,000 families, at a price of 500 Turkish pounds per family: a family was defined as 'blood relations living under one roof', which in the Kosovo countryside would include many three-generation households of more than ten members. The treaty also specified that a Yugoslav government commission would draw up the list of emigrants, and that all their land would pass immediately to the Yugoslav state. Curiously, one clause specifically excluded the urban population from the scheme: while this provision would have allowed some Albanians to remain, it also confirmed that the main object of the policy was to remove the Albanians and not the Turkish-speakers (the great majority of whom lived in towns). The entire process was meant to take six years, from 1939 to

1944. Fortunately for the Albanians of Kosovo, the Second World War prevented it from ever coming into effect.[47]

Many Albanians had not waited to be formally expelled. There was a large emigration from Kosovo during the inter-war period; although the exact figures are a matter of much dispute and speculation, it is clear that many thousands went to Albania and many tens of thousands to Turkey. One recent analysis puts the total emigration of Muslims (including Bosnian former muhaxhirs, and other Muslim Slavs) from Kosovo during the inter-war period at 77,000. But this calculation takes as its statistical base the census figures for 1921 which, as many observers argued at the time, understated the total number of Albanians. The three Catholic priests who petitioned the League of Nations in 1930 wrote that since 1912 10,000 had fled to Albania and 130,000 to Turkey – evidently a very rough estimate on their part, since no precise figures had been compiled by any authority. Modern Albanian historians have suggested much higher figures: Hakif Bajrami, for example, proposes a total emigration of 240,000 between 1918 and 1941, but gives no detailed evidence to support this calculation.[48] Assuming that the figure of 77,000 is an underestimate, and that the three priests were including generous estimates for the years 1912–18 when they made their case in 1930, we may suppose that the figure for the emigration of Albanians and other Muslims from Kosovo in the entire period 1918–41 was in the region between 90,000 and 150,000.

More reliable figures relate, as before, only to specific times and places. One official report in 1926 said that in the previous two years 32,000 people had emigrated to Turkey and 6,000 to Albania. In early 1927 Aubrey Herbert, who was involved in relief operations for refugees in Albania, noted that at least 1,150 families (perhaps 6,000 people) from Kosovo had settled there since 1924.[49] An interesting insight into the methods used to promote emigration comes from a letter written by a former Albanian consular official in Bulgaria, who found 2,000 Albanians from Kosovo stranded in Sofia in the summer of 1923, under the leadership of a Muslim cleric, Hoxha Mulla Rrahman. 'Later,' wrote the official, 'I understood that he was a spy, who had sold himself to the Serbs, and had been charged with the clearance of the Albanian Moslems from Prishtina by inducing them to emigrate to Asia Minor, the seat of their "Baba" [head of a dervish order], where he assured them the Turks had prepared great mounds of pilaf against their arrival.' He also learned that 'many thousands' of Albanians had passed through Sofia already. What he found most disturbing, however, was that when he tried to persuade them to go to Albania instead, he met with opposition not only from the Yugoslav authorities, but also from his own government in Tirana: 'Zogou [Zogolli, then Minister of the Interior] and his party were of the same mind, and even more fanatically so than the Serbs.'[50]

Zog's hostility to the pro-Kosovo lobby in Albania continued after his seizure of power in December 1924. He had promised Belgrade that he would suppress the Kosovo Committee; several of its leading members, such as Hasan Prishtina, fled to Vienna. Zog organized an attempt to assassinate him there in 1928, which was unsuccessful; Hasan Prishtina arranged a counter-plot to kill Zog, which also failed, and he was condemned to death *in absentia* in the same year. The politics of rivalry and intrigue now became exceptionally complex, as Zog's initially good relations with his benefactors, the Belgrade government, rapidly soured, and the Albanian regime became more and more dependent on Italy, Yugoslavia's chief rival in the Adriatic region. Italy, unlike Yugoslavia, could supply large-scale capital investment; and Mussolini ruthlessly exploited his country's growing economic influence to turn Albania into a virtual Italian protectorate. Since Mussolini was also keen to destabilize Yugoslavia, this new alignment of Albanian policy meant that Zog was now required to play the irredentist card on Kosovo: when, for example, he had himself declared King in 1928, the title he chose – with Rome's approval – was not 'King of Albania' but 'King of the Albanians'. For the same reason Hasan Prishtina was paid a large monthly subsidy by an Italian intelligence agent in Vienna. Zog's personal hatred of him, nevertheless, continued unabated, and in 1933 he finally succeeded in having Hasan Prishtina assassinated: an Albanian joined him for a drink at the Café Astoria in Salonica, then took out a revolver and fired six shots into his body. All the leading figures of the great Kosovar revolt of 1912 were now dead; all had been shot except, curiously, the one who was purely a military leader, Idriz Seferi, who died peacefully in his bed in 1927.[51]

By the late 1930s Mussolini was seriously considering the annexation of Albania. A strong stimulus to this policy came from Hitler's *Anschluss* with Austria: Mussolini saw this not only as a model but also as a threat of more direct German interference in Albania, given the traditional Austrian–Albanian connections in areas such as the activities of the Catholic Church.[52] In discussions with Stojadinović's government in Belgrade in 1938 and early 1939, the Italians suggested a partitioning of Albania, with the Yugoslavs gaining the Shkodra area, Greece getting part of the south, and the rest being taken by Italy, which would thenceforth renounce all claims to Kosovo. But after the fall of Stojadinović's government in February 1939, the Italians decided to go ahead with full annexation.[53] An ultimatum was presented to Zog in late March, and on 7 April Albania was invaded by a 30,000-strong Italian army. Zog quickly fled; a puppet government was installed, and the Albanian crown was humbly offered by a so-called 'Constituent Assembly' to Vittorio Emanuele III, thus creating a 'personal union' between the two realms. An Albanian Fascist Party was formed, and in order to establish some ideological rapport with their subjects the Italian administrators tried hard to identify themselves with at least some of the traditional demands of irredentist Albanian nationalism. The first opportunity to gain credit on those grounds came in October 1940, when the Italian army launched its attack on Greece: the Albanians were told that this was a crusade to recover the lost province of Çamëria, in northwestern Greece, which had a significant Albanian population. The second opportunity would come less than six months later, when the Axis powers launched a devastating *Blitzkrieg* against Yugoslavia. Italy, the ruler of Albania, would now become the co-conqueror of Kosovo.

15

Occupied Kosovo in the Second World War:
1941–1945

HITLER HAD TWO options where Yugoslavia was concerned. He could either coerce it into becoming an ally, or conquer it by force. The first policy seemed to have reached a successful conclusion when, on 25 March 1941, the Yugoslav government reluctantly joined the Axis pact. But on the following day the government was overthrown by a popular coup in Belgrade; Hitler, informed of this and of the anti-German demonstrations in the streets of the Yugoslav capital, decided on an immediate punitive invasion. On 28 March the German Military Attaché in Rome told the Italians that the attack would begin on 2 or 3 April, and asked for their help in taking Skopje. The Germans had already built up a force of their own on Bulgarian territory, apparently in preparation for the invasion of Greece (though the Italian military afterwards suspected that the operation against Yugoslavia had also been planned long in advance); an initial move to block the north–south communication links in Macedonia was essential, in order to cut off the Yugoslav army from any contacts with the Greek army or the British forces in Greece.[1]

For the Italians, still bogged down in their operations against the Greeks in the south of Albania, this was unwelcome news. They calculated that the Yugoslav army had roughly 170,000 men in Kosovo and Macedonia, and 70,000 in Montenegro: if these forces went to war against the smaller and poorly equipped Italian army in Albania, they argued, the Italians would be 'overpowered in a short time'. So they promised Berlin merely that they would take a defensive position and try to hold the frontier until the German troops arrived.[2] The Yugoslav army, meanwhile, was beginning to organize itself, but with fatal slowness and inefficiency. On 30 March its 'Kosovo Division' was ordered to prepare for a general mobilization on 7 April. Although 25,000 Albanians in Kosovo had done military service, call-up papers were not sent to them, on the grounds that they could not be trusted. Of those Serbs who were summoned, roughly one-quarter did not turn up; particularly unresponsive were those who were meant to supply transport to the Yugoslav army, which ended up depending mainly on ox-carts. Sluggishness on the ground was matched by stupidity at the head-quarters: even though the Yugoslav army commanders must have been aware that any war against Germany would involve large-scale attacks on Yugoslavia from several directions, they nevertheless decided to put into action their war plan 'R-41', which was a plan for a Yugoslav invasion of Albania.[3]

And so it was that soon after the war had begun – to the complete surprise of the Yugoslav High Command – with massive bombing raids on Belgrade and other targets on 6 April, the order went out to the soldiers of the Kosovo Division to advance deep into Albania. On 7 April they crossed the frontier; the very next day news came of a German advance on Skopje; and two days later the Germans were on the outskirts of Prizren. Only then were the Yugoslav soldiers recalled from Albania to fight a brief rearguard action in Western Kosovo. The Italian army followed on their heels, quickly switching from defensive to offensive operations and taking Prizren on 14 April; and on the following day the commander of the Yugoslav Third Army ordered his men to stop fighting. The whole of Kosovo had been conquered in precisely one week; only briefly, in Prizren and Suha Reka, did locally based forces make any real attempt to halt the invaders. Resistance in other parts of Yugoslavia had collapsed with equal rapidity, and an unconditional surrender was signed on 17 April 1941.[4]

After the conquest came the partition, which brought about a three-way division of Kosovo. Most of Macedonia and parts of south-eastern Serbia were annexed by Bulgaria; also included in Bulgarian territory was a thin strip of land in Eastern Kosovo, including Kaçanik but skirting just to the east of Gjilan. Two battalions of Bulgarian occupation troops were quickly installed in this area. The Bulgarian policy was a virtual repetition of what had happened in the First World War: all the new officials were people brought in from Bulgaria, and Bulgarian replaced Serbo-Croat as the official language for all purposes, including education.

A law promulgated at the end of 1941 threatened the death penalty for any form of 'propaganda against the Bulgarian state'. This area under Bulgarian control would be extended to include some further districts of northern Kosovo later in the war, as Germany became more and more dependent on its ally for occupation troops in the former Serbian-ruled territories.[5]

Albania, in theory a separate kingdom that just happened to be ruled by the King of Italy, was given the lion's share of Kosovo. Most of Kosovo had in fact been conquered by German troops, but at a meeting of the Italian and German foreign ministers in Vienna on 21 April it was agreed that the largest part of this Albanian-inhabited territory should be put under Italian control and joined to Albania, in order to prevent Albanian ethnic irredentism from becoming the driving force of an anti-German resistance movement. Italy was of course eager to get the whole of Kosovo, because of the area's rich mineral resources: a detailed report prepared for Mussolini by a mining expert on 20 April noted that if Italy controlled the Trepça mine it would become the leading exporter of lead and zinc in the whole of Europe. Accordingly, the Italian viceroy in Albania had already gathered a group of Albanian politicians-in-exile from Kosovo and encouraged them to send off a 'telegram for the liberation of the Kosovo region' to Mussolini. (These included Rexhep Mitrovica, who had been Albanian Minister of Education in 1923–4, and Bedri Peja, who had been a member of the Albanian parliament in 1922–4.)[6] But of course the Germans were equally keen to have the mines of the Trepça district, as well as being anxious about control of the railway line between Mitrovica and Kaçanik. Eventually it was agreed that the northern tip of Kosovo, including Trepça, Mitrovica and Vuçitërn, would be in German-occupied territory, but that the Italians could have Prishtina (which they took over in June 1941) on condition that the Germans would have their own personnel on the railway line.[7]

The areas of Kosovo given to Italy – together with a north-western strip of Macedonian territory including the town of Debar – stayed under military rule until July 1941; then it was announced, to great public acclamation in Tirana, that they would come under civil admin-istration as part of the kingdom of Albania. They were entrusted first to a 'Civil Commissioner' and then, from late 1941 until early 1943, to a 'Ministry for the Liberated Areas' in Tirana. In practice, of course, the

Italians still depended on a large number of occupation troops: the main formations were the Puglia (Apulia) and Firenze (Florence) divisions of the Italian army, based respectively in Kukës (just inside the former Albanian frontier) and Debar. Carabinieri and Italian 'finance police' were also deployed in Kosovo, which was divided into three administrative districts: Prishtina, Prizren and Peć. In total, the Italians had roughly 20,000 armed men in Kosovo. The attempt to unite or reunite Kosovo with Albania was made in earnest: by decrees of October 1941 and February 1942 all the inhabitants of Italian-occupied Kosovo (including, under the second decree, the Slav ones) became Albanian citizens. The Italians also made real efforts to introduce education in the Albanian language, setting up at least 173 new elementary schools in Kosovo and western Macedonia. But a less popular measure was their reintroduction of feudal dues on the peasantry, who were required to pay one-fifth of their produce to the former landowners; the Italian administrators knew that rural Kosovo was still a very traditional society, in which little could be achieved without the compliance of the old land-owning families.[8]

While the areas given to Bulgaria and Albania were formally annexed by those countries, the small German-occupied part of Kosovo was the one area which remained part of the rump Serbian state, which was under German military occupation but governed by Serbian officials from Belgrade. (Rump Serbia was all that was left of Yugoslavia: Slovenia was partitioned between Italy and Germany, Montenegro was made nominally independent but put under Italian occupation, and Croatia and Bosnia were combined as a separate puppet state, the so-called Independent State of Croatia.) The main town in northern Kosovo, Mitrovica, became the headquarters of an Austrian infantry division (of 8,000 men) which covered most of the Sandžak as well. However, some special arrangements were made to acknowledge the overwhelmingly Albanian nature of northern Kosovo's population.

A few days after the conquest, on 21 April 1941, the German divisional commander, General Eberhardt, held a meeting with local Albanian leaders in Mitrovica. There were representatives from several towns, but the leading figure from Mitrovica itself was a man who would figure largely in the history of occupied Kosovo: Xhafer Deva, who, it is frequently alleged, had been working for German intelligence for some time before the war. At this meeting it was agreed that the Albanians would take over the local government in the Albanian-inhabited occupied areas, and that they would have the right to organize education 'according to their own wishes'. The Serbian quisling government in Belgrade (first under the former Minister of the Interior Milan Aćimović, then from August 1941 under the army general Milan Nedić) objected strongly to any such recognition of the Albanian character of this region, and German officials in Belgrade suspended the agreement; but elements of it were later reinstated, and at least forty Albanian elementary schools were created in the Mitrovica region during the following two years. Xhafer Deva himself became the chief of the local administration in Mitrovica. The Germans also restored feudal dues; and, in another concession to Albanian traditionalism, they permitted a council of elders and bajraktars to issue a set of rules based on the şeriat and the Kanun of Lek Dukagjin. These rules included a new system of fines for the settlement of blood-feuds: by the summer of 1944, a total of 652 feuds had been settled in this way.[9]

One of the main topics discussed at the meeting between General Eberhardt and the Albanian notables on 21 April 1941 was the expulsion of the Serbian and Montenegrin colonists from Kosovo. Eberhardt promised to help with their removal, but insisted that 'There must be no sudden adoption of hasty measures, and it is to be expected that everything in this respect will be done in a reasonable and peaceful way.'[10] Such expectations, unfortunately, were already proving illusory. Attacks by Albanians on Serb villages had begun during the invasion of Kosovo: in some cases these may have been retaliations for actions by the Yugoslav army (which had seized Albanian hostages and launched its own attacks on Albanian villages), but the general aim was simply to get rid of the colonists and take back the confiscated land which had been given to them.[11] In late May 1941 an Italian officer noted that a large number of Montenegrin colonists from the area round Peć had been driven out by the local Albanians, 'not without many episodes of bloodshed and violence', within days of the fall of Yugoslavia. The Germans, who had controlled the area at first, not only permitted this but formally ordered the Montenegrins to get out within twenty-four hours; when the Italians took over the area they told them they could return, but the majority were too frightened to do so. The first 'Civil Commissioner', Carlo Umiltà, who arrived in Kosovo at the end of May, was immediately struck by the large number of burnt-out houses in the countryside. He noted that the destruction had not been a purely one-sided affair ('Slavs and Albanians had burnt down one another's houses, had killed as many people as they could, and had stolen livestock, goods and tools'); but clearly the Montenegrins and Serbs were the principal victims. It has been estimated that in the first two or three months 20,000 of them fled; up to 10,000 houses were burnt down; and all the colonist villages were abandoned except for two, Vitomirica and Dobruša, which held out until the autumn. Only in late October did conditions for the colonists (and many other rural Serbs) improve somewhat in the German-occupied area, when a formal besë was made between Albanian and Serbian leaders, promising at least the peaceful evacuation of all those who wished to leave.[12] In the Italian-occupied territory, however, fighting between Albanians and Serbs intensified in October and November; Carlo Umiltà noted that the Italian military authorities and the ordinary Italian soldiers openly took the Serb side in this conflict.[13]

Another element of General Eberhardt's discussion with the Albanian notables in April 1941 was an agreement to set up an Albanian police force. This was to be the first of several collaborationist formations. Roughly 1,000 men were recruited to a so-called 'Albanian gendarmerie', which was placed under the command of a member of Isa Boletin's family, Pajazi or Bajazit Boletin; and in addition to these uniformed officers, roughly 1,000 volunteer auxiliaries were also raised through the activities of a movement called the 'Albanian Popular League' in Mitrovica. In the summer of 1942, however, at the insistence of the Serbian government in Belgrade, this police force was absorbed into the 18,000-strong 'Serbian State Guard', an armed gendarmerie created by Nedić (the quisling ruler of Serbia) with the support of the SS general in Belgrade. This was an unwelcome development for the Albanians, since the ideology of the Serbian State Guard was strongly in favour of the creation of a Greater Serbia.[14]

The Germans' first attempts to recruit Albanians into military formations came in early 1943 – though these recruitments were intended only to strengthen forces acting against local insurgents, and were never for the purpose of fighting on war fronts elsewhere. In March of that year the German commander in Belgrade, General Bader, planned to set up a 'Muslim Battalion' of up to 170 men, to be based in Mitrovica and Novi Pazar and consisting of both Albanians and Muslim Slavs. The two most important Albanian political leaders in Mitrovica, Xhafer Deva and Ali Draga, both agreed to help in its recruitment. In the following month, however, the project was cancelled on the grounds that a decision had just been made to start recruiting a Muslim SS division in Bosnia: all Muslim volunteers, it was now said, should be put at the disposal of that division. Had the battalion ever been formed, its status would have been similar to that of the four battalions which already made up the 'Serbian Volunteer Corps', a formation in occupied Serbia that took part not only in military actions against the Communist Partisans but also in reprisals against civilians.[15] Following this setback, the Germans tried to enlist Albanians as auxiliaries in the locally based German units; a recruitment drive took place in April and May, but the population was unenthusiastic, and in some areas people were threatened with imprisonment if they refused to join up. Of 200 'volunteers' collected in Podujevo and sent to Vuçitërn under armed guard, fifty deserted en route.[16] Only in the following year was any more ambitious attempt made to create a large-scale Albanian military formation, the so-called Skanderbeg Division: this will be described in the last part of this chapter, after the watershed of the Italian capitulation in September 1943.

In the Italian-occupied part of Kosovo similar recruitment efforts were also made. The initial strategy of the new rulers of Albania, after their conquest of it in 1939, had been to absorb Albanians as far as possible into Italian formations. From 1940 to early 1941 the Albanian armed forces had been merged with the Italian army; then, as a sop to Albanian pride, a separate Albanian army group was established, known as the 'Skanderbeg Group' (not to be confused with the later German-organized Skanderbeg Division). Just one battalion of this group was stationed in Kosovo, while roughly 3,000 local men were also recruited to serve as auxiliaries to the Puglia division of the Italian army.[17] An Albanian Fascist Party had been formed soon after the conquest of Albania, and one Blackshirt battalion, recruited through this organization, was established at Prizren; plans to raise two more battalions (one for each of the two other administrative divisions of Kosovo) were dropped, however, because of a lack of public support. Reports by a local Communist organizer in March and August 1942 said that collaboration was strong in the towns of Kosovo, and that the occupiers controlled the countryside through the compliance of the bajraktars; he estimated that there were between 4,000 and 5,000 volunteers in quisling formations in Kosovo, but he also noted that no Albanians, apart from mercenaries, were willing to fight outside their own territory.[18]

Other evidence suggests, as we shall see, that many of the local Albanian leaders were basically opposed to the Axis powers. One Italian army report in early 1943 noted that until recently (when a number of Albanian officials had been dismissed from their posts in Kosovo) the area had suffered from 'the defeatism created by the leading figures in Kosovo's public life, who were stirring up hatred and a spirit of rebellion against the Italians'.[19] Collaboration certainly existed at many levels, but its driving force was neither ideological sympathy with Fascism or Nazism, nor any interest in the wider war aims of the Axis powers, but simply the desire of many Albanians to seize the opportunity offered by the collapse of Yugoslavia to gain more power over their own territory and reverse the colonizing and Slavicizing policies of the previous two decades.

There was, in the circumstances, an awkward paradox at the heart of the official Italian position: Italy was appealing whenever possible to Albanian nationalism, which aimed at independence and self-government, but doing so in order to persuade people to accept their status as *de facto* colonial subjects, governed by Italians and absorbed into Italian institutions. This paradox was becoming less and less acceptable to the population of both Kosovo and Albania, not least because of the poor conditions which Italian rule had created. In 1942 there were serious food shortages, and an Italian report in early 1943 described the economic situation as 'disastrous', with goods which cost 1 lira in Italy being sold for more than 6 lire in Albania. (German economic mismanagement was almost equally bad, with severe shortages and roaring inflation.) The same Italian report also summarized the situation in Kosovo and Albania as 'the total bankruptcy of our experiment in the political-administrative field ... the triumph of corruption, personal wheeler-dealing and intrigue'.[20] In February 1943 the Italian viceroy in Tirana, Francesco Jacomini, flew to Rome and told Mussolini that he must choose between military rule and a political solution in the

Albanian lands: local leaders, especially the northern chiefs, demanded a much more equal relationship with Italy, which would involve respecting Albanian autonomy and substituting an Albanian nationalist movement, to be called the 'Greater Albanian Guard', for the discredited Fascist Party. This policy was duly adopted. A new Albanian gendarmerie, with Albanian officers, was set up immediately, and the Albanian Fascist Party was disbanded; but the Greater Albanian Guard was not a success, and an Italian official noted in April that the idea had failed to gain much sympathy among the people. Later that year, in August, the Italians embarked on a more desperate attempt to recruit Albanian fighters, setting up an 'Albanian Volunteer Militia'. By then, however, the Italian war effort was already on the point of collapse.[21]

In some ways, the overall situation in Kosovo during the Second World War was not very different from that in Serbia itself: many officials and public servants continued to work for the new regime, and a small proportion of men of military age joined collaborationist formations. (In Serbia, roughly 25,000 had joined the Serbian State Guard, Border Guard and Volunteer Corps by early 1943.)[22] That the proportion was higher in Kosovo is not surprising, given that most Albanians had felt no loyalty to the previous Yugoslav regime, and had viewed the Axis conquest as, at least potentially, a kind of liberation. The main difference between the situation in Kosovo and that in other parts of Yugoslavia was that the two resistance movements which sprang up in the early part of the war – the Četniks and the Communists – were peculiarly weak in Kosovo, and this was for the simple reason that both of them were viewed as almost exclusively Slav-based organizations. The Communists were of almost no military significance in Kosovo until the final months of the war; the Četniks were never militarily important there, and by the second half of the war they had in any case become a broadly collaborationist movement, a Serbian nationalist counterpart in some respects to the Albanian movement led by Xhafer Deva.

The term 'Četnik' has sometimes been a source of confusion. Originally, as we have seen, it was just a general word for a member of a četa or band of fighters. Since the 1920s Kosta Pećanac had led an official Četnik organization, based on veterans of the guerrilla formations he had led in the First World War, which supported a policy of hard-line Serbian nationalism. Pećanac's personal stronghold was in the upper

Morava valley, just to the east and north-east of Kosovo; he gathered a force of several thousand men there in the first two months of Axis occupation, but his political views were so dominated by anti-Communism that, after Hitler's invasion of Russia in late June 1941, he ordered his men to refrain from anti-German actions. In September he made a formal agreement with the Germans; his men were 'legalized' and paid salaries, to act as an anti-Communist militia inside Serbia, by the quisling government in Belgrade. This remained their principal function, though they also engaged in some sporadic fighting against Albanian bands on the fringes of Kosovo.[23]

In Yugoslav Second World War history, however, the term 'Četnik' usually refers to a separate movement created by the Yugoslav army Colonel Draža Mihailović (later promoted to general and appointed Minister of War by the government-in-exile). He began to organize resistance to the Germans from a base in the hill country of western Serbia immediately after the conquest of Yugoslavia; his support was strongest in Serbia and Montenegro. Politically, Mihailović represented a broadly conservative position, loyal to the monarchy and formally committed to restoring the old Yugoslavia. But many of the activists in his movement, including most of his regional commanders and his own chief advisers, were hard-line Serb nationalists, advocates of a Greater Serbia from which undesirable elements such as Muslims and Albanians would have to be 'cleansed'. (The word *čišćenje*, meaning 'cleansing', was used by one of his advisers, Stevan Moljević, who in 1942 advocated sending all 'non-Serb elements' to Albania or Turkey.) After some initial attempts at open military resistance, Mihailović adopted a more passive policy towards the occupiers, for two reasons: first, because the government-in-exile instructed him to do so, and secondly, because of the savage programme of reprisals adopted by the German authorities. A third reason quickly emerged: political rivalry with the Communist Partisans, a rivalry which developed, from late 1941 onwards, into open warfare between the two movements. As the Axis occupiers were eager to encourage the Četniks in this direction, Mihailović was gradually drawn into a morass of accommodations, 'parallel actions' and finally direct collaborations, first with the Italians and then, in 1943, with the Germans too.[24]

Mihailović made little headway in Kosovo. One of his men visited

Prishtina in September 1941 and organized a small group of Yugoslav army officers there, but their activities – if there were any – have left no trace. Another emissary, a student called Ljubo Jovanović, travelled to the Prishtina district in April 1942 and set up a 'Gračanica brigade', which, in an extraordinarily short space of time, seemed to have acquired fourteen battalions, numbering 6,500 men; these battalions probably existed on paper only, the products of sheer imagination.[25] A more senior figure, Captain Jovan Miladinović, was sent there in the summer of 1942, and claimed to have set up three military units. In September he was given the grandiose title of 'Commander of the Kosovo Corps'. But in the final months of that year the Communists embarked on an assassination campaign against the Četniks in Kosovo, and Miladinović fled in fear of his life, reassembling his 'Kosovo Corps' in the Jablanica district, north of Kosovo. A second 'Kosovo Corps' was formed in early 1943 among Serb refugees from Western Kosovo who had gathered in the hill country to the north of the province, and was placed under the command of another army captain, Živojin Marković; both of these formations would remain outside Kosovo for the rest of the war. Only occasional raids would be made by Četniks from Montenegro, such as a large attack on Albanian villages near Peć in November 1943.[26] For those Četnik sympathizers who stayed in Kosovo, assassination by Communists was not the only threat; they were also at risk from the local Albanian authorities who, as one Italian report noted in February 1943, hounded them mercilessly. The official who wrote this report suggested that 'the pro-Mihailović elements could be useful to us, for the purpose of persecuting Communism in Kosovo more effectively'; and some links with them were eventually established by the ever-active chief of Italian military intelligence in Kosovo, Captain Angelo Antica.[27]

The rivals and enemies of the Četniks, the Communist Partisans, were also very weak in Kosovo. As a political movement they had been completely insignificant there ever since the Communist Party had been formally banned in 1920. Kosovo had just a handful of Party cells in the 1930s; one was at the English-owned Trepça mine, where its members helped to organize strikes in 1937 and 1939. (They also chose forty-nine men to go and fight in the Spanish Civil War; but in the end only one actually went.)[28] To anyone who looks only at the theoretical pronouncements of the Yugoslav Communist Party in the period just before the war, it may seem that the Communist programme was ideally designed to attract the Albanians of Kosovo. Communist slogans denounced the 'Greater-Serbian bourgeoisie', criticized the colonization programme and demanded equal rights for Albanians. At the Fifth National Congress of the Party, held in October 1940, the local committee for Kosovo was separated from the regional committee for Montenegro (under which it had been placed up till then) and given a separate status of its own, which strongly implied that the territory of Kosovo itself was regarded as a distinct unit. The discussion paper on the national question in Kosovo prepared by one leading Party member, Moša Pijade, and accepted by that conference, went even further: 'the solution', it proposed, 'can be attained through the formation of a free workers' and peasants' republic of Kosovo, by means of the revolutionary overthrow of the Greater-Serbian fascist-imperialist regime.'[29]

But since the Communist Party in Kosovo was in fact just a small offshoot of an overwhelmingly Slav organization, it was regarded there mainly as a Slav entity. By the summer of 1940 there were just 239 Party members in Kosovo, and of those only twenty-five were Albanians; by the outbreak of war in the following year the total had risen to 270, but the number of Albanians had dropped to twenty. In Western Kosovo the members of the Party consisted mainly of colonists; its first 'regional committee' meeting during the war was actually held in the colonist village of Vitomirica.[30] Given that the Party was both numerically weak and closely linked to a minority which was being hounded by the majority population, it is not surprising that its range of activities was very slight. As elsewhere in Yugoslavia, the Communists in Kosovo made no active resistance until after Hitler's invasion of the Soviet Union. Then, in July 1941, they received instructions from the Central Committee to begin acts of sabotage, especially against the Trepça mine. This was a well-chosen target, not only because there were some Communists working there, but also because it was of vital economic importance to the Germans: from the beginning of that month Trepça had been sending a daily train-load of 500 tons of lead and zinc concentrate to Germany's munitions factories. Eventually an attempt was made to blow up two of the pillars supporting the 'téléphérique' which carried the hoppers of ore. One pillar was slightly damaged, but was repaired within twelve hours. Thereafter, the Trepça mine continued to function throughout the war, supplying roughly 40 per cent of Germany's consumption of lead.[31]

During 1942 the Communists tried hard to increase their membership in Kosovo. The Italian military intelligence service was equally industrious, and in Peć (one of the main centres of the Party) sixty out of the ninety members were arrested during that year. Albanians were still a tiny minority in the Party, but their numbers included several activists – notably Fadil Hoxha and Emin Duraku – who had been involved in Marxist groups in Albania and had returned to Kosovo in 1939. In September 1942 the first all-Albanian Partisan group was formed, called the Zejnel Ajdini unit; it immediately launched a successful attack on a mine near Kumanovo, and in January 1943 it ambushed a German column on the road south of Prishtina, killing (reportedly) roughly thirty men. This was the first properly active Partisan unit on Kosovo's soil; others had existed only on paper, apart from a detachment recruited in Kosovo which operated in the Kopaonik mountains, north of Kosovo's border. And in early 1943 another Albanian unit was formed as an offshoot from it, the 'Emin Duraku' unit, which was also unusually active, attacking an Italian column on the road west of Prizren in its first action and killing twenty-three soldiers.[32]

But this period also brought many setbacks to the Communist cause. Emin Duraku himself had been killed in late 1942; two other leaders, Boro Vukmirović and Ramiz Sadiku, were captured in Gjakova and executed in April 1943. An Italian report, commenting on their capture, said that the general population was becoming more collaborative 'in order to prevent the Slav element from regaining power over this region' (even though Ramiz Sadiku was Albanian), and contentedly observed: 'Even in Gjakova, the stronghold of Kosovo Communism, there have indeed been episodes of spontaneous collaboration on the part of the citizens, making possible the arrest of dangerous Communists.'[33] But these Italian reports would swing from one extreme to the other in their interpretation of the local mood; just one month later the Italian officials were complaining that the Albanian authorities in Kosovo were doing their best to help the Communist movement, since they were expending all their energies persecuting 'the nationalist Serbs who assist our anti-Communist action', while never troubling 'the real dangerous subversives', who 'live in complete freedom'. One thing at least remains clear:

the dominant factor was the Albanian–Serb national question, not political philosophy or feelings for or against the occupying powers. As one despairing Communist report put it in August 1943, 'The movement in Kosovo is very weak, almost dead. It is completely cut off from the Albanian masses ... Among the Albanian masses, the Communists are regarded as having sold themselves to the Serbs.'[34]

In the circumstances, one might have expected the Communist Party of Albania to step into the breach, supplying to the Kosovo Albanians a form of Communist propaganda adapted to their national tastes. But this was not done, mainly because the Albanian Communist Party was more or less a puppet of Tito, who jealously guarded his own Yugoslav Party's right to be the sole operator on Yugoslav soil. As late as 1941 there was no real Communist Party in Albania, merely a scattering of Marxist cells; these were gathered into a party in the late autumn of that year under the tutelage of two Yugoslav Communist emissaries, Dušan Mugoša and Miladin Popović. The degree to which all early decision-making in the Albanian Party was controlled by these two Yugoslavs is only now beginning to emerge, with the publication of hitherto secret documents from the Party archives. As Enver Hoxha, the Party leader, admitted in an internal discussion in 1944, 'When the Party was formed our reliance on those two comrades, Miladin and Dušan, was great, because I was without experience and without clear views on organization or policy.' At the founding meeting of the Albanian Communist Party in November 1941 the question of Kosovo was simply not mentioned, and complete silence also descended on the issue at the first national conference of the party in March 1943.[35] In late 1942 one leading Albanian Communist, Koço Tashko, had sent a bitter letter of complaint about this to Moscow: on Kosovo, he said, 'the Party has been systematically silent, while saying – these are Comrade Miladin's words – that this question does not concern us, but only concerns the Communist Party of Yugoslavia.' Miladin Popović had turned down his request to set up a special Communist organization for Kosovo, thereby losing a valuable opportunity: 'The hatred and fear of the Kosovars for the Serbs and Montenegrins is very great, but let us not forget that they also have a great hatred for the fascist Italians, whom they call "weaklings" and "infidels".'[36]

The main beneficiary of this Albanian Communist policy (or lack of it), apart from the Italian and quisling authorities, was the anti-Communist resistance movement in Albania, known as Balli Kombëtar ('the National Front'). Founded in late 1942, this was a movement based on the old opposition to King Zog; Communist historians depict it as a reactionary landowners' party, but in fact its political programme was republican, anti-feudal and generally left-of-centre, reflecting the views of the supporters of Fan Noli who had been driven out by Zog in 1924. Balli Kombëtar also had strong nationalist credentials: its leader was the elderly Midhat Frashëri (son of Abdyl, the intellectual driving force of the League of Prizren) and its programme included the traditional Albanian national claims to the whole Albanian 'ethnic territory', which now roughly coincided with the Greater Albania created by Mussolini. The attitude of the Communists towards Balli Kombëtar was cold and hostile from the outset: they were particularly irked by the fact that the 'Ballists' refused to join the broader 'National Liberation Movement' which they had set up as a kind of Communist-controlled front.[37]

Nevertheless, in early August 1943 a meeting was held between the National Liberation Movement and Balli Kombëtar in the village of Mukje, north of Tirana, at which a common programme was agreed. As the chief Communist representative at the meeting, Ymer Dishnica, wrote in his report to Enver Hoxha, the question of creating an 'ethnic Albania' (i.e. one including Kosovo) was one of two main stumbling-blocks, the other being the call for Albanian independence, on which the Ballists refused to compromise. (Communist policy at this stage favoured the idea of setting up a Balkan federation.) In the end, Dishnica reported, 'We got over the obstacle of "ethnic Albania" with a neutral formula.' The wording they chose was as follows: 'Struggle for an independent Albania and, through the application of the principle – which is universally known and guaranteed by the Atlantic Charter – of the self-determination of peoples, for an ethnic Albania.' This was too much for Miladin Popović, who condemned the proclamation issued by the Mukje conference; and Enver Hoxha wrote a furious letter to Dishnica in which he insisted: 'You must proclaim war against fascism, not independence.' It was their rejection of the Mukje agreement that marked, in effect, the declaration of war by the Communist leadership against Balli Kombëtar:

in the conflict which developed over the next two years the Ballists were pushed into a collaborationist position, similar in the end to the one adopted by the Četniks in Yugoslavia.[38]

One month after the Mukje conference, however, the political and military situation changed dramatically in Albania and Kosovo, with the announcement of Italy's capitulation on the evening of 8 September 1943. Just after midnight an order was sent from Rome, directing the Italian troops to withdraw towards the ports of Albania and Montenegro. The commander of all Italian forces in Greater Albania informed the Germans that he would order his men to resist any attempt to disarm them, and to fire, if necessary, in self-defence.[39] But the Germans quickly took control, sending fast-moving units from Prishtina to block the withdrawal of the Puglia division from Kosovo, moving a German column rapidly to Elbasan and using parachutists to capture the Italian High Command in Tirana. The Italian commander was then forced to order the deportation of the troops from Kosovo into Bulgarian- or German-occupied territory, under German military law and only carrying personal weapons. But several senior Italian officers had other ideas. The commander of the Firenze division, based in Debar, made an agreement with elements of the non-Communist resistance, including two British liaison officers; at the end of September he also agreed to let his men fight on the Communist side. Some did so, forming the 'Antonio Gramsci' Partisan battalion; others were killed or stripped of their equipment by the Partisans. Many Italian soldiers who escaped the German round-up were put to work in the fields, being bought and sold by local Albanians and treated simply as slaves.[40]

The German policy towards the newly acquired territory of Kosovo and Albania was to court the sympathy of the population by using the rhetoric of Albanian nationalism and Albanian independence – in other words, a further step down the path which Italian policy had taken in February 1943. At the end of September the Germans officially recognized Albania (within the borders established by Mussolini) as an independent country; like the Austro-Hungarians when they occupied it in the First World War, they maintained the fiction that Albania was just a friendly neutral state. Accompanying the recognition of independence was a proclamation which said: 'The German Army has come only to defend your land from English occupation. The governmental and political organization of the country must be decided only by the Albanian people.' In fact, of course, the government was carefully selected and controlled by the German authorities. One of their first moves was to make their most trusted servant, Xhafer Deva, Minister of the Interior: he moved to Tirana, where he began to recruit an Albanian security force to fight against Communists and other insurgents.[41]

In the first days after the Italian capitulation, before the German policy towards Kosovo and Albania had become clear, a group of leading Albanian officials in Kosovo (including Deva) had decided to form a movement to campaign for ethnic unification. Their main aim was to ensure that Kosovo and Albania would remain united, together with the other areas added to Albania since 1941, such as Debar; they also campaigned, unsuccessfully, for the transfer of the northern tip of Kosovo to the ethnic Albanian state. In mid-September they held a large public meeting in Prizren, at which they proclaimed themselves the 'Second League of Prizren'. An executive committee was set up, with Rexhep Mitrovica as chairman, and statutes were drafted which gave as their aim 'the defence of the liberated areas [i.e. liberated from Yugoslavia] and of other areas of the former Yugoslavia'.[42]

The Second League raised its own volunteers, and by late November it was engaged in fighting against Montenegrins and Serbs in the countryside near Peć. According to the account of the Second League written by one of its leaders, this was a defensive action against Četnik raids on Albanian villages; but it is hard to disentangle the activities of the League from the new wave of expulsions of Serbs and Montenegrins which took place in the winter of 1943–4. When General Nedić, the head of the quisling Serbian government, sent in his resignation in February 1944 he gave the German failure to stop these expulsions as one of the reasons for his decision: there were, he said, 120 railway waggons full of women and children who had fled from Lipljan, and 600 families had recently been expelled from the Mitrovica area. By April the chief German political officer in Belgrade, Hermann Neubacher, was demanding that the expulsions be halted; he calculated that since 1941 40,000 Serbs and Montenegrins had been driven out of Kosovo.[43]

Since the leaders of the Second League of Prizren were all people who had collaborated with the Italians and the Germans, the growth of this movement, which is said to have reached a total membership of between

12,000 and 15,000, may seem to show that the Kosovo Albanians were becoming more actively collaborationist in the final period of the war. But the appeal of the Second League was primarily to Albanian nationalism (and, as a by-product of that, to anti-Communism, given that the Communists were seen as aiming at the restoration of Yugoslav rule), and not to pro-German sentiment as such. Nor was the Second League the only Albanian movement active in Kosovo at this time. Balli Kombëtar, whose leaders were still broadly pro-English, had many supporters there: in the words of a later Balli Kombëtar memorandum, 'By direct orders of the Minister of the Interior, Xhafer Deva, our members were severely persecuted in Kosova and our propaganda was much thwarted. People were threatened, imprisoned and beaten if they were caught spreading or even reading our leaflets.' And another Albanian movement, the pro-Zog Legalitet ('legality') party, was also active, especially among the military: one Communist report in February 1944 estimated that two-thirds of the Albanian officers in Kosovo were Legalitet supporters.[44] Legalitet was in principle pro-English (Zog had spent the war in London), and its military chief, Abaz Kupi, had cooperated actively with British officers in northern Albania. Behind the smooth facade of collaboration, therefore, there was a much more complex pattern of political activity. Some sense of the oddity of the situation can be gained from the memoirs of Peter Kemp, a British officer who made two brief visits to Kosovo in December 1943 and January 1944 in an attempt to organize resistance there. He was offered help by the Chief of Police at Peć, and the commander of the Albanian army garrison there agreed to put his men at Kemp's disposal in the event of an Allied invasion; he also had a secret meeting, under the noses of the German security police, with the Mayor of Gjakova and the Colonel-Commandant of the Albanian army in Kosovo.[45]

Kemp found that the strongest pro-Allied support among the Kosovo notables came from the Kryeziu family of Gjakova: of the three surviving sons of Riza bey Kryeziu, one (Hasan) had stayed in Gjakova throughout the war, while the other two (Gani and Said) had been interned on a remote Italian island, being suspected – correctly – of pro-British activities. After the Italian capitulation they made their way back to Kosovo, arriving there in mid-January 1944. Both, Kemp found, were 'impatient to go into action with us against the Germans'; they already had 100 armed men, and thought they could quickly raise 1,000. This was not an idle boast, as the Kryezius were a powerful family and Gani bey was a charismatic figure, highly regarded as a military leader. Three days after he had agreed with them on a plan to prepare a general insurrection in Kosovo, however, Kemp was ordered by his superiors in SOE (Special Operations Executive) to break off all contact with them, on the grounds that the Communist Partisans were objecting to Kemp's dealings with non-Communist resistance leaders. 'Our relations with Jugoslav Partisans', said the message from SOE, 'are of overriding importance.'[46]

The Communists now had two main strategies where the Albanians of Kosovo were concerned. On the one hand they made some slight policy concessions towards Albanian nationalism; and on the other hand they ruthlessly suppressed the development of any non-Communist Albanian national resistance movement. The concessions were small but potentially significant. The slogan of 'self-determination' was allowed to creep into some of the official statements of the Albanian Communist Party in relation to Kosovo: the strongest of all these statements, in a tract issued by the Party in December 1943 (with the permission of the Yugoslav Communists in Kosovo), advocated self-determination 'up to and including secession'. This was, apparently, a tactical ploy to counter the propaganda of the Second League. Miladin Popović had come round to the idea that the Communists could make progress among the Kosovo Albanians only if they took this line; in early December he was ticked off by Tito for suggesting that they campaign on the basis of the eventual annexation of Kosovo by Albania.[47]

The most important statement of this position was made at a special conference of delegates from the two local committees of the Yugoslav Communist Party in Kosovo, which covered 'Kosovo' (i.e. Eastern Kosovo) and the Metohija (i.e. Western Kosovo). The latter had changed its name in late 1943 to the 'Dukagjin' committee, 'Rrafsh i Dukagjinit', the 'Dukagjin plateau', being the Albanian name for 'Metohija'. From 31 December 1943 to 2 January 1944 the delegates met at the village of Bujan, near Tropoja in north-eastern Albania. Altogether forty-nine people took part, of whom forty-two were ethnic Albanians. They agreed to set up a new regional council for the whole 'Kosovo-Metohija' or 'Kosovo-Dukagjin' area, and they also issued a 'Resolution' and a 'Proclamation'. One key passage in the Resolution stated:

> Kosovo-Metohija is an area with a majority Albanian population, which, now as always in the past, wishes to be united with Albania ... The only way that the Albanians of Kosovo-Metohija can be united with Albania is through a common struggle with the other peoples of Yugoslavia against the occupiers and their lackeys. For the only way freedom can be achieved is if all peoples, including the Albanians, have the possibility of deciding on their own destiny, with the right to self-determination, up to and including secession.[48]

The Yugoslav Central Committee was not happy about this part of the Resolution, and in late March Tito's right-hand man, Milovan Djilas, sent a letter (on behalf of the Central Committee) to the regional committee, in which he complained: 'In fact, any raising of the question of changing the borders helps the Germans to set one people against another.' But the wording of this criticism was notably mild; and, in strict logic, it would have applied equally to any promise to restore the old Yugoslav–Albanian border. The Resolution remained the official policy of the regional committee, and indeed was not changed until long after the Germans had left.[49]

While the Party adapted its rhetoric in this way, at least at the regional level, it was also making strenuous efforts to suppress any Albanian national resistance of a non-Communist kind. In December 1943 the Albanian Communists had tried hard to prevent Peter Kemp from making contact with the resident Kryeziu brother in Gjakova; when he insisted on going to meet him, they secretly informed the Gestapo in Gjakova about his visit. The British policy of cold-shouldering the Kryezius remained in force from January until June 1944, when contact was renewed and plans for organizing resistance in Kosovo were formed once again; this enraged both Tito and Enver Hoxha, who, as one modern study puts it, 'must already have resolved that it would be better from their point of view if there was no resistance in Kosovë rather than a successful movement led by Gani Kryeziu with British support'. In August and September Hoxha ordered his forces to attack Kryeziu's men and to kill Kryeziu himself (who was in the end captured by Yugoslav

Partisans and put in gaol); he likewise ordered the destruction of another popular leader in the Luma region, Muharem Bajraktar, who had actively resisted the Italians and the Germans but had refused to become a member of the 'National Liberation Movement'.[50]

The Communists were able to flex their muscles in this way because they were gaining in military strength during this period – particularly the Albanian Partisans, who benefited from Allied deliveries of money and equipment. Yet the scale and scope of military activities by the Yugoslav Partisans in Kosovo remained disappointingly slight; the most significant actions in the first half of 1944 were some minor sabotage attacks on the important chrome mines in the Gjakova-Kukës region. By June, however, production of chrome ore had risen to a new peak of 8,000 tons, and in August it achieved its all-time record of 9,267 tons. More damage was done to the ore transportation system by Allied air attacks than by any Partisan actions on the ground. Indeed, bombing raids were now playing an important role, politically as well as militarily, in Kosovo. As one Communist report put it in May 1944: 'The development of the political situation is changing from day to day. The causes are the progress of the Red Army, and above all the Allied bombings, which make a great impression on the Albanian masses. Because of this situation the Albanian masses do not respond to the mobilization. The deadline for mobilization is constantly being postponed.'[51]

Those plans by the Germans to institute a general mobilization of the Albanians in Kosovo never came to anything. There was, however, one large-scale recruitment effort: the creation of the 'Skanderbeg' volunteer SS division. This sprang from discussions between the German authorities and Bedri Peja, who offered to raise a large military force to fight against the Communists; at one point he claimed he could gather up to 150,000 men. But the recruitment drive, carried out in early 1944, was a disappointment: in the whole period up to the beginning of the German withdrawal only 6,491 men joined the division. According to the commanding officer's report, the main obstacle had been 'the invisible resistance of the beys and agas, which resulted in inactivity on the part of the prefects and mayors who were controlled by the beys, and in a whispering campaign of propaganda against recruitment'.[52] The Skanderbeg division was never a significant combat force. In a very jaundiced

description of Albanian fighting skills the divisional commander wrote
that the Albanians would fight only in traditional bands, not in proper
military formations, and that 'When it rains, the Albanian leaves his
post, and when it gets dark, he abandons his position in the field and
goes into the village to drink raki.' By May some of the Skanderbeg
division troops were deployed in the Gjakova area to guard the mines
and carry out arrests; in the middle of that month they took part in the
most shameful episode of Kosovo's wartime history, the round-up and
deportation of 281 Jews.[53] But during the summer their morale deteriorated; according to their commander, the hostile propaganda of the beys
intensified, based on 'the hope ... that the English will be able to replace
the Germans before the Bolsheviks enter Albania'. In September the
commander of Army Group 'E' (which covered German formations in
the southern Balkans) was informed that the Skanderbeg division was of
no military value; by early October its numbers had fallen to 3,500, and
it was reported that 'the division is without any particular will to fight.'[54]
Nevertheless, it would play some part in assisting the German withdrawal
during the next two months.

The German retreat from Greece, using the main railway lines through
Macedonia, Kosovo and Serbia, began in early September. On 8 Septem-
ber Soviet troops entered Bulgaria, and on the following day the
Bulgarian 'Fatherland Front' took over the government there, declaring
that Bulgaria was now a Soviet ally and at war with Germany. The
Germans took quick action to disarm or expel the Bulgarians from
Macedonia and Eastern Kosovo. But by early October Soviet and
Bulgarian forces were breaking through into eastern Serbia: Niš fell to
them on 14 October, and a Bulgarian column moved south-west from
there towards Kosovo. Since the main railway route to Belgrade was now
cut, most of the German forces had to retreat through Kosovo, either
taking the roads over the mountains of northern Albania and Montenegro, or using the old trade route through Novi Pazar to Bosnia. Two
defensive groups were formed to cover this retreat: one, under General
Müller, in central Serbia, and the other, under Major-General Scholz, in
eastern Kosovo and northern Macedonia.[55]

By 23 October the Bulgarians had reached the vicinity of Podujevo, in
the north-eastern corner of Kosovo; another Bulgarian force was also
closing on Kumanovo, a strategically important town just to the north-

east of Skopje. For a crucial period of a fortnight, however, this front remained more or less static. This was thanks to two factors: the disruption of the Bulgarian army by the sudden removal (at Russian insistence) of its old officer corps, and the dogged resistance of the Scholz Group, which was assisted by up to 5,000 Albanians in the Prishtina–Mitrovica area (of whom some belonged to the security force recruited in Albania by Xhafer Deva, and 700 were members of the Skanderbeg division) as well as some local Četnik formations. The Germans formed a plan for the orderly evacuation of their forces, which they were able to carry out on schedule, abandoning Skopje on 11 November, destroying installations at the Trepça mine on the 12th and leaving Prishtina on the 19th, from where they retreated north-westwards into Bosnia.[56]

Accounts of these events published in post-war Yugoslavia give the impression that the Germans were driven out by the Partisans, who 'liberated' the cities of Kosovo by force. There was some fighting by a combined force of Yugoslav and Albanian Partisans in Western Kosovo, mainly against the remnants of the Skanderbeg division; but these actions were quite insignificant compared with the Soviet–Bulgarian advance. The war diary of the commander of the German Army Group 'E', with its detailed day-by-day record of military actions in Kosovo, contains hardly any references to Partisan actions at all. The general pattern was that the towns in Western Kosovo were 'liberated', i.e. taken over by Partisan forces, only after the Germans and their auxiliaries had left; in Eastern Kosovo it was the Soviet and Bulgarian forces (with some Yugoslav Partisans attached to them) who took over, also after the Germans had got out. Altogether the Germans succeeded in evacuating 350,000 men and 10,000 vehicles from Greece and Albania, the majority of them through the territory of Kosovo.[57]

While most of the remnants of the Skanderbeg division retreated to Bosnia, some armed groups raised by the Second League of Prizren did remain in Kosovo at the end of November. Orders issued by Miladin Popović decreed that anyone suspected of organizing resistance in the villages was to be subjected to a summary trial, and his property confiscated. Some armed resistance nevertheless continued: on 1 December a group of several hundred Albanians tried to seize the town of Ferizaj from the Partisans, and a month later a similar attack was made, also unsuccessfully, against Gjilan. More alarming for the Communists, perhaps, was the fact that some of their own Albanian soldiers turned against them. One Albanian Partisan commander, Shaban Polluzha, rejected an order to take his men to the front in Srem (the Croatian region west of Belgrade), saying that he wanted to stay and defend his home region of Drenica against attacks on Albanians by Četnik bands. His force, composed of roughly 8,000 men, was then attacked by other Partisan units; fighting in the Drenica region lasted until March, and forty-four villages were destroyed there. It has been estimated that more than 20,000 local Albanians joined Polluzha's force; in the end the revolt was completely suppressed. A smaller rebellion in the Mitrovica region in late January was more quickly crushed, but in some remoter parts of Kosovo resistance to the Communists would continue until the 1950s. Lingering resistance was a phenomenon encountered in many parts of Yugoslavia. Nowhere, however, did it last as long as in Kosovo.[58]

According to the later account written by one of the leaders of the Second League, a total of 47,300 Albanians were killed by the Communists (in battle or by execution), 28,400 of them within the borders of Kosovo. This figure is repeated by some modern Albanian writers, but more thorough recent research suggests that it is an exaggeration. Even more inflated is the claim by one modern Serbian writer that 60,000 Serbs and Montenegrins were killed in Kosovo during the war.[59] Two scholars – one Serb, one Croat – have carried out detailed investigations of Yugoslav losses in the Second World War: their figures for Kosovo's war dead for the whole period of 1941–5 are 10,000 and 24,000 respectively. In an ethnic breakdown of those totals, the Serb historian supposes that 3,000 Albanians and 4,000 Serbs and Montenegrins were killed; the Croat's estimate is 14,000 Albanians and 3,000 Serbs and Montenegrins. A more recent revision of their figures by two other Serb historians raises the total number of war dead in Kosovo to 25,000, of whom 12,000 were Albanian and 10,000 Serb or Montenegrin. Compared with most other areas of Yugoslavia, this represents an unusually low proportion of the population; indeed, Macedonia and Kosovo were the only parts of Yugoslavia to register a slight rise in population between 1940 and 1948.[60]

Serbian nationalists account for this rise by saying that huge numbers of Albanians flooded into Kosovo from Albania during the war; the figure of 100,000 has been claimed for 1941–5, and a petition of Kosovo Serbs in 1985 claimed that 260,000 had entered Kosovo since 1941 (mainly between 1941 and 1948). These figures, however, are pure fantasy. No evidence of any such mass migration during the war can be found in any of the documents of the occupying powers. It is likely that a few thousand people did move from Albania into Kosovo: some of these were officials brought in by the Italians or Germans, and some were Kosovars who had moved to Albania during the inter-war years.[61] What is certain, on the other hand, is that tens of thousands of Serbs and Montenegrins – mainly colonists, but including some of the long-established Slavs of Kosovo – were expelled from the area during the war. Estimates range from an over-modest 30,000 to an exaggerated 100,000. The estimate of a senior German official, Hermann Neubacher, has already been noted: he put it at 40,000, which is less than the total number of colonists who had come to Kosovo by the late 1930s.[62] Many of these never came back, for reasons which will be explained in the next chapter.

16

Kosovo under Tito: 1945–1980

TITO IS STILL remembered with genuine affection by many Albanians in the former Yugoslavia. They see him as the man who halted or reversed the most objectionable policies of the previous Yugoslav régime – the colonization programme and the suppression of the Albanian language – and who gave the territory of Kosovo a form of autonomy which, by the 1970s, had come close to attaining equal status with the other federal units of the Yugoslav state. It is understandable that, looking back from a vantage-point after 1989, the Albanians of Kosovo should view the Tito years with somewhat rosy-tinted indulgence. But a more complete judgement on Tito's Kosovo policy must also be a much more heavily qualified one. Some of his measures to respect the rights of the Albanians were only half-measures; some developed only under the pressure of circumstances (including the pressure of unsatisfied Albanian demands); and some were made for pragmatic reasons quite uncon-nected with the needs of Kosovo itself (such as the desire to divert Serb colonists to the Vojvodina instead). The first two decades of Communist rule in Kosovo were particularly harsh, and the dominance of Serbs and Montenegrins in the Party and State security apparatus meant that the Albanians there still had very much a second-class position. The resentments created by this initial imbalance of power set up an oscillating dynamic of reaction and counter-reaction – Albanian reaction to the Slavs after 1966, and Slav counter-reaction in the 1980s – which made Kosovo's internal politics all the more bitter and intractable. Nor should it be forgotten that it was Tito's legacy of a stultified political system and a collapsing economy that created the conditions under which a politician such as Slobodan Milošević could rise to power and manipulate Serbian nationalism to his own destructive advantage.

The essential question of the status of Kosovo in the new Communist Yugoslavia was decided – like all essential questions – from above. The basic structure of the state, as a federation of six republics, had been agreed by the Communist leadership as early as 1943; but the position of Kosovo in that structure had remained unclear for a long time thereafter. In March 1944 Tito had written that Vojvodina and other similar areas 'will obtain a broader autonomy, and the question of which federal unit they are joined to will depend on the people themselves, through their representatives, when the issue is decided by a definitive ruling after the war'. (The term 'representatives' here was a useful weasel-word, by means of which any concept of popular self-determination could be neutralized: the only representatives who mattered would be Communist ones, carrying out the wishes of the Party.) Some discussion did take place among senior Communists in 1944 and early 1945 about which federal unit Kosovo should be joined to: both Montenegro and Macedonia put in their bids, but the dominant idea was always to join Kosovo to Serbia. At a late stage in these debates in February 1945, one of Tito's closest advisers, Edvard Kardelj, added one interesting qualification when supporting that idea: 'The best solution', he told a Central Committee meeting, 'would be if Kosovo were to be united with Albania, but because neither foreign nor domestic factors favour this, it must remain a compact province within the framework of Serbia.'[1]

Accordingly, in April 1945 two delegates from the 'National Liberation Council' of Kosovo (Dušan Mugoša and Mehmet Hoxha) attended the 'Anti-Fascist National Liberation Assembly of Serbia' and said that Kosovo wished to be made a province within Serbia. A formal request was deferred, however, until there was a meeting of Kosovo's own 'Regional People's Council'. This duly occurred in early July, when one of the items on the agenda was a 'draft resolution for the annexation of Kosovo-Metohija to federal Serbia'. The members of this unelected body, which represented only the 2,250 members of the Communist Party in Kosovo, were pointedly reminded that there were more than 50,000 troops in Kosovo who were willing to defend the gains of the war. Such reminders may hardly have been necessary, since only thirty-three out of the 142 members of the council were Albanians. The resolution was passed by acclamation, without a vote and without a single speech on the subject.[2]

On the basis of this decision, the presidency of the 'People's Assembly' of Serbia passed a law on 3 September 1945 establishing the 'Autonomous Region of Kosovo-Metohija', and declaring that it was a 'constituent part' of Serbia. A similar law two days previously had set up the 'Autonomous Province of Vojvodina': the difference between a region (*oblast*) and a province (*pokrajina*) was never legally defined or officially explained, but the nuance was evidently that a province was a little higher up the pecking order. Two months later Yugoslav-wide elections were held; the Communist-dominated 'Popular Front' won more than 90 per cent of the votes, and the assembly thus elected then passed a new Yugoslav constitution in January 1946, confirming the federal arrangements and the existence of the two autonomous units in Serbia. Exactly one year later Serbia issued its own constitution, which supplied more detail about the 'autonomous' rights of Kosovo to direct its own economic and cultural development, prepare a plan for its own budget, protect the rights of its citizens, and so on. These autonomous powers were, it said, 'secured by the constitution of the People's Republic of Serbia, in agreement with the constitution of the Federative People's Republic of Yugoslavia'.[3]

Serbian and Albanian legal theorists have argued long and hard about the significance of this whole sequence of events. Serbs like to emphasize that Kosovo was already 'annexed' by Serbia several months before the promulgation of the federal Yugoslav constitution, suggesting that it belongs primarily to Serbia and only in the second place to Yugoslavia. Albanians can point out, on the other hand, that the resolution passed in the Regional People's Council in Kosovo was in favour of annexation by a 'federal Serbia' – 'federal' here meaning that Serbia was defined as a federal unit of Yugoslavia. (It did not mean that Serbia was itself a federation: for that, the term would have been 'federative Serbia'.) They also emphasize that that same Regional People's Council picked its own delegates to represent Kosovo directly in the third meeting of the 'Anti-Fascist Council for the National Liberation of Yugoslavia' (AVNOJ) in August 1945, which implies that at a key stage in the formation of the new Yugoslavia Kosovo acted as a primary political unit, not just a part of Serbia. And they observe too that Kosovo's Regional People's Council continued to meet for three years, not holding any new election after the annexation and merely coopting a few new members at the end of 1945:

again, this seems to suggest that the political legitimacy of post-annexation Kosovo depended on continuity with its own pre-annexation institutions.[4] The reality, however, is that all these legal arguments are artificial, since they accept the validity of decisions made by utterly unrepresentative bodies, whether in Kosovo or in Serbia itself. Power in Yugoslavia had come out of the barrel of a gun – Tito's own guns and those of his Soviet sponsor. Whatever system he wished to impose was imposed, and whether the legal niceties were carried out in one order or another was a matter of the purest formality.

While these technicalities were being worked out, conditions in Kosovo were becoming somewhat more peaceful. The widespread resistance in early 1945 had so alarmed the Communists that they had imposed martial law in February, lifting it only four months later after the uprising in the Drenica region had been crushed. (Also during that period one of the leading Communists in the region, Miladin Popović, was assassinated in his office in Prishtina: the organizer of the plot was himself a captain in the Partisans, and the motive may have been as much personal as political.) While suppressing resistance in the countryside, the Communist authorities took the opportunity to 'requisition' large quantities of foodstuffs from the Kosovo peasantry: 3,763,000 kilograms of corn and 1,157,000 of meat were taken in April and May alone.[5]

It was as a direct result of the Albanian resistance in the spring of 1945 that Tito made one decision for which he is heavily blamed by Serbian writers: on 16 March he issued a 'provisional decree' banning the return of Slav colonists to their farms in Kosovo. This fact is lodged in Serbian folk-memory, which tends to assume that Tito's decree was absolute and final, and that a massive injustice was therefore done to tens of thousands of Serbs and Montenegrins who had already suffered grievously during the war. But the 'provisional decree' was indeed only provisional. Just two weeks later Tito changed his mind completely and decided to send all the colonists back; this caused such alarm among the Albanians – and, therefore, among the Communist administrators in Kosovo – that a compromise was eventually made. A law passed in August 1945 said that all colonists could return, unless they had either taken their land originally from peasants who were actually working on it, or taken the property of political émigrés (some of whom were

Communists), or been gendarme officers or absent *rentiers*. A 'Commission for the Revision of the Agrarian Reform' was also set up, which considered 11,168 contested cases by the time it completed its work in 1947. In 4,829 of these the colonists had their rights fully confirmed; in 5,744 they lost some of their previous land-holding; and in just 595 cases they lost everything. Nearly 16,000 hectares were given back to Albanians. After the violence directed against them during the war, not all colonists had wished to return at all. Approximately 4,000 colonist families are known to have settled in other parts of Yugoslavia: just over half of these were given land in Vojvodina, where the Communist authorities, having driven out the large ethnic German population and many of the Hungarians, were keen to engage in some ethnic engineering of their own to ensure an eventual Serb majority.[6]

While Albanian wishes were only partly met on the question of the removal of the colonists, another of the main demands of the Kosovo Albanians in the inter-war years, the free use of the Albanian language in official life and education, would eventually be more fully satisfied. Some of the more petty forms of linguistic Serbianization were quickly halted, such as the inter-war policy of Serbianizing Albanian names, either by adding '-ić' ('Berišić', 'Hotić') or by translating into Serbian (Kryeziu, which means 'black head', had been turned into 'Crnoglavić'). In theory, Albanian was given equal status with Serbo-Croat in official and legal matters; but since most of the key officials and judges were Slavs, there was little immediate change in practice. In the sphere of education there was, however, some progress. Before the war there had been just 252 schools in Kosovo, teaching only in Serbian. By the end of 1945 there were 392, containing 357 classes in Serbian and 279 in Albanian. The practical difficulties here were considerable. A survey carried out in 1948 found that, thanks to the combined effects of Ottoman and pre-war Yugoslav policies, 74 per cent of all Kosovo Albanians over the age of ten were illiterate. There was a real shortage of teachers, and indeed of professionally qualified Albanians of all kinds. Just over 300 Albanian schoolteachers were employed in 1945; these were supplemented by nearly fifty recruited from Albania itself.[7]

As this last detail shows, there was some real cooperation between Yugoslavia and Albania during these years: the border between the two

states would become hermetically sealed only after Tito's falling-out
with Stalin in 1948. Indeed, the master–servant relationship established
between Tito and Enver Hoxha during the war continued unabated in
the period from 1945 to 1948. One early incident illustrated this, when a
column of newly recruited men from Kosovo was marched (with
Hoxha's permission) across northern Albania to reach the Montenegrin
port of Bar in April 1945. When a Slav soldier was drowned while the
group was crossing the river Buena, the Slav soldiers, thinking he had
been killed deliberately, panicked and opened fire indiscriminately on
the Albanian recruits: many were killed but some managed to escape.
These Albanians were later rounded up by the Albanian Sigurimi (secret
police) and sent back to Yugoslavia, probably to their deaths.[8]

The full extent of Hoxha's subservience to Tito is only now beginning
to become clear, as hitherto secret documents are released from the
Party archives in Tirana. At a special meeting of his Party Plenum in
December 1946 Hoxha asked rhetorically: 'Is it in our interests to ask for
Kosovo? That is not a progressive thing to do. No, in this situation, on
the contrary, we must do whatever is possible to ensure that the
Kosovars become brothers with the Yugoslavs.' Earlier in the year the
two countries had established a 'Treaty of Friendship' and an economic
agreement which provided for the removal of all customs barriers
between them.[9] Some modern writers assume that after the passing of
this customs agreement the border simply disappeared between the two
states; this notion is then used to support Serbian claims about a large
influx of Albanians into Kosovo in the period 1945–8. In fact police
controls continued to operate at the border; and one whole year after
the agreement was signed, the Albanian Politburo was informed that it
had not yet been implemented where customs were concerned. At that
Politburo meeting in December 1947 Hoxha's enthusiasm for Tito
remained undimmed: he insisted that more should be done to 'popular-
ize' Yugoslavia among the Albanians, and fiercely reproved one Politburo
member, Nako Spiru, for suggesting that his pro-Yugoslav policy could
jeopardize Albania's independence. As Hoxha made clear, the long-term
aim of the policy (as laid down by Moscow) was to merge Albania with
Yugoslavia and Bulgaria in a 'Balkan Federation'. For this purpose he
was already involved in planning the unification of the Albanian and

Yugoslav armies; in a letter to Tito in March 1948 he agreed warmly with the idea of unifying the two states, and urged him to take more concrete measures to achieve this goal.[10]

It was this issue of Yugoslav–Albanian unification that provided the catalyst for Stalin's move against Tito in 1948. When Tito's trusted aide Milovan Djilas was summoned to Moscow in January of that year, he was questioned closely by Stalin on this project. (Djilas later claimed to have regarded it as a union of equal partners, and to have had only the most high-minded reasons for supporting it, above all the belief that it was the best way to solve the problem of Kosovo. He was shocked to be told in blunt terms by Stalin: 'You ought to swallow Albania – the sooner the better.') Over the next few months, however, Stalin issued a stream of contradictory counter-commands and complaints about the whole 'Balkan Federation' project, the overall purpose of which was apparently to test Tito's obedience and curb his tendency to present himself as a regional, rather than national, Communist leader. The final break came in June 1948, when Cominform (the recently established successor-organization to Comintern) formally expelled Yugoslavia from its ranks.[11]

The break with Moscow may have made possible some later 'liberal-izing' policies, but in the short term it had ill-effects both on Yugoslavia in general and on Kosovo in particular. The Communist system of control was tightened, as more power was given to the security apparatus to conduct its hunt for 'Cominformists' (pro-Moscow elements); and at the same time Tito seems to have made his own policies more Stalinist, as if to show that his ideological purity could not be faulted. Collectiv-ization was increased; a graph of grain production in Kosovo, accordingly, shows dramatic falls in 1949, 1951 and 1953. Serious food shortages developed in many parts of Yugoslavia by 1950.[12] The more damaging consequence of the break for Kosovo, however, was at the political level. Enver Hoxha trumpeted his own loyalty to Moscow and became a vociferous critic of Tito's policies, especially on the subject of Yugoslav rule in Kosovo. The Yugoslav secret police – known by the acronym 'Udba' – suspected Hoxha of infiltrating agents and saboteurs into Kosovo, and the whole Albanian population there began to be viewed as a potential nest of fifth-columnists and traitors. One sign of this approach in the mid-1950s was a growing obsession with hunting for weapons among the Kosovo Albanians; whole villages would be cordoned off and the menfolk interrogated or beaten. So severe was the treatment of those who failed to hand over a gun that many Albanians would prudently buy a weapon in order to have something to surrender. And since the Udba officers in Kosovo were, according to statistics for 1956, 58 per cent Serb, 28 per cent Montenegrin and only 13 per cent Albanian, their operations could only add to the increasingly bitter sense of ethnic polarization in the province.[13]

The most dramatic – and mysterious – instance of this policy was the so-called 'Prizren trial'. In 1956 the Udba chiefs in Kosovo claimed to have discovered a network of spies and agents who had been infiltrated into the province from Albania since 1950. The evidence of infiltration seems to have been particularly flimsy, involving as it did a bizarre claim about the joint involvement of the Albanian government and émigré organizations in America; but the main interest of the Udba men was not in the spies themselves but in the Kosovo Albanians who were alleged to have had contacts with them. These included first of all a group of three influential dervish sheikhs, and secondly a number of people with links to senior Albanian members of the Yugoslav Communist Party (now renamed the League of Communists of Yugoslavia). One suspect was the nephew of Mehmet Hoxha, who was now a minister in the republican government of Serbia; another person who seemed to be implicated was Nijazi Maljoku, a former Secretary of the Regional Committee of the Party; and several other leading Communists, including the wartime Partisan commander Fadil Hoxha, were also named by suspects under interrogation. The Udba chiefs wanted to arrest all these Communist dignitaries but were apparently overruled by the Foreign Ministry in Belgrade, which was conducting a rapprochement with Krushchev and did not want a new 'Cominformist' scandal on its hands.

Eventually a small trial was held *in camera* in Prizren in June and July 1956; no material evidence of any kind was produced, and the prosecution rested entirely on oral evidence supplied by the accused and other arrested suspects (including one of the dervish sheikhs). The nine accused men, who received long prison sentences, included the senior Communist Maljoku, the editor of *Rilindja* (Kosovo's Albanian-language newspaper), the nephew of Mehmet Hoxha and several illiterate peasants. Twelve years later all of them were released and proclaimed innocent, and Kosovo's Assembly passed a resolution declaring the trial 'staged and mendacious'. Since all the original records of the trial had been destroyed soon after it ended, it is difficult to judge whether there was any grain of truth in any of the accusations. The earliest subversive pro-Tirana movement known to have operated in Kosovo, the 'Revolutionary Movement for the Unification of the Albanians', was not founded until the early 1960s; its leader, Adem Demaçi, claimed to have attracted a membership of roughly 300, many of whom were arrested (with him) in 1964. But the significance of the Prizren trial eight years earlier lies in what it tells us about the attitude taken by the security services towards every sector of the Albanian population.[14]

In such an atmosphere of hostility and suspicion it is not surprising that the thoughts of many Kosovo Albanians turned once again to emigration. An additional reason for some Albanians must have been the restrictions imposed on Islam since the Communist take-over. The şeriat courts had been suppressed in 1946, the mektebs (Koranic elementary schools) abolished and the teaching of children in mosques made a criminal offence in 1950, and the dervish orders officially closed down in 1952.[15] While these changes were happening the Yugoslav authorities took unusually active measures to enable and encourage people in Kosovo and Macedonia to identify themselves as 'Turks' by nationality: given the traditional overtones of the word 'Turk' in the region (where it had been used as a general term for Muslims), this move may have held a special attraction for the more devout elements of the Muslim Albanian population. As a result, the number of people registered as 'Turks' in Kosovo jumped from 1,315 in the 1948 census to 34,583 in 1953. Strong pressure was put on the Kosovo authorities by Belgrade in 1951 to encourage this process by declaring the Turks a national minority there and opening new Turkish schools. To some extent this may have been merely an application of the principle of 'divide and rule'. But in 1953, when Yugoslavia signed a new treaty with both Turkey and Greece and large-scale emigration of Yugoslav 'Turks' to Turkey was permitted, it began to seem that a long-prepared policy had been at work, aimed at the complete removal of large numbers of Albanians.

The leading advocate of such a policy in the pre-war period, Vasa Čubrilović, had made a seamless transition in his own career from

Serbian nationalist to Communist adviser, and had submitted another report to the Communist leadership in November 1944 urging that 'The only correct solution of the question of minorities for us is emigration.' Large-scale emigration began in 1953 with, according to some reports, 13,000 'Turks' leaving Yugoslavia for Turkey. It has been estimated that between 1945 and 1966 roughly 246,000 people emigrated to Turkey from the whole of Yugoslavia. More than half of that total was probably from Macedonia (where the recorded population of 'Turks' had jumped from 95,940 in 1948 to 203,000 in 1953); some of those who left may have been Muslim Slavs, and some, indeed, may have been ethnic Turks. Detailed figures for Kosovo are not recorded, but a total in the region of 100,000 for the whole of that period may not be an unreasonable guess.[16]

The 1950s and early 1960s formed, from the Albanian point of view, the nadir of the whole period of Tito's rule. A strong ethnic imbalance remained in place: Serbs and Montenegrins, who were 27 per cent of the population of Kosovo according to the 1953 census, accounted for 50 per cent of the Party membership and 68 per cent of 'administrative and leading' positions. In the factories they also made up roughly 50 per cent of the workers.[17] Industrial development was slow: it was only after 1957 that Kosovo began to receive investment funds for industrialization under the federal budget. By 1958 there were forty-nine industrial enterprises in the whole of Kosovo, employing 16,000 people; Slovenia, by comparison, had 465. Throughout the Titoist period the absolute improvement in levels of production and income in Kosovo was outstripped by higher rates of growth in other parts of Yugoslavia (of which Slovenia was the most advanced), so that the population of Kosovo became relatively poorer: the average income in Slovenia was three times larger than that in Kosovo in 1946, and five times greater in 1964. And most of the investment in Kosovo was concentrated in 'primary' industrial projects such as mines, basic chemical works and power stations, which supplied raw materials or energy for use elsewhere in Yugoslavia. This primary industry was capital-intensive but not labour-intensive, which was also unfortunate, given that Kosovo was the area of Yugoslavia with the fastest-growing population.[18]

To add to these economic and social problems, the 'autonomous' status of Kosovo was also reduced to its absolute nadir by the new Yugoslav constitution of 1963. Although it promoted Kosovo to the title of Autonomous 'Province' ('pokrajina'), this constitution stated that republics could form autonomous provinces on their own initiative, and that the provinces of Kosovo and Vojvodina had been created by the decision of the Serbian Assembly. For the first time, Kosovo's constitutional status seemed to have been completely eliminated at the federal level and made a mere function of the internal arrangements of the republic of Serbia.[19]

The turn-around came in 1966. At the Party Plenum held on Brioni (Tito's personal resort-island) the Minister of the Interior, Serbian strongman Aleksandar Ranković, who had directed the harshly anti-Albanian security policy of the previous decades, was abruptly dismissed. Tito had apparently been persuaded to use his loyal henchman as a scapegoat for various policy failures; but, in addition, Ranković had been opposing the new tendency in Tito's thinking, which was to abandon the attempt to create a homogeneous 'Yugoslavism' and encourage more elements of national self-direction instead. That, indeed, was probably the purpose of the changes in the 1963 constitution, which aimed at treating Serbia as a single 'national' unit. The difference after 1966, however, was that this principle of decentralization was extended to the autonomous provinces as well.

Various concessions to the Albanians now followed. In March 1967 Tito paid his first visit to Kosovo for sixteen years, and made some public criticisms of conditions there. 'One cannot talk about equal rights', he declared, 'when Serbs are given preference in the factories ... and Albanians are rejected although they have the same or better qualifications.' In the following year it was announced that the Serbian word 'Šiptar', a version of the Albanian 'shqiptar' (meaning 'Albanian') but with pejorative connotations, would no longer be used: the correct term would be 'Albanac' instead.[20] More significantly, during 1968 high-level meetings were held to discuss changes to the 1963 constitution, and several major amendments were finally promulgated in mid-December. Amendment VII said that the autonomous provinces belonged both to Serbia and to the federal structure; and the name 'Kosovo-Metohija' or 'Kosmet', which had always irritated Albanians, was reduced to plain 'Kosovo'. Most importantly of all, Amendment XVIII defined the autonomous provinces as 'socio-political communities' (the same term that was used in the definition of the republics), and stated that they would carry out all the tasks of a republic apart from those tasks which were of concern to the republic of Serbia as a whole. Kosovo was now firmly established as a legal entity at the federal level, with the potential for exercising any or perhaps even all of the powers of a republic. From now on the political ambitions of the Kosovo Albanians would be directed at what seemed to be the natural next step – a Kosovo Republic. In fact the call for a republic had already been made, at least rhetorically and by implication, when the senior Communist Mehmet Hoxha asked in April 1968: 'Why do 370,000 Montenegrins have their own republic, while 1.2 million Albanians do not even have total autonomy?'[21]

The first time that the slogan 'Kosovo – republic!' was heard on the streets was on 27 November 1968, when several hundred demonstrators marched through Prishtina. Other slogans chanted by them (and by people taking part in smaller demonstrations in Gjilan, Ferizaj and Podujevo) included 'We want a university!', 'Down with colonial policy in Kosovo!', 'Long live Albania!' and 'Long live Enver Hoxha!' The police reacted forcefully, and one demonstrator was killed; in the following month forty-four people were given prison sentences.[22] But the official reaction was more conciliatory than would have been thought possible at almost any time in the previous twenty-odd years; the issuing of a new batch of amendments to the constitution (including the crucial Amendment XVIII) in mid-December was evidently intended to placate public opinion and defuse the situation. For most of the previous two decades, shouting 'Long live Enver Hoxha' would also have been a treasonable offence; but here too the official policy had changed. Albania had lost its status as an ideological ally of Russia (and recipient of large Soviet subsidies) in 1961, and had been making tentative gestures aimed at a reconciliation with Yugoslavia since 1962.[23] The Soviet invasion of Czechoslovakia in 1968 seems to have alarmed Tito and made him feel that he needed all the anti-Russian allies in the Balkans that he could get.

And so it was that a new period began of rapprochement between the two states, of which the Kosovars were in some ways the beneficiaries. From 1969 Kosovo Albanians were permitted to fly, as their own 'national' emblem, the Albanian flag – an unusual gesture on the part of the Yugoslav government, and one which only intensified the fears of the Kosovo Slavs about the growth of 'separatism' or 'irredentism'. In

April of that year Belgrade and Tirana signed an agreement about road transport between the two countries, and a fuller commercial agreement was made in the following year. Most importantly for Kosovo, the decision was made in late 1969 that the handful of higher education 'faculties' which already existed there (and which had been set up as off-shoots of the University of Belgrade) should be converted, and expanded, into a fully-fledged University of Prishtina, with teaching in Albanian as well as Serbo-Croat. In 1970 this new university signed an agreement with the University of Tirana; more than 200 teachers from Tirana would be brought in during the next five years to set up Albanian-language courses in Prishtina, using textbooks printed in Albania. The growth of the university was extraordinarily rapid. Within ten years the number of students attending it was put officially at 47,000, which would have made it one of the largest in Europe; it was later admitted that this figure was an exaggeration, aimed at getting more funds out of the federal budget, but the real number of students was still believed to be roughly 30,000, studying under more than 1,000 lecturers. Also significantly, the proportion of ethnic Albanians among Kosovo's student population rose between 1968 and 1978 from 38 to 72 per cent.[24]

With the growth of a new class of highly educated Albanians – indeed, a class which greatly exceeded the number of posts available for such personnel in Kosovo's still rudimentary economic system – the ethnic imbalance in some areas of public life was partially corrected. This process took time; in 1971, while Serbs and Montenegrins made up 21 per cent of the population, they still occupied 52 per cent of the managerial positions. In fact the overall imbalance in public employment was never overcome: in 1980 it was calculated that one in five Serbs had a state-salaried job, but only one in eleven Albanians. But where the Albanians made most progress was in entering the ranks of the Party and the local administration. By the late 1970s the proportion of Albanians in the League of Communists in Kosovo had risen to roughly two-thirds; and by 1981 it was claimed that the police and other security forces were three-quarters Albanian.[25] Serbs would later complain that this rapid Albanianization of the organs of local power had resulted in widespread anti-Slav discrimination. No doubt there were cases where Serbs or Montenegrins came under pressure from Albanian-speaking officials or policemen, and found it a new and unpleasant experience.

But to describe the change from the 1950s and 1960s to the 1970s in purely symmetrical terms (Slav oppression of Albanians followed by Albanian oppression of Slavs) would be misleading. There was no intimidation on the scale of the massive searches for weaponry in the mid-1950s, and nothing like the atmosphere of surveillance created under Ranković, when every Albanian who bought the official Albanian-language newspaper *Rilindja* was registered by the secret police and dossiers were drawn up on more than 120,000 people.[26]

If 1963 was the nadir of Albanian national interests in Titoist Kosovo, then 1974 was the zenith, at least where matters of constitutional theory were concerned. The new Yugoslav constitution of 1974 – which would remain in force until the final break-up of Yugoslavia – gave the autonomous provinces of Kosovo and Vojvodina a status equivalent in most ways to that of the six republics themselves, with their own direct representation on the main federal Yugoslav bodies. Incorporated in this constitution were some important changes already made by another batch of amendments issued in 1971: these had given the autonomous provinces equal status with the republics in most forms of economic decision-making, and even in some areas of foreign policy. Amendment XXXVI had stipulated that the Presidency of Yugoslavia would be a collective body with two representatives from each republic and one from each autonomous province. The 1974 constitution added another important right, which was that the autonomous provinces could issue their own constitutions. (Up till then, their constitutions or 'statutes' had been handed down to them by the Serbian Assembly.) So, although the 1974 constitution continued to assert that Kosovo and Vojvodina were parts of Serbia, by most criteria of constitutional law they were at the same time fully-fledged federal bodies.[27]

Why, then, was the final step not taken of turning these 'autonomous provinces' into republics? To this there were two answers, one theoretical, the other practical. The theoretical objection had always been that the whole basis of the Yugoslav federal system, as laid down by the Communist leadership at their meeting in Jajce in 1943, was that republics were entities for 'nations' as opposed to 'nationalities'. This distinction, which has never come across very clearly in English terminology, was a piece of Communist doctrine developed in the Soviet Union. A nation (Srb.: *narod*) was potentially a state-forming unit – or at least, its 'working people' were – and therefore retained some ultimate right of secession when it formed a republic in a federation. A nationality (Srb.: *narodnost*), on the other hand, was a displaced bit of a nation, the main part of which lived elsewhere: it could not be a constituent nation in a federation, and could not have a federal unit of its own. The Kosovo Albanians were a nationality, because the 'nation' of Albanians had its own state in Albania; and the same applied to the Hungarians of Vojvodina.

It was hard to see why such a rule should have the force of prescription when it so clearly failed as a description of reality. On such grounds the Romanian-speaking population of Moldova, adjoining the north-east of Romania, should never have been given a republic of its own in the Soviet Union. But in any case the rule itself was tacitly abandoned in the text of the 1974 constitution, which described Yugoslavia as 'a federal republic of free and equal nations and national-ities' and announced, in an important new statement of principle, that 'The working people, and the nations and nationalities, shall exercise their sovereign rights in the Socialist Republics, and in the Socialist Autonomous Provinces.'[28] The main theoretical objection to a Kosovo Republic – the idea that nationalities are not equal to nations, and cannot hold sovereign rights – thus quietly withered away.

Practical political reasons, naturally enough, were the real driving force behind the policy of denying republican status to Kosovo. The primary fear was that a Kosovo Republic would secede from Yugoslavia and join itself to Albania. How popular such a move would have been among Kosovo Albanians at that time is hard to judge, in the complete absence of opinion polls. It is true that some of the demonstrators in 1968 had shouted pro-Tirana slogans (as others would do in the larger protests in 1981). But on the other hand there was some general understanding of the miserable conditions that now prevailed in Albania; and the formal suppression of all forms of religion by Enver Hoxha in 1967 would not have endeared his rule to the great mass of rural Albanian Muslims in Kosovo, for whom religious practices were still an essential part of ordinary life. One possible line of policy for the Yugoslav authorities might have been to emphasize (or manufacture) differences in identity between the Albanians of Kosovo and those of Albania, following the example of Soviet policy where the Romanians of Moldova were concerned. In matters of language, for example, Kosovo could have been given a distinct identity by codifying the special features of the Geg version of Albanian, in contradistinction to the mainly Tosk version which had been made the official language of Albania in 1972. But such a policy was never even attempted in Kosovo, where Tirana's 'unified literary Albanian' was automatically adopted.

Conversely, another fear which was strongly felt by the Communist leadership in Belgrade was that granting republican status to either or both of the autonomous provinces would cause fierce political resentment in Serbia itself, as well as among the Serbs who lived in Kosovo. In private, many Serbs had always resented the existence of the two autonomous provinces, regarding their creation as some sort of punitive truncation of Serbia by the half-Croat, half-Slovene Josip Broz Tito. (In fact Vojvodina had never belonged to Serbia, having joined the Yugoslav kingdom in 1918; and at the level of legal theory, as we have seen, Kosovo had also been incorporated into the Yugoslav kingdom, and not into the previous Serbian one.) Such feelings would not be expressed in public until after Tito's death; but their existence was not a secret in ruling circles. One of the chief representatives of Serbian national *ressentiment*, the novelist and senior Communist Dobrica Ćosić, complained bitterly about the direction of policy in Kosovo at a meeting of the Serbian Central Committee in 1968, and as a result was dismissed from that body later in the year.[29]

Also at that meeting Ćosić had raised an issue which would loom large in all discussions of Kosovo during the 1970s and 1980s: the expulsion, or emigration, of Serbs and Montenegrins from the province. Extremely high figures came to be bandied about: in the early 1980s it was often claimed in the Serbian press that 200,000 had left Kosovo during the previous twenty years; in 1984 a prominent Orthodox priest, Archimandrite Atanasije Jevtić, wrote that 200,000 had fled in the last fifteen years; and by 1990 it was being alleged that the loss in the previous two decades was 400,000.[30] More realistic figures could be obtained from the official censuses, which recorded the number of Serbs and Montenegrins in Kosovo as follows: 264,604 (1961); 259,819 (1971); 236,526 (1981); 215,346 (1991). A pattern of demographic decline was clearly present, but not on the scale alleged by Serbian publicists. The true picture is of course more complicated than these figures suggest, since there was also a small element of immigration of Serbs and Montenegrins into Kosovo; and overall demographic loss is affected not only by changes in the birth-rate, but also by such questions as whether the emigrants are young people looking for work (who have their child-producing years ahead of them) or old people moving in retirement. Taking such factors into account, the most careful modern study of this issue concluded that there was a net emigration of between 80,000 and 100,000 between 1961 and 1981. This estimate is in line with the evidence of the 1981 census, which found that 110,675 people living in inner Serbia or 'Serbia proper' (Serbia minus the autonomous provinces) had moved there from Kosovo, of whom 85,636 had come in the period 1961–81.[31]

In the Yugoslavia of the later Tito years, however, Serbs from Kosovo were not the only people engaging in internal migration. From the early 1960s onwards there was a large-scale flow from all the under-developed areas to the more developed or developing ones. Bosnia-Hercegovina, for example, the second poorest part of Yugoslavia after Kosovo, had suffered proportionately an even larger outflow of its population by 1981; understandably enough, this basically economic phenomenon also had a national colouring to it, with Bosnian Croats moving mainly to Croatia and Bosnian Serbs to Serbia. Inner Serbia may not have been as prosperous as some other regions, such as Slovenia, but thanks to the expansion of Belgrade and the industrial development of Serbian cities such as Kragujevac it attracted a higher net immigration, from all parts of Yugoslavia, than any other area. In 1981 the population of inner Serbia included 111,828 people who had moved there from Bosnia, 110,704 from Croatia (mainly from poor Serb-inhabited rural areas), 50,011 from Macedonia, and so on.[32]

Set against this broader background, the figures for Kosovo no longer seem quite so startling or exceptional. Economic causes were the dominant factor for many of the Serbs and Montenegrins who left Kosovo, just as they were for the 45,000 Albanians who left the province between 1971 and 1981.[33] Nevertheless, it would probably be wrong to attribute the emigration of the Slavs to economic causes alone. There is at least anecdotal evidence, widely circulated from the early 1980s onwards, of people leaving because they either were threatened or felt threatened – and the sometimes sensational publicity given to these stories helped to ensure that all the Slavs in Kosovo did feel at least potentially under threat. As such an atmosphere developed, wrongdoings of the sort that occur in any rural society, such as the theft of livestock or damage to property, began to be interpreted (whenever the victim was a Slav) as political acts, part of a deliberate campaign to drive out the Serb and Montenegrin population.

In the mid-1980s the Serbian Academy of Sciences commissioned a survey of 500 households of Serbs who had migrated to inner Serbia from Kosovo. Many of the people interviewed thought that there was a political dimension to the deterioration of conditions for the Slavs in Kosovo: 60 per cent dated the breakdown of relations between Slavs and Albanians to the period 1966–8, immediately after Ranković's fall. When giving the reasons for their migration, 41 per cent mentioned 'indirect pressure' from the Albanians, and 21 per cent referred to direct pressure: that last category was composed of verbal abuse (8.5 per cent), material damage (7.5 per cent) and personal injury (5 per cent). However, it must be borne in mind that the Serbian Academy of Sciences commissioned this survey only because it had already embarked on a polemical publicity campaign against Albanian 'atrocities' in Kosovo; the selection of the interviewees, and perhaps the prompting of them by the interviewers, may have been less than scientific. Official reports on the reasons given for emigration from Kosovo by the 14,921 Serbs who left in the period 1983–7 present a very different picture. In 95 per cent of all cases the emigrants cited either economic or family reasons; in only eleven individual cases (less than 0.1 per cent) were pressures from Albanians given as the main cause of emigration.[34]

The departure of Serbs and Montenegrins was one reason, but not the only one, for a steady rise in the proportion of Albanians in the population of Kosovo from the 1960s onwards. The ratio had remained quite constant between 1948 and 1961, at roughly 28 per cent Serbs and Montenegrins and 67 or 68 per cent Albanians; but in subsequent censuses the Serb–Montenegrin element dwindled steadily, reaching 11 per cent in 1991, while the Albanian proportion rose to an officially estimated 82 per cent by that year.[35] Apart from Slav emigration, the main reason for this was the high birth-rate of the Albanians – something which also received much hostile publicity in Serbia, where it was portrayed as a deliberate and politically motivated policy on the part of the Albanian population. Once again, a study of the statistics makes possible a rather less sensationalist interpretation of the facts.

The Albanians of Kosovo do have a very high birth-rate: the highest, in fact, in present-day Europe. They are still a mainly agricultural society, and life in the villages is strongly traditional; the tradition of large families developed through many centuries as a response to the death-toll of disease and blood-feuds on the one hand, and general conditions of insecurity on the other. What has happened in the twentieth century is that mortality (from feuds, infectious diseases and perinatal problems) has been quite sharply reduced, while the tradition of large families has been eroded much more slowly. In the post-war years the Albanian birth-rate in Kosovo has come down from forty-six births per 1,000 head of population in the early 1950s to roughly twenty-nine in the late 1980s. What these overall figures conceal, however, is that birth-rates vary among the Albanians, as among any modern population, in accordance with the socio-economic status of the mother: in 1981 rural housewives would have on average 6.7 children, but urban working women only 2.7. The idea that Albanians breed as part of a political campaign is rather neatly disproved by this evidence, since the urban couples are much more likely to be politicized than their counterparts in remote villages.[36]

One other element of the statistical evidence which is often overlooked is that all ethnic groups in Kosovo have relatively high birth-rates; the 1981 census showed that a Serb woman in Kosovo would have on average 3.4 children by the end of her child-bearing years, while her equivalent in inner Serbia would have only 1.9. In these matters, as in many others, the Serb population in Kosovo had a traditional way of life quite similar to that of its Albanian neighbours. In the early 1950s the Serbs had a birth-rate almost as high as the Albanians (forty-one per 1,000), and since their mortality rate was much lower, their net rate of population growth was actually greater (2.7 per cent growth per year, as opposed to the Albanians' 2.1).[37] The most important single element in any proper explanation of the relative changes since then, therefore, has to be the extraordinarily steep decline in the Serbs' own birth-rate. One general reason for that must be the much greater degree of urbanization among the Serbs in Kosovo, which has exposed them to more rapid processes of social change. But one special reason must also be mentioned, namely the very high rate of abortion among the Serbs. By 1994 it was reported that Serbia had the highest abortion rate in the whole of Europe. For every 100 live births in inner Serbia there were 214 abortions; the equivalent figure for the whole population of Kosovo (i.e. calculated on a statistical base which is more than 80 per cent Albanian) was just twenty. While Albanian women were hostile on religious and cultural grounds to abortion, it had become an accepted part of cultural normality among the Serbs. On this point at least, it could be said that they had only themselves to blame.[38]

17

Kosovo after the death of Tito: 1981–1997

AT LUNCHTIME ON 11 March 1981, in the eating-hall of the University of Prishtina, a student found a cockroach in his soup. Disgusted, he hurled his tray of food on to the floor. Other students present felt equally fed up with their conditions of life at the University, and quickly joined in the protest. Soon there were at least 500 of them demonstrating in the street outside the main administrative building, chanting the words 'Food!' and 'Conditions!' The police moved in and arrested some of them, whereupon the slogan changed to 'We want our comrades!' By now the centre of Prishtina was full of young people who had just attended a football match; the crowd grew, to between 3,000 and 4,000, and the slogans turned to more general criticism of the authorities: 'Some people sit in armchairs, others have no bread!' More arrests were made, stones were hurled at the police, and rioting continued through the night, until the crowds were finally dispersed with tear-gas in the morning.[1]

Exactly two weeks later, the streets of Prishtina were full of spectators awaiting the arrival of the runners in the all-Yugoslav 'Youth relay-race', one of the national sporting events which had been established in the Tito years to encourage a feeling of 'brotherhood and unity'. During the morning many of the students in this crowd gathered together to chant renewed demands for better conditions, as well as the release of those students who had been arrested. Gradually, however, some openly political slogans crept in, such as 'Who does Trepça work for?' And according to a later report compiled by the Belgrade newspaper *Politika*, the students then started shouting 'Kosovo – Republic!', 'We are Albanians – not Yugoslavs!' and 'Unification with Albania!' The police moved in with tear-gas and baton charges again, injuring thirty-two students and arresting many more. Two days later the University authorities tried to defuse the situation by promising new student hostels and improvements at the canteen; but the protests were already turning into something more seriously political. High-school students from Podujevo came to Prishtina on 1 April to join the protesters there, and the slogans now included 'Long live Adem Demaçi' (the campaigner for Kosovo's secession who had begun his third prison sentence in 1975 and would be released only in 1990). On the following day tanks appeared in the streets; but this did not stop several thousand construction workers from making a protest of their own, which led to more violent clashes with the police. Over the next forty-eight hours there would be demonstrations in Podujevo, Vuçitërn, Gjilan, Gjakova, Ferizaj and Mitrovica: at the last of these, workers from the metal-working factories joined in. The authorities were seriously alarmed. Special units of security police were brought in from other parts of Yugoslavia, curfews were imposed, and a general state of emergency in Kosovo was now declared.[2]

The psychological impact of these events, in a country where such forms of open protest were virtually unknown, was enormous. Had the rioting been fully reported in the Yugoslav media it would have been even greater, but the fact that much information about the demonstrations was suppressed is itself a sign of how worried the governing circles were. To this day there is widespread disagreement about the number of people killed. The official figure was nine demonstrators and one policeman, but one later estimate (based apparently on local hearsay, which must surely have exaggerated) puts the number of dead at more than 1,000.[3] More than 2,000 Albanians were arrested at the time of the demonstrations; trials were held mostly *in camera*, and prison sentences were handed down which varied from one month to fifteen years. By early June it was officially reported that 479 people had been sentenced; another wave of trials took place in the autumn. Further arrests in connection with the demonstrations continued over many months. A survey of the subsequent clampdown drawn up by the Belgrade magazine *NIN* in 1986 concluded that 1,200 people had been given substantial prison sentences, and another 3,000 sent to gaol for up to three months.[4]

The repercussions at the political level were also on a large scale, though it was some time before any heads began to roll. At first, the senior Communists in both Prishtina and Belgrade blamed everything on a combination of 'hooligans' and sinister 'counter-revolutionary organizations'. (This last explanation, which usually also implied support for the 'counter-revolutionaries' by agents from Tirana, became the main preoccupation of the security clampdown and the trials: secret organizations and cells were constantly being named, and the authorities seemed obsessed with locating a 'general command' which was assumed to have coordinated them all.) Albanian Communist leaders in Kosovo such as Mahmut Bakalli and Fadil Hoxha issued fierce denunciations of Albanian chauvinism, separatism and the machinations of Tirana; the Albanian deputy chairman of the Yugoslav federal assembly, Sinan Hasani, also gave a long interview to the Belgrade newspaper *Borba* concentrating on these themes. But in meetings of the Central Committees of Kosovo, Serbia and Yugoslavia some more deep-lying causes began to be discussed. Hasani criticized the local Party leadership for nepotism, careerism and 'monopolism', and Bakalli (who was president of the Party in Kosovo) engaged in a little 'self-criticism' for failing to anticipate the crisis. The most germane comments, however, came from a member of the Serbian Central Committee, Tihomir Vlaškalić, who argued that the root cause of the problem was the long-term mismanagement of Kosovo's economy. He criticized the emphasis on heavy industry at the expense of investment in agriculture, and he noted that the huge expansion of higher education had become used simply as a safety-valve for unemployment.[5]

Gradually the pressure grew in these circles for what was euphemistically called a 'differentiation' process – in other words, a purge of Party officials. Bakalli was expelled from the Party presidium in July; the president of the provincial presidium, Xhavid Nimani, was forced to resign; and another Albanian member of that body, the head of Kosovo Radio, was also pushed out on the obscure charge of having taken down some posters bearing Tito slogans in Dečani. An energetic Communist youth leader, Azem Vllasi, was brought into the provincial leadership; before long he was complaining that the 'differentiation' process had already gone too far, but the purge continued and by August more than 500 Party members had been expelled.[6]

In the final analysis, the political reaction to the crisis in Kosovo did little to improve the situation and much to harm it. The differentiation process that was really needed, differentiating carefully between the various social, economic and political grievances of the protesters, was never attempted; instead, all complainants were lumped together as 'counter-revolutionaries', and the assumption was blithely made that a call for a Kosovo Republic was identical with a call for unification with Enver Hoxha's Stalinist state. (Most foreign observers at the time found little enthusiasm for Hoxha's Albania in Kosovo, and many of the protesters would later insist that the slogans in favour of Enver Hoxha and Marxism–Leninism had been shouted by *agents provocateurs* working for the security police.)[7] The serious economic and social problems mentioned by Vlaškalić were never properly addressed; statistics about the high level of investment by federal funds in Kosovo were repeatedly quoted, but it was widely understood that the main objects of these funds were primary industries whose products (metals, chemicals and electricity) were then supplied at artificially low prices to processing industries elsewhere in Yugoslavia. The unemployment level in Kosovo was the highest in the whole country: officially 67,000 people were registered as unemployed, but observers estimated the actual figure at 250,000. Out of a population of 1.5 million, only 178,000 had jobs in all forms of state-run enterprises (civil service, schools, hospitals, factories and so on); and a significant ethnic imbalance was still in place, with the Serbs and Montenegrins, who formed 15 per cent of the population, holding 30 per cent of these jobs.[8]

But the most damaging effect of the political reaction in 1981 was the way in which it unleashed a new round of accusations and counter-accusations about Albanian and Serbian nationalism. The question of the 'flight' of Serbs and Montenegrins from Kosovo was raised publicly; one Serb politician, Dušan Ristić, the chairman of the provincial assembly, resigned after being accused of Serbian nationalism because of his campaign on this issue. Several Albanian intellectuals, meanwhile, were attacked on the grounds of 'nationalist' tendencies in their writings: the most prominent of them, Professor Ali Hadri, was forced to relinquish his post as head of the Historical Institute. Three years later arguments about historical and cultural nationalism flared up again: the Kosovar historian Hajredin Hoxha published a study of the 1943–4 Bujan Conference – where, it will be remembered, the right to secession had been asserted – which was fiercely attacked by Serbian writers, and Serbian intellectuals were enraged by a book published in Slovenia which contained essays by Kosovar writers criticizing the whole history of Serbian policy. What might be called the culture war was now in full swing. In 1985 an openly polemical survey of the history of Kosovo, Dimitrije Bogdanović's *Knjiga o Kosovu* ('A Book about Kosovo'), was published, which accused the Albanian population there of working to create an 'ethnically pure' province. During the rest of the 1980s a stream of books would pour from the printing presses of Belgrade, including works written or edited by respected historians such as Radovan Samardžić and Dušan Bataković, presenting the whole history of the Serbs in Kosovo as an unending chronicle of ethnic martyrdom.[9]

It was not only the intellectuals who became caught up in such disputes. With the gradual erosion of both press controls and traditional taboos in the mid-1980s, more and more polemical or sensational materials were appearing in the popular press. The most dramatic instance of this was the 'Martinović case', which became a national scandal thanks to the writings of a campaigning journalist on the Belgrade news magazine *NIN*. Djordje Martinović was a fifty-six-year-old Serb farmer (and civilian employee of the Yugoslav Army) from a village near Gjilan, who apparently suffered a particularly unpleasant and humiliating assault: on 1 May 1985 he was rushed to hospital in Prishtina, where a beer-bottle was removed from his anus. The bottle had broken, and the injuries were severe. He claimed that he had been attacked by two masked Albanians in a field near his house, who had tied him up and inflicted this injury on him; and he said that the probable motive was to drive him out of the district, in order to take his land. Albanian sources, however, offered a different explanation, which was that he was a homosexual who had had an accident while engaging in an act of self-gratification. The authorities in Kosovo seemed to favour this second explanation, evidently hoping that the scandal created by the initial news reports would die down; but the Belgrade press continued its campaign, and enough publicity was generated to ensure that the case was debated in the Yugoslav federal assembly in July 1985 and again in February 1986. Later in 1986 the *NIN* journalist who had led the campaign on this issue published a 485-page book entitled *Slučaj Martinović* ('The Martinović Case'). The fact that the initial print-run of this book was 50,000 copies gives some idea of what a fever-pitch Serbian public opinion had now reached.[10]

The association of ideas between Albanian aggression and intimate personal degradation was strengthened by another theme taken up by the Serbian media: the rape of Serb women in Kosovo by Albanian men. The Orthodox archimandrite Atanasije Jevtić, for example, made 'the rape of girls and old women in villages and nunneries' one of his leading complaints in a book published in Belgrade in 1984. As one Albanian writer later noted, the impression given by many Serbian publications was 'that Albanians rape anyone they can get hold of, old women, children, married women, teenagers, and that they rape them in the houses, in public places, in the street . . .'[11] The only serious study of this issue was carried out by an independent committee of Serbian lawyers and human rights experts in 1990. Analysing all the statistics on rape and attempted rape for the 1980s, they found first of all that the frequency of this crime was significantly lower in Kosovo than in other parts of Yugoslavia: while inner Serbia, on average, had 2.43 cases per year for every 10,000 men in the population, the figure in Kosovo was 0.96. They also found that in the great majority of cases in Kosovo (71 per cent) the assailant and the victim were of the same nationality. Altogether the number of cases where an Albanian committed or attempted the rape of a Serbian woman was just thirty-one in the whole period from 1982 to 1989: an average of fewer than five per year.[12]

Cool factual analysis of this sort could do little, however, to halt the progress of what had become a fervent campaign of complaint among parts of the Kosovo Serb community. One local activist, Kosta Bulatović – who was in fact originally from Montenegro – organized a petition in the autumn of 1985 which became known as 'petition 2,016', after the number of signatures it attracted: the text contained not only demands for protection, but also a gross historical claim about the presence of 300,000 Albanians who had crossed into Kosovo from Albania since 1941 (the implication being that they should all be sent back). In February 1986 a group of 160 Serbs and Montenegrins from Kosovo presented their complaints to the federal assembly in Belgrade; two months later there was a well-publicized 'peasants' march' on Belgrade to protest at Bulatović's recent arrest, and a large demonstration in his home town of Kosovo Polje. With a heavy heart the Serbian Party president, Ivan Stambolić, went down to Kosovo to negotiate with them. The reason for his reluctance, as he later revealed, was that he had been privately informed that a hostile 'scenario' was being planned for him in Kosovo by the real directors of the movement, whom he described as the 'nationalist central organization' in Belgrade.[13]

What Stambolić apparently meant by this term was a group of Serbian nationalist intellectuals with high-level positions or contacts in the Party, the army and the Church. Playing a dominant role among them was the novelist Dobrica Ćosić who, as mentioned in the last chapter, had been expelled from the Party presidency in 1968 because of his opposition to the post-Ranković change of policy in Kosovo. The first public sign of the activities of this group was a petition presented to the Yugoslav assembly in January 1986 and signed by 216 prominent intellectuals, which complained that the Serbs were suffering 'genocide' and declared: 'The case of Djordje Martinović has become that of the whole Serb nation in Kosovo'. Later in the year some fragments began to appear in the Serbian press of a more important document, a 'Memorandum' drawn up by members of the Serbian Academy of Sciences; this had apparently been produced as an advisory document for the government by a group under Ćosić's direction in 1985, and the full text was eventually published in 1989.[14]

All the old themes of Serbian nationalist *ressentiment* against Tito were gathered together in this Memorandum, but its most bitter criticism was reserved for the 1974 constitution which, it said, had carved Serbia into three parts. 'The relations between Serbia and the autonomous provinces', it argued, 'cannot be reduced, either solely or mainly, to formal or juridical questions about the interpretation of constitutions. It is a matter above all of the Serbian people and their state.' Since 1981, it claimed, the Albanians in Kosovo had made 'war' against the Serbs. What it called the 'physical, political, juridical and cultural genocide' of the Serb population there represented, it said, Serbia's worst defeat since 1804. The Martinović case was duly mentioned as part of this 'genocide'; it was described as 'reminiscent of the blackest periods of Turkish impalings'. Also included was the bogus statistic of 200,000 emigrating Serbs in the previous two decades. The conclusion drawn at the end of this section of the Memorandum was that the government must establish 'objective and lasting conditions for the return of the exiled people'. And the general conclusion was that the 'integrity of the Serbian people' must be the overriding concern of future policy.[15] With good reason, this

Memorandum has been seen in retrospect as a virtual manifesto for the 'Greater Serbian' policies pursued by Belgrade in the 1990s.

Many senior Communists were still sufficiently imbued with Titoist sentiments to be shocked by this document when it first became public in 1986. But one ambitious younger member of the Serbian Central Committee, Slobodan Milošević, showed no such alarm, and actually persuaded his colleagues on the Committee not to issue a formal condemnation.[16] Possibly he had already sensed the political advantage that could be gained from linking this intellectual–political movement with the advancement of his own career. It was indeed the issue of Kosovo that brought about his transformation from little-known Party *apparatchik* into demagogic political leader. But while the incident that catapulted him to fame did show signs of planning, the planning was not his; what happened seems to have taken him almost as much by surprise as it did the rest of his colleagues.

In April 1987 news came from Kosovo that the group of Serb and Montenegrin activists round Bulatović was intending to bring another large protest to Belgrade. They asked the Serbian Party president, Stambolić, to come and speak to them first in the town of Kosovo Polje; reluctant to enter such a hostile bear-pit (he had already made several speeches criticizing Serbian nationalism), he sent his deputy, Slobodan Milošević, instead. As Stambolić later recalled, Milošević had never shown any interest in Kosovo, and had even said to him on one occasion: 'Forget about the provinces, let's get back to Yugoslavia.' But the events in Kosovo Polje on 24 April 1987 were to change all that. While Milošević listened to angry speeches by local spokesmen in the 'House of Culture', fighting broke out between the large crowd of Serbs outside and the police, who responded with their batons. The fighting had been carefully planned by one of the local Serb leaders, Miroslav Šolević (local, at least, in the sense that he lived there: he had moved to Kosovo from the Serbian city of Niš): as he later admitted, he had arranged for a truck full of stones to be parked outside the building, to give the Serbs a copious supply of ammunition. Milošević broke off the meeting and came out to speak to the crowd, where he uttered – luckily for him, on camera – the words on which his entire political future would be built: 'No one should dare to beat you!' The crowd, enraptured by these words, began chanting 'Slobo, Slobo!' With a skill which he had never displayed before, Milošević made an eloquent extempore speech in defence of the sacred rights of the Serbs. From that day, his nature as a politician changed; it was as if a powerful new drug had entered his veins.[17]

By exploiting the issue of Kosovo Milošević quickly turned himself into a 'national' leader, a role which enabled him to quell all opposition to his takeover of the Communist Party machine. He had two valuable sources of support: Radio Television Belgrade, which broadcast his speech at Kosovo Polje over and over again, and the hard-line activists in Kosovo, who organized protest meetings of thousands of angry demonstrators in Belgrade and other cities. Another chance event also played into his hands: in early September a young Albanian conscript went berserk at a barracks in central Serbia, shooting four other recruits (two Bosniacs, i.e. Bosnian Muslims, one Croat and one Serb) before killing himself. Although this was clearly an individual case of mental breakdown, the Serbian media gave it great prominence as yet another example of the Albanian policy of 'genocide' against the Serbs, and the Minister of Defence solemnly warned that 'The enemy has switched to new methods of destabilization.' Up to 20,000 people attended the Serb recruit's funeral; many of them then broke off from the procession to make a pilgrimage to Ranković's grave, where slogans such as 'Albanians out of Yugoslavia!' were shouted. Later that month, Milošević was able to use the issue of Kosovo to launch an attack on his friend and political patron, Ivan Stambolić. By the end of 1987, Stambolić was dismissed from power and Milošević took over as president of the Serbian League of Communists.[18]

The next year was spent in extending and consolidating Milošević's power, both in Serbia and in neighbouring Montenegro. Mass rallies, based mainly on the issue of Kosovo (described as 'Meetings of Truth') and involving bussed-in crowds paid for by the state and organized by Šolević and other Kosovo hard-liners, were an essential part of the mechanism he used to crush his opponents. In this way he forced the resignation of the local Party leadership first in Vojvodina, then in Montenegro, installing his own supporters in their place.[19] By the autumn of 1988 Kosovo was very evidently the next on his list. The first step he took was to arrange the removal of the two leading Albanians in the provincial Party machine, Azem Vllasi and Kaqusha Jashari, in order to replace them with more compliant figures who would cooperate in the dismantling of Kosovo's autonomy. As news of this move spread, mass protests quickly developed; unlike the mass rallies in Vojvodina and Montenegro, these were protests in defence of a local Party leadership – and, what is more, they had not been organized from above, paid for, or bussed in. On 17 November the miners of Trepça emerged from their pit at dawn and started to march the 30 miles to Prishtina. There they were joined on the 18th by factory workers, students and schoolchildren; even Radio Television Belgrade estimated the number of protestors at 100,000. Nevertheless, in its meeting that day the Provincial Committee agreed to accept the resignations of the two leaders. (The highly unpopular police chief, Rrahman Morina, was later installed as the new Party president in Kosovo.) *Force majeure* was on Milošević's side – as symbolized by his holding in Belgrade on the following day the biggest of all his mass rallies, attended by at least 350,000 people. 'Every nation has a love which eternally warms its heart,' Milošević told the crowd. 'For Serbia it is Kosovo.'[20]

Early in the following year the Serbian assembly began preparing amendments to the Serbian constitution which would severely restrict Kosovo's powers: they would give Serbia control over Kosovo's police, courts and civil defence, as well as such matters as social and economic policy, educational policy, the power to issue 'administrative instructions' and the choice of an official language.[21] Under the existing constitution such amendments could be proposed by Serbia, but had to be accepted by the Kosovo assembly itself. Realizing that the extinction of Kosovo's autonomy was fast approaching, the Albanian population there embarked on a new series of protests. The leading role, once again, was played by the miners of Trepça, who barricaded themselves in the depths of their mine (many of them on hunger strike) and issued a list of demands: the dismissal of Rrahman Morina and the reversal of Milošević's 'discriminatory policies' were included, but the first item on the list was 'No retreat from the fundamental principles of the 1974 constitution'. Other strikes and mass-meetings spread throughout the province. After eight days the authorities appeared to give way, announcing the resignation of Morina, and the miners ended their protest; but under instructions from Belgrade Morina then 'suspended' his resignation. Meanwhile troops had been sent into Kosovo, a state of emergency was declared, and the crackdown began. Hundreds of people who had made protests or gone on strike were arrested; among those seized was Azem Vllasi, who was formally charged with 'counter-revolutionary endangering of the social order', an offence which could carry the death penalty.[22]

On 23 March 1989 the provincial assembly of Kosovo met under unusual circumstances, with tanks and armoured cars parked in front of it. Large numbers of 'guests', both members of the security police and Communist Party functionaries from Serbia, mingled with the delegates inside the building, and according to several accounts some of the officials from Serbia actually took part in the voting. Under these conditions the constitutional amendments were passed, although without the two-thirds majority normally required for such changes. The final confirmation of the amendments was then voted through in an unusually festive session of the Serbian assembly in Belgrade on 28 March: Kosovo's 'autonomy' was now reduced to a mere token.[23] Milošević had won. This was a significant moment not only for Kosovo, but also for the whole of Yugoslavia. Thanks to the forces of Serbian nationalism which he had so carefully cultivated, Slobodan Milošević now seemed an unstoppable force: the adulation he received at the massive Serbian celebration of the 600th anniversary of the battle of Kosovo on 28 June was comparable, in Yugoslav experience, only to the cult of Tito. With the votes of Serbia, Kosovo, Vojvodina and Montenegro in his pocket, Milošević now had merely to take over one other republic to gain a controlling majority on the federal presidency. It was the increasing fear of this prospect felt by political leaders in Slovenia and Croatia, combined with a growth of Croatian nationalism in response to Serbia's new style of nationalist politics, that would lead to the final break-up.

In Kosovo the reaction was immediate and intense. On the day of the vote, 3,000 people demonstrated and threw stones in the centre of Prishtina; a larger demonstration in Ferizaj was crushed by riot police; and over the next five days major protests took place in at least nine Kosovo towns, including a particularly intense conflict with the police in Podujevo, where firearms were used by both sides. The official death-toll by the end of March was twenty-one demonstrators and two policemen; by the end of April it may have been as high as 100. Once again there were arrests on a large scale: more than 1,000 workers were put on trial in Ferizaj alone. Many members of the Albanian élite – intellectuals, officials, directors of enterprises – were arrested, and more than 200 were held in solitary confinement, without access to defence lawyers, for several months.[24] Later in the year a new wave of demonstrations, including another underground sit-in at the Trepça mine, was sparked by the impending trial of Vllasi, which began on 30 October. More violent clashes with the police took place in January 1990: demonstrators demanded the resignation of the provincial leadership (which still had Morina at its head) and the ending of the state of emergency. This time at least fourteen people were shot dead.[25]

In an unusual softening of the policy line, the Serbian authorities did agree to lift the state of emergency in April, and during that month they also released not only Vllasi and his co-defendants, but also the veteran political prisoner Adem Demaçi. Yet the remission in policy was little more than symbolic. New security measures were at the same time introduced, in connection with the public reaction to a curious episode which has never been fully explained: the so-called mass poisoning of Albanian children. In a series of mysterious cases in March and April 1990, thousands of children were taken to hospital suffering from stomach pains, headaches and nausea; a rumour sprang up that they were being deliberately poisoned at the schools (where separate teaching sessions for Serbs and Albanians had been introduced). Most observers at the time believed that this was merely a case of mass hysteria. A UN expert on toxicology did later conclude, however, from analyses of blood and urine samples, that the substances Sarin or Tabun (used in chemical weapons) were present, and in 1995 evidence emerged that the Yugoslav army had manufactured Sarin. Whatever the true explanation, most Albanians did believe that their children were being poisoned, and in some parts of Kosovo they attacked the homes of local Serbs. This gave the authorities the excuse they needed for another crackdown, involving the transfer of 25,000 policemen from Serbia to the province – which prompted the resignation of seven Albanian ministers from the provincial government in protest.[26]

Even more important than this, however, was the series of new measures decreed by the Serbian assembly in March 1990 under the somewhat Orwellian title of the 'Programme for the Realization of Peace and Prosperity in Kosovo'. Acting in accordance with a so-called 'Yugoslav Programme of Measures to be Taken in Kosovo' (passed by the federal assembly in January), this included a wide range of devices to shore up the position of the Serbs: creating new municipalities for them, concentrating new investment in Serb-majority areas, building new houses for Serbs who returned to Kosovo, encouraging Albanians to seek work in other parts of Yugoslavia, introducing family planning for Albanians, and annulling, retrospectively, sales of property to Albanians by departing Serbs. Already, under new Serbian laws passed in 1989, Albanians in Kosovo were forbidden to buy or sell property without obtaining special permission from the authorities. And on 26 June 1990 a new wave of decrees, officially described as 'temporary measures', was made possible by a 'Law on the Activities of Organs of the Republic in Exceptional Circumstances'. These temporary measures, which have remained permanent, would include the suppression of the Albanian-language newspaper *Rilindja*, the closing of the Kosovo Academy of Arts and Sciences, and the dismissal of many thousands of state employees.[27]

During this long process of political and legislative attrition, the attitude taken by the Albanian members of the provincial assembly had been, for the most part, one of inglorious submission under pressure. But in late June a large group of these delegates showed a surprising sense of initiative, when they attempted to block the new Serbian constitution and put forward a scheme of their own for a Kosovo republic. The Serb president of the assembly quickly adjourned the meeting, and promised to reconvene it on 2 July; subsequently he announced a postponement to 5 July. Nevertheless, on 2 July 114 out of the 123 Albanian members of the assembly did meet, gathering in the street outside the locked-up assembly building, and passed a resolution declaring Kosovo 'an equal and independent entity within the framework of the Yugoslav federation'. This vote, like the one in the assembly on 23 March 1989, was probably invalid on procedural grounds, but it sent out an unexpectedly strong symbolic signal. In response, the Serbian authorities dissolved both the assembly and the government, thus removing almost the last vestiges of Kosovo's autonomous status. (One vestige, nevertheless, was kept in place: the representative of Kosovo on the federal presidency, whose vote Milošević still required.) Three weeks later, in a final twist of the screw, the Serbian assembly passed a special law on 'labour relations' in Kosovo, which made possible the subsequent expulsion of more than 80,000 Albanians from their jobs.[28]

Many of the Albanian delegates who had taken part in the vote on 2 July held another meeting in the little town of Kaçanik on 7 September, in conditions of great secrecy. There they agreed on the proclamation of a constitutional law for a 'Republic of Kosovo', a document which contained provisions for a new assembly and an elected presidency of the republic. All other laws (emanating from Serbia and Yugoslavia) would, it proudly declared, be valid only insofar as they were in harmony with this new republican constitution. Such a proclamation might have seemed an act of pure fantasy; but that is not how it was regarded by the Serbian authorities, who made strenuous efforts to track down and prosecute the participants.[29] And as the months passed, the fantasy began to look more and more like a shadowy reality. In September of the following year the Albanians in Kosovo succeeded in organizing a referendum, this time to consider a decision (by members of the underground assembly) to declare Kosovo a sovereign and independent republic; it was claimed that 87 per cent of voters took part, and that 99 per cent voted in favour. And on 24 May 1992 Kosovo-wide elections were held, using private houses as polling-stations under the noses of the Serbian authorities, to create a new republican assembly and government.[30]

As this sequence of events shows, a resilient and increasingly sophisticated political culture had grown up among the Kosovo Albanians since 1989. Its roots were to be found not so much in the old political class of functionaries in the Titoist system, as in the intellectual circles that developed round the University of Prishtina in the late 1980s. Two organizations played a key role: the Association of Philosophers and Sociologists of Kosovo, and the Association of Writers of Kosovo. The former became a centre of intellectual protest against the Serbian policy, organizing many public meetings and petitions (one of which, entitled 'For Democracy, Against Violence', was signed by 400,000 people). And the latter was galvanized into a political role by a mass resignation of its Serb members in 1988, who wanted to be members of a purely Serb organization; in the public quarrel which followed, the Association presented a statement of Albanian national political aims which attracted wide support, turning the Association of Writers into the nucleus of a popular movement. It was in this way that the president of the Association, Dr Ibrahim Rugova, a specialist in literary history and aesthetics (and author of an authoritative study of the works of the seventeenth-century Archbishop Pjetër Bogdani) became the leader of the political movement which was officially founded in December 1989. This was the 'Democratic League of Kosovo' (known by its Albanian initials as the LDK): the word 'League' was deliberately chosen to convey some of the historic resonances of the League of Prizren. As it developed it came to function, rather like Solidarity in Poland, as a cross between a party and a mass movement; its membership, officially but implausibly put at 700,000, hugely overshadows that of any other party. But other political parties do exist – Social Democrats, Christian Democrats, Liberals and many more – and in theory the LDK is merely *primus inter pares*, with its majority of elected members in the shadowy assembly of 1992 and its leader, Rugova, occupying the post of elected President of the Kosovo 'Republic'.[31]

The basic policy pursued by Rugova and the LDK since 1990 has been a three-fold one: to prevent violent revolt; to 'internationalize' the problem, which means seeking various forms of international political involvement (ranging from diplomatic mediation to the setting up of a UN Trusteeship over Kosovo); and to deny systematically the legitimacy of Serbian rule, by boycotting elections and censuses and creating at least the outlines of the state apparatus of a Kosovo 'Republic'. The first of these three aims has been successful to an extent that could hardly have been imagined by anyone who knew the warlike traditions of the Albanians and their long history of armed uprisings. The second has involved Rugova in innumerable visits to foreign capitals, but has achieved little beyond some resolutions by bodies such as the United Nations or the European Parliament. Both the second and third policy aims are directed against the idea – which is still accepted in principle by all the major Western powers – that the status of Kosovo is just an internal question for Serbia. By setting up the institutions of a separate republic, the Albanians of Kosovo have engaged in a strategy of political 'as if'. To behave as if Kosovo were not part of Serbia might seem, in the short term, sheer make-believe; but if the strategy were persisted in for long enough, foreign governments might eventually feel obliged to admit that they were the ones who were engaging in fiction when they continued to treat Kosovo as a mere region of the Serbian state. The question for the Albanians, therefore, was: how long was long enough, and how much suffering would they have to endure during that time?

To produce an adequate survey of the human rights abuses suffered by the Albanians of Kosovo since 1990 would require several long chapters in itself. Every aspect of life in Kosovo has been affected. Using a combination of emergency measures, administrative fiats and laws authorizing the dismissal of anyone who had taken part in a one-day protest strike, the Serb authorities have sacked the overwhelming majority of those Albanians who had any form of state employment in 1990. Most Albanian doctors and health workers were also dismissed from the hospitals; deaths from diseases such as measles and polio have increased, with the decline in the number of Albanians receiving vaccinations. Approximately 6,000 school-teachers were sacked in 1990 for having taken part in protests, and the rest were dismissed when they refused to comply with a new Serbian curriculum which largely eliminated the teaching of Albanian literature and history. In some places the Albanian teachers were allowed to continue to take classes (without state pay) in the school buildings, but strict physical segregation was introduced – with, for example, separate lavatories for Albanian and Serb children – and equipment or materials, including in one case the window-glass, was removed from the areas they used. For both healthcare and education the Albanians have organized their own 'parallel' system of clinics and schools, mainly in private premises; the doctors and teachers are paid by the 'Republic' (in practice, by the LDK) out of an income tax of three per cent levied, on a voluntary basis, in the diaspora. In this way teaching is arranged for more than 400,000 children; the teachers and organizers are, however, frequently subjected to arrest, intimidation and beatings by the Serb police.[32]

Arbitrary arrest and police violence have become routine. Serbian law allows the arrest and summary imprisonment for up to two months of anyone who has committed a 'verbal crime' such as insulting the 'patriotic feelings' of Serbian citizens. It also permits a procedure known as 'informative talks', under which a person can be summoned to a police station and questioned for up to three days: in 1994 15,000 people in Kosovo were questioned in this way, usually without being told the reason for the summons. Serbian law does not, of course, permit the beating up of people in police custody; but many graphic testimonies exist of severe beatings with truncheons, the application of electric shocks to the genitals, and so on. Also widely violated in Kosovo are the official rules for the lawful search of people's houses: homes are frequently raided without explanation, and goods and money confiscated (i.e. stolen) by the police. In 1994 alone the Council for the Defence of Human Rights and Freedoms in Kosovo recorded 2,157 physical assaults by the police, 3,553 raids on private dwellings and 2,963 arbitrary arrests.[33]

Such methods were already being applied before the outbreak of the war in the former Yugoslavia in the summer of 1991. At first the war had little direct effect on conditions in Kosovo apart from increasing the reluctance of young Albanians to do their military service in the Yugoslav – now, in practice, Serbian – army. The most important effect of the outbreak of the war was on the thinking of Albanian political circles in Kosovo: it was the declarations of independence of Slovenia and Croatia in June 1991 that led the LDK to change its aims from republican status within Yugoslavia to full sovereignty and independence. But in terms of practical life, the only group that felt immediately affected by the Serbian-Croatian war was the small population of so-called 'Kosovo Croats', the Catholic Slavs who lived in Janjevo and a small group of villages to the south of that town. More than half of the Janjevo Catholics fled to Croatia (mainly to Zagreb) by the end of 1991, and the inhabitants of villages such as Letnica followed in 1992. (These villagers seem to have been the objects of two-fold manipulation: first by local Serbs, who pressured them to leave, and then by the Croatian authorities, who placed them in houses abandoned by Serbs in Western Slavonia.)[34]

With the launching of Serbia's war of territorial expansion against Bosnia in April 1992, however, the position of the Albanians in Kosovo worsened significantly. The rhetoric of Serbian nationalism now concentrated on the Islamic 'threat'; speeches made by extremist leaders such as Radovan Karadžić referred to the 'demographic aggression' (i.e. high birth-rate) of the Bosnian Muslims in terms identical with those used about the Albanians, and the Serbian media often alluded to the threat of an 'Islamic crescent' extending from Bosnia through the Slav Muslim territory of the Sandžak to the predominantly Muslim Albanians of Kosovo. All these populations, it was suggested, were hotbeds of 'fundamentalism', and in a gross inversion of reality it was claimed that they were all plotting an aggressive 'holy war' against the Orthodox Slavs. In fact the Bosnian and Kosovar political movements had had little contact with each other; and although Islam, in a non-fundamentalist form, did play a part in the political awakening of the Bosnian Muslims, its political role in Kosovo was so slight as to be quite invisible. Indeed, so untroubled are the Kosovars by religious politics that no one there thinks it strange to have a 'Christian Democrat' party in which the overwhelming majority of the members are Muslims.[35]

In practical terms the Bosnian war had another serious effect on Kosovo, in the form of the international economic sanctions which were eventually imposed on Serbia and Montenegro. This led to the closing of the Kosovo–Macedonian border to most forms of direct trade, and it also further depressed the ramshackle Serbian economy. Already Milošević's own economic mismanagement, combined with his policy of paying soldiers by merely printing money, had led to galloping inflation. The economic collapse which Serbia experienced during these years affected ordinary Serbs, of course, as well as Albanians; in some ways the local economy of agriculture and private trading developed by the Albanians was actually more resilient than the conditions of state-salaried employment under which so many of Kosovo's Serbs now lived. But there was also massive poverty among ordinary Albanians; the 'Mother Teresa' charity reported in 1993 that it was supplying basic foodstuffs to 50,000 Albanian families (*c*.250,000 people) who would otherwise be below subsistence level.[36]

One important development that accompanied the economic collapse in Serbia was the increasing gangsterization of the economy, with Mafia-style gangs taking over the trade in foreign goods and hard currency. This was at the same time a social, political and even military phenomenon, based on the paramilitary groups raised (with the approval and, initially, the financial help of the Belgrade government) to fight in Croatia and Bosnia. Two of the leaders of these organizations, Željko Ražnatović (known as Arkan) and Vojislav Šešelj, also developed political careers, for which purpose they made frequent use of the Kosovo issue to whip up nationalist support. Arkan was even elected to the Serbian assembly to represent a Kosovo constituency, in a poll boycotted by the Albanians. He explained his policy on Kosovo in one of his speeches:

only those who recognized the authority of Belgrade could be permitted
to live there, and in any case it was well known that 1.5 million of the
Albanians had crossed into Kosovo from Albania during the previous
fifty years. They should be regarded, he said, as 'tourists'. The implication
was quite clear.[37]

In this way as in so many others, the Serb policies (and rhetoric) of
the 1990s were uncannily reminiscent of those carried out, or at least
proposed by extremists such as Čubrilović, in the 1920s and 1930s. The
same overall strategy of persuading Albanians to leave by rendering their
conditions of life intolerable was in operation; so too was the policy of
'Serbianizing' the region by imposing the Serbian language, suppressing
most Albanian-language publications, changing local place-names and
destroying Albanian cultural institutions. In early 1996, for example, all
the Albanian street-names in Gjakova (a town with a 97 per cent
Albanian population) were changed to commemorate Serbian saints and
heroes: 'League of Prizren Street' became 'King Peter the Liberator
Street', and so on. The Institute of Albanian Studies in Prishtina was
closed down by administrative decree and its academic staff evicted by a
gang of armed men in plain clothes; the main reading-rooms of the
National Library in that city were turned over to a Serbian Orthodox
school; large quantities of Albanian-language materials from that library
were reportedly sent to Serbia, possibly for pulping, as were many boxes
of documents from the state archives in Prishtina; and in Prizren the
Museum of the League of Prizren, in an Ottoman quarter of the town
declared a World Heritage site by UNESCO, had its exhibits taken away
and was converted into a hostel for Serb refugees from Croatia.[38]

This last detail introduces the final resemblance between the 1990s
and the period between the two World Wars: the renewed programme
of colonization. The first attempts were made in the summer of 1991,
when a law was passed giving Serbs or Montenegrins who returned to
Kosovo the right to 5 hectares of land, to be supplied free of charge out
of municipal land-holdings. This scheme met with little public interest.
But one important effect of the wars in Croatia and Bosnia was to create
a huge new pool of potential colonists. By the autumn of 1994 roughly
6,000 Serb refugees from those countries had been sent to Kosovo by the
Serbian authorities; and in the summer of 1995, after the Croatian
army's successful action against the Serb-held 'Krajina' region, the state-

run media in Belgrade announced that at least 20,000 of these Krajina Serbs would now be settled in Kosovo. This total seems not to have been achieved, partly because most refugees had no wish to move to an impoverished Serb-minority region; in one famous incident, when a bus-load of refugees only discovered en route that they were being taken to Kosovo, they put a gun to the driver's head and forced him to turn back to Belgrade. Nevertheless, the official total of Serb refugee-colonists in Kosovo had risen to 19,000 by the summer of 1996.[39]

Such numbers, although representing a massive investment in house-building (in an area which was already the most densely populated in the former Yugoslavia), were still quite insignificant in changing the overall ethnic balance. More important than the influx of Serbs was the outflow of Albanians, which increased sharply during the war-years: surveys of Kosovo Albanians in Western European countries yielded the total of 217,000 in early 1992, and 368,000 in 1993.[40] But many Serbs too were leaving Serbia during the war; and the whole idea of creating an ethnic 'balance' in an area with a population of 200,000 Serbs and nearly two million Albanians remained as illusory as it had always been.

The ending of the war in Bosnia brought no end to the crisis in Kosovo. This fact alone was a blow to Rugova's prestige: he had spent four years telling his people, in effect, that they must be patient until the international community imposed a final settlement on ex-Yugoslavia, in which their interests would also be respected. But that settlement, worked out by the Americans at Dayton, Ohio, in November 1995, left the Albanians of Kosovo exactly where they were. The only nod in Kosovo's direction was an agreement by the UN Security Council that the 'outer wall' of sanctions against Serbia (involving such things as denial of access to the International Monetary Fund) would remain in place until Belgrade reformed its human rights record in Kosovo. Otherwise the Dayton settlement had the general effect of strengthening Milošević's rule in Serbia: Western diplomats made it clear that they were grateful to him for his 'peace-making' efforts, and that they regarded him as a constructive force in the region, whose removal might lead to 'instability'. The only serious challenge to Milošević, therefore, came not from the West but from his own internal opposition, which mounted a lengthy series of popular street-protests during the winter of 1996–7. But this was of little value to the Kosovo Albanians, since the two dominant members of the Serbian opposition coalition, Vuk Drašković and Zoran Djindjić, were leading representatives of Serbian nationalism, strongly committed to the defence of 'Serb land'.

As criticism of Rugova's policy grew in Kosovar political circles, it tended to take two forms. Some argued that his absolute refusal to negotiate with Belgrade (unless in an international forum) was unrealistic. They believed that Kosovo could escape from its present plight only by entering a long process of emancipation, in which the first step would be to become a federal unit in a new federation with Serbia, Montenegro, Vojvodina and, perhaps, the Bosnian 'Republika Srpska'. Others criticized him for not being absolute enough in his rejection of Belgrade, and wanted a more active policy of protest. And some of his critics, confusingly, seemed to combine both lines of criticism at once. Interwoven in many of these complaints was a feeling that the LDK had become too much of a monolith, too content with its own power over the local population. To widespread surprise, Rugova did negotiate with Milošević in September 1996, through the mediation of an Italian Catholic charity, and signed an agreement under which school and university buildings (but not state salaries) would be made available to the Albanian parallel education system. But when the Serbian authorities, more than six months later, had completely failed to implement this agreement, it appeared that Milošević had done little more than engage in a clever manoeuvre to undermine Rugova's credibility.[41]

Two other factors also contributed to the weakening of Rugova's position. One was the political crisis in Albania in the spring of 1997, where, after the failure of several large financial pyramid schemes, an insurrection broke out which aimed at the overthrow of the President, Sali Berisha. Dr Berisha had given moral and political support to the LDK (his was the only government to recognize the Kosovo 'Republic'), and his political opponents had not been pleased by the strong expressions of support for Berisha's party made by Rugova in return. Any post-Berisha government was likely to be less willing to come to the aid of the Kosovo Albanians; and the Albanian army had in any case undergone a complete collapse in 1997, with its weapons stores being looted in many parts of the country.

The other factor, of more immediate concern to Kosovo, was the development of new forms of direct action: shootings and bomb attacks against Serb institutions and officials. For many years the Serb media had referred to Albanian 'terrorism', usually meaning students throwing stones; now, for the first time since the Serb clampdown of 1989–90, there were signs of genuine terrorist activities. Several attacks took place from the summer of 1996 onwards, including the shooting of two policemen in Mitrovica, a bomb blast in Podujevo and an attack on the Serb Rector of Prishtina University; no organization claimed responsibility, and many Albanians assumed that these were artificial acts of provocation. But by the summer of 1997 a spokesman for something calling itself the 'Kosovo Liberation Army' was giving interviews in Switzerland, in which he said that his organization was responsible for several recent shootings of Serb policemen, and declared: 'This is the movement people support now.'[42] Whatever degree of support this 'army' did receive would have to be interpreted as an expression of popular frustration at the apparent inability of Ibrahim Rugova to gain any new recognition of Kosovo's interests from the outside world in the aftermath of Dayton.

And yet, no matter how powerless the Kosovar leadership might be in the short or medium term, the most important and most long-term weakness of all lay on the Serbian side. Quite simply, Serbia had already lost Kosovo – lost it, that is, in the most basic human and demographic terms. The Serbs who lived in Kosovo remained a small minority; and the vast majority of Serbs in the rest of Serbia had no wish to go and live in this already densely inhabited territory. The Serb birth-rate had continued to decline during the war (when, according to one Serbian gynaecologist, out of every 100 babies born in the whole of Serbia, sixty-four were non-Serbs), and it was now being predicted that by the middle of the next century the Serbs would be a minority in the entire Serbian republic. It was because of such calculations that the President of the Serbian Academy of Arts and Sciences, Aleksandar Despić, called in June 1996 for a public debate on the idea of negotiating a 'peaceful and civilized secession' for Kosovo.[43] The uproar which greeted this proposal was loud and predictable. Nevertheless, the thing had been said, and an important taboo had been broken.

Whether Kosovo is brought, in the end, to a peaceful solution, or plunged into a conflict potentially even more deadly than that which was created in Bosnia, will depend to a large extent on the ability of ordinary Serbs to challenge the fixed pattern of thought which has held them in its grip for so long. Both sides in this conflict have developed blinkered views of the history of Kosovo, of course; but the constricted understanding of the Serbs is the more serious impediment of the two, for the simple reason that it is Serbia that holds, for the time being at least, the power to make change or to block it.

Not everything the Serbs have been told about the history of Kosovo is false; what is needed, however, is an ability to accept that there are other truths which they have not been told. According to the mythic history of the Serbs, what happened in Kosovo in 1912 was an act of liberation which rescued an oppressed people from a kind of alien, colonial rule. There is an element of truth in this, but it is very much less than the whole truth. Serbs will never understand the nature of the Kosovo question unless they recognize first that the territory conquered in 1912 already had a majority non-Serb population, and secondly that the experience of alien, colonial rule is precisely what Serbian policy inflicted on that majority population during most of the next eighty-five years. Who, in the end, benefited from that policy? Among the direct beneficiaries were a few Serbian politicians of the inter-war years, and, more recently, Milošević, Šešelj and Arkan; indirectly, the policy was of some benefit to Mussolini and Hitler. Beneficiaries certainly do not include the ordinary indigenous Serbs of Kosovo, whose lives have been darkened and distorted by unnecessary political conflict; nor, obviously, the Kosovo Albanians; nor even the Serbs of Serbia proper, whose hopes of genuine democratic development have been poisoned by the constant reintroduction from above of a politics of fantasy and hatred. When ordinary Serbs learn to think more rationally and humanely about Kosovo, and more critically about some of their national myths, all the people of Kosovo and Serbia will benefit – not least the Serbs themselves.

Notes

Introduction

1 For details of this memorandum see Dogo, *Kosovo*, p. 54.
2 Letter to Sir John Myres, 21 Dec. 1943, Bodl. MS Myres 12, fo. 163ʳ.

1. Orientation: places, names and peoples

1 Wilkinson, *Maps and Politics*, p. 28.
2 Mladenov, 'Bemerkungen', p. 44.
3 Montenegro, the modern republic and former kingdom, is, as its Italian-derived name suggests, also called 'Crna Gora' in Serbian; to avoid confusion with Montenegro, the 'Skopska Crna Gora' is usually referred to with its qualifying adjective (from the nearby city of Skopje). In Albanian Montenegro is called 'Mal i Zi', which also means 'Black Mountain'.
4 More curiously, one little stream, the Neredimka, is said to feed both a tributary of the Morava, which flows north into the Danube, and a tributary of the Vardar, which flows south into the Aegean. Local peasants used to say that it sends water to the Black Sea and the White Sea (a name for the Mediterranean): Muir Mackenzie and Irby, *Travels*, vol. 1, p. 181 n.
5 Rizaj, *Kosova gjatë shekujve*, p. 273. Perhaps because of the 'Kosova' in Albania (there is a village of this name near Gjirokastra), Rizaj suggests that the true origins of the word lie in Illyrian or Thracian rather than Serbian; but, as we shall see, there are many Slav place-names in Albania. Another Albanian scholar, Muharem Cërabregu, tries to derive Kosovo from an Illyrian root *kasa*, meaning a deep valley, and the Albanian word *va*, meaning ford (*Gjeo dhe hartolinguistika*, p. 236); this is very unconvincing.
6 Rizaj (*Kosova gjatë shekujve*, pp. 215–16) identifies the town with Belasica, near Trepça; von Hahn (*Reise von Belgrad*, p. 84) and Anhegger (*Beiträge*, vol. 1, p. 160) place it near Janjevo. The early Ottoman administrative unit

was a kadılık in the sancak of Vuçitërn: Stojan Novaković located this too at Janjevo ('Hadži-Kalfa', p. 58).

7 For a precise geographical description of the Kosovo depression see Urošević, *Etnički procesi*, p. 8. Further geographical and geological information is given in Maletić, ed., *Kosovo*, pp. 5–25.

8 Maletić, ed., *Kosovo*, p. 26; Krasniqi, *Savremene promene*, pp. 107–9.

9 Hadri, *Lëvizja*, pp. 97–9; Schlarp, *Wirtschaft*, pp. 175–8.

10 Čerskov, *Rimljani*, pp. 49–52.

11 On Novo Brdo see Pertusi, *Martino Segono*, pp. 204–7 n., and the plates between pp. 16 and 17.

12 Murphey, 'Silver Production', p. 79.

13 von Hahn, *Reise von Belgrad*, p. 43. There was, however, a little silver and gold still being mined at Janjevo, south of Prishtina, and some mercury extraction further south: Wiet, 'Mémoire', p. 275.

14 On the various routes discussed here, see Čerskov, *Rimljani*, pp. 44–7, and Stadtmüller, *Forschungen*, pp. 96–112 (Roman period); Jireček, *Handelsstrassen*, pp. 74–87, and Škrivanić, *Putevi*, pp. 72–4 and the map facing p. 40 (medieval period); Yerasimos, *Les Voyageurs*, pp. 36–41 (early Ottoman); Boué, *La Turquie*, vol. 4, pp. 507–52 (late Ottoman, with route-timings).

15 Muir Mackenzie and Irby, *Travels*, vol. 1, p. 194; Glück, *Albanien*, p. 55; for Bulgarian claims see the ethnographic map in Marenin, *Albanija*; Čilev, 'Obikolka'; and Mladenov, 'Bemerkungen', pp. 56–60.

16 Knight, *Albania*, p. 123.

17 'Malësi' and 'malësor' are the standard spellings in modern Albanian. Other spellings are 'Malsi, malsor' or 'Malci, malcor', and in texts by West European writers one may encounter 'Maltsi' and 'maltsor' or 'malissor'.

18 The religious history of Montenegro is complex, however; in modern times it has developed its own Montenegrin Orthodox Church, and Venetian and Austrian influence on its coastal territories gave it, in the past, a significant Catholic population: see Draganović, 'Massenübertritte'.

19 On this whole question see Durham, *Tribal Origins*, pp. 1–59. Another common factor in the ethnic history of these populations was the Vlach element: see Kaser, *Hirten, Kämpfer*, pp. 85–92. (On the Vlachs see above, pp. 25–7, 202–5.) In a private letter, Edith Durham commented on the Albanian and Montenegrin custom of reciting (in church, once a year) family pedigrees, which often went back thirteen generations: 'the Montenegrin pedigree matter is of interest for it goes to prove a point of which I am more & more certain viz: that the Montenegrins are not Slavs but Albanian & Vlah by origin. So far as I know the reading of the pedigrees in church is *not* a Serbian custom ... I should think that the keeping of pedigrees so jealously certainly indicates always strict marriage laws. In this case exogamy ...' (letter to Sir John Myres, 21 Mar. 1931: Bodl. MS Myres

12, fo. 158). This is too sweeping a claim about all the Montenegrins, but may well apply to some of the mountain clans.

20 See Charanis, 'Town and Country', p. 119. The classic Serbian study of the village is S. Novaković, *Selo*. For valuable studies of twentieth-century village life, see Lodge, *Peasant Life*, and Erlich, *Family*.

21 *High Albania*, p. 251; see also pp. 283–4, with a diagram of a zadruga at Gračanica. Mijatović noted the rapid disappearance of the zadruga in Serbia: *Servia*, p. 177. Lodge studied a forty-member zadruga (of Montenegrin origin) in a village near Novi Pazar in 1930: for a diagram and full family tree, see the end-papers to her *Peasant Life*. The best general studies are Sicard, *La Zadruga*, and the essays by Philip Mosely in Byrnes, ed., *Zadruga*.

22 Gavazzi, 'Mehrfamilien'; Kaser, *Hirten, Kämpfer*, pp. 102–4.

23 See Erlich, 'The Last Big Zadrugas'; Lutovac, *La Metohija*, pp. 37–9; Sestini, 'La Metochia', p. 33; Barjaktarović, 'Dvovjerske zadruge'; Krasniqi, *Lugu i Baranit*, pp. 39–40, and his 'Organizimi', which describes an Albanian zadruga near Peć, of eighty-three members, in sixteen families, all derived from a common ancestor in five generations.

24 This argument is not meant to imply, of course, that the traditions of critical thinking developed in Western Christianity are a sufficient guarantee of democratic or responsible politics: gross aberrations in the histories of several Western countries prove that they are not.

25 *Servia*, p. 38.

26 On the vestiges of a clan system in the South, known as *fara* or *gjeri*, see Kaser, *Hirten, Kämpfer*, p. 30.

27 For a useful summary of the linguistic differences, see Pipa, *Politics*, pp. 8–20; for an important study of the local varieties of Geg speech found in Kosovo, see Tagliavini, 'Le parlate'.

28 Pipa, *Politics*, is a powerful study of the political basis and theoretical inadequacies of 'unified literary Albanian'. For British readers, the Scottish–English analogy may be misleading here, since the dominance of southern literary English is based on a long history of literary production in the south, as well as administrative centralization. Albania had no centralized administration of its own until 1912, and the power-house of literary Albanian, from the sixteenth century to the early twentieth, was the work of Geg-speaking Catholics in the north.

29 The vëllazëri could also be called a *mëhallë*, from the Turkish word for houses grouped together. For a good description of a vëllazëri in 1890 see Valentini, ed., *La legge*, pp. 46–7. On the clan system in general see Durham, *Tribal Origins*, pp. 13–59; Kaser, *Hirten, Kämpfer*, pp. 26–9; and Baxhaku and Kaser, eds., *Stammesgesellschaften*, pp. 272–98 (reproducing an important text by Nopcsa).

30 Some anthropologists explain exogamy in functionalist terms, as a device

for bringing new genes into the clan's gene pool. But with two neighbouring clans exchanging brides over the centuries and caring little about relatedness through female lines, exogamy was in fact no protection against in-breeding (see Durham, *High Albania*, p. 21).

31 Coon, *Mountains of Giants*, pp. 30–2, gives a very confused account in an attempt to correct Edith Durham's classification.

32 Krasniqi, *Lugu i Baranit*, pp. 44–6. The best survey of the role of the bajraktar is M. Hasluck, *Unwritten Law*, pp. 115–29.

33 See pp. 120–1.

34 The traditional identification is with Lek III Dukagjin (1410–81), though the great Albanian writer Fan Noli chose Pal Dukagjin instead (d. 1446): Pupovci, 'Origjina', pp. 104–5. Edith Durham preferred Lek II Dukagjin (ruled 1444–59): *Tribal Origins*, p. 65.

35 Castelletti, 'Consuetudini', pp. 64–72.

36 See von Thallóczy, 'Kanun', pp. 409–10.

37 Some elements of the Kanun were summarized by von Hahn in 1854 (*Albanesische Studien*, vol. 1, pp. 176–82); more materials, gathered by a government commission, were printed in the Turkish-language journal *Prizren* in 1871 (Kaleshi, 'Türkische Angaben', p. 107); an Italian priest issued an account in 1890, which was then plagiarized by the Austro-Hungarian vice-consul at Shkodra (Libardi, *Primi moti*, part 1, p. 2); and a Serbian summary appeared in 1901 (Pupovci, 'Burimet', p. 83).

38 Gjeçov, *Kanuni*, now printed with a valuable parallel translation by Leonard Fox. Details of Gjeçov's sources (of whom the most important were from the Catholic clan of Mirdita) are given by Schirò, who also demonstrates that Gjeçov's text contained both genuine proverbial sayings and more artificial definitions of his own devising: 'Gjeçov e la prosa', esp. pp. 185–201.

39 *Tribal Origins*, pp. 64–5.

40 Gjeçov, *Kanuni*, arts. 315–40 (blacksmiths, millers), 892–3 (fines), 1044–111 (jurors, etc.), 1187–94 (execution). M. Hasluck, *Unwritten Law*, covers many aspects of the Kanun, including a chapter on the rights and duties of people attacked by dogs – an important issue, as anyone who has walked in the Balkans will know.

41 Valentini, ed., *La legge*, pp. x-xi.

42 Gjeçov, *Kanuni*, arts. 598, 601.

43 Brown, *Winter*, p. 209.

44 M. Hasluck, *Unwritten Law*, p. 25.

45 On the sworn virgins see von Hahn, *Reise durch Drin und Wardar*, pp. 31–2; Steinmetz, *Vorstoss*, p. 50; Durham, *High Albania*, pp. 80, 85, 101–2; Nopcsa, *Šala und Klementi*, pp. 12–13; and, with more recent examples, Filipović, *Has*, p. 59.

46 *High Albania*, pp. 37–8.

47 Durham, *Tribal Origins*, pp. 162–71. The fullest account of the blood-feud system is M. Hasluck, *Unwritten Law*, pp. 219–60. Blood-feuds had previously existed also among the Slavs, and survived longest in the patriarchal-pastoral societies of the mountain regions, especially Montenegro: see Miklosich, 'Die Blutrache', and Simić, 'Blood Feud'.
48 Siebertz, *Albanien*, p. 211.
49 Dumont, *Le Balkan*, pp. 304–5.
50 Naval Intelligence Division, *Albania*, p. 132.
51 Siebertz, *Albanien*, p. 91.

2. Origins: Serbs, Albanians and Vlachs

1 Fine, *Early Medieval Balkans*, pp. 26–7; Obolensky, *Byzantine Commonwealth*, pp. 85–6; Goldstein, *Hrvatski rani srednji vijek*, pp. 88–90.
2 Velkov, *Cities in Thrace*, pp. 31–46, gives a good summary; V. Popović, 'L'Albanie', p. 259, discusses the Goth attacks on Albania in 459 and 479.
3 The Bulgar language disappeared by the mid-ninth century: Runciman, *Bulgarian Empire*, p. 93. From then on, the term 'Bulgarian' can be used generally to refer to the political unit which the Bulgars created, to its mainly Slav population, and to their Slav language.
4 Velkov, *Cities in Thrace*, p. 49; Skok, *Dolazak Slovena*, p. 105; Hammond, *Migrations*, p. 66 (suggesting that they entered Macedonia through the Kaçanik pass).
5 Runciman, *Bulgarian Empire*, pp. 22–4 (traditional view); Fine, *Early Medieval Balkans*, p. 28 (new evidence).
6 Fine, *Early Medieval Balkans*, pp. 49–59. Goldstein, *Hrvatski rani srednji vijek*, pp. 87–92, gives a more hesitant treatment of Constantine's story, and Whittow, *Orthodox Byzantium*, p. 263, rejects it.
7 Fine, *Early Medieval Balkans*, p. 57; on the social organization of the early Serbs see Gimbutas, *Slavs*, pp. 140–1.
8 Makushev, *O Slavianakh*, p. 2; Stadtmüller, *Forschungen*, p. 128.
9 Nopcsa, 'Beiträge', p. 238; Ducellier, *Façade*, pp. 70, 196; Selishchev, *Slavianskoe naselenie*, pp. 73–85.
10 Lemerle, ed., *Les Plus Anciens Recueils*, vol. 1, p. 186; Velkov, *Cities in Thrace*, pp. 52–3; Howard-Johnston, 'Urban Continuity'; Whittow, *Orthodox Byzantium*, pp. 267–8.
11 Jireček, 'Die Romanen'; Šufflay, 'Städte und Burgen', p. 36; Stadtmüller, *Forschungen*, p. 129.
12 Whittow, *Orthodox Byzantium*, p. 268; V. Popović, 'L'Albanie', pp. 269–72.
13 Nopcsa, 'Beiträge', p. 238 (Dalmatians in Albania); Mirdita, 'Balkanski Vlasi', pp. 75–6 (citing and analysing the statement by the eleventh-century writer Kekaumenos).

14 For good general studies of the Vlachs, see Wace and Thompson, *Nomads*; Weigand, *Aromunen*; and Winnifrith, *Vlachs*.
15 Weigand, 'Albanische Einwanderung', p. 225.
16 For a powerful presentation of the evidence see Schramm, 'Frühe Schicksale'.
17 E.g. Niederle, *Slovanské starožitnosti*, vol. 2, map opposite p. 296; Angelov, *Obrazuvane*, map on p. 155.
18 See van Wijk, 'Taalkunde gegevens'; quotation from p. 71. The modern dialect of Serbo-Croat which borders Macedonian and Bulgarian territory, the 'Timok-Prizren' dialect, does have some transitional features; but research has shown that it picked them up only after the medieval expansion of the Serbian state into Kosovo and the Morava valley, which brought its speakers into closer contact with Bulgarian (*ibid.*, pp. 62, 71).
19 Runciman, *Bulgarian Empire*, pp. 88–93, 127–38; Selishchev, *Slavianskoe naselenie*, p. 61; Stadtmüller, *Forschungen*, pp. 129–32.
20 Whittow, *Orthodox Byzantium*, pp. 387–8. Hilferding, *Geschichte*, p. 35 n., notes that after Samuel's death in 1014, the local Slav tribes in Eastern Kosovo formally submitted to Byzantine rule.
21 Stadtmüller, *Forschungen*, pp. 162–4.
22 Grégoire and de Keyser, 'La *Chanson*'; Grégoire, 'La Chanson'; Hammond, *Migrations*, p. 56.
23 Šufflay, 'Städte und Burgen', p. 203; *duca* is the Italian title.
24 Jireček, 'Albanien', p. 69; Šufflay, 'Povijest', p. 227.
25 For slightly different eleventh-century locations see Stadtmüller, *Forschungen*, pp. 167–73, and Ducellier, *Façade*, p. 80; the twentieth-century name was noted by Father Gjeçov, and reported in Dema, 'Shqypnija katolike', p. 532 n.
26 The same root gave rise to 'Albion', an early name for Britain, and another name derived from it, 'Albany'. There is also a territory known to classical geographers as Albania in the Caucasus; some earlier writers, such as the French diplomat de Pouqueville, supposed that the Balkan Albanians came from there, but there is no connection between the two areas.
27 This probably derives from another version of the place-name, Arbëria, a term for the highlands between Vlora, Gjirokastra and the sea: see Stadtmüller, *Forschungen*, p. 177.
28 Šufflay, 'Povijest', p. 200 (documents); Stadtmüller, *Forschungen*, p. 70 (eagle). The 'he who understands' argument may possibly be the wrong way round; in Hungarian, for example, *magyarázni* means 'to explain', but only because its original meaning was 'to put into Magyar'. Çabej notes that the presumed derivation of *shqipoj* from Latin *excipere* is very doubtful ('Zur Charakteristik', p. 194). Another derivation of *shqip*, suggested by Skok, from the place-name Scupi (Skopje; Alb.: Shkup), requires some unusual sound-changes (see Schramm, *Eroberer*, p. 361).

29 Curiously, it is treated as authentic by Hammond, *Migrations*, pp. 56–7. But the document, a Ragusan chronicle written probably in the fourteenth century and surviving only in an eighteenth-century copy, evidently described much more recent events: see Makushev, 'Issledovaniia', pp. 204, 303–32.

30 E.g. Çabej, 'Problem of place', p. 79.

31 Skënder Anamali has argued the Illyrian-Albanian case in a series of articles: see 'Problemi i kulturës' and 'De la civilisation'. But as Vladimir Popović points out, the finds at Koman and the Kruja necropolis are similar to those at other semi-isolated Romano-Byzantine towns of this period in Corfu and Dalmatia: 'L'Albanie', pp. 269–72.

32 Durham, 'Antiquity'; for a strong argument against tribal continuity see Kaser, *Hirten, Kämpfer*, pp. 39–43.

33 Stadtmüller, *Forschungen*, pp. 138–9, 145–7; Selishchev, *Slavianskoe nase-lenie*, pp. 176–81; Jokl, 'Slaven und Albaner', pp. 291–7, 315.

34 Schramm, *Anfänge*, p. 151. The best evidence is from the area of Debar and the Black Drin.

35 Stipčević, *Iliri*, pp. 27–30; Wilkes, *Illyrians*, p. 68; Wiesner, *Thraker*, p. 27.

36 Stipčević, *Iliri*, p. 30 and n.; Mirdita, *Studime dardane*, pp. 7–46; Papazoglu, *Central Balkan Tribes*, pp. 210–69. As Papazoglu notes, most ancient sources classify Dardanians as Illyrians. Her reasons for rejecting this identification in a later essay, 'Les Royaumes', are obscure. There were Thracian names in the eastern strip of Dardania, but Illyrian names dominated the rest; Katičić has shown that these belong with two other Illyrian 'onomastic provinces' (see his summary in *Ancient Languages*, pp. 179–81, and the evidence in Papazoglu, 'Dardanska onomastika').

37 Dečev, *Sprachreste*, pp. 575, 579 (by Dečev and Georgiev respectively).

38 Katičić, *Ancient Languages*, pp. 169–70.

39 *Ibid.*, p. 171 (cloud); Dečev, *Sprachreste*, pp. 543, 544 (blackberry). Çabej notes a Swiss (Rhaetoromance) word for a raspberry, *mani*, and suggests that the term was originally an Illyrian word, which spread both west into Alpine Latin and east into Thracian ('L'Illyrien', p. 52). Cimochowski also argues that 'mantia' could be Illyrian: 'Prejardhja', p. 38. The oft-cited link claimed by Weigand between the Thracian word for 'thyme' and the Albanian for 'peas' is now rejected: see Weigand, 'Albanische Einwande-rung', p. 209; Philippide, *Originea Romînilor*, vol. 1, p. 375; Dečev, *Spra-chreste*, p. 554.

40 Mladenov, 'Albanisch', p. 183 (Carlo, Lodovico).

41 Çabej, 'Problem of place'; Schramm, *Eroberer*, p. 293; Huld, *Basic Etymolo-gies*, pp. 48, 121–2.

42 For this important argument see Gjinari, 'De la continuation'. On Thracian compound names see Georgiev, 'Thrace et illyrien', p. 73; Katičić, *Ancient Languages*, pp. 139–41.

43 The best discussions of this issue are Pisani, 'Les Origines'; Cimochowski, 'Prejardhja', pp. 41–5. See also Mayer, *Sprache der Illyrier*, vol. 1, p. 12; Katičić, *Ancient Languages*, pp. 174, 184. One more recent attempt to prove that Illyrian was centum is by Schramm, *Anfänge*, pp. 26–7. But his argument rests only on one speculative etymology for a river-name, connecting it with an Indo-European root for 'knee': this does not match the known derivation from that root in Albanian (see Huld, *Basic Etymologies*, p. 70).

44 Katičić, *Ancient Languages*, p. 163; Rosetti, 'Thrace, daco-mésien', p. 81.

45 Polomé, 'Position'; Hamp, 'Position', p. 111. Based on the assumed Messapian link was another argument, about the accentuation of the first syllable in place-names (Brindisi, for example, preserves the Messapian accent): some Albanian names do this and others do not. Dropping the Messapian–Illyrian connection removes this problem from the agenda.

46 See Huld, *Basic Etymologies*, pp. 159–61. Huld finds the classification particularly unhelpful for Albanian, which differs in some ways from satem languages without being identifiable as centum.

47 Georgiev, 'Albanisch, dakisch-mysisch'. See Hamp, 'Position'; Rosetti, 'Thrace, daco-mésien'; and, for the fullest demolition, di Giovine, 'Tracio, dacio ed albanese'.

48 Çabej, 'Problem of Autochthony', p. 43; Katičić, *Ancient Languages*, p. 186; Mihăescu, 'Les Éléments', p. 325.

49 This claim is put forward as a prime argument against the 'Illyrian' origins of the Albanians by Schramm: *Eroberer*, pp. 33–4; *Anfänge*, p. 23. It had already been answered by Çabej, who pointed out that the shift to 'h' belonged to a much earlier (pre-Roman) period of Albanian: 'Problem of Autochthony', p. 44. Schramm's case can be disproved by a series of Albanian borrowings from Latin, such as *shkorsë* (rug) from *scortea*, *shkëndijë* (spark) from *scantilla*, *shkëmb* (rock-formation) from *scamnum*, and *shkop* (staff) from *scopae*: see Capidan, 'Raporturile', pp. 546–8; Philippide, *Originea Romînilor*, vol. 2, pp. 653–4; Çabej, 'Zur Charakteristik', p. 177; and the entries in Meyer, *Etymologisches Wörterbuch*.

50 Jokl, 'Slaven und Albaner', pp. 287, 618, 627.

51 Weigand, 'Sind die Albaner?', p. 233.

52 See Çabej, 'L'Illyrien', p. 46, and the comments in Hamp, 'Position', p. 98.

53 It is sometimes imagined that the shepherds of the northern Albanian mountains must always have grazed their flocks on the coastal plains in the winter, but this is not correct. Many move only from summer pastures in the mountains to winter pastures in nearby valleys: see Kaser, *Hirten, Kämpfer*, pp. 57–67.

54 Skok, *Dolazak Slovena*, p. 22 (Plovdiv area); Schramm, 'Frühe Schicksale', (ii), p. 104 (Ohrid area); Schramm, *Eroberer*, pp. 115–30 (mountain areas). St Jerome referred to Illyrian-speakers in Dalmatia or Pannonia in the fifth

century, but their location is uncertain: Mirdita, 'Çështja e etnogenezës', pp. 638–9.

55 Schramm, *Anfänge*, p. 232. In later Byzantine usage, 'Bessoi' became a general name for Vlachs (see Cankova-Petkova, 'La Survivance'). Perhaps because of this, Tomaschek argued ('Die alten Thraker', (i), p. 77) that these monks were speaking a Balkan Latin, and that *bessam* was just added in the manuscript as a gloss on *latinam*; but this is refuted by the evidence of the two earliest MSS (see Milani, ed., *Itinerarium*, p. 204). There is other evidence of Christian 'Bessi' in Constantinople and Jerusalem: Schramm, *Anfänge*, pp. 112–20. Irfan Shahîd's attempt to identify Bessan here with Arabic is unconvincing (*Byzantium and Arabs, Fourth Century*, pp. 320–1), but his location of Lakhmids in the region (*ibid.*, pp. 31–60, and *Byzantium and Arabs, Sixth Century*, p. 979) must overturn a recent claim that the 'Lachmienses' at Sinai were Vlachs (Nandriş, 'Jebaliyeh').

56 Schramm, *Anfänge*, pp. 149–56.

57 *Ibid.*, pp. 48–77. Even the Goths held out for a long time: a small Gothic-speaking population existed in the Crimea as late as the sixteenth century.

58 For useful listings see Haarmann, *Der lateinische Lehnwortschatz*, pp. 105–8; Philippide, *Originea Romînilor*, vol. 1, pp. 665–76.

59 Schramm, *Anfänge*, pp. 94–5.

60 There are two common Albanian words for flock, *kope* and *tufë*.

61 Jireček, 'Die Romanen', (i), p. 13; Philippide, *Originea Romînilor*, vol. 1, pp. 70–2; Papazoglu, 'Les Royaumes', pp. 193–5. Albanian does preserve a very small quantity of borrowings from ancient Greek: see Thumb, 'Altgriechische Elemente'; Jokl, 'Altmakedonisch'; Çabej, 'Zur Charakteristik', p. 182. This low level of borrowing from Greek is a further argument against the identification of Albanians with Bessi, part of whose tribal territory was Hellenized: see Philippide, *Originea Romînilor*, vol. 1, pp. 11, 283; Velkov, 'La Thrace', p. 188.

62 Stadtmüller, *Forschungen*, pp. 118–22; Zeitler, 'Das lateinische Erbe'.

63 Schramm gives a valuable survey of the literature and the evidence: 'Frühe Schicksale', esp. pp. 112–15. See also Pipa's comments on the symbiosis in *Albanian Literature*, pp. 62–75.

64 On substratum vocabulary see Capidan, 'Raporturile', pp. 457–83. For an etymology of *copil* see Reichenkron, 'Vorrömische Elemente', pp. 242–3. One key word, *vatra* (hearth), suggests that the original substratum may have been a widespread 'Albanoid' group, of which Albanian is the only survivor: Hamp, 'Distribution'. But below that there may have been a sub-substratum of pre-Indo-European words: for examples (connected with Basque) see Polák, 'Die Beziehungen', pp. 213–15.

65 On Dalmatian, which was recorded just in time from its last speaker in the 1890s, see Mihăescu, *La Romanité*, pp. 91–130.

66 Weigand, 'Sind die Albaner?', pp. 231–2.

67 Earlier studies linked Albanian exclusively with Romanian; more recent
    ones have tried to prise them apart, especially if written by Albanians trying
    to keep Albanian origins in Albania, or Romanians trying to keep Romanian
    origins in Romania: see Çabej, 'Zur Charakteristik'; Mihăescu, 'Les Élé-
    ments'. Mihăescu uses Latin Christian vocabulary in Albanian to emphasize
    its divergence from Romanian, but this is highly misleading: Romanian has
    a different vocabulary here simply because Romanians were later brought
    under the Orthodox Church.
68 Jireček, *Geschichte der Bulgaren*, pp. 112–13 (admitting some agriculture
    too); Howard-Johnston, 'Urban Continuity', p. 251 (towns only).
69 Capidan, 'Românii nomazi', pp. 205–8.
70 Dinić, 'Dubrovačka trgovina'.
71 The Montenegrin highlands are rather neglected in most studies of these
    issues; but they clearly had a well-established Vlach population by the early
    fourteenth century, when Vlach place-names are recorded there: see Šufflay,
    Srbi i Arbanasi, p. 75; Radusinović, *Stanovništvo*, p. 31 (and for Albanian
    names in Montenegro, see above, n. 24).
72 Capidan, 'Raporturile'; Schramm, 'Frühe Schicksale'. Weigand, 'Albanische
    Einwanderung', shows that some Albanians went with the Romanians into
    Transylvania.
73 Čerskov, *Rimljani*, p. 54; Mirdita, 'Rreth problemit'.
74 Čerskov, *Rimljani*, p. 55.

3. Medieval Kosovo before Prince Lazar: 850s–1380s

1 Gelzer, *Patriarchat*, p. 4; Gjini, *Ipeshkvia*, pp. 79–80.
2 Mirdita, *Historia e kishës*, pp. 18–20.
3 Nopcsa, 'Beiträge', pp. 238–9; Ducellier, *Façade*, pp. 108–9. Šufflay describes
   the medieval Albanian nobility as leading an 'amphibious' religious life:
   'Kirchenzustände', p. 241.
4 Gjini, *Ipeshkvia*, p. 77; Grafenauer, Perović and Šidak, *Historija*, pp. 248–9.
   On the Roman Church in Dioclea see Fine, *Early Medieval Balkans*, pp. 215,
   223. Jireček notes that it was the Serbs of Dioclea who placed Shkodra
   under the Roman Archbishopric of Bar in the eleventh century: 'Skutari',
   p. 104.
5 Mirdita, *Historia e kishës*, p. 20. There is also an obscure reference to a
   Bishop of 'Prinateuns' in *c*.1100, which some have identified with Prizren:
   Mirdita, 'Alcuni aspetti', p. 179.
6 Fine, *Early Medieval Balkans*, pp. 219–20.
7 Šufflay, 'Kirchenzustände', p. 198 (Prizren); Jireček, 'Staat und Gesellschaft',
   (i), p. 64.

8   Charanis, 'Town and Country'; Ostrogorsky, *Féodalité*, pp. 13–29.
9   Ostrogorsky, *Féodalité*, pp. 187–90; Vlainac, *Verhältnisse*, pp. 79–80.
10 On the complex history of Dioclea and Rascia in this period, see Fine, *Early Medieval Balkans*, pp. 202–37.
11 On all these events see Fine, *Late Medieval Balkans*, pp. 7–9, 25–6.
12 Hafner, ed. and tr., *Serbisches Mittelalter*, vol. 1, p. 87.
13 Stojan Novaković suggested that he lost these areas in 1194: *Il campo d'azione*, pp. 45–6. The best discussion of this complex issue is R. Novaković, 'O nekim pitanjima', pp. 195–207.
14 R. Novaković, 'O nekim pitanjima', pp. 208–12.
15 Hafner, ed. and tr., *Serbisches Mittelalter*, vol. 1, p. 76.
16 On all these events see Slijepčević, *Istorija crkve*, vol. 1, pp. 78–91, 105; Obolensky, *Byzantine Commonwealth*, pp. 314–15; Fine, *Late Medieval Balkans*, pp. 116–17.
17 On the promises (by Stefan Uroš I, Milutin and Dušan), see Jireček, 'Staat und Gesellschaft', (i), p. 53.
18 Hafner, *Studien*, pp. 40–52.
19 Ćirković, Korać and Babić, *Studenica*, p. 16.
20 Kouri, *Die Milutinschule*, pp. 8–11. Greek architects, on the other hand, seem not to have been used until the end of the thirteenth century: Ćurčić, *Gračanica*, p. 141.
21 The Cumans were a Turkic tribe which had settled in Romania and Bulgaria. The archbishopric had property outside Peć, and built a church there in the mid-thirteenth century; a new church and other buildings were added to it in the early fourteenth century, creating what became the Patriarchate complex. The traditional date of 1253 for the move from Žiča to Peć is incorrect. See Ćirković, 'Kosovo u srednjem veku', p. 31. Nor was Peć the exclusive seat of the Patriarch. Žiča was rebuilt, and Patriarch Spiridon (d. 1389) and his successor Danilo both resided there: Radojičić, 'Izbor patrijarha'.
22 Fine, *Late Medieval Balkans*, p. 204.
23 Mavromatis, *La Fondation*, pp. 15–28. For simplicity's sake, Milutin's popular name is used here, rather than his official title (Stefan Uroš II).
24 For this dating (revising earlier accounts) see *ibid.*, pp. 34–5. For the Greekness of Skopje see Jireček, 'Staat und Gesellschaft', (i), p. 26.
25 Patriarch Danilo II, in Hafner, ed. and tr., *Serbisches Mittelalter*, vol. 2, pp. 176–94. Ćurčić, *Gračanica*, is a valuable architectural study.
26 Mošin, 'Vizantiski uticaj', pp. 147–9.
27 Report by Theodore Metochites, in Sathas, ed., *Mesaiônikê vivliothêkê*, vol. 1, pp. 165–6 (courtiers), 173 (clothes, furnishings).
28 The 'blinding' of Dečanski (official title: Stefan Uroš III) is discussed in Fine, *Late Medieval Balkans*, p. 263. This is one of the many cruel

punishments, fratricides, etc., which prompted even the Slavophile scholar Gilferding to complain that the early Serbian lives of the Nemanjids were a dismal catalogue of crimes in cold blood: see Hafner, *Studien*, pp. 1–3.

29　Fine, *Late Medieval Balkans*, pp. 273–4. On the differing early accounts of these events, see Mavromatis, *La Fondation*, pp. 82–3. Shkodra's population was mainly Albanian in the fourteenth century: see Šufflay, 'Städte und Burgen', p. 37. Nerodimlje was a royal court (at modern Sarajište) in south-central Kosovo.

30　Jireček, 'Staat und Gesellschaft', (i), p. 75; Hammond, *Migrations*, pp. 57–61.

31　Slijepčević, *Istorija crkve*, vol. 1, pp. 173–5.

32　Soulis, *Serbs and Byzantium*, pp. 79–80, 120–1.

33　Fine, *Late Medieval Balkans*, pp. 345–62. The origins of the Balsha are obscure: the story that they were descended from a son of Bertrand de Baux, who accompanied Charles d'Anjou when he seized the kingdom of Naples, is probably pure legend (Lenormant, *Turcs et monténégrins*, pp. 4–10; Gelcich, *La Zedda*, pp. 28–9). Šufflay thought they were originally Vlach ('Povijest', p. 204); an Albano-Vlach origin is confirmed by Weigand, who noted 'Balşa' among a group of early Albanian family names in Romania ('Albanische Einwanderung', p. 223). Possibly the name comes from the ancient town of Balletium, and/or the village Balëz, near Shkodra: Gegaj, *L'Albanie*, p. 16; Rizaj, *Kosova gjatë shekujve*, pp. 20–1.

34　Fine, *Late Medieval Balkans*, p. 363; T. Popović, *Prince Marko*.

35　On all these developments see Fine, *Late Medieval Balkans*, pp. 377–89; Kojaković, *Borba Jugoslovena*, pp. 1–13; Dinić, *Srpske zemlje*, pp. 148–77.

36　Jireček, 'Staat und Gesellschaft', (i), p. 65; Rizaj, *Kosova gjatë shekujve*, p. 249.

37　Jireček, 'Staat und Gesellschaft', (i), pp. 6–7; Ćirković, 'Kosovo u srednjem veku', pp. 30–1.

38　A chrysobull was the highest form of royal charter; its Greek name means 'golden seal'.

39　Vlainac, *Verhältnisse*, pp. 59–80; Jireček, 'Staat und Gesellschaft', (i), pp. 43–4.

40　Radojčić, ed., *Zakonik* (tr. Burr, 'Code of Dušan'), art. 68. On meropahs and free peasants see Vlainac, *Verhältnisse*, pp. 143–212; on slaves see Grafenauer, Perović and Šidak, *Historija*, p. 422, and Jireček, 'Staat und Gesellschaft', (i), p. 73 (noting that the recorded names of slaves are mainly Slav, but include some Vlachs and Albanians).

41　Vlainac, *Verhältnisse*, pp. 206–57; Jireček, 'Staat und Gesellschaft', (ii), pp. 70–1.

42　Inalcık, 'Ottoman Decline', p. 338.

43　Radojčić, ed., *Zakonik* (tr. Burr, 'Code of Dušan'), arts. 53, 54, 97, 107, 145,

207. One historian, commenting on these provisions, describes the medieval Serbian system as 'severe oppression': Hehn, 'Man and State'.
44 Škrivanić, *Putevi*, pp. 37–9.
45 Jireček, 'Staat und Gesellschaft', (iii), p. 31.
46 Radojčić, ed., *Zakonik* (tr. Burr, 'Code of Dušan'), art. 85.
47 *Ibid.*, arts. 6, 10.
48 Theiner, ed., *Vetera monumenta Hungariae*, vol. 1, pp. 359–61 (letters to Helena and Milutin), 375 (confessor), 408 (parishes), 831 (persecution); *Vetera monumenta slavorum*, vol. 1, pp. 124 (letter to Milutin), 128 (envoys). For evidence of the persecution of Catholics in the early fourteenth century see Xhufi, 'Albanian Heretics'; Ducellier, 'Have the Albanians?', p. 64.
49 Gjini, *Ipeshkvia*, pp. 95–6.
50 He was bishop from *c.*1363 to *c.*1375: *ibid.*, pp. 117, 218.
51 Mehlan, 'Über die Bedeutung', p. 386; Kovačević-Kojić, *Priština*, p. 46.
52 Quotation from Mehlan, 'Über die Bedeutung', p. 399. See also Jireček, 'Staat und Gesellschaft', (i), pp. 65–8; (ii), pp. 43–6; Takács, 'Sächsische Bergleute'; Dinić, *Srpske zemlje*, pp. 113–20, 400–9.
53 Jireček, 'Staat und Gesellschaft', (ii), pp. 63–4. The reference is in *Paradiso*, canto 19, lines 140–2: for the text of a Venetian decree against Serbian imitations of Venetian grossi, see Toynbee, *Dictionary*, s.v. 'Rascia'. These coins were in fact from the first Serbian mint, at Brskovo, in Montenegro.
54 Radojčić, ed., *Zakonik* (tr. Burr, 'Code of Dušan'), arts. 82 (herdsmen in villages), 197 (winter grazing), 183 (shepherds before judges); the suggestion is by Burr, p. 138 n.
55 *Ibid.*, art. 77. The construction here is ambiguous: it need not mean only the brawling of Vlachs against Albanians, but could also mean any brawling among Vlachs or Albanians.
56 Dragomir, 'Vlahii din Serbia', pp. 280, 287; Buda *et al.*, *Burime*, vol. 2, pp. 142 n., 147.
57 Dragomir, 'Vlahii din Serbia', p. 285; Vlainac, *Verhältnisse*, pp. 260–75.
58 Buda *et al.*, *Burime*, p. 141. Possibly the daughters of rich Vlach shepherds had dowries big enough to tempt the sons of minor landowners.
59 Dragomir, 'Vlahii din Serbia', p. 283 (charter); Buda *et al.*, *Burime*, vol. 2, p. 145 (Surdul).
60 Vlainac, *Verhältnisse*, pp. 275–6.
61 See the listings in Vukanović, *Srbi na Kosovu*, vol. 1.
62 D. Kostić, 'Miloš Kopilić', pp. 241–2.
63 For a summary presentation of this argument see Pulaha, 'On the Presence'.
64 S. Stanojević, 'Lična imena'. An example of the power of fashion might be the popularity of the name 'Natasha' in late twentieth-century England. But this name entered English culture from books, films and television programmes; personal contacts with Russians were not needed. It is hard to

imagine how a fashion for Vlach and Albanian names could have arisen among medieval Serbs except from personal contacts with Vlachs and Albanians.

4. The Battle and the Myth

1 Emmert, *Serbian Golgotha*, pp. 25–6 (discussing the views of Jireček and Ostrogorsky).
2 Jireček, *Geschichte der Bulgaren*, pp. 329–31 (Marica); T. Popović, *Prince Marko*, p. 18.
3 See above, Chapter 3, n. 21. Lazar also persuaded the Greek Church finally to recognize the legitimacy of the Serbian Patriarchate.
4 On all these complexities see Fine, *Late Medieval Balkans*, pp. 382–96.
5 Reinert, 'From Niš to Kosovo', p. 192.
6 Decei, *Istoria imperiului*, p. 52.
7 Oikonomides, 'Turks in Europe', pp. 159–62.
8 Jireček, 'Staat und Gesellschaft', (ii), p. 58 n. 'Yeni' means 'new' in Turkish; 'Yunan' means 'Greece'. Lipljan is the town south of Prishtina.
9 Mavromatis, *La Fondation*, p. 75 (2,000 Cumans); Jireček, 'Staat und Gesellschaft', (i), p. 78.
10 Fine, *Late Medieval Balkans*, pp. 293–309, 322–6.
11 Reinert, 'From Niš to Kosovo', pp. 170–9. (Reinert's marvellously detailed study supersedes all previous accounts.) On Neşri, the most influential Ottoman historian (not only on Ottomans, but also, thanks to the large-scale borrowing from him by the sixteenth-century Dutch historian Leunclavius, on all European writers), see Babinger, *Geschichtsschreiber*, pp. 38–9; Ménage, *Neshri's History*.
12 Aktepe, 'Kosova', p. 870.
13 Reinert, 'From Niš to Kosovo', pp. 191–4.
14 Hopf, *Chroniques*, p. 273.
15 Islami and Frashëri, *Historia e Shqipërisë*, p. 238; Pollo and Buda, *Historia e popullit*, vol. 1, p. 222 (Albanian historians); Reinert, 'From Niš to Kosovo', pp. 170–2 (Neşri); Gelcich, *La Zedda*, pp. 154–6 (Ulcinj). The Balshas were probably of Albanian stock (see above, Chapter 3, n. 33), but culturally Serbianized to a large degree: they had been Orthodox for a long time, and only converted to Catholicism once or twice for political reasons (Jireček, 'Skutari', pp. 239–40).
16 Olesnicki, 'Turski izvori', pp. 64, 73; Pulaha, ed., *Lufta shqiptaro-turke*, p. 80. See also Leunclavius (using Neşri), *Historiae*, p. 297. The popular tradition that a contingent of Croats also took part, under their Ban, Ivan Horvat (Jireček, *Geschichte der Bulgaren*, p. 343), is not supported by these texts.

Later Ottoman historians also added Poles: Pulaha, ed., *Lufta shqiptaro-turke*, pp. 143, 255. Their presence is accepted by one modern Turkish military historian: Mükerrem, *Türk ordusunun*, p. 23.

17 Bašagić, 'Najstarija vijest', p. 97.

18 Pulaha, ed., *Lufta shqiptaro-turke*, p. 84 (Leunclavius, *Historiae*, pp. 293–4).

19 E.g. Jireček, *Geschichte der Bulgaren*, p. 343; Decei, *Istoria imperiului*, p. 54. They certainly took part in a later battle, in 1395, at which they were both killed.

20 Minerbetti, 'Cronica', in Tartinius, ed., *Rerum italicarum scriptores*, vol. 2, cols. 182, 184.

21 Reinert, 'From Niš to Kosovo', p. 203.

22 Braun, *Kosovo: die Schlacht*, p. 30.

23 Boué, *La Turquie*, vol. 3, pp. 192–3 (Mirdita story); Hecquard, *Histoire*, pp. 183–4, 233–4 (Këlmendi and Mirdita stories, suggesting the former refers to participation in Vuk Branković's treason, and doubting the latter); Agaj, *Miloshi*, p. 14 (relating Mirdita story told by Gjon Mark Gjonaj, 'kapidan' of the Mirdita). Another writer, however, recorded the tradition that the Këlmendi fought against Murat: Seiner, *Gliederung*, p. 14.

24 Pulaha, ed., *Lufta shqiptaro-turke*, pp. 83 (Neşri), 42 (Uruc).

25 Mükerrem, *Türk ordusunun*, pp. 22–3; Decei, *Istoria imperiului*, p. 54; Shaw and Shaw, *History*, vol. 1, p. 21.

26 Estimates by Tomac and Škrivanić: Emmert, *Serbian Golgotha*, p. 56; Fine, *Late Medieval Balkans*, p. 410 (the leading authority). The figure of 100,000 apparently derives from the chronicler Şukrullah, who wrote in 1457: Pulaha, ed., *Lufta shqiptaro-turke*, p. 31; Olesnicki, 'Turski izvori', p. 73. There are some valuable comments about the sizes of armies in the following century in Rázsó, 'Mercenary Army', pp. 129–30, pointing out that Charles VII's French army in 1445 had fewer than 30,000 men, and that Charles the Bold of Burgundy (the richest ruler in Europe) fought with 10–15,000.

27 Pulaha, ed., *Lufta shqiptaro-turke*, pp. 85–6; Leunclavius, *Historiae*, pp. 291–2. Camels may not have been such a novelty to the Serbs (or their horses): their use had spread through the Byzantine Empire as far as Prilep in Macedonia (Jireček, 'Staat und Gesellschaft', (ii), p. 28). On Gazi Evrenoz, member of a leading military family from Karası (on the Anatolian side of the Dardanelles), see Mélikoff, 'Ewrenos'.

28 Emmert, *Serbian Golgotha*, p. 46 (letter); Blagojević, 'Vojno-istorijske rekon-strukcije', pp. 16–17 (military practice, summarizing the studies by Tomac and Škrivanić).

29 Pulaha, ed., *Lufta shqiptaro-turke*, p. 86 (Leunclavius, *Historiae*, p. 297).

30 The letters (one of them written as if by Murat) are described in Langlès, 'Notice', pp. 671–2; translated in Wickerhauser, *Wegweiser*, pp. 232–9;

accepted as genuine by Gibbons, *Foundation*, p. 181, and D. Subotić, *Yugoslav Ballads*, p. 75; and were shown to be forgeries by Olesnicki (see Beldiceanu-Steinherr, *Recherches*, pp. 43–4).

31 Pulaha, ed., *Lufta shqiptaro-turke*, pp. 87–9 (Leunclavius, *Historiae*, pp. 299–301).

32 Emmert, *Serbian Golgotha*, pp. 73–4. Zirojević dates this text of the Peć chronicle to 1402: 'Kosovo u pamćenju', p. 10. If, however, Braun is right in suggesting that it was written soon after 1391 (*Kosovo: die Schlacht*, pp. 30–1), then we should remember that Peć was still under the rule of Vuk Branković at that time.

33 Pacheco, ed., *Història de Jacob*, p. 147, ll. 21–6.

34 Konstantin of Kostenec, *Den serbiske Despot*, p. 93; Ćirković, 'Serbia on the Eve', p. 4.

35 Mihailović, *Memoirs*, p. 47.

36 This source is the anonymous Italian translation of the Byzantine chronicler Ducas: see Emmert, *Serbian Golgotha*, pp. 98–100; Spremić, 'Die Kosovo-Schlacht', p. 249 (coins).

37 Zirojević, 'Kosovo u pamćenju', p. 11.

38 See for example the 'Popijevka o kosovskom boju', the earliest recorded Kosovo poem, in Miletich, ed. and tr., *Bugarštica*, pp. 12–31.

39 Emmert, *Serbian Golgotha*, p. 196. In the German's account there is no mention of treachery; the sons-in-law argue about who will fight best against the Turks, and one of them assassinates Murat in order to win the argument.

40 Rački, 'Izvještaj Marina Bizzia', p. 121. On the confusions between 1389 and 1448 see Koljević, *Epic*, pp. 59, 155.

41 On Vuk's vassalage, and on conflicting stories of his death, see Fine, *Late Medieval Balkans*, pp. 412, 425.

42 On all these events see Spremić, 'Die Kosovo-Schlacht', pp. 240–8.

43 Bašagić, 'Najstarija vijest', p. 97 (Olesnicki, 'Turski izvori', p. 61).

44 Olesnicki, 'Turski izvori', p. 65.

45 *Ibid.*, pp. 94–5. The rest of Olesnicki's theory, involving a 'court' tradition and a 'popular' tradition in the town of Edirne, seems over-elaborate; for sensible criticisms of it see Emmert, *Serbian Golgotha*, pp. 91–2.

46 Miletich, ed. and tr., *Bugarštica*, p. 25.

47 Braun, *Kosovo: die Schlacht*, p. 70.

48 Konstantin of Kostenec, *Den serbiske Despot*, p. 88.

49 Rootham, *Kossovo*, p. 18; for other examples see D. Kostić, 'Starost pes-ništva', p. 12.

50 Ćorović, 'Siluan i Danilo', esp. p. 89 (tr. in Matejić and Milivojević, eds. and trs., *Anthology*, pp. 122–5). The influence of the epic is identified by Kämpfer, 'Der Kult', p. 94.

51 Emmert, *Serbian Golgotha*, p. 46.

52 Braun, *Kosovo: die Schlacht*, p. 89.

53 Tartinius, ed., *Rerum italicarum scriptores*, vol. 2, cols. 183–4.

54 Emmert, *Serbian Golgotha*, p. 58.

55 Miquel y Planas, ed., *La Història*, pp. viii–ix (based on a historical text, perhaps Greek); Pacheco, ed., *Història*, p. 10 (its historical fidelity is 'almost absolute, down to the smallest details'); Carbonell *et al.*, *Literatura catalana*, p. 135 (Ottoman customs); Molas and Massot i Muntaner, *Diccionari*, p. 313 (based on a Greek or Turkish chronicle); Badia, ed., *La Història*, p. 13 (based on an anti-Bayezit Turkish text). Another writer suggests, on linguistic grounds, that it was based on an original text in Arabic: Sola-Solé, 'La Història'.

56 Pacheco, ed., *Història*, pp. 141–7.

57 See Wertner, 'Herren von Gara', pp. 80–4.

58 Miletich, ed. and tr., *Bugarštica*, p. 14: 'Od ugarske gospode i od braće Ugovića' ('From the Hungarian lords and from the Ugović brothers'). Koljević comments on this 'close acoustic connection': *Epic*, p. 159. In this poem Lazar is described as leading a Hungarian army, which again suggests a confusion with the battle of 1448. Possibly all the Hungarian elements in this song could be explained on that basis. But on the other hand, if there had already been a Hungarian element in the story of the battle of 1389, this would help to explain why the stories of the two battles were so liable to amalgamation.

59 Bogdan, 'Ein Beitrag', p. 529.

60 Chalcocondylas, *Historiarum*, p. 54; Mihailović, *Memoirs*, p. 46; Leunclavius, *Historiae*, p. 304; Kuripešić, *Itinerarium*, p. 47; Ljubić, ed., *Commissiones*, vol. 3, p. 170; Palerne, *Peregrinations*, p. 506; Evliya Çelebi, *Putopis*, p. 267. The form 'Comnene' given by Palerne probably arises from a confusion with a Mihailo Komnen Crnojević, lord of Novo Brdo under the Turks in 1502, who apparently claimed descent from the Byzantine Comnenus dynasty (Urošević, *Etnički procesi*, p. 35).

61 Drançolli, 'Njoftime burimore', (i), notes that the change was first made in 1765; see also Subotić, *Yugoslav Ballads*, p. 88. This bogus etymology was supported by Vuk Karadžić in his Serbian dictionary of 1818 (*Dela*, vol. 5, pp. 476–7).

62 D. Kostić, 'Miloš Kopilić'; Drançolli, 'Njoftime burimore'.

63 D. Subotić, *Yugoslav Ballads*, p. 88.

64 Elezović, ed. and tr., *Ogledalo sveta*, p. 70, n. 3; Pulaha, ed., *Lufta shqiptaro-turke*, p. 86. Pulaha identifies him with a northern Albanian nobleman, Dhimitër Jonima (p. 75); but there is no clear reason for this, beyond the shared first name and the rough similarity of 'Jon-' and 'Yund'. Olesnicki's suggestion that 'Yund' might be a scribal error for 'Jug' is also unconvincing: 'Turski izvori', pp. 81–2.

65 For this information about Hungarian shamanism I am indebted to Dr

Marian Wenzel, who has some important unpublished work on the subject. She also tells me that the earliest Hungarian tombstones bear a feature which is probably a stylized version of a horse's head.

66 Miletich, ed. and tr., *Bugarštica*, pp. 28–9.

67 Pulaha, ed., *Lufta shqiptaro-turke*, p. 54; Braun, *Kosovo: die Schlacht*, p. 30.

68 Pacheco, ed., *Història*, p. 147, referring to 'Enabechsu Bey': on Ayna beg or Ayna bey see Mükerrem, *Türk ordusunun*, p. 23.

69 Emmert, *Serbian Golgotha*, pp. 46 (Tvrtko), 49–50 (de Mézières); Grégoire, 'L'Opinion byzantine', and Ćirković, 'Dimitrije Kidon' (Byzantines); Radojičić, 'Pohvala', p. 248 (pohvalas); Kuripešić, *Itinerarium*, p. 49 (Slovene).

70 Ćorović, 'Siluan i Danilo', p. 94 (religious text); Braun, *Kosovo: die Schlacht*, p. 12, and Mihaljčić, *Lazar Hrebeljanović*, p. 121 (chronicles).

71 Konstantin of Kostenec, *Den serbiske Despot*, p. 88; Pertusi, *Martino Segono*, p. 92.

72 On the early development of the cult see Radojičić, 'Izbor patriarha', and Mihaljčić, *Lazar Hrebeljanović*, pp. 127–40; on the texts see Kämpfer, 'Der Kult'. Key texts are translated in Matejić and Milivojević, eds. and trs., *Anthology*, pp. 112–26. Some scholars place the reburial of Lazar in the period 1392–8: see Fine, *Late Medieval Balkans*, p. 414.

73 Emmert, *Serbian Golgotha*, p. 63 (from the 'slovo' attributed to Patriarch Danilo, on which see Kämpfer, 'Der Kult', p. 94).

74 Mihaljčić, *Lazar Hrebeljanović*, pp. 177–8.

75 Zirojević, 'Kosovo u pamćenju', p. 16.

76 See Koljević, *Epic*, pp. 12–30; D. Kostić, 'Starost pesništva'; Gorup, 'Kosovo and Epic Poetry'.

77 Braun, *Kosovo: die Schlacht*, p. 101.

78 On Karadžić see Wilson, *Life and Times*, esp. pp. 190–207; on Njegoš see Emmert, *Serbian Golgotha*, pp. 123–4. Also important was Jovan Sterija Popović (1806–59), on whom see Mihalovich, 'Tradition of Kosovo', p. 147.

79 Zirojević, 'Kosovo u pamćenju', pp. 19–20 (1889), 21 n. (film). For studies of the way in which the 1889 anniversary was used to arouse nationalist feelings among the Serbs of Bosnia and Croatia, see Kraljačić, 'Der 500. Jahrestag', and Pejin, 'Die Begehung'.

80 Karadžić, *Dela*, vol. 2, p. 214.

81 Emmert, *Serbian Golgotha*, p. 107.

82 See Zirojević, 'Kosovo u pamćenju', p. 12.

83 Bataković, *Kosovo Chronicles*, p. 35.

5. The last years of Medieval Serbian Kosovo: 1389–1455

1 N. Pavlović, *Despot Stefan*, pp. 47–8; Fine, *Late Medieval Balkans*, pp. 411–12.

2 Gibbons, *Foundation*, p. 183 (claiming, incorrectly, that this was the last occasion on which a Sultan contracted a formal marriage).

3 N. Pavlović, *Despot Stefan*, p. 50; Gibbons, *Foundation*, p. 183.

4 Fine, *Late Medieval Balkans*, pp. 424–5; Shaw and Shaw, *History*, vol. 1, p. 33.

5 Konstantin of Kostenec, *Den serbiske Despot*, p. 97.

6 Kovačević-Kojić, 'Priština', p. 46.

7 Dinić, *Srpske zemlje*, pp. 159–60; Purković, *Knez i despot*, p. 35 (suggesting the expulsion may have been as early as 1394); Fine, *Late Medieval Balkans*, p. 425.

8 Dinić, *Srpske zemlje*, pp. 163–4.

9 Jireček, 'Staat und Gesellschaft', (iv), pp. 9–10 (Zvečan, Trepça); Kovačević-Kojić, 'Priština', p. 49 (Gluhavica).

10 See Beldiceanu, 'Les Roumains', p. 443. The early Ottoman chronicles quoted by Beldiceanu refer to the soldiers of 'Laz-oğlu' (i.e. the son of Lazar) and 'Wlq-oğlu' (i.e. the son of Vuk); Beldiceanu misinterprets 'Wlq' as a reference to Vlachs or Wallachians.

11 Marlowe, *Tamburlaine the Great, Part I*, III. iii. 162–3.

12 Gibbons, *Foundation*, p. 256 (quotation); S. Stanojević, 'Die Biographie', p. 428 (ransom).

13 Konstantin of Kostenec, *Den serbiske Despot*, p. 106.

14 On all these events see S. Stanojević, 'Die Biographie', pp. 429–44; Fine, *Late Medieval Balkans*, pp. 500–6; on the Hungarian raid against Prishtina see Kovačević-Kojić, 'Priština', p. 48.

15 Fine, *Late Medieval Balkans*, pp. 508–9, 516–17, 522–5.

16 Jireček, 'Staat und Gesellschaft', (iv), p. 8; Dinić, *Srpske zemlje*, p. 174.

17 Purković, *Knez i despot*, p. 20 (book-lover); Lazarević, *Slova i natpisi* (texts).

18 On Konstantin see S. Stanojević, 'Die Biographie'; on all these authors see Pertusi, *Martino Segono*, pp. 24–6.

19 Konstantin of Kostenec, *Den serbiske Despot*, p. 110.

20 de la Broquière, *Voyage*, p. 214 and n. The Serbian 'Novo Brdo' and German 'Neuberg' both mean 'new mountain'; 'Berg' also means 'mine', as in 'Bergmann', 'miner'.

21 K. Kostić, *Naši novi gradovi*, pp. 134–5; Rizaj, *Kosova gjatë shekujve*, pp. 219–20.

22 Dinić, *Iz dubrovačkog arhiva*, vol. 1, pp. 35–90 (names on pp. 48, 50, 51, 64, 69). It is almost incomprehensible that the Serbian scholar Atanasije Urošević can refer to this source (*Etnički procesi*, p. 25) and yet state, in the same work (p. 17), that there were no Albanians in Eastern Kosovo before the end of the seventeenth century.

23 Kaleshi, 'Shenime', pp. 503–4.

24 Kovačević-Kojić, 'Priština', pp. 49, 57–60, 67–8.

25 Dinić, *Iz dubrovačkog arhiva*, vol. 1, p. 2; Rizaj, *Kosova gjatë shekujve*, p. 256; Kovačević-Kojić, 'Priština', p. 72.

26 On all these events see Fine, *Late Medieval Balkans*, pp. 526–31; Dinić, *Srpske zemlje*, pp. 174–5.

27 Mirdita, 'Sudjelovanje vojske', esp. p. 15.

28 Engel, 'János Hunyadi', pp. 106–7.

29 Ćirković, 'Kosovo u srednjem veku', p. 45.

30 Fine, *Late Medieval Balkans*, pp. 550–1.

31 Islami and Frashëri, *Historia e Shqipërisë*, p. 268. For the traditional story see Gegaj, *L'Albanie*, pp. 45–6; otherwise Gegaj's book remains one of the most valuable accounts of Skanderbeg's career.

32 Pall, 'Skanderbeg et Janco', p. 92.

33 *Ibid.*; Pall, 'Les Relations', pp. 127–8; Radonić, *Zapadna Evropa*, pp. 255–6. Necati Salim gives Hunyadi a total of 50–100,000 (*Türk ordusunun*, p. 8), but most other historians agree on 30–34,000. However, the contemporary report by Pasquale de Sorgo from Hunyadi's camp says 72,000: M. Kostić, 'Opis vojske', p. 84. I have not been able to locate a copy of the only monograph on Hunyadi's army, Aurel Decei's *Oastea lui Iancu Huniade*; but Decei's conclusions are presented in his *Istoria imperiului*, p. 96, where he puts the estimated figure at 50,000.

34 Engel, 'János Hunyadi', pp. 112–13.

35 M. Kostić, 'Opis vojske'. Kostić notes that Hunyadi later complained to the Ragusan Senate that Sorgo had betrayed him, and that the Senate, accepting the charge, made new regulations about Ragusans acting in the service of foreign powers (p. 90).

36 *Ibid.*, pp. 85, 86.

37 Chalcocondylas, *Historiarum*, p. 355; Pall, 'Skanderbeg et Janco', p. 94; Radonić, *Zapadna Evropa*, pp. 256–7. Radonić puts the Turkish army at 150,000; the early chronicler Bonfini gave it as 80,000 (*Rerum ungaricarum*, vol. 3, p. 161); Salim says 50–150,000 (*Türk ordusunun*, p. 7).

38 Pall, 'Skanderbeg et Janco', p. 95.

39 Chalcocondylas, *Historiarum*, pp. 358–9; Bonfini, *Rerum ungaricarum*, vol. 3, pp. 160–6.

40 Radonić, *Zapadna Evropa*, p. 260; Decei, *Istoria imperiului*, p. 96.

41 Mihailović, *Memoirs*, pp. 9, 218 n. 4. It should also be noted that in Aug. 1453 Branković sent envoys to the Sultan's court to give alms to the Christian prisoners and pay a ransom for 100 Orthodox nuns: Babinger, *Mehmed*, p. 103.

42 Babinger, *Mehmed*, p. 109; Mihailović, *Memoirs*, p. 219 n. 1.

43 Babinger, *Mehmed*, pp. 126–7; Mihailović, *Memoirs*, p. 99 (eye-witness).

44 Kaleshi, 'Shenime', p. 498; Babinger, *Mehmed*, p. 127. This is the traditionally accepted date. According to Yastrebov, Prizren was taken in 1455

by Ahmet-bey, the son of Evrenoz ('Stara Serbiia', p. 50). Birken states that a sancak of Prizren was established in 1455: *Die Provinzen*, p. 58. However, some writers date the conquest of Prizren to 1458 (e.g. Mehlan, 'Über die Bedeutung', p. 401). Skënder Rizaj has suggested that it was conquered several times, and finally in 1459; and the town of Peć, which may have been under the Dukagjin family, was finally brought under direct Ottoman rule in 1462: *Kosova gjatë shekujve*, pp. 32–3, 60.

45 On these events see Fine, *Late Medieval Balkans*, pp. 268–75; Babinger, *Mehmed*, pp. 138–44, 163–4.

6. Early Ottoman Kosovo: 1450s–1580s

1 On the askeri–raya distinction see Vasić, 'Social Structure', p. 45; Rizaj, 'Pravni položaj', p. 199; Faroqhi, *Kultur*, p. 72.

2 The best general study is Goodwin, *Janissaries*; on the devşirme see also Papoulia, *Ursprung*.

3 See Kunt, 'Ethnic Solidarity'.

4 Sugar, *Southeastern Europe*, p. 58. A document of 1646/7 extended this privilege to Muslim Albanians too (Rizaj, *Kosova gjatë shekujve*, p. 373); but by then the devşirme system was beginning to break down, and the Janissaries were already starting to turn into a hereditary Muslim social caste.

5 Goodwin, *Janissaries*, p. 40 (uprising); Rizaj, 'Pravni položaj', p. 203 (Novo Brdo).

6 Rizaj, *Kosova gjatë shekujve*, pp. 285–6, 293. For further details of prominent Albanian officials, including Mehmet II's tutor, see Rizaj, 'Transferimet, deportimet', p. 149.

7 Faroqhi, 'Rural Society' (ii), pp. 125–6. On the general legal-administrative conditions see Cvetkova, *Les Institutions*, pp. 8–17; Mutafčieva, *Agrarian Relations*, pp. 13–50.

8 Inalcık, 'Od Stefana Dušana', pp. 36 (Albania), 31 (Skopje), 32 (Vuk). These registers have been published respectively by Inalcık (*Sûret-i defter-i*), Šabanović (*Krajište Isa-bega*) and Hadžibegić *et al.* (*Oblast Brankovića*). See also Inalcık, 'Timariotes chrétiens', and Rizvanolli, 'Disa të dhëna'.

9 Inalcık, 'Timariotes chrétiens', p. 130.

10 Kiel, *Art and Society*, p. 69.

11 Inalcık, *Ottoman Empire*, pp. 70–5.

12 Heyd, *Studies*, pp. 95–131 (pp. 102–3 on the discount for 'unbelievers').

13 Kiel, *Art and Society*, p. 59.

14 Heyd, *Studies*, pp. 177 (quotation), 212 (Heyd's judgement). Machiel Kiel declares: 'I am convinced that the Ottoman system of administrating law in

the Classical period of the Empire (1300–1600) compares favourably with that of feudal Europe': *Art and Society*, p. 59. On Celalzade see Rizaj, *Kosova gjatë shekujve*, p. 265.

15 The best account of all these changes is Rizaj, *Kosova gjatë shekujve*, pp. 42–65; on inclusion in the eyalet of Buda see Kaleshi, 'Shenime', p. 501. For the period 1550–1650 see also Kunt, *Sancaktan eyalete*, pp. 125–7. Some of the details given in Birken, *Die Provinzen*, pp. 54–60, are not reliable.

16 The figure for 1490 is from Rizaj, *Kosova gjatë shekujve*, p. 400. Rizaj also gives a figure of 264,810 Christians for the 1480s (p. 398), but then allows *c*.240,000 for the missing categories, to produce a total estimate of *c*.500,000; this seems excessive. Zirojević gives the figure of 61,718 Christian households for 1488/9: 'Prvi vekovi', p. 92. Pulaha gives a much lower figure of 28,037 households for this period (*Popullsia*, pp. 640, 648); the discrepancy has not been explained.

17 Pulaha, *Popullsia*, p. 650.

18 Cvetkova, *Les Institutions*, p. 45; Mutafčieva, *Agrarian Relations*, p. 155 (quoting definition by Ömer Lütfi Barkan).

19 Mutafčieva, *Agrarian Relations*, pp. 174–7; Thëngjilli, *Renta feudale*, pp. 51–74. Thëngjilli notes (p. 67) that in the sixteenth century the ispence was 22 akçes; in the fifteenth century it was 25 (Inalcık, *Osmanlı imparatorluğu*, p. 56). This was slightly less than the cost of one sheep (Rizaj, 'Pravni položaj', p. 206).

20 Cvetkova, *Les Institutions*, p. 48. Cvetkova discusses the Byzantine origins of several feudal dues and taxes in 'Influence', pp. 245–8.

21 Thëngjilli, *Renta feudale*, pp. 79–91 (feudal dues, market), 95–114 (poll-tax), 122–47 (extraordinary taxes). Inalcık gives a slightly different classification of the feudal dues: *Osmanlı imparatorluğu*, pp. 31–54. Sućeska notes that the extraordinary taxes were collected every five years until the end of the sixteenth century, becoming more frequent and oppressive thereafter: 'Promjene', pp. 79–80.

22 Inalcık, 'Ottoman Decline', pp. 338–40.

23 Cvetkova, *Les Institutions*, pp. 58–9; Thëngjilli, *Renta feudale*, pp. 76–7; Inalcık, *Ottoman Empire*, p. 111.

24 Mutafčieva, *Agrarian Relations*, p. 157.

25 *Ibid.*, p. 140 (citing Barkan).

26 Hadžibegić *et al.*, eds., *Oblast Brankovića*, vol. 2, p. ix.

27 McGowan, 'Food Supply and Taxation' (surplus); Aymard, *Venise*, pp. 49–50 (Ragusan merchants), 125–6 (prohibitions).

28 Rizaj, *Kosova gjatë shekujve*, pp. 90–3.

29 Zirojević, 'Prvi vekovi', p. 77; for the prohibition in Süleyman's code see Heyd, *Studies*, p. 111.

30 Vasić, *Martolosi*, and 'Social Structure', pp. 60–2; Stojanovski, *Raja*,

pp. 14–41; Adanır, 'Heiduckentum', pp. 80–1; Kiel, *Art and Society*, pp. 74–5.

31 Stojanovski, *Dervendžistvoto*; Kiel, *Art and Society*, pp. 93–101; Zirojević, 'Prvi vekovi', pp. 58–9 (Kaçanik, Rugova, Këlmendi); Thëngjilli, *Renta feudale*, pp. 43, 206 (Malësi). Adanır notes similar road-guarding duties in Dušan's code: 'Heiduckentum', p. 91.

32 Stojanovski, *Raja*, pp. 80–111 (falconer status); Zirojević, 'Prvi vekovi', p. 66 (falconers in Kosovo); Vasić, 'Social Structure', pp. 65–6 (miners, ammunition-makers).

33 Babinger, *Mehmed*, p. 127.

34 Anhegger, *Beiträge*, vol. 1, pp. 90–103; Rizaj, 'Rudari'; Kiel, *Art and Society*, p. 120.

35 Elezović, ed. and tr., *Turski spomenici*, pp. 39–43.

36 Zirojević, 'Prvi vekovi', p. 71; Anhegger, *Beiträge*, vol. 1, pp. 58–60, 80–1. Other local mints were at Skopje and Kratovo: Rizaj, *Kosova gjatë shekujve*, pp. 157–76.

37 Rizaj, *Kosova gjatë shekujve*, p. 223 (efforts); Zirojević, 'Prvi vekovi', p. 75 (Prizren); Anhegger, *Beiträge*, vol. 1, pp. 8–18 (laws), vol. 2 (texts of laws); Rizaj, *Rudarstvo*, p. 35 (1536).

38 Murphey, 'Silver Production', p. 84.

39 Rizaj, *Kosova gjatë shekujve*, p. 194; Tadić, 'Dubrovčani'. Rizaj also notes a Ragusan colony in Trepça in the 1540s (p. 258).

40 Pulaha, *Popullsia*, p. 650.

41 Rizaj, *Kosova gjatë shekujve*, pp. 249–50 (Prizren, Kukli-bey), 263–5 (Vuçitërn); Kaleshi and Rexhep, 'Prizrenac Kukli Beg'.

42 Pulaha, 'Qytetet', p. 14.

43 Rizaj, *Kosova gjatë shekujve*, p. 178.

44 Zirojević, 'Prvi vekovi', pp. 82–3; Shkodra, *Esnafet*, pp. 63–4.

45 Šufflay, 'Städte und Burgen', p. 47; Zirojević, 'Prvi vekovi', p. 82.

46 Šufflay, 'Städte und Burgen', p. 46 (coastal towns); Shkodra, *Esnafet*, p. 144 (lonca); Halimi, 'Esnafet', p. 111 (Sarajevo). Zija Shkodra, the leading authority on this subject, comes down in favour of the continuity thesis. He also notes a tradition which says that when Mehmet II conquered Albania he issued a decree that the existing guilds be allowed to continue (p. 83).

47 On the peculiarities of the Ottoman vakıf see Barnes, *Introduction*, esp. pp. 39–49.

48 Lleshi, *Prizren, Priština*, part 1, pp. 87 n., 88.

49 See Elsie, *History*, vol. 1, pp. 91–2 (Mesihi); Kaleshi, *Kontributi*, pp. 22–5 (Mesihi, Suzi); Olesnicki, 'Suzi Čelebi'; Mujezinović, 'Natpisi' (Suzi); Rizaj, *Kosova gjatë shekujve*, p. 265 (Celalzade). See also Redžepagić, *Zhvillimi*, pp. 42–3.

50 Kaleshi and Rexhep, 'Prizrenac Kukli Beg', p. 165.

51 Željazkova, *Razprostranenie*, pp. 118–20.
52 Rizaj, *Kosova gjatë shekujve*, pp. 221–3; Tërnava notes, however, that the Muslim mahalles in Novo Brdo were larger than the Christian ones: 'Përhapja', p. 47.
53 Tërnava, 'Përhapja', p. 48; Pulaha, *Popullsia*, p. 621.
54 Some historians believe that German was still being spoken in these mines in the late sixteenth century: Mehlan, 'Über die Bedeutung', p. 392. German family names can be found in the tax registers of the 1570s, such as the 'Šuman' (Schumann) family of Trepça (Pešikan, 'Imenoslov kosovskih sredešta', p. 126); but the evidence of their first names suggests they had already been Slavicized.
55 Pulaha, 'Qytetet', p. 26.
56 Inalcık, 'Osmanlı imperatorluğunun kuruluş', p. 641.
57 Rizaj, *Kosova gjatë shekujve*, pp. 345–6. The northernmost Yürük settlement was at Ovče Polje, in Macedonia (Truhelka, 'Über die Yürüken', p. 92; cf. Sokolski, 'Islamizacija', p. 80), though a few were later recorded in the Novi Pazar district (Gökbilgin, *Rumeli'de Yürükler*, pp. 268–9). On the Yürüks see also the discussion of Kosovo's Turkish minority in Chapter 11.
58 Sokolski, 'Islamizacija', pp. 81–4. Sokolski notes (p. 86) that this method probably underestimates the true number of converts. Tërnava lists 185 Abdullahs or sons of Abdullah from a register of the sancak of Vuçitërn of 1566–74: 'Përhapja', pp. 49–54. On the convention see Lowry, 'Changes', p. 29.
59 Babinger, ed., *Dernschwam's Tagebuch*, pp. 140–1.
60 Željazkova, *Razprostranenie*, p. 161.
61 *Ibid.*, pp. 57–9, noting also that the vakıfs acted as centres for Muslim proselytizing. Vakıfs were important estate-owners in Macedonia, but much less so in Kosovo and the Serb lands: Mutafčieva and Dimitrov, 'Agrarverhältnisse', p. 693.
62 See Cahen and Hardy, 'Djizya'; Hadžibegić, 'Džizja'.
63 Hupchick, *Bulgarians*, p. 35.
64 Heyd, *Studies*, p. 287; Heyd notes that this rule was reconfirmed a century later, in 1587.
65 See Cahen, 'Dhimma'; Tritton, *Caliphs*; Vryonis, *Decline*, pp. 224–6; Lewis, *Jews of Islam*, pp. 1–66.
66 Kaleshi, 'Shenime', p. 498; Zirojević, *Crkve*, p. 25; Rizaj, *Kosova gjatë shekujve*, p. 236.
67 Kiel, *Art and Society*, p. 168. Zirojević adds that fortified churches were especially liable to conversion: *Crkve*, p. 25.
68 Tritton, *Caliphs*, pp. 37–60, and Heyd, *Studies*, p. 284 (regulations); Zirojević, *Crkve*, pp. 27–31 (Patriarchate).
69 Kiel, *Art and Society*, pp. 152–5. Some of the properties of the monastery of Ravanica were made into an ecclesiastical timar, with an income of 4,000

akçes and the duty of providing one armed soldier: Djurdjev, 'Serbian Church', p. 294.

70 Mihaljčić, *Lazar Hrebeljanović*, pp. 347–8; Palerne, *Peregrinations*, p. 508. For similar accounts of Mileševa and Peć see Slijepčević, *Istorija crkve*, vol. 1, pp. 306–7.

71 On all these questions see L. Stanojević, 'Srpska crkva'; Slijepčević, *Istorija crkve*, vol. 1, pp. 310–23; Djurdjev, 'Serbian Church'.

72 Jireček, 'Der Grossvezier'; Samardžić, *Mehmed Sokolović*; Slijepčević, *Istorija crkve*, vol. 1, pp. 325–42 (criticizing Jireček for the 'sentiment' theory).

73 Kiel, *Art and Society*, p. 151 n.

74 See the studies by Muhamet Tërnava and Selami Pulaha listed in the Bibliography.

75 P. Contarini, *Diario*, p. 20. Some (but surely not all) of these may have been Albanian too.

76 Tërnava, 'Migrimet e popullsisë', pp. 304–9; Pulaha, 'Qytetet', pp. 36–7 (towns: some of the Bosnians were Orthodox, others Muslim).

77 Pulaha, 'Qytetet', pp. 35–6, and *Popullsia*, pp. 647–8.

78 Hadžibegić *et al.*, eds., *Oblast Brankovića*, vol. 1, pp. 24, 78. For a discussion of the Albanian names in this register see Handžić, 'Nekoliko vijesti', pp. 202–4.

79 Pulaha, 'Qytetet', p. 29.

80 *Ibid.*, p. 27 (Peć); Pulaha, 'Të dhëna për krahinën e Opoljes', p. 105 (Gjon, Gjonja). For Orthodox names in Albanianized forms see Pulaha, 'Krahinat verilindore', p. 205.

81 Pulaha, 'Të dhëna për krahinën e Hoçës', pp. 138, 141, and 'Qytetet', pp. 25, 33.

82 Pulaha, 'Të dhëna për krahinën e Hoçës', p. 145, and 'Krahinat verilindore', p. 205. These refer only to those cases where the Muslim name retains some previous component; most Muslim names are of the form 'Hasan, son of Ahmet', and yield no such information.

83 The Serbian historian Mitar Pešikan agrees with this last point ('Imenoslov kosovskih sredešta', p. 126), though he confines the Albanian population of Western Kosovo to the Gjakova-Prizren area (p. 123).

84 Nopcsa, 'Beiträge', pp. 248–50; Durham, *Tribal Origins*, pp. 15–29.

85 Kaser, *Hirten, Kämpfer*, pp. 107–11; Pulaha, 'Formation des régions'; Thëngjilli, *Renta feudale*, pp. 43–5.

86 Stevenson, *Alasdair MacColla*, pp. 11–12. Large parts of Stevenson's valuable discussion of the emergence of the Scottish clans (pp. 8–14) could be applied almost unaltered to the Albanian phenomenon.

7. War, rebellion and religious life: 1580s–1680s

1 Goodwin, *Janissaries*, pp. 147–8; Faroqhi, 'Crisis and Change', p. 414; Pamuk, 'Money', pp. 960–1.

2 Adanır, 'Heiduckentum', esp. pp. 88–91; Faroqhi, 'Crisis and Change', pp. 413–14.

3 Inalcık, 'Military and fiscal transformation', p. 288.

4 Heyd, *Studies*, pp. 212–13.

5 Inalcık, 'Ottoman Decline', p. 344.

6 Thëngjilli, *Renta feudale*, pp. 122–47 (state taxes), 166–72 (local pashas); Sućeska, 'Promjene u sistemu'.

7 BN MS f.fr. 17193, fo. 13 (from an anonymous 'Discours sur la puissance […] de l'Empire des Turcs' (1683), a well-informed analysis of Ottoman military weakness).

8 On this complex phenomenon see Veinstein, 'Çiftlik Debate'; Inalcık, 'Emergence of Big Farms'. Çiftliks were much more common in Macedonia than in Kosovo: see Faroqhi, 'Crisis and Change', p. 450.

9 Kaleshi, 'Alcuni dati', p. 206.

10 Adanır, 'Heiduckentum', pp. 101–2; Hupchick, *Bulgarians*, p. 35.

11 PRO SP 97/19, fo. 76^v (William Winchilsea, 4/14 April 1669). This practice was also recorded in northern Albania in the seventeenth century: Gjini, *Ipeshkvia*, p. 139.

12 Giannelli, 'Documenti inediti', pp. 31–2. It is often claimed that the Archbishop, Giovanni Bruni, died in an Ottoman prison: Stadtmüller, 'Islamisierung', p. 410. In fact he was made into a galley slave, and the galley was captured by Christians who, mistaking him for a Turk, cut off his head: Jačov, ed., *Spisi tajnog arhiva*, p. 133.

13 de Gubernatis and de Turre, *Orbis seraphicus*, pp. 564b–566b (1645); Farlati, *Illyrici sacri*, vol. 7, p. 131 (1649); Radonić, *Rimska kurija*, p. 275 (1652).

14 Elezović, ed. and tr., *Turski spomenici*, pp. 337–47; cf. Tadić, 'Dubrovčani', p. 199.

15 Rizaj, 'Pravni položaj', p. 208, and *Kosova gjatë shekujve*, pp. 481–2.

16 Rizaj, *Kosova gjatë shekujve*, pp. 484, 486. For details of other tax revolts and/or hajduk actions in this period see also Rizaj, 'Pravni položaj', pp. 208–10; Zirojević, 'Prvi vekovi', pp. 98–100; and the documents in Pulaha, ed., *Qëndresa e popullit*, pp. 95–9.

17 The best survey of all the factors involved is Adanır, 'Heiduckentum'; for a valuable study of the Anatolian evidence see Barkey, *Bandits*. On the Hungarian origins see Rácz, *A Hajdúk*, pp. 12–13, 16–23.

18 Lenormant, *Turcs et monténégrins*, pp. 312–15. For general accounts of the Këlmendi see Hecquard, *Histoire*, pp. 98–107, 175–97; Bartl, 'Die Këlmendi'.

For the use of Këlmendi as Ottoman auxiliaries see de Gubernatis and de Turre, *Orbis seraphicus*, p. 567b; Thëngjilli, *Renta feudale*, pp. 206–7.

19 Tričković, 'U susret iskušenjima', p. 120; Zamputi, 'Bashkimi i maleve', pp. 76–94.

20 BAV MS Cod. Urb. Lat. 839, fos. 71ᵛ–72ᵛ.

21 Floristán Imízcoz, *Fuentes para la politica*, pp. 424–46. See also Ugolini, 'Pagine di storia', pp. 18–19. The best general study of all these projects and their diplomatic context is Bartl, *Der Westbalkan*.

22 Bartl, 'Die Albaner-Versammlung', p. 8; Zamputi, ed., *Dokumente*, vol. 3, p. 228 (1608), and 'Bashkimi i maleve', p. 75 (1620). For the text of the detailed plan drawn up in 1620 see Zamputi, ed., *Dokumente*, vol. 3, pp. 364–75.

23 Ugolini, 'Pagine di storia', pp. 19–25.

24 Islami and Frashëri, *Historia e Shqipërisë*, pp. 358–61; Theiner, ed., *Vetera monumenta slavorum*, vol. 2, pp. 111–13 ('Nicolaus Mechaensi').

25 Bartl, 'Die Albaner-Versammlung', p. 8.

26 The biography was written by a Croatian priest, Rafael Levaković, and survives in MSS in Udine and Split: see Antoljak, '"Sultan Jahja"', pp. 111–13. Antoljak emphasizes that many details can be confirmed by other archival sources. The only full-length modern biography is Catualdi, *Sultan Jahja*, which correlates Levaković's claims with many contemporary documents. (Catualdi's book, which was privately published in Trieste, is extremely rare; there are copies in the library of the Archivio di Stato, Venice, and the Bibliothèque Nationale, Paris. The latter's catalogue states that 'Catualdi' was a pseudonym for O. de Hassek.)

27 Catualdi, *Sultan Jahja*, pp. 12–97.

28 Antoljak, '"Sultan Jahja"', pp. 116 n., 117–19. For details of Jovan's negotiations with Spain and Savoy see Zamputi, ed., *Dokumente*, vol. 3, pp. 171–4, 188, 203–4, 237–41.

29 Catualdi, *Sultan Jahja*, pp. 98–101; Levaković's account is given on pp. 394–400, and reprinted in Zamputi, ed., *Dokumente*, vol. 3, pp. 306–11.

30 BAV MS Cod. Barb. Lat. 5372, fos. 139–41. This document, attributed to 'Alessandro Greco', was apparently unknown to Catualdi.

31 On the Balkan plans of the duc de Nevers, Charles de Gonzaga, who fantasized about becoming Sultan himself, see Papadopoulos, *Hê kinêsê tou douka tou Never*.

32 Ugolini, 'Pagine di storia', pp. 26–9 (details). For the other events described here see Catualdi, *Sultan Jahja*, pp. 103–4; Levaković's account is on pp. 400–6, and reprinted in Zamputi, ed., *Dokumente*, vol. 3, pp. 312–15.

33 The letter is printed in Catualdi, *Sultan Jahja*, pp. 506–10, and Zamputi, ed., *Dokumente*, vol. 3, pp. 350–9.

34 Catualdi, *Sultan Jahja*, pp. 119–212.

35 Zamputi, ed., *Relacione*, vol. 1, pp. 296–310 (Budi); Farlati, *Illyrici sacri*, vol. 7, p. 126 (Bardhi); Jačov, ed., *Spisi tajnog arhiva*, pp. 140–1 (Bogdani).

36 Giannelli, 'Documenti inediti', pp. 54–5; this number was certainly an exaggeration (p. 44). The names of the signatories are mainly Slav, but include three Albanians (p. 59).

37 See for example a report of 1599 in Cordignano, 'Geografia ecclesiastica', p. 233, and a report of 1623/4 in Zamputi, ed., *Relacione*, vol. 1, p. 336.

38 Many are published in Zamputi, ed., *Relacione*; Bartl, ed., *Quellen und Materialen*; Jačov, ed., *Spisi kongregacije*; but many remain unpublished, especially from the eighteenth and nineteenth centuries. For a valuable overview of this material see Bartl, 'Kosova and Macedonia'.

39 Cordignano summarizes these activities: 'Geografia ecclesiastica', pp. 264–5. For a report of 1650, with details of the 'ospizio' at Gashi which served Prizren, see Zamputi, ed., *Relacione*, vol. 2, pp. 392–402. These activities came under the Franciscan Province of Albania, which had been declared in 1593: Mihačević, *Schematismus*, p. 27. The fullest account of the Franciscan missions is de Gubernatis and de Turre, *Orbis seraphicus*, pp. 466–595.

40 Gjini, *Ipeshkvia*, pp. 117–18 (Prizren); Radonić, *Rimska kurija*, pp. 244–5, 373, and Dujčev, *Cattolicesimo in Bulgaria*, pp. 59–61, 70–2 (Skopje). Pjetër Bogdani's appointment was decreed in 1679, and he received the pallio in 1680 (ASCPF SOCG 482, fo. 285^r).

41 Redžepagić, *Zhvillimi i arësimit*, p. 46 (Loreto, Clementinum); de Gubernatis and de Turre, *Orbis seraphicus*, p. 504a (Bologna); Bartocetti, 'Il Collegio' (Fermo).

42 Fermendžin, 'Izprave', pp. 171–2 (Peć); ASCPF SOCG 431, fo. 154 (Janjevo). Redžepagić thinks the teaching at Janjevo was 'doubtless' in Albanian (*Zhvillimi i arësimit*, p. 49); but the Catholic community at Janjevo was mainly Slav (see above, n. 36).

43 ASCPF SOCG 482, fos. 286^v–291^r.

44 Elsie, *History*, vol. 1, pp. 59–62 (Budi), 66–70 (Bardhi), 71 (Bogdani); de Gubernatis and de Turre, *Orbis seraphicus*, p. 540b (Cittadella).

45 See Elsie, *History*, vol. 1, pp. 71–7; Rugova, *Vepra e Bogdanit*; Xholi, 'Pjetër Bogdani'.

46 Pjetër Mazrreku in Fermendžin, ed., *Acta Bosnae*, p. 398.

47 Jačov, ed., *Spisi kongregacije*, p. 345; this complaint was echoed by Andrija Zmajević, Archbishop of Bar, later in the century, who gave the ignorance of the clergy as the main reason for apostasy: Arnold, *Preaching of Islam*, p. 190.

48 ASCPF SOCG 309, fo. 64^r ('attende troppo alla crapula bevendo questo sino all'omissione della raggione exclusive').

49 BN MS f.ital. 1168, pp. 56 ('assai negligente'), 58–9 ('per essere stato inquieto, e per dubio della sua Fede'). Ndre Bogdani was by now in his eighties; he resigned later in 1677.

50 Lamansky, *Secrets d'état*, appendix, p. '064'.
51 Radonić, *Rimska kurija*, pp. 340–2. The problem recurred three times in the 1670s (pp. 347–8, 370).
52 ASCPF SOCG 309, fo. 102ʳ. In a report of 1670 he said that the Catholics were in fact paying tribute to the Patriarch: ASCPF SOCG 431, fo. 157ʳ.
53 The main exception, of course, was the Russian Church. The Ottomans grew suspicious of any attempts by the Serbs to make contacts with Moscow; Patriarch Gavril, who went there in 1654, was executed by the Ottomans (on a charge of inciting Russia to attack the Empire) in 1657 (Radonić, *Rimska kurija*, pp. 316, 331).
54 Kiel, *Art and Society*, p. 148 n. (1578, annual tax); Hadrovics, *L'Église serbe*, pp. 75–83 (other taxes); Jačov, ed., *Spisi kongregacije*, p. 481 (de Leonardis).
55 Hadrovics, *L'Église serbe*, p. 50.
56 Evans, *Making of Habsburg Monarchy*, p. 421 (Ruthenes); Hofmann, 'Il Beato Bellarmino' (Serbs), and 'Griechische Patriarchen' (Constantinople).
57 Gjini, *Ipeshkvia*, p. 165; Radonić, *Rimska kurija*, pp. 176, 301–7; Zamputi, ed., *Relacione*, vol. 2, p. 374; Fermendžin, 'Izprave', pp. 181–5.
58 de Gubernatis and de Turre, *Orbis seraphicus*, pp. 479a, 491a (Franciscans, Cherubino); Farlati, *Illyrici sacri*, vol. 7, p. 130 (Dalmatia).
59 This phenomenon is described in a report by Matija Gundulić of 1675, printed in Banduri, *Imperium*, vol. 2, part 2, p. 58.
60 Above, n. 36 (1578); Cordignano, 'Geografia ecclesiastica', p. 233 (1599); Zamputi, ed., *Relacione*, vol. 2, p. 170 (1638/9).
61 See for example Cordignano, 'Geografia ecclesiastica', p. 233.
62 ASCPF SOCG 309, fos. 60ʳ ('dotto ed a bene'), 84–5.
63 Jačov, ed., *Spisi kongregacije*, p. 656.
64 *Ibid.*, p. 482.
65 Radonić, *Rimska kurija*, p. 168 (Dečani); Zamputi, ed., *Relacione*, vol. 2, pp. 442–4 (funeral practices).
66 de Gubernatis and de Turre, *Orbis seraphicus*, p. 588b; Stadtmüller, 'Das Nationalkonzil', p. 71; Vryonis, 'Religious Changes', p. 174. On the magical properties of baptism for Muslims see F. Hasluck, *Christianity and Islam*, vol. 1, pp. 31–6; Hasluck's book contains a wealth of information about Muslim and Christian folk religion.
67 Zamputi, ed., *Relacione*, vol. 2, p. 116 (baptisms); de Gubernatis and de Turre, *Orbis seraphicus*, p. 492b (welcome).
68 Fermendžin, 'Izprave', p. 175. Pjetër Bogdani preached passionately against recourse to 'witches' in 1680: ASCPF SOCG 482, fo. 286ᵛ.
69 ASCPF SOCG 482, fos. 288ᵛ–289ʳ: 'ivi tutta la notte se la passano, con Tamburi, Siffare, balli, e Canti. Passata la mezza notte principiano una confusa Processione Turchi, Serviani, e Greci con candele di cera accese à misura della propria vita longhe. Circondano la Cima del più alto monte per spatio di tre hore à piedi scalzi alcuni de Turchi principali à cavallo . . .'

Gregor Mazrreku gave a very similar description in 1651, though the festival he described was the feast of St Anne (26 July); he also noted that many Muslim women placed copper coins on the altar: Fermendžin, 'Izprave', p. 177.

70 Clayer, *L'Albanie*, pp. 22, 171 (Sarı Saltık); Nušić, *S Kosova*, p. 35 (Pantaleimon). On Sarı Saltık more generally see Norris, *Islam*, pp. 146–57.

71 Zamputi, ed., *Relacione*, vol. 2, pp. 97, 440; Gaspari, 'Nji dorshkrim', p. 386.

72 Zamputi, ed., *Relacione*, vol. 2, pp. 440–2.

73 Jačov, ed., *Spisi tajnog arhiva*, p. 38.

74 Thëngjilli, *Renta feudale*, p. 96; Limanoski, *Islamizacijata*, pp. 137–8 (noting the pairings Bogdan-Hasan, Nikola-Mustafa, etc.: these villagers were or had been Orthodox).

75 For examples of double names from the nineteenth and twentieth centuries see Valentini, ed., *La legge*, p. 24; Libardi, *Primi moti*, part 1, p. 33; Coon, *Mountains of Giants*, p. 36.

76 Botero, *Le relationi*, part 3, p. 116; Zamputi, ed., *Dokumente*, vol. 3, pp. 50–1.

77 See the Venetian report of 1579 in Albèri, ed., *Relazioni*, ser. 3, vol. 1, p. 454, which says this was very common in Bosnia, Serbia and Thrace.

78 Zamputi, ed., *Relacione*, vol. 2, p. 442.

79 For the texts of all of these see Farlati, *Illyrici sacri*, vol. 7, pp. 136, 145–8, 172–6, 188–9. On the 1703 Synod see Stadtmüller, 'Das Nationalkonzil'. On two other texts, issued by the Holy Office in 1724 and 1730, see Rostagno, 'Note sulla simulazione', pp. 157–60. See also Skendi, 'Crypto-Christianity', pp. 237–8; Gjini, *Ipeshkvia*, pp. 147–9.

80 ASCPF SC Servia 1, fo. 318ʳ.

81 de Gubernatis and de Turre, *Orbis seraphicus*, p. 590. The Catholics did celebrate Fridays because of the Muslims, and their bishops had promoted the cult of 'Sancta Veneranda' in order to assimilate this practice (p. 591a).

82 Zamputi, ed., *Relacione*, vol. 2, p. 398. A seventeenth-century German author also noted that those who live among Muslims and observe their daily piety and good works 'will come to think that they are good people and will very probably be saved': Arnold, *Preaching of Islam*, pp. 165–6.

83 For examples of reconversion see de Gubernatis and de Turre, *Orbis seraphicus*, pp. 479a, 518b, 570b; Radonić even records that Ndre Bogdani converted some Muslims secretly to Christianity: *Rimska kurija*, p. 559.

84 For general studies of the orders see Trimingham, *Sufi Orders*; A. Popović, *Derviches balkaniques*; Ćehajić, *Derviški redovi*; Lifchez, ed., *Dervish Lodge*; Norris, *Islam*, pp. 82–137. On the Bektashi see Birge, *Bektashi Order*; F. Hasluck, *Christianity and Islam*, vol. 2, pp. 483–596. The classic study of the role of dervishes in the early Ottoman expansion is Barkan, 'Osmanlı imperatorluğunda'; but Barkan's material is mainly Anatolian.

85 T. Djordjević, *Naš narodni život*, vol. 10, p. 70.

86 Kaleshi and Rexhep, 'Prizrenac Kukli Beg', p. 144 (Kukli-bey); Kaleshi, *Kontributi*, p. 40, and Clayer, *Mystiques*, p. 174 (Prizren); Evliya Çelebi, *Putopis*, pp. 267–78 (Mitrovica, Vuçitërn, Sinan Pasha, Kaçanik); Kissling, 'Zur Frage' (Albania). On the late development of Bektashism in Kosovo see Ćehajić, *Derviški redovi*, pp. 171–2. For details of Sinan Pasha's foundation of a mosque, school and imaret at Kaçanik see Tričković, 'U susret iskušenjima', p. 116.

87 All these details are from Shkodra, *Esnafet*, which is by far the best study. For useful brief summaries see R. Lewis, *Everyday Life*, pp. 145–9; Hupchick, *Bulgarians*, pp. 40–3. For a marvellous description of the annual procession of the guilds in Istanbul see Evliya Çelebi, *Narrative*, vol. 1, part 2, pp. 225–49. On the growth of the Kadiri order in Kosovo (whose Prizren tekke was founded in 1655) see Ćehajić, *Derviški redovi*, p. 137.

88 Zamputi, ed., *Relacione*, vol. 1, p. 168 (Bizzi, 1610); ASCPF SOCG 431, fo. 161ʳ (1670); Evliya Çelebi, *Putopis*, pp. 276 (Prishtina), 338 (Gjakova); Zamputi, vol. 1, p. 336 (Prizren, 1624: clearly an underestimate).

89 BN MS f.fr. 17193, fo. 13ʳ ('ils ne vivent plus dans la rigueur de l'ancienne discipline, parce qu'on permet à la plus part de negocier et de demeurer avec leurs familles'). On this change see also Sugar, *Southeastern Europe*, pp. 227–8.

90 Rizaj, *Rudarstvo*, pp. 44–8 (general causes of decline); Zamputi, ed., *Relacione*, vol. 1, p. 342 (1624), vol. 2, p. 260 (1642); Jačov, ed., *Spisi tajnog arhiva*, p. 141 (1685).

91 See above, n. 43, and Zamputi, ed., *Relacione*, vol. 2, pp. 96–100.

92 Evliya Çelebi, *Putopis*, p. 274.

93 Zamputi, ed., *Relacione*, vol. 1, p. 170 (1610); Cordignano, 'Geografia ecclesiastica', p. 236 (1577); route-timings from Boué, *La Turquie*, vol. 4, pp. 548, 551; Grisebach, *Reise*, vol. 2, p. 323.

94 Zamputi, ed., *Relacione*, vol. 1, p. 342 (1624); vol. 2, p. 100 (1637); Fermendžin, 'Izprave', p. 174 (1651).

95 Zamputi, ed., *Relacione*, vol. 2, pp. 264–6.

8. The Austrian invasion and the 'Great Migration' of the Serbs: 1689–1690

1 Respectively: Belgrade TV broadcast, 1982, cited in Rizaj, 'Mbi të ashtuquajturën dyndje', p. 85; Picot, *Les Serbes de Hongrie*, p. 75; Gopčević, *Makedonien*, p. 223.

2 For such claims see Jovan Tomić, *Les Albanais*, p. 33; Veselinović, 'Die "Albaner"'; Tričković, 'Velika seoba'. For Serbian claims about the 'Invitation' see Hadrovics, *L'Église serbe*, p. 139.

3 For such claims see Rizaj, *Kosova gjatë shekujve*, pp. 511–19, and 'Mbi të ashtuquajturën dyndje'; K. Frashëri, 'Pjetër Bogdani'.

4　The arguments are surveyed in M. Kostić, 'Prilozi'.

5　Radonić, *Rimska kurija*, p. 377; Tričković, 'Velika seoba', p. 129 n.

6　ASCPF SC Servia 1, fo. 185ʳ ('Furono serrate le chiese; dispersi li Sacerdoti; fugiti li Popoli'; 'seguito da una moltitudine dei fideli, fugendo per li Monti mi servino di matterazzo della neve').

7　*Ibid.*, fo. 185ᵛ.

8　On Yeğen's career and rebellion see Inalcık, 'Fiscal and military transformation', pp. 299–302; Rizaj, *Kosova gjatë shekujve*, pp. 500–6 (order quoted on p. 506); Aktepe, 'Kosova', p. 873; Külçe, *Osmanlı tarihinde Arnavutluk*, p. 100; Zamputi and Pulaha, eds., *Dokumente*, vol. 4, pp. 118–20, 157–8.

9　SOAS PP MS 4, box 11, bundle 51(i), item I/64 (report from Sofia, 20/30 Sept. 1689)

10　PRO SP 97/20, fos. 143 (1st quotation), 150ʳ, 151, 152ʳ (2nd quotation).

11　AMAE Corr. pol., Autriche, vol. 65, fos. 108ʳ, 114ʳ.

12　Zamputi and Pulaha, eds., *Dokumente*, vol. 4, pp. 169–70.

13　Röder von Diersburg, *Des Markgrafen von Baden Feldzüge*, vol. 2, p. 195.

14　C. Contarini, *Istoria*, vol. 2, p. 167; Foresti *et al.*, *Mappamondo*, vol. 6, part 2, p. 367.

15　Zamputi and Pulaha, eds., *Dokumente*, vol. 4, p. 229.

16　AMAE Corr. pol., Autriche, vol. 65, fo. 114ʳ ('abondant en vivres de bouche pour hommes et chevaux').

17　BNM MS IT. VII. 1068, fo. 141ʳ ('Con il buon ordine, e con altri allettamenti, procurava di rittirare a quella parte gl' habitanti, ch' anco andavano rittornando e prestavano giuramento per viver fideli all' Imperatore, essendo la maggior parte, di ritto Greco'), printed with many inaccuracies in de Hurmuzaki, ed., *Documente*, vol. 5, part 2, p. 178.

18　C. Contarini, *Istoria*, vol. 2, p. 166.

19　ASCPF SOCG 506, fo. 251ᵛ ('sopravenendo in queste parti l'essercito vittorioso del nostro Cesare andò personalmente ad incontrarlo & rintazzare l'orgoglio della soldatesca a non inoltrarsi alli danni e straggi delli Cattolici, et il tutto felicemente ottenne').

20　Tomoski, 'Eden izguben dokument', p. 122 n.

21　Rácz, *A hajdúk*, pp. 30–1 (term in Hungary); Schwicker, *Politische Geschichte*, p. 4 (immigrants); G. Stanojević, *Srbija*, pp. 119, 123 (Rascian regiment, Niš).

22　Cvetkova, 'Novi dokumenti', p. 255 (petition).

23　Soranzo, *L'Ottomanno*, p. 148.

24　Babinger, ed., *Dernschwam's Tagebuch*, p. 8.

25　HHSA Illyrico-Serbica, 1 (1611–1738), Konv. B, fo. 14, endorsement (Invitatorium); Hadrovics, 'A Magyarországi szerb kérdés', p. 330 (court style).

26　AMAE Corr. pol., Autriche, vol. 51, fo. 174ʳ ('in Pristina 5000 m. Arnauti rebuttati à Turchi').

27 Slightly different chronologies are given in Tomoski, 'Eden izguben dokument', pp. 123–4, and AMAE Corr. pol., Autriche, vol. 51, fo. 174ᵛ (which
corresponds to the account in Zamputi and Pulaha, eds., *Dokumente*, vol.
4, p. 258).

28 Röder von Diersburg, *Des Markgrafen von Baden Feldzüge*, vol. 2, p. 165:
report by Baden to Emperor, 29 Oct.

29 AMAE Corr. pol., Autriche, vol. 51, fo. 175ʳ (composition); ASVat Dispacci,
Nunziatura di Venezia, ISSSV microfilm 134, fo. 431ʳ (death toll).

30 AMAE Corr. pol., Autriche, vol. 51, fos. 175ᵛ–176; C. Contarini, *Istoria*, vol.
2, pp. 167–8.

31 C. Contarini, *Istoria*, vol. 2, p. 168.

32 Boethius *et al.*, *Des Glantz-erhöheten und Triumphleuchtenden Kriegs-
Helms* ... , vol. 4 (1691), p. 1199, printed in Brlić, ed., *Die freiwillige
Theilname*, p. 71; Anon., *Der neu-eröffneten Pforten Fortzetzung*, p. 517b.

33 Veselinović, 'Die "Albaner"', p. 205 (geographical usage). The Këlmendi
were the dominant clan in the group of northern malësors and brdjani.
Kristo Frashëri claims that Bogdani was promoting a plan to elevate his title
to that of 'Patriarch', but this seems to be pure speculation: 'Pjetër Bogdani',
pp. 72–3.

34 KA FA (Türkenkrieg), 1689–13–1, 'Annotationes No. 5'. This MS is printed
with an Albanian translation in Zamputi and Pulaha, eds., *Dokumente*, vol.
4, pp. 256–301; unfortunately, some serious mistranscriptions (such as
'Türckhen' for 'Teutschen') make this printing unreliable.

35 Veselinović, 'Die "Albaner"', p. 207. Veselinović engaged in a long-running
dispute with the Montenegrin historian Gligor Stanojević on this point: see
N. Samardžić, 'Savremena štampa', p. 79. John Stoye agrees with Veselinović: *Marsigli's Europe*, p. 87.

36 AMAE Corr. pol., Autriche, vol. 51, fos. 8–378, entitled 'Origine della
guerra fra l'Imperatore dei Christiani, e quello de Turchi l'Anno 1682'. One
section of this text, describing the battle of Kaçanik (fos. 181–4) was printed
in Veterani, *Memorie*, pp. 105–13.

37 AMAE Corr. pol., Autriche, vol. 65, fos. 122ᵛ–123ʳ.

38 *Ibid.*, fo. 123ʳ; Boethius, obviously drawing on the same source, gives a
similar account: Brlić, *Die freiwillige Theilname*, p. 71.

39 AMAE Corr. pol., Autriche, vol. 51, fo. 177ʳ ('Non mancava il Conte di
consultare coll' Arcivescovo, et altri Capi Allemanni').

40 For biographical details see Veselinović, 'Die "Albaner"', pp. 221–2;
M. Kostić, 'O ulozi'; ASCPF SC Servia 1, fo. 116 (autobiographical account
by Raspasani, 1682). He was born in Letnica (Zefiq, *Mihael Summa*, p. 65),
and his family lived in Prishtina (ASCPF SOCG 431, fo. 160ʳ). An Ottoman
document described him as Vicar to the Archbishop in 1680: Zamputi and
Pulaha, eds., *Dokumente*, vol. 4, pp. 18–20.

41 Veterani, *Memorie*, p. 50; KA Exp. Prot. 1690, fo. 41ʳ.

42 Jačov, ed., *Spisi tajnog arhiva*, p. 141 (report of 1685).

43 AMAE Corr. pol., Autriche, vol. 51, fo. 177ʳ.

44 Röder von Diersburg, *Des Markgrafen von Baden Feldzüge*, vol. 2, p. 165.

45 Jačov, ed., *Spisi tajnog arhiva*, p. 140; AMAE Corr. pol., Autriche, vol. 51, fo. 177ʳ.

46 BUB MS Marsigli 103, fo. 6ᵛ; MS Marsigli 54, fo. 355ʳ.

47 Veselinović, 'Die "Albaner"'.

48 AMAE Corr. pol., Autriche, vol. 51, fos. 177ʳ ('Stavano fuori di Priseren 6000 e più Albanesi, e di quelli medesimi altre volte assoldati da Turchi nominati Arnauti'), 180ʳ ('quale teniva tutti quei Popoli, e la più gran part degl' Arnauti in freno, et alla devozione di Sua Maiestà Cesarea').

49 ASVat Dispacci, Nunziatura di Venezia, ISSSV microfilm 134, fo. 408ʳ ('gli Albanesi, Arnotti, et altri Popoli di quelle reggioni tanto Turchi che Cristiani stavano in trattati col Generale Piccolomini'); Anon., *Der neu-eröffneten Pforten Fortsetzung*, p. 517b.

50 Zamputi, 'Bashkimi i maleve', p. 86 (1638); de Gubernatis and de Turre, *Orbis seraphicus*, p. 569a (1692); Pulaha, ed., *Qëndresa e popullit*, pp. 184–5.

51 AMAE Corr. pol., Autriche, vol. 51, fo. 177ᵛ (Piccolomini); ASCPF SOCG 506, fo. 251ᵛ (Bogdani).

52 ASVat Dispacci, Nunziatura di Venezia, ISSSV microfilm 136, fo. 35ʳ ('Arnotti Albanesi'); AMAE Corr. pol., Autriche, vol. 65, fo. 126, describing it as a 'test of loyalty' of the 'militias of Albania' ('preuve de fidelité', 'les milices d'Albanie').

53 C. Contarini, *Istoria*, vol. 2, p. 169; AMAE Corr. pol., Autriche, vol. 51, fo. 180ʳ. Many of the Luma people remained Slav-speaking and Orthodox until the nineteenth century: see Kanitz, 'Die fortschreitende Arnautisirung'.

54 AMAE Corr. pol., Autriche, vol. 51, fos. 180ᵛ ('avaritia, e superbia'), 179ᵛ ('cosa insoportabile à quella nazione libera e bellicosa'), 182ᵛ (3,000 'Arnauti'); ASVat Dispacci, Nunziatura di Venezia, ISSSV microfilm 136, fo. 78ʳ (Papal envoy).

55 von Hammer, *Geschichte*, vol. 6, p. 546; Külçe, *Osmanlı tarihinde Arnavutluk*, p. 105 (akçes).

56 All the above details are from AMAE Corr. pol., Autriche, vol. 51, fos. 181–182ʳ (printed in Veterani, *Memorie*, pp. 105–7). The council of war is dated 27 Nov. by N. Samardžić ('Savremena štampa', p. 86) and 27 Dec. by Sesser ('Die Denkwürdigkeiten', p. 92); the former is clearly incorrect, and Sesser gives no evidence for the latter.

57 ASVat Dispacci, Nunziatura di Venezia, ISSSV microfilm 136, fo. 35ʳ ('era in tanto arrivato colà il Patriarcha di quel Paese, et ammesso alla presenza di S. A., fece instanza per un passaporto, per potersi condurre alla Corte Cesarea e rapresentare alla medesima lo stato di quel Paese, e l'intentione, che alimentano quei popoli à pr[op]ò della Christianità'); 'Christianità',

when Catholic authors of this period write about the Orthodox Church, means only Roman Catholicism.

58 Feigius, *Wunderbarer Adlers-Schwung oder fernere Geschichte-Fortsetzung Ortelii*, cited in Jovan Tomić, 'Patriarah Arsenije', p. 121 n.; N. Samardžić, 'Savremena štampa', p. 85.

59 Kahnè, 'L'azione politica', pp. 275, 283 (quotations), 298–300 (arrest).

60 Theiner, *Vetera monumenta slavorum*, vol. 2, pp. 225–6; Giannelli, 'Lettere', p. 70, and Kahnè, 'A proposito'.

61 On Ragusan policy see Zlatar, *Between Eagle and Crescent*, pp. 128–74; on Venetian policy, Jovan Tomić, *Crna Gora*, pp. 153–9.

62 Ongania, ed., *Il Montenegro*, pp. 42–3, 47; ASVen Provv. t. e m., filza 529, Molin report, 1 Oct. 1689 (hostages). See also ASVen Collegio, relaz. di amb., vol. 67, fos. 11–12, for a special report of July 1689 discussing the risk that the highland clans might side with Austria. Ongania's book, which was privately published, is extremely rare; the copy I have used is in the Biblioteca Casanatense, Rome.

63 ASVen Provv. t. e m., filza 529, Molin report, 10 Oct. 1689, with the texts of the two documents ('li perseguiterà sino alla loro distruttione'). On Arsenije's departure from Peć see *ibid.*, Molin report of an interview with the monk Nikon, 7 Oct. 1689 (partly printed in Jovan Tomić, 'Patriarah Arsenije', pp. 103–4); Radonić, *Rimska kurija*, pp. 396–7; and (with an elaborate theory of intrigue) Kahnè, 'L'azione politica', pp. 276–82.

64 The monk Nikon used the term 'confederatione': ASVen Provv. t. e m., filza 529, Molin report of interview, 7 Oct. 1689; Provveditore Duodo's report, 7 Sept. 1689, in Ongania, ed., *Il Montenegro*, pp. 49–52.

65 Zamputi and Pulaha, eds., *Dokumente*, vol. 4, p. 247 (Istanbul); BNM MS IT VII 1068, fo. 160ᵛ (Vienna); ASVen Provv. t. e m., filza 530, Molin report, 5 Mar. 1690 (Montenegro).

66 ASVen Provv. t. e m., filza 529, Zmajević to Molin, 22 Nov. 1689 (Bijelo Polje), and filza 530, Molin report, 5 Mar. 1690 ('Li popoli di quei Monti ... stan sempre coll' Armi alla Mano. Alcuni d'essi nella vicinanza de gl' Imperiali s'uniscono alle loro partite contro gl' Ottomani, altri le praticono per se stessi'). The Albanian clans mentioned above at n. 50 were not part of the Këlmendi-Montenegrin grouping.

67 ASVen Provv. t. e m., filza 529, Molin report, 26 Nov. 1689 ('Che i Popoli del rito greco, prese le parti di Cesare'); Arsenije letter to Bolizza, 'scritta li 4 Nov alla Vechia, sono 14'; translation of letter from Igumen Visarion *et al.*, 28 Oct. 1689. The first two items are printed in Ongania, ed., *Il Montenegro*, pp. 53–4.

68 See Ongania, ed., *Il Montenegro*, pp. 55–6; Kahnè, 'L'azione politica', p. 310; Zlatar, *Between Eagle and Crescent*, pp. 179, 298.

69 ASVen Provv. t. e m., filza 529, letter from Capt. Zmajević to Molin, 22

Nov. ('Al presente il Patriarca s'attrova a Nixichi'); letter from Igumen
Viktor to Giovanni Bolizza, 29 Nov. ('ne credo che l'istesso Patriarca potrà
andare'). Gligor Stanojević suggests, however, that Arsenije went straight
back to Peć, arriving on *c.*21 Nov.: *Srbija*, p. 136.

70 AMAE Corr. pol., Autriche, vol. 51, fos. 183–4 (printed in Veterani,
    Memorie, pp. 108–11).

71 This claim, made by the anonymous writer (see above, n. 70), was repeated
    in an early brochure about the battle, cited in N. Samardžić, 'Savremena
    štampa', pp. 89–91.

72 SOAS PP MS 4, box 11, bundle 51(ii), item II/26, Porphyrita report, 17/27
    Feb. 1690 ('doppo un combattimento di 6 hore essendo dal detto numero
    li 400 à Cavallo fuggirono e lasciarono li 800 che era la fantaria, la quale
    non potendo resistere à tanto numeroso Esercito del inimico, volendo
    ancora questi fugire si sono persiguiti'). The total of 1,200 matches that of
    the anonymous Italian account, though the proportions of foot to horse are
    reversed. (A Venetian report mentions losses of 800 cavalry and 200
    infantry: ASVen Senato, dispacci, Germania, filza 165, fo. 365^r.) If the
    prisoners' account is accurate, then evidently the cavalry were successfully
    pursued as well: no horsemen returned to the Austrians.

73 KA Reg. Prot. 1690, fo. 32^r.

74 ASCPF SC Albania 5, fo. 160^v ('mio Zio essendo stato ritrovato già morto,
    e sepolito fù nulladimeno cavato fuori dalla sepoltura, e dato à pasto, e cibo
    dei Cani in mezzo la Piazza di Prisctina con la Mitra in Testa').

75 ASCPF SOCG 515, fo. 343^r ('Io sono scappato nudo e crudo dalli Turchi
    sopr' un Cavallo, havendo loro particolarmente teso di attrapparmi'); the
    evacuation and its route are described in a Venetian report from Vienna of
    Mar./Apr. 1690: ASVen Senato, dispacci, Germania, filza 165, fo. 402^r.

76 Ongania, ed., *Il Montenegro*, p. 57 (horse-loads, reoccupation); ASVen
    Provv. t. e m., filza 530, letter from Igumen Viktor and Ivan Iliković to
    Molin, 25 Feb. 1689/90 ('tagliato a pezzi').

77 ASCPF SC Servia 1, fo. 189^r ('da Prisreno e da Pechia non è pottuto
    scampare nissuno, ma tutti sono restati praedi del Barbaro'; 'il Paese con li
    Paesani fu affatto distrutto, trucidato dalla Barbara gente').

78 SOAS PP MS 4, box 11, bundle 51(ii), item III/91 ('che forse mai più
    potranno rihaversi se non per gran spatio di tempo'); ASVat Dispacci,
    Nunziatura di Venezia, ISSSV microfilm 136, fos. 69^r ('abruciando, e
    rovinando il Paese'), 124^r ('hanno fatto barbaro macello di quei infelici
    Abitanti, e gran numero condotto seco nella schiavitù').

79 AMAE Corr. pol., Autriche, vol. 51, fo. 187^r (describing Kaçanik, absurdly,
    as a large town abandoned before 6 December); Veterani, *Memorie*,
    pp. 55–6, and Gerba, 'Die kaiserlichen', pp. 167–8 (raids); ASVen Provv. t.
    e m., filza 530, Bolizza report, 27 Apr. 1690 ('Cossovo distrutto dall due

Eserciti giacesse trà li medesimi deserto, non vedendosi alcuno per quella Campagna').

80 Document printed in Veterani, *Memorie*, pp. 130–1.

81 HHSA Illyrico-Serbica 1 (1611–1738), Konv. B, fo. 15ᵛ ('animare i suoi Popoli in Albania, Rascia di prender armi contro i Turchi'), printed very inaccurately in M. Kostić, 'Prilozi', p. 19. On Marsigli's mission see Stoye, *Marsigli's Europe*, pp. 89–90; M. Kostić, *Završni bilans*, pp. 9–10. Both Kostić (in 'Prilozi') and Stoye assume that this memorandum was based on information supplied by Raspasani; but it contains inaccuracies which Raspasani would never have been guilty of, such as the statement that Patriarch Arsenije had been very helpful to Piccolomini.

82 HHSA Illyrico-Serbica 1 (1611–1738), Konv. B, fo. 14ʳ ('Ad Patriarchum Rascianorum animatio, ut populos illos ad insurrectionem contra Turcos excitet'); the rough draft is fos. 38–9, and another copy is fos. 40ʳ–42ʳ. The statement in this document that Arsenije was very helpful to Piccolomini (fo. 14ʳ) is clearly taken from Marsigli's mistaken remark (see above, n. 81). A reliable printing of the text is given in Radonić, *Histoire des Serbes*, pp. 203–5; Radonić's theory that the text was based on proposals by the seventeenth-century adventurer Djuradj Branković for a semi-autonomous Serb state (p. 167) is, however, baseless. On the omission of 'non' see Hadrovics, *L'Église serbe*, p. 139; see also M. Kostić, 'O postanku'.

83 N. Samardžić, 'Savremena štampa', p. 96 (399, from an Ottoman source); D. Popović, *Velika seoba*, pp. 32–3 (4,000).

84 D. Popović, *Velika seoba*, p. 29.

85 Radonić, *Histoire des Serbes*, pp. 170–2 (negotiations); D. Popović, *Velika seoba*, p. 30 (dignitaries).

86 BNM MS IT VII 1068, fo. 454ʳ; SOAS PP MS 4, box 11, bundle 51(ii), item II/63; PRO SP 80/17, fo. 93ᵛ; ASVat Dispacci, Nunziatura di Venezia, ISSSV microfilm 137, fo. 194ʳ. Von Hammer notes that, according to Ottoman sources, the Ottomans lost 15,000 men and the Austrians 30–45,000: *Geschichte*, vol. 6, p. 557.

87 Ćidić and Lazić, *Očevici*, p. 26 (Atanasije Daskal, writing before 1699).

88 HHSA Illyrico-Serbica 1 (1611–1738), Konv. B, fo. 48 ('sono venuti in Strigonia, Comora, e Buda, huomini con le loro mogli e figli totalmente spogliati, e nudi, che in tutto saranno più che 30 m. anime'); Grujić, *Kako se postupalo*, p. 46 (40,000); N. Samardžić, 'Savremena štampa', p. 101 (news-sheet).

89 Stojanović, *Stari srpski zapisi*, no. 5283.

90 D. Popović, *Velika seoba*, p. 55 (10,000); KA Exp. Prot. 1691, fos. 211ᵛ–212ʳ (2,000); KA Reg. Prot. 1693, fo. 237ᵛ (Szent Endre, Pest). Szent Endre would remain an important Serb settlement, and was for a time the seat of a Serb Orthodox bishopric: Berki, *Hê en Oungaria ekklêsia*, p. 12.

91 Tričković, 'Velika seoba', p. 137 (tax registers); T. Djordjević, *Naš narodni život*, vol. 4, pp. 114–38 (other evidence).

92 ASCPF SOCG 515 fo. 341ʳ ('dove parte di fame, e parte di malatia la maggior parte è creppata').

93 KA Reg. Prot. 1690, fo. 585ᵛ; Exp. Prot. 1691, fo. 140ᵛ; Exp. Prot. 1693, fo. 82ʳ ('die grosse anzahl Rätzen, worunter auch Türckhen sein sollen'). For other evidence of Arnauts in Imperial service or on Habsburg soil see de Hurmuzaki, ed., *Documente*, vol. 5, part 2, p. 217; T. Djordjević, *Naš narodni život*, vol. 4, p. 116.

9. Recovery and decline: 1690–1817

1 Rizaj, *Kosova gjatë shekujve*, p. 126.

2 Tričković, 'Velika seoba', p. 136.

3 Hadrovics, *L'Église serbe*, pp. 147–8; Radonić, *Rimska kurija*, pp. 473–9; Slijepčević, *Istorija crkve*, vol. 1, pp. 376–7, 395. M. Kostić interprets the appointment of Kalinik as a move to stop further emigration: 'Ustanak', p. 207.

4 Kahnè, 'L'azione politica', p. 303.

5 D. Popović, *Velika seoba*, pp. 45, 130.

6 KA Exp. Prot. 1693, fos. 162ᵛ ('Ratz. Rauber', 'grosse insolenzien'), 334ᵛ–335ʳ (traders); KA Reg. Prot. 1693, fos. 208ᵛ, 212ᵛ, 222ᵛ, and Schwicker, *Politische Geschichte*, p. 17 (other offences).

7 Langer, 'Nord-Albaniens Unterwerfungs-Anerbieten', p. 246.

8 de Gubernatis and de Turre, *Orbis seraphicus*, p. 569b.

9 Kaleshi, 'Shenime', p. 509 n. (1695); Bartl, ed., *Quellen und Materialen*, vol. 2, pp. 6, 136–8; Rostagno, 'Note sulla simulazione', p. 155.

10 Radonić, *Rimska kurija*, p. 503.

11 Zamputi and Pulaha, eds., *Dokumente*, vol. 4, pp. 472–3 (1698); Jovan Tomić, 'Gradja', p. 57 (house sacked). Raspasani noted that the Këlmendi resumed their habit of demanding contributions in July 1690, causing great fear in Peć: M. Kostić, 'Prilozi', p. 20.

12 Jovan Tomić, 'Gradja', pp. 58–9; Bartl, 'Die Këlmendi', p. 132.

13 Bartl, ed., *Quellen und Materialen*, vol. 2, p. 133.

14 Tërnava, 'Migrimet', p. 322. This document is misrepresented by Tričković as a general order to settle Albanians in the Vuçitërn sancak: 'Ustanci, seobe', p. 144.

15 Bartl, ed., *Quellen und Materialen*, vol. 2, p. 139; ASCPF SC Servia 1, fo. 253ʳ (Karadžić).

16 Jovan Tomić, 'Gradja', p. 60 (1707); Theiner, ed., *Vetera monumenta slavorum*, vol. 2, p. 241 (1711). The renewed Ottoman-Këlmendi hostilities continued into 1708, with another attempt to starve them out: Pulaha, ed.,

Qëndresa e popullit, pp. 245–6. There were 1,000 Catholic Këlmendi still in the Pešter area in 1713, 2,000 in 1719, and 2,500 in 1735: ASVat Vis. ad lim., vol. 728, item 1 (Karadžić report, 12 Dec. 1713); Jačov, ed., *Spisi tajnog arhiva*, p. 246; ASVat Vis. ad lim., vol. 728, item 9 (Suma report, 16 Dec. 1735).

17 ASCPF SOCG 515, fo. 341ᵛ.

18 Radonić, *Rimska kurija*, p. 419 (successor); ASVat Vis. ad lim., vol. 56, Zmajević report, May 1692 (three priests).

19 Gjini, *Ipeshkvia*, p. 198; Radonić, *Rimska kurija*, pp. 501–2. The Archbishop's name is given by Albanian writers as 'Karagić' or 'Karagiq'; but such spellings are taken from Italian documents, in which 'Karagich' was merely a transcription of 'Karadžić', with the Italian soft 'g'.

20 Bartl, ed., *Quellen und Materialen*, vol. 2, p. 139.

21 *Ibid.*, p. 127: Nikolaos Mavrokordatos, Chief Dragoman (interpreter), who was appointed ruler of Moldavia in 1711. On the dispute over the firman see Radonić, *Rimska kurija*, pp. 476–7.

22 Bartl, ed., *Quellen und Materialen*, vol. 2, pp. 137–8.

23 Jačov, ed., *Spisi tajnog arhiva*, p. 245; ASVat Vis. ad lim., vol. 728, item 8, Karadžić report, 20 May 1710 ('faccio venire da Venetia tanti candelieri, specchi grandi, confeti, zuccari, e belli bechieri').

24 ASVat Vis. ad lim., vol. 728, item 9, Karadžić report, 12 June 1716. One priest died in prison: he was the elderly Croat Petar of Vukovar, who had won the confidence of Hudaverdi's mother: Radonić, *Rimska kurija*, p. 534.

25 Pulaha, ed., *Qëndresa e popullit*, pp. 311–12.

26 Tričković, 'Ustanci, seobe', pp. 149–51 (rising, emigration, taxes); Kahnè, 'L'azione politica', p. 279 n. (firman); M. Kostić, 'Ustanak', p. 208 (letter to Karlovci).

27 M. Kostić, 'Ustanak', pp. 208–10; Zefiq, *Mihael Summa*, p. 67.

28 Langer, 'Nord-Albaniens Unterwerfungs-Anerbieten', pp. 267–9.

29 On all these events see M. Kostić, 'Ustanak', pp. 212–17; von Schmettau, *Geheime Nachrichten*, pp. 20–9 (p. 28: Te Deum). For the Bosnian–Ottoman chronicle see Bosnavi, *Tarih-i Bosna*, pp. 84–5.

30 M. Kostić, 'Ustanak', pp. 216–25; Zefiq, *Mihael Summa*, pp. 69–70.

31 ASVat Vis. ad lim., vol. 728, final item (Suma letter from Belgrade, 1739) ('Io con la Misione di Pestera siamo ritirati nel Dominio Austriaco allor che si ritirno gl'Imperiali, e l'istesso ha fatto anche la Capelaria di Novi Pazar e molti altri Cristiani che potevano fugire').

32 M. Kostić, 'Ustanak', pp. 226–7; Tkallac, 'Kostumet të Kelmendeve'; ASCPF SC Servia 1, fo. 299 (letter from the two chiefs, Deda and Fat, 1742), and SC Servia 2, fos. 155–6 (letter from Mazarek on a request for a priest, 1771).

33 von Thallóczy, 'Die albanische Diaspora', p. 321 (1900); Cana, *Shpalime historike*, p. 194 (1968); Kandić, ed., *Spotlight*, pp. 3–6 (1992).

34 Tričković, 'Ustanci, seobe', p. 160 (Ottoman report); ASVat Vis. ad lim., vol. 728, final item (exile, slavery and murder: Suma letter, 1739); ASCPF SC Servia 1, fo. 325ᵛ (murder, slavery: Nikollë report, 1743).

35 Tričković, 'Ustanci, seobe', p. 161 (edict); Jovan Tomić, *Les Albanais*, pp. 49–50 (campaigns, Vasojević); Slijepčević, *Istorija crkve*, vol. 1, p. 384 (Patriarch).

36 Pitton de Tournefort, *Relation*, vol. 1, pp. 100–1.

37 ASCPF SOCG 792, fo. 143ʳ (Mazarek report).

38 Radonić, *Rimska kurija*, p. 665; Slijepčević, *Istorija crkve*, vol. 1, pp. 462–79 (arguing it was an act of force, but citing evidence to the contrary).

39 Bremer, *Ekklesiale Struktur*, pp. 17, 108.

40 ASCPF SC Servia 2, fos. 242ᵛ ('Mehmet aga mio grande amico'), 243ᵛ ('Allora soggiunse Mehmet aga Badate dunque ò Patriarca alli fatti vostri, e non imbrogliate le carte'). Perhaps because of such references to a 'Patriarch', there is some confusion over the date of the closure: Radonić, for example, gives it as 1788 (*Rimska kurija*, p. 664).

41 The name may come from any of several villages called Mazrrek: in northern Albania (Urošević, 'Janjevo', p. 197), near Elbasan (Rizaj, 'Transferimet, deportimet', p. 153 n.), or near Prizren (Rizaj, *Kosova gjatë shekujve*, p. 376); the name of the third may have been transferred to Kosovo by people from the first or second. The Archbishop signed himself 'Masarech' and stated that Albanian was not his native tongue: ASCPF SOCG 872, fo. 140ʳ (report of 1785).

42 ASCPF SOCG 792, fo. 146ʳ ('continuamente vengono molte Familie Cattoliche dalle Montagne di Albania, li quali per esser di natura calida, iraconda, e superba, facilissimi alli omicidii, non sofrano di esser calpestrati dalli Turchi come ci insegna il santo Evangelio, non umiliandosi al tributo Ottomano, sempre di giorno, e di notte vanno armate, per un minimo affronto di parole, e di fatti si amazzano . . .').

43 ASCPF SOCG 895, fos. 73ᵛ–74ʳ ('empito, e predominato'; 'la razza più che si multiplica . . . cento case'; 'capiscono, e si informano di notte, e di giorno di tutto quello, che si parla et opera per tutto il Mondo, tutta la notte si radunano in una casa della citta, o della villa, e fanno conciliaboli e consili'); 81ᵛ (prayer).

44 ASCPF SOCG 792, fo. 146ʳ.

45 ASCPF SOCG 872, fo. 139ʳ ('cinque case di grosse famiglie cattolici occulti').

46 ASVat Proc. consist., vol. 114, fo. 617ᵛ ('et multae aliae animae fideles sunt dispersae inter domicilia Turcharum et sunt a nobis administrata sacramenta'); ASCPF SC Servia 1, fo. 318ʳ (Gjon Nikollë or Nikolović, 1743).

47 Farlati, *Illyrici sacri*, vol. 7, pp. 172–6 (text of encyclical *Inter omnigenas calamitates*); ASCPF SOCG 792, fo. 149ᵛ (Mazarek report, 1760).

48 ASVat Vis. ad lim., vol. 728, 2nd report (1725).

49 All these details are from the fullest description, a summary of the report by Nikollë in 1743: ASCPF SC Servia 1, fos. 317–23.

50 *Ibid.*, fo. 303^r, Gjin Logoreci report, 1742 ('essendo loro privi de' Sacramenti, vogliono che le loro donne ancora restino prive dicendo: Dove andaremo noi, è bene che venghino ancora le nostre Donne').

51 ASCPF SC Servia 2, fos. 149–50 (Krasniqi report, 1770: death-threats), and SOCG 895, fo. 74^v, Mazarek report, 1791 ('li peggiori persecutori delli Catolici').

52 ASCPF SOCG 895, report of 1791, fos. 77^v (Peć), 75^r ('certa curiosa malatia donesca'), and SOCG 872 (report of 1785), fo. 130^r ('visitar i loro malati, ed anche nell'esorcizare, e benedire i loro animali').

53 ASCPF SOCG 872, fo. 144^v ('guerre orribili fra li turchi'), and SOCG 895, report of 1791, fo. 70^r ('delle continue, e generali sanguinose guerre Civili frà li Governatori Ottomani quasi per ogni città di Servia').

54 Rizaj, *Kosova gjatë shekujve*, pp. 297–8.

55 Shkodra, *La Ville albanaise*, p. 40; Mikić, *Društvene prilike*, pp. 15–16.

56 Pollo and Puto, *History*, pp. 95–7; Zavalani, *Histori*, vol. 1, pp. 251–2.

57 Gurakuqi, 'Kronikë', pp. 22–3.

58 ASCPF SC Servia 3, fos. 19^r: letter, 1788 ('Christiani'); 194^r: letter, 1796 ('hà preso borse infinite delli serviani, e l'ha spogliata di tutta la robba, viveri, et animali, e portato il tutto in Scuttari').

59 AMAE Mém. et doc., Turquie, vol. 136, fos. 274^v (hills); 282^r ('ce Pays n'est pas peuplé le quart de ce qu'il devrait être'); 276^v ('De loin, c'est quelque chose. De près, c'est un amas de rues boueuses & de maisons de terre'); 285^r ('Puissent mes ennemis vivre & mourir à Katchanizza!').

60 Lleshi, *Prizren, Priština*, part 1, p. 103.

61 Rizaj, *Kosova gjatë shekujve*, p. 262; Anhegger, *Beiträge*, vol. 1, p. 153.

62 Shkodra, *Esnafet*, pp. 299, 217–18.

63 Clayer, *Mystiques*, pp. 210–11 (Halveti), and *L'Albanie*, pp. 163–72 (Sa'di); Filipović, *Has*, pp. 63–4 (conversion).

64 ASCPF SOCG 792, fo. 153^r ('fine arti').

65 P. Kostić, *Prosvetno-kulturni život*, p. 5; Hadži-Vasiljević, *Prosvetne prilike*, p. 4.

66 ASCPF SOCG 895, fo. 71^r ('superbi Greci e scismatici').

67 ASCPF SC Servia 2, fo. 169^v ('et anche li istessi turchi, i quali fra di loro si mangiano, si amazzano, e saccheggiano uno l'altro'; 'tanto delli cattolici, scismatici, quanto delli turchi sono affatto esterminati, spopolati').

68 Kosančić, *Novo-Pazarski Sandžak*, pp. 6–8.

69 Gaston Gravier, quoted in Midhat Frashëri, *Albanais et Slaves*, p. 31 n.

70 ASCPF SC Servia 2, fo. 170^r ('ma di nuovo sono molti').

71 Urošević, *Etnički procesi*, pp. 18–20, 22–3.

72 Bataković, 'Od srpske revolucije', p. 175 (Andrija *et al.*); Brestovci, *Marrëdhëniet*, p. 39 (Bajraktari).

73 Hrabak, 'Srpski ustanici'; Bataković, 'Od srpske revolucije', pp. 176–8.
74 Jelavich, *History*, vol. 1, pp. 194–204.

10. Reform and resistance: 1817–1878

1 On the military (and associated educational) reforms see B. Lewis, *Emergence*, pp. 76–103.
2 On this whole episode see Nakičević, *Revolt* (quotation from p. 27).
3 *Ibid.*, pp. 24–5 (petition); P. Kostić, 'Prizrenski mutesarifi', p. 159 (ploy); Bataković, 'Od srpske revolucije', p. 179 (churches).
4 P. Kostić, 'Prizrenski mutesarifi', pp. 159–61. The Turkish sport of wrestling, *pehlivanlık*, was especially popular in Prizren: see Yastrebov, 'Stara Serbiia', p. 88.
5 Hecquard, *Histoire*, pp. 446–7; D. Pavlović, *Pokret u Bosni*, pp. 69–72.
6 D. Pavlović, *Pokret u Bosni*, pp. 72–8.
7 *Ibid.*, pp. 22–3, 81–3; Stojančević, *Jugoslovenski narodi*, pp. 49–60; Aličić, *Pokret*, pp. 233–5.
8 Thëngjilli, ed., *Kryengritjet*, pp. 45–6.
9 *Ibid.*, pp. 262–3, 294–7, 318–20; Mikić, *Društvene prilike*, p. 18. Mikić's claim that Mahmut was executed is false; his statement that Jashar met the same fate is contradicted by Boué, who wrote in 1839 that the paşalık of Prishtina 'seems to have been quite well administered for several years now by Jashar pasha': *La Turquie*, vol. 3, p. 187.
10 Müller, *Albanien*, p. 2 (military rule); Thëngjilli, ed., *Kryengritjet*, pp. 320–1 (conscription); AMAE Mém. et doc., Turquie, vol. 23, fo. 426, report by de Boislecomte, 1835 (revolts against uniform); Boué, *La Turquie*, vol. 3, p. 193 (other revolts); Ippen, 'Beiträge', p. 357, and Shkodra, *Shqipnia*, p. 32 (1839).
11 B. Lewis, *Emergence*, pp. 106–9; Davison, *Reform*, pp. 36–45.
12 Ippen, 'Beiträge', pp. 357–60; Shkodra, *Shqipnia*, pp. 39–40.
13 Wiet, 'Mémoire', p. 283.
14 ASCPF SC Albania 34, fo. 1018ᵛ ('quei luoghi possono considerarsi come in una permanente rivoluzione ed anarchia'). The English traveller Edmund Spencer, who visited Kosovo in 1850, refers to another revolt over conscription in 1847 (*Travels*, vol. 1, p. 384); this may perhaps be an error for 1845.
15 Kaleshi and Kornrumpf, 'Das Wilajet', p. 181.
16 ASCPF SOCG 922, fo. 333 (Krasniqi report, 1820). In Sept. 1820 Rome began a 'processo informativo' on the Rugovo martyrs (fos. 314–15).
17 All these details are from ASCPF SC Servia 4, fos. 172–3 (report by Fra Dionisio d'Afragola), and fos. 178–80 (report by Gaspër Krasniqi): 'perchè

i Fantesi non sono stati mai disturbati nei loro affari di Religione?'; 'dispersi tra i Villaggi tutti Turchi' (fo. 172ᵛ).

18 ASCPF SC Servia 4, fos. 209–10 (letter from Archbishop Bogdanović), 237 (visitation report by Bogdanović, giving the figure of 158 people); Gjini, *Ipeshkvia*, pp. 190–3; Gjergj-Gashi, *Martirët*, pp. 61–5, 82–92 (with 148 names and other statistics).

19 ASCPF SC Servia 4, fos. 350–2, 368–70 (Bogdanović reports, 1849, 1850).

20 Davison, *Reform*, pp. 55–6; text in Šopov, *Les Réformes*, pp. 48–54 (quotation p. 51).

21 Archbishop Bucciarelli noted the continuation of crypto-Catholicism in his report of 1872 (ASCPF SC Servia 5, fo. 589ᵛ); some declared themselves soon after 1856 (von Hahn, *Reise von Belgrad*, p. 83), but some did so only in the 1920s or '30s (Gjini, *Ipeshkvia*, p. 153).

22 Redžepagić, *Zhvillimi*, pp. 114, 117; Wiet, 'Mémoire', p. 283; Spuler, *Minderheitenschulen*, p. 84.

23 P. Kostić, *Prosvetno-kulturni život*, p. 6; Redžepagić, *Zhvillimi*, pp. 94, 152–4. Gopčević gives later dates for some of the Serb schools, and adds Janjevo, Lipljan and Orahovac from 1866: *Makedonien*, pp. 320–1.

24 Spuler, *Minderheitenschulen*, pp. 51, 59.

25 P. Kostić, *Prosvetno-kulturni život*, pp. 86–7 (SS. Basil, George), 43–4 (seminary).

26 Muir Mackenzie and Irby, *Travels*, vol. 1, pp. 202, 225, and P. Kostić, *Prosvetno-kulturni život*, p. 47 (unpopularity); Stojančević, *Jugoslovenski narodi*, p. 89 (price); Hadži-Vasiljević, *Prosvetne prilike*, p. 140 (Musulin).

27 Hadži-Vasiljević, *Prosvetne prilike*, p. 23 (Garašanin); Čilingirov, *Pomoravija*, pp. 36–7 (committee, schools); Stanković, *Beleške*, pp. 54–6 (Milojević).

28 Pavlowitch, 'Society in Serbia', p. 144 (violence); T. Djordjević, 'Arnauti' (Miloš).

29 Brestovci, *Marrëdhëniet*, pp. 81–7, 136–7, 152, 161; Stojančević, *Jugoslovenski narodi*, pp. 292–3; Senkevich, *Albaniia*, pp. 53–8; Bartl, 'L'attività', pp. 410–11 (Doçi).

30 Spencer, *Travels*, vol. 1, p. 193 (mayor); vol. 2, pp. 6 (Peć), 10 (Prizren).

31 On the guardians see Zirojević, *Crkve*, p. 36; Rizaj, *Kosova gjatë shekujve*, p. 477; Djuričić, *Običaji*, pp. 675–94. A report of 1899 said that Devič was protected in this way 'until recently': Peruničić, ed., *Zulumi*, p. 161. For examples of Muslim veneration of churches see von Hahn, *Reise von Belgrad*, p. 48; Muir Mackenzie and Irby, *Travels*, vol. 2, p. 88.

32 Brestovci, *Marrëdhëniet*, p. 104.

33 Stojančević, *Jugoslovenski narodi*, p. 314.

34 Shkodra, *Shqipnia*, pp. 53–4; see also Clayer, 'Bektachisme'.

35 Davison, *Reform*, pp. 105–6.

36 Midhat Bey, *Life of Midhat*, p. 37.

37 Davison, *Reform*, pp. 146–8; Birken, *Die Provinzen*, pp. 22–5.
38 On the transfer of the Prizren-Skopje eyalet see Wiet, 'Mémoire', p. 284. Midhat Bey implies mistakenly that Prizren had been under his father's rule in the period 1861–4 (*Life of Midhat*, p. 37).
39 Davison, *Reform*, pp. 151–4. There is an interesting description of Midhat's administration by the Albanian politician Ismail Qemal Vlora, who worked under him in Bulgaria in 1866–7: Vlora, *Memorie*, pp. 38–41.
40 Midhat Bey, *Life of Midhat*, p. 37; Kaleshi, 'Türkische Angaben', p. 110.
41 For the text of the Vilayet law of 1867, and further legislation of 1870, see Šopov, *Les Réformes*, pp. 114–30, 137–68.
42 Senkevich, *Albaniia*, p. 53, referring to documents in the Russian Central Military–Historical Archive.
43 Ippen, 'Beiträge', pp. 367–8; Brestovci, *Marrëdhëniet*, p. 169; Senkevich, *Albaniia*, p. 51.
44 Shkodra, *Shqipnia*, pp. 57–8.
45 P. Kostić, *Prosvetno-kulturni život*, pp. 77–9; Stanković, *Beleške*, pp. 32–6 (Stanković was co-editor and translator from Turkish to Serbian). On the enlarged Kosovo vilayet see Rizaj, 'Struktura', p. 95.
46 Wiet, 'Mémoire', p. 286.
47 Gounaris, *Steam*, pp. 42–6; Engin, *Rumeli demiryolları*, pp. 88–110.
48 Shkodra, *La Ville albanaise*, pp. 72–9 (hides, silk), 85–9 (metal, guns); Wiet, 'Mémoire', p. 288 (Serbia).
49 Shkodra, *Esnafet*, pp. 317–19, 335 n.
50 von Hahn, *Reise durch Drin und Wardar*, p. 80 (1863); Glück, *Albanien*, p. 52 (1891); Shkodra, *La Ville albanaise*, p. 93; Rahimi, *Vilajeti*, pp. 36–7 (Mitrovica, Prishtina). There was later a rope-factory in Prizren: Shkodra, *Esnafet*, p. 340.
51 Kaleshi and Kornrumpf, 'Das Wilajet', p. 202. Both these authors and Stojančević ('O stanovništvu', p. 216) take these figures as referring to the populations of the whole kazas of Prizren, Prishtina, etc., not just the towns; but Yastrebov, who served as a consular official in Prizren in the 1870s, was quite certain that the figures for Prizren (35,628 Muslims, 8,300 non-Muslims) referred only to the town ('Stara Serbiia', p. 40). These figures also match other reports from the 1860s on the town of Prizren: see Wiet, 'Mémoire', p. 276; von Hahn, *Reise durch Drin und Wardar*, p. 79.
52 Anon., *Detailbeschreibung*, pp. 80–1 (omitting Luma, Berane, Trgovište and Preševo, and counting 10,000 of the Gypsies as Muslim). This text incorporates material by Ippen, and may be largely his work.
53 Müller, *Albanien*, p. 12.
54 Yastrebov, 'Stara Serbiia', pp. 5–9, 52–92.
55 See the discussion of the Kosovo Polje area in Klaić, *Kosovo*, p. 11.
56 A report by Archbishop Bucciarelli in 1872 gave the total of Catholics in the archdiocese of Skopje as 10,848: ASCPF SC Servia 5, fo. 616ʳ.

57 Midhat Frashëri, *Albanais et Slaves*, p. 19 (fifty families).
58 The Austrian statistics give a total of 9,650, of whom 6,400 were in Prizren (Anon., *Detailbeschreibung*, pp. 80–1); but Nušić wrote that in 1894 there were no more than fifteen genuine Turkish families in Prizren (*S Kosova*, p. 32), and Petar Kostić put it at a maximum of twenty families (Hadži-Vasiljević, *Muslimani*, p. 24)
59 On the Gora see Yastrebov, 'Stara Serbiia', pp. 91–6, and *Obichai*. On the date and cause of conversion see Kanitz, 'Die Arnautisirung', pp. 39–40 (post-1766); Hadži-Vasiljević, *Muslimani* (post-1766); Yastrebov, 'Stara Serbiia', pp. 95–6 (pre-1766); Nušić, *S Kosova*, p. 39 (both).
60 Stojančević, *Jugoslovenski narodi*, p. 331 (1,123 households); Ippen, *Novibazar*, p. 147 (Prishtina); Müller, *Albanien*, p. 82.
61 Mikić, *Društvene prilike*, p. 22; Hadži-Vasiljević, *Muslimani*, p. 33 (Jews).
62 Elezović, *Rečnik* (absent); Karadžić, *Dela*, vol. 5, col. 11.
63 Mihačević, *Po Albaniji*, p. 64; Nušić, *S Kosova*, p. 37.
64 Yastrebov, 'Stara Serbiia', pp. 80–1 (Opoja); Nušić, *S Kosova*, p. 25; Kosančić, *Novo-Pazarski Sandžak*, p. 22.
65 Pipa, 'Rapsodi albanesi', pp. 392, 399.
66 Čilev, 'Obikolka', p. 108 (Catholics); Hadži-Vasiljević, *Muslimani*, p. 33 (relations).
67 Yastrebov, *Obichai*, pp. 1–22 (saints, slava), 'Stara Serbiia', p. 89 (Yule-log).
68 Schneeweis, *Serbokroatische Volkskunde*, pp. 114–16 (log), 148–54 (slava); Heim, *Gopčević*, p. 101 (slava); on the pre-Christian origins of many of these practices see Stadtmüller, 'Altheidnische Volksglaube'.
69 Müller, *Albanien*, p. 73; KA K.I.a.30, fo. 14ʳ. This MS was printed by Ivić ('Rumiljski vilajet': here p. 124), but without noticing the relation to Müller's book.
70 Milojević, *Putopis*, vol. 2, p. 114 (Geg claim); Wilkinson, *Maps and Politics*, p. 93 (Macedonian forgeries); Cvijić, *Remarques*, p. 44 n. ('propagandist'); on Cvijić's own drift into propaganda see Grimm, 'Ethnographic Maps', pp. 47–8.
71 Gopčević, *Makedonien*, pp. 209, 217, *Das Fürstentum*, p. 1.
72 Wilkinson, *Maps and Politics*, p. 103 ('father' quotation); Heim, *Gopčević*, esp. pp. 92–114. Gopčević's other activities included publishing a bogus correspondence with Gladstone after the latter's death, and conducting an anti-semitic campaign in Vienna.
73 Stern, *Das alte Rascien*, pp. 19–20; Ippen, *Novibazar*, pp. 41–2.
74 Hozier, ed., *Russo-Turkish War*, vol. 2, p. 795; Bataković, *Kosovo Chronicles*, p. 56.
75 Hrabak, 'Prvi izveštaji', p. 253.
76 Stern, *Das alte Rascien*, pp. 20–1.
77 For a concise account of the war and the treaties, see Jelavich and Jelavich, *Establishment*, pp. 141–57.

11. Kosovo's other minorities: Vlachs, Gypsies, Turks, Jews, and Circassians

1 Urošević, *Etnički procesi*, p. 14 (place-names, with other examples); Nopcsa, 'Beiträge', p. 236 (traditions).
2 Zirojević, 'Prvi vekovi', p. 63 (1488/9); Rizaj, *Kosova gjatë shekujve*, p. 264 (1490/1).
3 Beldiceanu, 'Sur les valaques', p. 97 (tax); Rizaj, *Kosova gjatë shekujve*, p. 357 (mines).
4 Capidan describes the case of a Vlach village, Stanišor, near Gjilan, where all the inhabitants were Slavicized: 'Românii nomazi', p. 333.
5 Hadžibegić *et al.*, eds., *Oblast Brankovića*, vol. 1, p. 209 (register); Burileanu, *I romeni*, p. 36 (traditions).
6 See Kaser, *Hirten, Kämpfer*, pp. 31, 48, 225 (though incorrectly describing the Gorans as Albanian-speakers).
7 Ippen, *Skutari*, p. 37; Shkodra, *Esnafet*, p. 206; Evliya Çelebi, *Narrative*, vol. 1, part 2, pp. 225, 230–2.
8 The best study is Peyfuss, *Die Druckerei*, esp. pp. 23–41; see also Wace and Thompson, *Nomads*, pp. 214–15 (Vienna), and Papathanasiou, *Historia tôn vlachôn*, pp. 46–51 (citing the figure of 12,000 houses, which Peyfuss rejects).
9 Peyfuss, *Die Druckerei*, pp. 41–6 (destruction); Martinianos, *Hê Moschopolis*, pp. 180–2 (towns, including Prizren); Shuteriqi, 'Shqiptarët' (church at Ráckeve, 30 km south of Budapest). A few Vlachs remained at Moschopolis: in 1905 there were roughly eighty families still there (Burileanu, *I romeni*, p. 129).
10 In 1858 von Hahn noted a Vlach village near Vranje: *Reise von Belgrad*, p. 47. In the 1890s the Serbian writer Branislav Nušić (himself of Vlach origin: 'Nuşi') observed pastoral Vlachs wearing fustanellas (kilts) in the market at Ferizaj: *S Kosova*, p. 17. On the Vlach community in Ferizaj see a report by the Serbian consul in 1899: Peruničić, ed., *Zulumi*, pp. 159–60.
11 Čilev, 'Obikolka', p. 109 (three villages); Müller, *Albanien*, pp. 22, 82.
12 Lleshi, *Prizren, Priština*, part 1, p. 98 (mahala); P. Kostić, *Prosvetno-kulturni život*, p. 23, and Nušić, *S Kosova*, pp. 30–1 (church, school).
13 Rakić, *Konzulska pisma*, pp. 114–15.
14 Gopčević, *Makedonien*, pp. 215–16; Yastrebov, 'Stara Serbiia', p. 39; Čilev, 'Obikolka', p. 109.
15 Fraser, *Gypsies*, p. 57; Crowe, *History*, p. 196.
16 Fraser, *Gypsies*, p. 57. For the derivation of this word (from Grk.: *tzanga*, shoe), see Jireček, 'Staat und Gesellschaft', (ii), p. 42 n.
17 Jireček, 'Staat und Gesellschaft', (i), p. 71 (and cf. Vlainac, *Verhältnisse*, p. 212); Rizaj, *Kosova gjatë shekujve*, pp. 417–18 (village). The derivation of 'magjup' (Alb.: *magjypë*) is uncertain. Margaret Hasluck proposed a

derivation from the 'gyp' element from a word for 'Egyptian' plus the Albanian prefix 'ma-', meaning bald or stripped; but this seems highly speculative.

18 Rizaj, *Kosova gjatë shekujve*, p. 349 (mining); Zirojević, 'Cigani', pp. 68 (1491), 72–3 (smithing, mines).

19 Zirojević, 'Cigani', pp. 69–70, 76.

20 *Ibid.*, p. 68, and Rizaj, *Kosova gjatë shekujve*, p. 418 (sancak); Barkan, *XV ve XVI inci asırlarda*, pp. 249–50 (tax, prohibition).

21 Mujić, 'Položaj cigana', pp. 146–55 (general rights); Thëngjilli, *Renta feudale*, p. 215 (exemption).

22 Browne, *Brief Account*, pp. 70 (quotation), 49.

23 Željazkova, *Razprostranenie*, p. 74.

24 Mujić, 'Položaj cigana', p. 149.

25 Müller, *Albanien*, pp. 82–3; ASCPF SC Albania 34, fo. 1024ʳ; Wiet, 'Mémoire', pp. 266, 277–8, 280.

26 Filipović, *Has*, pp. 51–2, and M. Hasluck, 'Gypsies' (language, professions); Jäckh, *Im Kriegslager*, p. 59 (quotation).

27 M. Hasluck, 'Gypsies'; Lutovac, *La Metohija*, p. 72 (farms); Urošević, *Kosovo*, pp. 48, 103–4, 109 (language, religion, intermarriage).

28 Petrović, 'Contributions' (slava, St George's Day, and Yule-log too).

29 von Hahn, *Reise von Belgrad*, p. 48.

30 Kanitz, *Das Königreich*, vol. 1, p. 649.

31 T. Djordjević, *Die Zigeuner*, p. 24 (campaign). A fascinating recent study discusses the ambivalence of Serbian culture towards Gypsy music, describing how Serbs both distance themselves from it as a form of the primitive, and cherish it as something in which they can participate: van de Port, *Het einde*.

32 Crowe, *History*, pp. 213–14.

33 Vučković and Nikolić, *Stanovništvo*, pp. 105 (war deaths, summarizing the findings of Kočović and Žerjavić), 108 (censuses).

34 See Duijzings, 'Egyptians'.

35 Rizaj, *Kosova gjatë shekujve*, pp. 345–6 (mines); Gökbilgin, *Rumeli'de Yürükler*, pp. 268–9 (1691: I am assuming that the kaza of Karadağ here is Montenegro, not Skopska Crna Gora).

36 Željazkova, *Razprostranenie*, pp. 70–5 (Yürük categorization); Hadžibegić et al., eds., *Oblast Brankovića*, vol. 1, p. 209 (Novo Brdo).

37 Urošević, 'Janjevo', p. 198.

38 *Ibid.*

39 Kaleshi, *Kontributi*, pp. 28–9.

40 Rizaj, *Kosova gjatë shekujve*, p. 448, giving several examples from Peć.

41 Stojančević, *Jugoslovenski narodi*, p. 329 (Sakate, near Gjakova); A. Popović, *L'Islam*, p. 307 (Dobrčani, near Gjilan, and Mamuša, near Prizren).

42 Müller, *Albanien*, pp. 73, 78, 82; von Hahn, *Reise von Belgrad*, p. 74.

43 Hadži-Vasiljević, *Muslimani*, p. 24.
44 Vučković and Nikolić, *Stanovništvo*, pp. 79, 108.
45 S. Goldstein, ed., *Jews in Yugoslavia*, p. 27.
46 Matkovski, *History*, pp. 11 (Salonica), 32 (Skopje); Hrabak, 'Jevreji u Albaniji', p. 58 (Durrës).
47 Jireček, 'Staat und Gesellschaft', (ii), p. 52.
48 On the general conditions see B. Lewis, *Jews of Islam*; Shaw, *Jews of Ottoman Empire*; Benbassa and Rodrigue, *Juifs des Balkans*. The late application of zimmi status is emphasized by Epstein, *Ottoman Jewish Communities*, pp. 27, 47.
49 Matkovski, *History*, pp. 37–41; Shaw notes further expulsions in the sixteenth century: *Jews of Ottoman Empire*, p. 35.
50 Rizaj, *Kosova gjatë shekujve*, pp. 223, 417 (registers); Epstein, *Ottoman Jewish Communities*, pp. 112 (minting), 71 (directing refugees).
51 Dželetović Ivanov, *Jevreji*, pp. 34 (Prishtina), 41 (Prizren); Hrabak, 'Jevreji u Albaniji' (Albania).
52 Kolonomos, *Poslovice*, p. 51 (1544); AMAE Corr. pol., Autriche, vol. 51, fo. 175^v (3,000, out of a total population of 60,000).
53 Spencer, *Travels*, vol. 2, p. 10 (Prizren); Wiet, 'Mémoire', pp. 278 (Prishtina), 280 (Gjakova); von Hahn, *Reise von Belgrad*, p. 19 (Prokuplje).
54 Midhat Frashëri, *Albanais et Slaves*, p. 10 (citing Bulgarian figures of 1903); Ippen, *Novibazar*, p. 20 (Spanish); Dželetović Ivanov, *Jevreji*, p. 43 (3,000). The anonymous *Detailbeschreibung*, however, gave a total of only 500 in 1899 (pp. 80–1).
55 Shaw, *Jews of Ottoman Empire*, pp. 193–4; P. Cohen, *Serbia's Secret War*, pp. 65–8.
56 Dželetović Ivanov, *Jevreji*, p. 43.
57 P. Cohen, *Serbia's Secret War*, pp. 71–2; Matkovski, *History*, pp. 81–2.
58 Dželetović Ivanov, *Jevreji*, pp. 59, 70–4, 83. This writer gives the figure of more than 400 arrested by the Skanderbeg division (p. 59), but the official report by the divisional commander stated 281: see Chapter 15, n. 53.
59 Rizaj, *Kosova gjatë shekujve*, p. 367.
60 See the account of these events, with a valuable summary of Circassia's social and political background, in Henze, 'Circassian Resistance'.
61 *Ibid.*, p. 63 (Jordan); Andrews, *Türkiye'de etnik gruplar*, pp. 236–7 (Turkey).
62 Bullemer gives this figure: 'Tscherkessendorf', p. 234; T. Djordjević says 40,000 families: 'Čerkezi', p. 144. Özbek suggests the inclusion of Abkhaz: *Erzählungen*, p. x.
63 Županić lists nineteen villages ('Etnološki značaj', p. 224), and T. Djordjević adds three others ('Čerkezi', p. 145); Uka gives the total of thirty ('Vom Kaukasus', p. 119). The figure of 12,000 is given by Županić, correcting a commonly quoted figure of 40,000.

64 T. Djordjević, 'Čerkezi', pp. 147–8 (epidemics, trades); Bullemer, 'Tscherkessendorf', p. 236 (rebellion); Ippen, *Novibazar*, p. 58 (Tula silver).
65 T. Djordjević, 'Čerkezi', p. 151 (quotation); Urošević, *Etnički procesi*, pp. 80–2 (explanation).
66 Bullemer, 'Tscherkessendorf', p. 236.
67 *Ibid.*, pp. 237–8.
68 Uka, 'Vom Kaukasus', p. 123 (fifty-two families); Özbek, *Erzählungen*, pp. xiii–xv.

12. From the League of Prizren to the Young Turk revolution: 1878–1908

1 Ippen, 'Beiträge', p. 367.
2 Boué, *La Turquie*, vol. 4, p. 126.
3 Bartl, 'L'attività', pp. 410–11 (1876); Baxhaku and Kaser, eds., *Die Stammesgesellschaften*, pp. 70–5 (1877, Austrian interests), 81–2 (petition, 1878); Selishchev, *Slavianskoe naselenie*, pp. 110–11 (Italian incitements, 1873, 1876); Senkevich, *Albaniia*, pp. 73–6 (Arbëresh delegation).
4 Hadži-Vasiljević, *Arbanaska liga*, p. 27.
5 Unfortunately there is no general study of the Albanian diaspora. Brief accounts were given in a series of articles in 1915–16: Anon., 'Colonies albanaises'; see also Azemi and Halimi, *Shqiptarët* (Egypt); Norris, *Islam*, pp. 196–211 (Arab lands); Dërmaku, 'Mbi veprimtarinë' (Romania); Sokolova, *Albanski pečat* (Bulgaria).
6 Sokolova, *Albanski pečat*, p. 43.
7 On the Frashëri brothers see Bartl, *Die albanischen Muslime*, pp. 132–41; Elsie, *History*, vol. 1, pp. 226–48. Extracts from Naim Frashëri's work on the Bektashi were published in French translation: see N. Frashëri, 'Le Livre'.
8 Skendi, *Albanian Awakening*, p. 88; Rahimi, *Lufta*, p. 24.
9 K. Frashëri, *Abdyl Frashëri*, pp. 83–103; Skendi, *Albanian Awakening*, p. 55.
10 For specimens of these petitions see Pollo and Pulaha, eds., *Akte*, pp. 12–32; the proclamation is on pp. 18–19.
11 The French consul in Shkodra, Colonna Ceccaldi, reported on 4 May that Ali pasha and the Muslims of several areas had formed 'a sort of league ... to oppose, with armed force, the occupation of their country by the Montenegrins' ('une sorte de ligue ... pour s'opposer, par les armes, à l'occupation de leur pays par les Monténégrins'), and that the towns of Prizren and Gjakova were considering whether to join it: AMAE Corr. pol. du cons., Turquie, Scutari d'Albanie, vol. 21, fo. 78ᵛ.
12 Bartl, *Albanien*, pp. 94–5; Belegu, *Lidhja*, p. 20 (fragment). For a list of delegates see Külçe, *Osmanlı tarihinde Arnavutluk*, pp. 249–50.

13 Pollo and Pulaha, eds., *Akte*, pp. 18–19. Belegu states that another meeting, on 15 June, threatened to declare Albanian independence if an inch of land was ceded to a foreign state (*Lidhja*, p. 21); this is quite out of character with the League's other declarations at this stage, and corroborating evidence for it is lacking. Kristo Frashëri states that the document of 18 June (the 'Kararname') was replaced by another document, the 'Kanun', on 2 July, which set out an authentically autonomist programme (*Abdyl Frashëri*, p. 195). But the Kanun was not a plan for an autonomous government, merely a system of military organization and recruitment; it was also passed on 18 June, and was seen as complementary to the Kararname: see Dako, *Liga*, pp. 37–42; Pollo and Pulaha, eds., *Akte*, pp. 43–8.

14 Skendi, *Albanian Awakening*, pp. 38–9. Three Mirdita men had taken part in the meeting at Prizren, and one from the Catholic clan of Gruda; but the other Catholic malësors remained aloof at this stage: AMAE Corr. pol. du cons., Turquie, Scutari d'Albanie, vol. 21, fos. 159, 177ʳ (Pons reports, 1 July and 2 Aug. 1878). Cf. an Italian report of Sept., saying that only the Catholics of Shkodra really wanted autonomy: Hrabak, 'Prvi izveštaji', p. 262.

15 Rizaj, 'Nëntë dokumente', pp. 199, 201. 'Ulema' is a collective term for Muslim clergy and scholars; 'the Porte' is the traditional term for the Ottoman government. In 1879 the British consul in Shkodra described the Leaguers in Kosovo as 'fanatical Muslims': Knight, *Albania*, p. 115.

16 Ippen, 'Beiträge', pp. 381–2; Choublier, *La Question*, pp. 182–4; Belegu, *Lidhja*, p. 17; Bartl, *Die albanischen Muslime*, p. 112.

17 Hadži-Vasiljević, *Arbanaska liga*, p. 50 n.; Schanderl, *Die Albanienpolitik*, p. 43; von Moltke, *Unter dem Halbmond*, p. 32.

18 Hadži-Vasiljević, *Arbanaska liga*, p. 53 (mosque); Hrabak, 'Prvi izveštaji', p. 266 (disarmament).

19 Senkevich, *Albaniia*, pp. 111–12 (white flag); Hadži-Vasiljević, *Arbanaska liga*, p. 56 (eight Albanians); AMAE Corr. pol. du cons., Turquie, Scutari d'Albanie, vol. 21, fos. 200ʳ ('piquée sur un picu fut promenée en triomphe dans les bazars de la ville'), 201ᵛ (estimates).

20 Pollo and Pulaha, eds., *Akte*, pp. 62–3.

21 *Ibid.*, pp. 59–62 (Ioannina), 65–6 (Debar). Kristo Dako later described the Debar declaration as the key document of the League: *Liga*, pp. 43–5. The importance of the Bektashi was pointed out by Mehdi Frashëri (*Lidhja*, p. 34), but was minimized in Albanian historiography of the period 1945–91. But the political role of the Bektashi sheikhs in the Debar region in the 1850s was noted by Zija Shkodra: *Shqipnia*, pp. 53–4 (cf. above, p. 190). See also Clayer, 'Bektachisme'.

22 Ippen, 'Beiträge', pp. 372–3; Plava, *Plava e Gucia*, pp. 63–83; Skendi, *Albanian Awakening*, pp. 60–5.

23 Ippen, 'Beiträge', p. 372 (Oct. 1878); Hadži-Vasiljević, *Arbanaska liga*, p. 93; AMAE Mém. et doc., Turquie, vol. 95, fos. 201–207ʳ (de Ring report, 2 Oct. 1879).

24 Hadži-Vasiljević, *Arbanaska liga*, p. 100 (Shkodra); British Government, *Accounts and Papers*, part 2, pp. 180–1. Fitzmaurice was supported by Lord Goschen, the Ambassador in Istanbul. See also Schanderl, *Die Albanienpolitik*, pp. 47–8.

25 K. Prifti, ed., *Lidhja*, pp. 76–9, 84–5, 99–103, 110–11.

26 PRO FO 195/1324, fo. 27 (Blunt report, Aug. 1880).

27 K. Prifti, ed., *Lidhja*, pp. 168–9.

28 Rizaj, ed., *Lidhja*, p. 281; PRO FO 195/1360, fo. 136 (Blunt report, 8 Feb. 1881). These impressions are confirmed by a report in the Russian archives from a leading Serb in Prishtina: see Senkevich, *Albaniia*, p. 147.

29 Ippen, 'Beiträge', pp. 377–8; HHSA PA XII 263, Liasse VIII B, Waldhart reports, 4 and 18 Jan. 1881.

30 PRO FO 195/1360, fos. 167ᵛ–168ʳ, Blunt report, 20 Feb. 1881 (conditions), 219ᵛ–220ᵛ, Blunt report, Mar. 1881 (Frashëri); AMAE Corr. pol. du cons., Turquie, Scutari d'Albanie, vol. 22, fo. 205ᵛ, le Rée report, 5 March 1881 (army plans).

31 Ippen, 'Beiträge', pp. 378–9.

32 K. Prifti, ed., *Lidhja*, pp. 180–1 (arrest); K. Frashëri, *Abdyl Frashëri*, pp. 316–29 (imprisonment, last years).

33 Rahimi, *Vilajeti*, p. 73; Braha, *Idriz Seferi*, p. 42 (4,000, Shuajip); K. Prifti, ed., *Lidhja*, pp. 251–72 (Voksh). Stulli gives the figure of 3,000 Albanians deported to Anatolia: 'Albansko pitanje', pp. 384–5.

34 Rahimi, *Lufta*, pp. 61 n., 67.

35 Bartl, *Die albanischen Muslime*, pp. 146–7, and Rahimi, *Lufta*, p. 58 (émigrés, schools); Redžepagić, *Zhvillimi*, pp. 160–4 (Albanian-language schools in Kosovo).

36 Rahimi, *Vilajeti*, pp. 12–14; Ippen, *Novibazar*, p. 50. There were several other changes, including, at one stage, the removal of the sancaks of Prizren and Debar, which were attached to the vilayet of Monastir: see Rizaj, 'Struktura stanovništva', p. 100.

37 Davison, *Reform*, pp. 386–90 (constitution); Ippen, *Novibazar*, p. 52 (1892 quotation); Anon., *Detailbeschreibung*, p. 64 (1899).

38 Pllana, 'Les Raisons', pp. 189–90 (quotation); Uka, *Dëbimi*, vol. 1, pp. 25–7 (110,000); Şimşir, ed., *Rumeli'den Türk göçleri*, vol. 1, p. 737 (60,000 families); Rizaj, 'Nëntë dokumente', p. 198 (60–70,000).

39 Şimşir, ed., *Rumeli'den Türk göçleri*, vol. 2, p. 516 (Niš); AMAE Mém. et doc., Turquie, vol. 95, fo. 172ʳ ('Le matériel provenant de ces démolitions, tel que pierres, bois, etc., a été vendu: de façon qu'à notre retour dans nos foyers nous ne trouverons plus aucun abri'). A tiny number of families did eventually go back: Kanitz, *Das Königreich*, vol. 2, p. 322.

40　Hadži-Vasiljević, *Arbanaska liga*, pp. 12–13 (Vranje); AMAE Mém et doc., Turquie, vol. 95, fo. 183ᵛ, de Ring report, 29 Sept. 1879 (Yastrebov). Hadži-Vasiljević is a somewhat rare example of a writer who was a Serbian nationalist without being anti-Muslim. (He was not a Muslim himself: the prefix 'Hadži-' was used by Orthodox Serbs if an ancestor had made the pilgrimage to Jerusalem.) His own explanation of the policy was that it followed the dictum of the poet Njegoš, 'to cleanse [*očistiti*] the land of the infidel' (p. 12). The Serbian nationalist term *čišćenje*, 'cleansing', probably originates from this Njegoš quotation.

41　Mikić, *Društvene prilike*, p. 26 (Eastern Kosovo); PRO FO 195/1360, fo. 114ᵛ, Blunt report, 2 Feb. 1881.

42　Ippen, *Novibazar*, p. 17 (Nikšić); Lleshi, *Prizren, Priština*, part 1, pp. 98–100 (Prizren).

43　Mikić, *Društvene prilike*, p. 27; Hadži-Vasiljević, *Muslimani*, p. 35.

44　Županić ['Gersin'], *Altserbien*, p. 29. This figure has been used more recently by the Serb émigré scholar Aleksandar Popović, who introduces it with the phrase 'on cite...' ('the figure is cited of...'): *L'Islam*, p. 307; and by Dušan Bataković, who extends the starting-date to 1850: *Kosovo Chronicles*, p. 59.

45　Nušić, *S Kosova*, p. 26.

46　AMAE Mém. et doc., Turquie, vol. 95, fo. 184ᵛ, de Ring report, 30 Sept. 1879; Bartl, *Die albanischen Muslime*, p. 54.

47　Vučković and Nikolić, *Stanovništvo*, p. 58; Midhat Frashëri, *Albanais et Slaves*, p. 7.

48　Bataković, 'Ulazak', pp. 233, 237.

49　For texts see Šopov, *Les Réformes*, pp. 380 (art. 23), 600–603 (Organic Statute), 528–30 (1896 decree).

50　Cvijić, *Remarques*, pp. 9–10; Hadži-Vasiljević, *Muslimani*, p. 37 ('naš jezik'); Mihačević, *Po Albaniji*, p. 16 ('naški').

51　Vojvodić, ed., *Dokumenti*, p. 973.

52　K. Prifti, *Le Mouvement*, pp. 149–50.

53　Rahimi, *Vilajeti*, pp. 80–3, 89–94.

54　Anon., 'Un interview', p. 158.

55　See for example K. Prifti, *Le Mouvement*, pp. 158–80.

56　HHSA PA XII 312, Liasse XXXIII, fo. 18ʳ, report by 'Musani' from Skopje, 6 Jan. 1899 ('unirsi tutti in una *bessa* generale per poter tener fronte ai bulgari, serbi e montenegrini, e rifiutare ogni altra qualità di riforme').

57　*Ibid.*, Liasse XXXIII, fos. 40ʳ ('Nous désirons restaurer l'ancienne Albanie'; 'avec délice'), 44ᵛ.

58　*Ibid.*, Liasse XXXIII, fos. 89–90, Rappoport report, 5 Feb. 1899 (listing twelve points), 89ᵛ ('mit feierlichem Eide auf den Koran'); a list of five points was later published: Pollo and Pulaha, eds., *Akte*, p. 137. See also Rahimi, *Lufta*,

p. 86 n. (translating the twelve points); Skendi, *Albanian Awakening*, p. 196 (adding details of the Muslim committees, from another Austrian report).

59 Rahimi, *Vilajeti*, pp. 97–100.

60 Abdyli, *Lëvizja*, pp. 34–6.

61 Bataković, 'Pogibija konzula', pp. 314–19. The very different version of this story believed by Edith Durham seems to have been mere hearsay: 'You need not waste pity on Stcherbina for he undoubtedly was killed while serving a gun on behalf of the Serbs' (SRO DD/DRU 47, letter to Aubrey Herbert, 19 Oct. 1922).

62 Lamouche, *Quinze ans*, pp. 41–4.

63 Dogo, *Kosovo*, p. 85 (1898, medal); Peruničić, ed., *Zulumi*, pp. 157–9 (1899); Cana, *Lëvizja*, p. 235 n. (1912).

64 Oestreich, 'Reisen', p. 316 (1898); Bataković, *Dečansko pitanje*. For a description of Dečani by a Russian visitor in 1908 see Bashmakov, *Through Montenegro*, pp. 76–90.

65 Rakić, *Konzulska pisma*, p. 58.

66 *Ibid.*, pp. 50–1, 97–105 (quotation from p. 101).

67 Hadži-Vasiljević, *Četnička akcija*, pp. 18–20; Peruničić, ed., *Zulumi*, pp. 370–2 (Velika Hoča), 396–7 (Pasjan); Rakić, *Konzulska pisma*, p. 338 n. (Pasjan).

68 Rahimi, *Lufta*, p. 140.

69 For a summary see B. Lewis, *Emergence*, pp. 194–207; for the Nationality Law see Davison, *Reform*, p. 262.

70 Skendi, *Albanian Awakening*, pp. 335–9; Bartl, *Die albanischen Muslime*, pp. 152–5.

71 Mikić, 'Shqiptarët', pp. 138–52; Bashmakov, *Through Montenegro*, p. 8.

72 Avramovski, 'Izveštaji', pp. 323–8.

73 *Ibid.*, p. 335 (Austrian report); E. Vlora, *Die Wahrheit*, p. 7; Skendi, *Albanian Awakening*, p. 343 (promises); Külçe, *Firzovik toplantısı*, pp. 56–9 (Draga, Curri), 60–1 (telegram); I. Vlora, *Memorie*, p. 263. Isa Boletin, however, refused to come to Ferizaj out of loyalty to the Sultan: see Külçe, p. 56, and Anon., Interview with Boletin.

74 Avramovski, 'Izveštaji', pp. 334–5; Louis-Jaray, *L'Albanie*, p. 99.

75 Durham, 'Scutari', p. 300; cf. her *High Albania*, pp. 223–31, and *Twenty Years*, pp. 188–90; Libardi, *Primi moti*, part 1, pp. 15–18.

13. The great rebellions, the Serbian conquest and the First World War: 1908–1918

1 Skendi, *Albanian Awakening*, pp. 344–51; Elsie, *History*, vol. 1, pp. 336–7. (Two alphabets were in fact agreed at Monastir, and another conference was held in 1910.)

2 Bartl, *Die albanischen Muslime*, pp. 168–9.

3 Durham, *Twenty Years*, pp. 191–2.

4 Rahimi, *Vilajeti*, p. 132.

5 B. Lewis, *Emergence*, pp. 214–17 (coup); Cana, *Lëvizja*, p. 51 (Riza bey); Anon., Interview with Boletin; Bartl, *Die albanischen Muslime*, p. 171 (rebellion).

6 Cana, *Lëvizja*, pp. 56–8, 64–6 (campaigns); Rakić, *Konzulska pisma*, pp. 163 (quotation), 164 (previous humiliation); E. Vlora, *Die Wahrheit*, pp. 24–5 (Luma, wedding). The official requirement was merely to enlarge the windows of the kullës, but Cavit's preferred way of doing this was by artillery fire: he boasted that he had destroyed sixty (Louis-Jaray, *L'Albanie*, p. 41). On the kullë see Nopcsa, *Haus und Hausrat*, pp. 38–50.

7 Jäckh, *Im Kriegslager*, pp. 26–39; Bartl, *Die albanischen Muslime*, p. 172; Cana, *Lëvizja*, pp. 91–115, 127; Braha, *Idriz Seferi*, pp. 81–129; Libardi, *Primi moti*, part 1, p. 23. Given the mainly Muslim nature of the Kosovo resistance to the Young Turks, it is worth noting that Idriz Seferi was a crypto-Catholic: see Rakić, *Konzulska pisma*, p. 239.

8 Jäckh, *Im Kriegslager*, pp. 23 (proclamation), 41 (40,000); Libardi, *Primi moti*, part 1, pp. 55–69 (campaign, martial law); E. Vlora, *Die Wahrheit*, p. 36 (guns).

9 Rakić, *Konzulska pisma*, pp. 235–8 (estimate); Durham, *Twenty Years*, p. 214, and Baxhaku and Kaser, eds., *Die Stammesgesellschaften*, pp. 173–6 (Catholics).

10 Cana, *Lëvizja*, pp. 120–1, 148–9; Rahimi, *Lufta*, p. 177.

11 Murzaku, *Politika*, p. 49 (founding, branches, Radenković); Cana, *Shpalime*, pp. 17–18 (alphabet), and *Lëvizja*, pp. 141–3 (Narodna Odbrana agreement).

12 Libardi, *Primi moti*, part 2, pp. 7–8, 38–9, 52–3; Durham, *Struggle*, pp. 23–42; Cana, *Lëvizja*, pp. 152–3; Rahimi, *Lufta*, p. 176.

13 Text in Puto, ed., *La Question*, vol. 1, pp. 365–70; see also Skendi, *Albanian Awakening*, pp. 416–18; Cana, *Lëvizja*, pp. 163–5; Sokolova, *Albanski pečat*, p. 76.

14 Durham, *Struggle*, pp. 68–80; Skendi, *Albanian Awakening*, p. 419–20; Bartl, *Die albanesischen Muslime*, pp. 177–8.

15 Rakić, *Konzulska pisma*, pp. 245–50; Cana, *Lëvizja*, pp. 157–60.

16 Cana, *Lëvizja*, pp. 170–8. Italy toyed with the idea of invading Albania, but was warned off by Austria-Hungary, and confined itself to shelling one small port: Durham, *Struggle*, p. 106.

17 Graves, *Storm Centres*, pp. 252–64, gives a vivid account. Local opinion was noted by Peckham, vice-consul in Skopje: 'It is argued that Albanian schools opened today may be shut the moment the elections are over' (PRO FO 195/2406/988). Edith Durham found the exercise incompetent as well as cynical (PRO FO 195/2406/2105, letter from Shkodra, 28 Mar. 1912).

18 Kaleshi, 'Hasan Prishtina', pp. 485–6 (family, career); Nuro and Bato, eds., *Hasan Prishtina*, pp. 22–43 (schools, speeches).
19 Peckham reports, 28 Apr. 1912: PRO FO 195/2406/1983 and 195/2406/ 2049. Prishtina's own account of this meeting is given in his memoir, *Nji shkurtim*, pp. 11–12: he asked for British support for an uprising, and eventually received the reply that Britain had no interest in the matter.
20 Peckham report, 29 June 1912: PRO FO 195/2406/3086; another version of this text is in Libardi, *Primi moti*, part 2, pp. 282–3.
21 Mantegazza, *L'Albania*, p. 219.
22 Bartl, *Die albanesischen Muslime*, p. 180; Cana, *Lëvizja*, pp. 202–13 (early revolt, Junik); Pollo and Pulaha, eds., *Akte*, pp. 234–5 (12 points).
23 Prishtina, *Nji shkurtim*, pp. 17–19; Cana, *Lëvizja*, pp. 213–20; PRO FO 195/ 2406/2759 (Peckham report, 7 June 1912, on clash at Junik).
24 PRO FO 195/2406/3186, 195/2407/3311 (wives); 195/2407/3489 (water-closet) (Peckham reports, 7, 12, 22 July 1912).
25 PRO FO 195/2407/3576 (25,000 men: Peckham report, 27 July 1912); Braha, *Idriz Seferi*, p. 175 (20,000); Skendi, *Albanian Awakening*, pp. 433–4 (parley, dissolution).
26 Four different texts are in Pollo and Pulaha, eds., *Akte*, pp. 248–53. See also Skendi, *Albanian Awakening*, pp. 435–7.
27 PRO FO 195/2407/3873–5 (arrivals in Skopje), 195/2407/3905 (16,000; quotation): Peckham reports, 14–16 Aug. 1912. Bartl gives the figure of 30,000 men (*Die albanischen Muslime*, p. 182); Swire thought 20,000 (*Albania*, p. 123); but Peckham's figure was confirmed by a French observer in Skopje, Jean Brunhes, who also commented on the high degree of discipline: see Godart, *L'Albanie*, p. 116 n.
28 Cana, *Lëvizja*, pp. 246–58; PRO FO 195/2407/4322 (Ottoman version, 20 Aug. 1912).
29 SRO DD/DRU 33, part 2, memorandum, 4 Jan. 1918; for a similar judgement see Swire, *Albania*, pp. 124–5.
30 Herbert, *Ben Kendim*, pp. 200, 205.
31 Puto, ed., *La Question*, vol. 1, pp. 373–6 (text); Murzaku, *Politika*, pp. 73–4.
32 Helmreich, *Diplomacy*, pp. 85–9.
33 Swire, *Albania*, p. 133 (Montenegro); Cana, *Lëvizja*, pp. 190 (early 1912), 239–40 (Draga); Murzaku, *Politika*, pp. 108 (publicity), 116 (Curri); Vojvodić, ed., *Dokumenti*, pp. 1022–3 (Curri negotiations with Pašić and Milojević).
34 Swire, *Albania*, pp. 127–9 (envoys, Apis); Dogo, *Kosovo*, pp. 110–12 (Boletin); HHSA PA XXXVIII 405, Prochaska report, 27 Aug. 1912 (arms to Boletin); Wirth, *Der Balkan*, p. 145 (rumour of subsidy). Arms deliveries from Serbia continued in Sept.: see AMAE n.s. Turquie, vol. 234, fo. 174^{r} (report from Skopje, 10 Sept. 1912).

35	Helmreich, *Diplomacy*, pp. 96–7, and Swire, *Albania*, pp. 130–2 (Montenegrin incidents); Murzaku, *Politika*, p. 112 (četniks); PRO FO 195/2407/4714 (Peckham report, 24 Sept.).

36	AMAE n.s. Turquie, vol. 235, fos. 188 (complaint), 192 (Ottoman withdrawal), 213–17 (mobilization); Murzaku, *Politika*, p. 111 (low strength); Helmreich, *Diplomacy*, p. 99 (purge); AMAE n.s. Turquie, vol. 236, fos. 174–175^r, Carlier report, 4 Oct. 1912 (untrained, sent home).

37	Swire, *Albania*, p. 134; Helmreich, *Diplomacy*, pp. 140–5. Edith Durham had a simpler explanation: 'Montenegro hoped by rushing in first to occupy the coveted Kosova land, especially Prizren, before the Serbs got going' (Destani, ed., *Albanian Question*, p. 18).

38	Murzaku, *Politika*, p. 111, and Rushiti, *Rrethanat*, p. 22 (army strengths); Mantegazza, *L'Albania*, pp. 269–71 n. (report, 12 Oct., from *Corriere d'Italia* correspondent in Skopje); AMAE n.s. Turquie, vol. 239, fos. 62^v–63^r ('qu'on prétendait acheté par la Serbie, fait une propagande acharnée contre ce pays et il a armé 1,000 de ses gens de bons fusils "Mauser"').

39	Jaša Tomić, *Rat*, p. 103 (journalist); Murzaku, *Politika*, pp. 128–32 (campaign, Mitrovica); Rushiti, *Rrethanat*, p. 23 (1,448); Anon., Interview with Boletin (withdrawal). Serbian sources quoted a telegram from Ali Riza pasha to Isa Boletin, allegedly found in the post office in Prishtina, complaining 'you have done nothing': this must be either a sign of Ali Riza's ignorance, or a fabrication (see Martinović, 'Qëndrimi', p. 248).

40	Murzaku, *Politika*, pp. 132–4 (Ferizaj, army movements); Braha, *Idriz Seferi*, pp. 190–4 (Seferi); Jasă Tomić, *Rat*, pp. 132–7, and Trevelyan, 'Servian Army', p. 602 (Kumanovo).

41	Külçe, *Osmanlı tarihinde Arnavutluk*, pp. 423–4, and Gjergj-Gashi, *Kosova*, p. 92 (Prizren); Murzaku, *Politika*, pp. 135 (Gjakova), 143–51 (Malësi); Rushiti, *Rrethanat*, p. 30 (Peć).

42	Jaša Tomić, *Rat*, p. 120 (Kosovo Polje); Miller, *Ottoman Empire*, p. 503; for many examples of the medievalist ideology see K. Subotić, ed., *Ilustrovana kronika*.

43	Trevelyan, 'Servian Army'; Cana, *Socialdemokracia*, p. 127 (approval of left); Trotsky, *Balkan Wars*, pp. 120, 286.

44	Cana, *Socialdemokracia*, pp. 128–9; Tucović, *Srbija i Arbanija*, esp. pp. 97–114 (criticizing the occupation of northern Albania); see also the extracts from Tucović's writings in Stefan, ed., *Srbija i Albanci*, vol. 1 pp. 22–51.

45	Durham letter to Myres, 31 Jan. 1944: Bodl. MS Myres 12, fo. 165^r; Durham, 'Frontiers', p. 643.

46	Freundlich, *Albaniens Golgotha*, p. 9 (Danish report; pp. 12–15 also give a version of Mjeda's report); Bodl. MS Myres 12, fo. 164^r (Durham letter, 1944, quoting *Telegraph* report); Gjergj-Gashi, *Kosova*, pp. 89–100 (Mjeda report, quotation from p. 93; the Austrian consul in Skopje wrote that where he had direct evidence, it confirmed Mjeda's account: pp. 101–6); Halaçoğlu, *Balkan harbi sirasinda*, p. 37 (20,000 estimate).

47 Carnegie Endowment, *Report*, p. 151.

48 Gjergj-Gashi, *Kosova*, pp. 113–15 (Austrian consul); Krasniqi, *Lugu i Baranit*, p. 29; Martinović, 'Qëndrimi', p. 274 (Mjeda complaint). On the Palaj affair see Cana, *Socialdemokracia*, pp. 148–9, Durham, *Twenty Years*, pp. 235–6, and Freundlich, *Albaniens Golgotha*, p. 29.

49 Rushiti, *Rrethanat*, p. 91 (Prishtina); Freundlich, *Albaniens Golgotha*, p. 27.

50 Helmreich, *Diplomacy*, p. 209–24 (Pašić quotation, p. 224); PRO FO 195/2438/6757, Greig report, 8 Nov. 1912, from Monastir (where Nušić had been appointed 'civil governor'); Hrabak, *Britanska diplomatija*, p. 13 (British position).

51 Rushiti, *Rrethanat*, p. 71 (Serbian census); Kolea, 'Les Massacres', p. 49 (Russian report); Mladenov, 'Bemerkungen', pp. 57–8 (Bulgarian census).

52 Helmreich, *Diplomacy*, pp. 251–93; Hrabak, *Britanska diplomatija*, pp. 42–55.

53 A copy of the proceedings of the commission, a typescript volume of 124 pp., is contained in HHSA PA XIV 46, Liasse IL/1, 2, with other documents, including the Austrian proposal for one or more neutral zones (telegram of 8 Jan. 1914).

54 Rushiti, *Rrethanat*, p. 53 (agreement); Dogo, *Kosovo*, p. 54 (Serbian declaration).

55 Martinović, 'Qëndrimi', pp. 253–5 (royal decree, weapons); Rushiti, *Rrethanat*, p. 56 (Aug. decree); Carnegie Endowment, *Report*, pp. 160–2 (Sept. decree, full text).

56 HHSA PA XXXVIII 405, von Pözel report, 28 June 1913 (kaçaks), and Kohlruss report, 18 Sept. 1913 (Fshaj); Cana, *Socialdemokracia*, p. 147 n. (Fshaj); Rushiti, *Rrethanat*, pp. 161–4 (revolt); Wirth, *Der Balkan*, pp. 171–2 (Serb actions, ultimatum).

57 HHSA PA XXXVIII 405, Kohlruss report, 27 Jan. 1914.

58 Babić, 'Migracije', p. 165 (11,000), and 'Iseljavanje', p. 314 (16,000).

59 Krause, 'Das Problem', p. 350 (Bosnian figures, reproducing a document in the Kriegsarchiv); Bajrami, 'Konventa', p. 243 (120,000).

60 Rushiti, *Rrethanat*, p. 169 (8,481); Anon., 'Dans l'engrenage', quoting a report by the Italian journalist Magrini (50,000). After the war a petition to the League of Nations from the Albanian 'Dëshira' society of Sofia noted that Albanians had been 'forced' ('contraints') to serve in the Serbian army: PRO FO 371/9961/5193.

61 Rushiti, *Rrethanat*, p. 172; for the complex Albanian political circumstances which prompted this adventure see Pollo and Puto, *History*, pp. 163–5.

62 Immanuel, *Serbiens Untergang*, p. 36, and Rushiti, *Rrethanat*, pp. 173–4 (Bulgarian campaign); Bojović, *Odbrana*, pp. 29–31 (withdrawal), 32, 48 (kaçaks), 53 ('disorders').

63 Boppe, *A la suite*, p. 41 (council); Immanuel, *Serbiens Untergang*, p. 51 (welcome).

64 Bojović, *Odbrana*, p. 75 (decision); Immanuel, *Serbiens Untergang*, pp. 52–4 (advance, prisoners).

65 Boppe, *A la suite*, p. 100 (dignitaries); H. Schwanke, 'Zur Geschichte', p. 54 (horses, cannibalism); SRO DD/DRU 47, undated Durham memorandum; see also the comments in Kolea, 'Les Massacres'.

66 Kolea, 'Les Massacres', p. 34 n. (communiqués); Schanderl, *Die Albanien- politik*, e.g. pp. 59–63; HHSA PA I 991, Liasse Krieg 47, report from Mitrovica, 11 Jan. 1916 (Prishtina: on his recruits and their subsequent operations in Albania see H. Schwanke, 'Zur Geschichte', pp. 75–9); Haxhiu, *Shota dhe Azem*, pp. 38–9 (Draga). On the welcome to the Austrians given by Hasan Prishtina and the Albanians of Vuçitërn see also Stern, *Das alte Rascien*, p. 88.

67 Lange, 'Curri', p. 344; Herbert, *Ben Kendim*, p. 213, and Anon., 'Iç Boletine' (two slightly different accounts of Boletin's death).

68 Redžepagić, *Zhvillimi*, p. 259 (schools in Kosovo); San Nicolò, *Die Verwal- tung*, pp. 1–4 (Albania not conquered), 144–5 (permission needed), 233–4, 248–9 (schools, literary commission in Albania); R. Schwanke, 'Das Schul- wesen', p. 63 n. (army's preference); HHSA PA I 874, draft of telegram by Burián to Prince Hohenlohe, 2 Feb. 1916.

69 HHSA PA I 874 contains the Austrian documents on this dispute, including a telegram from Conrad to Burián, 12 Feb. 1916, relating Ferdinand's claim ('dass ... ein grosser Teil der Bevölkerung bulgarisch sei'). For a full treatment of this issue, and of later Bulgarian claims over Kosovo, see Avramovski, 'Pretendimet'.

70 Rushiti, *Rrethanat*, pp. 180–4 (conditions, labour, famine); Interallied Commission, *Report*, pp. 7 (Metropolitan), 18 (1,000 dead), 22–4 (Bulgarianization).

71 Braha, *Idriz Seferi*, pp. 219–23; Haxhiu, *Azem dhe Shota*, pp. 49–55, and Rushiti, *Rrethanat*, pp. 197–9.

72 The best account of the whole withdrawal is Kirch, *Krieg*, pp. 101–31; see also Rushiti, *Rrethanat*, p. 199 (Bejta); Reith, *Von Monastir*, p. 53 (fortunate encounter); SRO DD/DRU 33, part 2, Herbert letter from Vlora, 30 Oct. 1918 (Italian advance from Prizren).

14. Kaçaks and colonists: 1918–1941

1 For the 1903 text see Dareste de la Chavanne, *Les Constitutions*, vol. 2, p. 260.

2 On all these points see Pop-Kosić, *Étude juridique*, pp. 23–4, 88–90.

3 *Ibid.*, pp. 105–15.

4 Rushiti, *Lëvizja*, p. 247; PRO FO 371/6194/7963, Young report, April 1921 (concessions); FO 371/6194/13729, Strang report, June 1921 (vote).

5 Text in International Documentation on Macedonia, *Harold Nicolson*, pp. 127–30 (arts. 2, 8 and 9); the Yugoslav government refused at first to sign this treaty, but did so under international pressure on 5 Dec. 1921 (Dogo, *Kosovo*, pp. 230–1).

6 Pirraku, 'Kulturno-prosvetni pokret', p. 358 (closures, mektebs); Beard and Radin, *Balkan Pivot*, pp. 253 (newspapers for Germans, etc., citing a report by the US consul), 255 (Montenegro); Bisak, Kurti and Gashi, *Gjendja*, pp. 73–85 (schools, teachers, catechism, poster); Redžepagić, *Zhvillimi*, pp. 194–6 (Lumezi).

7 Pirraku, 'Kulturno-prosvetni pokret', p. 357 n. (statement); Clissold, ed., *Short History*, p. 165, and Vučković and Nikolić, *Stanovništvo*, p. 79 (statistics).

8 Baldacci, *Studi*, vol. 1, p. 273; Popp, 'Minoritatea', p. 365. Most Albanian sources used the figure of 800,000: see Kokalari, *Kosova*, p. 90. For the other linguistic groups in the 1921 census see Clissold, ed., *Short History*, p. 165: Serbs, Croats and Bosnians were treated as speakers of the same language, and so too were Macedonians.

9 V. Djordjević, *Les Albanais*, pp. 8–9 (tails), 60 (Skanderbeg); for a valuable discussion of these ideological contradictions see Banac, *National Question*, pp. 292–6.

10 Bajrami, *Rrethanat*, p. 182, and A. Popović, *L'Islam*, p. 330 (name, foundation); Pirraku, 'Kulturno-prosvetni pokret', p. 361 (Slavicizing policy); Anon., 'The Moslems' (demands agreed at Skopje). I do not know on what grounds Bajrami gives the name of the party in Albanian as 'Shoqëria e mbrojtjes së të drejtave shqiptare', 'The Association for the Defence of Albanian Rights' (p. 182).

11 Bajrami, *Rrethanat*, p. 190 (Kosovo statistics: registration, voters and seats); Naval Intelligence Division, *Jugoslavia*, vol. 2, pp. 324 (suffrage), 340 (total in Assembly). Dogo states that eight Xhemijet deputies were elected (*Kosovo*, p. 136); this may perhaps be a confusion with the number of ethnic Albanians.

12 PRO FO 371/6193/1923, Stonehewer Bird report from Skopje, 2 Jan. 1921 ('The success of the Communist party in Southern Serbia was due to Bulgarian intrigue ... The Communist party here is not numerically strong enough to have met with any success at the recent elections, had it stood for the principles of Communism alone'); Beard and Radin, *Balkan Pivot*, p. 113 (various answers). See also Banac, *National Question*, pp. 153–89 (Radicals, Democrats), 328–39 (Communists).

13 PRO FO 371/6203/2832, translation of report in *Agramer Tageblatt*, 2 Feb. 1921 (inquisition quotation); Verli, *Reforma*, p. 154 (Apr. 1922, Sept. 1923); Rushiti, *Lëvizja*, p. 249 (Pašić wooing); Bajrami, *Rrethanat*, p. 216 (budget).

14 Bajrami, *Rrethanat*, pp. 212–14 (Draga complaint), 219–20 (split); Rushiti, *Lëvizja*, p. 257 (Croatian visit).

15 Bajrami, *Rrethanat*, pp. 139 (Gafuri), 228–33 (Račić mission, arrest, party collapse), 241 (1927 sentence); Banac, *National Question*, p. 377 (Tetovo candidature); Dogo, *Kosovo*, p. 264 (Hak closure, arrests); Borshi, 'Les Albanais', p. 18 (Gafuri). The charge against Draga was that he had killed eighteen Serbs during the First World War; Serb reports in 1918 had in fact said that he had protected the Serbs, before being interned by the Austrians (Rushiti, *Lëvizja*, p. 237).

16 Rushiti, *Lëvizja*, p. 205 (private schools); Verli, *Reforma*, pp. 158–60 (White Drin, Gjeçov, continued Xhemijet activity, education in Albania); Pirraku, 'Kulturno-prosvetni pokret', p. 359 (sports clubs, etc., Agimi); Elsie, *History*, vol. 1, p. 304, and Bisak, Kurti and Gashi, *Gjendja*, pp. 43–7 (Gjeçov).

17 Rushiti, *Lëvizja*, pp. 70–81 (resistance, clashes); Dogo, *Kosovo*, pp. 68–9 (Montenegrins); Gjergj-Gashi, *Kosova*, p. 331 (statistics).

18 Rushiti, *Lëvizja*, pp. 79 (foundation), 90 (Feb. protest); Nuro and Bato, eds., *Hasan Prishtina*, pp. 99–100 (telegram to Woodrow Wilson); Swire, *Albania*, pp. 280, 287, 295 (Peace Conference, frontiers).

19 Rushiti, *Lëvizja*, pp. 94–101 (rules, 1919 campaign); Bajrami, *Rrethanat*, pp. 143–4 (demands).

20 Rushiti, *Lëvizja*, pp. 104–43; Bajrami, *Rrethanat*, pp. 99–118; Haxhiu, *Shota dhe Azem*, pp. 122–7, 144–5.

21 PRO FO 371/6193/4351 and 5870, Stonehewer Bird reports, 17 Feb. 1921 (text of proclamation), 16 Mar. (2,000); FO 371/6194/7962, Stonehewer Bird report, 4 Apr. 1921 (internment).

22 PRO FO 371/5725/7856 and 11284, Eyres report, Durrës, 16 Apr. (first quotation), and Young report, Belgrade, 25 May (quoting article by Jovan Cirković, *Politika*, 23 May); Rushiti, *Lëvizja*, p. 171 (Bejta return).

23 Kaleshi, 'Hasan Prishtina', p. 488; Fischer, *King Zog*, p. 20 (Kadri); Dogo, *Kosovo*, p. 133 (Curri).

24 Fischer, *King Zog*, pp. 20 (Shkodra), 28–9 (Mirdita); SRO DD/DRU 35, part 2, statement by delegation from Lushnja Conference (request for Peć etc.); DD/DRU 33, part 3, letter from Mr Abraham, League of Nations, 8 Oct. 1921 (new frontiers); Swire, *Albania*, pp. 280 (map of frontier changes), 354–70 (Mirdita rebellion, international response, frontiers); Milo, *Shqipëria*, pp. 134–5 (Mirdita rebellion).

25 Fischer, *King Zog*, pp. 32–7.

26 Rushiti, *Lëvizja*, pp. 187–221 (death sentence, neutral zone, besë, death of Azem), 233 (Curri), 239 (Shota); Fischer, *King Zog*, pp. 70–5 (Zog's Yugoslav troops). Milo writes that Zog had received secret subsidies from Belgrade during the entire period 1920–4: *Shqipëria*, p. 151.

27 PRO FO 371/5725/11103, letter from Midhat Frashëri to League of Nations,

29 Apr. 1921 (2,000); FO 371/6194/17975, Strang report, 8 Sept. 1921 (Čaušević interview, Aug.); Bajrami, 'Konventa', p. 243 (Kosovo Committee).

28 Verli, *Reforma*, pp. 148–52 (discouraging colonists): Verli notes that colonization hardly began in the Drenica region until after Azem Bejta had been killed.

29 The best general studies of the colonization programme are Obradović, *Agrarna reforma*, and Verli, *Reforma* (p. 106 on the Wrangel plan: discussed also in a letter from Hasan Prishtina to the British Foreign Secretary in Jan. 1921, PRO FO 371/5725/2613). See also the useful summary in Roux, *Les Albanais*, pp. 191–203, and the place-by-place statistical survey in Sekulić, *Seobe*, pp. 61–86.

30 Obradović, *Agrarna reforma*, pp. 23–33; Verli, *Reforma*, pp. 13–20; Babić, 'Migracije', pp. 167–8.

31 Ivšić, *Les Problèmes*, pp. 103, 177–9; Verli, *Reforma*, pp. 30–2; Obradović, *Agrarna reforma*, pp. 92–5.

32 Verli, *Reforma*, pp. 37–8, 53–5.

33 Obradović, *Agrarna reforma*, p. 127; Roux, *Les Albanais*, p. 194.

34 Verli, *Reforma*, pp. 87–8, 143 (statistics), 136 (hostility of local Serbs); Krstić, *Kolonizacija*, p. 81 (quotation).

35 Larnaude, 'Un village', p. 323.

36 Verli, *Reforma*, pp. 59 (unpublicized decisions, expulsions), 102 (foreign charities); Krstić, *Kolonizacija*, p. 3 (Vitomirica).

37 Verli, *Reforma*, p. 116 (1928–9 figures); Dragnich and Todorovich, *Saga of Kosovo*, p. 120 ('The new government was not a wealthy uncle...', etc.). Equally bizarre is the attempt of these two authors to present the entire colonization programme as a 'relief' operation. Their statement that 'Most of the land available for homesteading [the authors' term for colonization] belonged to Turks who had left with the Turkish army...' (p. 121) is false; so too is their claim that none of the colonists in Kosovo were Serbs from Serbia (p. 122). A total of 3,671 colonist families – roughly 18,000 people – were from Serbia proper, excluding Vojvodina: see Obradović, *Agrarna reforma*, p. 221.

38 Roux, *Les Albanais*, p. 195; Verli, *Reforma*, pp. 95–6, 138; Obradović, *Agrarna reforma*, p. 221; Krstić, *Kolonizacija*, p. 81.

39 Ivšić, *Les Problèmes*, p. 220 (lack of tools, etc., malaria, kaçaks); Larnaude, 'Un village', p. 323 n. (malaria); Verli, *Reforma*, pp. 150–2 (kaçaks), 161 (corruption). Krstić admitted that many 'mistakes' had been made: *Kolonizacija*, pp. 42–3.

40 Ristić, 'Naseljavanje', pp. 36 (return), 37 (quotation).

41 Obradović, *Agrarna reforma*, p. 165 (Peć, Istok); Bajrami, *Rrethanat*, pp. 77–8 (letter).

42 'R. R.', 'Qui sont les Banus?'; Matijević, 'Yougoslavie', noted that the division of Kosovo was designed to make the Albanians a minority in each of the three new units.

43 Verli, *Reforma*, pp. 70–6 (policy, upper Drenica); Pirraku, 'Kulturno-prosvetni pokret', pp. 365, 366 n. (quotation). Hajredin Hoxha notes that in some parts of Kosovo in 1937–40 even the figure of 0.4 ha. was not respected, and that families of more than ten members were left with less than 2 ha.: 'Elemente', p. 330.

44 H. Hoxha, 'Politika', pp. 432–4.

45 Čubrilović, 'Expulsion', pp. 12–15.

46 H. Hoxha, 'Politika', p. 437 (fines); Bajrami, *Rrethanat*, pp. 142–3 (mosques, graveyard, report).

47 H. Hoxha, 'Politika', pp. 436–7; Bajrami, 'Konventa'. Earlier negotiations had occurred in 1926, when Yugoslavia asked Turkey to take 300–400,000 Albanians: Bajrami, *Rrethanat*, pp. 153–4. Another prominent intellectual who worked in the Yugoslav Foreign Ministry, the novelist Ivo Andrić, also supported the policy of sending all Muslim Albanians to Turkey: see Krizman, 'Elaborat', p. 89.

48 Roux, *Les Albanais*, pp. 223–4 (77,000); Bisak, Kurti and Gashi, *Gjendja*, p. 54; Bajrami, *Rrethanat*, p. 177.

49 Rushiti, *Lëvizja*, p. 155 (1926); SRO DD/DRU 35, part 2, Herbert typescript, Mar. 1927.

50 PRO FO 371/9961/14470, Eyres report, 3 Sept. 1924: translation of article by Gjergj Bubbi in *Shqipëria e re* (Constanţa), 24 Aug. 1924. Cf. Čubrilović's recommendation in his policy paper: 'we must first of all win over their clergy … either by money, or by threats … They must describe the beauties of the new territories in Turkey, the easy and pleasant life there' ('Expulsion', p. 14).

51 See Dogo, *Kosovo*, pp. 170–7 (exile politics, subsidies), 216–17 (assassination attempts), 306–12 (subsidies, death of Prishtina); Fischer, *King Zog*, pp. 82–152 (pp. 145–6 on the title).

52 Jacomini, *La politica*, p. 84.

53 *Ibid.*, p. 85; Ciano, *Diary*, pp. 12–14, 23–7; Stojadinović, *La Yougoslavie*, pp. 199–204.

15. Occupied Kosovo in the Second World War: 1941–1945

1 NA T-821, reel 128, frames 171–2, notes on discussion between Italian Supreme Command and von Rintelen, 28 Mar. 1941; Roatta, *Otto milioni*, p. 161 (Italian suspicions). On the Belgrade coup and Hitler's Balkan policy see Jelavich, *History*, vol. 2, pp. 233–6.

2 NA T-821, reel 129, frame 852, memorandum by Italian Supreme Command, 28 Mar. 1941 ('in breve tempo sopraffatto'); reel 128, frame 157, note by Italian Supreme Command of briefing given to von Rintelen, 30 Mar. 1941.

3 Hadri, *Lëvizja*, pp. 78–9.

4 *Ibid.*, pp. 80–4; Bianchini and Privitera, *6 aprile*, pp. 53–4. On Prizren and Suha Reka see F. Hoxha, 'Prve jedinice', p. 137.

5 Hadri, 'Okupacioni sistem', p. 57, and *Lëvizja*, p. 140; Mitrovski, Glišić and Ristovski, *Bulgarian Army*, pp. 30–5.

6 Schlarp, *Wirtschaft*, pp. 92–3 (Vienna meeting, fears of irredentism); NA T-821, reel 129, frames 470–6 (mining report, by Dino Gardini); and T-120, reel 120, frames 66218–19 (German consul's report on telegram, from Tirana, 19 Apr. 1941).

7 Schlarp, *Wirtschaft*, pp. 93–4 (mining interests, railway); NA T-821, reel 128, frame 137, von Rintelen report, 24 Apr. 41 (railway); and T-501, reel 245, frame 418, Kriegstagebuch of German commander in Serbia (Prishtina).

8 On all these measures see Hadri, 'Okupacioni sistem', pp. 45–54, and *Lëvizja*, pp. 105–16; see also Jacomini, *La politica*, p. 279 (July acclamation).

9 Hadri, 'Okupacioni sistem', pp. 54–6, and *Lëvizja*, pp. 123–38; NA T-501, reel 249, frames 1054–6, text of agreement between Gen. Eberhardt and Albanian notables, 21 Apr. 1941 (frame 1056: 'nach eigenen Wünschen'). On Deva see Hoti, *Çështja*, pp. 27–8, Shukriu, 'Situacija', p. 759, and Djaković, *Sukobi*, pp. 168–9; on the council of elders, Bajrami, *Batalioni*, pp. 68–74.

10 NA T-501, reel 249, frame 1055, text of agreement ('Es dürfen daher keinen voreiligen Massnahmen ergriffen werden, und es wird erwartet, dass sich alle in vernünftiger und ruhiger Weise in diesem Sinne einsetzen').

11 Hadri, *Gjakova*, p. 61; for an example of an unprovoked attack by Yugoslav soldiers see Kemp, *No Colours*, p. 210.

12 NA T-821, reel 129, frame 478, Italian War Ministry report on Kosovo, 26 May 1941 ('non senza numerosi episodi di sangue e di violenza'); Umiltà, *Jugoslavia*, p. 112; Hadri, *Lëvizja*, p. 148 (20,000); Glišić, 'Albanization', p. 298 (houses, Vitomirica, Dobruša); Bajrami, *Batalioni*, pp. 63–4 (besë).

13 Umiltà, *Jugoslavia*, pp. 134–5, 140; the explanation he offered for this phenomenon (which, as he said, went against Italian policy) was that the Italian soldiers and officials found it much easier to form sexual relations with the Serbian women; Albanian women, on the other hand, were 'jealously guarded by their menfolk' (p. 141).

14 NA T-501, reel 249, frame 1055, text of agreement, 21 Apr. 1941; Hadri, *Lëvizja*, p. 128; Jovičević, 'Politička situacija', p. 222; on the Serbian State Guard see P. Cohen, *Serbia's Secret War*, pp. 39–40.

15 NA T-501, reel 249, frames 21, 109, 147, 166, 196, Bader's Kriegstagebuch (Muslim battalion plans); frames 115, 142 (Serbian Volunteer Corps); see also P. Cohen, *Serbia's Secret War*, pp. 37–9.

16 Bajrami, *Batalioni*, pp. 75–7. Bajrami notes that some of the deserters were assisted by local Serb families.

17 British Government, *Albania*, part 2, p. 37; Hadri, *Lëvizja*, p. 321; Jacomini, *La politica*, p. 299.

18 Hadri, *Lëvizja*, p. 110 (Blackshirts); Vojnoistorijski institut, *Zbornik*, pp. 67–8, 135 (reports).

19 NA T-821, reel 248, frame 69, Italian army report, Apr. 1943 ('il disfattismo fatto dai maggiorenti della vita pubblica Kossovana che fomentavano l'odio e lo spirito di ribellione contro gli italiani').

20 Jacomini, *La politica*, p. 301 (1942); NA T-821, reel 248, frames 58–9, report from Tirana, 10 Apr. 1943 ('Fallimento totale del nostro esperimento nel campo politico-amministrativo ... trionfo della corruzione, dell'affarismo personale e dell'intrigo ... situazione economica disastrosa'); Wuescht, *Jugoslawien*, p. 219 (German conditions).

21 Jacomini, *La politica*, pp. 315–17; NA T-821, reel 248, frame 60, report from Tirana, 10 April 1943; Hadri, 'Okupacioni sistem', p. 50 (volunteer militia).

22 P. Cohen, *Serbia's Secret War*, p. 39.

23 Tomasevich, *Chetniks*, pp. 115–22; Manoschek, '*Serbien ist judenfrei*', pp. 110–11; Lawrence, *Irregular Adventure*, pp. 84, 104.

24 For good general treatments see Tomasevich, *Chetniks*; Milazzo, *Chetnik Movement*. For the Moljević text see Dedijer and Miletić, *Genocid*, pp. 33–4.

25 Medenica, 'Četnički pokret', pp. 348–50; Djaković, *Sukobi*, p. 173.

26 Medenica, 'Četnički pokret', pp. 353–5, 363, 389–94; Zaimi, *Lidhja*, p. 52 (Peć raid).

27 NA T-821, reel 248, frames 118–19, Foreign Ministry report, 15 Feb. 1943 ('gli elementi mihailoviciani potrebbero esserci utili per perseguire, con migliori resultati, il comunismo del Kossovo'); Medenica, 'Četnički pokret', pp. 367–8 (Antica).

28 Hadri, *Lëvizja*, pp. 33–8 (1930s); Pllana, 'Greva' (Trepça).

29 Djaković, *Sukobi*, pp. 24–8 (slogans); Lukač, *Radnički pokret*, p. 367 (Fifth Conference, Pijade text). Djaković also notes (p. 37) that the Fourth Party Congress in 1928 had decided that the Communists should cooperate with the (Albanian) 'Kosovo Committee', which was campaigning for the secession of Kosovo.

30 Hadri, *Gjakova*, pp. 49–50 (1940 figures), 75 (Vitomirica); F. Hoxha, 'Prve jedinice', p. 136 (1941 figures).

31 Hadri, *Lëvizja*, pp. 179–80, 273–4; Schlarp, *Wirtschaft*, pp. 176–8; Djaković, *Sukobi*, p. 56.

32 Hadri, *Lëvizja*, p. 167 (Peć arrests); Djaković, *Sukobi*, pp. 77, 193–4 (units); Hadri, 'Aradhet', pp. 20–2 (Kopaonik detachment).

33 Djaković, *Sukobi*, pp. 70, 268; NA T-821, reel 248, frames 69–70, report of Apr. 1943 ('per impedire che l'elemento slavo possa riacquistare il dominio di quella regione' ... 'Si sono infatti avuti nella stessa Gjakova, roccaforte del comunismo kossovano, episodi di spontanea collaborazione da parte dei cittadini che hanno favorito l'arresto di pericolosi comunisti'). Italian and German intelligence had many other successes during this period: see Hoti, *Lëvizja*, pp. 132–5, 170–2.

34 NA T-821, reel 248, frame 75, Foreign Ministry report on Kosovo, 28 May 1943 ('ai nazionalisti serbi che affiancano la nostra azione anticomunista' ... 'i veri e pericolosi sovversivi vivono in piena libertà'); Plasari and Malltezi, *Politike*, p. 229 (report by Ymer Dishnica, 3 Aug. 1943).

35 Dedijer, *Jugoslovensko-albanski odnosi*, pp. 11–20; Plasari and Malltezi, *Politike*, p. 153 (Hoxha quotation); Plasari, 'Politika', p. 79.

36 Plasari and Malltezi, *Politike*, pp. 183–4.

37 On Balli Kombëtar see Bartl, *Albanien*, pp. 237–8; Amery, *Sons of the Eagle*, pp. 57–8; Davies, *Illyrian Venture*, pp. 79–92.

38 Plasari and Malltezi, *Politike*, pp. 220, 226 (Dishnica report), 234 (Hoxha letter). These newly published documents overturn all modern accounts of Hoxha's wartime policies, which, based on his own retrospective self-justifications, or on the documents he permitted to be printed, present him as struggling for national independence throughout the war. On the policy of a Balkan federation see Petranović, 'Kosovo', pp. 343–8.

39 Serra, *Albania*, p. 34 (order from Rome); NA T-501, reel 259, frame 31, German report on German-Italian relations (Rosi's statement).

40 Serra, *Albania*, pp. 35–42, 99; Anon., *Les Italiens*, pp. 11–16 (agreements); NA T-501, reel 259, reports on Italian-German relations, frame 37 (new orders); frame 39 also reports that many units of the Firenze division were joining Communist bands.

41 Serra, *Albania*, p. 68 (proclamation); NA T-501, reel 258, survey of occupation policy in Balkans, frames 613 (fiction of neutrality), 625 (Deva); T-311, reel 183, Kriegstagebuch of Army Group 'E', 1944, frame 170 (Deva's recruiting efforts).

42 Zaimi, *Lidhja*, pp. 35–45; Djaković, *Sukobi*, p. 120.

43 Zaimi, *Lidhja*, p. 52 (Second League); T-501, reel 256, frame 885, Nedić resignation letter; Hadri, *Lëvizja*, p. 330 (Neubacher).

44 Glišić, 'Albanization', p. 301 (12–15,000); NA T-501, reel 258, survey of occupation policy in Balkans, frames 624, 626 (pro-English leadership); SRO DD/DRU 35, part 1, memorandum entitled 'Some Instances of Persecution', p. 1 (quotation); Vojnoistorijski institut, *Zbornik*, p. 437 (Communist report).

45   Kemp, *No Colours*, pp. 199, 207.

46   *Ibid.*, pp. 213–17; on the pro-British role of the Kryeziu brothers and Abaz Kupi in 1940 see Amery, *Approach March*, pp. 162–5: at that time, Amery noted, the brothers were 'worth two thousand rifles at short call' (p. 162).

47   Plasari, 'Politika', pp. 81–2; Dizdarević, *Albanski dnevnik*, p. 45.

48   On the Bujan conference see Hadri, *Gjakova*, pp. 179–84; Djaković, *Sukobi*, pp. 201–10; Horvat, *Kosovsko pitanje*, pp. 80–7; Rajović, *Autonomija*, pp. 206–10, 433–7 (text of Resolution: quotation from p. 435, from a Serbian translation of the original Albanian, which presumably used 'Dukagjin' instead of 'Metohija'). The Proclamation is printed in Vojnoistorijski institut, *Zbornik*, pp. 376–82.

49   Rajović, *Autonomija*, p. 439 (quotation); Hibbert, *Albania's Struggle*, p. 91.

50   Kemp, *No Colours*, pp. 196–9; Hibbert, *Albania's Struggle*, p. 164 (quotation); Plasari and Malltezi, *Politike*, pp. 26 n., 31, 136, 161, 328.

51   Avramovski, 'Eksploatimi', pp. 155–61 (mines); Vojnoistorijski institut, *Zbornik*, p. 547.

52   Hadri, *Lëvizja*, pp. 321–2; Djaković, *Sukobi*, pp. 121–5; NA T-354, reel 160, frame 3805941, divisional commander's report, Oct. 1945 ('auf den unsichtbaren Widerstand der Beg und Agas, der sich in der Passivität der beghörigen Präfekten und Bürgermeister und einer aufstellungsfeindlichen Flüsterpropaganda auswirkte').

53   NA T-354, reel 160, frames 3805940 ('Wenn es regnet, verlässt der Albaner seinen Posten; wenn es dunkel wird, geht er von seiner Feldstellung ins Dorf und trinkt Raki'), 3805943 (Jews); Avramovski, 'Eksploatimi', p. 158, and Hadri, *Gjakova*, p. 199 (Gjakova); Dželetović Ivanov, *Jevreji*, p. 70 (Jews).

54   NA T-354, reel 160, frame 3805944 ('die Hoffnung . . . dass die Engländer die Deutschen ablösen mögen, bevor die Bolschewiken in Albanien einrücken'); T-311, reel 183, Army Group 'E' Kriegstagebuch, 24 Sept. and 10 Oct., frame 52 ('Die Division ist ohne besondere Kampfwillen').

55   Schmidt-Richberg, *Der Endkampf*, pp. 35–48; NA T-311, reel 183, frame 99.

56   Schmidt-Richberg, *Der Endkampf*, pp. 49–65; NA T-311, reel 183, frames 105–228.

57   Hadri, *Lëvizja*, pp. 403–14; NA T-311, reel 183 (for a rare reference to the Partisans see frame 191, 10 Nov., which merely states that the Prizren-Gjakova road was 'threatened' ('bedroht') by the First Kosovo Brigade); Schmidt-Richberg, *Der Endkampf*, p. 74 (totals).

58   Zaimi, *Lidhja*, pp. 76–8 (Ferizaj, Gjilan), 87 (Polluzha, 44 villages); Djaković, *Sukobi*, pp. 232 (Popović order), 238–47 (Ferizaj, Gjilan, Drenica, Mitrovica); Qosja, *La Question*, p. 168 (support by peasants); Glišić, 'Albanization', p. 303 (till 1950s); Djilas, *Tito*, pp. 76–8 (resistance elsewhere).

59 Zaimi, *Lidhja*, p. 93, accepted by Nasi, 'Eight Months', p. 229; Živančević, *Emigranti*, p. 47 (60,000).

60 The figures of Bogoljub Kočović (Serb) and Vladimir Žerjavić (Croat) are presented by Vučković and Nikolić, *Stanovništvo*, pp. 104–5, together with their revision. Roux, *Les Albanais*, p. 150, gives figures for Yugoslav regions in 1940 and 1948.

61 Vučković and Nikolić, *Stanovništvo*, cite the figure of 100,000 but do not support it, arguing that the main groups were officials and returning émigrés (p. 102); for the figure of 260,000 see Živančević, *Emigranti*, p. 39.

62 Vučković and Nikolić, *Stanovništvo*, pp. 96–100; above, n. 43 (Neubacher).

16. Kosovo under Tito: 1945–1980

1 Saliu, *Lindja*, p. 30 (Tito quotation, from article in *Nova Jugoslavija*); Braha, *Gjenocidi*, pp. 469–70 (Montenegro, Macedonia); Bajraktari, 'Serbia's Annexation', p. 117 (Kardelj quotation).

2 Rajović, *Autonomija*, pp. 233–5; Bajraktari, 'Serbia's Annexation', p. 118.

3 Rajović, *Autonomija*, pp. 238, 249–54; Auty, 'Yugoslavia', pp. 59–62.

4 For the Albanian case see Saliu, *Lindja*, pp. 31–6; elements of the Serbian case are presented in Rajović, *Autonomija*, pp. 238–50.

5 Djaković, *Sukobi*, pp. 273–4 (Popović); Braha, *Gjenocidi*, p. 482 (requisitions).

6 Živančević, *Emigranti*, pp. 24 (provisional decree), 31 (statistics); Rajović, *Autonomija*, p. 264 (change of mind); Verli, *Reforma*, pp. 181–2 (Aug. law, Commission, statistics).

7 Krasniqi, *Savremene promene*, p. 40 (names); Rajović, *Autonomija*, p. 262 (pre-war schools); Braha, *Gjenocidi*, p. 483 (school statistics); Roux, *Les Albanais*, pp. 280–2 (illiteracy).

8 Nasi, 'Eight Months', p. 232; statements by Lt.-Col. Zoi Themeli, prepared for the trial of Koçi Xoxe in 1949, now displayed in the National Historical Museum, Tirana.

9 Plasari and Malltezi, *Marrëdhëniet*, pp. 44–7 (treaty), 62–5 (agreement), 73 (Plenum quotation).

10 *Ibid.*, pp. 140–5 (Politburo), 149–53 (army plan), 415–17 (letter). Nako Spiru shot himself, or was shot, in Nov. 1947; he was then enthusiastically denounced by Hoxha (pp. 153–99). In his own later (post-1948) version of these events Hoxha presented himself as a heroic ally of Spiru battling for Albania's independence, who was merely obliged by political pressures to denounce 'anti-Yugoslavism' for appearance's sake: see his *The Titoites*, and, following him, Pollo and Puto, *History*, pp. 260–2.

11 Djilas, *Conversations*, p. 112; for a valuable discussion of the Stalin–Tito

break, see Pavlowitch, *Tito*, pp. 54–7. On the arguments about the Balkan Federation, see Petranović, 'Kosovo', pp. 413–21.

12 Rusinow, *Yugoslav Experiment*, pp. 35–6; Krasniqi, *Savremene promene*, p. 51 (graph).

13 von Kohl and Libal, *Kosovo*, p. 59 (searches); Horvat, *Kosovsko pitanje*, p. 90 (statistics).

14 The fullest account, by a Serb journalist convinced of the guilt of the accused and depending mainly on the recollections of Udba officers and other Serb officials, is Bulatović, *Prizrenski proces*: see esp. pp. 9–21, 53, 86–111. On Demaçi's movement see Demaçi, *Republika*, pp. 7, 16–17.

15 A. Popović, *L'Islam*, pp. 347–53.

16 Qosja, *La Question*, pp. 180–1; Shtylla, 'Deportation' (development of policy, details for 1953); Čubrilović, 'Problem of Minorities'; Islami, 'Demografski problemi', p. 52 (246,000).

17 Reuter, *Die Albaner*, p. 47 (Party); L. Cohen, *Socialist Pyramid*, p. 350 (positions).

18 P. Prifti, 'Kosova's Economy', esp. p. 137 (federal budget, primary industries); Krasniqi, *Savremene promene*, p. 99 (enterprises); L. Cohen, *Socialist Pyramid*, pp. 352–3, and Roux, *Les Albanais*, pp. 300–18 (industrialization, relative decline).

19 Yugoslav Government, *Constitution*, pp. 68–9 (arts. 111–12); Saliu, *Lindja*, pp. 48–51; Repishti, 'Evolution', pp. 211–13.

20 L. Cohen, *Socialist Pyramid*, p. 356 (quotation); Reuter, *Die Albaner*, p. 46 (Šiptar).

21 Saliu, *Lindja*, pp. 52–5, and Rajović, *Autonomija*, pp. 292–4 (amendments); L. Cohen, *Socialist Pyramid*, p. 356 (Hoxha).

22 Reuter, *Die Albaner*, pp. 48–9; von Kohl and Libal, *Kosovo*, pp. 67–8; Pipa, *Albanian Stalinism*, p. 162.

23 Institut d'étude, *Les Relations*, p. 25.

24 Pipa, *Albanian Stalinism*, p. 157 (flag); Djaković, *Sukobi*, pp. 313–14 (faculties). Roux, *Les Albanais*, p. 282, accepts the official figures; L. Cohen, *Socialist Pyramid*, p. 363, notes the exaggeration.

25 L. Cohen, *Socialist Pyramid*, pp. 359–66 (managers, Party, police); Reuter, *Die Albaner*, p. 63 (employment).

26 Reuter, *Die Albaner*, pp. 44–5.

27 Rajović, *Autonomija*, pp. 302–10; Saliu, *Lindja*, pp. 56–8; Repishti, 'Evolution', p. 202; Shoup, 'Government', p. 234.

28 Repishti, 'Evolution', pp. 199–200. For a statement of the traditional arguments against allowing a 'narodnost' to form a republic, see Vučinić, *Zašto Kosovo ne može*, pp. 211–16.

29 Bataković, *Kosovo Chronicles*, p. 25.

30 Jevtić, 'Od Kosova do Jadovna', reprinted in Vladisavljević, *Kosovski nesrbi*, p. 9; Roux, *Les Albanais*, p. 389.

31 Vučković and Nikolić, *Stanovništvo*, p. 108 (statistics); Roux, *Les Albanais*, p. 390 (modern study); Islami, *Fshati*, p. 100 (1981 census).
32 Islami, 'Demografski problemi', p. 47.
33 P. Prifti, 'Kosova's Economy', p. 129.
34 Petrović and Blagojević, *Migration*, pp. 110, 179 (Serbian Academy figures); Islami, 'Demografski problemi', pp. 62–3 (official figures).
35 Vučković and Nikolić, *Stanovništvo*, p. 108: 'officially estimated' because the 1991 census was boycotted by the Albanians. Their proportion in 1981 was 77.4 per cent; by the mid-1990s some Albanian demographers were claiming a figure of 90 per cent.
36 Roux, *Les Albanais*, pp. 151–3; Islami, 'Demografski problemi', pp. 40–1.
37 Roux, *Les Albanais*, p. 152; Islami, 'Demografski problemi', pp. 41–2.
38 Mališić, 'Svi Srbi', p. 6 (statistics, quoting Dr Mirjana Rašević of the Centre for Demographic Research, Belgrade; the figures for Kosovo must be treated with caution, since most Albanian women had by now ceased to receive medical treatment in Kosovo hospitals). On Albanian cultural attitudes to contraception and abortion see Vučković and Nikolić, *Stanovništvo*, pp. 120–2.

17. *Kosovo after the death of Tito: 1981–1997*

1 *Financial Times*, 13 Mar. 1981; *Times*, 14 Mar. 1981. The fullest account of this and subsequent events published in the West is Magnusson, 'Nationalitets problem' (here p. 70), which is based on contemporary Yugoslav materials.
2 Magnusson, 'Nationalitetsproblem', pp. 72–82; Horvat, *Kosovsko pitanje*, pp. 139–41 (slogans); *Observer*, 29 Mar. 1981 (University concessions); *Financial Times*, *Times*, 3 and 4 Apr. 1981.
3 Gesellschaft für bedrohte Völker, *The Albanians*, p. 27 (official); Reuter, *Die Albaner*, p. 82 (1,000).
4 *Financial Times*, 8 Sept. 1981 (2,000 arrests); Gesellschaft für bedrohte Völker, *The Albanians*, p. 33 (official report, June); Magnusson, 'Serbian Reaction', p. 11 n. (*NIN*).
5 Magnusson, 'Nationalitetsproblem', pp. 6–7, 11–16, 40–52; S. Hasani, *Kosova* (Borba interview).
6 Magnusson, 'Nationalitetsproblem', pp. 131–3, 151. Final estimates of the number of expulsions from the Party ranged from 900 to 4,000: see Gesellschaft für bedrohte Völker, *The Albanians*, p. 33.
7 Gesellschaft für bedrohte Völker, *The Albanians*, pp. 26–9.
8 Reuter, *Die Albaner*, pp. 54–70; P. Prifti, 'Kosova's Economy', pp. 134–7, 142–4; the best analysis of the investment policy is Verli, *Shfrytezimi*.
9 Magnusson, 'Nationalitetsproblem', pp. 106–7 (Hadri), 141–3 (Ristić), and

'Serbian Reaction', pp. 18–19 (Hajredin Hoxha; Slovene book); Bogdanović, *Knjiga*, esp. pp. 249–56.

10 Spasojević, *Slučaj Martinović*, pp. 11–59 (first reports), 101–15, 365–73 (debates in assembly); Cviić, 'Culture of Humiliation'. Cviić notes that it is still not possible to be certain which explanation was correct, but that the fact that the Serb authorities made no attempt to reopen the case after their takeover of Kosovo in 1989 suggests that real doubts existed about Martinović's story.

11 Vladisavljević, *Kosovski nesrbi*, pp. 6–7 (Jevtić); Bobi, 'Kosovska "drama"', p. 143 (quotation).

12 Popović, Janča and Petovar, *Kosovski čvor*, pp. 37–57.

13 Živančević, *Emigranti*, p. 24, and Gesellschaft für bedrohte Völker, *The Albanians*, p. 30 (petition); Magnusson, 'Serbian Reaction', pp. 14–15 (assembly, peasants' march); Stambolić, *Put*, p. 166.

14 Magaš, *Destruction*, pp. 50–1 (petition); Grmek, Gjidara and Simac, *Le Nettoyage*, pp. 232–5 (Memorandum).

15 Grmek, Gjidara and Simac, *Le Nettoyage*, pp. 247–56.

16 *Ibid.*, p. 233.

17 Stambolić, *Put*, p. 165; Silber and Little, *Death*, pp. 37–8; Judah, *Serbs*, p. 162. Before this, the only time Milošević had shown any interest in the Kosovo issue was at a meeting with Party officials in Kragujevac in Dec. 1986, when he called for the unification of Serbia but also warned against Serbian nationalism: see Milošević, *Les Années*, pp. 98–9.

18 Gesellschaft für bedrohte Völker, *The Albanians*, p. 42; Stambolić, *Put*, pp. 181–5; Silber and Little, *Death*, pp. 41–7.

19 Meier, *Wie Jugoslawien*, pp. 132–9; and see the valuable account of these events, and of the wider power struggle in the Serbian Party, in Magaš, *Destruction*, pp. 197–208.

20 Magaš, *Destruction*, pp. 208–9; *Times*, 19 Nov. 1988; Silber and Little, *Death*, pp. 62–3.

21 Omari, 'Constitutional Changes', pp. 290–2; *Daily Telegraph*, 24 Mar. 1989.

22 Magaš, *Destruction*, pp. 180–9; Poulton, *Balkans*, pp. 67–8.

23 von Kohl and Libal, *Kosovo*, p. 116; Gashi, *Denial*, pp. 102–3.

24 von Kohl and Libal, *Kosovo*, pp. 116–19; *Daily Telegraph*, 24, 28, 29, 31 Mar. 1989; Salvoldi and Gjergji, *Resistenza*, p. 65 (100 dead); *Der Spiegel*, 26 June 1989.

25 Poulton, *Balkans*, p. 68; *Daily Telegraph*, 31 Oct. 1989, 29 Jan., 1 Feb. 1990.

26 Poulton, *Balkans*, pp. 68–9; *Daily Telegraph*, 23 Mar., 4 Apr. 1990 (children); *Independent*, 19 Apr. 1990; *Kosova Communication*, 5 Dec. 1995 (Sarin).

27 Rugova, *La Question*, pp. 92, 105–6; Gashi, *Denial*, pp. 130–4, 138.

28 Poulton, *Balkans*, p. 69; Gashi, *Denial*, pp. 103–4; *Independent*, 3, 6 July 1990; K. Prifti *et al.*, eds., *Truth*, p. 329 (text of 2 July resolution).

29 Poulton, *Balkans*, p. 70; K. Prifti *et al.*, eds., *Truth*, pp. 331–3 (text of the

15-article constitutional law adopted at Kaçanik); for the later full text of the constitution see Kuvendi i Republikës, *Kushtetuta*.

30 Rugova, *La Question*, pp. 107–8; Judah, *Serbs*, pp. 331–2; *Daily Telegraph*, 25 May 1992.

31 Maliqi, 'Albanian Movement', pp. 144–7; on Rugova's biography (he was born in Dec. 1944, and his father was killed three weeks later by the Yugoslav Partisans), see Rugova, *La Question*, pp. 185–202.

32 See the two very thorough reports issued by the 'Humanitarian Law Center' in Belgrade, published in Kandić, ed., *Spotlight*, pp. 42–55, and Fond za humanitarno pravo, *Spotlight Report*; Helsinki Watch, *Human Rights*; Gashi, *Denial*; X. Hasani, *Shkolla*, pp. 11–15.

33 See the reports listed in n. 32, especially Gashi, *Denial*, pp. 311–12 (extract from Helsinki Watch report, 1991) and Fond za humanitarno pravo, *Spotlight Report*, pp. 15–18, 25–6 (testimonies), 27–30 (violation of legal procedures). See also Selmeci, 'Kosova', p. 18 (1994 statistics), and the Amnesty International reports on police violence listed in the Bibliography.

34 Duijzings, 'The Exodus'.

35 For an important study of the development of Serbian anti-Muslim rhetoric see Cigar, *Genocide*, pp. 62–106 (e.g. the remark about a 'demographic jihad' by the academic Darko Tanasković, quoted on p. 69). Islam does, of course, remain a living presence in ordinary life, especially in rural Kosovo; see the account in Norris, *Islam*, pp. 271–7.

36 Judah, *Serbs*, pp. 259–74 (economy, inflation); *Guardian*, 20 Oct. 1992 (plight of salaried Serbs); Salvoldi and Gjergji, *Resistenza*, pp. 81–2 (Mother Teresa).

37 Judah, *Serbs*, pp. 255–8 (gangsterization); Salvoldi and Gjergji, *Resistenza*, p. 52 (Arkan quotation).

38 Ruston, 'Kosovo'; Gashi, *Denial*, pp. 144–7; *Kosova Communication*, 11 Sept., 16 Oct. 1995, 8 Jan. 1996; Fond za humanitarno pravo, *Spotlight Report*, pp. 7–8.

39 *Kosova Communication*, 17 Oct. 1994, 15 Aug., 5 Sept., 1995, 17 June 1996.

40 Blaku, *Hintergründe*, p. 55.

41 *Kosova Communication*, 3, 9, 16 and 24 Sept. 1996.

42 *Kosova Communication*, 24 June 1996; *Albania, gazeta e Bashkësisë Shqiptare 'Faik Konitza'* (London), no. 3 (Aug. 1996); *New York Times International*, 11 May 1997.

43 *NIN*, 8 Nov. 1996 (gynaecologist, noting also that the abortion rate had quadrupled during the war); *Kosova Communication*, 17 June, 3, 29 July 1996.

Glossary

aga originally, Janissary officer; generally, a term for an Ottoman landowner, ranking lower than bey.

akçe Ottoman coin, originally containing 3 grams of silver, but subject to frequent devaluation (to 0.68g in 1580, 0.32 in 1600 and 0.23 in 1680). A sheep cost 25 akçes in 1546 and 80 in 1604. A coin worth 120 akçes, introduced in *c*. 1690, contained 18.8g of silver then; this fell to 13.7 in 1740, 5.9 in 1790 and 1 in 1844.

Arbëresh Albanian-speaking population in parts of southern Italy.

Arnaut term for Albanian, used especially for Muslim Albanians and/or ones serving in Ottoman forces.

Arnautaš term for Albanianized Slav; the 'Arnautaš thesis' supposes that most or all Kosovo Albanians are Albanianized Slavs.

askeri military–administrative class of Ottoman subjects.

bajrak Ottoman military–administrative territorial division.

bajraktar local leader (usually hereditary) with responsibility for a bajrak.

besë word of honour, promise, truce (especially one suspending a blood-feud).

bey 'lord', Ottoman landowner.

beylerbeyi governor of an eyalet.

brdjanin highlander, member of Montenegrin mountain clan.

četa band of fighters.

Četnik traditional term for member of a četa, used particularly for (i) members of organization led by Kosta Pećanac, (ii) members of forces under Draža Mihailović in Second World War.

chrysobull medieval Serbian royal charter.

çift peasant's plot of land, in virtual hereditary ownership.

çiftçi peasant working on a çiftlik.

çiftlik originally, the 'home farm' component of a timar; generally, a large private non-timar estate.

cizye graduated poll-tax on non-Muslims.

derbend category of village given tax privileges in return for guarding mountain roads.

dervish member of a Sufi order.

devşirme levy of Christian youths, taken for training as Janissaries and imperial servants.

esnaf craft guild.

eyalet province, the largest administrative division of the Ottoman Empire.

firman Ottoman imperial decree.

fis Albanian clan.

Geg inhabitant (or dialect) of both northern half of Albania and Kosovo.

hajduk originally, irregular fighter used by Austrians in Hungarian frontier region; generally, outlaw or brigand in South Slav lands.

hamam public baths.

haraç originally a land-tax on non-Muslims, but later merged with the cizye.

hoca Muslim religious teacher.

imaret soup-kitchen for the poor.

ispence fixed annual land-tax on non-Muslims, equivalent of the resm-i çift.

Janissary Ottoman regular soldier, originally recruited through devşirme, but from mid-seventeenth century recruited from ordinary Muslims.

kaçak generally, outlaw or bandit; after 1912, Albanian fighters rebelling against Slav rule in Kosovo.

kadı judge.

kadılık area administered by a kadı.

kanun law code.

Kanun of Lek Dukagjin code of Albanian customary law.

katun shepherding settlement.

kaymakam governor of a kaza (after 1864).

kaza originally, a kadılık; after 1864, administrative sub-division of a sancak.

kullë Albanian fortified stone tower-house.

kuvend gathering of clan elders.

magjup Albanian sedentary Gypsy.

mahalle quarter, small sub-division of a town.

Malësi highlands of northern Albania.

malësor highlander, inhabitant of the Malësi.

medrese Muslim seminary.

mekteb Muslim elementary school.

meropah peasant in medieval Serbian feudal system.

mufti senior Muslim cleric and expert on şeriat.

muhaxhir Muslim refugee.

mutesarif after 1864, governor of a sancak.

nahiye administrative sub-division.

paşalık area governed by a pasha (usually a sancak).

pasha general term for Ottoman territorial governor or other high-ranking official.

perper medieval Serbian monetary unit.

pohvala eulogy-commemoration in the Serbian Church.

Porte, the traditional term for the Ottoman government.

pronoia Byzantine feudal estate.

provveditore Venetian governor–commander.

raya tax-paying, non-military, non-administrative class of Ottoman subjects.

resm-i çift fixed annual land-tax on Muslims.

sancak military–administrative district, sub-division of an eyalet.

sancakbeyi governor of a sancak.

şeriat Islamic sacred law.

slava family saint's day.

spahi Ottoman feudal knight.

tekke dervish lodge.

timar Ottoman military–feudal estate.

Tosk inhabitant (or dialect) of southern half of Albania.

vakıf Islamic religious–charitable foundation, holding property in perpetuity.

vali governor of a vilayet.

vëllazëri brotherhood, group of blood-related families.

vilayet originally, a small taxation district; after 1864, a large province (replacing the eyalet).

vojvod chief of clan; more generally, war-leader.

zadruga large communal family.

zimmi protected status of Christians and Jews under Muslim rule.

župa early Serb tribal territory.

župan ruler of a župa.

List of manuscripts

This list is confined to those manuscripts which have been quoted or referred to in this book. The archives are listed by the abbreviations which have been used for them in the notes, in alphabetical order.

AMAE *Archives du Ministère des Affaires Étrangères, Paris*

Correspondance politique, Autriche, vol. 51: 'Origine della guerra . . .'
Correspondance politique, Autriche, vol. 65: reports from Vienna, 1689
Correspondance politique du consulat, Turquie, Scutari d'Albanie, vol. 21: Colonna Ceccaldi report, Pons reports, all 1878
Correspondance politique du consulat, Turquie, Scutari d'Albanie, vol. 22: le Rée report, 1881
Mémoires et documents, Turquie, vol. 23: de Boislecomte report, 1835
Mémoires et documents, Turquie, vol. 95: de Ring report, Albanian petition, 1879
Mémoires et documents, Turquie, vol. 136: report, 1813
Nouvelle série, Turquie, vol. 234: report from Skopje, 1912
Nouvelle série, Turquie, vol. 235: reports from Belgrade, Skopje, 1912
Nouvelle série, Turquie, vol. 236: Carlier report, 1912
Nouvelle série, Turquie, vol. 239: Carlier report, 1912

ASCPF *Archivio della Sacra Congregazione della Propaganda Fide, Rome*

SC Albania 5: G. Bogdani letter, 1698
SC Albania 34: Bogdanović report, 1853
SC Servia 1: Raspasani report, 1682; P. Bogdani report, 1685; Raspasani letter, 1690; Karadžić report, 1706; Deda and Fat letter, 1742; Logoreci report, 1742; Nikollë report and summary, 1743
SC Servia 2: A. Krasniqi report, 1770; Mazarek letters, 1771–2; Mazarek report, 1774
SC Servia 3: Mazarek letters, 1788, 1796

SC Servia 4, d'Afragola report, 1845; G. Krasniqi report, 1845; Bogdanović letter, 1846; Bogdanović reports, 1846, 1849, 1850
SC Servia 5: Bucciarelli report, 1872
SOCG 309: P. Bogdani report, 1661
SOCG 431: A. Bogdani report, 1670
SOCG 482: P. Bogdani report, 1680
SOCG 506: G. Bogdani letter, 1689
SOCG 515: Raspasani letter, 1693
SOCG 792: Mazarek report, 1760
SOCG 872: Mazarek report, 1785
SOCG 895: Mazarek report, 1791
SOCG 922: G. Krasniqi report, 1820

ASVat *Archivio Segreto Vaticano, Vatican City*

Dispacci, Nunziatura di Venezia, microfilms in Istituto per la storia della società e dello stato veneziano ('ISSSV'), Fondazione Giorgio Cini, Venice:
  microfilm 134: reports from Vienna (via Venice), 1689
  microfilm 136: reports from Vienna (via Venice), 1690
  microfilm 137: reports from Vienna (via Venice), 1690
Processus consistoriales, vol. 114: Suma process, 1728
Visitationes ad limina, vol. 56: Zmajević report, 1692
Visitationes ad limina, vol. 728: Karadžić reports, 1713, 1716, 1725; Suma report, 1735; Suma letter, 1739

ASVen *Archivio di Stato, Venice*

Collegio, relazioni di ambasciatori, vol. 67: Cornaro report, 1689
Provveditori da terra e da mar, filza 529: Molin reports; Baden documents; Arsenije to Bolizza; Igumen Visarion to Arsenije; Igumen Viktor to Bolizza; Capt. Zmajević to Molin; all 1689
Provveditori da terra e da mar, filza 530: Molin reports; Igumen Viktor and Iliković to Molin; all 1690
Senato, dispacci, Germania, filza 165: Venier reports, 1690

BAV *Biblioteca Apostolica Vaticana, Vatican City*

Cod. Barb. Lat. 5372: Jahja proposal, c.1616
Cod. Urb. Lat. 839: Komulović report, c.1590

BN *Bibliothèque Nationale, Paris*

f.fr. 17193: 'Discours sur la puissance [. . .] de l'Empire des Turcs', 1683
f.ital. 1168: Cerri, 'Stato della religione', 1677

BNM *Biblioteca Nazionale Marciana, Venice*

IT VII 1068: Venier reports, 1689–90

Bodl. *Bodleian Library, Oxford*

Myres 12: Durham letters, 1931, 1943, 1944

BUB *Biblioteca Universitaria, Bologna*

Cod. Marsigli 54: Marsigli notes
Cod. Marsigli 103: Marsigli notes

HHSA *Haus-, Hof- und Staatsarchiv, Vienna*

Illyrico-Serbica 1 (1611–1738), Konv. B: Marsigli memorandum, 1690; Leopold
    I exhortation, 1690; Arsenije letter, 1690
PA I 874: Burián telegram, Conrad telegram, 1916
PA I 991, Liasse Krieg 47: report from Mitrovica, 1916
PA XII 263, Liasse VIII B: Waldhart reports, 1881
PA XII 312, Liasse XXXIII: Musani report, von Calice report, Rappoport report;
    all 1899
PA XIV 46, Liasse IL/1, 2: border commission proceedings, 1913; telegram, 1914
PA XXXVIII 405: Prochaska report, 1912; von Pözel report, 1913; Kohlruss
    reports, 1913, 1914

ISSSV see **ASVat**

KA *Kriegsarchiv, Vienna*

Exp. Prot. 1690: summaries of documents, 1690
Exp. Prot. 1691: summaries of documents, 1691
Exp. Prot. 1693: summaries of documents, 1693
FA (Türkenkrieg), 1689–13–1: 'Annotationes und Reflexiones', n.d.
Karten I.a.30: Müller notes, 1838
Reg. Prot. 1690: summaries of documents, 1690
Reg. Prot. 1693: summaries of documents, 1693

NA *National Archives, Washington (at College Park, Maryland)*

Captured German and Italian documents, microfilm collection:
T-120, reel 120: German consul in Tirana, report, 1941
T-311, reel 183: Army Group 'E' Kriegstagebuch, 1944
T-354, reel 160: Skanderbeg division, commander's report, 1944
T-501, reel 245: German commander in Serbia, Kriegstagebuch, 1941

T-501, reel 249: Eberhardt report, Bader Kriegstagebuch, both 1941
T-501, reel 256: Nedić resignation letter, 1944
T-501, reel 258: survey of German occupation policy in Balkans, 1945
T-501, reel 259: reports on German–Italian relations in Albania, 1943
T-821, reel 128: Italian Supreme Command, briefing and discussion notes; von Rintelen report; all 1941
T-821, reel 129: Italian Supreme Command, memorandum; Gardini report; Italian War Ministry report; all 1941
T-821, reel 248: Italian army and Foreign Ministry reports, 1943

PRO *Public Record Office, London*

FO 195/1324: Blunt report, 1880
FO 195/1360: Blunt reports, 1881
FO 195/2406: Peckham reports, Durham letter, 1912
FO 195/2407: Peckham reports, 14 points text, 1912
FO 195/2438: Greig report, 1912
FO 371/5193: Dëshira petition, 1923
FO 371/5725: Eyres report, Young report, Frashëri letter, Prishtina letter; all 1921
FO 371/6193: Stonehewer Bird reports, 1921
FO 371/6194: Young report, Strang reports, Stonehewer Bird report; all 1921
FO 371/6203: *Agramer Tageblatt* article, 1921
FO 371/9961: Eyres report, 1924
SP 80/17: Paget report, 1690
SP 97/19: Winchilsea report, 1669
SP 97/20: Trumbull reports, 1689

SOAS *School of Oriental and African Studies, London*

PP MS 4 (Paget papers), box 11, bundle 51: Porphyrita reports, 1689–90

SRO *Somerset Record Office, Taunton*

DD/DRU 33: Herbert memorandum, letter, 1918; Abraham letter, 1921
DD/DRU 35: Lushnja Conference statement, 1920; Herbert typescript, 1927; Balli Kombëtar memorandum, 1945
DD/DRU 47: Durham letter, 1922; Durham memorandum, n.d.

Bibliography

This bibliography is confined to listing those works which have been quoted or referred to in this book (except news reports, for which full references have been given in the notes). It is not intended as a general bibliography; useful printed bibliographies, listing many items relevant to the history of Kosovo, will be found in the entries for Daniel, Destani and Horecky. Serbian Cyrillic is given in Serbo-Croat (Latin) transcription; Russian and Greek are given in English transcription; Macedonian is given in Serbo-Croat transcription, and Bulgarian in Serbo-Croat transcription with the additional character 'ŭ'. The alphabetical order is English; all diacritical marks are disregarded for the purposes of this ordering, and so too are double consonants. The latter are also disregarded in the formation of initials: thus Shtjefën is abbreviated as 'S.', Ljubomir as 'L.'

Abbreviations Used in the Bibliography

AASJE *Arhiv za arbanasku starinu, jezik i etnologiju*

AFSP *Archiv für slavische Philologie*

AOBDIA *L'Albanie: organe bi-mensuel de défense des intérêts albanais*

ATT A. Buda *et al.*, *The Albanians and their Territories* (Tirana, 1985)

BA *Balkan-Archiv*

BE *Balkansko ezikoznanie*

BUSTSS *Buletin i Universitetit shtetëror të Tiranës, seria shkencat shoqerore*

DKAWP-H *Denkschriften der kaiserlichen Akademie der Wissenschaften in Wien* [continued as: *Denkschriften der Akademie der Wissenschaften in Wien*], *philosophisch-historische Classe*

DO *Dissertationes orientales*

EI2 *The Encyclopaedia of Islam*, 2nd edn., ed. H. A. R. Gibb, J. H. Kramers, E. Lévi-Provençal and J. Schacht (Leiden, 1960–)

FB *La Fédération balkanique*

GASH *Gjurmime albanologjike, seria e shkencave historike*

GSKA *Glas srpske kraljevske akademije*

GSND *Glasnik skopskog naučnog društva*

HD *Hylli i dritës*

IAF L. von Thallóczy, ed., *Illyrisch-albanische Forschungen*, 2 vols. (Munich, 1916)

IGA M. Korkuti, S. Anamali and J. Gjinari, eds., *Les Illyriens et la genèse des Albanais* (Tirana, 1971)

JAZU Jugoslovenska Akademija Znanosti i Umjetnosti

JIČ *Jugoslovenski istorijski časopis*

IČ *Istorijski časopis*

KBNP N. Tasić, ed., *Kosovska bitka 1389 godine i njene posledice* (Belgrade, 1991)

KLMB W. S. Vucinich and T. A. Emmert, eds., *Kosovo: Legacy of a Medieval Battle* (Minneapolis, Minnesota, 1991)

KMSI R. Samardžić, ed., *Kosovo i Metohija u srpskoj istoriji* (Belgrade, 1989)

KSGA G. Reichenkron and A. Schmaus, eds., *Die Kultur Südosteuropas: ihre Geschichte und ihre Ausdrucksformen* (Wiesbaden, 1964)

MÖS *Mitteilungen des österreichischen Staatsarchivs*

n.d. no date of publication

n.p. no place of publication

n.s. new series

OC *Orientalia christiana*

OCP *Orientalia christiana periodica*

POF *Prilozi za orijentalnu filologiju i istoriju jugoslovenskih naroda pod turskom vladavinom*

RIEB *Revue internationale des études balkaniques*

SA *Studia albanica*

SAN Srpska Akademija Nauka

SANU Srpska Akademija Nauka i Umetnosti

SH *Studime historike*

SJAZU *Starine Jugoslovenske Akademije Znanosti i Umjetnosti*

SOF *Südost-Forschungen*

SOK A. Pipa and S. Repishti, eds., *Studies on Kosova* (New York, 1984)

SPS I. Ajeti *et al.*, eds., *Simpoziumi për Skënderbeun: Simpozijum o Skenderbegu (9–12 maj 1968)* (Prishtina, 1969)

SSKA *Spomenik srpske kraljevske akademije*

TOK K. Prifti *et al.*, eds., *The Truth on Kosova* (Tirana, 1993)

UNJ M. Djurović, ed., *Ustanak naroda Jugoslavije 1941: zbornik*, 6 vols. (Belgrade, 1962–4)

VAK *Vjetar i arkivit të Kosovës*

ZFB *Zeitschrift für Balkanologie*

Abdyli, T., *Lëvizja kombëtare shqiptare 1900–1903*, 2nd edn. (Prishtina, 1982)

Adanır, F., 'Heiduckentum und osmanische Herrschaft: sozialgeschichtliche Aspekte der Diskussion um das frühneuzeitliche Räuberwesen in Südosteuropa', *SOF*, vol. 41 (1982), pp. 43–116

Agaj, A., *Miloshi heroi i Kosovës: legjendë mbledhur e përthyer* (n.p., n.d.)

Aktepe, M. M., 'Kosova', in *Islâm ansiklopedisi*, vol. 6 (Istanbul, 1955), pp. 869–76

Albèri, E., ed., *Relazioni degli ambasciatori veneti al senato*, 15 vols. (Florence, 1839–63)

Aličić, A., *Pokret za autonomiju Bosne od 1831. do 1832. godine* (Sarajevo, 1996)

Amery, J., *Sons of the Eagle: A Study in Guerrilla War* (London, 1948)

—, *Approach March: A Venture in Autobiography* (London, 1973)

Amnesty International, *Yugoslavia: Ethnic Albanians: Victims of Torture and Illtreatment by police in Kosovo Province* (London, 1992)

—, *Yugoslavia: Ethnic Albanians: Trial by Truncheon* (London, 1994)

—, *Yugoslavia: Police Violence in Kosovo Province: The Victims* (London, 1994)

Anamali, S., 'Problemi i kulturës së hershme mesjetare shqiptare në driten e zbulimeve të reja arkeologjike', *SH*, vol. 21 (1967), no. 2, pp. 29–40

— 'De la civilisation haute-médiévale albanaise', in *IGA*, pp. 183–99

Andrews, P. A., *Türkiye'de etnik gruplar* (Istanbul, 1992)

Angelov, D., *Obrazuvane na bŭlgarskata narodnost* (Sofia, 1971)

Anhegger, R., *Beiträge zur Geschichte des Bergbaus im osmanischen Reich*, I: 'Europäische Türkei', 2 vols. (Istanbul, Zurich, 1943–4)

Anon., *Der neu-eröffneten Ottomanischen Pforten Fortsetzung oder: continuirter historischer Bericht betreffend der Türkischen Monarchie Staats-Maximen* (Augsburg, 1701)

—, 'Un interview avec Riza bey', *La Revue albanaise*, vol. 'A' (1897–8), pp. 157–8

—, *Detailbeschreibung des Sandžaks Plevlje und des Vilajets Kosovo* (Vienna, 1899)

—, Interview with Isa Boletin, *Daily Telegraph*, 5 May 1913

—, 'Colonies albanaises', *AOBDIA*, (i): year 1, no. 5 (16 Nov. 1915), pp. 33–4; (ii): year 1, no. 6 (1 Dec. 1915), pp. 41–2; (iii): year 2, no. 8 (1 Jan. 1916), p. 57

—, 'Dans l'engrenage', *AOBDIA*, year 1, no. 5 (16 Nov. 1915), pp. 34–6

—, 'Iç Boletine', *AOBDIA*, year 2, no. 8 (1 Jan. 1916), p. 67

—, 'The Moslems of Yugoslavia', *The Near East*, vol. 17, no. 454 (16 Jan. 1920), p. 74

—, *Les Italiens en Albanie après le 8 septembre 1943* (n.p., n.d. [c.1946])

Antoljak, S., '"Sultan Jahja" u Makedoniji', *Godišen zbornik, filozofski fakultet na univerzitetot Skopje, istorisko-filološki oddel*, vol. 13 (1962), pp. 109–66

Arnold, T. W., *The Preaching of Islam: A History of the Propagation of the Muslim Faith*, 3rd edn. (London, 1935)

Auty, P., 'Yugoslavia', in R. R. Betts, ed., *Central and South East Europe 1945–1948* (London, 1950), pp. 52–104

Avramovski, Ž., 'Izveštaji austrougarskih konzula u Kosovskoj Mitrovici, Prizrenu i Skoplju o odborskoj skupštini u Ferizoviću 5–23 jula 1908 godine', *VAK*, vols. 2–3, for 1966–7 (1970), pp. 303–42

—, 'Pretendimet territoriale austrohungareze-bullgare në pjesën qendrore të ballkanit më 1916–1918, me një vështrim të posaçëm ndaj Shqipërisë', *GASH*, vol. 6, for 1976 (1977), pp. 145–91

—, 'Eksploatimi Gjerman i minierave të xehës së kromit në rajonin e Gjakovës dhe të Kukësit pas kapitulimit të Italisë (1943–1944)', *GASH*, vol. 9, for 1979 (1980), pp. 221–35, and vol. 10, for 1980 (1981), pp. 149–72

Aymard, M., *Venise, Raguse et le commerce du blé pendant la seconde moitié du XVIe siècle* (Paris, 1966)

Azemi, E., and S. Halimi, *Shqiptarët e Egjiptit* (Skopje, 1993)

Babić, B., 'Migracije u novooslobodjenim krajevima Crne Gore 1912–1915', *JIČ* (1973), nos. 3–4, pp. 163–70

—, 'Iseljavanje Muslimana iz novih krajeva Crne Gore u proljeće 1914. godine', *JIČ* (1978), nos. 1–4, pp. 311–24

Babinger, F., ed., *Hans Dernschwam's Tagebuch einer Reise nach Konstantinopel und Kleinasien (1553/55)* (Munich, 1923)

—, *Die Geschichtsschreiber der Osmanen und ihre Werke* (Leipzig, 1927)

—, *Mehmed the Conqueror and His Time*, ed. W. C. Hickman, tr. R. Manheim (Princeton, NJ, 1978)

Badia, L., ed., *La Història de Jacob Xalabín* (Barcelona, 1982)

Bajraktari, J., 'Serbia's Annexation of Kosova in 1945', in Bajraktari *et al.*, eds., *The Kosova Issue: A Historic and Current Problem* (Tirana, 1996), pp. 115–20

Bajrami, H., *Rrethanat shoqërore dhe politika në Kosovë më 1918–1941* (Prishtina, 1981).

—, 'Konventa jugosllavo-turke e vitit 1938 për shpërnguljen e shqiptarëve', *GASH*, vol. 12, for 1982 (1983), pp. 243–71

—, *Batalioni partizan 'Meto Bajraktari'* (Prishtina, 1988)

Baldacci, A., *Studi speciali albanesi*, 3 vols. (Rome, 1932–7)

Banac, I., *The National Question in Yugoslavia: Origins, History, Politics* (Ithaca, NY, 1984)

Banašević, N., 'O postanku i razvoju Kosovskog i Markova ciklusa', *Srpski književni glasnik*, n.s., vol. 47 (1936), pp. 523–34, 611–22

Banduri, A., *Imperium orientale, sive antiquitates constantinopolitanae*, 2 vols. (Venice, 1729)

Barjaktarović, M., 'Dvovjerske šiptarske zadruge u Metohiji', SAN, *Zbornik radova*, vol. 4 (= Etnografski Institut, vol. 1) (1950), pp. 197–209

Barkan, Ö. L., 'Osmanlı imparatorluğunda bir iskân ve kolonizasyon metodu olarak vakıflar ve temlikler. I: Istilâ devirlerinin kolonizatör Türk dervişleri ve zâviyeler', *Vakıflar dergisi*, vol. 2 (1942), pp. 279–386

—, *XV ve XVI inci asırlarda Osmanlı imparatorluğunda ziraî ekonominin hukukî ve malî esasları*, vol. 1, 'Kanunlar' (Istanbul, 1943)

Barkey, K., *Bandits and Bureaucrats: The Ottoman Route to State Centralization* (Ithaca, NY, 1994)

Barnes, J. R., *An Introduction to Religious Foundations in the Ottoman Empire* (Leiden, 1987)

Bartl, P., *Die albanischen Muslime zur Zeit der nationalen Unabhängigkeitsbewegung (1878–1912)* (Wiesbaden, 1968)

—, 'Die Albaner-Versammlung von Dukagjin im Jahre 1608', in H.-G. Beck and A. Schmaus, eds., *Beiträge zur Südosteuropa-Forschung* (Munich, 1970), pp. 7–14

—, *Der Westbalkan zwischen spanischer Monarchie und osmanischem Reich: zur Türkenkriegsproblematik an der Wende vom 16. zum 17. Jahrhundert* (Munich, 1974)

—, ed., *Quellen und Materialen zur albanischen Geschichte im 17. und 18. Jahrhundert*, 2 vols. (Munich, 1975–9)

—, 'Die Këlmendi: zur Geschichte eines nordalbanischen Bergstammes', *Shêjzat (Le Pleiadi)* (1977), pp. 123–38

—, 'L'attività politica e culturale di Mons. Prenk Doçi, Abate della Mirdizia', in A. Guzzetta, ed., *Etnia albanese e minoranze linguistiche in Italia: atti del IX Congresso Internazionale di Studi Albanesi* (Palermo, 1983), pp. 409–21

—, 'Kosova and Macedonia as Reflected in Ecclesiastical Reports', in SOK, pp. 23–39

—, *Albanien: vom Mittelalter bis zur Gegenwart* (Regensburg, 1995)

Bartocetti, V., 'Il Collegio Illirico di San Pietro e Paolo di Fermo (1663–1746)', *Studia Picena*, vol. 11 (1935), pp. 133–62

Bašagić, S., 'Najstarija turska vijest o kosovskom boju', *Glasnik zemaljskog muzeja u Bosni i Hercegovini*, vol. 36 (1924), pp. 95–9

Bashmakov ['Baschmakoff'], A., *Through Montenegro to the Land of the Guègues* (n.p., n.d. [St Petersburg, c.1915])

Bataković, D., 'Pogibija ruskog konzula G. S. Ščerbine u Mitrovici 1903. godine', *IČ*, vol. 34 (1987), pp. 309–25

—, *Dečansko pitanje* (Belgrade, 1989)

—, 'Od srpske revolucije do istočne krize: 1804–1875', in KMSI, pp. 171–208

—, 'Ulazak u sferu evropskog interesovanja', in *KMSI*, pp. 209–47

—, *The Kosovo Chronicles* (Belgrade, 1992)

Baxhaku, F., and K. Kaser, eds., *Die Stammesgesellschaften Nordalbaniens: Berichte und Forschungen österreichischer Konsuln und Gelehrter (1861–1917)* (Vienna, 1996)

Beard, C. A., and G. Radin, *The Balkan Pivot: Yugoslavia, A Study in Government and Administration* (New York, 1929)

Beldiceanu, N., 'Les Roumains à la bataille d'Ankara: quelques données sur leur organisation militaire dans la péninsule balkanique', *SOF*, vol. 14 (1955), pp. 441–9

—, 'Sur les valaques des balkans slaves à l'époque ottomane (1450–1550)', *Revue des études islamiques*, vol. 34 (1966), pp. 83–132

Beldiceanu-Steinherr, I., *Recherches sur les actes des règnes des sultans Osman, Orkhan et Murad I* (Munich, 1967)

Belegu, X., *Lidhja e Prizrenit* (Tirana, 1939)

Benbassa, E., and A. Rodrigue, *Juifs des Balkans: espaces judéo-ibériques XIVᵉ–XXᵉ siècles* (Paris, 1993)

Berki, F., *Hê en Oungaria orthodoxos ekklêsia* (Salonica, 1964)

Bey, Midhat, *see* Midhat

Bianchini, S., and F. Privitera, *6 aprile 1941: l'attacco italiano alla Jugoslavia* (Milan, 1993)

Birge, J. K., *The Bektashi Order of Dervishes* (London, 1937)

Birken, A., *Die Provinzen des Osmanischen Reiches* (Wiesbaden, 1976)

Bisak, G., Kurti, S., and L. Gashi, *Gjendja e Shqiptareve në Jugosllavi: promemorie e paraqitur në Lidhjen e Kombeve (1930)*, tr. S. Koçi (Tirana, 1995)

Blagojević, M., 'Vojno-istorijske rekonstrukcije Kosovske bitke', in S. Ćirković, ed., *Kosovska bitka u istoriografiji* (Belgrade, 1990), pp. 11–22

Blaku, R., *Hintergründe der Auswanderung von Albanern aus Kosova in die westeuropäischen Staaten: Möglichkeiten der Wiedereinbürgerung in der Heimat* (Vienna, 1996)

Bobi, G., 'Kosovska "drama" i kominternovski "greh"', in S. Gaber and T. Kuzmanić, eds., *Zbornik Kosovo – Srbija – Jugoslavija* (Ljubljana, 1989), pp. 137–48

Bogdan, J., 'Ein Beitrag zur bulgarischen und serbischen Geschichtsschreibung', *AFSP*, vol. 13 (1891), pp. 480–543

Bogdanović, D., *Knjiga o Kosovu* (Belgrade, 1985)

Bojović, P., *Odbrana Kosovoga Polja 1915. g. i zaštita odstupanja srpske vojske preko Albanije i Crne Gore* (Belgrade, 1990)

Bonfini ['de Bonfinis'], A., *Rerum ungaricarum decades*, ed. I. Fógel, B. Iványi and L. Juhász, 4 vols. (Leipzig, 1936–41)

Boppe, A., *A la suite du gouvernement serbe de Nich à Corfou 20 octobre 1915 – 19 janvier 1916* (Paris, 1917)

Borshi, L., 'Les Albanais du Kossovo: les serfs du régime panserbe', *FB*, year 7, no. 140(1) (Nov. 1930), pp. 17–19

Bosnavi, Ö., *Tarih-i Bosna der zaman-ı Hekimoğlu Ali paşa*, ed. K. Su (Ankara, 1979)

Botero, G., *Le relationi universali*, new edn. (Venice, 1602)

Boué, A., *La Turquie d'Europe*, 4 vols. (Paris, 1840)

Braha, S., *Idriz Seferi në lëvizjet kombëtare shqiptare* (Tirana, 1981)

—, *Gjenocidi serbomadh dhe qëndresa shqiptare (1844–1990)* (Gjakova, 1991)

Braun, M., *Kosovo: die Schlacht auf dem Amselfelde in geschichtlicher und epischer Überlieferung* (Leipzig, 1937)

Bremer, T., *Ekklesiale Struktur und Ekklesiologie in der Serbischen Orthodoxen Kirche im 19. und 20. Jahrhundert* (Würzburg, 1992)

Brestovci, S., *Marrëdhëniet shqiptare-serbo-malazeze (1830–1878)* (Prishtina, 1983)

British Government, *Accounts and Papers*, 1880, vol. 42 (Turkey), c.2703, c.2703–1 (London, 1880)

—, *Albania: Basic Handbook*, 2 parts (London, 1943)

Brlić, T., *Die freiwillige Theilnahme der Serben und Kroaten an den vier letzten österreichisch-türkischen Kriegen* (Vienna, 1854)

de la Broquière, B., *Le Voyage d'Outremer*, ed. C. Schefer (Paris, 1892)

Brown, H. A., *A Winter in Albania* (London, 1888)

Browne ['Brown'], E., *A Brief Account of Some Travels in Hungaria, Servia, Bulgaria, Macedonia, Thessaly, Austria, Styria, Carinthia, Carniola, and Friuli* (London, 1673)

Buda, A., Zamputi, I., Frashëri, K., and P. Pepo, eds., *Burime të zgjedhura për historinë e Shqipërisë*, vol. 2 (Tirana, 1962)

Bulatović, L., *Prizrenski proces* (Novi Sad, 1988)

Bullemer, G., 'Ein Tscherkessendorf auf dem Amselfeld', *Mitteilungen der geographischen Gesellschaft in Wien*, vol. 75 (1932), pp. 232–8

Burileanu, C. N., *I romeni di Albania* (Bologna, 1912)

Burr, M., 'The Code of Stephen Dušan, Tsar and Autocrat of the Serbs and Greeks', *The Slavonic (and East European) Review*, vol. 28 (1949–50), pp. 198–217, 514–39

Byrnes, R. F., ed., *The Zadruga: Essays by Philip E. Mosely and Essays in His Honor* (Notre Dame, Indiana, 1976)

Çabej, E., 'Zur Charakteristik der lateinischen Lehnwörter im Albanischen', *Revue [roumaine] de linguistique*, vol. 7 (1962), pp. 161–99.

—, 'L'Illyrien et l'albanais: questions de principe', in *IGA*, pp. 41–52

—, 'The Problem of the Autochthony of the Albanians in the Light of the Albanian Language and Place Names', in *ATT*, pp. 33–48

—, 'The Problem of the Place of Formation of the Albanian Language', in *ATT*, pp. 63–99

Cahen, C., 'Dhimma', in *EI2*, vol. 2, pp. 227–31

—, and P. Hardy, 'Djizya', in *EI2*, vol. 2, pp. 559–67

Cana, Z., *Lëvizja kombëtare shqiptare në Kosovë 1908–1912* (Tirana, 1982)

—, *Shpalime historike* (Prishtina, 1982)

—, *Socialdemokracia serbe dhe çështja shqiptare 1903–1914* (Prishtina, 1986)

Cankova-Petkova, G., 'La Survivance du nom des Besses au moyenne [*sic*] âge', *BE*, vol. 6 (1963), pp. 93–6

Capidan, T., 'Raporturile albano-române', *Dacoromania: buletinul 'muzeului limbei române'*, vol. 2 (1921–2), pp. 444–554

—, 'Românii nomazi: studiu din viaţa Românilor din sudul Peninsulei Balcanice', *Dacoromania: buletinul 'muzeului limbei române'*, vol. 4 (1924–6), pp. 183–352

Carbonell, A., Espadaler, A. M., Llovet, J., and A. Tayadella, *Literatura catalana dels inicis als nostres dies* (Barcelona, 1979)

Carnegie Endowment for International Peace, *Report of the International Commission to Inquire into the Causes and Conduct of the Balkan Wars* (Washington, 1914)

Castelletti, G., 'Consuetudini e vita sociale nelle montagne albanesi secondo il Kanun i Lek Dukagjinit', *Studi albanesi*, vols. 3–4 (1933–4), pp. 61–163

Catualdi, V. [pseudonym of O. de Hassek], *Sultan Jahja, dell'imperial casa ottomana, od altrimenti Alessandro Conte di Montenegro ed i suoi discendenti in Italia: nuovi contributi alla storia della questione orientale, e delle relazioni politiche fra la Turchia e le potenze cristiane nel secolo XVII* (Trieste, 1889)

Ćehajić, D., *Derviški redovi u jugoslovenskim zemljama sa posebnim osvrtom na Bosnu i Hercegovinu* (Sarajevo, 1986)

Çelebi, Evliya: *see* Evliya

Çërabregu, M., *Gjeo dhe hartolinguistika: hartografia II* (Prishtina, 1990)

Čerskov, E., *Rimljani na Kosovu i Metohiji* (Belgrade, 1969)

Chalcocondylas, L., *Historiarum libri decem*, ed. I Bekker (Bonn, 1843)

Charanis, P., 'Town and Country in the Byzantine Possessions of the Balkan Peninsula during the Later Period of the Empire', in H. Birnbaum and S. Vryonis, eds., *Aspects of the Balkans: Continuity and Change* (The Hague, 1972), pp. 117–37

Choublier, M., *La Question d'Orient, depuis le traité de Berlin: étude d'histoire diplomatique* (Paris, 1897)

Ciano, Count Galeazzo, *Ciano's Diary 1939–1943*, ed. M. Muggeridge (London, 1947)

Ćidić, L., and D. Lazić, eds., *Očevici o velikoj seobi Srba* (Kruševac, 1990)

Cigar, N., *Genocide in Bosnia: The Policy of 'Ethnic Cleansing'* (College Station, Texas, 1995)

Čilev, P., 'Obikolka iz albanski selišta vŭ Prištinsko, Prizrensko, Debŭrsko i Ohridsko', *Izvestija na narodnija etnografski muzei vŭ Sofija*, vol. 6 (1926), pp. 107–12

Čilingirov, S., *Pomoravija po srbski svidetelstva: istoričeski izdirvanija s edna karta* (Sofia, 1917)

Cimochowski, W., 'Prejardhja e gjuhës shqipe', *BUSTSS*, vol. 12 (1958), no. 2, pp. 37–53

Ćirković, S., 'Dimitrije Kidon o kosovskom boju', *Zbornik radova vizantološkog instituta*, vol. 13 (1971), pp. 213–19

—, 'Kosovo i Metohija u srednjem veku', in *KMSI*, pp. 21–45

—, 'Serbia on the Eve of the Battle of Kosovo', in *KLMB*, pp. 1–17

—, Korać, V., and G. Babić, *Studenica Monastery* (Belgrade, 1986)

Clayer, N., *L'Albanie, pays des derviches: les ordres mystiques musulmans en Albanie à l'époque post-ottomane (1912–1967)* (Berlin, 1990)

—, *Mystiques, état et société: les Halvetis dans l'aire balkanique de la fin du XVᵉ siècle à nos jours* (Leiden, 1994)

—, 'Bektachisme et nationalisme albanais', in A. Popović and G. Veinstein, eds., *Bektachiyya: études sur l'ordre mystique des Bektachis et les groupes relevant de Hadji Bektach* (Istanbul, 1995), pp. 277–308

Clissold, S., ed., *A Short History of Yugoslavia* (Cambridge, 1968)

Cohen, L. J., *The Socialist Pyramid: Elites and Power in Yugoslavia* (London, 1989)

Cohen, P., *Serbia's Secret War: Propaganda and the Deceit of History* (College Station, Texas, 1996)

Contarini, C., *Istoria della guerra di Leopoldo Primo Imperadore e de' principi collegati contro il Turco*, 2 vols. (Venice, 1710)

Contarini, P. *Diario del viaggio da Venezia a Costantinopoli di M. Paolo Contarini, che andava bailo per la repubblica veneta alla porta ottomana nel 1580*, ed. V. Lazari (Venice, 1856)

Coon, C. S., *The Mountains of Giants: A Racial and Cultural Study of the North Albanian Mountain Ghegs* (Cambridge, Mass., 1950)

Cordignano, F., 'Geografia ecclesiastica dell'Albania dagli ultimi decenni del secolo XVI⁰ alla metà del secolo XVII⁰', *OC*, vol. 36, no. 99 (1934), pp. 229–94

Ćorović, V., 'Siluan i Danilo II, srpski pisci XIV–XV veka', *GSKA*, vol. 136 (1929), pp. 13–103

Crowe, D. M., *A History of the Gypsies of Eastern Europe and Russia* (New York, 1994)

Čubrilović, V., 'The Expulsion of the Albanians by the Serbs', in *That Was Yugoslavia: Information and Facts*, nos. 4–5 (1993), pp. 6–28

—, 'The Problem of Minorities in the New Yugoslavia', in *TOK*, pp. 301–6

Ćurčić, S., *Gračanica: King Milutin's Church and its Place in Late Byzantine Architecture* (University Park, Pennsylvania, 1979)

Cvetkova, B., 'Influence exercée par certaines institutions de Byzance et des Balkans du moyen âge sur le système féodal ottoman', *Byzantinobulgarica*, vol. 1 (1962), pp. 237–57

—, 'Novi dokumenti za istoriata na osvoboditelnite dviženija v Bŭlgarskite zemi prez XVII v.', *Izvestija na Instituta za Istorija, Bŭlgarska Akademija na Naukite*, vol. 19 (1967), pp. 243–62

—, *Les Institutions ottomanes en Europe* (Wiesbaden, 1978)

Cviić, C. [K.], 'A Culture of Humiliation', *The National Interest*, no. 32 (Summer 1993), pp. 79–82

Cvijić, J., *Remarques sur l'ethnographie de la Macédoine*, 2nd edn. (Paris, 1907)

Dako, K., *Liga e Prizrenit e para lëvizje kombtare për të mprojtur tërësine toksore të atdheut dhe për të fituar independencën e Shqipërisë* (Bucharest, 1922)

Daniel, O., *Albanie, une bibliographie historique* (Paris, 1985)

Dareste de la Chavanne, F. R., *Les Constitutions modernes*, 3rd edn., 2 vols (Paris, 1910)

Davies, Brig. 'Trotsky', *Illyrian Venture: The Story of the British Military Mission to Enemy-occupied Albania 1943–4* (London, 1952)

Davison, R. H., *Reform in the Ottoman Empire 1856–1876* (Princeton, NJ, 1963)

Decei, A., *Oastea lui Iancu Huniade înainte de batalia de la Kosovo* (Bucharest, 1946)

—, *Istoria imperiului otoman pînă la 1596* (Bucharest, 1978)

Dečev ['Detschew'], D., *Die thrakischen Sprachreste* (Vienna, 1957)

Dedijer, V., *Jugoslovensko-albanski odnosi (1939–1948)* (Belgrade, 1949)

—, and A. Miletić, *Genocid nad Muslimanima, 1941–1945: zbornik dokumenata i svedočenja* (Sarajevo, 1990)

Dema, B., 'Shqypnija katolike në vjetë 1671 (xjerrë prej dokumentit të Vizitatorit D. Shtjefën Gasparit)', *HD*, vol. 8 (1932), pp. 410–24, 518–37

Demaçi, A., *Republika e Kosovës është shpallur në zemrën e popullit tim* (n.p., 1990)

Dërmaku, I., 'Mbi veprimtarinë politike-kulturale të shqiptarëvet në Rumani gjatë rilindjes shqiptare', *VAK*, vols. 2–3, for 1966–7 (1970), pp. 57–81

Destani, B., *Selektivna bibliografija knjiga o Albaniji* (Belgrade, 1986)

—, ed., *The Albanian Question* (London, 1996)

Dinić, M. J., 'Dubrovačka srednjevekovna karavanska trgovina', *JIČ*, vol. 3 (1937), pp. 119–45

—, 'Dva savremenika o boju na Kosovu', *GSKA*, vol. 182 (= 2nd ser., vol. 92) (1940), pp. 131–48

—, *Iz dubrovačkog arhiva*, 3 vols. (Belgrade, 1957–67)

—, *Srpske zemlje u srednjem veku: istorijsko-geografske studije*, ed. S. Ćirković (Belgrade, 1978)

Dizdarević, N., *Albanski dnevnik* (Zagreb, 1988)

Djaković, S., *Sukobi na Kosovu* (Belgrade, 1984)

Djilas, M., *Conversations with Stalin* (Harmondsworth, 1963)

—, *Tito: The Story from Inside* (New York, 1980)

Djordjević ['Gjorgjević'], T., *Die Zigeuner in Serbien: ethnologische Forschungen*, 2 vols. (Budapest, 1903–6)

—, 'Arnauti u Srbiji za vlade Kneza Miloša (1815–1839)', *AASJE*, vol. 1 (1923), pp. 197–201

—, 'Čerkezi u našoj zemlji', *GSND*, vol. 3 (1928), pp. 143–53

—, *Naš narodni život*, 10 vols. (Belgrade, 1930–4)

Djordjević ['Georgevitch'], V., *Les Albanais et les grandes puissances*, tr. A. Karadjordjević (Paris, 1913)

Djurdjev, B., 'The Serbian Church in the History of the Serbian Nation under the Ottoman Rule (till the Reinstatement of the Patriarchate of Peć in 1557)', *DO*, vol. 40 (1978), pp. 288–304

Djuričić, M., *Običaji i verovanja Albanaca* (Belgrade, 1994)

Dogo, M., *Kosovo: albanesi e serbi: le radici del conflitto* (Lungro di Cosenza, 1992)

Draganović, K. S., 'Massenübertritte von Katholiken zur "Orthodoxie" im kroatischen Sprachgebiet zur Zeit der Türkenherrschaft', *OCP*, vol. 3 (1937), pp. 181–232

Dragnich, A. N., and S. Todorovich, *The Saga of Kosovo: Focus on Serbian–Albanian Relations* (New York, 1984)

Dragomir, S., 'Vlahii din Serbia în sec. XII–XV', *Anuarul institutului de istorie naţională*, vol. 1 (1921–2), pp. 279–99

Drançolli, J., 'Njoftime burimore rreth origjinës së Milosh Kopiliqit', (i): *Illyria*, no. 441 (3 Oct. 1995), p. 14; (ii): *Illyria*, no. 442 (5 Oct. 1995), p. 13

Ducellier, A., *La Façade maritime de l'Albanie au moyen age: Durazzo et Valona du XIᵉ au XVᵉ siècle* (Salonica, 1981)

—, 'Have the Albanians Occupied Kosova?', in *TOK*, pp. 63–8

Duijzings, G., 'Egyptians in Kosovo and Macedonia', in E. Hardten, A. Stanisavljević and D. Tsakiris, eds., *Der Balkan in Europa* (Frankfurt, 1996), pp. 103–21

—, 'The Exodus of Letnica – Croatian Refugees from Kosovo in Western Slavonia. A Chronicle', in J. Kirin and M. Povrzanović, eds., *War, Exile, Everyday Life: Cultural Perspectives* (Zagreb, 1996), pp. 147–70

Dujčev, I., *Il Cattolicesimo in Bulgaria nel sec. XVII secondo i processi informativi sulla nomina dei vescovi cattolici* (Rome, 1937)

Dumont, A., *Le Balkan et l'Adriatique: les bulgares et les albanais; l'administration en Turquie; la vie des campagnes; le panslavisme et l'hellénisme*, 2nd edn. (Paris, 1874)

Durham, M. E., *High Albania* (London, 1909)

—, 'Scutari, Albania, and the Constitution', *The Fortnightly Review*, n.s., vol. 85 (1909), pp. 295–302

—, 'Frontiers and Fanaticism', *The Nation*, vol. 13, no. 17 (26 July 1913), pp. 642–4

—, *The Struggle for Scutari (Turk, Slav, and Albanian)* (London, 1914)

—, 'The Antiquity of Albania', *The Near East*, vol. 14, no. 352 (1 Feb. 1918), pp. 95–6

—, *Twenty Years of Balkan Tangle* (London, 1920)

—, *Some Tribal Origins, Laws, and Customs of the Balkans* (London, 1928)

Dželetović Ivanov, P., *Jevreji Kosova i Metohije* (Belgrade, 1988)

Elezović, G., *Rečnik kosovsko-metohiskog dijalekta*, 2 vols. (Belgrade, 1932–5)

—, ed. and tr., *Turski spomenici*, bk. 1, vol. 1 (1348–1520) (Belgrade, 1940)

—, ed. and tr., *Ogledalo sveta ili istorija Mehmeda Nešrije* (Belgrade, 1957)

Elsie, R., *History of Albanian Literature*, 2 vols. (New York, 1995)

Emmert, T. A., *Serbian Golgotha: Kosovo, 1389* (New York, 1990)

Engel, P., 'János Hunyadi: The Decisive Years of His Career, 1440–1444', in J. M. Bak and B. K. Király, eds., *From Hunyadi to Rákóczi: War and Society in Late Medieval and Early Modern Hungary* (New York, 1982), pp. 103–23

Engin, V., *Rumeli demiryolları* (Istanbul, 1993)

Epstein, M. A., *The Ottoman Jewish Communities and their Role in the Fifteenth and Sixteenth Centuries* (Freiburg, 1980)

Erlich, V. S., *Family in Transition: A Study of 300 Yugoslav Villages* (Princeton, NJ, 1966)

—, 'The Last Big Zadrugas: Albanian Extended Families in the Kosovo Region', in R. F. Byrnes, ed., *The Zadruga: Essays by Philip E. Mosley and Essays in His Honor* (Notre Dame, Indiana, 1976), pp. 244–51

Evans, R. J. W., *The Making of the Habsburg Monarchy 1550–1700: An Interpretation* (Oxford, 1979)

Evliya Çelebi ['Evliya Efendi'], *Narrative of Travels in Europe, Asia, and Africa*, tr. J. von Hammer, 2 vols. (London, 1850)

— ['Evlija Čelebi'], *Putopis: odlomci o jugoslavenskim zemljama*, ed. and tr. H. Šabanović (Sarajevo, 1967)

Farlati, D., *Illyrici sacri*, 8 vols. (Venice, 1751–1819)

Faroqhi, S., 'Rural Society in Anatolia and the Balkans during the Sixteenth Century', *Turcica*, (i): vol. 9 (1977), pp. 161–95; (ii): vol. 11 (1979), pp. 103–53

—, 'Crisis and Change, 1590–1699', in H. Inalcık and D. Quataert, eds., *An Economic and Social History of the Ottoman Empire, 1300–1914* (Cambridge, 1994), pp. 411–636

—, *Kultur und Alltag im Osmanischen Reich: vom Mittelalter bis zum Anfang des 20. Jahrhunderts* (Munich, 1995)

Fermendžin, E., ed., *Acta Bosnae potissimum ecclesiastica cum insertis editorum documentorum regestis ab anno 925 usque ad annum 1752* (Zagreb, 1892)

—, 'Izprave god. 1579–1671 tičuće se Crne Gore i stare Srbije', *SJAZU*, vol. 25 (1892), pp. 164–200

Filipović, M. S., *Has pod Paštrikom* (Sarajevo, 1958)

Fine, J. V. A., *The Early Medieval Balkans: A Critical Survey from the Sixth to the Late Twelfth Century* (Ann Arbor, Michigan, 1983)

—, *The Late Medieval Balkans: A Critical Survey from the Late Twelfth Century to the Ottoman Conquest* (Ann Arbor, Michigan, 1987)

Fischer, B. J., *King Zog and the Struggle for Stability in Albania* (New York, 1984)

Floristán Imízcoz, J. M., *Fuentes para la política oriental de las Austrias: la documentación griega del Archivo de Simancas (1571–1621)*, 2 vols. (Leon, 1988)

Fond za humanitarno pravo, *Spotlight Report*, no. 16 (Feb. 1995)

Foresti, A., et al., *Mappamondo istorico, cioè, ordinata narrazione dei quattro sommi imperii del mondo*, 11 vols. (Rome, 1711–22)

Fraser, A., *The Gypsies* (Oxford, 1992)

Frashëri, K., *Abdyl Frashëri (1839–1892)* (Tirana, 1990)

—, 'Pjetër Bogdani dhe lëvizja çlirimtare në shekullin e 17-të', in A. Kostallari, ed., *Pjetër Bogdani dhe vepra e tij* (Tirana, 1991), pp. 53–83

Frashëri, Mehdi, *Lidhja e Prizrenit edhe efektet dipllomatike të saj* (Tirana, 1938)

Frashëri, Midhat ['Lumo Skendo'], *Albanais et Slaves* (Lausanne, 1919)

Frashëri, N. ['N. H. F.'], 'Le Livre des Bektachis', tr. anon., *La Revue albanaise*, vol. 'A' (1897–8), pp. 174–6, 193, 212–13

Freundlich, L., *Albaniens Golgotha: Anklageakten gegen die Vernichter des Albanervolkes* (Vienna, 1913)

Gashi, A. A., *The Denial of Human and National Rights of Albanians in Kosova* (New York, 1992)

Gaspari, S., 'Nji dorshkrim i vjetës 1671 mbi Shqypni', *HD*, vol. 6 (1930), pp. 377–88, 492–8, 605–13; vol. 7 (1931), pp. 154–61, 223–7, 349–55, 434–47, 640–4, 699–703; vol. 8 (1932), pp. 48–50, 98–104, 208–10, 265–7, 310–14

Gavazzi, M., 'Die Mehrfamilien der europäischen Völker', *Ethnologia europaea*, vol. 11 (1980), pp. 158–90

Gegaj, A., *L'Albanie et l'invasion turque au XVe siècle* (Paris, 1937)

Gelcich, G., *La Zedda e la dinastia dei Balšidi: studî storici documentati* (Split, 1899)

Gelzer, H., *Der Patriarchat von Achrida: Geschichte und Urkunden* (Leipzig, 1902)

Georgiev, V., 'Albanisch, dakisch-mysisch und rumänisch: die Herkunft der Albaner', *BE*, vol. 2 (1960), pp. 1–19

—, 'Thrace et illyrien', *BE*, vol. 6 (1963), pp. 71–4

Gerba, Captain, 'Die Kaiserlichen in Albanien', *Mittheilungen des k. k. Kriegs-Archivs*, n.s., vol. 2 (Vienna, 1888)

Gesellschaft für bedrohte Völker, *The Albanians in Kosovo* (Göttingen, 1988)

Giannelli, C., 'Documenti inediti sullo stato di alcune comunità cattoliche della Serbia meridionale nel 1578', *Ricerche slavistiche*, vol. 2 (1953), pp. 29–59

—, 'Lettere del Patriarca di Peć Arsenio III e del Vescovo Savatije all' Arcivescovo di Antivari Andrea Zmajević', *OCP*, vol. 21 (1955), pp. 63–78

Gibbons, H. A., *The Foundation of the Ottoman Empire: A History of the Osmanlis up to the Death of Bayezid I (1300–1403)* (Oxford, 1916)

Gimbutas, M., *The Slavs* (London, 1971)

di Giovine, P., 'Tracio, dacio ed albanese nella prospettiva genealogica', in *Actes du deuxième Symposium International de Thracologie* (Rome, 1980), pp. 137–46

Gjeçov, S., ed., *Kanuni i Lekë Dukagjinit: The Code of Lek Dukagjin*, with tr. by L. Fox (Bakersfield, Calif., 1989)

Gjergj-Gashi, G., *Martirët shqiptarë gjatë viteve 1846–1848* (Zagreb, 1994)

—, ed., *Kosova: altari i Arbërisë 1910–1941*, vol. 3 (Tirana, 1996)

Gjinari, J., 'De la continuation de l'illyrien en albanais', in *IGA*, pp. 173–81

Gjini, G., *Ipeshkvia Shkup-Prizren nëpër shekuj* (Zagreb, 1992)

Glišić, V., 'Albanization of Kosovo and Metohija', in A. Mitrović, ed., *Srbi i Albanci u XX veku* (Belgrade, 1991), pp. 293–308

Glück, L., *Albanien und Macedonien: eine Reiseskizze* (Würzburg, 1892)

Godart, J., *L'Albanie en 1921* (Paris, 1922)

Gökbilgin, M. T., *Rumeli'de Yürükler, Tartarlar ve Evlâd-ı Fâtihân* (Istanbul, 1957)

Goldstein, I., *Hrvatski rani srednji vijek* (Zagreb, 1995)

Goldstein, S., ed., *Jews in Yugoslavia* (Zagreb, 1989)

Goodwin, G., *The Janissaries* (London, 1994)

Gopčević, S., *Makedonien und Alt-Serbien* (Vienna, 1889)

—, *Das Fürstentum Albanien, seine Vergangenheit, ethnographischen Verhältnisse, politische Lage und Aussichten für die Zukunft*, 2nd edn. (Berlin, 1914)

Gorup, R. J., 'Kosovo and Epic Poetry', in *KLMB*, pp. 109–21

Gounaris, B. C., *Steam over Macedonia, 1870–1912: Socio-Economic Change and the Railway Factor* (New York, 1993)

Grafenauer, B., Perović, D., and J. Šidak, *Historija naroda Jugoslavije*, vol. 1 (Zagreb, 1953)

Graves, Sir Robert, *Storm Centres of the Near East: Personal Memories 1879–1929* (London, 1933)

Grégoire, H., 'L'Opinion byzantine et la bataille de Kossovo', *Byzantion*, vol. 6 (1931), pp. 247–51

—, 'La Chanson de Roland de l'an 1085: Baligant et Califerne ou l'étymologie du mot "Californie"', *Bulletin de la classe des lettres et des sciences morales et politiques de l'Académie Royale de Belgique*, 5th ser., vol. 25 (1939), pp. 211–73

—, and R. de Keyser, 'La *Chanson de Roland* et Byzance: ou de l'utilité du grec pour les romanistes', *Byzantion*, vol. 14 (1939), pp. 265–316

Grimm, G., 'Ethnographic Maps of the Kosova Region from 1730 to 1913', in *SOK*, pp. 41–53

Grisebach, A., *Reise durch Rumelien und nach Brusa im Jahre 1839*, 2 vols. (Göttingen, 1841)

Grmek, M., Gjidara, M., and N. Simac, eds., *Le Nettoyage ethnique: documents historiques sur une idéologie serbe* (Paris, 1993)

Grujić, R., *Kako se postupalo sa srpskim molbama na dvoru ćesara avstrijskog poslednje godine života patriarha Arsenija III Čarnojevića* (Novi Sad, 1906) de Gubernatis, D., and A. M. de Turre, *Orbis seraphicus: historia de tribus ordinibus a seraphico patriarcha S. Francisco institutis deque eorum progressibus per quatuor mundi partes [. . .] tomus secundus*, ed. M. a Civetia and T. Domenichelli (Quaracchi, 1886)

Gurakuqi, G., 'Kronikë mbi Mahmud Pashen, Brahim Pashen e Mustaf Pashen', *HD*, vol. 8 (1932), pp. 19–28, 109–17

Haarmann, H., *Der lateinische Lehnwortschatz im Albanischen* (Hamburg, 1972)

Hadri, A., 'Aradhet e para partizane në Kosovë-Metohi', *Përparimi*, vol. 6 (1960), pp. 15–28

——, 'Okupacioni sistem na Kosovu i Metohiji 1941–1944', *JIČ* (1965), no. 2, pp. 39–60

——, *Lëvizja nacionalçlirimtare në Kosovë (1941–1945)* (Prishtina, 1971)

——, *Gjakova në lëvizjen nacionalçlirimtare* (Prishtina, 1974)

Hadrovics, L., 'A Magyarországi szerb kérdés Balkáni gyökerei', *A Magyar történettudományi intézet évkönyve* (1942), pp. 327–66

——, *L'Église serbe sous la domination turque* (Paris, 1947)

Hadžibegić, H., 'Džizja ili harač', *POF*, (i): vols. 3–4 (1952–3), pp. 55–135; (ii): vol. 5 (1954–5), pp. 43–102

——, Handžić, A., and E. Kovačević, eds., *Oblast Brankovića: opširni katastarski popis iz 1455. godine*, 2 vols. (Sarajevo, 1972)

Hadži-Vasiljević, J., *Arbanaska liga – arnautska kongra – i srpski narod u turskom carstvu (1878–1882)* (Belgrade, 1909)

——, *Muslimani naše krive u Južnoj Srbiji* (Belgrade, 1924)

——, *Četnička akcija u staroj Srbiji i Maćedoniji* (Belgrade, 1928)

——, *Prosvetne i političke prilike u Južnim Srpskim oblastima u XIX v. (do srpsko-turskih ratova 1876–78)* (Belgrade, 1928)

Hafner, S., ed. and tr., *Serbisches Mittelalter: altserbische Herrscherbiographien*, 2 vols. (Graz, 1962–76)

——, *Studien zur altserbischen dynastischen Historiographie* (Munich, 1964)

von Hahn, J. G., *Albanesische Studien*, 3 vols. (Jena, 1854)

—— *Reise von Belgrad nach Salonik* (Vienna, 1861)

—— *Reise durch die Gebiete des Drin und Wardar im Auftrage der k. Akademie der Wissenschaften, unternommen im Jahre 1863* (Vienna, 1869)

Halaçoğlu, A., *Balkan harbi sirasinda Rumeli'den Türk göçleri (1912–1913)* (Ankara, 1994)

Halimi, K., 'Esnafet në Kosovë-Metohi', *Përparimi*, vol. 4 (1958), pp. 109–18

von Hammer, J., *Geschichte des Osmanischen Reiches*, 10 vols. (Pest, 1827–35)

Hammond, N. G. L., *Migrations and Invasions in Greece and Adjacent Areas* (Park Ridge, NJ, 1976)

Hamp, E. P., 'The Position of Albanian', in H. Birnbaum and J. Puhvel, eds., *Ancient Indo-European Dialects* (Berkeley, Calif., 1966), pp. 97–121

——, 'On the Distribution and Origin of Vatra', in H. D. Pohl and N. Salnikow, eds., *Opuscula slavica et linguistica* (Klagenfurt, 1976), pp. 201–10

Handžić, A., 'Nekoliko vijesti o Arbanasima na Kosovu i Metohiju sredinom XV vijeka', in *SPS*, pp. 201–9

Hasani, S., *Kosova, të vërtetat dhe maskat: intervistë e Sinan Hasanit dhënë gazetës 'Borba'* (Prishtina, 1981)

Hasani, X., *Shkolla dhe arsimi shqip ndër viset shqiptare në Kosovë, Maqedoni dhe Mal të Zi përballë shovinizmit serb, maqedon e malazez (1945–1994)* (Vienna, 1995)

Hasluck, F. W., *Christianity and Islam under the Sultans*, ed. M. M. Hasluck, 2 vols. (Oxford, 1929)

Hasluck, M. M., 'The Gypsies of Albania', *Journal of the Gypsy Lore Society*, vol. 17 (1938), pp. 49–61; vol. 17 (1938), Jubilee no., pp. 18–30, 110–22

—, *The Unwritten Law in Albania*, ed. J. H. Hutton (Cambridge, 1954)

Haxhiu, A., *Shota dhe Azem Galica* (Tirana, 1976)

Hecquard, H., *Histoire et description de la Haute Albanie ou Guégarie* (Paris, n.d. [1858])

Hehn, P., 'Man and the State in Serbia, from the Fourteenth to the Mid-Nineteenth Century: A Study in Centralist and Anti-Centralist Conflict', *Balkan Studies*, vol. 27 (1987), pp. 3–27

Heim, M., *Spiridion Gopčević: Leben und Werk* (Wiesbaden, 1966)

Helmreich, E. C., *The Diplomacy of the Balkan Wars 1912–1913* (Cambridge, Mass., 1938)

Helsinki Watch, *Human Rights Abuses in Kosovo, 1990–1992* (New York, 1992)

Henze, P. B., 'Circassian Resistance to Russia', in M. Bennigsen Broxup, ed., *The North Caucasus Barrier: The Russian Advance towards the Muslim World* (London, 1992), pp. 62–111.

Herbert, A., *Ben Kendim: A Record of Eastern Travel*, ed. D. MacCarthy (London, 1924)

Heyd, U., *Studies in Old Ottoman Criminal Law*, ed. V. Ménage (Oxford, 1973)

Hibbert, Sir Reginald, *Albania's National Liberation Struggle: The Bitter Victory* (London, 1991)

Hilferding [Gilferding], A., *Geschichte der Serben und Bulgaren*, 2 vols. (Bautzen, 1856–64)

Hofmann, G., 'Il Beato Bellarmino e gli orientali', *OC*, vol. 8, no. 6 (1927), pp. 261–307

—, 'Griechische Patriarchen und römische Päpste: Untersuchungen und Texte', *OC*, vol. 25, no. 2 (1932), pp. 225–304

Hopf, C., *Chroniques gréco-romanes inédites ou peu connues* (Berlin, 1873)

Horecky, P. L., ed., *Southeastern Europe: A Guide to Basic Publications* (Chicago, 1969)

Horvat, B., *Kosovsko pitanje* (Zagreb, 1989)

Hoti, I., *Lëvizja ilegale antifashiste në Kosovën lindore 1941–1945* (Prishtina, '1980' [1990])

—, *Çështja e Kosovës gjatë luftës së dytë botërore* (Prishtina, 1997)

Howard-Johnston, J. D., 'Urban Continuity in the Balkans in the Early Middle Ages', in A. G. Poulter, ed., *Ancient Bulgaria*, 2 vols. (Nottingham, 1983), vol. 2, pp. 242–54

Hoxha, E., *The Titoites* (Tirana, 1982)

Hoxha, F., 'Prve partizanske jedinice na Kosovu i u Metohiji', in *UNJ*, vol. 1, pp. 134–48

Hoxha, H., 'Elemente të presionit ekonomik ndaj shqiptarëve në Jugosllavinë e vjetër', *Përparimi*, vol. 16 (1970), pp. 309–33

—, 'Politika e eliminimit të shqiptarëve nga trualli i Jugosllavisë së vjetër', *Përparimi*, vol. 16 (1970), pp. 430–6

Hozier, H. M., ed., *The Russo-Turkish War: Including an Account of the Rise and Decline of the Ottoman Power, and the History of the Eastern Question*, 2 vols. (London, n.d. [1879])

Hrabak, B., 'Jevreji u Albaniji od kraja XIII do kraja XVII veka i njihove veze sa Dubrovnikom', *Jevrejski Istorijski Muzej, Beograd, zbornik*, vol. 1 (1971), pp. 55–97

—, 'Prvi izveštaji diplomata velikih sila o Prizrenskoj Ligi', *Balcanica*, vol. 9 (1978), pp. 235–89

—, *Britanska diplomatija o razgraničenju severne Albanije* (Titograd, 1986)

—, 'Srpski ustanici i Novopazarski sandžak (Raška) 1804–1813 godine', *IČ*, vols. 40–1 (1993–4), pp. 95–137

Huld, M. E., *Basic Albanian Etymologies* (Los Angeles, 1983)

Hupchick, D. R., *The Bulgarians in the Seventeenth Century: Slavic Orthodox Society and Culture under Ottoman Rule* (Jefferson, North Carolina, 1993)

de Hurmuzaki, E., ed., *Documente privitóre la istoria Românilor*, vol. 5, part 2 (Bucharest, 1886)

Immanuel, Oberst [Colonel], *Serbiens und Montenegros Untergang: ein Beitrag zur Geschichte des Weltkrieges*, 2nd edn. (Berlin, 1916)

Inalcık, H., 'Osmanlı imperatorluğunun kuruluş ve inkişafı devrinde Türkiye'nin iktisadi vaziyeti üzerinde bir tetkik münasebetiyle', *Belleten*, vol. 15 (1951), pp. 629–90

—, 'Timariotes chrétiens en Albanie au XV. siècle d'après un registre de timars ottoman', *MÖS*, vol. 4 (1951), pp. 118–38

—, 'Od Stefana Dušana do osmanskog carstva', *POF*, vols. 3–4 (1952–3), pp. 23–53

—, ed., *Sûret-i defter-i sancak-i Arvanid* (Ankara, 1954)

—, 'The Ottoman Decline and its Effects upon the *reaya*', in H. Birnbaum and S. Vryonis, eds., *Aspects of the Balkans: Continuity and Change* (The Hague, 1972), pp. 338–54

—, *The Ottoman Empire: The Classical Age, 1300–1600* (London, 1973)

—, 'Military and Fiscal Transformation in the Ottoman Empire, 1600–1700', *Archivum ottomanicum*, vol. 6 (1980), pp. 283–337

—, 'The Emergence of Big Farms, *Çiftliks*: State, Landlords and Tenants', in

J.-L. Bacque-Grammont and P. Dumont, eds., *Contributions à l'histoire économique et sociale de l'Empire ottoman* (Louvain, 1983), pp. 105–26

—, *Osmanlı imparatorluğu: toplum ve ekonomi* (Istanbul, 1993)

Institut d'étude sur l'Albanie socialiste, *Les Relations albano-yougoslaves 1912–1982*, Les Cahiers de l'INEAS, 1/1983 (Paris, 1983)

Interallied Commission, *Report of the Interallied Commission on the Violation of the Hague Convention and of the Principles of the International Law Committed in 1915–1918 by the Bulgarians in Occupied Serbia* (Paris, 1919)

International Documentation on Macedonia, *Harold Nicolson and the Balkans*, 1st sub-series, 'League of Nations', nos. 10–12 (Geneva, 1979)

Ippen, T., *Novibazar und Kossovo (das alte Rascien)* (Vienna, 1892)

—, *Skutari und die nordalbanische Küstenebene* (Sarajevo, 1907)

—, 'Beiträge zur inneren Geschichte Albaniens im XIX. Jahrhundert', in *IAF*, vol. 1, pp. 342–85

Islami, H., *Fshati i Kosovës: kontribut për studimin sociologjiko-demografik të evolucionit rural* (Prishtina, 1985)

—, 'Demografski problemi Kosova i njihovo tumačenje', in S. Gaber and T. Kuzmanić, eds., *Zbornik Kosovo – Srbija – Jugoslavija* (Ljubljana, 1989), pp. 39–66

Islami, S., and K. Frashëri, *Historia e Shqiperisë*, 2nd edn., vol. 1 (Tirana, 1967)

Ivić, A., 'Rumilijski vilajet u godini 1838', *Prilozi za književnost, jezik, istoriju i folklor*, vol. 13 (1933), pp. 117–26

Ivšić, M., *Les Problèmes agraires en Yougoslavie: par la liberté vers l'organisation sociale et économique* (Paris, 1926)

Jäckh, E., *Im türkischen Kriegslager durch Albanien: Bekenntnisse zur deutsch-türkischen Freundschaft* (Heilbronn, 1911)

Jacomini, F., *La politica dell'Italia in Albania* (Rocca San Cacciano, 1965)

Jačov, M., ed., *Spisi tajnog vatikanskog arhiva XVI–XVIII veka* (Belgrade, 1983)

—, ed., *Spisi kongregacije za propagandu vere u Rimu o Srbima 1622–1644*, vol. 1 (Belgrade, 1986)

Jelavich, B., *History of the Balkans*, 2 vols. (Cambridge, 1983)

—, and C. Jelavich, *The Establishment of the Balkan National States, 1804–1920* (Seattle, Washington, 1977)

Jireček, K. ['C.'], *Geschichte der Bulgaren* (Prague, 1876)

—, *Die Handelsstrassen und Bergwerke von Serbien und Bosnien während des Mittelalters: historisch-geographische Studien* (Prague, 1879)

—, 'Der Grossvezier Mehmed Sokolović und die serbischen Patriarchen Makarij und Antonij', *AFSP*, vol. 9 (1886), pp. 291–7

—, 'Die Romanen in den Städten Dalmatiens während des Mittelalters', *DKAWP-H*, (i): vol. 48 (1902), no. 3; (ii–iii): vol. 49 (1904), nos. 1–2

—, 'Staat und Gesellschaft im mittelalterlichen Serbien', *DKAWP-H*, (i): vol. 56 (1912), no. 1; (ii): vol. 56 (1912), no. 2; (iii): vol. 58 (1914), no. 2; (iv): vol. 64 (1919), no. 2

—, 'Albanien in der Vergangenheit', in *IAF*, vol. 1, pp. 63–93

—, 'Skutari und sein Gebiet im Mittelalter', in *IAF*, vol. 1, pp. 94–124

Jokl, N., 'Altmakedonisch-Griechisch-Albanisches', *Indogermanische Forschungen: Zeitschrift für indogermanische Sprach- und Altertumskunde*, vol. 26 (1910), pp. 1–20

—, 'Slaven und Albaner', *Slavia: časopis pro slovanskou filologii*, vol. 13 (1934–5), pp. 281–325, 609–45

Jovičević, P., 'Politička situacija i rad partijske organizacije na Kosovu i u Metohiji pred rat i u 1941. godini', in *UNJ*, vol. 2, pp. 204–48

Judah, T., *The Serbs: History, Myth and the Destruction of Yugoslavia* (New Haven, Conn., 1997)

Kadare, I., *Broken April*, tr. anon. (New York, 1990)

Kahnè, S., 'A proposito della lettera del patriarca di Peć Arsenio III all' arcivescovo di Antivari Andrea Zmajević', *OCP*, vol. 22 (1956), pp. 41–58

—, 'L'azione politica del patriarca di Peć Arsenio Črnojević dal 1682 al 1690', *OCP*, vol. 23 (1957), pp. 267–312

Kaleshi, H., 'Shenime nga e kaluemja e Prizrenit gjatë periodës turke', *Përparimi*, vol. 7 (1961), pp. 497–510

—, 'Türkische Angaben über den Kanun des Leka Dukadjini', in *KSGA*, pp. 103–12

—, 'Alcuni dati delle cronache ottomane sulle guerre albano-turche del XV secolo', in Centro internazionale di studi albanesi presso l'Università di Palermo, *V. Convegno internazionale di studi albanesi* (Palermo, 1969), pp. 203–20

—, 'Hasan Prishtina', in M. Bernath, F. von Schroeder and K. Nehring, eds., *Biographisches Lexikon zur Geschichte Südosteuropas*, 4 vols. (Munich, 1974–81), vol. 3, pp. 485–9

—, *Kontributi i Shqiptarëve në dituritë Islame* (Prizren, 1991)

—, and H.-J. Kornrumpf, 'Das Wilajet Prizren: Beitrag zur Geschichte der türkischen Staatsreform auf dem Balkan im 19. Jahrhundert', *SOF*, vol. 26 (1967), pp. 176–238

—, and I. Rexhep ['Redžep'], 'Prizrenac Kukli Beg i njegove zadužbine', *POF*, vols. 8–9 (1958–9), pp. 143–68

Kämpfer, F., 'Der Kult des heiligen Serbenfürsten Lazar: Textinterpretationen zur Ideologiegeschichte des Spätmittelalters', *SOF*, vol. 31 (1972), pp. 81–139

Kandić, N., ed., *Spotlight on Human Rights Violations in Times of Armed Conflict* (Belgrade, 1995)

Kanitz, F., 'Die fortschreitende Arnautisirung und Muhamedanisirung Alt-Serbiens', *Österreichische Monatsschrift für den Orient*, year 14, no. 3 (March 1888), pp. 37–41

—, *Das Königreich Serbien und das Serbenvolk von der Römerzeit bis zur Gegenwart*, 3 vols. (Leipzig, 1904–14)

Karadžić, V. S., *Dela*, ed. V. Nedić, P. Ivić, *et al.*, 12 vols. (Belgrade, 1969)

Kaser, K., *Hirten, Kämpfer, Stammeshelden: Ursprünge und Gegenwart des balkanischen Patriarchats* (Vienna, 1992)

Katičić, R., *Ancient Languages of the Balkans*, 'part 1' (Paris, 1976)

Kemp, P., *No Colours or Crest* (London, 1958)

Kiel, M., *Art and Society of Bulgaria in the Turkish Period* (Assen, 1985)

Kirch, P., *Krieg und Verwaltung in Serbien und Mazedonien 1916–1918* (Stuttgart, 1928)

Kissling, H. J., 'Zur Frage der Anfänge des Bektašitums in Albanien', *Oriens*, vol. 15 (1962), pp. 281–6

Klaić, V., *Kosovo: geografsko-historijske crtice* (Zagreb, 1889)

Knight, E. F., *Albania: A Narrative of Recent Travel* (London, 1880)

von Kohl, C., and W. Libal, *Kosovo: gordischer Knoten des Balkan* (Vienna, 1992)

Kojaković, V., *Borba Jugoslovena za svoj opstanak prije kosovske bitke* (Dubrovnik, 1934)

Kokalari, H., *Kosova, djepi i shqiptarizmit* (Rome, 1962)

Kolea, S. ['S. K.'], 'Les Massacres serbes', *AOBDIA*, 2nd ser., no. 4 (25 Aug. 1918), pp. 26–8; no. 5 (25 Sept. 1918), pp. 34–8; no. 6 (25 Nov. 1918), pp. 45–9

Koljević, S., *The Epic in the Making* (Oxford, 1980)

Kolonomos, Ž., *Poslovice, izreke i priče sefardskih jevreja Makedonije* (Belgrade, 1978)

Konstantin of Kostenec ['Konstantin fra Kostenec'], *Den serbiske Despot Stefan Lazarevićs liv og levned*, ed. and tr. G. Svane (Copenhagen, 1975)

Kosančić, I., *Novo-Pazarski Sandžak i njegov etnički problem* (Belgrade, 1912)

Kostić, D., 'Starost narodnog epskog pesništva našeg', *Jugoslovenski filolog*, vol. 12 (1933), pp. 1–72

—, 'Miloš Kopilić – Kobilić – Obilić', *RIEB*, vols. 1–2 (1934–5), pp. 232–54

Kostić, K. N., *Naši novi gradovi na jugu* (Belgrade, 1922)

Kostić, M., 'Prilozi istoriji srpsko-arbanaskog ustanka 1689–1690 g.', *AASJE*, vol. 2 (1924), pp. 11–20

—, 'Opis vojske Jovana Hunjadija pri polasku u boj na Kosovo', *GSND*, vol. 1 (1925), pp. 79–91

—, 'Ustanak Srba i Arbanasa u Staroj Srbiji protiv Turaka 1737–1739 i seoba u Ugarsku', *GSND*, vols. 7–8 (1930), pp. 203–35

—, 'O postanku i značenju tzv. 'Invitatorije' Leopolda I balkanskim narodima od 6 aprila 1690', *IČ*, vol. 2, for 1949–50 (1951), pp. 144–56

—, 'O ulozi franjevca Toma Raspasanovića u austro-turskom ratu na kosovskom i ugarsko-erdeljskom frontu krajem XVII veka', *Istorijski glasnik*, vols. 3–4 (1957), pp. 81–7

—, *Završni bilans polemike o srpsko-arbanaskom ustanku protiv Turaka uz austrijsku vojsku 1689/90* (Belgrade, 1962)

Kostić, P., 'Prizrenski mutesarifi i valije u XVIII. i XIX. veku', *GSND*, vol. 5 (1929), pp. 157–64

—, *Prosvetno-kulturni život pravoslavnih Srba u Prizrenu i njegovoj okolini u XIX i početkom XX veka (sa uspomenama pisca)* (Skopje, 1933)

Kouri, E. I., *Die Milutinschule der byzantinischen Wandmalerei in Serbien, Makedonien, Kosovo-Metohien und Montenegro (1294/1295–1321)* (Helsinki, 1982)

Kovačević-Kojić, D., 'Priština u srednjem veku', *IČ*, vol. 22 (1975), pp. 45–74

Kraljačić, T., 'Der 500. Jahrestag der Kosovo-Schlacht in Bosnien und Herzegowina', in *KBNP*, pp. 355–62

Krasniqi, M., 'Organizimi i jetës shoqnore në një familje të madhe në rrethin e Pejës', *Përparimi*, vol. 5 (1959), pp. 303–13

—, ['Krasnići'], *Savremene društveno-geografske promene na Kosovu i Metohiji* (Prishtina, 1963)

—, *Lugu i Baranit: monografi etno-gjeografike* (Prishtina, 1984)

Krause, A., 'Das Problem der albanischen Unabhängigkeit in den Jahren 1908–1914', Phil. diss., Vienna, 1970 (copy in Kriegsarchiv library, Vienna)

Krizman, B., 'Elaborat dra Ive Andrića o Albaniji iz 1939. godine', *Časopis za suvremenu povijest*, vol. 2 (1977), pp. 77–89

Krstić, D., *Kolonizacija u Južnoj Srbiji* (Sarajevo, 1928)

Külçe, S., *Osmanlı tarihinde Arnavutluk*, printed with *Firzovik toplantısı ve meşrutiyet* (Smyrna, 1944)

Kunt, I. M., 'Ethnic-Regional (*Cins*) Solidarity in the Seventeenth-Century Ottoman Establishment', *International Journal of Middle Eastern Studies*, vol. 5 (1974), pp. 233–9

—, *Sancaktan eyalete: 1550–1650 arasında Osmanlı ümerası ve il idaresi* (Istanbul, 1978)

Kuripešić ['Curipeschitz'], B., *Itinerarium der Botschaftsreise des Josef von Lamberg und Niclas Jurischitz durch Bosnien, Serbien, Bulgarien nach Konstantinopel 1530*, ed. E. Lamberg-Schwarzenberg (Innsbruck, 1910)

Kuvendi i Republikës së Kosovës, *Kushtetuta e Republikës së Kosovës* (Prishtina, 1990)

Lamansky, V., *Secrets d'état de Venise: documents, extraits, notices et études servant à éclaircir les rapports de la Seigneurie avec les Grecs, les Slaves et la Porte Ottomane à la fin du XVᵉ et au XVIᵉ siècle* (St Petersburg, 1884)

Lamouche, Colonel, *Quinze ans d'histoire balkanique (1904–1918)* (Paris, 1928)

Lange, K., 'Bajram Curri', in M. Bernath, F. von Schroeder and K. Nehring, eds., *Biographisches Lexikon zur Geschichte Südosteuropas*, 4 vols. (Munich, 1974–81), vol. 1, pp. 344–5

Langer, J., 'Nord-Albaniens und der Herzegowina Unterwerfungs-Anerbieten an Österreich, 1737–1739', *Archiv für österreichische Geschichte*, vol. 62 (1881), pp. 239–304

Langlès, L. M., 'Notice d'un recueil de pièces en turk, en arabe et en persan, formant le Nᵒ 79 des Mss. Turks de la Bibliothèque nationale', *Notices et extraits des manuscrits de la Bibliothèque Nationale et autres bibliothèques, publiés par l'Institut National de France*, vol. 5, year 7 (1798–9), pp. 668–88

Larnaude, M., 'Un village de colonisation en Serbie du sud', *Annales de géographie*, vol. 39 (1930), pp. 320–4

Lawrence, C., *Irregular Adventure* (London, 1947)

Lazarević, Despot Stefan, *Slova i natpisi*, ed. D. Bogdanović (Belgrade, 1979)

Lemerle, P., ed., *Les Plus Anciens Recueils des miracles de Saint Démétrius et la pénétration des Slaves dans les Balkans*, 2 vols. (Paris, 1979–81)

Lenormant, F., *Turcs et monténégrins* (Paris, 1866)

Leunclavius, J., *Historiae musulmanae Turcorum, de monumentis ipsorum exscriptae, libri XVIII* (Frankfurt, 1591)

Lewis, B., *The Emergence of Modern Turkey*, 2nd edn. (London, 1968)

—, *The Jews of Islam* (Princeton, NJ, 1984)

Lewis, R., *Everyday Life in Ottoman Turkey* (London, 1971)

Libardi, C., *I primi moti patriottici albanesi nel 1910–1911–1912, specie nei Dukagini*, 2 parts (Trento, 1935)

Lifchez, R., ed., *The Dervish Lodge: Architecture, Art, and Sufism in Ottoman Turkey* (Berkeley, Calif., 1992)

Limanoski, N., *Islamizacijata i etničkite promeni vo Makedonija* (Skopje, 1993)

Ljubić, S., ed., *Commissiones et relationes venetae*, vol. 3 (1553–1571), Monumenta spectantia historiam slavorum meridionalium, vol. 11 (Zagreb, 1880)

Lleshi, Q., *Prizren, Priština i Kosovska Mitrovica: geografske osnove razvoja* (Prishtina, 1975)

Lodge, O., *Peasant Life in Jugoslavia* (London, 1942)

Louis-Jaray, G., *L'Albanie inconnue* (Paris, 1913)

Lowry, H., 'Changes in Fifteenth-Century Ottoman Peasant Taxation: The Case Study of Radilofo', in A. Bryer and H. Lowry, eds., *Continuity and Change in Late Byzantine and Early Ottoman Society* (Birmingham, 1986), pp. 23–37

Lukač, D., *Radnički pokret u Jugoslaviji i nacionalno pitanje 1918–1941* (Belgrade, 1972)

Lutovac, M., *La Metohija: étude de géographie humaine* (Paris, 1935)

McGowan, B., 'Food Supply and Taxation on the Middle Danube (1568–1579)', *Archivium ottomanicum*, vol. 1 (1969), pp. 138–96

Magaš, B., *The Destruction of Yugoslavia: Tracking the Break-up 1980–92* (London, 1993)

Magnusson, K., 'Nationalitetsproblem i Jugoslavien: krisen i Kosovo', *Bidrag till öststatsforskningen*, vol. 9 (1981), no. 2

—, 'The Serbian Reaction: Kosovo and Ethnic Mobilization among the Serbs', *Nordic Journal of Soviet and East European Studies*, vol. 4, no. 3 (1987), pp. 3–30

Makushev, V., 'Issledovaniia ob istoricheskikh pamiatnikakh i bytopisateliakh Dubrovnika', *Zapiski Imperatorskoi Akademii Nauk*, vol. 11 (1867), prilozheniia, no. 5, pp. 1–446

—, *O Slavianakh v Albanii* (Warsaw, 1871)

Maletić, M., ed., *Kosovo nekad i danas: Kosova dikur e sot* (Belgrade, 1973)

Maliqi, S., 'The Albanian Movement in Kosova', in D. A. Dyker and I. Vejvoda, eds., *Yugoslavia and After: A Study in Fragmentation, Despair and Rebirth* (London, 1996), pp. 138–54

Mališić, V., 'Svi Srbi u jednoj legendi', *Duga*, 28 May–10 June 1994, pp. 4–7

Manoschek, W., *'Serbien ist judenfrei': militärische Besatzungspolitik und Juden-vernichtung in Serbien 1941/42* (Munich, 1993)

Mantegazza, V., *L'Albania* (Rome, 1912)

Marenin, N. [pseudonym of A. Šopov], *Albanija i albanicite* (Sofia, 1902)

Marlowe, C., *Tamburlaine the Great*, ed. J. S. Cunningham (Manchester, 1981)

Martinianos, I., *Hê Moschopolis 1330–1930* (Salonica, 1957)

Martinović ['Martinoviq'], S., 'Qëndrimi i ushtrisë serbe ndaj Shqiptarëve në viset e pushtuara në vitet 1912–1913', *GASH*, vol. 7, for 1977 (1978), pp. 247–78

Matejić, M., and D. Milivojević, eds. and trs., *An Anthology of Medieval Serbian Literature in English* (Columbus, Ohio, 1978)

Matijević ['Matijévitch'], M., 'Yougoslavie – Grande-Serbie', *FB*, year 6, no. 123 (1 Nov. 1929), pp. 2709–10

Matkovski, A., *A History of the Jews in Macedonia* (Skopje, 1982)

Mavromatis, L., *La Fondation de l'empire serbe: le kralj Milutin* (Salonica, 1978)

Mayer, A., *Die Sprache der alten Illyrier*, 2 vols. (Vienna, 1957–9)

Medenica, G., 'Četnički pokret na Kosovu i Metohiji u vreme II svetskog rata', *VAK*, vols. 10–11, for 1974–5 (1979), pp. 347–425

Mehlan, A., 'Über die Bedeutung der mittelalterlichen Bergbaukolonien für die slavischen Balkanvölker', *RIEB*, vol. 3, nos. 1–2 (1937–8), pp. 383–404

Meier, V., *Wie Jugoslawien verspielt wurde* (Munich, 1995)

Mélikoff, I., 'Ewrenos', in *EI2*, vol. 2, p. 720

Ménage, V. L., *Neshri's History of the Ottomans* (London, 1964)

Meyer, G., *Etymologisches Wörterbuch der albanischen Sprache* (Strasbourg, 1891)

Midhat Bey, A. H., *The Life of Midhat Pasha: A Record of his Services, Political Reforms, Banishment, and Judicial Murder* (London, 1903)

Mihačević, L., *Schematismus almae provinciae missionariae Albaniae St. Mariae Annuntiatae ordinis fratrum minorum S.P.N. Francisci* (Sarajevo, 1908)

—, *Po Albaniji: dojmovi s puta* (Zagreb, 1911)

Mihăescu, H., 'Les Éléments latins de la langue albanaise', *Revue des études sud-est européennes*, vol. 4 (1966), pp. 5–33, 323–53

—, *La Romanité dans le sud-est de l'Europe* (Bucharest, 1993)

Mihailović, K., *Memoirs of a Janissary*, tr. B. Stolz, ed. S. Soucek (Ann Arbor, Michigan, 1975)

Mihaljčić, R., *Lazar Hrebeljanović: istorija, kult, predanje* (Belgrade, 1984)

Mihalovich, V., 'The Tradition of Kosovo in Serbian Literature', in *KLMB*, pp. 141–58

Mijatović, Č. ['Mijatovich, C.'], *Servia of the Servians*, 2nd edn. (London, 1911)

Mikić, D. ['Mikiq, G.'], 'Shqiptarët dhe projektet hekurudhore të Austro-Hungarisë dhe Serbisë në Turqi në vitet 1908 dhe 1909', *GASH*, vols. 4–5, for 1974–5 (1977), pp. 137–63

—, *Društvene i ekonomske prilike kosovskih Srba u XIX i početkom XX veka (od čifčijstva do bankarstva)* (Belgrade, 1988)

Miklosich, F., 'Die Blutrache bei den Slaven', *DKAWP-H*, vol. 37 (1887), no. 1

Milani, C., ed., *Itinerarium Antonini Placentini: un viaggio in Terra Santa del 560–570 d.C.* (Milan, 1977)

Milazzo, M., *The Chetnik Movement and the Yugoslav Resistance* (Baltimore, 1975)

Miletich, J. S., ed. and tr., *The Bugarštica: A Bilingual Anthology of the Earliest Extant South Slavic Folk Narrative Song* (Urbana, Illinois, 1990)

Miller, W., *The Ottoman Empire and its Successors, 1801–1927* (Cambridge, 1936)

Milo, P., *Shqipëria dhe Jugosllavia 1918–1927* (Tirana, 1992)

Milojević, M., *Putopis dela prave (stare) Srbije*, 2 vols. (Belgrade, 1871–2)

Milošević, S., *Les Années décisives* (Lausanne, 1990)

Miquel y Planas, R., ed., *La Història de Jacob Xalabín* and *La Filla de l'Emperador Contastí* (Barcelona, 1910)

Mirdita, Z., 'Çështja e etnogenezës së shqiptarëve', *Përparimi*, vol. 16 (1970), pp. 626–44

—, 'Rreth problemit të romanizimit të dardanëve', *Përparimi*, vol. 19 (1973), pp. 1–11

—, *Studime dardane* (Tirana, 1981)

—, 'Alcuni aspetti del cristianesimo fra gli Albanesi in epoca bizantina', in *Le minoranze etniche e linguistiche: atti del 2° congresso internazionale, Piana degli Albanesi, 7/11 settembre 1988* (Palermo, 1989), pp. 173–80

—, *Historia e Kishës në popullin Shqiptar: material për historinë e Kishës kombëtare në Institutin Katekistik Kombëtar në Shkodër, 1994/5* (Shkodra, 1994)

—, 'Sudjelovanje vojske Hrvatskoga Kraljevstva u bitci naroda kod Varne', *Povijesni prilozi*, vol. 13 (1994), pp. 9–25

—, 'Balkanski Vlasi u svijetlu podataka Bizantskih autora', *Povijesni prilozi*, vol. 14 (1995), pp. 25–115

Mitrovski, B., Glišić, V., and T. Ristovksi, *The Bulgarian Army in Yugoslavia 1941–1945* (Belgrade, 1971)

Mladenov ['Mladenoff'], S., 'Bemerkungen über die Albaner und das Albanische in Nordmakedonien und Altserbien', *BA*, vol. 1 (1925), pp. 43–70

—, 'Albanisch und Thrako-Illyrisch (kritische Bemerkungen zu einer vermeintlichen Streitfrage)', *BA*, vol. 4 (1928), pp. 181–94

Molas, J., and J. Massot i Muntaner, eds., *Diccionari de la literatura catalana* (Barcelona, 1979)

von Moltke, H., *Unter dem Halbmond: Erlebnisse in der alten Türkei 1835–1839*, ed. H. Arndt (Stuttgart, 1984)

Mošin, V., 'Vizantiski uticaj u Srbiji u XIV veku', *JIČ*, vol. 3 (1937), pp. 147–59

Muir Mackenzie, G., and A. P. Irby, *Travels in the Slavonic Provinces of Turkey-in-Europe*, 3rd edn., 2 vols. (London, 1877)

Mujezinović, M., 'Natpisi na nadgrobnim spomenicima Suzi-Čelebija i Neharija u Prizrenu', *POF*, vols. 12–13 (1962–3), pp. 265–8

Mujić, M., 'Položaj cigana u jugoslovenskim zemljama pod osmanskom vlašću', *POF*, vols. 3–4 (1952–3), pp. 137–91

Mükerrem, Binbaşı [Major], *Türk ordusunun eski seferlinden bir imha muharebesi: Kosova 1389* (Istanbul, 1931)

Müller, J., *Albanien, Rumelien und die österreichische-montenegrinische Grenze* (Prague, 1844)

Murphey, R., 'Silver Production in Rumelia, According to an Official Report circa 1600', *SOF*, vol. 39 (1980), pp. 75–104

Murzaku, T., *Politika e Serbisë kundrejt Shqipërisë gjatë luftës ballkanike 1912–1913* (Tirana, 1987)

Mutafčieva ['Moutafchieva'], V., *Agrarian Relations in the Ottoman Empire in the 15th and 16th Centuries* (Boulder, Colorado, 1988)

—, and S. Dimitrov, 'Die Agrarverhältnisse im osmanischen Reiche im XV–XVI Jh.', in *Actes du premier congrès international des études balkaniques et sud-est européennes* (Sofia, 1969), vol. 3, pp. 689–702

Nakičević, O., *Revolt i protestni marš stanovnika Kosova 1822. godine* (Prishtina, 1969)

Nandriş, J. G., 'The Jebaliyeh of Mount Sinai, and the Land of Vlah', *Quaderni di studi arabi*, vol. 8 (1990), pp. 45–90

Nasi, L., 'Eight Months in the History of the Albanian Population in Yugoslavia', in *TOK*, pp. 222–32

Naval Intelligence Division, *Jugoslavia*, 3 vols. (London, 1944)

—, *Albania* (London, 1945)

Niederle, L., *Slovanské starožitnosti*, oddíl 1, díl 2, 2 vols. (Prague, 1906–10)

Nopcsa, F., *Aus Šala und Klementi: albanische Wanderungen* (Sarajevo, 1910)

—, 'Beiträge zur Vorgeschichte und Ethnologie Nordalbaniens', *Wissenchaftliche Mitteilungen aus Bosnien und der Herzegowina*, vol. 12 (1912), pp. 168–253

—, *Haus und Hausrat im katholischen Nordalbanien* (Sarajevo, 1912)

—, *see also* Baxhaku and Kaser, eds.

Norris, H. T., *Islam in the Balkans: Religion and Society between Europe and the Arab World* (London, 1993)

Novaković, R., 'O nekim pitanjima područja današnje Metohije krajem XII i početkom XIII veka', *Zbornik radova Vizantološkog Instituta*, vol. 9 (1966), pp. 195–215

Novaković, S., *Il campo d'azione di Nemanja: studio storico-geografico* (Split, 1878)

—, 'Hadži-Kalfa ili Ćatib-Čelebija, turski geograf XVII veka, o balkanskim poluostrvu', *SSKA*, vol. 18 (1892), cols. 1–132

—, *Selo* (Belgrade, 1965)

Nuro, K., and N. Bato, eds., *Hasan Prishtina (përmbledhje dokumentesh) 1908–1934* (Tirana, 1982)

Nušić, B., *S Kosova na sinje more: beleške s puta kroz Arbanase 1894. godine* (Belgrade, 1902)

Obolensky, D., *The Byzantine Commonwealth: Eastern Europe 500–1453* (London, 1971)

Obradović, M., *Agrarna reforma i kolonizacija na Kosovu (1918–1941)* (Prishtina, 1981)

Oestreich, K., 'Reisen im Vilajet Kosovo', *Verhandlungen der Gesellschaft für Erdkunde zu Berlin*, vol. 26 (1899), pp. 305–19

Oikonomides, N., 'The Turks in Europe (1305–13) and the Serbs in Asia Minor (1313)', in E. Zachariadou, ed., *The Ottoman Emirate (1300–1389)* (Rethymnon, 1993), pp. 159–68

Olesnicki, A., 'Suzi Čelebi iz Prizrena, turski pesnik-istorik XV–XVI veka (prilog biografiji)', *GSND*, vol. 13 (1934), pp. 62–82

—, 'Turski izvori o kosovskom boju: pokušaj kritičke analize njihova sadržaja i uzajamne konsekutivne veze', *GSND*, vol. 14 (1935), pp. 59–99

Omari, L., 'The Constitutional Changes and the Autonomy of Kosova', in *TOK*, pp. 286–95

Ongania, F., ed., *Il Montenegro da relazioni dei provveditori veneti (1687–1735)* (Rome, 1896)

Ostrogorsky ['Ostrogorskij'], G., *Pour l'histoire de la féodalité byzantine*, tr. H. Grégoire and P. Lemerle (Brussels, 1954)

Özbek, B., *Erzählungen der letzten Tscherkessen auf dem Amselfeld* (Bonn, 1986)

Pacheco, A., ed., *La Història de Jacob Xalabín* (Barcelona, 1964)

Palerne, J., *Peregrinations [. . .] où est traicté de plusieurs singularités, & antiquités* (Lyon, 1606)

Pall, F., 'Les Relations entre la Hongrie et Scanderbeg', *Revue historique du sud-est européen*, vol. 10 (1933), nos. 4–6, pp. 119–41

—, 'Skanderbeg et Janco de Hunedoara (Jean Hunyadi)', in A. Kostallari, ed., *Deuxième conférence des études albanologiques*, 2 vols. (Tirana, 1969), vol. 1, pp. 87–104

Pamuk, Ş., 'Money in the Ottoman Empire', in H. İnalcık and D. Quataert, eds., *An Economic and Social History of the Ottoman Empire, 1300–1914* (Cambridge, 1994), pp. 947–85

Papadopoulos, S. I., *Hê kinêsê tou douka tou Never Karolou Gonzaga yia tên apeleutherôsê tôn valkanikôn laôn (1603–1625)* (Salonica, 1966)

Papathanasiou, Y. A., *Hê historia tôn vlachôn* (Salonica, 1991)

Papazoglu, F., 'Dardanska onomastika', *Zbornik filozofskog fakulteta, Beogradski univerzitet*, vol. 8 (1964), pp. 49–75

—, 'Les Royaumes d'Illyrie et de Dardanie: origines et développement, structures, hellénisation et romanisation', in M. Garašanin, ed., *Iliri i Albanci* (Belgrade, 1988), pp. 173–99

—, *The Central Balkan Tribes in Pre-Roman Times: Triballi, Autariatae, Dardanians, Scordisci and Moesians*, tr. M. Stansfield-Popović (Amsterdam, 1978)

Papoulia, B. D., *Ursprung und Wesen der 'Knabenlese' im osmanischen Reich* (Munich, 1963)

Pavlović, D. M., *Pokret u Bosni i u Albaniji protivu reforama Mahmuda II* (Belgrade, 1913)

Pavlović, N. D., *Despot Stefan Lazarević* (Subotica, 1968)

Pavlowitch, S. K., 'Society in Serbia, 1791–1830', in R. Clogg, ed., *Balkan Society in the Age of Greek Independence* (London, 1981), pp. 137–56

—, *Tito: Yugoslavia's Great Dictator* (London, 1992)

Pejin, J., 'Die Begehung des 500. Jahrestages der Kosovo-Schlacht und die Verbreitung der Kosovo-Legende', in *KBNP*, pp. 363–91

Pertusi, A., *Martino Segono di Novo Brdo, vescovo di Dulcigno: un umanista serbo-dalmata del tardo quattrocento* (Rome, 1981)

Peruničić, B., ed., *Zulumi aga i begova u kosovskom vilajetu* (Belgrade, 1989)

Pešikan, M., 'Imenoslov kosovskih varoških i rudarskih sredešta u drugoj polovini XVI veka', *Kosovsko-metohijski zbornik*, vol. 1 (1990), pp. 123–31

Petranović, B., 'Kosovo in Yugoslav-Albanian Relations and the Project of a Balkan Federation', in A. Mitrović, ed., *Srbi i Albanci u XX veku* (Belgrade, 1991), pp. 341–72, 399–422

Petrović, A., 'Contributions to the Study of the Serbian Gypsies', *Journal of the Gypsy Lore Society*, 3rd ser., vol. 17 (1938), pp. 31–8, 61–70; vol. 17 (1938), Jubilee no., pp. 67–74

Petrović, R., and M. Blagojević, *The Migration of Serbs and Montenegrins from Kosovo and Metohija: Results of the Survey Conducted in 1985–1986* (Belgrade, 1992)

Peyfuss, M. D., *Die Druckerei von Moschopolis, 1731–1769: Buchdruck und Heiligenverehrung im Erzbistum Achrida* (Vienna, 1989)

Philippide, A., *Originea Romînilor*, 2 vols. (Iaşi, 1923–7)

Picot, A. E., *Les Serbes de Hongrie: leur histoire, leurs privilèges, leur église, leur état politique et social* (Prague, 1873)

Pipa, A., *Albanian Literature: Social Perspectives* (Munich, 1978)

—, 'Rapsodi albanesi in serbocroato: il ciclo epico di frontiera', in A. Guzzetta, ed., *Etnia albanese e minoranze linguistiche in Italia: atti del IX Congresso Internazionale di Studi Albanesi* (Palermo, 1983), pp. 371–408

—, *The Politics of Language in Socialist Albania* (Boulder, Colorado, 1989)

—, *Albanian Stalinism: Ideo-political Aspects* (New York, 1990)

Pirraku, M., 'Kulturno-prosvetni pokret Albanaca u Jugoslaviji (1919–1941)', *JIČ* (1978), nos. 1–4, pp. 356–70

Pisani, V., 'Les Origines de la langue albanaise: questions de principes et de méthode', *SA* (1964), no. 1, pp. 61–8

Pitton de Tournefort, J., *Relation d'un voyage du Levant, fait par ordre du Roy*, 2 vols. (Paris, 1717)

Plasari, N., 'Politika e udheheqjes së PKSH dhe e Enver Hoxhës ndaj çështjes së Kosovës gjatë luftës së dytë botërore', *SH*, vol. 29, for 1992 (1995), nos. 1–4, pp. 79–92

—, and L. Malltezi, *Marrëdhëniet shqiptaro-jugosllave 1945–1948* (Tirana, 1996)

—, and L. Malltezi, *Politike antikombetare e Enver Hoxhës: plenumi i 2të i KQ të PKSH, Berat, 23–27 nëntor 1944* (Tirana, 1996)

Plava, E., *Plava e Gucia në lëvizjen kombëtare shqiptare (kujtime dhe dokumente historike)* (Tirana, 1995)

Pllana, E., 'Greva e dytë dhe e tretë e xehtarëvet të Trepçës', *Përparimi*, vol. 9 (1963), pp. 38–42

—, 'Les Raisons et la manière de l'exode des refugiés albanais du territoire du sandjak de Nish à Kosove (1877–1878)', *SA* (1985), no. 1, pp. 179–200

Polák, V., 'Die Beziehungen des Albanischen zu den europäischen Substratsprachen mit Rücksicht auf die balkanische Situation', in *KSGA*, pp. 207–17

Pollo, S., and A. Buda, eds., *Historia e popullit shqiptar*, 2 vols. (Prishtina, 1969)

—, and S. Pulaha, eds., *Akte të Rilindjes Kombëtare Shqiptare 1878–1912* (Tirana, 1978)

—, and A. Puto, *The History of Albania from its Origins to the Present Day*, tr. C. Wiseman and G. Hole (London, 1981)

Polomé, E. G., 'The Position of Illyrian and Venetic', in H. Birnbaum and J. Puhvel, eds., *Ancient Indo-European Dialects* (Berkeley, Calif., 1966), pp. 59–76

Pop-Kosić, Ž. ['Pop-Kocitch, J.'], *Étude juridique sur l'incorporation de territoires macédoniens à la Serbie: contribution à l'étude de l'annexion* (Paris, 1935)

Popović, A., *L'Islam balkanique: les musulmans du sud-est européen dans la période post-ottomane* (Berlin, 1986)

—, *Les Derviches balkaniques hier et aujourd'hui* (Istanbul, 1994)

Popović, D., *Velika seoba Srba 1690: Srbi seljaci i plemići* (Belgrade, 1954)

Popović, S., Janča, D., and T. Petovar, eds., *Kosovski čvor: drešiti ili seći?* (Belgrade, 1990)

Popović, T., *Prince Marko: The Hero of the South Slavic Epics* (Syracuse, NY, 1988)

Popović, V., 'L'Albanie pendant la basse antiquité', in M. Garašanin, ed., *Iliri i Albanci* (Belgrade, 1988), pp. 251–83

Popp, N., 'Minoritatea româno-albaneză din Jugoslavia', *Buletinul societății regale române de geografie*, vol. 50 (1931), pp. 353–70

van de Port, M., *Het einde van de wereld: beschaving, redeloosheid en zigeunercafés in Servië* (Amsterdam, 1994)

Poulton, H., *The Balkans: Minorities and States in Conflict*, 2nd edn. (London, 1993)

Prifti, K., ed., *Lidhja shqiptare e Prizrenit në dokumentet osmane 1878–1881* (Tirana, 1978)
—, *Le Mouvement national albanais de 1896 à 1900: la Ligue de Pejë* (Tirana, 1989)
—, *et al.*, eds., *The Truth on Kosova* (Tirana, 1993)
Prifti, P., 'Kosova's Economy: Problems and Prospects', in *SOK*, pp. 125–65
Prishtina, H., *Nji shkurtim kujtimesh mbi kryengritjen shqiptare të vjetit 1912*, 2nd edn. (Tirana, 1995)
Pulaha, S., ed., *Lufta shqiptaro-turke në shekullin XV: burime osmane* (Tirana, 1968)
—, 'Krahinat verilindore të sanxhakut të Dukagjinit – Hassi dhe popullsia e tyre në gjysmën e dytë të shekullit XVI', *GASH*, vol. 2, for 1972 (1974), pp. 185–336
—, 'Të dhëna ekonomike dhe demografike për krahinën e Opoljes (Opoja) në gjysmën e dytë të shek. XVI', *SH*, vol. 12 (1975), pp. 101–35
—, 'Formation des régions de selfgovernment dans les Malessies du sandjak de Shkodër aux XV–XVIIᵉ siècles', *SA*, vol. 13 (1976), no. 2, pp. 173–9
—, 'Të dhëna ekonomike dhe demografike për krahinën e Hoçës – regjistrimi kadastral i vitit 1591', *SH*, vol. 13 (1976), (i): no. 1, pp. 137–208; (ii): no. 2, pp. 85–139
—, ed., *Qëndresa e popullit shqiptar kundër sundimit osman nga shek. XVI deri në fillim të shek. XVIII: dokumente osmane* (Tirana, 1978)
—, 'Qytetet e Rrafshit të Dukagjinit dhe të Kosovës gjatë gjysmës së dytë të shek. XVI në dritën e të dhënave të reja të regjistrimeve kadastrale osmane', *GASH*, vol. 9, for 1979 (1980), pp. 11–43
—, *Popullsia shqiptare e Kosovës gjatë shekujve XV–XVI (studime dhe dokumente)* (Tirana, 1983)
—, 'On the Presence of Albanians in Kosova during the 14th–17th Centuries', in *TOK*, pp. 33–47
Pupovci, S., *Gradjanskopravni odnosi u zakoniku Leke Dukadjina* (Prishtina, 1968)
— 'Burimet për studimin e Kanunit të Lekë Dukagjinit', *SH* (1971), no. 2, pp. 75–98
— 'Origjina dhe emri i Kanunit të Lekë Dukagjinit', *SH* (1972), no. 1, pp. 103–28
Purković, M., *Knez i despot Stefan Lazarević* (Belgrade, 1978)
Puto, A., ed., *La Question albanaise dans les actes internationaux de l'époque impérialiste*, 2 vols. (Tirana, 1985–8)
Qosja, R., *La Question albanaise* (Paris, 1995)
R., R., 'Qui sont les nouveaux Banus?', *FB*, year 6, no. 123 (1 Nov. 1929), p. 2710
Rački, F., 'Izvještaj barskog nadbiskupa Marina Bizzia o svojem putovanju god. 1610 po Arbanaskoj i staroj Srbiji', *SJAZU*, vol. 20 (1888), pp. 50–156

Rácz, I., *A hajdúk a XVII. században* (Debrecen, 1969)

Radojčić, N., ed., *Zakonik cara Stefana Dušana 1349 i 1354* (Belgrade, 1960)

Radojičić, D. S., 'Izbor patrijarha Danila III i kanonizacija kneza Lazara', *GSND*, vol. 21 (1940), pp. 33–81

—, 'Pohvala knezu Lazaru sa stihovima', *IČ*, vol. 5 (1954–5), pp. 241–53

Radonić, J., *Zapadna Evropa i balkanski narodi prema turcima u prvoj polovini XV. veka* (Novi Sad, 1905)

—, *Histoire des Serbes de Hongrie* (Paris, 1919)

—, *Rimska kurija i južnoslovenske zemlje od XVI do XIX veka* (Belgrade, 1950)

Radusinović, P., *Stanovništvo Crne Gore do 1945 godine: opšta istorijsko-geografska i demografska razmatranja* (Belgrade, 1978)

Rahimi, S., *Vilajeti i Kosovës më 1878–1912* (Prishtina, 1969)

—, *Lufta e Shqiptarëve për autonomi 1897–1912* (Prishtina, 1978)

Rajović, R., *Autonomija Kosova: istorijsko-pravna studija* (Belgrade, 1985)

Rakić, M., *Konzulska pisma 1905–1911*, ed. A. Mitrović (Belgrade, 1985)

Rázsó, G., 'The Mercenary Army of King Matthias Corvinus', in J. M. Bak and B. K. Király, eds., *From Hunyadi to Rákóczi: War and Society in Late Medieval and Early Modern Hungary* (New York, 1982), pp. 125–40

Redžepagić ['Rexhepagiq'], J., *Zhvillimi i arësimit dhe i sistemit shkollor të kombësisë shqiptare në teritorin e Jugosllavisë së sotme deri në vitin 1918* (Prishtina, 1970)

Reichenkron, G., 'Vorrömische Elemente im Rumänischen', in *KSGA*, pp. 237–53

Reinert, S. W., 'From Niš to Kosovo Polje: Reflections on Murad I's Final Years', in E. Zachariadou, ed., *The Ottoman Emirate (1300–1389)* (Rethymnon, 1993), pp. 169–211

Reith, W., *Von Monastir durchs Amselfeld: Rückzug 1918* (Berlin, n.d.)

Repishti, S., 'The Evolution of Kosova's Autonomy Within the Yugoslav Constitutional Framework', in *SOK*, pp. 195–231

Reuter, J., *Die Albaner in Jugoslawien* (Munich, 1982)

Ristić, K., 'Naseljavanje Vojvodjana na Kosovu izmedju prvog i drugog svetskog rata', in J. F. Trifunoski and K. Ristić, *Vojvodjani van Vojvodine* (Novi Sad, 1961), pp. 25–40

Rizaj, S., 'Rudari (madendžije) u sistemu privilegija i dužnosti ('muaf ve müsellem reâya')', *Glasnik muzeja Kosova i Metohije*, vol. 19, for 1964 (1965), pp. 213–36

—, *Rudarstvo Kosova i susednih krajeva od XV do XVII veka* (Prishtina, 1968)

—, 'Transferimet, deportimet dhe dyndjet e Shqiptarëvet në kohën e Skënder-beut', in *SPS*, pp. 145–53

—, 'Struktura stanovništva kosovskog vilajeta u drugoj polovini XIX stoleća', *Vranjski glasnik*, vol. 8 (1972), pp. 91–113

—, ed., *Lidhja shqiptare e Prizrenit në dokumente angleze (1878–1881)* (Prishtina, 1978)

—, 'Pravni i stvarni položaj raje rumelijskog ejaleta od sredine XVI do sredine XVII veka', *JIČ* (1978), nos. 1–4, pp. 198–214

—, 'Nëntë dokumente angleze mbi Lidhjen Shqiptare të Prizrenit (1878–1880)', *GASH*, vol. 10, for 1980 (1981), pp. 181–206

—, *Kosova gjatë shekujve XV, XVI dhe XVII: administrimi, ekonomia, shoqëria dhe lëvizja popullore* (Prishtina, 1982)

—, 'Mbi të ashtuquajturën dyndje e madhe serbe nga Kosova në krye me Patrikun Arsenije Çarnojeviq (1690)', *GASH*, vol. 12, for 1982 (1983), pp. 81–103

Rizvanolli, M., 'Disa të dhëna mbi spahite e krishterë në shekullin XV në Shqiperi, në Kosovë dhe në Rrafshin e Dukagjinit', in *SPS*, pp. 155–70

Roatta, M., *Otto milioni di baionette: l'esercito italiano in guerra dal 1940 al 1944* (n.p., 1946)

Röder von Diersburg, P., *Des Markgrafen Ludwig Wilhelm von Baden Feldzüge wider die Türken*, 2 vols. (Karlsruhe, 1839–42)

Rootham, H., ed. and tr., *Kossovo: Heroic Songs of the Serbs* (Oxford, 1920)

Rosetti, A., 'Thrace, daco-mésien, illyrien, roumain et albanais: quelques précisions', *BE*, vol. 20 (1977), nos. 1–2, pp. 79–82

Rostagno, L., 'Note sulla simulazione di fede nell'Albania ottomana', in G. Calasso *et al.*, *La bisaccia dello sheikh: omaggio ad Alessandro Bausani islamista nel sessantesimo compleanno* (Venice, 1981), pp. 153–63

Roux, M., *Les Albanais en Yougoslavie: minorité nationale, territoire et développement* (Paris, 1992)

Rugova, I., *Vepra e Bogdanit* (Prishtina, 1990)

—, *La Question du Kosovo: entretiens avec Marie-Françoise Allain et Xavier Galmiche* (Paris, 1994)

Runciman, S., *A History of the First Bulgarian Empire* (London, 1930)

Rushiti, L., *Lëvizja kaçakë në Kosovë (1918–1928)* (Prishtina, 1981)

—, *Rrethanat politiko-shoqerore në Kosovë 1912–1918* (Prishtina, 1986)

Rusinow, D., *The Yugoslav Experiment, 1948–1974* (Berkeley, Calif., 1978)

Ruston, U., 'Kosovo: Where Journalism is a Crime', *Index on Censorship*, vol. 21, no. 2 (Feb. 1992), pp. 18–20

Šabanović, H., ed., *Krajište Isa-bega Išakovića* (Sarajevo, 1964)

Salim, N., *Türk ordusunun eski seferlerinden bir imha muharebesi: ikinci Kosova 1448* (Istanbul, 1932)

Saliu, K., *Lindja, zhvillimi, pozita dhe aspektet e autonomitetit të krahinës socialiste autonome të Kosovës në Jugosllavinë socialiste* (Prishtina, 1984)

Salvoldi, V., and L. Gjergji, *Resistenza nonviolenta nella ex-Jugoslavia* (Bologna, 1993)

Samardžić, N., 'Savremena štampa o velikoj seobi Srba 1690. godine', *IČ*, vol. 32 (1985), pp. 79–103

Samardžić, R., *Mehmed Sokolović* (Belgrade, 1971)

San Nicolò, M., *Die Verwaltung Albaniens durch die k.u.k. österreichisch-ungarischen Truppen in den ersten zwei Jahren der Besetzung des Landes an der Hand der ergangenen Befehle* (Vienna, 1918)

Sathas, K. N., ed., *Mesaiônikê vivliothêkê*, 7 vols. (Venice, 1872–94)

Schanderl, H. D., *Die Albanienpolitik Österreich-Ungarns und Italiens 1877–1908* (Wiesbaden, 1971)

Schirò, G., 'P. Gjeçov e la prosa del *Kanûn di Lek Dukagjini*', in F. Ercole, ed., *Le terre albanesi redente I: Kossovo* (Rome, 1942), pp. 177–201

Schlarp, K.-H., *Wirtschaft und Besatzung in Serbien 1941–1944: ein Beitrag zur nationalsozialistischen Wirtschaftspolitik in Südosteuropa* (Stuttgart, 1986)

von Schmettau, F., *Geheime Nachrichten von dem Kriege in Ungarn in den Feldzügen 1737, 1738 und 1739* (Frankfurt, 1788)

Schmidt-Richberg, E., *Der Endkampf auf dem Balkan: die Operationen der Heeresgruppe E von Griechenland bis zu den Alpen* (Heidelberg, 1955)

Schneeweis, E., *Serbokroatische Volkskunde: Volksglaube und Volksbrauch* (Berlin, 1961)

Schramm, G., *Eroberer und Eingesessene: geographische Lehnnamen als Zeugen der Geschichte Südosteuropas im ersten Jahrtausend n. Chr.* (Stuttgart, 1981)

—, 'Frühe Schicksale der Rumänen: acht Thesen zur Lokalisierung der lateinischen Kontinuität in Südosteuropa', *ZFB*, (i): vol. 21 (1985), no. 2, pp. 222–41; (ii): vol. 22 (1986), no. 1, pp. 104–25; (iii): vol. 22 (1986), no. 2, pp. 78–94.

—, *Anfänge des albanischen Christentums: die frühe Bekehrung der Bessen und ihre langen Folgen* (Freiburg im Breisgau, 1994)

Schwanke, H., 'Zur Geschichte der österreichisch-ungarischen Militärverwaltung in Albanien (1916–1918)', phil. diss., Vienna, 1982 (copy in Kriegsarchiv library, Vienna)

Schwanke, R., 'Das albanische Schulwesen und Österreich-Ungarn während des I. Weltkrieges', in P. Bartl, M. Camaj and G. Grimm, eds., *Dissertationes albanicae* (Munich, 1971), pp. 62–77

Schwicker, J. H., *Politische Geschichte der Serben in Ungarn* (Budapest, 1880)

Seiner, F., *Die Gliederung der albanischen Stämme* (Vienna, 1922)

Sekulić, T., *Seobe kao sudbina* (Prishtina, 1994)

Selishchev, A. M., *Slavianskoe naselenie v Albanii* (Sofia, 1931)

Selmeci, A., 'Kosova: Apartheid mitten in Europa: immer brutaler geht Serbien gegen die Albaner vor', *Pogrom: Zeitschrift für bedrohte Völker*, no. 184 (Aug./Sept. 1995), pp. 18–19

Senkevich, I. G., *Albaniia v period vostochnogo krizisa (1875–1881 gg.)* (Moscow, 1965)

Serra, A., *Albania 8 settembre 1943 – marzo 1944* (Milan, 1974)

Sesser, A., 'Die Denkwürdigkeiten des kaiserlichen Feldmarschalls Grafen Friedrich Veterani', phil. diss., Vienna, 1932 (copy in Kriegsarchiv library, Vienna)

Sestini, A., 'La Metochia', *Bolletino della reale società geografica italiana*, ser. 7, vol. 7 (1942), pp. 29–35

Shahîd, I., Byzantium and the Arabs in the Fourth Century (Washington, DC, 1984)

—, Byzantium and the Arabs in the Sixth Century (Washington, DC, 1995)

Shaw, S. J., The Jews of the Ottoman Empire and the Turkish Republic (London, 1991)

—, and E. K. Shaw, History of the Ottoman Empire and Modern Turkey, 2 vols. (Cambridge, 1976–7)

Shkodra, Z., Shqipnia në kohën e Tanzimatit (Tirana, 1959)

—, Esnafet shqiptare (shekujt XV–XX) (Tirana, 1973)

—, La Ville albanaise au cours de la renaissance nationale (Tirana, 1988)

Shoup, P., 'The Government and Constitutional Status of Kosova: Some Brief Remarks', in SOK, pp. 233–8

Shtylla, Z., 'The Deportation of Albanians in Yugoslavia after the Second World War (1950–1966)', in TOK, pp. 233–41

Shukriu ['Šukrija'], A., 'Situacija 1941. na području Kosovske Mitrovice', in UNJ, vol. 2, pp. 757–67

Shuteriqi, D. S., 'Shqiptarët në Hungari', B[UST]SS, (1957), no. 2, pp. 236–42

Sicard, É., La Zadruga sud-slave dans l'évolution du groupe domestique (Paris, 1943)

Siebertz, P., Albanien und die Albanesen: Landschafts- und Charakterbilder (Vienna, 1910)

Silber, L., and A. Little, The Death of Yugoslavia, 2nd edn (London, 1996)

Simić, A., 'The Blood Feud in Montenegro', in W. G. Lockwood, ed., Essays in Balkan Ethnology (Berkeley, Calif., 1967), pp. 83–94

Şimşir, B. N., ed., Rumeli'den Türk göçleri: belgeler, 2 vols. (Ankara, 1968–70)

Skendi, S., 'Crypto-Christianity in the Balkan Area under the Ottomans', Slavic Review, vol. 26 (1967), pp. 227–46

—, The Albanian National Awakening 1878–1912 (Princeton, NJ, 1967)

Skok, P., Dolazak Slovena na Mediteran (Split, 1934)

Škrivanić, G., Putevi u srednjovekovnoj Srbiji (Belgrade, 1974)

Slijepčević, D., Istorija srpske pravoslavne crkve, 2 vols. (Munich, 1962–6)

Sokolova, B., Albanski vŭzrŭždenski pečat v Bŭlgarija (Sofia, 1979)

Sokolski, M., 'Islamizacija u Makedoniji u XV i XVI veku', IČ, vol. 22 (1975), pp. 75–89

Sola-Solé, J. M., 'La Història de Jacob Xalabín i el món àrab', in J. Gulsoy and J. M. Sola-Solé, eds., Catalan Studies: estudis sobre al Català (Barcelona, 1977), pp. 213–22

Šopov ['Schopoff'], A., Les Réformes et la protection des chrétiens en Turquie 1673–1904 (Paris, 1904)

—, see also Marenin

Soranzo, L., L'Ottomanno, dove si dà pieno ragguaglio [. . .] di varii popoli, siti, città, e viaggi (Milan, 1599)

Soulis, G. C., *The Serbs and Byzantium during the Reign of Tsar Stephen Dušan (1331–1355) and his Successors* (Athens, 1995)

Spasojević, S., *Slučaj Martinović* (Belgrade, 1986)

Spencer, E., *Travels in European Turkey, in 1850, through Bosnia, Servia, Macedonia, Thrace, Albania, and Epirus; with a Visit to Greece and the Ionian Isles*, 2 vols. (London, 1851)

Spremić, M., 'Die Kosovo-Schlacht: ein Problem des Verrats', in *KBNP*, pp. 239–53

Spuler, B., *Die Minderheitenschulen der europäischen Türkei von der Reformzeit bis zum Weltkrieg* (Breslau, 1936)

Stadtmüller, G., *Forschungen zur albanischen Frühgeschichte* (Budapest, 1942)

—, 'Altheidnische Volksglaube und Christianisierung in Albanien', *OCP*, vol. 20 (1954), pp. 211–46

—, 'Die Islamisierung bei den Albanern', *Jahrbücher für Geschichte Osteuropas*, n.s., vol. 3 (1955), pp. 404–29

—, 'Das albanische Nationalkonzil vom Jahre 1703', *OCP*, vol. 22 (1956), pp. 68–91

Stambolić, I., *Put u bespuće: odgovori Ivana Stambolića na pitanja Slobodana Inića* (Belgrade, 1995)

Stanković, T., *Beleške o Staroj Srbiji – Maćedoniji* (Niš, 1915)

Stanojević, G., *Srbija u vreme bečkog rata 1683–1699* (Belgrade, 1976)

Stanojević, L., 'Srpska crkva u medjuvremenu od patriarha Arsenija II do Makarija (oko 1459–63 do 1557)', *GSKA*, vol. 106 (1923), pp. 76–93

Stanojević, S., 'Die Biographie Stefan Lazarević's von Konstantin dem Philosophen als Geschichtsquelle', *AFSP*, vol. 18 (1896), pp. 409–72

—, 'Lična imena i narodnost u Srbiji srednjega veka', *Južnoslovenski filolog*, vol. 8 (1928–9), pp. 151–4

Stefan, L. ['Korsika, B.'], ed., *Srbija i albanci: pregled politike Srbije prema albancima*, 3 vols. (Ljubljana, 1989)

Steinmetz, K., *Eine Reise durch die Hochländergaue Oberalbaniens* (Vienna, 1904)

—, *Ein Vorstoss in die nordalbanischen Alpen* (Vienna, 1905)

Stern, G., *Das alte Rascien: der Sandschak Novipazar und dessen Anland unter der k.u.k. Militärverwaltung* (Vienna, 1916)

Stevenson, D., *Alasdair MacColla and the Highland Problem in the Seventeenth Century* (Edinburgh, 1980)

Stipčević, A., *Iliri: povijest, život, kultura*, 3rd edn. (Zagreb, 1991)

Stojadinović ['Stoyadinovitch'], M., *La Yougoslavie entre les deux guerres: ni le pacte, ni la guerre* (Paris, 1979)

Stojančević, V., *Jugoslovenski narodi u osmanskom carstvu od jedrenskog mira 1829. do pariskog kongresa 1856. godine* (Belgrade, 1971)

—, 'O stanovništvu u prizrenskom vilajetu pred srpsko-turske ratove 1876–1878 godine', *Kosovsko-metohijski zbornik*, vol. 1 (1990), pp. 213–27

Stojanović, L., *Stari srpski zapisi i natpisi*, 6 vols. (Belgrade, 1902–26)

Stojanovski, A., *Dervendžistvoto vo Makedonija* (Skopje, 1974)

—, *Raja so specijalni zadolženija vo Makedonija (vojnuci, sokolari, orizari i solari)* (Skopje, 1990)

Stoye, J., *Marsigli's Europe 1680–1730: The Life and Times of Luigi Ferdinando Marsigli, Soldier and Virtuoso* (New Haven, Conn., 1994)

Stulli, B., 'Albansko pitanje (1875–1882)', *Rad JAZU*, vol. 318 (1959), pp. 287–391

Subotić, D., *Yugoslav Popular Ballads: Their Origin and Development* (Cambridge, 1932)

Subotić, K., ed., *Ilustrovana ratna kronika* (Novi Sad, 1912–13)

Sućeska, A., 'Promjene u sistemu izvanrednog oporezivanja u Turskoj u XVII vijeku i pojava nameta tekâlîf-i şâkka', *POF*, vols. 10–11 (1960–1), pp. 75–112

Šufflay, M., 'Die Kirchenzustände im vortürkischen Albanien: die orthodoxe Durchbruchzone im katholischen Damme', in *IAF*, vol. 1, pp. 188–281

—, 'Povijest sjevernih Arbanasa (sociološka studija)', *AASJE*, vol. 2 (1924), pp. 193–242

—, 'Städte und Burgen Albaniens hauptsächlich während des Mittelalters', *DKAWP-H*, vol. 63 (1924), no. 1

—, *Srbi i Arbanasi (njihova simbioza u srednjem vijeku)* (Belgrade, 1925)

Sugar, P., *Southeastern Europe under Ottoman Rule, 1354–1804* (Seattle, Washington, 1977)

Swire, J., *Albania: The Rise of a Kingdom* (London, 1929)

Tadić, J., 'Dubrovčani po Južnoj Srbiji u XVI stoleću', *GSND*, vols. 7–8 (1930), pp. 197–202

Tagliavini, C., 'Le parlate albanesi di tipo ghego orientale (Dardania e Macedonia nord-occidentale)', in F. Ercole, ed., *Le terre albanesi redente I: Kossovo* (Rome, 1942), pp. 1–82

Takács, M., 'Sächsische Bergleute im mittelalterlichen Serbien und die "sächsische Kirche" von Novo Brdo', *SOF*, vol. 50 (1991), pp. 31–60

Tartinius, F., ed., *Rerum italicarum scriptores ab anno aerae christianae millesimo ad millesimum sexcentesimum*, 2 vols. (Florence, 1748–70)

Tërnava, M., 'Migrimet e popullsisë në territorin e sotëm të Kosovës gjatë shekujve XIV–XVI', *Kosova/Kosovo*, vol. 5 (1976), pp. 289–325

—, 'Përhapja e islamizmit në territorin e sotëm të Kosovës deri në fund të shekullit të XVII', *GASH*, vol. 9, for 1979 (1980), pp. 45–69

von Thallóczy, 'Die albanische Diaspora', in *IAF*, vol. 1, pp. 299–341

—, 'Kanun i Lekës: ein Beitrag zum albanischen Gewohnheitsrecht', in *IAF*, vol. 1, pp. 409–60.

Theiner, A., ed., *Vetera monumenta historica Hungariam sacram illustrantia*, 2 vols. (Rome, 1859–60)

—, ed., *Vetera monumenta slavorum meridionalium historiam illustrantia*, 2 vols. (Rome, Zagreb, 1863–75)

Thëngjilli, P., ed., *Kryengritjet popullore në vitet 30 të shekullit XIX (dokumente osmane)* (Tirana, 1978)

—, *Renta feudale dhe evoluimi i saj në vise Shqiptare (shek. XVII – mesi i shek. XVIII)* (Tirana, 1990)

Thumb, A., 'Altgriechische Elemente des Albanischen', *Indogermanische Forschungen: Zeitschrift für indogermanische Sprach- und Altertumskunde*, vol. 26 (1910), pp. 1–20

Tkallac, K., 'Kostumet popullore të Kelmendeve të Sremit në Hërtkovc dhe Nikinc', *Përparimi*, year 16 (1970), pp. 162–3

Tomaschek, W., 'Die alten Thraker: eine ethnologische Untersuchung', *Sitzungsberichte der philosophisch-historischen Classe der kaiserlichen Akademie der Wissenschaften*, (i): vol. 128 (1893), no. 4; (ii): vol. 130 (1894), no. 2

Tomasevich, J., *The Chetniks: War and Revolution in Yugoslavia, 1941–1945* (Stanford, Calif., 1975)

Tomić, Jaša, *Rat na Kosovu i Staroj Srbiji 1912. godine* (Novi Sad, 1913)

Tomić, Jovan, 'Gradja za istoriju gornje Arbanije', *SSKA*, vol. 42 (= 2nd ser., vol. 37) (1905), pp. 51–77

—, 'Patriarah Arsenije III Crnojević prema mlečićima i ćesaru 1685–1695', *GSKA*, vol. 70 (= 2nd ser., vol. 43) (1906), pp. 66–161

—, *Crna Gora za morejskog rata (1684–1699)* (Belgrade, 1907)

— ['I. Tomitch'], *Les Albanais en Vieille-Serbie et dans le Sandjak de Novi-Bazar* (Paris, 1913)

Tomoski, T., 'Eden izguben dokument za avstriskata vojna vo Makedonija vo 1689 godina', *Godišen zbornik na filozofski fakultet na univerzitetot Skopje, oddel istorija i istorija na umetnosta*, vol. 15 (1963), pp. 121–32

Toynbee, P., *A Dictionary of Proper Names and Notable Matters in the Works of Dante*, revd. C. S. Singleton (Oxford, 1968)

Trevelyan, G. M., 'The Servian Army and its Turkish Victories', *The Nation*, vol. 13, no. 16 (19 July 1913), pp. 601–3

Tričković, R., 'U susret najtežim iskušenjima: XVII vek', in *KMSI*, pp. 115–26

—, 'Velika seoba Srba 1690. godine', in *KMSI*, pp. 127–41

—, 'Ustanci, seobe i stradanja u XVIII veku', in *KMSI*, pp. 143–69

Trimingham, J. S., *The Sufi Orders in Islam* (Oxford, 1971)

Tritton, A. S., *The Caliphs and their Non-Muslim Subjects: A Critical Study of the Covenant of Umar* (London, 1930)

Trotsky, L. [pseudonym of L. Bronshtein], *The War Correspondence of Leon Trotsky: The Balkan Wars*, tr. B. Pearce (New York, 1981)

Truhelka, Ć., 'Über die Balkan-Yürüken', *RIEB*, vols. 1–2 (1934–5), pp. 89–99

Tucović, D., *Srbija i Arbanija: jedan prilog kritici zavojevačke politike srpske buržoazije*, 2nd edn. (Belgrade, 1946)

Ugolini, L. M., 'Pagine di storia veneta ai tempi di Scanderbeg e dei suoi successori (con due documenti inediti)', off-print from *Studi albanesi*, vols. 3–4 (1933–4)

Uka, S., 'Vom Kaukasus aufs Amselfeld', tr. J. Knobloch, in B. Özbek, *Erzählungen der letzten Tscherkessen auf dem Amselfeld* (Bonn, 1986), pp. 116–31
—, *Dëbimi i Shqiptarëve nga sanxhaku i Nishit dhe vendosja e tyre në Kosovë*, 2nd edn., 2 vols. (Prishtina, 1994)
Umiltà, C., *Jugoslavia e Albania: memorie di un diplomatico* (Milan, 1947)
Urošević, A., 'Janjevo: antropogeografska ispitivanja', *GSND*, vol. 14 (1935), pp. 187–200
—, *Kosovo* (Belgrade, 1965)
—, *Etnički procesi na Kosovu tokom turske vladavine* (Belgrade, 1987)
Valentini, G., ed., *La legge delle montagne albanesi nelle relazioni della missione volante 1880–1932* (Florence, 1969)
Vasić, M., *Martolosi u jugoslovenskim zemljama pod turskom vladavinom* (Sarajevo, 1967)
—, 'Social Structure of Yugoslav Countries under the Ottoman Rule till the End of the 17th Century', *DO*, vol. 40 (1978), pp. 45–77
Veinstein, G., 'On the Çiftlik Debate', in C. Keyder and F. Tabak, eds., *Landholding and Commercial Agriculture in the Middle East* (New York, 1991), pp. 35–53
Velkov, V., *Cities in Thrace and Dacia in Late Antiquity (Studies and Materials)* (Amsterdam, 1977)
—, 'La Thrace et la Mésie Inférieure pendant l'époque de la basse antiquité (IV–VI ss.)', in A. G. Poulter, ed., *Ancient Bulgaria*, 2 vols. (Nottingham, 1983), vol. 2, pp. 177–93
Verli, M., *Reforma agrare koloniquese në Kosovë (1918–1941)* (Bonn, 1992)
—, *Shfrytëzimi ekonomik i Kosovës 1970–1990* (Tirana, 1994)
Veselinović, R., 'Die "Albaner" und "Klimenten" in den österreichischen Quellen zu Ende des 17. Jahrhunderts: historisch-geographische und ethnographische Abhandlung', *MÖS*, vol. 13 (1960), pp. 195–230
Veterani, F., *Memorie del maresciallo Conte Federico Veterani, dall' anno 1683. sino all' anno 1694. concernenti l'operazioni militari da lui fatte in Ungaria, e provincie adiacenti* (Vienna, 1771)
Vladisavljević, V., *Kosovski nesrbi* (Paris, 1984)
Vlainac ['Wlainatz'], M., *Die agrar-rechtlichen Verhältnisse des mittelalterlichen Serbiens* (Jena, 1903)
Vlora, Eqrem bey ['E. b. V.'], *Die Wahrheit über das Vorgehen der Jungtürken in Albanien* (Vienna, 1911)
Vlora, Ismail Qemal ['Kemal'], *Memorie*, tr. N. V. Falaschi (Vlora, 1992)
Vojnoistorijski institut, *Zbornik dokumenata i podataka o narodnooslobodilačkom ratu Jugoslovenskih naroda*, series 1, vol. 19: 'Borbe na Kosovu 1941–1944' (Belgrade, 1969)
Vojvodić, M., ed., *Dokumente o spoljnoj politici kraljevine Srbije 1903–1914*, vol. 5, part 1 (Belgrade, 1984)

Vryonis, S., *The Decline of Medieval Hellenism in Asia Minor and the Process of Islamization from the Eleventh through the Fifteenth Century* (Berkeley, Calif., 1971)

—, 'Religious Changes and Patterns in the Balkans, 14th-16th Centuries', in H. Birnbaum and S. Vryonis, eds., *Aspects of the Balkans: Continuity and Change* (The Hague, 1972), pp. 151–76

Vučinić, M., *Zašto Kosovo ne može da bude republika* (Belgrade, 1990)

Vučković, M., and G. Nikolić, *Stanovništvo Kosova u razdoblju od 1918. do 1991. godine* (Munich, 1996)

Vukanović, T., *Srbi na Kosovu*, 3 vols. (Vranje, 1986)

Wace, A., and M. A. Thompson, *The Nomads of the Balkans: An Account of Life and Customs among the Vlachs of the Northern Pindus* (London, 1914)

Weigand, G., *Die Aromunen: ethnographisch-philologisch-historische Untersuchungen über das Volk der sogenannten Makedo-Romänen oder Zinzaren*, 2 vols. (Leipzig, 1894–5)

—, 'Albanische Einwanderung in Siebenbürgen', *BA*, vol. 3 (1927), pp. 208–26

—, 'Sind die Albaner die Nachkommen der Illyrer oder der Thraker?', *BA*, vol. 3 (1927), pp. 227–51

Wertner, M., 'Die Herren von Gara und die Ellerbach von Magyorókerék (Eberau)', *Jahrbuch der k. k. heraldischen Gesellschaft 'Adler'*, n.s., vol. 7 (1897), pp. 66–116

Whittow, M., *The Making of Orthodox Byzantium, 600–1025* (London, 1996)

Wickerhauser, M., *Wegweiser zum Verständniss der türkischen Sprache: eine deutsch-türkische Chrestomathie* (Vienna, 1853)

Wiesner, J., *Die Thraker: Studien zu einen versunkenen Volk des Balkanraumes* (Stuttgart, 1963)

Wiet, É., 'Mémoire sur le pachalik de Prisrend', *Bulletin de la société de géographie*, ser. 5, vol. 12 (1866), pp. 273–89

van Wijk, N., 'Taalkundige en historiese gegevens betreffende de oudste betrekkingen tussen Serven en Bulgaren', *Mededeelingen der Koninklijke Akademie van Wetenschappen, afdeeling letterkunde*, vol. 55, ser. A (1923), pp. 55–76

Wilkes, J., *The Illyrians* (Oxford, 1992)

Wilkinson, H. R., *Maps and Politics: A Review of the Ethnographic Cartography of Macedonia* (Liverpool, 1951)

Wilson, D., *The Life and Times of Vuk Stefanović Karadžić, 1787–1864: Literacy, Literature, and National Independence in Serbia* (Oxford, 1970)

Winnifrith, T. J., *The Vlachs: The History of a Balkan People* (London, 1987)

Wirth, A., *Der Balkan: seine Länder und Völker in Geschichte, Kultur, Politik, Volkswirtschaft und Weltverkehr*, 4th edn. (Stuttgart, 1914)

Wuescht, J., *Jugoslawien und das Dritte Reich: eine dokumentierte Geschichte der deutsch-jugoslawischen Beziehungen von 1933 bis 1945* (Stuttgart, 1969)

Xholi, Z., 'Pjetër Bogdani – humanisti ynë i shquar', in A. Kostallari, ed., *Pjetër Bogdani dhe vepra e tij* (Tirana, 1991), pp. 85–114

Xhufi, P., 'Albanian Heretics in the Serbian Mediaeval Kingdom', in *TOK*, pp. 48–54

Yastrebov [Iastrebov], I. S., *Obichai i pesni turetskikh serbov (v Prizren, Ipek, Morav i Dibr)* (St Petersburg, 1886)

—, 'Stara Serbiia i Albaniia', *SSKA*, vol. 41 (1904)

Yerasimos, S., *Les Voyageurs dans l'empire ottoman (XIVᵉ–XVIᵉ siècles): bibliographie, itinéraires et inventaire des lieux habités* (Ankara, 1991)

Yugoslav Government, *The Constitution of the Socialist Federal Republic of Yugoslavia Adopted on April 7th 1963* (Belgrade, 1963)

Zaimi, T., *Lidhja e II e Prizrenit dhe lufta heroike e popullit për mbrojtjen e Kosovës* (Brussels, 1964)

Zamputi, I., 'Bashkimi i maleve shqiptare në fillim të shekullit të XVII-të: expedita e Vuço Pashës mbi Këlmand me 1638', *B[UST]SS* (1957), no. 3, pp. 63–95

—, ed., *Relacione mbi gjendjen e Shqipërisë veriore e të mesme në shekullin XVII*, 2 vols. (Tirana, 1963–5)

—, ed., *Dokumente të shekujve XVI–XVII për historinë e Shqipërisë*, vols. 1–3 (Tirana, 1989–90)

—, and S. Pulaha, eds., *Dokumente të shekujve XVI–XVII për historinë e Shqipërisë*, vol. 4 (Tirana, 1990)

Zavalani, T., *Histori e Shqipnis*, 2 vols. (London, n.d.)

Zefiq, F., *Mihael Summa, nadbiskup skopski (1695–1777)* (Osijek, 1994)

Zeitler, W., 'Das lateinische Erbe im Albanischen und die älteren Wohnsitze der Albaner: zur Methode und zum gegenwärtigen Stand der Forschung', *ZFB*, vol. 14 (1978), pp. 200–7

Željazkova, A., *Razprostranenie na isljama v zapadnobalkanskite zemi pod osmanska vlast, XV–XVIII vek* (Sofia, 1990)

Zirojević, O., 'Cigani u Srbiji od dolaska Turaka do kraja XVI veka', *JIČ* (1976), nos. 1–2, pp. 67–78

—, *Crkve i manastiri na području pećke patriaršije do 1683. godine* (Belgrade, 1984)

—, 'Prvi vekovi tudjinske vlasti', in *KMSI*, pp. 47–113

—, 'Kosovo u istorijskom pamćenju (mit, legende, činjenice)', *Republika* (1–15 Mar. 1995), pp. 9–24

Živančević, P., *Emigranti: naseljavanje Kosova i Metohije iz Albanije* (Belgrade, 1989)

Zlatar, Z., *Between the Double Eagle and the Crescent: The Republic of Dubrovnik and the Origins of the Eastern Question* (New York, 1992)

Županić, N. ['Gersin, K.'], *Altserbien und die albanesische Frage* (Vienna, 1912)

—, 'Etnološki značaj kosovskih Čerkeza', *Etnologa, glasnik etnografskog muzeja u Ljubljani*, vol. 6 (1933), pp. 217–53

Index